A
Documentary and Genealogical History
of the
Family of
Andrew McElwain
and
Mary Mickey
of Cumberland County,
Pennsylvania

Wilbur J. McElwain

HERITAGE BOOKS
2012

HERITAGE BOOKS

AN IMPRINT OF HERITAGE BOOKS, INC.

Books, CDs, and more—Worldwide

For our listing of thousands of titles see our website
at
www.HeritageBooks.com

Published 2012 by
HERITAGE BOOKS, INC.
Publishing Division
100 Railroad Ave. #104
Westminster, Maryland 21157

International Standard Book Numbers
Paperbound: 978-0-7884-0682-9
Clothbound: 978-0-7884-9221-1

PREFACE

These are the researches of Wilbur J. McElwain, which he publishes, in the hope of thereby preserving from decay the remembrance of what men have done, and of preventing the great and wonderful actions of our American ancestors from losing their due meed of glory.

Herodotus, in the passage which I have presumed to use (with some slight and obvious changes) referred, of course, to the actions of the Greeks and the Persians in that great war by which the Greeks preserved the western civilization which they had begun to develop. There are no actions here to compare with the charge at Marathon or the stand at Thermopylae. Rather what is described is the part, small but still important, played by a typical family in the transfer of that western civilization preserved by the Greeks to the vast area that now is the United States.

Fernand Braudel, the great French historian of everyday life, somewhere remarks that the great political events which are the subject of academic studies are but froth on the surface of the great ocean of the life and activities of the uncounted millions who lead useful and productive lives without achieving any kind of fame, and often not leaving behind any remembrance of their existence. This book, a simple family history, records the story of people, mostly humble, some eminent, but none famous, who took part in the settlement and expansion of this country. What I have been able to learn of their part in this movement is recorded. I hope that the reader will find reason to admire and to honor his forebears here recorded and that this admiration and honor will help each of us to shape our conduct so that it will contribute a small addition to the continuing development of our unique civilization.

This work is intended to serve several purposes. First, it provides a genealogy as complete as it has been possible to compile with the materials I have been able to uncover. It also attempts to gather together such documents as are available concerning the life of the early generations of the McElwain family in this country, and to link these together with a narrative. Finally, it endeavors to set forth how some genealogical and historical conclusions were reached and to suggest to future family historians research which might prove fruitful and problems which might arise.

I would like to spend a year (or five years) more in research and would also like to go over the text of my book several more times to remove errors both of fact and of typing—not to mention inelegancies, ambiguities, and imprecisions (and probably other ins-, ams-, and ims-) that are no doubt in it.

But time passes and age accumulates, and with age eyes grow dim, fingers stiffen, and the flow of energy ebbs. And so it is time to publish.

Since I have so freely borrowed from others in beginning this section, I will do so to end it, using the words of Peter Roget in his Preface to the First Edition (1852) of the *Thesaurus of English Words and Phrases*. When I read this I was much struck with the parallels with the writing of this book. He expresses my feelings much better than I could myself. Of course, I do not compare either his great with my much more narrow task, or his splendid with my very limited achievement.

"Since my retirement, finding myself possessed of more leisure, I resolved in an undertaking which, for the past three or four years has given me incessant occupation, and has, indeed, imposed upon me an amount of labor very much greater than I had anticipated. Notwithstanding all the pains I have bestowed on its execution, I am fully aware of its numerous deficiencies and imperfections, and of its falling far short of the degree of excellence that might be attained. But, in a work of this nature, where perfection is placed at so great a distance, I have thought it best to limit my ambition to that moderate share of merit which it may claim in its present form; trusting to the indulgence of those for whose benefit it is intended, and to the candor of critics who, while they find it easy to detect faults, can at the same time duly appreciate difficulties."

Wilbur J. McElwain
10122 NE 126 Street
Kirkland, WA 98034

July 24, 1996

CONTENTS

Preface   iii

Introduction   vii

THE HISTORY

Chapter I   Biographical Sketches   1

Chapter II   Related Families   33

Chapter III   The McIlvaine Family of Sussex County,   45
                 Delaware

Chapter IV   Areas of Early Settlement   57

Chapter V   The McElwain Institute   72

Chapter VI   The Churches of Cumberland County   81

Chapter VII   The McIlvaine Family of Grimet, Scotland   89

Chapter VIII   Sources   96

THE GENEALOGY

Genealogy of the Family of Andrew McElwain and   107
  Mary Mickey

Index to the History   331

Index to the Genealogy   337

MAPS AND ILLUSTRATIONS

Land Warrants Issued to James McElwain and
    Andrew, Robert, and William McElwain, 1786   62

Surveys of the Plantations of James McElwain
    and of Andrew, Robert, and William McElwain   63

The Wills of Andrew McElwain and James McElwain   64

Mercer County in 1873   66

The Borough of New Lebanon, Pennsylvania   67

Sandy Lake Borough, Pennsylvania   68

Program for a Musical Recital at the
    McElwain Institute   78

Program for a Public "Entertainment" at the
    McElwain Institute   79

Two Graduation Programs from McElwain Institute   80

The Big Spring Presbyterian Church (plan)   83

Illustrations from the History of Mercer County   106
    The Fairfield Presbyterian Church
    Portrait of John T. McElwain
    Residence of Gen. J. M. Carnahan

INTRODUCTION

This work consists of two parts, a History and a Genealogy, separately organized and indexed, but paged consecutively.

THE HISTORY

The first part, the History, combines documents and a connective narrative to present what I have been able to learn of the early history of the McElwain family. Most of the documents are presented in full, although this involves including material which possibly could have been omitted. My aim, however, to give both every bit of information available and to provide the little details which help to give full body and flavor to the story, caused me to provide more rather than too little.

By first presenting brief lives of the early family members and of members of certain related families, and then proceeding to provide material on the land in which they lived and the institutions which they knew, I hope to give not merely dry details, but to provide as full a possible a picture as possible of their life and times.

The two parts of the book, where it seemed useful, are keyed to each other by the insertion of serial numbers of individuals in the History, and by notes in the Genealogy.

The source of each document transcribed is stated along with the document. The numerous other sources used are not individually cited. An overall discussion of sources appears in Chapter VIII.

The documents are transcribed exactly as written, except where it is noted otherwise. Spelling has not been changed; spellings which differ from modern usage may be those common at the time, or, probably more often, are the misspelling of the writer or the official transcriber, if it can be said that there is such a thing as misspelling at a time when orthography was considered of comparatively little importance. Abbreviations typical of the period have been written as in the original. The reader will note particularly the habit of using a small raised final letter (or two) of an abbreviation. Another common custom was that of substituting an apostrophe for the letter "e" in a past tense, as in "appear'd". The custom no doubt indicated that the "ed" was not pronounced as a separate syllable.

THE GENEALOGY

Presenting a large volume of data in a concise and convenient form creates unavoidable conflict between completeness and economy. The genealogy here presented reflects the compromises that this makes necessary, but, it is hoped, nevertheless provides sufficient information.

The format is simple. Each family is presented in a separate entry listing the husband and wife (singular or plural as necessary) and the children. Persons who married or had children (whether married or not) appear twice, first in the entry for their parents, and then in an entry for their own families. Persons who did not marry and have no children appear only in the listing with their parents.

Each entry begins with a serial number followed by the family name in capital letters. Two or more family names appear when a woman married more than once. The spouses are then listed, with the name of the descendent of Andrew and Mary Mickey McElwain invariably first. Multiple spouses are designated "s", "t", and so forth immediately preceding the name.

Children are listed only by given name, are arranged, where it is possible, in the order of birth, and are numbered consecutively. If there is more than one spouse, the parent of the child is designated in one of two ways. If the father has more than one wife, the mother of each child is designated by the letters (s, t, etc.), placed in the next to last space in the name column, corresponding to the letter assigned in the spouse section. If the wife has more than one husband, the surname of the father is added to that of the child and is underlined. Children who marry or have children are designated by an asterisk in the last space of the name column, indicating that a subsequent entry provides additional information.

Dates and places are provided in columnar form for births, marriages, and deaths. The place designated is the most precise location known: for example, a person born in Newville would have that designated as the birth place rather than the less definite Cumberland County. Only town, state, and nation designations are used.

Where information could be obtained on the life of an individual it appears either immediately after the parent section or after the section on the children, as appropriate.

The system of serial numbers is of my own devising, although, since the time of its creation, I have learned that similar systems are employed by others.

Numbers are based on descent from Andrew McElwain and Mary Mickey, who were assigned #000000000. Each of their children was assigned a number based on their supposed date of birth. Thus Elizabeth, the presumed eldest child, is #100000000, James the second child, #200000000, and so forth. For succeeding generations the process is repeated. For example, to James' number are added digits to designate his children, again in order of birth, #210000000, #220000000, and so forth. Since some early families had many children it is necessary to use letters to designate digits above nine; thus ten is represented by "a", eleven by "b", and so on. Zeroes are added to the numbers to facilitate computer operations by providing a standard nine-digit serial number.

The serial number enable the user to move backward or forward in the table to find ancestors or descendents with a minimum of inconvenience. To find the parent of a person numbered 123456000, simply go back to serial number 123450000; to find children of that same person, go forward to numbers 123456100, 123456200, and so forth.

The serial numbers indicate the number of generations from Andrew and Mary McElwain. The number of digits other than trailing zeroes is the number of generations. Thus I (#226323100) am of the seventh generation from the founders.

ABBREVIATIONS

Abbreviations I view with considerable aversion, but they are necessary to keep the tables within the boundaries imposed by margins. Most of those used are standard or self-explanatory, but several are the fruits of my imagination and need explanation.

Geographical abbreviations

States -- standard postal two-letter abbreviations

Foreign countries and sub-divisions thereof

Australia	AU	Japan	JP
Canada	CN	Korea	KO
Alberta	AB	Mexico	MX
British Columbia	BC	Sweden	SW
Saskatchewan	SK	Switzerland	SZ
Costa Rica	CR	United Kingdom	UK
Denmark	DN	England	EN
Finland	FN	Northern Ireland	NI
France	FR	Scotland	ST
Germany	GY	Venezuela	VZ

Date abbreviations and symbols

Months are given by the first three letters without a final period.

Approximation symbols (The end position of "c", and the use of the other two of these symbols are unique to this book.)

symbol = to be read as

c = "about" (circa)
< = "or before"
> = "or later"

Thus 1850c should be read "about 1850", and 1850>, "1850 or later". The same rule applies to months: 1850 Sep< should be read "September 1850 or before".

These time symbols are placed immediately following the part of the date to which they relate. The practical reason for this placement is that the dates are taken directly from a data base and the placement in the final position permits sorting by date without interference from the symbol.

Multiple spouses

s = first spouse
t = second spouse
u = third spouse
(no symbols are used when there is but one spouse)

Place of interment

In the death column, "i" is used to indicate the place of interment when it is known and the place of death is not.

SAMPLE ENTRY

    The following illustration will make the format clear.

SERIAL #   SURNAME / ADDITIONAL SURNAME
  McElwain descendent   !date and place of birth   !date and place of marriage   !date and place of death
s spouse   !date and place of birth   ! name of parents of spouse   !date and place of death
t second spouse   !date and place of birth   !date and place of 2nd marriage!date and place of death
                    !   ! name of parents of 2nd spouse!
    biographical and other information related to the parents or the entire family
1 first child   s !date and place of birth   !date and place of 1st marriage!date and place of death
2 second child   t*!date and place of birth   !date and place of 1st marriage!date and place of death
    biographical and other informatiion related to children for whom there is no subsequent entry.

    If the person of McElwain descent was a woman the children's section would appear as illustrated below.

1 first child <u>surname</u>   s !date and place of birth   !date and place of 1st marriage!date and place of death
2 second child <u>surname</u>   t*!date and place of birth   !date and place of 1st marriage!date and place of death

    An asterisk in the rightmost space of the first column indicates a subsequent entry for persons who married or had children.

CHAPTER I

BIOGRAPHICAL SKETCHES

ANDREW AND MARY MCELWAIN (#000000000)

The ancestry of Andrew McElwain, who came to Cumberland County about 1745, continues to elude the efforts of researchers, but there are some clues which may yet provide a solution.

It is probable that Andrew came from Sussex County in what is now Delaware. His will provides the information that his wife was Mary Mickey, and, since there were numerous Mickeys and McIlvaines in Sussex County, it is not unreasonable to regard that area as the original home. Nevertheless, it should be remembered that several sources state that Chester County, Pennsylvania was the place of Andrew's origin.

Apart from Andrew McIlvaine of Cool Spring, whose sons are known not to be ancestors of this Cumberland County Andrew, there were at least three others of the name (in one or another of its spellings) in Sussex County in 1726. It was in that year that Andrew McIlvaine made his will, witnessed by Francis Muckelvane, which left a yearling to Alexander Muckelvane, and 30 acres to Andrew McCalvaine. Andrew McCalvaine might possibly be the person who married Mary Mickey, or any one of the three might be the parent of our Andrew, but no information has been found to prove or to disprove any of these possibilities.

Of the Andrew McCalvaine who received the thirty acres of land nothing certain is known. What is known, however, is that Andrew McElwain of Cumberland County was closely associated with George McElwain, the youngest son of Andrew McIlvaine of Cool Spring, Delaware since he served as an executor of George's estate. There is also some information provided by an early genealogist, Gustav Anjou.

from the *Complete History*, page 100a

Anjou Record
p. 73 [of the Anjou Record]
    The first settlers in Mifflin came there between 1734 and 1738, following the streams and in 1744 three brothers-in-law from Lancaster and Chester Counties, Robert Mickey, William Thompson, and Andrew McIlvaine, who located on Brandy Run on the tract known as the Lusk farm. He was the son of Andrew McIlvain, referred to in his father's will.
p. 85
    The lands of the Kittochinny or Cumberland Valley were purchased from the Indians in October, 1736, but as early as 1730 Andrew McIlvain had received a license for settlement of such lands beyond the Susquehanna as might please him, and his son Andrew availed himself thereof and received a patent to the lands afterward. Most of the settlers came from Lancaster and Chester Counties.

The context of the quoted section poses some problems. It occurs in a section on Andrew McIlvain of Drumore township, Lancaster County (another of the innumerable Andrews), and it is not easy to ascertain whether Anjou is suggesting that the Andrew mentioned as claiming land long after his father is related to Andrew of Drumore or not, but it seems probable that he was not.

A very neat solution to the whole problem would be to take the Andrew who received thirty acres in the Sussex County will to be the father who obtained the original authorization, and his son to be the Andrew who married Mary Mickey, moved to Cumberland County, and is presently causing so much difficulty. But neatness does not replace documentation. The will in which the father mentions his son has not been found, and no information has been uncovered on the family or fate of Andrew McCalvaine and his thirty acres.

Two other possible sources of information on Andrew's ancestry are his supposed sisters. William Thompson, one of the three brothers-in-law in the migration story, married, some sources say, Eleanor McElwain, Andrew's sister. No one has produced a document to sustain this, but the lady must have been either a McElwain or a Mickey. Another sister of Andrew supposedly married a Williamson, but if he or any other Williamson did have a McElwain for a wife, there seems to be no document which mentions that fact. Investigation of these two families might produce some clues.

Once he was established in Cumberland County, Andrew is much less a mystery. There are tax documents which mention him, several anecdotes of his life survive, and, most important of all, his will is readily available and is written in such a manner that it provides a good deal of family information.

Andrew and Mary McElwain settled a tract of almost 400 acres in Hopewell (later Upper Mifflin) township of Cumberland County. Their farm, on Brandy Run, a small creek which flows south into Conodoguinet Creek, was located near the present day community of Heberlig, five or six miles northwest of Newville. There they raised ten children to maturity. The births occurred over a considerable period of time: James, the eldest boy, was born about 1752 and William, the youngest, about 1767. It is probable that Elizabeth was born before James, since she was married in 1770, when James was but eighteen years of age. It is also possible that some of the other girls were born before 1752, but we have no definite information except the order in which the names are mentioned in the will. Apart from Elizabeth, who is mentioned separately, the girls are named in the order Prudence, Ruth, Hannah, Mary, and Elenor. Elenor, who married James Stewart, appears in the 1789 membership list of the Big Spring Church as being 22, which provides a birth year of about 1767. This agrees well with the birth order assumed from the will. The boys are named in order of their birth (James also being separately mentioned): Andrew, Robert, and William. The approximate years of the birth of three of the boys can be calculated from a Big Spring Presbyterian Church census taken about 1789. From the ages given there the approximate dates are James (1752), Andrew (1756), and Robert (1766). William did not appear on the list, but the *Complete History* states that a William McIlvaine was born in Cumberland County in 1767, although without stating a source. That year has been adopted for William since it fits the order of the names in the will, and because none of the other McElwains or McIlvaines in Cumberland County had a son named William so far as is known.

During the years spent in clearing and operating the farm and raising ten children, Andrew and Mary had at least one dangerous brush with Indians, an incident related below.

A reading of the will of Andrew, printed below in its entirety, reveals several bits of information. First, the daughter Elizabeth, whose married name, Nicholson, is mentioned, was willed only 7 shillings 6 pence, and was specifically excluded from any share of the residue of the estate. What disgrace she might have fallen into is not stated. The language of the will makes it seem unlikely that she is excluded because, as was common practice in those days, she had previously, perhaps upon her marriage, been given her part of the estate.

The will also proves that a son Thomas, mentioned in *Torrence and Allied Families*, never existed. This mention repeated in the *Complete History*, and the further mention there of a Thomas McElwayne killed in the assault on Quebec in 1779, has resulted in an erroneous entry in many genealogies listing, as a child of Andrew and Mary, Thomas McElwain, "killed in the Revolution". Andrew's will was written in 1770, five years before the outbreak of the Revolution, and it mentions no son Thomas. It is not possible that a living son who was to be excluded from an inheritance would not be mentioned by Andrew, who meticulously provided Elizabeth with a token inheritance and then specifically excluded her from anything further.

A tantalizing phrase in the will reading "...if all my family should agree to go out to the late purchase..." indicates that there had been a recent acquisition of property, probably, judging by the "go out to" phrase, at some distance. Whether this was the property in Westmoreland County which was later in the possession of Robert and William is not presently known.

Only James received land under the terms of the will. He was about eighteen year old at the time, and did not come into full possession until he became of age. The remainder of the property was to be held until the remarriage or death of Mary, and then sold, with the proceeds to be distributed to Andew, Robert, and William. In the course of time, however, the portion of the farm not willed to James, about 277 acres, came into the possession of Andrew.

Mary Mickey appears in the Big Spring census as age 70. That would place her birth around 1719, if the age is accurate. This is

4

a reasonable date; her brother Robert is supposed to have been born in 1721. It also indicates that her childbearing extended to age 48, assuming the age for William is correct. She was the daughter of Robert Mickey, the fellow traveller and purchaser with Andrew McIlvaine of the property at Cool Spring, Sussex County, Delaware. Since her father arrived in America in 1719, Mary may have been born in Sussex Co.

Little is known of Mary's life, apart from the incident with the Indians. When she died is not known.

Concerning the documents transcribed here some comments are in order. The article on the migration by "Jasper" has about it an air of fiction; one wonders how the writer got such intimate details on events of a century and a quarter earlier.

Both the "Jasper" article and the selection from the History of Cumberland County place the date of the migration too early. James B. Scouler, in the *History of Cumberland County* gives 1744 as the year, Cochrane's *History of Juniata Valley* says the date was about 1745, and Frank C. McElvain, in the *Complete History* remarks that the 1745 date is probably correct. Since Mary Mickey was born about 1719 and Robert Mickey about 1721, they could not have come to Cumberland County as married persons in 1729 or even 1732.

[article from the Newville *Valley Star*, December 16, 1858, signed "Jasper"]

By your request, I shall transfer from memory to paper what little I have heard concerning the early settlement of this neighborhood. About the spring of 1732, Wm. Thompson of Dauphin County, (then Lancaster) conceived the idea that a trip farther west might be attended with great advantages, and accordingly "packed his kit," and came as far as Harris Ferry, now Harrisburg, and was brought over the Susquehanna by Mr. Harris, father of the founder of our State Capital. He then proceeded on until he arrived some three miles west of Newville. He was received cordially by the Indians, who were quite numerous in the district. He threw together a few poles, and covered them with leaves and clay, which answered the purpose of a summer residence. He prepared a piece of ground and planted it in corn, and another in potatoes, of which he took great care during the summer. He built himself a corn-house from rough poles cut near by, and when ripe he husked and stowed away. The summer's labor being over, and his crops secured, he returned to his home and family. He had many an incident to relate to his friends as they sat around their blazing hearths during the winter. It was agreed that he together with his two brothers-in-law, Robert Mickey and Andrew McElvain should return to the new valley. Many were the preparations made during the winter that as soon as the spring opened they, with their families, might at once repair to their western home.

We find them all, toward the latter part of March, pushing forward, unmolested, until suddenly checked by the great river. Again were the services of Mr. Harris required, and the whole party was carefully transported by means of the ferry boat. They finally arrived at their destination, viz: Mr. Thompson's former retreat. Behold the great disappointment of that weary band on discovering a total destruction of Mr. T's crops, the work of foxes, rabbits, rats, etc. They were kindly received by the natives and supplied with provisions until their crops had again produced. Those worthy ancients had big ideas, and thought, being the first settlers, they could claim just as much land as they pleased; so, in belief thereof, they included some forty or fifty square miles of land, which they called their own--Mr. Mickey the southern part of what is now Newton township; Mr. McElwain the northwestern part of Mifflin, and Mr. Thompson occupying a large area between the two former, along Conodoguinet Creek, claiming possession from the south to the north mountain of our valley.

Grand, great-grand, and great-great-grand children of these worthies remain in Cumberland Valley. More anon.

[from *History of Cumberland County* pp. 308-310]

The time of the first settlement in Mifflin is earlier than has been supposed. We have in our possession a letter from Mr. W. C. Koons, a descendent of the maternal side of the Carnahans, who were among the earliest settlers in the township, which we will lay before the reader.

"The first settlers in Newton and Mifflin Townships, then included in Hopewell, were Robert Mickey, William Thompson, and Andrew McElwain. They were brothers-in-law and came at the same time to make their home in this part of Cumberland Valley. Robert Mickey located near the source of the west branch of Green Spring, in Newton Township, William Thompson in the great bend of the Conodoguinet Creek, and Andrew McElwain (or McIlvain) on the "Fountain of Health" Farm, both in Mifflin Township. There is uncertainty as to the particular year of their settlement, but by receipts given to Robert Shannon by John Penn, dated respectively 1732, 1733, and 1734, and a deed on full payment, dated 1735, it is certain that their coming was not later than 1729, as they had preceded Shannon by three years. Still, as the papers indicate that it was not unusual for the settlers to occupy their lands for years before warrants or patents were issued, it is quite possible that the settlements may have been made several years previous to 1729. Soon after they were joined by Stevenson, Shannon, the Carnahans, Nicholsons, Williamsons, and others. These were all Presbyterians, and during hostilities with the Indians they were in the habit of carrying their fire arms with them to church for protection in case of assault.

The Williamson Massacre "The Williamson Massacre, as to date and details, is a matter of tradition. We find it put down as having occurred in 1753 or 1754. The family lived on the farm adjoining Andrew McElwain's tract on the east side. The evening preceding the massacre several men from the Carnahan Fort were stopping at Andrew McElwain's, distant about three miles from the fort. About dusk, Mrs. McElvain went out to look after some cattle. Nearing the stock yard she heard the sound of footsteps, as of men getting over the fence at the opposite side. Believing them to be Indians, she returned to the house and informed the men of what had occurred. The men from the fort remained, keeping watch during the night. About daylight the sound of guns was heard from beyond the hill, in the direction of the Williamsons, nearly a mile distant. Immediately all started for the fort, and after proceeding a little way, it was discovered that a babe had been left in the cradle. Two of the men returned, brought the child away, and all reached the fort in safety. Shortly after their arrival a number of men was sent out from the fort to look after the Indians. Reaching the Williamson farm, they found that the whole family, some eight or nine persons, Mrs. Williamson excepted, had been murdered. I may add, that the only material difference between this and other versions of this bloody affair which have come to my notice, is that Mrs. Williamson, carrying a child with her, escaped.

6

[Will of Andrew McElvain   (transcribed from the original document now in the possession of the Cumberland County Historical Society)]

          In the name of God, Amen.   I Andrew Mc Elvain of the township of Newton in county of Cumberland in province of Pennsylvania farmer being very sick in body but in perfect mind and memory do this fifth day of June one thousand seven hundred seventy make and declare this to contain my last will and Testament in manner and form following that is to say after paying all my lawful debts and funeral charges I leave and bequeath unto my well beloved son James McElvain the lower end of my Plantation the partition line to cross from the Brode or Mody Dulick [the handwriting at this point is quite clear, but the significance of the previous four words is certainly not clear] to a corner of Samuel Williamsons line but not to be given into his possession until he comes to the years of twenty one or marries and two years after he comes of age I allow him to give his executor hereafter to be mentioned twenty pounds but if the land be got to it that is in dispute between me and Hugh Allon then he is to pay thirty pounds which is to be divided in following.   I also give unto my Daughter Elizabeth Nicholson seven shillings and six pence. I also give unto my true and beloved wife Mary McElwane all the rest of my real and personal Estate during her Widowhood for Bringing up Maintainance and Education of my Children, but if she marries before she dies I allow her a bed with the clothing her wheel saddle and bridle and the best riding creature about the house and the one third of all my personal estate beside the Articles above mentioned.   But if any of my daughters should marry before her marriage or decease I allow them their equal part of my personal estate according to the apprisment Elizabeth excepted.   I allow my Executors to Warrant and survey all my Land as soon as they get money to do it with and at the time of my loving wifes marriage or decease which ever happens first I allow and impower my executors to sell the part of my Plantation that I live on and divide the money equally between my three sons Andrew Robert and William also at the same time I allow all the rest of my personal estate to be equally divided between my five daughters Viz Prudence Mary Hannah Ruth and Elonor if they have not got their part before but if all my family should agree to go out to the late purchase I allow my executors to sell all my real and personal estate and divide it as above James equal shares with his Brothers in the Real Estate and I do hereby nominate and appoint my true and loving Brother in law Robert Mickey and my dear and loving wife Mary McElvain Executors of this my last Will and testament hereby revoking all former Wills & testaments by me made and declare this to be my last will and testament   In Witness Whereof I have hereunto set my hand and seal the day and date above writing Signed sealed Published and declared in the presence of us
          William Tomson
          Alex Laughlin   Andrew McElvain SEAL

Cumberland County LS
     Personally appear'd before me John Armstrong Esq. Deputy Register for the probate of wills and granting Letters of Administration for the County of Cumberland, William Tomson & Alexander Laughlin the two subscribing Witnesses to the within instrument of writing who on their solemn oath respectively do say that they were personally present & saw Andrew McElvain the testator therein named Sign Seal publish & declare the same as and for his Testament & last will that at the doing thereof he was of sound and disposing mind and that they subscribed their names as Witnesses to the same in the presence of the Testator and of each other
     Sworn & Subscribed   )
     at Carlisle the 31st day of Aug⁼ᵗ 1770)   William Tomson
     Before   John Armstrong   Alexander Laughlin

Be it remembered that on the 31st day of August 1770 Letters Testamentary issued in common form to Robert Mickey and Mary McElvain Executors named in the Last Will and Testament of Andrew McElvain dec d of which this record is a true Copy Inventory and Account to be [exhibited] at the time appointed by Law Witness my hand and seal the day and year above said.

ELIZABETH MCELWAIN (#100000000)

Apart from the information in her father's will that she married a Nicholson and that she was disinherited, nothing certain is known of Elizabeth. Torrence names her husband as William Nicholson, without giving any source. Frank McElvain further confuses the issue. He lists as a child of Andrew a Mary Elizabeth, married to William Nicholson. Since the will of Andrew names both Elizabeth and Mary, it is evident that Frank has merged two separate women into one. Mary McElwain married John Nicholdson July 29, 1794 at the Big Spring Church; perhaps the similarity of the surnames produced this error.

A microfilm collection of genealogical items published in the Boston Transcript (undated but fairly early in the twentieth century), deals with an Elizabeth McIlvaine Nicholson. Although there are some points of similarity, the apparent existence of a marriage prior to that with William Nicholson would seem to eliminate the possibility that this was the daughter of Andrew, since that daughter must have been young when she married Nicholson, even if she was the oldest of the children. The Cumberland County couple mentioned could well be the daughter of Andrew and her husband. The Westmoreland Nicolsons are the basis of a book, *Nicholson, Bruner, and Getz Family History* by James B. Nicholson; the extensive genealogy begins with William and Elizabeth McIlvaine Nicholson, but offers no solution to the identity. This work was privately printed by the author in 1930; it is probably quite rare, but a copy does exist in the Seattle Public Library.

[Item 982, The *Boston Transcript* genealogy collection]

A William Nicholson came to Westmoreland County, Pennsylvania in the early days of the settlements there. His wife was Elizabeth McElvain. She died about 1800 and the family scattered. The father married again. In the Westmoreland records is found a release of dower interest in the estate of Hugh Park, the first husband of Elizabeth Nicholson, dated August 18, 1798. This release was made to John Willis for 38 pounds and 15 shillings.

Earlier a William Nicholson was in Newton Township, Cumberland County. In 1777 he purchased land from John Kismer and in 1787 he sold this same land to Andrew Patterson, wife Elizabeth signing. Very substantial tradition gives William Nicholson and Elizabeth McElvain twelve sons. The 1790 census records a William Nicholson, six sons, three above sixteen, three younger, living in Franklin Township, Westmoreland County. This looks like the same William. Perhaps some of the sons were married as there was a James Nicholson in Cumberland County, 1786-1795.

8

JAMES MCELWAIN (#200000000)

James was the eldest son of Andrew McElwain and Mary Mickey. He was born about 1752, as computed from the 1789 census of the Big Spring Presbyterian Church, in which he was listed as being 37 years of age. He was again listed as a member of the church in 1808.

On the death of his father in 1770, James was the only son to be willed land. He received a tract of 130 acres and 30 perches, which constituted the southern third of the family farm. James married Mary Nicholson, the daughter of Richard Nicholson, some time prior to 1776. He and Mary had four children, Mary, John, Ruth, and Richard. Mary died before 1789, a date determined by her absence from the membership list of the Big Spring Church. Some time thereafter James married Margaret, surname unknown, by whom he had a fifth child, Margaret. There is no documentary source either for the second marriage or for the birth of the child, but that this is what actually occurred is established with reasonable certainty in the discussion which follows.

James died in 1816 and his sons John and Richard were named as executors in his will, but long before that time John had moved to Mercer County in western Pennsylvania. The details are obscure, but it appears that Richard, who had remained in Cumberland County, administered the estate without John, and, apparently, not to John's satisfaction, because, in 1824, John filed a complaint which resulted in cancellation of Richard's authority, and in new Letters of Administration being issued to John.

The McElwain family histories compiled in the late nineteenth and early twentieth century by descendents of James' grandson John Thompson McElwain, contain many errors concerning James. He was not born in 1729, as they state, and did not come to America in 1750. These histories are also incomplete in mentioning only Margaret as his spouse. They give her the full name of Margaret Bell, which may or may not be correct. There is no documentation that Margaret is a Bell; however, Andrew, the younger brother of James, did marry as his second wife a Margaret Bell. It is possible that the early researchers somehow confused the two women.

The will of James McElwain provides many helps in working out the circumstances of his life. Early genealogies listed Margaret as his wife and made no mention of a first marriage. The fact of the first marriage was eventually worked out from several clues. The will of Richard Nicholson, written in 1791, provided one of these. Richard mentions four of James' children as his grand-children, but makes no mention of a granddaughter Margaret. James, in his will, mentions Margaret as "her" (his wife's) daughter, which he does not do for any of the other four. He does elsewhere also call Margaret "my" daughter. The will of James' wife, Margaret, adds additional weight to the two-wife theory. She does not mention any child as hers except Margaret, and all of her personal property is left to that daughter. The circumstance that first suggested the two wife theory was that in the 1789 Big Spring membership list James appears with no wife being listed for him, although both his brothers have wives listed. Since it is known that children of James were grandchildren of Richard Nicholson, and the Nicholsons were members of the Big Spring Church, it would be remarkable if James' wife was not. Thus it seems evident that she had died before that time. The evidence of the membership list as far as the children are concerned is doubtful. Mary, John, and Ruth are listed, but Richard and Margaret are not. The three children listed were ages 12, 10, and 7. The absence of Richard and Margaret is explained by the fact that children of a very tender age were not listed as members because they had not passed the required theological examination.

Nowhere is there mention of Mary Nicholson, not even in her father's will, in which, if he had been a good will writer, he would have mentioned his grandchildren as "children of my deceased daughter". And so Mary, who is missing entirely from all documents, has been conjured up as James's first wife.

A phrase in the will bequeathing one hundred pounds "to my grandson John McElwains son James McElwain" caused Frank McElwain (Complete History, p. 454) to add a sixth child, James, to the family. How he fell into this error is not evident.

Will of James McElwain   (transcribed from the original document now in the possession of the Cumberland County Historical Society)

In the name of God Amen I James McElwain Weak and Indisposed in Body though blessed be God I feel myself of a sound disposing judgement and memory calling to mind the mortality of My body and knowing that it is appointed for all men once to die do this Twenty Eighth day of March in the year of our Lord one Thousand Eight Hundred and Twelve do make and ordain this to be my Last will and Testament the first place resign my Soul to god who gave it and my Body at death to be Buried in a decent Christian way and maner at the discretion of my Executors and respecting what worldly goods it hath pleased god to bless me with after my lawful debts are discharged I do give and bequeath in the manner following   Imprimus to my beloved wife Margaret I do give and Bequeath the first choise of all my horse creatures and as many of the Cow or Cattle kine as She chooses to keep and what remains of my moveable property that my wife Margaret does not chose to keep I allow to be sold at publick Sale and all my Lawful debts to be Paid out of the moneys ariseing from the Sale and what money remains after discharging the debts I allow My wife to keep for her own and her Daughter Margarets use and further I allow my wife to have the whole of the benefits & profits arising from the real property I now live on to be for her use during her natural life and For a home to my daughter Margaret as long as she and her mother incline to live together but I allow my wife to live on the place I now live on as long as she wishes so to do and at the death of my wife I allow the place to be sold I Bequeath to my Daughter Mary Steel fifty pounds and to my daughter Ruth Carnahan I Bequeath one hundred and fifty pounds and my daughter Margaret McElwain I Bequeath two hundred pounds and I bequeath to my grandson John McElwains son James McElwain one hundred pounds out of the last sales of the land to be lifted [?] by his father and kept for his use until he is of age and further I Bequeath to my two Sons John and Richard McElwain All the remainder of the money arising from the sale of my land Equally divided between them and all the Legatees to be equal sharers in the payments of the legacies agreeably to the Bequeathments and to receive a

10

proportionable Sums out of the moneys Paid in hand and the sales agreeable to the sale of the land and I allow my son Richard McElwain to cut and put into the Barn all the fall grain that is now in the ground him to get one third divided in the shock and my wife Margaret to receive the two parts I allow my Son Richard to cut the meadow and put the hay either in the barn or in sufficient stacks him geting the one half of the hay and my wife the other half   I do by these presents constitute and appoint my two sons John McElwain and Richard McElwain my whole and Sole Executors of this my Last will and Testament but in case any one of them should die I allow my other heirs to choose and to have one appointed in his place I do by these presents constitute make and ordain this to be my last will and testament in witness hereof I have hereunto set my hand and Seal this Twenty Eighth day of March one Thousand Eight Hundred and Twelve

Test Brice Sterrett
      Robert McElwain   Jas. McElwain SEAL

        Cumberland County LS [?]
     Before me George Kline Register for the Probate of wills granting Letters of administration in and for Cumberland County personally appeared Robert McElwain one of the subscribing witnesses to the foregoing instrument of writing and being duly sworn according to law deposeth and sayeth that he saw James McElwain the testator in the same named sign seal publish prounounce and declare the same as and for his last will & testament that at the time of his so doing the said James McElwain was of a sound and disposing mind and memory that he wrote his name thereto as a witness at the request of the testator and in his presence and in the presence of Brice J. Sterret the other subscribing witness who signed at the same time
Sworn and subscribed
This 21st day of Nov. 1816   Robert McElwain
Before me Geo. Kline, Register

        Cumberland County LS [?]
     Before me George Kline Register for the Probate of wills and granting Letters of Administration in and for Cumberland County personally appeared Walter Bell and who being duly sworn according to law deposeth and sayeth that upon examination of the handwriting of Brice Sterret one of the subscribing witnesses to the within instrument of writing is the proper hand writing of Brice Sterret he this deponent being well acquainted with his hand writing having frequently seen him write his name & further sayeth that he believes that the whole instrument is in the handwriting of Brice J. Sterret to which he Brice J. Sterret is a subscribing witness.
Sworn and subscribed
this 22nd day of Nov.   Walter Bell
Before me Geo. Kline Reg'r

Proven 22nd day of Nov 1816

     Letters issued January 20th 1824 to Richard McElwain in the will named John McElwain the other executor named not living this state.
     13th March 1824 in pursuance of a decree of the Registers court the Letters issued to Rich^d McElwain were by the decree of said court vacated and Letters testamentary directed to issue to John McElwain the other executor within named.

     The will of Margaret, wife of James lends credence to the idea that the daughter Margaret was the only child of James and his second wife.   The omission of any reference to the older children would hardly have occurred if they were her own children.

Will of Margaret McElwain, wife of James   (transcribed from the official copy on file in the
        Cumberland County courthouse)

Last Will & Testament) I Margaret McElwain of the Township
        of   ) of Mifflin being Weak of body but of
Margaret McElwain   ) Sound mind and Recollection do make
 Deceased   ) and ordain this my last will &
                        Testament viz 1st I give and bequeath to my daughter Margaret one cow,
one feather bed, Bolster & Pillows under bed and bedstead Two fine Sheets & two course ones,
all the Table Clothes I have all my calico quilts one flannel quilt & one coverlid one pair of
blankets and all my wool and woolen yarn. Four chairs one little pot & Pot Hooks all my
drepor [?] & Cupboard Furniture, Two hogs (her own choice) all my geese my wheel & Saddle.
2nd the grain in the barn the corn in the ground my cow cattle (after Peggy gets her choice)
my sheep & the residue of my hogs & my mare I allow to be disposed of by my executor in the
way he may think most Profitable for the payment of my debts and funeral expenses & should
there be any remainder after these are paid I Leave it likewise to Margaret and do hereby
constitute and appoint David Ralston my sole executor of this my Last Will & Testament.
In witness whereof I have hereunto set my hand & seal the 31st day of July 1823.

Signed in presence of Wm. Lusk   Margaret McElwain (Seal)

Cumberland County Pa
        Before me Frederick Sharrett Regr. for the probate of wills and granting Letters of
administration in and for said county personally came William Lusk the subscribing witness to
the within will and being duly sworn according to Law deposeth and saith that he saw & heard
the Testatrix Margaret McElwain sign seal publish pronounce and declare the within instrument
of writing as & for her Testament & Last Will that at the time of her so doing she was of a
sound and disposing mind memory & understanding to the best of his knowledge observation and
belief   That he subscribed his name thereto at the request of the Testatrix and in her
presence.
Sworn & subscribed   Wm Lusk
September 27th 1823 before me F. Sharrett

Cumberland County Pa
        Before me Frederick Sharrett Register for the probate of wills & granting Letters of
administration in and for said County Personally came Richard McElwain and being duly sworn as
the law directs deposeth and saith that he was well acquainted with Margaret McElwain the
Testatrix in the within will named and that he was well acquainted with her handwriting having
often seen her write and that the name Margaret McElwain signed to said will the deponent
verily believes to be the proper hand writing of said Testatrix & further saith not
Sworn and subscribed October 19th 1823)   Richard McElwain
before me F. Sharrett, Regr.   )
Be it remembered that on the 26 day of September 1823 the last will and Testament of Margaret
McElwain Decd. was duly proven & Letters Testamentary issued the 17th day of October A D 1823
to the executor therein named.   Inventory and account to be exhibited in the Time appoined
by law.
            Witness my hand F. Sharrett, Register

    Margaret, the child of James and Margaret McElwain survived
her mother only five years. She had never married and therefore
distributed her worldly goods to various female relatives.   She
specifies the relationship of her sister-in-law Rosanna and a
niece, Margaret.   As there was no niece Margaret in Cumberland

12

County at that time, it might be conjectured that the person referred to was Margery, a child of Rosanna born in 1822, although what a young child would do with an adult-sized coat is hard to say. The several misspellings of McElwain, which indicate a careless copyist, lend some weight to this possibility. Elizabeth B. McElwain is another child of Rosanna. The lack of information on the Nicholson family makes it impossible to identify Elizabeth H. Nicholson. The mention of Margaret Steel, however, provides a clue concerning the family of Mary, the eldest of the children of James and his first wife Elizabeth Nicholson, as is discussed in the section on Mary.

Will of Margaret McElwain, daughter of James and Margaret McElwain   (transcribed from the official copy on file at the Cumberland County courthouse).

The last will and }   I Margaret McIwane of the township
Testament of   }   of Mifflin do make and ordain this
Margaret McElwaine)   my last will & testament. First it
  ~~~~~~~~~   is my will I bequeath to my sister in Law Rosanna McIwane my crape dress my best flannel frock and white Linnen under coat and to my niece Margaret McIwane my coat. And to Elizabeth H. Nicholson my white frock and white cotton petticoat and to Elizabeth B. McIwane my Bonnet, and any other of my clothing not mentioned I leave to Rosanna McIwane to be divided among her children.   I bequeath to Margaret Steel a flannel quilt a tow sheet a table cloth and my wheel. To Elizabeth H. Nicholson a calico quilt a fine linnen sheet and a table cloth.   And further I bequeath to my Brother Richard a good suit of clothes out of the remainder if there is any thing left after all the expences is paid out.   And further to Margaret McElvane my Bed the remainder of my Bedding and all other of my personal property not otherwise mentioned.   And also I allow my executor to purchase half an acre whereon the Buildings stand the Buildings excepted and if this purchase is made the Lot and any remainder of money is to be divided equally among the female heirs of Richard McElvane after him and his wifes decease.   And I do hereby constitute and appoint William Brown Jr. executor of this my last will & testament.
In Witness whereof I have hereunto set my hand and Seal this seventeenth day of April 1828.
Signed, Sealed and }
acknowledged   }   Margt. McElvain (Seal)
in presence of   }
David Ralston   }

Cumberland County, Pa
        This fourth day of February 1829.   Before one Abraham Hendel Deputy for Jacob Hendel Esq. Register for the probate of wills and granting Letters of Administration in & for said County, personally came David Ralston the subscribing witness to the within instrument of writing and being duly sworn according to Law, deposeth and saith that he was present and saw and heard the testatrix Margaret McElvain, acknowledge the same as and for her testament and last will, that at the time of so doing she was of perfect and sound mind, memory and understanding to the best of his knowledge, observation and belief.   That he signed his name thereto as a witness at the request and in the presence of the Testatrix.   Deponent further saith that Rosanna McElvain (wife of Richard McElvain) was present when the acknowledgement above mentioned was made by the Testatrix, and that he deponent did not know it was necessary to have two witnesses thereto.   David Ralston
Sworn and Subscribed Before me Abm. Hendel for Jacob Hendel, Reg.

Cumberland County, Pa
     This thirty first day of March 1829.   Before me Jacob Hendel Esq. Register for the probate of wills and granting Letters of Administration in and for said County, personally came Letitia McCulloch and being duly sworn according to Law, deposeth and saith that about six months previous to the death of Margaret McElwain in the foregoing instrument named, she said Margaret requested this deponent to call on William Brown Junr. in said instrument named and request him to come and write her will;   In two or three days after said Margaret told deponent that said Brown had drawn her will and that she was now satisfied, that said Margaret died some time in October last; Deponent Further Saith that said Margaret at the time refered to was of sound and disposing mind, memory & understanding, and continued so, Deponent having often visited her during that time.

Sworn and Subscribed }   her
  Before me   }   Letitia X McCulloch
Jacob Hendel Reg: }   mark

     Be it remembered that on the thirty first day of March A D One thousand eight hundred and twenty nine, the last will and testament of Margaret McElwain late of Mifflin township in the County of Cumberland decd. was legally proved, and that Letters Testamentary were issued same day to William Brown Junior the executor in the said will named. Inventory and account to be exhibited in the time appointed by Law.
     Witness my hand Jacob Hendel Regr.

MARY McELWAIN STEEL (#210000000)

    Mary was the eldest child of James McElwain and Mary Nicholson. Three of her younger brothers and sisters moved to Mercer County, and when their descendents in the late nineteenth and early twentieth centuries compiled the family histories she was not mentioned. That fact would lend support to the idea that she lived out her life in Cumberland County and had faded from the collective memory of her western relatives.

    Her existence and her marriage is documented by the will of her father who refers to her as Mary Steel. The name of her husband has not been positively established, but a grave marker in the cemetery of the Big Spring Church for Robert and Mary Steel, she being born Feb 1, 1776, makes it highly probable that this is James' daughter and her husband. In the 1789 membership list for the church Mary's age is given as twelve. This makes a not quite exact match, but since there is some question as to the actual date of the list it is close enough to provide some support for this relationship.

    Further circumstantial evidence for this conclusion is provided by the 1850 census which lists Mary (age 74) and Margaret (age 32) Steel as residents of Newville. The 1828 will of Margaret McElwain, who never married, left various items of personal property to several females, one of whom was Margaret Steel. Unfortunately, Margaret is the only person whose relationship to her she does not specify, but if Margaret Steel is

Mary Steel's daughter, she would be the niece of Margaret McElwain, a logical person to be among the list of female relatives named.

In the abstract of the will of Robert Steel given here the name of the daughter "Marret" is probably an copyist's error for Margaret. Robert was survived by three sons and two daughters. This branch of the family has never been contacted by any McElwain researcher and it is not known if there are any living descendents of Mary and Robert Steel. Margaret does appear in the 1860 census for Cumberland County, still unmarried, but having in her household two young persons also named Steel, John, age 15, and Mary, age 12, both born in Illinois. No indication of relationship appears in this census.

Abstract of the will of Robert Steel

personal property to wife Mary, and the house; the house to be sold after her death, and the proceeds to be divided between daughter Letchea [Leticia?] and stepson John Nickerson, son Robert Steel, and daughter Marret Steel. $1.00 to son Matthew Steel and $1.00 to son James Steel to be paid one year after the property is sold, if demanded. Executors Joseph McKibben and son James Steel.
dated July 25, 1831; proved September 3, 1836
The executors renounced the executorship, and Letters of Administration were issued to James McCandless.

JOHN S. MCELWAIN (#220000000)

John was born about 1779 in Cumberland County, Pennsylvania. He married Hannah Thompson, the daughter of Andrew Thompson and Elizabeth Bell, at the Middle Spring Presbyterian Church on March 21, 1805. The couple moved to Mercer County, Pennsylvania in 1806, where they lived the rest of their lives. They had eleven children, nine of whom attained maturity, Hannah died May 5, 1829 at age 42; John died on Nov. 14, 1845 at age 66. Both are buried in the Fairfield Cemetery at the Fairfield Presbyterian Church in New Vernon township, Mercer County. Neither a will nor estate papers have been found for John.

John was a farmer, but records of Mercer County show a John P. McElwain as town supervisor in 1808 and a John S. McElwain as constable in 1809. Whether the John P. is a mistake or a an entirely different person has not been determined.

When James McElwain died in 1816, naming his sons John and Richard as executors of his will, John was not able to be present at the probate session and Letters of Administration were issued to Richard. Apparently John eventually became dissatisfied with this arrangement, for in 1824 he filed a complaint with the Register for Probate of Wills and Granting Letters of Administration of

Cumberland County. The result was that John was appointed administrator in Richard's stead. The delay from November 1816 until January 1824 may be explained by the fact that Margaret McElwain, James' second wife, died about September of 1823, and John may have been reluctant to complain while she remained alive. What is known of the story is told in a document of the Register.

CUMBERLAND COUNTY, SS

By the tenor of these Presents:

I, FREDERICK SHARRETTS, Esquire, Register for the Probate of Wills and Granting Letters of Administration in and for the County of Cumberland in the Commonwealth of Pennsylvania, Do make known unto all men, that on the day of the date hereof at Carlisle before me was Proved, Approved and Insinuated the last Will and Testament of James McElwain Deceased (a true copy whereof is to these presents annexed) having whilst he lived, and at the time of his death, divers goods and chattels, rights and credits, within the said commonwealth, by reason whereof the approbation and insinuation of the said last Will and Testament and the committing the Administration of all and singular the goods and chattels, rights and credits which were of the said deceased, and also the Auditing, the Accounts, Calculation and Reckoning of the said Administration, and a final dismission from the same to me are manifestly known to belong: And that administration of all and singular the goods, chattels, rights and credits of the said deceased, any way concerning his last Will and Testament was committed to John McElwain and Richard McElwain the said John not being present the said Richard in the said Testament named only having been first sworn well and truly to administer the goods, chattels, rights and credits of the said deceased, and make a true and perfect inventory thereof: And exhibit the same into the Register's Office in the borough of Carlisle, on or before the twentieth day of February next ensuing, and a just and true account, calculation and reckoning of your administration, to render at or before the twentieth day of January in the year of our Lord one thousand eight hundred and twenty five or when thereunto lawfully required.

In Witness Whereof I have hereunto set my Hand and Seal of Office at Carlisle the twentieth day of January in the year of our Lord one thousand eight hundred and twenty four.

F. Sharrett, REGISTER

[Inserted at this point is the text of James' will, identical to that transcribed in the above section on James McElwain (#200000000)]

Cumberland County, SS

Whereas at a Registers Court to held at the Registers Office in the Borough of Carlisle for the said County on Saturday the thirteenth day of March 1824 before Jacob Hendel Esquire Register for the Probate of Wills and granting Letters of Administration in and for the said County and the Honourable John Reed Esquire President and James Armstrong Esquire Associate Judges of the Court of Common Pleas for the said County an application of John McElwain one of the executors named in the Testament and last will of James McElwain deceased That Letters Testamentary had issued by Frederick K. Sharrett Esquire late Register for Probate of Wills and granting Letters of administration for said County to Richard McElwain the other executor in said will named, on the twentieth day of January A. D. 1824, which said Letters Testamentary it is alleged issued illegally.

Whereas notice having been given by citation to the said Richard McElwain to appear before this Court on Saturday the thirteenth day of March AD 1824 at two oclock in the afternoon of the same day to shew cause why said Letters Testamentary so issued as aforesaid should not be revoked and new Letters Testamentary issued and proof being made of the due service of the said citation.

And whereas it appearing to the said court that the said Letters Testamentary had issued illegally to the said Richard McElwain It is ordered and decreed that the same Letters Testamentary be revoked and further it is ordered that new Letters Testamentary on the said testament and last will of the said James McElwain deceased be issued by the said Register of Probate of Wills and granting Letters of Administration for said County.

Jacob Hendel, Reg^r
John Reed   ) Judges of the
James Armstrong) Common Pleas

JOHN THOMPSON MCELWAIN (226000000)

John Thompson McElwain spent most of his working life as a business man in the town of New Lebanon, Mercer County, PA. He owned a general store and had various other interests, which made him one of the more prosperous citizens of his community. His life story can be gleaned from several documents reproduced here.

A generous benefaction to an educational institution resulted in it being named in his honor. The McElwain Institute was housed in a handsome structure, and offered education at a level beyond the elementary grades. John served on the board of the Institute until his death. The Institute continued to operate for many years with varying fortunes, and finally closed when the modern public high school became common. The original structure still stands, but has declined from an educational into a religious function. Some historical material on the McElwain Institute is presented in a separate chapter.

Mary McCracken, John's wife, was the daughter of Joshua McCracken and Mary Zahniser. Separate sections are devoted to those two families in the "Related Families" chapter.

From *History of Mercer County, Pennsylvania* (1877), p. 143

JOHN MCELWAIN

Among the truly representative men of Mercer county, few, if any, have been more intimately associated with the material development of New Lebanon and vicinity, than John McElwain, the well-known merchant, farmer, and stock raiser. He has not only witnessed the transition of his native township from a thin settlement into a populous and prosperous region --but, in his own person has typified so admirably the agencies which wrought these changes, that no history of Mercer county would be complete without some sketch of his life, labors, and character.

Mr. McElwain was born on the 3d of December, 1817, on a farm in French Creek township, settled by his father about the year 1806. His early life, like that of most of our successful business men, was one of close application, self-reliance, and self-denial. From early boyhood to his twenty-first year, he worked by the day, and month, to help support a large family, early bereft of a mother's tender care. In 1838, he started out on his own account, seventy-five cents constituting his entire capital. He walked from his home to Sharon, a distance of thirty miles, without dinner, paid fifty cents for his supper and lodging, arose with the lark on the succeeding morning, and hired to a house joiner, before breakfast, at thirteen dollars a month. Here his faithful industry continued for a period of eleven years. In 1843, he married Miss Mary McCracken, a member of a highly respectable family, and a native of his own township. In 1849, he was stricken with a malignant kidney disease; but, nothing daunted, he mounted crutches, and went to teaching music and canvassing for books, in order to support his family. He then purchased a small farm, with the fruits of his economy. In April, 1852, he sold his farm advantageously, and then embarked in the merchandising, farming, and stock-raising business. Accurate knowledge, a venturesome disposition, and a quick mercantile apprehension enabled him to spread his operations with the best results, until, at the present time, he is one of the wealthiest men in the part of the county in which he resides.

The good fortune which has attended Mr. McElwain in all his transactions, was not, in any sense, accidental. It was a necessary consequence of untiring industry, good management of his interests, and, above all, of a firm, uncompromising spirit of personal honor and integrity. When he began trade, the speculative tendency, which has so conspicuously marked the conduct of mercantile pursuits in this country, of late years, was comparatively unknown; capital was limited, business principles few and simple, and the standard of individual rectitude severer than we find them in our day. Hard and persistent labor, diligence, punctuality in fulfilling engagements, and, to use a trite but expressive phrase, "square dealing" were then the prime factors of success. These Mr. McElwain possesses in a remarkable degree. The above is high praise, but it is only the reflex of the prominent facts in his history; and what, to the strange reader, may seem peculiarly the language of eulogy, will be readily recognized, by all who know him, as a mere statement of the salient points of his character, and features of his business career.

In politics, Mr. McElwain is a Republican, having been identified with the party since its formation. He was a firm supporter of the Administration during the Rebellion, and for its suppression gave liberally of his means. It is truly said of him that no soldier's wife or child ever left his store empty handed, and, while he suffered, in a pecuniary point of view, by his generosity, he consoles himself with the reflection that he did some good, and that he has enough of this world's fortune left. He doubtless realizes the truth of the Scriptural injunction: "Cast your bread upon the waters, for it shall return after many days." His elder son served through the war in a way alike creditable to himself and to the patriotism of his father.

In religion, Mr. McElwain is a Presbyterian, of which church he is a liberal supporter. He has raised a family of seven children--four sons and three daughters--all young men and women grown; the sons all Republicans, and the daughters intending to support that ticket so soon as "Women's Rights" shall be an established fact. The family of Mr. McElwain, under the blessings of Providence, are in the full enjoyment of excellent health, and are now reaping the benefits of his well-spent and industrious life. And he, too, is hale and hearty, and will doubtless live many years to partake of the blessings of his labors, and, dying, will leave behind him "footprints in the sands of time."

WILL OF JOHN THOMPSON MCELWAIN   (transcribed from the original document on file in the Mercer
    County courthouse)

Jan. 9th, 1883

        I John McElwain of Mill Creek Tp. Mercer Co. Pa.   Being of Sound Mind Memory & Under-
standing knowing of the uncertainty of Life and the Certainty of Death Do Make and Ordain this
My last Will and Testament.
Item 1st   That I desire and direct My Executors to pay all just debts and Funeral Expenses,
        together with a Monument Worth from one to two Hundred dolls. to be placed at my Grave.
Item 2nd   I leave the sum of Three Thousand dolls. for the use of my beloved wife to placed
        on interest which interest together with so much of the principal as necessary for her
        ample maintenance and comfort to be furnished her by my executors herein after Named and
        if necessary to draw further [two words illegible] the proceeds of my estate.
Item 3rd   I further direct that I give & bequeath My son Cyrus P. McElvain all my Oil [two
        lines illegible] together with all fixtures & Machinery connected with the mills and
        works.
Item 4th   I give and bequeath   My son David McElwain fifty acres of land situated in New
        Vernon Tp. Mercer Co. Pa Bounded by Wm. McGee on the West, Hoyt and Campbell on the North
        East [one word illegible] the same is conditional that he pay to my Executors a certain
        note of hand amounting to sixteen hundred dolls., together with accrued interest
        theron.
Item 5th   I give and bequeath my son Harvey McElwain the Farm designated as the old Homestead
        situated at the Village of New Vernon Mercer Co Pa containing some forty five acres more
        or less there being one Hundred dolls. rent due on same which is to be paid to the
        Executors. Said Farm is Valued at [four digIt figure is illegible]
Item 6th   I set apart Two Thousand dolls. to My son Allexander McElwain the interest of which
        is to be divided equally between him and his wife share and share alike during their life-
        times and at their decease the principal is to go to their children share and share alike
        all of which is to be arranged by my Executors [several words illegible]
Item 7th   I set apart the sum of Two Thousand dolls. to my son Watson the interest of which he
        is to Receive annually during his lifetime & in case and on condition he should take him-
        himself [one word illegible] go to work & become agreeable and of steady habits for the
        space of Two or more years I direct My Executors to pay the said Amt. to him. But in case
        he does not reform then and in that case the said Amt. is to be equally divided between
        his brothers and sisters share and share alike at his decease
Item 8th   I Give and bequeath to My son Adam McElwain My store house distilling house and Lot
        on which they are situated in the Borrow of New Lebanon Mercer Co Pa & also the Undivided
        one half of the Farm on which I now reside in   [boundaries are described,   but these six
        lines are illegible]
Item 9th   I Give and bequeath My son Wm. P. McElwain my stock and interest in the McElwain
        Institute at New Lebanon Mercer Co Pa and also the Undivided one half interest of the farm
        on which I now reside situated in Mill Creek Tp. sd Farm containing about 60 as. Balance
        of the same divised to my son Adam before instructed in this will [several words illeg-
        ible] share and share alike & also one thousand dolls. less the amt of the notes which I
        hold against him
Item 10th   I give and bequeath My daughters Theresa & Emma McElwain the fifty acres of land
        situated partly in Mill Creek & partly in New Vernon Tps Mercer Co Pa Bounded East H.Reed
        West by Hills McCracken & [illegible] and valued at $2000 dolls   I also bequeath Theresa
        My Dwelling House in the Borrow of New Lebanon & the lot on which it is situated [remain-
        der of page is almost all illegible, but it appears that Theresa is also given $400 and
        Emma another house and lot]   I also Bequeath Emma the sum of $500 dolls. and is to have
        the right to have such furniture out of the house or household goods she may wish which is
        not taken by Theresa to be [counted?] out of the Five Hundred dolls.

Item 11th I Also Bequeath to my Daughter Melinda Miller the sum off Fifteen Hundred dolls. in
    addition to what she has already recd.
Item 12th I also give and bequeath My Daughter Anna Bell McElvain the sum of seventeen Hundred
    dolls. & the Pianna.
Item 13th I also give & Bequeath My Grandson John McElvain the sum of one Hundred dolls.

    I hereby require My Executors to pay the amounts herein Bequeathed in the order in which
they are left or bequeathed as soon as practicable after my decease and I further authorize
direct and require the same Executors to make Execute & deliver to the heirs heretofore mentioned the pieces of land or town lots to each as is herein specified to them their heirs or
assigns the same as I might or could do if living.
    In Witness Whereof I John McElvain hereunto set my hand & seal to this My Last Will and
Testament & hereby select & appoint James Lindsay & W. P. McElvain my Executors.

            John McElvain (ss)

    We James Lindsey & J. F. McCormick parties being present & at his request do hereby
witness this the last Will & testament of John McElvain & did sign the same as such as being
signed by him in our presence.   James Lindsay
                                      J. F. McCormick

RUTH MCELWAIN CARNAHAN (#230000000)

    Ruth married Adam Carnahan on February 5, 1802 at the Big
Spring Presbyterian Church in Newville, Pennsylvania, and the
couple apparently moved to Mercer County shortly afterward.

    According to the *History of Mercer County, Pennsylvania* Adam
had settled a tract in Sandy Lake township in 1797, but it turned
out that the land had already been claimed by another. The
following year he took up a tract near Milledgeville. In 1799,
desiring to return to civilization for a time, he persuaded a
family to live on his land and hold the land for him. As might
have been expected, when he returned to claim his land, the other
family refused to move, feeling he had no better claim than they.
In 1800 he finally found a permanent place in French Creek
township. He must thereafter have returned to Cumberland County
to marry. *The History* mentions a daughter born to Adam in 1801 as
possibly the second white child born in the County. This
information conflicts with date for the marriage. Because the
marriage date is from the records of the Big Spring Church it is
almost certainly correct. Either the story of the birth is in
error, or the child must have been born and died in late 1802.

    Adam was a farmer. He and his wife raised their family on
the property he originally settled in French Creek township.
Their presence in Mill Creek township in the 1850 census is the
result, not of a move, but of a new township being created.

    Ruth died on June 23, 1853 at age seventy two, and Adam on
August 25 of the same year, three months before his seventy-sixth
birthday.   Adam's death certificate was registered by a son-in-

law William Zahniser; it gives the date of death as August 26, and the cause as "piles".

The will of Adam discloses, as do so many of the wills in this volume, an evident problem with a son. A bequest of $500 was given into the control of the wife of his son Adam, Junior. That wife, Mariah in the will, appears in most records as Mary Jane. The young couple had no children at the time, so the strange word "speci" which appears in the transcript of the will should very probably be "issue", which would make sense of the passage.

[Mercer County, Pennsylvania, Vol. 3, page 432, transcribed by O. D. Carnahan from an abstract on film #878,967 in the LDS Family History Library]

to my son James M. I give and bequeth 5 dollars, and to my son Adam I give and bequeath 500 dollars or rather it is my intention that his wife Mariah shall have the above named few hundred dollars for her use and under her control during my son Adam's life and at his decease it is my will that if he should die without speci [sic] then the said five hundred dollars to be divided equally among all my other children and to my daughter-in-law Mariah I give and bequeth one hundred dollars for her own use and benifit. To my daughters Margaret Walker, Mariah Rhodes, Elizabeth Thompson and Ruth Zahniser I give and bequeath one hundred dollars each, and to my daughter Nancy Hannah I give and bequeath forty dollars, also a judgement note I hold again John Hannah of the docket of the Prothenitary of mercer county also it is my will and desire that the nett proceeds arising from my estate from my decease until said estate can be sold to advantage it all be equally divided among all my children also I direct the residue of my estate after the aforesaid sums have all been paid be divided equally between my sons John and William S. I likewise make and constitute and appoint William Zahniser and Adam Thompson to be executors of this my last will and testament.

RICHARD MCELWAIN (#240000000)

Richard married Rosanna Thompson, a sister of Hannah, the wife of his brother John. Richard and Hannah remained in Cumberland County for many years after John had moved to Mercer County, according to the McElwain Family Histories, but a document, dated 1808 transferring their interest in the land inherited by Rosanna from her father, gives their place of residence as Mercer County. Other documents, dated 1818 place them in Cumberland County. Census records show them in Cumberland County in 1810, 1820, and 1830, and in Mercer County in 1840. It appears that they may have moved to Mercer County for a time and then returned to take over the Cumberland County family farm between 1808 and 1810.

The 1812 will of James gives Richard authorization to cut the grain and hay in the fields and retain a portion for himself, clearly indicating that Richard was in Cumberland County. Richard also appeared at the proving of the will of his step-mother, Margaret McElwain, in 1823.

Just what happened after the death of James is not at all

clear, but in 1818, parts of the farm were sold at a sheriff's
auction in satisfaction of debt. In 1824 there arose some
difficulty concerning the administration of James's estate and
Letters of Administration which had been issued to Richard were
cancelled and new letters were issued to John.

Some of the McElwain Family Histories state that Richard and
Rosanna were buried at the Fairfield Presbyterian Church
graveyard, but there is no record of this in the Mercer County
Cemetery Records, Volume VIII. There is no reason to doubt the
statement, however, since markers sometimes are never placed on a
grave, and sometimes they crumble away or sink into the ground.

[Sale by Richard and Rosanna McElwain of land inherited from Andrew Thompson (pp. 141-143 of an
unspecified Cumberland County deed book)

Deed Richard McElwain et uxor To Joseph Culbertson

This Indenture made this second day of January in the year of our Lord one thousand Eight
hundred and Eight Betwixt Richard McElwaine and Rosanna his wife of Mercertown in Mercer
County and the State of Pennsylvania of the one part and Joseph Culbertson [several words
illegible] of Franklin County and state aforesaid beginning [several words illegible] John
McKees thence by the same lands north Eighty one degrees west one hundred and sixty perches
and a half thence south twenty two degrees west one hundred and seventy nine perches and three
fourths to a Post, thence south seven degrees west one hundred and twenty two perches to a
dogwood thence south eighty three degrees East seventy perches and one half to a post thence
north seven degrees East one hundred and two perches to a post thence north forty two degrees
East fifty three perches and a half to a post thence south Eighty three degrees East one
hundred and fifteen perches to a Chestnut oak and thence north forty one degrees East one
hundred and thirty two perches to a white oak thence North fifty three degrees west sixty three
perches & thence West fifty six perches to the Place of Beginning, which said decedent did
by his last will and Testament devise and bequeath unto his six daughters, viz Jean Elizabeth
Sarah Prudence Hannah and Rosanna Reference being had to said will it will more fully appear,
which the aforesaid Rosanna did sell to the aforesaid Joseph Culbertson being bound by an
Instrument of writing bearing date December the 20th 1804 to convey it at the period of
arriving at full age which said Rosanna is since intermarried with the aforesaid Richard
McElwaine NOW KNOW Ye that the aforesaid Richard McElwain and Rosanna his wife, Heirs at
law of the said Andrew Thompson deceased hath granted bargained and sold and by these presents
doth grant Bargain sell alien enfeoff release and confirm unto the aforesaid Joseph Culbertson
their full sixth part of the above described tract or parcel of land Containing two hundred and
sixty acres and ninety seven perches and allowances to which the said Richard McElwain and
Rosanna his wife could by will by law or Equity have claimed (subject nevertheless to the sixth
part of the widows dower yearly during her natural life and the Residue of the purchase money
and fees of Patenting to be defrayed by the said Joseph Culbertson) and the aforesaid Richard
McElwain and Rosanna his wife doth by these presents for and in the consideration of one
hundred and forty pounds to them in hand paid the Receipt of which is hereby acknowledged and
themselves therewith fully satisfied before the Ensealment and delivering of these presents
hath granted Bargained sold Aliened Enfeoffed and confirmed unto the aforesaid Joseph
Culbertson his heirs and assigns and to the only use and behoof of him the aforesaid Joseph
Culbertson his heirs and assigns forever and the aforesaid Richard McElwain and Rosanna his
wife doth covenant and agree to warrant and defend the aforesaid sixth part of the before
described tract or parcel of land and their claim or Right of the Building Improvements woods

ways water courses and hereditaments thereunto belonging unto or appertaining will forever
warrant and defend from all manner of Persons setting up any claim from through by or under
them or Either of them and defend by these presents, And In testamony of and in Confirmation
of the above the parties have Interchangeably set their hands and affixed their seals the day
and year above written.
In presence of   Richard McElvain {Seal}
William Ritchvan [?] Robert Shannon   Rosanna McElvain {Seal}
            Received the day of the above date one hundred and forty pounds the full
consideration money above mentioned I say received by us
      Test   John McKee   Richard McElvain Rosanna McElvain
Cumberland County LS
            Be it Remembered that on the date of the above Instrument came before me
the subscriber one of the Justices of the peace in and for said County Richard McElvain and
Rosanna McElvain (she being apart Examined by me) and acknowledged the above instrument of
writing to be their act and deed in order that the same may be Recorded as such In testimony of
which I have set my name and seal of office the above date.
John McKee {Seal}
That Martha Thompson Widow and Relict of Andrew Thompson Hath Released of Dower to the above
undivided sixth part of Richard McElvain above specified is certified by her signature in
presence of the subscribing witness.

                                             Martha Thompson
Recorded March the 28th 1808 & Compd by - Francis Gibson Recorder

Sheriff's Deed Book, Cumberland County, Pennsylvania, pages 331 and 337

1080 Deed Poll from Andrew Mitchell to Robert McElvain
    Came into Court Andrew Mitchell Esqr., High Sheriff of Cumberland County and produced a
Deed Poll from him to Robert McElvain of the township of Mifflin and County of Cumberland dated
the 6th day of January 1818 - For the one undivided third part of a certain Plantation and
Tract of land situate in Mifflin Township adjoining lands of Jacob High, John Allen, and others
- Containing one hundred and thirty acres more or less with a log dwelling house and double
barn thereon erected - also a large Apple orchard thereon (as the property of Richard
McElvaine) which was seized and taken in execution and sold as the property of Richard
McElvaine, at the suit of Andrew McElvaine by public vendue or outcry on the 7th day of
November 1817 to the said Robert McElvain for the sum of one hundred and thirty five dollars
lawful money of Pennsylvania, he being the highest and best bidder and that the highest and
best price bidden for the same - Which Deed Poll the said Sheriff acknowledged in open court
the 6th day of January 1818 to be his act and deed and desired the same might be recorded as
such. No. 137 January 7 [?] 1818

1102 Deed Poll from Andrew Mitchell to Isaac Creslip
    Came into Court Andrew Mitchell, High Sheriff of Cumberland County and produced a Deed
Poll from him to Isaac Creslip dated the 7th day of November A.D. 1818 - For the one
undivided sixth part of a certain Plantation or Tract of land situate in Mifflin Township
adjoining lands of Jacob High, Hugh McElhany and others, containing one hundred and thirty
acres more of less with improvements and subject to the Payment of certain specific legacies
with the Life Estate of the widow of James McElvain, decd., seized and taken in execution and
sold as the property of Richard McElvain and Margaret McElvain at the suit of Andrew McElvain
by public vendue or outcry on the 7th day of August A. D. 1818 to the said Isaac Creslip for
the sum of forty dollars of lawful money of Pennsylvania, he being the highest and best bidder
and that the highest and best price bidden for the same - which Deed Poll the said Andrew
Mitchell, Esq. as aforesaid acknowledged in open Court the 7th day of November A. D. 1818 to be
his act and deed and desired it might be recorded as such. No. 267 August 8, 1818

23

ANDREW MCELWAIN (#400000000)

Andrew's birth year is estimated from his age, 33, given in the 1789 Big Spring census. He appears there with his wife Elizabeth, age 30, and three children, Mary, Robert, and Jane. He appears also in a 1790 list as the holder of pew 75, and finally in 1808 as a member with four unnamed persons in his family.

At the time of the death of his father Andrew was about fourteen years of age. He received no land under the terms of the will; the land not willed to James, the eldest son, was to be sold eventually and the proceeds divided among the male heirs. Andrew and his two younger brothers, Robert and William, obtained a warrant for the 277 acres on November 16, 1786. This entire tract was listed as the property of Andrew in the roll for the 1798 United States Direct Tax. Robert and William, however, still had part ownership and in the following year half of the tract was was sold to Robert Lusk and the other half, by the surrender of the rights of the two younger brothers, became the property of Andrew.

A few years after the death of Andrew's elder brother, James, a judgement was obtained by Andrew against Richard McElwain, the son of James, which resulted in the sale of portions of the land which had belonged to James. A one-third interest in James' land was purchased at auction by Robert, the oldest son of Andrew, and a sixth part by Isaac Creslip. The text of the two documents appears in the section on Richard McElwain (#240000000).

Andrew married twice. His first wife was Elizabeth Shannon, daughter of Robert Shannon, who had been captain of the company in which Andrew had served in the Revolutionary War. Robert mentioned Andrew and two of Andrew's children in his will, proved in 1796. Andrew married a second time on August 26, 1790, so Elizabeth must have died between the time of the Big Spring census, in which she appears, and that date. There were seven children from this first marriage.

Andrew's second wife was Margaret Bell. There were numerous Bell families in Cumberland County at that time, but it has not been determined from which Margaret came. There were six children from this marriage.

About 1819 Andrew made an agreement to turn the farm over to his son Robert, reserving a portion for a retirement residence. Robert was required to construct a residence for Andrew and his wife, and it specifies in some detail just how the home was to be constructed. Andrew died before the project could be completed.

Agreement   ) Article of Agreement made and agreed upon
Andrew & Robert) between Andrew McElwain Senr and Robert
McElwain   ) McElwain Witnesseth that the said Andrew McElwain hath bargained and sold
to the said Robert McElwain the plantation he now lives on containing one hundred and thirty
eight acres & three fourths with allowance, on the following conditions viz at the rate of

sixteen dollars and fifty cents per acre exclusive of the allowance, one half to be paid on the first of April next (1820) viz Eleven hundred and forty four dollars & sixty nine cents & the other half in Eight equal yearly payments said Andrew McElwain is to give said Robert a clear right for said land clear of all encumbrances (excepting what is hereafter mentioned) with privilege to put in a crop this ensuing fall and full possession of the whole on the first of April next (excepting as hereinafter mentioned)   and whatever part of the hand money Robert McElwain does not advance on the first of April 1820 he is to pay interest for untill it is all paid (from that time)--and said Andrew reserves during his lifetime and the life of his wife Margaret two acres and one half of the aforesaid land next the cross roads one acre of plough land and one acre and a half of meadow ground to extend from the road at the run up the run and across towards & over the Newville road as far as it will require.   and said Robert McElwain doth bind himself to build on the aforesaid lot of two and & a half acres a good log house seventeen by twenty three feet one story and a half high with two floors a division on the first floor, convenient stairs to the loft a stone chimney a cellar under the house half the size of the house with a door to it, and sufficient light in the house and to put a good shingle roof on it all at his own expense.   And likewise to build a convenient stable on said lot sufficient to keep a horse and two cows in with a loft for hay and to give said Andrew McElwain during his life and the life of Margaret his wife pasture for two cows and one horse along with his own cows and horses -- And said Robert to fence off the aforesaid lot and to keep the fences and building in good repair during the lives of Andrew and Margaret McElwain who are to have full possession and use of the aforesaid lot with the buildings and improvements during their lives or either of them but they are not to put any of the buildings or improvements out of repair unnecessarily and at the death of Andrew & Margaret McElwain the aforesaid lot buildings improvements to be Roberts, said Andrew and Margaret is to have possession of the back room or stone part of the old house with liberty to cook at the kitchen fire and Robert is to keep them in firewood until the aforesaid building is completed with the fences which Robert is to do within one year after the first of April 1820.

Present Thomas McElwain   Andrew McElwain (Seal)
         Wm Lusk   Robert McElwain (Seal)

Received the day of the date of the foregoing article from Robert McElwain eighty dollars in part of the hand money therein mentioned.   Recd by me $80.00
         Test   Andrew McElwain
         Wm Lusk
Cumberland County, Ls
     Before me the subscriber one of the Justices of the Peace in and for said County personally came William Lusk and Thomas McElwain the subscribing witnesses to the aforesaid instrument of writing and being duly sworn as the law directs deposeth and saith that they were present at the execution of the aforegoing article of agreement and saw Andrew McElwain and Robert McElwain signing the same and that they subscribed their names thereto as witnesses and that the names William Lusk and Thomas McElwain are in the proper handwriting of deponents.
Sworn and Subscribed May 12th 1820   Wm Lusk
Before me Samuel Weise   Thomas McElwain
Entered May 13, 1820   Compared with the original

     The *Complete History* states that Andrew's estate was settled in 1820, but no will or administration papers have been found. There is extant, however, both a bill for Andrew's funeral expenses and a Vendue Paper, the report on the sale of his personal property which gives a detailed description of what sort of personal articles people of the time owned, and of their value.

(from *The Valley Times*, Newville, PA, Thursday, June 18, 1942)

The Estate of Andrew McElvain Debtor to Robert Peebles
for the Funeral, April 8, 1820.

21 Yards Muslin at 75 cents	$ 4.50	18 Black Handkerchiefs	13.50
10 Pair Silk Gloves	5.00	1 Pair Black Stockings	1.00
6 Pair Gloves	3.00	2 1/2 Yards Crepe	2.50
1 pair White Stockings	.50	1 Yard Muslin	.75
Silk and Thread	.25		
			$31.00

The Vendue Paper Of Andrew McElwain has been transcribed in a way that approximates its appearance as closely as possible, apart from the obvious difference in the appearance of handwriting and typewriting. The peculiarities of spelling, the abbreviations (including "Dᵒ" as well as ditto marks), and the abbreviation of given names with the elevation of the final letter, appear here as they do in the original. The handwriting differs markedly from modern style only in the use of the long, or medial, "s", which looks, to the unaccustomed eye, much like a modern "f" with the lower loop reversed. The pages were not numbered in the original.

The purchasers seem to be, for the most part, members of the family of the deceased. It is not certain if Andrew's second wife was alive in 1820, but the frequency of the purchases by a Margaret McElwain indicates that she was. The other McElwains were all children of Andrew: Robert, William, James, Thomas, and Sarah. That James was present indicates that he had not yet moved to Ohio. James Stewart was the husband of Andrew's daughter Jane. Thomas McKinney and Andrew Failer were probably relatives of husbands of Andrew's daughters. The remainder of the purchasers are neighbors.

Most of the items sold are familiar at least by name to modern readers, but a few may not be. A heckle (hackle) is a comb for dressing flax or hemp, a steelyard is a device for weighing objects, and a clevis is a U-shaped device for attaching a chain to a shaft. "Dastraff" is probably either a variant spelling or a misspelling of distaff, a stick used in spinning.

The appearance of a half cent in several of the prices gives the impression that there was a coin of that denomination in circulation, but the fact that the half-cent occurs only in the amount of 12 1/2 cents or a multiple of that amount indicates that the coin is probably a Mexican (Spanish) silver real, known as a "bit" which for some time circulated in the United States at the value of 12 1/2 cents.

Vendue Paper of the Property of Andrew McElwain, decᵈ this 10ᵗʰ day of May 1820

1

	Purchaser's Name	Article	Price
	Thoˢ McKinney	One Corn hoe	$ 0:41
	Robert McElwain	One Dᵒ	0:49
	Thoˢ McKinney	One Dᵒ	0:32
	Robert McElwain	One Dᵒ	0:20
Note	Wᵐ McElwain	One Dung Shovel	0:35
Note	Dᵒ	" Dᵒ Fork	0:61
	James Stewart	" Dᵒ Hook	0:59
	Robert McElwain	" Pair Mall Rings	0:30
	Dᵒ	" Iron wedge	0:40
	Thoˢ McKinney	" Pitchfork	0:27
	Robert McElwain	" Dᵒ	0:20
Note	Wᵐ McElwain	" Foot Adze	0:30
	Robert McElwain	" Handsaw	0:50
	Mathew Steel	" Scythe	0:12½
Note	Wᵐ McElwain	" Broad ax	0:15
Paid	Hugh McElhinny	Two Fishing Gigs	0:35
	Robert McElwain	One Log chain	0:75
	Thoˢ McKinney	" Half bushel	0:42
	Robert McElwain	" Pair double & Single Trees	0:79
	Margaret McElwain	" Ax	1:01
	Robert Shannon	" Drawing Knife	0:65
			9:18½

2

		One pair Andirons	0:41
	Margaret McElwain	One pair Andirons	0:41
	Dᵒ	" " Shovel & Tongs	0:76
Note	James McElwain	" " Horse Gears	2:25
	Robert McElwain	" set Plow Irons	3:00
	Dᵒ	" Plough	2:00
	Dᵒ	" pair Chains	0:37½
	Dᵒ	" Crosscut Saw	2:00
	Thoˢ McKinney	" Cutting Box	4:00
	James Stewart	" Waggan tire, pr lb, 4 cts 38 lbs	1:52
Note	Wᵐ McElwain	" Dᵒ 4 cts 34 lbs	1:36
	Robert McElwain	" Lot Iron Bands &	0:17
	James Stewart	" Do Boxes Iron &	0:36
	Robert McElwain	" Do Clevis	0:15
	Dᵒ	" Still, worm & Furnace Door	6:55
	Dᵒ	" Iron Square	0:30
Note	Wᵐ McElwain	" Gun	2:36
	Margaret McElwain	" Heckle	0:17
	Dᵒ	" Smoothing Iron	0:25
	Robert McElwain	" Painted chest	0:31
Note	Wᵐ McElwain	" Walnut Dᵒ	3:00
paid	Wᵐ Stevenson	" Plain pine Dᵒ	0:50
Note	Andʷ Failer	" Lot barrels	0:16
Note	James McElwain	" Cradle	2:57
			34.52½

3

		One Frying Pan	0:69
Note	Wᵐ McElwain	One Frying Pan	0:69
	Margaret McElwain	" Kettle & lid	0:75
	Dᵒ Dᵒ	" Dᵒ without lid	0:30
	Wᵐ Lusk	" Dᵒ broken	0:07
	Robert McElwain	" Griddle	0:33
	Elisha Carson	" Dinner Pot	0:78
	Margaret McElwain	" Large Dᵒ	2:01
	Dᵒ	" Barrel [?]	0:50
	Robert McElwain	" Pewter dish	0:38
	Thoˢ Allen	" Lanthern	0:41
Note	Andrew Failer	" Sorrel Mare	45:25
	Elisha Carson	" Saw	5:36
	Robert McElwain	Two Spotted Barrows	4:00
	Dᵒ	One splayed sow	1:80
	Dᵒ	Four Shoats	5:50
	Dᵒ	One Red Calf	4:25
	James Stewart	" Black Cow	10:00
	Margaret McElwain	" Red Cow & Calf	12:00
	Dᵒ	" Red & white Dᵒ	12:00
	Robert McElwain	" Sled	1:00
	Wᵐ Lusk	" Pair Steelyard	0:30
	Margaret McElwain	" Crook	1:00
	Robert McElwain	" Dᵒ	:55
			109:23

4

		Lot Chairs (6)	1:75
	Margaret McElwain	Lot Chairs (6)	1:75
	Robert McElwain	One Ewe and Lamb	2:00
Note	James McElwain	" Dᵒ " Dᵒ	2:50
	Robert McElwain	" Hogshead	0:30
	Margaret McElwain	" Lot wheat, 4 bush.	2:50
	Robert McElwain	" Remainder per bush. 65 cts, 4 bush	2:60
	Dᵒ	" Hogshead	0:30
	Margaret McElwain	A Butter Cask	0:50
	Dᵒ	one Cag	0:12½
Note	William McElwain	Three Barls	0:50
Note	Thomas McElwain	A Washing Mashin	0:39
	Miss Sarah McElwain	Womans Sadle & Bridle	15:50
	Margaret McElwain	A Can of Lard	0:25
	Dᵒ	" Dastraff [?]	0:76
	Robert McElwain	" Mans Sadle	0:60
	Margaret McElwain	" Reel	0:25
	Dᵒ	" Womans Sadelle	2:00
	Dᵒ	" Breakfast Table	0:75
	Robert McElwain	" Lot Logs	1:60
	James Stewart	" Calfskin	0:50
Note	Wm McElwain	" Dining Table	1:76
	Margaret McElwain	" Spinning Wheel	0:12½
	Dᵒ	" Dᵒ	1:00
	Wm McElwain	" Stove & Apparatus	16:25
	Margaret McElwain	" Looking Glass	0:75
			55:55

	Margaret McElvain	Bureau	4:00
	D°	One Bedstead, Bed &	
		bedding	30:00
	Sarah McElvain	" bed & bedding	29:00
Note	James McElvain	" Bed	6:00
	Margaret McElvain	" Chaff bag & matt	0:25
	Robert McElvain	" Bedstead & cord	1:00
	Margaret McElvain	" Sheet new	1:00
	D°	" Quilt	0:25
	D°	" Coarse Table cloth	0:50
Note	Tho° McElvain	" Sheet	0:80
	Margaret McElvain	" D°	1:26
Note	James McElvain	" D° new course	1:65
Note	Thomas McElvain	" D° " D°	1:96
	Margaret McElvain	" Table cloth fine	1:50
	D°	Two hand towels	0:50
	D°	One Blanket (coulered)	0:75
	James McElvain	Two Blankets	2:02
			82:44
			55:55½
			109:23
			34:52½
			9:18½
			290:93½

Andrew McElvain
estate

Vendue Paper

filed 29° Oct 1820

RUTH MCELWAIN (700000000)

Ruth married George McIlvaine who was the son of John McIlvaine, and the great-grandson of the Andrew McIlvaine who came to Sussex County in 1719. They married about 1779, lived for a time in Cumberland County, and then moved to Washington County. The time of the move is not certain. A note in Ordway's *The House of Grimet* would place the move between the births of their third and fourth children, or about 1785. As George appears in the 1790 census as a Washington County resident this date seems reasonable, although George himself, in a pension application made many years later, stated that it was 1791. He was eighty-two years of age at the time and may not have remembered accurately, although his other remembrances seem clear enough. The land warrant secured by George was issued in 1798, but that of his brother Greer, which included both his and George's land, was issued ten years earlier. Since settlers often occupied land for many years before seeking a warrant, the warrant date cannot be relied upon to determine the date of occupancy. A letter to Frank McElvain from Judge J. A. McIlvaine, written in 1903, puts the date at 1787, and another letter, written in 1914 by W. A. H. McIlvaine of Washington, Pa. moves it back to 1775. This last date is far too early, as George mentioned in his pension application that he was drafted into the Revolutionary Army at Shippensburg in August 1776. Both he and Greer were stated to be residents of Hopewell township (no doubt

28

Cumberland County, although there is a Hopewell township in Washington County) when they sold land in 1785.

Recorded in the *Complete History* are abstracts of documents describing the sale of the land inherited from John McIlvaine, and a veterans pension application made by George late in his life.

[Cumberland Co., Pa. Records, from Complete History, p. 429]

George McIlvane et al, to George Shoemaker, two deeds, dated April 25, 1785 and recorded Aug. 23, 1785 - Book H, Vol. I, p. 67.

George McIlvain, taylor, and Ruth his wife, and Grier McIlvain and Elizabeth, his wife, all of the township of Hopewell, one part and George Shoemaker, other part, farmer, ... By a Proprietory warrant dated the 26th day of July, 1744 to James McIlvaine for a tract of land called Cat's Cabin, in Hopewell township, then in Lancaster County, on the Conodoguinet Creek. James McIlvaine before his decease, made a will which was dated 8th April A D 1754 and gave the lands to his son John McIlvaine, including 300 acres (or in all 300 acres) called Cat's Cabin, record of which is on file in the Register's office at Lewes, Sussex Co., Delaware. The said John McIlvaine died and left a widow named Mary McIlvaine and issue, George McIlvaine, Grier McIlvaine and Catherine, married to Robert Luckey. Catherine and her husband released their share of the land to her brothers George and Grier McIlvaine and now they too sell the land for 963 pounds Pennsylvania Currency.

[Revolutionary War Records, Room 1851, Navy Building, Washington, D. C. The Pension Papers also bear No. 33336. (from Complete History, p. 429a)]

George McIlvaine, son of John McIlvaine, personally appeared and made application No. 6735 for a pension November 4, 1835; was about 82 years old; was a resident of Somerset township, Washington Co., Pennsylvania. That he was drafted in August 1776, at Shippensburg, Pa., where he was residing, as a private in the Company of Capt. Robert Culbertson, of the Regiment commanded by Colonel Davis of Carlisle, Pa. That he marched from Shippensburg to Carlisle, to Lancaster, Philadelphia, Trenton, New Jersey, New Brunswick, and Perth Amboy, where they engaged in repeling the landing of the British. Served three months. Was again drafted and served three months. A third time he was drafted and served as Lieutenant for one month against the Indians at Yellow Creek Station on the Ohio River, this time in the Company of Captain Edward Todd. Total service was seven months. He removed from Shippensburg to Somerset township Washington County, in June 1791, where he continued to reside. He further testified that he had no documentary evidence to produce as to his services in the Army, because he had at no time received a written discharge, but that his brother Greer McIlvaine, was familiar with his record. One Boyd Mercer, a clergyman, resident of Bethlehem Township testified to substantiate the facts given by George McIlvaine.

ROBERT AND WILLIAM MCELWAIN (#900000000 AND #a00000000)

The two younger sons of Andrew McElwain and Mary Mickey were born about 1766 and 1767. They both moved to Westmoreland County before 1799. Rather little has been learned about their lives.

Robert's birth in October 1766 is taken from an entry in the International Genealogical Index. Data obtained from that source must always be viewed with a certain amount of skepticism since anyone can submit material and it is not possible for the accuracy of the submission to be checked. However, Robert does appear in the 1789 census of the Big Spring Church as age 22, which would indicate a birth about 1766 or 1767. He was at that time living with Mary McElwain, age 70, no doubt his mother. A third member of the household was his wife Elizabeth, age 20. He also appears in the 1790 Federal Census. His household at that time consisted of himself and three females. The inadequate information provided in the early censuses does not make it possible to identify this third female; a reasonable guess would be a daughter of the young couple, but there is no corroborating evidence whatever.

Robert is also heard from in 1786 when he and his brothers Andrew and William warranted the 272 acres of the original homestead which were not left to James. Some time thereafter Robert and his wife moved to Westmoreland County. The Westmoreland County rolls for the United States Direct Tax of 1798 list two persons named Robert McElwain. It is not known which is our Robert, but it is probable that he is the one in Hempfield township, since there is also a William McElwain in that township, and it was common for relatives moving to distant places to locate close to each other.

Robert and Elizabeth signed a deed transferring the land in Cumberland County to Andrew McElwain and Robert Lusk in 1799. Thereafter we have no certain knowledge of him or his wife. The census of 1800 lists two Robert McElwains in Hempfield township, and a Robert McIlwain appears in North Huntington township in 1810 and 1830. It has not been possible to relate any of these to Robert, the son of Andrew McElwain.

William was the youngest of the four McElwain sons. He was born about 1767. The *Complete History* (p. 447) states, that a William McIlvaine was born in Cumberland County in that year, without offering either a source or any further details. None of the other William McElwains born in that area have births anywhere near that time, so this may be Andrew's son, despite the variant spelling of the name.

William does appear with Andrew and Robert on the land warrant for 277 acres issued in 1786. He was not on the membership list of the Big Spring Church in 1789, posssibly having gone to Westmoreland County by that time.

Information on William was entirely lacking until quite recently. Then there appeared in some correspondence information that William had married a woman named "Liddie", and this led to another clue which stated that he and his wife had a daughter Elizabeth who married John Love. Finally Debbie Hayes-Wolfe produced a list of the ten children of the John and Elizabeth Love, and from there it was a simple matter to search the census records and to compile at least skeleton outline of the family down to the early years of the twentieth century.

No researcher presently working on McElwain genealogy has had contact with any members of this family, but there are numerous persons of the name Love in the western counties of Jefferson, and Clarion, among others. Debbie Hayes-Wolfe has not made clear her relationship to this family.

[Sale of property to Robert Lusk (transcribed from a document in the Cumberland County Courthouse]

Deed of Conveyance   :   This Indenture made the second
And⁼ Rob* & W⁼ McElvaine :   day of October in the year of
to Robert Lusk   :   our Lord one thousand seven hundred and ninety nine between
Andrew McElvaine of the township of Mifflin in the County of Cumberland and the State of
Pennsylvania and Margaret his wife & Robert McElvaine of Westmoreland County of the state
aforesaid & Betty his wife & William McElvaine of said County and State aforesaid and Lidey his
wife of the one part & Robert Lusk of Mifflin township & County of Cumberland and state
aforesaid of the other part Witnesseth that the said Andrew McElvaine and Margaret his wife &
Rob* McElvain & Betty his wife & W⁼ McElvain and Lidey his wife for and in consideration of the
sum of ten hundred & thirty eight pounds eight shillings of Lawful money of Pennsylvania to
them in hand paid by the said Robert Lusk at and before the sealing and delivery hereof the
receipt whereof is hereby acknowledged, have granted, bargained sold aliened enfeoffed released
assigned & confirmed & by these presents do grant bargain sell alien enfeof release assign &
confirm to the said Robert Lusk his heirs and assigns forever a certain tract of land situate
in the township of Mifflin in the county of Cumberland & the state aforesaid bounded by the
following lines, to wit, Beginning at a dog-wood grub thence by land of Andrew Patterson north
forty nine degrees west sixty and a quarter perches to a post thence by land of Thomas Martin
north sixty four degrees east sixty nine perches and quarter to a white oak north 29 degrees
east forty eight perches to a chestnut tree north seventeen degrees west thirty one perches to
a hickory north twenty nine degrees east eighty six perches to a white oak north forty two
degrees east seventy perches to a post south fifty eight degrees east fifty one perches to a
white oak thence by land of John Morrow & of David Ramsey south fourteen degrees east forty
seven perches and a half to a hickory thence by land of D. Ramsey south twenty nine degrees
east thirty nine perches to a post, thence by land of Andrew McElvain south fifty degrees west
two hundred and fifty perches to the place of beginning Containing one hundred and thirty
eight acres & three quarters & allowances of six per cent for roads & it being one Moiety or
half part of two hundred and seventy seven acres and seventy three perches which said tract was
surveyed in performance of a warrant dated the 16th November 1786 granted to Andrew, Robert &
W⁼ McElwain with the appurtence to have and to hold the said tract or parcel of land, with the
apurtenance unto the said Andrew Robert & William McElwain & their heirs & assigns forever as
tenants in common with a patent granted to said Andrew Robert & W⁼ from the Commonwealth of
Pennsylvania bearing date the fifth day of September 1799, and the said Andrew McElvain &
Margaret his wife Robert McElvain & Betty his wife & William McElvain & Lidey his wife together

with all and singular the buildings improvements ways woods water water courses rights liberties hereditaments & appurtenances thereunto belonging or any wise appurtaining and the reversions & remainders rents and profits and all the estate rights title property claim and demand whatsoever them the said Andrew Robert & William McElwain & their wives or any of them of unto or out of the same to have and to hold the said messuage or tract of one hundred and thirty eight acres and one fourth and allowance of land hereditaments and premises hereby granted or mentioned so to be with the appurtenance, unto the said Robert Lusk his heirs and assigns for ever, free and clear of all restrictions and reservations, as to Mines royalties Quit rents or otherwise excepting reserving only the fifth part of all gold and silver Ore, for the use of the Commonwealth, to be delivered at the pits Mouth clear of all charges and the said Andrew Robert & William McElwain and their several wives for themselves their heirs executors administrators doth hereby covenant and agree and grant to and with the said Robert Lusk his heirs and assigns that them the said Andrew Robert & William McElwain and their wives & heirs to and against all & every other person & persons whatsoever laying any claim thereto shall and will warrant & forever defend by these presents-in witness whereof the said parties to these presents have hereunto Interchangeably set their hands and seals the day and year

	Andrew McElwain (Seal)
Sealed and delivered in presence	Margaret McElwain (Seal)
of John Curt-William Roseberry	Robert McElwain (Seal)
	Elizabeth McElwain (Seal)
	William McElwain (Seal)
	Lidey McElwain (Seal)

Received Octr the 19th one thousand seven hundred and ninety nine of the above named Robert Lusk the sum of ten hundred & thirty eight pounds eighteen shillings & 9^d which is the full consideration money above mentioned Rec^d by me being present Andrew McElwain - Jane Lusk Robt McElwain - Andrew McElwain

Westmoreland County, LS Be it remembered that on the day of the date of the above indenture Before me Wm Jack one of the associate Judges in and for said county came the above named Robert McElwain and Elizabeth his wife and William McElwain and Lidey his wife and severally acknowledged the above Indenture as their voluntary act and deed and desired the same may be recorded as such according to Law the said Elizabeth and Lidey by me being examined separately and apart from their said husbands declared they freely became parties to the above Indenture without any compulsion or coercion from their said husbands. In witness whereof I have hereunto set my hand and seal the day and year above written.

Wm Jack (Seal)

Cumberland County LS Be it remembered that on the nineteenth day of Octr one thousand seven hundred & ninety nine before me the subscriber one of the Justices of the Peace in and for the County came the above named Andrew McElwain and Margaret his wife she being of full age & being examined separately and apart from her husband & acknowledges the above Indenture to be their act & deed to the intent the same may be recorded as such according to law In witness whereof I have set my hand and seal. (Seal) Robert Patterson
Entered the 10th day of February 1800 Compared George Kline, Recorder

The 1800 census for Hempfield township of Westmoreland County, as mentioned, does have entries for two Robert McElwains and a William McElwain. Although it is not presently possible to relate these positively to the two sons of Andrew McElwain, the two who are adjacent in the census are probably the brothers. The other Robert, several pages away, has a wife too young to be Elizabeth McGlaughlin, Robert's wife. The ages for the adults match those of the families perfectly.

| Age | Robert | | William | | Approximate years |
	M	F	M	F	of birth
under 10	0	2	1	3	1791 or later
10-15	1	1	2	0	1785-1790
16-25	0	0	1	1	1775-1784
26-44	1	1	1	1	1756-1774
45 and +	0	0	0	0	1755 or before

If these are the correct Robert and William both probably had children. The male and female aged between 16 and 25 listed as members of William's household are unlikely to be his children as he was only 33 at the time. Elizabeth, the only child of William who is known was not born until two years later, and we have no idea how many other children there may be.

CHAPTER II

RELATED FAMILIES

RICHARD NICHOLSON (died 1793)

Richard Nicholson, the father of Mary Nicholson, lived on a 289 acre farm located on Whiskey Run, a small creek just east of Brandy Run. He was the son of Richard and Isabel Nicholson of Cumberland County. What little further is known of his genealogy is given in the family tree following his will.

The reader will no doubt be delighted by the stipulation in Richard's will by which he ensures that his most precious possession, his clock, will remain in the possession of some one in his legitimate blood line by leaving it to his son, James, with the proviso that if James does not have "issue of his own body lawfully begotten" the clock will then go to his son William. The value and rarity of clocks at that time is evident by his unwillingness to have the clock go to a wife who had not borne children, or to an illegitimate child.

Aside from this curious stipulation, Richard's will does provide some information and additional suggestions for research. The mention of only four of James' children provides strong evidence that the fifth child, Margaret, either was not yet born or that she was not Richard's grandchild. Richard did have a daughter named Margaret, but there is no evidence to indicate whether or not this might be James' second wife. The daughter was evidently unmarried at the time, and it would not be surprizing for James to have married the sister of his deceased wife. This idea could be quickly disproved if another husband could be found for Margaret, but no one has as yet offered any such evidence. If the second wife was Margaret Nicholson the marriage probably took place after Richard's death in early 1793, since he would have re-written the will under those circumstances.

THE WILL OF RICHARD NICHOLSON

Richard Nicholsons last will   In the name of God Aman I
and Testament   Richard Nicholson of the
                    Township of Newton in the County of Cumberland farmer calling to
mind the uncertainty of this Transitory life and knowing that it is appointed to all Men onc to
die Do this twenty Sixt of April in the year of our Lord one Thousand seven hundred and ninety
one make and ordain this Instrument of writting to contain my last will and Testament in form
and manner following that is to say after paying all my lawful debts and funeral charges. I
give and bequeath unto my dear and loving wife Mary Nicholson two Cows one Calf and a year old
Stear and all my household furnitor (only my clock) I also give and bequeath to my daughter
Margerey forty pounds lawfull Money, I likewise give and bequeath unto my Daughter Sarah Twenty
pounds lawfull Money--I also give and Bequeath unto my Daughter Ann twenty pounds lawfull money
--I likewise give and Bequeath unto my daughter Margaret forty pound lawfull Money to be given

her out of that Money that is coming to me from my son James, I give and bequeath unto my Son James my Clock but and if my said Son Should die without issue of his own body lawfully begotten then and in that case I allow and it is my will that he [?] be given to my son William or his hears I give and bequeath unto William Stevenson five pound to be paid him out of that money that is coming to me from my son James, I give and bequeath unto Mary Stevenson William Stevensons Daughter five pound to be paid her out of the Money that is coming to me from my son James, I give and bequeath unto my grandson Isaac Shannon ten pound to be paid him out of that Money that is coming to me from my son James. I also give and bequeath unto my two Gransons John and Richard McElvain five pound each to be paid them out of that Money that is coming to me from my son James. I also give and bequeath unto my two Grandaughters Mary and Ruth McElvain five pounds each to be paid them out of the Money that is coming to me from my son James. I likewise give and bequeath unto James Stevenson John Stevenson Deceased Son five pounds to be paid him out of that Money that is coming to me from my son James I likewise give and bequeath unto my grandson Benjamin Gamble ten pound lawfull Money to be paid him out of that Money that is coming to me from my son James -- I also give and bequeath unto my son William all my wearing Apperral both linning and wolling and also all the remender of my estate that I am possessed of now or Shall be possessed of at the time of Death and I do hereby Nominat constitute and appoint my true and loving Son James and my true and loving stepson William Stevenson to be my whole Executors of this my last will and Testament hearby revoking and disannulling all former wills and Testaments by me made and declare this to be my last In testimony whereof I have hereunto Set my hand and Seal the day and date aforesaid.

Signed Sealed and pronounced in presence)
of us Hugh Laughlin, Alexr Laughlin) Ric. Nicholson (SEAL)
N. B. I allow and it is my will that my son William Should give each of my son James Negroes seven shillings and sixpence out of his share

Be it remembered that on the 6th day of March 1793 the last will and Testament of Richard Nicholson Decd was legally proved of which the foregoing is a true copy and letters Testamentary issued in common form to James Nicholson Executor having resigned on the said 6th day of March 1793. Inventory and account to be exhibited into the registers office in the Burrough of Carlisle in the time appointed by law. Witness my hand
Willm. Lyon Regr.
[There appears to be a copyist error in the last paragraph. Perhaps it should say that William Stevenson resigned.]

ANDREW THOMPSON (died 1792)

Andrew Thompson lived in Hopewell Township, Cumberland County. He was the father of Hannah, who married John McElwain, and of Rosanna, who married Richard McElwain. He had five other daughters by his first wife, Elizabeth Bell.

The existence of Elizabeth was, until recently, not known, it being assumed that Martha, the wife named in Andrew's will, was the mother of his seven daughters. Some expressions in Andrew's will first raised questions concerning the wife he mentioned there. He stated that Martha was to have "all of the Goods and Chattles that she possessed at the time of our marriage", not something that one would say about a wife of sufficient years to have bourne seven children. He went on to say, "as long as she and my children can agree" they should continue to live together on his property, making it clear that the children were his, but not hers. Then the record of a marriage for a Thompson, first name not given, and Martha Denison was found. This, despite its incompleteness, seemed sufficient to justify further investigation. An article on the Bell family of Dauphin County by Raymond Bell seems to clear up the matter. Mr. Bell, who has collected a very large number of Bells in his publications lists Elizabeth Bell as the wife of Andrew Thompson. Although no documentation is given, Mr. Bell's credentials (F.A.S.G) and the obvious thoroughness of his research, combined with the use of Elizabeth Bell as given names for daughters of both Hannah and Rosanna was enough to convince both me and Carol Zapolnic (after we had discussed the matter in an extended correspondence).

Andrew's ancestry has not proved as easy to determine. He may be the son of Hugh Thompson who died in Hopewell township in 1761, leaving his property to his wife Mary, his son Andrew, and his daughter Mary. There is nothing, however, that makes the connection certain. There were a great number of Thompson families in Cumberland County at the time, though none can be connected with Andrew. A Joseph Thompson also died in Hopewell township in 1761, but his will establishes that he had no son named Andrew.

At the time of Andrew's death his eldest daughter, Mary, was married, but the others were minors. The birth year for Hannah has been established with some degree of certainty: her gravestone gives her date of death as May 5, 1829, age 42 years, which provides a birth year of about 1787. Raymond Bell gives 1783 as the birth year of Prudence. The relative ages of the girls can be determined from the order in which their names appear in the will and from court records relating to the administration of the will. Of course there is always conflicting data; here it is the age of 75 given for Rosanna in the 1860 census, which would place her birth in 1785.

It seems that Martha and the children did not agree, since in 1797 the farm was advertised for sale. It did not sell quickly and was advertised again in 1800. The property occupied 260 acres according to the advertisement, which agrees with the data given in the tax rolls for the United States Direct Tax of 1798.

WILL OF ANDREW THOMPSON

The Last will and Testament) In The Name of God Amen I
Andrew Thomson Decd   ) Andrew Thomson of the Town-
                 ship of Hopewell in the County of Cumberland and State of
Pennsylvania being very Low and weak in Body though Blessed be God of a Sound judgement and
memory now Calling to mind the Mortality of my Body and knowing that it is appointed for all
men once to Die Do this fourteenth Day of may in the year of our Lord one thousand Seven
hundred and ninty two make and ordain this my last will and Testament in the first place I
Recommend my Soul at Death to God who Gave it and my Body to be Buried in a Decent Christian
manner at the Discretion of my Executors and as touching what Worldly Goods it has pleased God
to bless me with I do Dispose of them as follows to wit I do allow one hundred acres of my Land

36

to be Solde in four years after my Decease and I do allow s⁴ hundred to be sold by my Executors
where John Wilson has his improvement and they are to have as full a pover to sell and transfer
s⁴ land as I Could or might have vere I present.
     Imprimus to my Beloved wife Martha I do Give and Bequeath my Sorrel horse and all and
Singular the Goods and Chattles that She posesed at the time of our Marriage and as Long as She
and my Children can agree and it [is] thought by the other Executors and her to be best for her
and them to live on the place that Such time She is to have the one thirds of the Benefits of
s⁴ place while the[y] live together and in Case it would answer them best to part and Quit the
place then She is to have in Lue of her Dover yearly and Every year During her Natural Life the
Sum of Eight pounds Current money of the State of Pennsylvania--Item to my Dutiful Daughter
Mary Wilson wife to John Wilson I do give and Bequeath the Sum of thirty pounds Lawful Money of
Pennsylvania two thirds of it to be paid in four years after my Decease and the Remainder to be
paid in one year after the first payment Item to my Dutiful Daughters Jean Elizabeth Sarah
Prudence Hannah and Rosanna I Do Give and Bequeath an Equal Share to each of them of my Real
and personal Estate after paying of the affsd Sums and Discharging what Debts may be against me
and the sum of Tventy pounds Specia that I Give and Bequeath to my Grand Son Andrew Wilsone to
be paid to him when he arives at twenty one years of age and if he Dies before that time it is
to be Equally Divided between his mother Brother and Sister and at the Expiration of Eight
Years after my Decease My Executors is to Sell the remainder of my Land at their Discretion and
I do give them as full pover to sell and transfer s⁴ Land as I Could or might vere I present
and my Six Daughters to witt Jean Elizabeth Sarah Prudence Hannah and Rosanna are to receive
Each an Equal Share of the [??ales] of both sales as they Come Due and further I Do Substitute
and appoint my beloved wife Martha to be my Exectrix and my trusty friends David Wills and John
Snody to be my Executors of this my Last will and Testament and I do by these presents
acknowledge this to be my Last will and Testament and I do Revoke all other wills by me
made Given under my hand and Seal the Day and year first above written---
                              Andrew Thomson (Seal)
Sealed and acknowledged in presence)
of Will⁰. Montgomery   Robert Bell)

Be it Remembered that on the 24th Day of May 1792 the Last will and Testament of Andrew Thomson
Decd was Legally proved of which this foregoing Record is a true Copy and Letters Testamentary
Issued in Common form to David Wills and John Snody Executors therein mentioned on the said
24th Day of May 1792 Inventory and account to be exhibited in time appointed by Lav-----Witness
my Hande
                         Will⁰. Lyon Regr

     Separate hearings were held for the appointment of guardians
for orphans over the age of fourteen.   The first report below is a
consolidation of the two reports in the court records.   Guardians
were appointed for the three younger children in a single hearing.

[Orphan Court, Docket #3, pp. 178-179, February 10, 1796]

     Came into Court [Elizabeth Thompson / Sarah Thompson] a minor, orphan daughter of Andrew
Thompson, deceased, above the age of fourteen years, and prayed the Court to appoint [William
Montgomery / John McKee] of Newton Township Guardian over her person and Estate. Whereupon the
Court did appoint the said [William Montgomery / John McKee] guardian over the person and
Estate of the said [Elizabeth Thompson / Sarah Thompson], minor Orphan daughter of the said
Andrew Thompson deceased during her minority or until another guardian be appointed in his
person.

Came into the Court David Wills and John Snoddy Executors of the last will and Testament of Andrew Thompson deceased and prayed the Court to appoint proper persons guardians over the persons and Estates of Prudence, Hannah, and Rosanna Thompson minors, Orphan Children of the said deceased under the age of fourteen years.   The Court on consideration did appoint William Montgomery and John McKee as guardians over the persons and Estates of the said Prudence, Hannah, and Rosanna Thompson minors orphan Children of the said Andrew Thompson deceased, or until other guardians are appointed in their room.

[Abstracts from South Central Pennsylvania newspapers, 1785-1800.   *Carlisle Gazette* #240]

Nov. 7, 1792
    All persons having claims against the estate of Andrew Thompson, deceased, to come and state their accounts. David Wills and John Snody, executors.

Feb. 22, 1797
    Tract for sale in Hopewell township, Cumberland County, adjoins lands of David Wills, and David McKinney, where Andrew Thompson, deceased, lived, and now occupied by Gilbert Kennedy. 260 A   John McKee, William Montgomery, guardians

[A second advertisment appeared on February 19, 1800.]

WALTER BELL

    Walter Bell, the father of Elizabeth Bell, was a resident of Hanover township, in that part of Lancaster County, PA which later became Dauphin County. He warranted a tract of 251 acres on March 16, 1737. His name appears on the 1750 tax list. In 1756 his name on the tax list is followed by "fled", indicating that he, like many other local residents, had departed because of Indian depredations during the French and Indian War. He evidently returned before the area was safe and lost his life in the manner described by an article from the *Pennsylvania Gazette*.

[from the *Pennsylvania Gazette* of October 5 1758]

    A letter from Fort Hunter dated the 15th. ult. mentions that a few Days before, one Walter Bell and his son, were killed and scalped by the Indians, in Hanover Township, Lancaster County, and that another Son of said Bell's, and a Soldier were carried off by them.

The inventory of Walter Bell's estate set its value at 484 pounds, 2 shillings, six pence. Eleven children were named in the will (Lancaster Co., Deed Book R, 45). Many of the children of Walter were later residents of Cumberland County.

    Most of the information in this section is taken from Raymond Martin Bell's article "The Bells in Dauphin County Before the Revolution", as is that in the Bell genealogy following.

Genealogy of the family of Walter Bell of Dauphin County

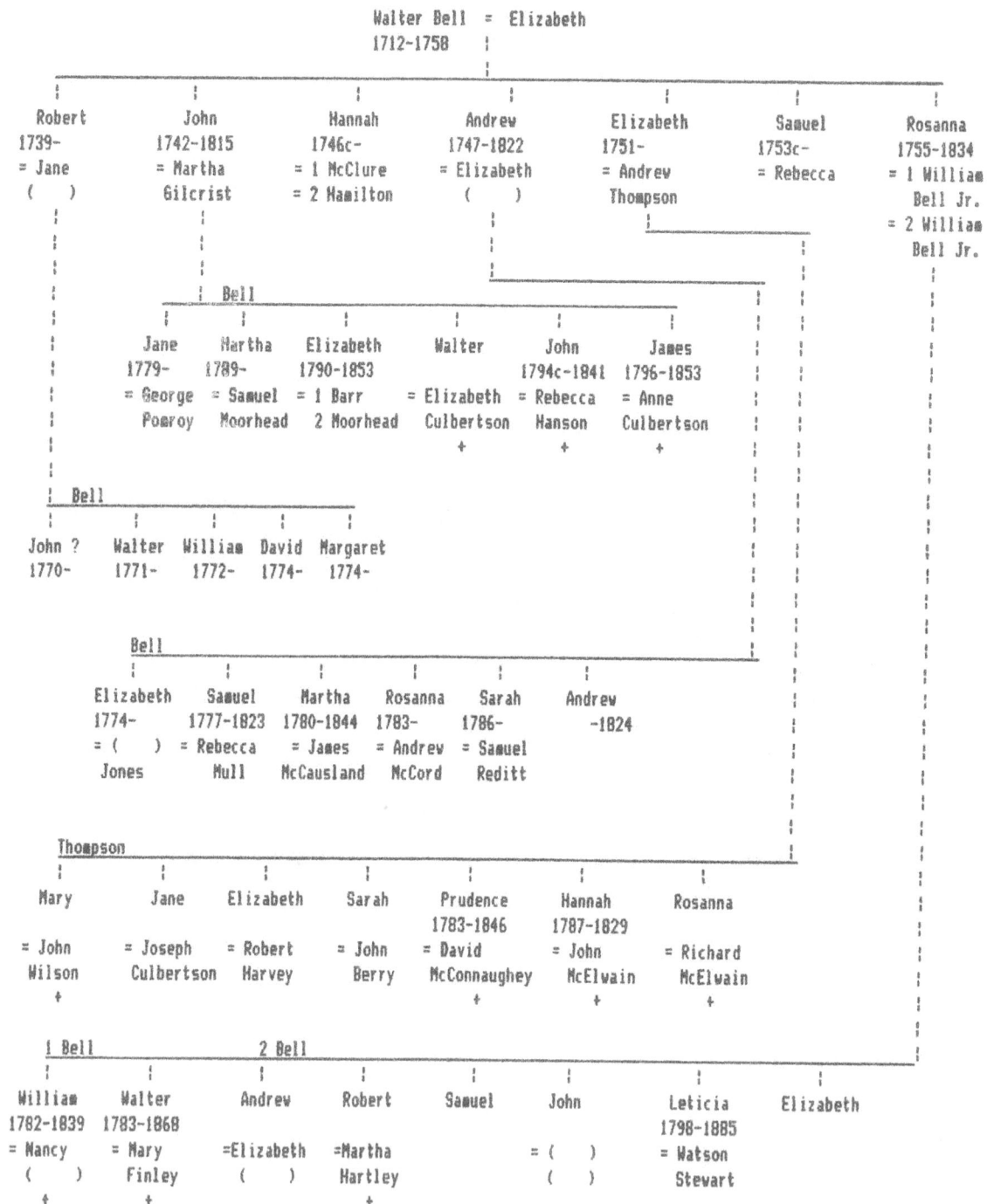

```
                              Walter Bell  =  Elizabeth
                              1712-1758    ¦
    _____
    ¦            ¦              ¦              ¦              ¦              ¦          ¦
  Robert       John          Hannah         Andrew        Elizabeth       Samuel    Rosanna
  1739-        1742-1815      1746c-         1747-1822     1751-           1753c-    1755-1834
  = Jane       = Martha       = 1 McClure    = Elizabeth   = Andrew        = Rebecca = 1 William
  (   )          Gilcrist     = 2 Hamilton   (     )         Thompson                  Bell Jr.
    ¦            ¦              ¦              ¦              _____          = 2 William
    ¦            ¦              ¦              ¦              ¦              ¦              Bell Jr.
    ¦            ¦            Bell             ¦              ¦              ¦          ¦
    ¦            _____         ¦          ¦
    ¦            ¦        ¦         ¦            ¦         ¦         ¦        ¦          ¦
    ¦          Jane     Martha   Elizabeth    Walter     John     James     ¦          ¦
    ¦          1779-    1789-    1790-1853               1794c-1841 1796-1853 ¦         ¦
    ¦          = George = Samuel = 1 Barr     = Elizabeth = Rebecca = Anne    ¦          ¦
    ¦            Pomroy   Moorhead  2 Moorhead  Culbertson  Hanson   Culbertson ¦        ¦
    ¦                                          +           +        +          ¦          ¦
    ¦                                                                          ¦          ¦
    ¦ Bell                                                                     ¦          ¦
    _____                                           ¦          ¦
    ¦        ¦        ¦        ¦        ¦                                       ¦          ¦
  John ?   Walter  William  David   Margaret                                  ¦          ¦
  1770-    1771-   1772-    1774-   1774-                                      ¦          ¦
                                                                              ¦          ¦
          Bell                                                                ¦          ¦
          _____        ¦          ¦
          ¦           ¦        ¦         ¦         ¦         ¦                 ¦          ¦
       Elizabeth    Samuel   Martha   Rosanna   Sarah     Andrew              ¦          ¦
       1774-        1777-1823 1780-1844 1783-    1786-      -1824              ¦          ¦
       = (   )      = Rebecca = James  = Andrew  = Samuel                      ¦          ¦
         Jones        Mull    McCausland McCord   Reditt                       ¦          ¦
                                                                              ¦          ¦
     Thompson                                                                 ¦          ¦
     _____  ¦          ¦
     ¦        ¦          ¦         ¦           ¦           ¦          ¦                   ¦
   Mary     Jane      Elizabeth  Sarah     Prudence    Hannah     Rosanna                ¦
                                           1783-1846   1787-1829                         ¦
   = John   = Joseph  = Robert   = John    = David     = John     = Richard              ¦
   Wilson     Culbertson Harvey   Berry    McConnaughey McElwain   McElwain              ¦
   +                                       +           +          +                      ¦
                                                                                        ¦
     1 Bell                  2 Bell                                                     ¦
     _____
     ¦        ¦          ¦         ¦           ¦           ¦          ¦          ¦
   William  Walter     Andrew    Robert     Samuel      John       Leticia   Elizabeth
   1782-1839 1783-1868                                             1798-1885
   = Nancy  = Mary     =Elizabeth =Martha               = (   )    = Watson
   (   )      Finley   (   )      Hartley               (   )        Stewart
   +         +                    +
```

+ = known to have had children   Five other children were born to Walter and Elizabeth Bell:
      Thomas (b. 1737c), James (b. 1740c), Walter (b. 1741c), [son] (1744c-1758), and George (b. 1749c).
      Rosanna Bell married different two men named William Bell, Jr.

THE ZAHNISER FAMILY

The McElwain family is connected to the Zahniser family at two points, as is illustrated by this family tree. The genealogy section lists more than 140 persons descended from William and Ruth Carnahan Zahniser (#230000000), and more than 260 from John and Mary McCracken McElwain (#226000000).

```
              Valentine Zahneisen  =  Juliana Clemens
                    d. 1753        :    1717-1801
                                   :
              Matthias Zahniser    =  Mary Lint
                  1749-1833        :   -1829
                                   :
        _____
        :                                             :
   Michael Zahniser                            Mary Zahniser
     1777-1852                                  1797-1825
   = Mary Mourer                              = Joshua McCracken
     1784-1876                                  1787-1847
        :                                             :
   William Zahniser                            Mary McCracken
     1811-1877                                  1820-1894
   =Ruth Carnahan                             = John McElwain
     1818-1894                                  1817-1883
```

Valentine Zahneisen lived near Landau, probably at Moersheim, near the Rhine River, in what is now the Rhineland Palatinate of Germany. He and his wife, Juliana Clemens, with two small boys, took ship for America in 1753. Valentine and one of the boys died during the voyage, and Juliana arrived in America a widow with a small child. She apparently had an adequate supply of money, and she managed to reach a German community in Lancaster County, Pennsylvania where she resided until 1790. The surviving son, Matthias, became a carpenter, and about 1774 married Mary Lint, by whom he had, over a period of many years, nine children.

The Zahniser family has taken a great interest in family history from a very early date. In 1875 a family reunion became the first of a series which continues today; each year the descendents of the family receive a notice summoning them to the Zahniser family picnic.

A bequest some years ago made possible the forming of the Zahniser Foundation which is devoted to preservation of family traditions, history, and genealogy. In 1906 a history of the family, written by Kate M. Zahniser and Charles Reed Zahniser and titled simply and aptly, *The Zahnisers*, was published. It was reissued with supplemental material in 1968, and the most recent Zahniser newsletter (July 1995) polled the family as to whether a new book should be published. In the meantime, the Foundation has continued to provide genealogical materials for anyone interested.

The current address is The Zahniser Foundation, % Mrs. Gordon Harrison, 7119 East State Street, Sharon, PA 16146. Doris McElwain Law (#3226327100) has served on the Board of Directors of the Foundation for a number of years.

Some of the history recorded in *The Zahnisers* deals with aspects of everyday life in the eighteenth and nineteenth century that is not commonly available. For that reason selected portions have been placed in this chapter as representative of what occurred in the lives of the Zahnisers and may well have occurred in the lives of any family of the time.

Selections from The Zahnisers

[These selections taken from several chapters of *The Zahnisers*. Matthias Zahniser came to Mercer county with his family eight or nine years before John S. McElvain.]

[During] the Revolutionary War the Zahnisers were not without a share of its hardships. Matthias' mother spun flax and carried the cloth to Philadelphia where she received $36 in Continental Currency. Shortly afterward the money was repudiated but she still preserved her hard-earned savings and most of it is still in the family. Matthias had some $600 of this money at the time of his death. Matthias was a soldier in the Revolutionary War, but it is not known in what organization or for how long a period.

In 1790 Matthias moved his family, including his mother to Allegheny County, and settled on a farm, though Matthias himself still worked at his trade and left the bulk of the farming to be done by the boys. The farm lies in Penn Township east of Pittsburgh and south of the Allegheny River and about one and one half miles south-west of the old town of Unity. The Mt. Hope Cemetery is on the farm and a few rods west of it is the old stone house in which Matthias probably lived. The western end of the structure carries a stone tablet that states it was built in 1812, but the eastern part is much older. The older part is virtually a three-storied affair and built directly over a large spring. The first story was used as a cellar and milk-house and the upper stories as a dwelling.

At the time when Matthias sold his farm in Allegheny County, the section of the state north of the Ohio and west of the Allegheny river had just been opened for settlement. The land had been purchased from the Indians in 1789 but they refused to vacate till General Wayne in the decisive battle of Fallen Timbers in 1794, convinced them that contracts are made to be kept and that the land was no longer theirs. The Legislature had in the meantime arranged to sell the land. Settlers were required to clear, fence, and cultivate at least two acres for every hundred they desired to purchase and to build a house in which they were to reside or cause others to reside for a period of five years. At the end of that time they were permitted to purchase the land at the rate of $20 for each hundred acres.

When Matthias Zahniser sold his farm in Allegheny County in 1796, he and his three oldest sons sought out a new location in the territory just opened. Going on the theory that the land which produced the largest trees would produce the best crops, he selected a place in what is now Lake Township, eight miles north-east of Mercer. Here they built a cabin, cleared five acres of land and planted an orchard.

With the coming of Winter, Matthias returned to Allegheny County but the three sons remained in the Wilderness with a few head of cattle which they fed chiefly on browse. Doubtless they would have returned with their father had it not been for the danger of thereby losing their claim to the land. By an unwritten law, universally observed among the settlers, if a claim was left without a person on it and without a fire in the cabin, it was considered abandoned and a new settlement could be made on it by any person who might choose to enter the vacant cabin.

During the winter of 1796-97, the two sons of Matthias who were staying in the cabin built the preceding summer worked in the timber during the day, leaving a fire in the cabin to hold their claim. One evening they returned to find that the cabin had taken fire and been entirely consumed, even their coats being burned and leaving them nothing but their axes and guns which they had with them. There were no neighbors and night was coming on.   Under the circumstances there was but one thing to do so, shouldering their guns they set out for Allegheny County and walked the entire distance to their father's home, some seventy miles.   Gathering a new set of supplies, they soon returned to their claim and built a new cabin, of course camping out despite the winter weather till their new home was completed.

At another time during the same winter when a heavy storm was raging, an Indian walked into their cabin.   He had lost his way and the customs of both Indians and frontiersmen entitled him to their protection and care till the weather should clear so that he could see the North Star which was to be his guide in finding his way home.   As long as he was their guest they were perfectly safe, even though he might come from a tribe intensely hostile.   There was never any trouble with hostile Indians, however, after the time when the Zahnisers settled.

On one occasion, Michael was aroused at night by the sound of his pigs squealing in their pens.   Going out to investigate, he found a huge bear helping himself to a mess of young pork. The bear was frightened away and in the morning was tracked to where he had taken refuge in a hollow tree.   As soon as the ax was applied to the tree, bruin came out to give battle but a bullet settled the controversy before he was entirely out of his hole.   Farmers in those days were often robbed of their pork in this manner though they were not always able to secure bear steak instead.

Small game of all kinds was abundant and constituted a large element in the regular food supply.   It was an ordinary thing for the women of that generation to send one of the boys out in the morning with his rifle to shoot half a dozen gray squirrels for breakfast.   Salt was very precious as what they obtained had to be carried on horseback from Erie or Pittsburgh. Cane-sugar was rare, but each farmer had a maple sugar grove in which a supply was made every spring for the ensuing year. Tropical fruits were not to be thought of.   Rice was one of the luxuries of the time, but so expensive that when a mother cooked a mess of it for a family of six or eight, it was customary to mold it in a tea cup.

The house [built by Matthias] was large and built of smoothly hewn logs with closely notched and dovetailed corners.   It was a two story structure, the second floor of which was little more than a loft and was used by the younger members of the family as sleeping quarters. There was but one room on the first floor.   From the uncovered joists overhead hung smoked sausages, dried beef, seed corn, and dried fruits and vegetables of various kinds.   At the eastern end was a huge stone chimney with the usual open fireplace.   Adjoining the western end of the house was a smaller addition called the stove room from the fact that it contained a real stove, a rare thing in the community then.   The stove was a huge ten-lid affair and the pride of the home for many years.

A few rods back of the house was a spring over which a good-sized spring-house was built, the upper story of which was used by Matthias as a carpenter shop.   Just north of the house were the peach, cherry, and apple trees and the currant bushes all red in autumn with their luscious fruit.   South of the house was the garden, and west of the spring-house was the big apple tree which bore an abundance of little apples just suited to the taste of the little grandsons.

JOSHUA MCCRACKEN

Joshua McCracken was the son of Thomas McCracken, who was born in Scotland in 1751. According to the *History of Mercer County*, Alexander McCracken, brother of Thomas, came to Mercer County in 1798, but nothing is said about the arrival of Thomas. Thomas died in January 1813 in Mercer County. His will is transcribed below

Joshua married Mary Zahniser, the daughter of Matthias Zahniser and Mary Lint. Mary was born in 1797, married Joshua on April 1, 1817, and died March 17, 1825, leaving four young children in the care of her husband. *The Zahnisers* says of Mary, "In her early life she had been the pet of the household at the old home and the cherished friend of her little nephews who, even as old men, never tired of recounting the graces of 'Aunt Polly'".

Joshua was for a short time, around 1816, a teacher in a common, log schoolhouse. The Mercer County history tells of a custom prevalent in the early settlements which permitted the school boys to lock the teacher out of school on Christmas Day and to admit him only when he agreed to "treat" them. The treat was not "to a good warming from a birch-switch, or a raw-hide as they deserved, but to apples or whiskey." Joshua managed to get into the school house while the student left on guard was asleep, and was able to dictate terms of peace which required the somnolent student to treat the crowd. The nature of this treat is not specified.

Mary McCracken, daughter of Joshua McCracken and Mary Zahniser, married John T. McElwain (226000000). Another child, Alexander, grew to maturity. A boy and a girl died in infancy.

Will of Thomas McCracken (Will Book I, page 40, Mercer
County, Pennsylvania

In the name of God Amen. I Thomas McCracken of Mercer County and State of Pennsylvania being sound in judgement and mind which I thank God for, do make my last Will and Testament in the manner following. First he allows his boddy be interred in a desant mannor and his soul to God ho gave it. I likevise bequeth all my reale and personal estate to my sons, Josuah and John with this proviso that said Josuah and John is at the expense of my funeral charges and likevise to keep their mother in a desant mannor with abundance of vitules and cloths and what rume in the house she chuses to live in, and if they appere harsh to her that the said Josuah and John pay there mother one hundred dollers anualey enduring her life but Josuah is to have of the whole estate one hundred dollers more than John shall and said Josuah and John is to keep in desant clothing induring the apprentiship of my son Alexander and at the death of there mother said Josh and John is to pay to James and Alexander McCracken there brothers fifty dollars each. I likevise leave one cow to each of James Gillilands two children when they come of age, and one dollar to said James Gilliland. I apoynt my sons Josuah and James to be the Executters of this my last Will and Testament--given under my hand this twelfth January one thousand eight hundred and thirteen.

Wits.   John Lindsay - John Gordon

Mercer County: Before me Bevan Pearson, Register for the probate of Wills - in and for Mercer County personally came John Lindsay and John Gordon the two subscribing witnesses to the within Will who being duly sworn according to law doth depose and say that they were personally present and saw Thomas McCracken the Testator within named sign (or order it to be signed) the within Will and as his act and deed deliver the same and for his last Will and Testament, and that he was of sound mind and memory at the time of so doing to the best of their knowledge. Sworn and subscribed before me the 20th of Jany. 1813.

Bevan Pearson, Regt.

ROBERT SHANNON

Robert Shannon was a Captain of the Company of the Second Class, First Battalion of the Cumberland County Militia during the Revolutionary War. Under him Andrew McElwain (#400000000) served as a sergeant, and Andrew later married Elizabeth Shannon, Robert's daughter.

Robert was a member of the Big Spring Presbyterian Church. He appears in the records as one of the parishioners who signed the call on March 21, 1786 to bring Samuel Wilson to the pastorship of the church. On that same day he subscribed one pound, 5 shillings toward the salary of the pastor. Big Spring records also record the marriage of two of his daughters, Sarah and Mary.

An abstract of the will of Robert Shannon is printed below. From this will a partial family tree has been deduced and appears on the following page.

Cumberland County, Pennsylvania Abstract of Wills, p. 433.

Robert Shannon   Newton
21 Nov. 1795   19 Feb. 1796

Wife Jean. Son Robert and his son Robert. Bound Boy, Samuel Baker, Son Samuel and his son Robert. Son Joseph and his son Robert. Son John. Son-in-law Samuel Fenton. Son-in-law Hugh McElhenny and his son Robert. Son-in-law John Patton. Son-in-law Elisha Carson, his step-sons William, Robert, and Joseph and his step-daughter Mary, his son Ezekiel and his daughter Margaret. Son-in-law Andrew McElwain and his son Robert and daughter Jenny McElwain. Son-in-law William Porterfield.

```
                              Family Tree of Robert and Jean Shannon


                                   Robert Shannon  =  Jean -----
                                    1722?-1795     :    1726-
                                                   :
    _____
    :        :        :           :        :          :          :          :          :           :          :
  Robert   Samuel   James       Joseph    John      Margaret    Sarah     Nancy Ann   Jane      Elizabeth     Mary
  b. 1749c    :     d. 1806     b. 1764   b. 1756c   b. 1756c    b. 1759c  b. 1759c    b. 1762c  b. 1759c      b. 1769c
  = Jane      :     = 1 Isabel  = Mary    = Margaret = Hugh      = John    = Samuel    = 1 Joseph = Andrew     = William
  McElhinny   :       McKee     McKee     (    )     McIlhenny   Patton    Fenton        McGoffin  McElwain     Porter-
    :         :     = 2 Elizabeth  :        :          :          :          :         = 2 Elisha  :            field
  Robert   Robert     Geese     :        :          :          two        :           Carson    :
                      (m. 1797)  :        : :          :         children    :           :         :
  Shannon_____:        : :          :                     :           :         :
    :    :       :        :         :     : :          :                     :           :         :
  John Jane  Margaret Elizabeth James Mary : :          :                     :           :         :
       1790-                            : :          :                     :           :         :
       1869                             : :          :                     :           :         :
  = Robert McElwain                     : :          :                     :           :         :
                                        : :          :                     :           :         :
    Shannon_____: :          :                     :           :         :
    :          :          :          :            :                     :           :         :
  Samuel    Martha     Margaret     Ann          :                     :           :         :
                                                   :                     :           :         :
    Shannon_____:            :                     :           :         :
    :          :                     :            :                     :           :         :
  Henry     Hugh          three other children    :                     :           :         :
                                                   :                     :           :         :
    McIlhenny_____:                     :           :         :
    :                     :                                               :           :         :
  Robert         six other children                                       :           :         :
                                                                          :           :         :
  = Margaret                                                              :           :         :
    Carnahan                                                              :           :         :
                                                                          :           :         :
         Fenton_____:           :         :
         :                     :                     :                     :          :         :
       James              Robert                Samuel                John            :         :
       b. 1776            b. 1770               b. 1780               b. 1782          :         :
                                                                                      :         :
    Carson_____:         :
    :          :          :          :            :          :          :            :         :
  William    Robert     Samuel      Mary        Ezekiel    Margaret   [child]         :         :
                                                                                      :         :
    McElwain_____:
    :     :     :       :      :         :        :       :          :       :        :        :       :        :
  Mary  Jane  Robert   Jane  Benjamin  Andrew   Thomas  Elizabeth  Sarah   Sarah   William   James   John    Stewart

       :_____:        :_____:
         children of Andrew and Elizabeth Shannon             children of Andrew and Margaret Bell
```

CHAPTER III

THE MCILVAINE FAMILY OF SUSSEX COUNTY, DELAWARE

ANDREW MCILVAINE OF COOL SPRING

Andrew McIlvaine is not an ancestor of the Andrew McElwain
who is the topic of this book, but he and his family are important
in this study because they were closely associated with Andrew
McElwain and can provide important backgound information about the
probable origins in Sussex County, in what later became Delaware.
Further because his great-grandson George McIlvaine married Andrew
McElwain's granddaughter Ruth McElwain, he is also an ancestor
about 40% of the known descendents of Andrew McElwain.

Andrew McIlvaine was the son of Alexander McIlvaine, a
younger son of John McIlvaine, Laird of Grimet and Attiquin in the
County of Ayr, Scotland. Alexander's elder brother Quentin
succeeded to the family estates in 1669. Alexander was born in
Ayreshire. He married a Miss McAdam, and at an undetermined time,
to escape religious persecution in Scotland, he moved to Ireland
and settled at Augnacloy in County Tyrone.

In 1719 Andrew McIlvaine emigrated from Ireland to Sussex
County, in what later became Delaware, bringing with him three
sons and a daughter. With him also came two brothers of his wife,
William and Andrew McAdam, a friend Robert Mickey, and another
person named Andrew McIlvaine. This second Andrew may be the
nephew of the first, and he may be the Andrew McCalvaine given
thirty acres in the will transcribed below.

Upon their arrival Andrew and Robert Mickey purchased together a tract of 550 acres. Andrew took 330 acres of this
property, and on his death in 1726, distributed it by will,
giving 100 acres t each son, and 30 acres to Andrew McCalvaine.
This latter fact would seem to support the idea that the other
Andrew McIlvaine mentioned in the account of the immigration was a
nephew rather than an uncle. One of two versions of the will in
the *Complete History* adds a thirty acre inheritance for his
daughter, but this may be a mistake. It is shown in parenthesis,
the significance o which is not clear. In the same variant
version a remark stating that the testator was "late of Ayr" also
appears in parenthesis, a does the mention of "my silver spoons".
Frank McElvain, in whose work the two versions appear, does not
explain the variations.

[from Complete History, page 374]

1719 - Deed Book D, p 410, Sussex Co., Del.

This indenture made the fourth day of February in the sixth year of our Sovereign Lord
over Great Britain, France, and Ireland, King and Defender of the Faith, Anno Domino 1719:
between John Russell, late of Somerset, in the Province of Maryland, but now of Sussex County,

Delaware, yeoman, party of the first part, and Andrew McIlvaine and Robert Mickey, late of the kingdom of Ireland, both of them, but now of the County aforesaid, of the other part...witnesseth... The fourth day of February, Ano. Dom. 1719, John Russell, yeoman, appeared in open court and acknowledged and delivered a certain deed of sale unto Andrew McIlvaine and Robert Mickey for five hundred and fifty acres of land, lying in the county and butted and bounded as said deed set forth, which bears date, the fourth day of February, ano Domini 1719, according to the contents of said deed." "Andrew McIlvaine, Sussex county on Delaware, hath for the ear-marks: for cattle, sheep, horses and hogs, a crop and two stittes on the right ear and a swallow's firk on the left."

Will of Andrew McIlvaine of Sussex County, Delaware, 1726 (Will record A-1, p. 208)

In the name of God, Amen, this fourth day of October Anno Domini, One Thousand Seven Hundred and Twenty-six, I Andrew Mucklevane, of Sussex county (late of Ayr, Scotland) yeoman being of perfect mind and memory (thanks be to God) do make this my last will and testament in manner and form following:

First, I bequeath my soul and spirit into the hands of Almighty God, my Heavenly Father, who gave it me, by whom of his and only Grace I hope to be received into Eternal rest through the death of my Savior, Jesus Christ and my body to be buried in a Christian decent-like manner at the direction of my executors hereafter named and as to what worldly estate it hath pleased by Almighty Father to endow me with, I dispose of the same as followeth.

Impr. - I will that all such debts as I owe shall be truly paid.

Item - I give unto my son, John McCalvaine, one hundred acres of land the plantation whereon he now liveth. Also my new suit of cloathes, he paying to my executor the sum of four pounds.

Item - I give and bequeath to my son James McCalvaine one hundred acres of land the plantation whereon he now liveth to him and his heirs forever.

Item - I give unto my daughter Martha McCalvaine (30 acres of land) three cows and two calves, my riding horse, my best feather bed, white rugg, Blanket, puter [pewter] and my Great Iron pot. (and my silver spns). Also my will is that my said daughter shall have privilege of the flax to make twenty yards of linen to purchase a side saddle and when my debts are paid my will is that my said daughter shall have the remainder of my house-hold goods, and to remain in the possession of my son James until she marry or is capable of taking the charge of herself.

Item - I give unto my son George One Hundred Acres of Land, being my part of the plantation whereon I now live together with all my iron work a Gun a Great Coat and one small pott. One Brown Rigg, one mare with her increase forever.

Item - I give unto Andrew McCalvaine thirty acres of land adjoining to the plantation that my son James lives on.

Item - I give unto Andrew McKee one Great Coat also to William McKee one small Iron Pott.

Item - I give unto Alexander Muckelvane one yearling.

Also I will and ordain that my son George, during his minority shall remain with my son James and that my son George shall at the age of Twenty-one years Take into his own possession what I have herein bequeathed.

Item - I will and ordain that my son James to be my full whole and sole executor of this my Last Will and Testament and I do Utterly Revoke all former Wills and testaments by me in any wise heretofore made or declared.

In witness hereof I have hereunto set my hand and seal that above written.

                         his
            ANDREW X MUCKLEVAINE (Seal)
                        mark

Signed, sealed, published pronounced, and delivered in sight and in presence of us.
 Daniel Mickey, Thos. Cokayne Francis X Mackelvaine (his mark)

Memorandum this 28th day of October, 1726.   Daniel Mickey appeared before me, Philip Russel
Deputy Register for the County of Sussex upon Delaware and made oath on the Holy Evangels that
in their sight presence and hearing the above Andrew McClevayne signed, sealed, published, and
declared the above and within written instrument to be his last Will and Testament and that at
the doing thereof the said testator was of sound disposing mind and memory (to the best of his
judgement) and also that he saw Thos. Cokayne and Francis Mucklevane sign with him as witness
to the same. Test. Philip Russell D-Register.

JAMES MCILVAINE OF COOL SPRING, DELAWARE

James, the second son of Andrew McIlvaine, was born in 1693.
He married Francis Mills.   Their son John received from his
father's will 300 acres "in the back country, called Cat's Cabin,"
a tract on Conodoguinet Creek in Cumberland County, Pennsylvania.
The grant "By the Proprietaries" to James Muckelvaine is dated July
26, 1744.   Interest on the mortgage was to begin as of March 1,
1737, a probable indication that the land had been occupied, or at
least claimed, since that time.   This piece of land eventually
came into the possession of John's three children, George (who
married Ruth McElwain), Greer, and Martha.

The will of James also establishes that he purchased the tract
of 100 acres which had been willed to his brother George.   George
moved to Cumberland County, where his son Andrew, through no fault
of his own, caused some early genealogists to make serious errors.

Extract from the will of James McElwain   (from *Torrence and Allied Families*, pp. 410-411)

I give, devise, and bequeath to my son James McIlvaine, and his heirs and assigns forever,
in fee simple, the plantation whereon he now dwells, and whereon I lately dwelt, in Indian
River Hundred, in aforsaid county [Sussex upon Delaware], which I bought of my brother George
McIlvaine....
I give, devise, and bequeath to my son John McIlvaine, his heirs and assigns forever, in
fee simple, three hundred acres of land and the buildings thereon, which I own in the back
country, called "Cat's Cabin".
... I have hereunto set my hand and seal, this eighth day of April, 1754.

GEORGE MCELWAIN OF CUMBERLAND COUNTY, PENNSYLVANIA

George, the youngest son of Andrew McIlvaine, was born about
1707, and was therefore about twelve years of age when the family
came to America.   At the time of the death of his father he was
not of age, and the will appointed his brother James as his
guardian. George received 100 acres from his father, which he
later sold to his brother and former guardian, James.   At some
time before 1744 George moved to Cumberland County.   This date is
established by an entry in the Session Book of the Middle Spring
Presbyterian Church which relates the story of a minor disorder and

48

the discipline imposed by the Church, upon George, whose name is spelled McElwain. A brief extract from the Minutes appears below.

George's surname appears in several forms on various documents, but usually, though not always, with the "w" rather than the "v". His descendents use the spelling McElwain.

In his will George left all of his land to his eldest son Andrew, who was then only about eight years of age. Some years later Andrew gave a portion of the land to his younger brother Joseph. All of the children of Andrew moved west, but descendents of Joseph still live in Cumberland County.

The will of George establishes several things of importance. First, the selection of Andrew McElwain as an executor shows that the connection between these two families was very close. Further, the will plainly indicates, by outlining an elementary educational curriculum for him, that the heir Andrew was very young at the time, making confusion of this Andrew with the older Andrew, who died twenty-two years later with ten children, hard to understand. The progenitor of this error was Robert Torrence in his *Torrence and Allied Families,* and the error has spread from Torrence into innumerable family trees and may never be entirely eradicated.

George's wife Margaret, not content with the terms of the will, filed an objection claiming dower rights of one-third of the whole estate. This "Caveat" is transcribed after George's will.

Extracts from the Session Book of the Middle Spring Presbyterian Church

Janry 16--1744/45   The sessions of Middle Spring & Big Spring Met conjunctly about a scandalous & riotous Quarrell wherein some Members of each congregation were concern'd.   Begun with prayer.   John McKee of Middle Spring, & David Killough of Big Spring absent.
The session proceeded to enquire into the Affair of the Quarrel.
Robert Finley complain'd that George McElvain assaulted him & tore his Handkerchief, which said George denies.
William Carnachan complain'd that William McCall assaulted him first, & ask'd him certain Questions, which it seems, said McCall says said Carnachan ask'd them at him. William McCall did not appear.   George McElvain being call'd solemnly declar'd that, to the best of his Knowledge, after there had been a skirmish at Andrew Culbertson's House, he, William Carnachan, & Francis McCall took Horse to go home, & having gone a little way, said McCall said as much as that he was displeas'd to see that William Carnachan shou'd be so much abus'd, they wou'd turn back, & get some more of their own company, the depnt. consented to go back, partly to prevent Robt. Finly from getting a Warrant; & partly to get some more company, in order to another Skirmish, upon which, they went back towards Shippensburgh, until they met their own company of Joseph Carnachan, James Laughlane Junr., James Jake, Saml. Smith, John Jake, John Smith, & Allexander Fairbairn; when they met, Joseph Carnachan, seeing his Brother Willm. bleeding & his shirt torn, was very angry, & said he wou'd have satisfaction of the currs that did it, then the whole company went towards Andrew Culbertson's, & met the other company; James Jake ask'd one who he was, & where he was going? The other reply'd his Name was Robt. Finley, & that he was going to the Justices.   Said Jake said it was a shame for Neighbors that cou'd'nt agree better in the dark night.   The Depont. saw no stroaks, nor hear any outcry; but after the others went away, he heard Joseph Carnachan, Jas. Jake, & Jas. Laughlane say they had struck,

but didn't say who.

Upon the whole this conjunct session apprehend they cannot come to a judgement about the first skirmish at Andrew Culbertson's, untill evidence be obtain'd between the parties concern'd in it, their Accounts of the Matter are so widely diferent; and therefore refer that part of the Matter to the session of Middle Spring at their next meeting, the persons chiefly concern'd in it, belonging to the congregation.

From George McElwain's Account of the affair the session judge, that George McElwain & Francis McCall were Accessorys to the Quarrel, in taking William Carnachan back after they had gone away, & James Laughlane in stricking, & that thereby they have violated the Law of God & given offence to the church; & appoint them to attend the next Meeting of the session of Big Spring, & there profess their sorrow for their sin, & be rebuk'd for it.

Order'd that William Lamond cite James Jake to attend then. Francis McCall order'd to attend the session of Middle Spring about the first skirmish at Andrew Culbertson's.

The Affair that was refer'd by the conjunct sessions, to the further consideration of this session resum'd.

Gustavus Henderson being call'd, solemnly declar'd that as he was walking in Andrew Culbertson's Floor, he heard Willm. Carnachan & Willm. McCall speaking pretty loud then going out he heard Willm. McCall say to Willm. Carnachan show me one word that I have said amiss, & I'll yeild. Upon which said Carnachan said, you believe in a rotten hearted fellow like yourself, & struck said McCall, & said McCall laying hold of him, they came both to the ground; after they were parted, while the Depnt. was speaking with Willm. McCall looking behind him he saw said Carnachan & George Finley having hold of each other & said Finley threw down said Carnachan; John Finley & the Depnt parted them; then said Carnachan going straight to Willm. McCall laid hold of him again, & both came to the ground, upon which the Depnt. went & loss'd said Carnachan's Arm from about said McCall's Neck; the Depnt. further says that said Carnachan's shirt was torn, but did'nt observe any wounds except that his Nose bled; & that there were none engag'd with said Carnachan but one at once.

Other evidences, who were cited about said Affair being not yet come, it is a little defer'd.

...

The other evidences concerning the Affair between Willm. Carnachan, & Willm. McCall, John, Robt. & George Finley not appearing, the session proceeded to consider the case, as now before them, & after serious Deliberation Judge, that notwithstanding it appears that Willm. Carnachan first began the Quarrel, & was principal in Carrying it on (tho it does not appear whether said Carnachan or McCall began the conversation) yet said McCall was to be blam'd for keeping up any conversation with him at such a time, about any Debate, & the other persons abov'd, for staying so late in the way of temptation: & that they be admonish'd for it.

Will of George McElwain (Will Book A-1 139: 1747B) (from *Complete History*, pp. 293a-294)

In the name of God, Amen the first day of January, 1748,
I George McElvain of the Township of Hopewell in the county of Lancaster in the Province of Pennsylvania a Farmer being very sick and weak in body but of perfect mind and memory thanks be given unto God therefore calling to mind the mortality of the body and knowing that it is appointed for all men once to die do make and ordain this my Last Will and Testament, that is principally and first of all I give and recommend my soul into the hands of almighty God that Gave it and my body I recommend to the Earth to be buried in Decent Christian Burial at the Discretion of my Executors Nothing Doubting but at the General Resurrection I shall receive it again by the Mighty Power of God and as touching such worldly Estate wherewith it has pleased God to Bless me in this life, I Give Demise and Dispose of the same in the following manner and form.

Item first I give and bequeath to Margaret my Dearly Beloved wife the third part of all my goods and Chattles after my Debts are paid Except my plantation and I allow her the Benefit of the Plantation During her widowhood and in Lew thereof She shall keep my two sons to wit Andrew and Joseph McElwein and put them to School During her widowhood or till they Can Read the Bible plain and Read and write Bills and Bonds and Work the Golden Rule in arethmetick perfect.

Item I Give unto my well beloved son Andrew McElwein all and singular my land messages and tenements by him freely to be possessed and enjoyed cleared out of the Land Office and if he dies before he comes of age I allow my son Joseph to become heir and if he does not learn to Read and write and Cypher before his mother Marrys I allow him to be put to school and taught as aforesaid

Item I Give to my beloved son Joseph McElwein the one third of my Moveable Estate after all my debts are paid by him freely to be possessed and if he Die before he comes of age I allow my son Andrew to be his Heir and Likewise constitute my well beloved friends William Thompson and Andrew McElwein my only sole executors of this my Last will and testament and I do hereby utterly Disallow Revoke and Dissannul all and Every former Testaments wills Legacies and Benefits and Exe's by me in any ways before named willed and Bequeathed Ratifying and Confirming this and no other to be my Last will and Testament in Witness whereof I have hereunto Set my hand and Seal the Day and year above written. George Mcc elwein [sic]

Signed Sealed published pronounced and Declared

By the said George MccElwein to be his Last will and

Testament in the presence of us the subscribers

William Lamond

Daniel X Mickie

    his mark

Lancaster County towit 7th March 17th [?]   Then personally appeared William Lamond and Daniel Mickie, two of the witnesses to the above Will and on their oaths declared they were present & they heard George McElvain the testator above named Sign Publish and Declare the above Writing to be his last Will and Testament & that at the doing that he was of sound mind and Memory to the best of their knowledge.

                 Before me   Tho. Cookson
                              D. R.

From court records of Sussex County, [Delaware]

    GEORGE McElwain, son of Andrew McIlvaine of Cool Springs, Del.
    Book 8, p. 215 Recorder of Deed, Sussex Co., Del., Georgetown, Del.

This indenture, made this 2nd day of November, 1748, between William [Thompson] and Andrew McIlvaine exrs. of the Testament and last will of George McIlvaine, who was admr., all and singular of the goods and chattels, Rights and credits of Daniel Mickie at the time of his death who dies intestate as its said, of the one part, and Thomas Carey of Sussex County on Delaware of the other part.   Whereas there is a certain tract of land in Angola Neck was legally conveyed to the Aforesaid Daniel McKee, dec'd, and whereas the aforesaid George McIlvaine at an Orphans Court held at Lewes for the County of Sussex, 8 of June 1738 obtained an order of the Court for sale of said land in order to satisfy his creditors and sold to John Simeton, Simeton transferred his right to John Block, who sold the same to Thomas Casey [sic], party to these presents.

Estate of George McElvaine afore'sd   William Thompson
who was admr of Daniel Mickey   Andrew McElvain

Pennsylvania Genealogical Magazine, Vol. XXIV, 1965-66. p. 28
    Philadelphia, Pa., published by the Genealogical Society
    of Pennsylvania.
Caveat entered by the Widow against probate of the will of George McElwain. I call to my assistance Edward Smout, Peter Morral, and James Galbraith, Esqrs. The Widow Claims her Thirds as Dower of the Whole.

ANDREW MCELWAIN (1740c-1793)

Andrew received by will the entire tract of land possessed by his father. He was at the time about eight years of age. Within the same year, on November 12, 1748, a Warrant was obtained in the name of Andrew McElwain for 316 acres and 54 perches of land on Conodoguinet Creek in Hopewell (later Mifflin) township, Cumberland County, Pennsylvania. Andrew in 1764 gave a portion of the land to his brother Joseph.

Andrew married and had five children. Like his father, he died in middle life, leaving minor children. His wife Mary shortly married William Lightcap. The children some time later moved to Darke County, Ohio, and the only son, another Andrew, eventually to Indiana. Some time after they had moved, several of them instituted a lawsuit against Lightcap, claiming that he had wrongfully converted the land of their father to his own use. The case dragged on for years and was finally resolved in favor of the defendant, but by that time almost all parties to the case were dead.

If any further proof is needed to establish that Andrew McElwain, the son of Andrew McIlvaine, is not the person who married Mary Mickey and died in 1770, the extract from the Orphans' Court records given below should do so. It deals with a deceased Andrew McElwain who, in 1797, twenty-seven years after the death of the older Andrew, has five children under the age of fourteen.

[gift of land from Andrew to Joseph, from *Complete History*, p. 441]

Cumberland Co., Pa. Records, Deed Book H, Vol. I, p. 419, Carlisle, dated Nov. 23, 1764
    (from *Complete History*, p. 441)

"In consideration of the love and good will which I bear to my loving brother, Joseph McIlvaone," the grantor, Andrew McIlvaine, transfers land in Hopewell Township, on the north side of Conodoguinet Creek." The deed states that both are farmers, both living in Hopewell Township. Witnesses, John Thompson, Alexander Scroggs, and Samuel Coveb. Name spelled Mcilwane and McLewan in deed.

[from Cumberland County, Pennsylvania Orphans' Court Docket Book 3, page 229, May 10, 1797]

Came into Court Joseph McElwain brother of Andrew McElwain, deceased, and prayed the Court appoint Samuel Fenton and John Shannon of Mifflin township, Yeomen, Guardians over the persons and estates of Isabella, Mary, Jannet, Rhuhama, and Andrew McElwain, minors, Orphan Children of Andrew McElwain, deceased, under the age of fourteen years, during their minority. The Court upon consideration appointed Samuel Fenton and John Shannon Guardians over the persons and estates of the said Isabella, Mary, Jannet, Rhuhama, and Andrew McElwain, minors and Orphan Children aforesaid during their minority until another Guardian or Guardians be appointed in their room.

By the Court

GENEALOGICAL TABLE OF THE MCILVAINE FAMILY OF DELAWARE

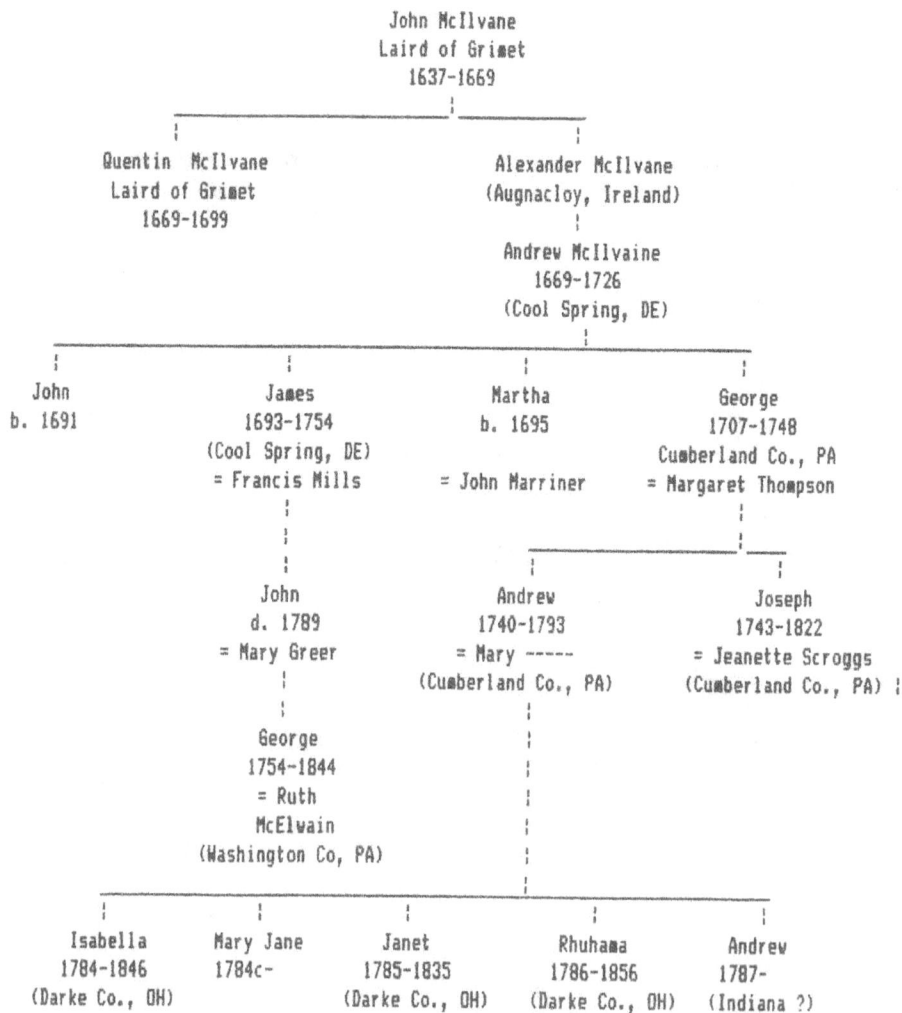

John McIlvane
Laird of Grimet
1637-1669

Quentin McIlvane
Laird of Grimet
1669-1699

Alexander McIlvane
(Augnacloy, Ireland)

Andrew McIlvaine
1669-1726
(Cool Spring, DE)

John
b. 1691

James
1693-1754
(Cool Spring, DE)
= Francis Mills

Martha
b. 1695

= John Marriner

George
1707-1748
Cumberland Co., PA
= Margaret Thompson

John
d. 1789
= Mary Greer

Andrew
1740-1793
= Mary -----
(Cumberland Co., PA)

Joseph
1743-1822
= Jeanette Scroggs
(Cumberland Co., PA)

George
1754-1844
= Ruth
McElwain
(Washington Co, PA)

Isabella
1784-1846
(Darke Co., OH)

Mary Jane
1784c-

Janet
1785-1835
(Darke Co., OH)

Rhuhama
1786-1856
(Darke Co., OH)

Andrew
1787-
(Indiana ?)

A partial genealogical table of the McIlvaine and McElwain relatives of George McElwain is included here, because of the close connection between his family and that of Andrew McElwain, and to provide aid in determining to which family an individual belongs.

GENEALOGY OF THE FAMILY OF GEORGE MCELWAIN OF CUMBERLAND COUNTY

Serial # and Name	Birth		Marriage		Death	
000000000 MCILVAINE						
Andrew McIlvaine	1669	Ayr	ST			
Martha Mickey						
Andrew came to Sussex County (Delaware) in or about 1719 and purchased a tract of land with Robert Mickey.						
1 John	1691					
2 James	*1693		IR		1754	
3 Martha	+1695					
4 George	*1707				1748	
John came to America with his family, but nothing in known of his life. Martha married John Marriner and lived in Delaware.						
20000000 MCILVAINE						
James McIlvaine	1693		IR		1754	Cool Spring DE
Frances Mills	1699				1733	DE
1 Robert	+1724				1764	
2 Andrew	+1728				1789	Sep 13
3 James	+ı	Cool Spring	DE		1787	
4 John	*ı				1789	
5 David	+ı	Cool Spring	DE		1828	
6 Prudence	+ı	Cool Spring	DE		1754	Apr 8
7 Mary	ı	Cool Spring	DE			
8 Frances	ı	Cool Spring	DE			
240000000 MCILVAINE						
John McIlvaine					1789	
Mary Greer			IR		1794	Mar 23
1 George	+1754				1844	Feb 8 Washington Co. PA
2 Greer	+1757				1845	
3 Catherine	+1759					
All three children moved to Washington County, PA. George married Ruth McElwain; their family is recorded in the Genealogy (#700000000). Greer married Elizabeth Morrow and Catherine married Robert Luckey.						
400000000 MCELWAIN						
George McElwain	1707		IR		1748	Cumberland Co. PA
Margaret Thompson						
George's name usually appears as McElwain, as does that of his ancestors.						
1 Andrew	*1740		PA		1793	
2 Joseph	*1743		PA		1822	
Both sons were probably born in Cumberland County, PA.						

Serial # and Name	Birth	Marriage	Death
410000000 McElwain			
Andrew McElwain	!1740	!	!1793
Mary -----	!	!	!
	!	!	!
1 Isabella	+!1783c Cumberland Co.	PA!1825 Jul 28 Cumberland Co. PA!1846 Dec 2 Darke Co. OH
2 Mary	!1784c Cumberland Co.	PA!never married	!
3 Jane	+!1785c Cumberland Co.	PA!1808 Dec 1 Cumberland Co. PA!1835
4 Ruhamma	+!1786 Cumberland Co.	PA!1821 Aug 3	!1856c
5 Andrew	!1787 Cumberland Co.	PA!	! ?IN

    Isabella married Daniel Duvall and Jane married Samuel Baker. All of the children moved west, the women to
Darke County, OH, and Andrew, eventually, to Indiana.

420000000 MCELWAIN			
Joseph McElwain	!1743	!	!
Jeanette Scroggs	!	! Alexander Scroggs &	!
	!	! ----- -----	!
1 Alexander	+!	!	!
2 Ebenezer	*!	!1801 Sep 24 Cumberland Co. PA!1825 Cumberland Co. PA
3 George	!	!	!
4 Jane	+!	!	!
5 Margaret	+!	!	!

    Jane married Joseph Graham; Margaret married George Crow. Alexander may have moved to Kentucky where his father
had property.

422000000 MCELWAIN			
Ebenezer McElwain	!	!1801 Sep 24 Cumberland Co. PA!1825 Cumberland Co. PA
Elizabeth Crow	!	!	!
	!	!	!
1 Jane	+!1802 Sep 21 Cumberland Co. PA!1827 Dec 6	!1877 Mar 10
2 Mary	!1806 Dec 5 Cumberland Co. PA!	!
3 Joseph	+!1808 Nov 20 Cumberland Co. PA!1848	!1888 Jan 18
4 Andrew	*!1810 Feb 24 Cumberland Co. PA!	!1855 Feb 2
5 William G.	!1813 Jul 13 Cumberland Co. PA!	!
6 Elizabeth	+!1815 Dec 5 Cumberland Co. PA!	!1893 Sep 2
7 Margaret	!1820 Mar 11 Cumberland Co. PA!	!
8 Ebenezer	!	!	!

    Jane married William Brown, Jr. and Elizabeth married David Haun.

4223000000 MCELWAIN			
Joseph McElwain	!1808 Nov 20 Cumberland Co. PA!1848	!1888 Jan 18
Elizabeth Cook	!1831	! James Cook & Elizabeth -----!
	!	!	!
1 Sarah Jane	+!1849c Cumberland Co. PA!	!
2 Amanda S.	+!1854c Oct Cumberland Co. PA!	!
3 Elizabeth	!1855 Oct 27 Cumberland Co. PA!	!
4 Margaret	+!1856c Cumberland Co. PA!	!
5 Joseph A.	!1865c Cumberland Co. PA!	!
6 John E.	!1869 Aug 22 Cumberland Co. PA!	!1869 Aug 25
7 Laura B.	!1871c Cumberland Co. PA!	!
8 Ebenezer	! Cumberland Co. PA!	!

    Sarah Jane married John Mowry; Amanda, Thomas Diven; and Margaret, Allumen Kuhn.

Serial # and Name	Birth	Marriage	Death
422500000 MCELWAIN			
Andrew McElwain	:1810 Feb 24 Cumberland Co. PA:		:1855 Feb 22
Elsie Jane Mitchell	:1823 Apr 22	: William Mitchell &	:1893 Dec 31
	:	: ----- -----	:
1 Mary H.	+:1846 Jan 12	:	:1905 Feb 22
2 Elizabeth	:1848 Oct 25	:	:1930 Dec 24
3 Andrew, Jr.	:1852 Oct 9	:	:1860 Feb 15
4 William M.	*:1854 Nov 29	:	:1928 Jan 22 Newville PA
Mary married Zeamer.			
422540000 MCELWAIN			
William M. McElwain	:1854 Nov 29	:1879 Feb 6	:1920 Jan 22 PA
Martha Jane Sharp	:1855 Nov 29	: Andrew Sharp &	:1884 Jun 15
	:	: Eliza E. Jacobs	:
1 Alexander Sharp	:1880 Jan 11	:	:1884 Dec
2 Andrew	*:1883 Jun 10	:1909 Jan 4 Carlisle	PA:1960 Dec 9 Newville PA
422541000 MCELWAIN			
Andrew McElwain	:1883 Jun 10	:1909 Jan 4 Carlisle	PA:1960 Dec 9 PA
s Esther Ellen Piper	:1885 Jul 27 Oakville	PA: John Miller Piper & --- --- :1911 Nov 7 Newville PA
t Kitty Clover Koser	:1886 Apr 6 Plainfield	PA:1914 Dec 28 Newville	PA:1956 Nov 26 Mercer PA
	:	: Howard Myers Koser &	:
	:	: Martha Ellen McCrae	:
1 John William	s+:1910 Oct 21	:1941 Apr 15	:
2 Guy Edward	t*:1916 Dec 9 Newville	PA:1942 Oct 10 Baltimore	MD:
3 Sharp McCrae	t*:1918 Jun 15	:1942 Apr 23 Ambridge	MA:
4 Martha Elizabeth	t+:1919 Oct 28	:1946 Aug 17	:1982 Dec 8 i. Beaver Cntr. PA
5 Jay Lawrence	t :1920 Nov 11	:1959 Dec 29	:
6 Clara Virginia	t+:1922 Jun 20 San Jose	CA:1947 Jun 20	:1962 Feb 12
7 Kitty Clover	t+:1924 Nov 10	:1949 Sep 10	:
8 Mary Jane	t+:1926 Aug 22	:1950 Apr 21	:
9 Barbara Ellen	t :1927 Sep 5	:	:1927 Feb 6
422541100 MCELWAIN			
Guy Edward McElwain	:1916 Dec 9 Newville	PA:1942 Oct 10 Baltimore	MD:
Elizabeth Ann Leisher	:1920 Dec 18 Chambersburg	PA: David Alan Leisher &	:
	:	: Laura Elizabeth Shade	:
1 Sally Ann Allen	+:1945 Apr 2 Baltimore	MD:1969 Aug 5 Newville	PA:
2 Guy Edward, Jr.	*:1949 Oct 29	:1976 Jun 13	:
3 Allen Andrew	*:1950 Mar 19	:1978 Aug 19	:
4 Barbara Ellen	+:1957 May 24	:1987 Apr 24	:
422541100 MCELWAIN			
Guy Edward McElwain, Jr.	:1949 Oct 29	:1976 Jun 13	:
Elizabeth Ann Wood	:1950 Jan 24	:	:
	:	:	:
1 Christopher Sean	:1979 Mar 1	:	:
2 Matthew David	:1982 Sep 2	:	:
3 Anna Elizabeth	:1984 Mar 15	:	:

Serial # and Name	Birth	Marriage	Death
422541200 MCELWAIN			
Allen Andrew McElwain	1950 Mar 19	1970 Aug 19	
Jo Ann Rhoads	1958 Mar 12		
1 Azile Rebecca	1984 May 30		
2 Elizabeth	1990		
442541200 MCELWAIN			
Sharp McCrae McElwain	1918 Jun 15	1942 Apr 23 Ambridge PA	
Elvira Esther Nippes	1916 Aug 1 Blairsville PA	William M. Nippes &	
		Martha Ellen Eppley	
1 Donna Kay	+1943 Jun 12	1964 Jun 8	
2 Paul Andrew	1947 May 10 Pittsburgh PA		

The format of this table is identical to that of the "Genealogy" section

* indicates a following entry for a family.

\+ indicates that the person married, but family information is not shown on this table.

i. = interred

CHAPTER IV

AREAS OF EARLY SETTLEMENT

CUMBERLAND COUNTY

The area that became Cumberland County was included the limits of Lancaster County when that county was erected in 1729. In 1750 Cumberland County was created, to include most of the southwestern part of the State. From time to time new counties were detached from Cumberland until 1820, when Perry County was created, the County assumed its present boundaries. The original County was divided into two townships, Pennsboro in the eastern part and Hopewell in the western. Hopewell was divided over the years, and the area settled by the McElwains became part of Mifflin township and finally of Lower Mifflin township.

The following brief history of Mifflin township is adapted from material written by James B. Schouller for a late nineteenth century History of Cumberland County, with some additional material which was presented at the Civic Club of Newville on July 9, 1942 by Mrs. E. Lee Oiler.

Mifflin was set off from Hopewell as a separate township in January 1797 and was called after Governor Mifflin. It is bounded on the north by North Mountain and on the south by the Conodoguinet Creek and contains some sixty square miles of territory. The soil is a mixture of clay, gravel, and slate; and is remarkably fertile with careful culture. The township is drained by four streams which run from the mountains to the Conodoguinet.

The Scouller family, which lived between the two eastern streams, from want of any other name, called the eastern the Big Run, and the other, which bounded the back part of the farm, the Back Run. The next stream west, which was settled at an earlier day, had no need of a mill, for there was one already at the mouth of Green Spring; so the first industry started by its inhabitants was the conversion of their surplus corn into whiskey, and a number of little distilleries started up, tradition says one on each farm, and the community, from a sense of the fitness of things, called it Whiskey Run. The next stream west, and only a mile distant, was jocosely called Brandy Run, because brandy is next and near to whiskey, and a little better. The western stream was called the Three Square Hollow Run, after the name of the gap in the mountain from which it issues. The triangular shape of the gap led some early Irish settlers to name it Three Square Hollow.

Before the days of white settlers there was an Indian trail through Doubling Gap, but it was used comparatively little and only for local purposes. The principal trail was through the Three Square Hollow, and was a branch of the great trail from the Ohio to the Susquehana, which crossed the Tuscarora mountains near the Burnt Cabins and went down Sherman Creek. This branch left the great trail in the corner of Franklin County, came through the Three Square Hollow, crossed the Conodoguinet near the mouth of Brandy Run, passed up the Green Spring to the head of Big Spring, and thence towards Dilsberg and York. The first settlements made in Mifflin were along this trail, and all the massacres during the Old French War were in its vicinity.

The probabilities are that the first settlers came to Mifflin between 1734 and 1736, but no family record or farm deed can now be found with a date earlier than 1744. In that year

58

three brothers-in-law came from Chester County; one, Mr. Robert Mickey, purchased on the
south side of the creek not far from the head of the Green Spring, and a numerous posterity
now dwell in that part of Newton township. Another, William Thompson, bought across the creek,
for 25 pounds, 11 shillings, 6 pence, the peninsula in the bend of the creek near the present
Thompson's bridge, and the third, Andrew McElwain, located on a tract on Brandy Run
subsequently known as the Lusk or Fountain of Health Farm, and now owned by Mrs. Gilmore.
Other early settlers in the Mifflin section included the Carnahans, Williamsons, Nicholsons,
Stevensons, Shannons, Laughlins, Porterfields, Lightcaps and other were settled, before 1751,
in this part of Mifflin. During the next fifteen years the McLaughlins, Browns, McElhennys,
Martins, Bells, Sterrits, Morrows, Agers, Bradys, and Lusks came in. There are but few of
these families now left--they have scattered in every direction, but mainly to the west.

All of the early settlers were Scotch and Irish with a small intermixture of English. It
is believed that the first Germans came about 1782 or 1783. The Germans came in freely after
1790, and being much more thrifty and economical than the Irish and Scotch, have supplanted the
descendents of the early settlers.

The Indian families which still remained in Mifflin when the first white settlers came,
and the bands which passed through on the great trail, were friendly and peaceable until about
1753 or 1754 when, with the tribes to which they belonged, they fell under the influence of the
French emissaries from Canada, and became very hostile. They committed a number of barbarous
massacres, most of which were in the region of Whiskey and Brandy Runs, or in the vicinity of
the great trail. Among these were the Williamson and the Nicholson massacres.

A number of block houses or forts were built at convenient places, to which the families
of the neighborhood could flee for safety when Indians were around. One of these was situated
on the creek, near the mouth of Brandy Run on the Carnahan farm. This was built at the
beginning of the French and Indian War. The others were probably of a later date, and designed
to give security during the Revolutionary War and the preceding ten years. One of these was on
the Lusk farm, near the Sulphur Spring.

Mifflin has never had within its bounds a post office, a resident physician, a lawyer, or
a clergyman, but has been dependent upon Newville for its mail facilities, its professional
visits, its purchase of house and farm necessities, and its sale of produce. In making these
necessary visitations, the Conodoguinet had to be passed and repassed, notwithstanding the
difficulties and dangers of its floods at all seasons, and its treacherous ice in the winter.
This difficulty has been partially removed by the building of three bridges. The first of
these on the state road leading to Doubling Gap, in the year 1824, and the original structure
is still in good condition. The second was at the Thompson crossing, some fifteen or twenty
years later; and the third still later, at the mouth of the Green Spring.

Tanning was one of the first industries started, and although bark has always been
convenient and cheap, yet the business has entirely died out. Distilleries were once very
numerous, but from a change in the method of conducting the business and a larger change in the
moral sentiment of the community in reference to the business itself, they have all long since
disappeared. Agriculture is the great business of the township, in addition to which the
following industries are now in successful operation: four flouring mills, six saw mills, one
woolen factory, two stores, five blacksmith shops, one cooper shop, and one brickyard.

The chart on page 58, taken from the rolls for the United
States Direct Tax of 1798 provides a picture of the businesses in
Cumberland County which were available to the sons and daughters
of Andrew and Mary Mickey McElwain.

COMMERCIAL STRUCTURES IN CUMBERLAND COUNTY BY TOWNSHIP, 1798

	ALLN	CARL	DICK	EPEN	FRAN	HOPE	MIDD	MIFF	NEWT	SHTN	WPEN	CNTY
apothecary shop										1		1
b. proof [?]							1					1
bar room											1	1
bark house		2						1	1	6		10
brew house		1										1
building										1		1
carpenter shop		3										3
counting house			1									1
coal house		2	1						1			4
cooper shop		3	1							1	1	6
currying shop		1								4		5
forge	1						2					3
fulling mill	2		1	1	1		2		1	1		9
furnace		2										2
granary	2		1		2							5
grist mill	5		6		1	2	13	1	2	5	6	41
hatter shop		4	1							2		7
hemp mill	2		1									3
joiner shop		1							2			3
kiln house		1		1								2
lumber house											1	1
malt house		1						1		2		4
merchant mill								4				4
milk house	3		9				2			3		17
mill	6	4		1						1		12
nursery							1					1
office		4	1									5
oil mill	3		1					1				5
paper mill										1		1
potash works		1	1									2
potter house		1										1
powder mill										2		2
printing office		1								1		2
sadler shop		1										1
saw mill	9		11	1	2	1	14	4	4	8	3	57
shade house		14				1						15
shop		16	1		4				7	16	1	45
slaughter house		3										3
slitting mill							1					1
smith shop	7	10	8		2	2	4	9	5	12	6	65
smoke house		7	3					1	3	1		15
still house	15	4	10	3	6	8	19	10	8	8	4	95
store house		10	1				2		3	3	1	20
tan house/yard	3	6		1	2	1		4		2	2	21
threshing floor		1										1
wagonmaker shop	1				1			2		1		5
weaver shop		2	2		1	1		3	1	1	1	12
wheelright shop		2										2
work shop		7	6								3	16
TOTAL STRUCTURES	59	113	69	8	20	18	60	41	44	76	29	537
1800 population	2077	2093	1475	881	2727	1092	2154	1409	1392	2078	1361	18739

THE PLANTATION OF ANDREW MCELWAIN

Andrew McElwain and Mary Mickey settled in what was then Hopewell township of Lancaster County, Pennsylvania, soon to be Cumberland County and later to be Mifflin township of that County. Their plantation encompassed about 400 acres and was located on Brandy Run, five or six miles north of its confluence with Conodoguinet Creek.

Andrew died in 1770, leaving about 123 acres to his eldest son James. The remaining property was to be held for the use of his wife and the nine other children, and eventually sold, with the proceeds to go to the three younger sons. This portion came into the possession of these three, and finally, after half had been sold to Robert Lusk, the remainder became the property of Andrew.

From the wording of the will it seems that the family dwelling must have been on the portion that was not given to James, and therefore that the house described in the tax roll for the United States Direct Tax of 1798 as that of James must have been erected at some time later. If this surmise is correct, the house belonging to Andrew must have been the original dwelling of Andrew and Mary.

A modern redrawing of surveys made in 1786 when both parts of the original tract were again warranted are reproduced on page 63. They give a good idea of the shape of each of the properties, and provide as well the names of the neighboring landowners. The two tracts join at the north end of James' property and the south of that of Andrew. Running through both is Brandy Run. The scale of the two surveys is not given, nor are they quite the same, but it is possible to see how the tracts join and to visualize the entire plantation of Andrew. The great irregularity of the tracts is typical of most tracts. Why such boundaries were set is difficult to say; they do not follow the stream line, but may be chosen for other natural features.

The original 1786 warrants authorizing the survey are reproduced on page 62. The area of the land on the warrant for the three younger brothers is easy to misread; it is two hundred seventy seven acres. Both warrants were issued on November 16, 1786. Using the rate stated on the warrants, James would have paid about 13 pounds for his land, and Andrew, Robert, and William slightly less than 28 pounds. The date when interest charges begin on the amount due differ greatly; for James they begin on March 1, 1764, for the others on March 1, 1774. In either case it would seem that a large amount of interest would have accrued. The value of a pound at that time is difficult to estimate, but seven years later, according to the estate inventory of Andrew McElwain, son of George, a cow sold for from two to three pounds, and a horse for twelve to twenty.

THE PLANTATIONS OF JAMES AND ANDREW MCELWAIN, 1798

The information in this chart is taken from the rolls for the United States Direct Tax of 1798.   In addition to the properties of James and Andrew, which together comprise the original plantation of their father Andrew, those of neighbors and related families are shown. Areas of the tracts differ slightly from that stated on the warrants.

Residences valued at more than $100 are classed as "house and lot"; two acres was arbitrarily assigned as the size of the house lot. Other residences are classed as "house" or "cabin".

Owner Tenant	Location Adjoining Owner	Structure Lot or Tract	Dim.	Descr.	Stories	Lights Windows		Area	Value
McElwain, Andrew		house & lot	27 x 16	wood	1 1/2	2	16	2 A	150.00
	Lusk, Robert	barn	75 x 20	wood					
		still house	16 x 16						
		tract						263 A	2606.85
McElwain, James		house & lot	42 x 19	wood & stone	1 1/2	1	12	2 A	180.00
	Williamson, David								
		barn	56 x 18	wood					
		tract						121 A	1179.75
Allen, Hugh,	on Three Square	house 1	24 x 20	wood					
heirs of	Hollow Road	house 2	20 x 20	wood	(total value for both houses)				80.00
Allen, John	Brison, Samuel	stable	22 x 22	logs					
		tract						200 A	1720.00
Lusk, Robert		house & lot	28 x 19	wood	2	5	27	2 A	280.00
	McElwain, Andrew	spring house	12 x 12	stone					
		barn	70 x 19	wood					
		tract						135 A	1551.15
McElwain, Andrew	on Conodoguinet Creek	house & lot	25 x 24	wood	2	4	34	2 A	270.00
heirs of	Gees, Conrad	kitchen		wood					
Lightcap, William		barn	60 x 20	wood					
		tract						269 A	3139.30
McElwain, Joseph	on Conodoguinet Creek	house & lot	27 x 17	wood	1 1/2	4	24	2 A	250.00
	Morrow, Samuel	pump house	small	wood					
		barn	60 x 20						
[Andrew and Joseph were sons of George]		tan vats		six vats					
		tract						100 A	1300.00
Morrow, John		house & lot	20 x 20	wood	1	1	9	2 A	100.25
	Felair, Andrew	barn	22 x 22	wood					
		tract						98 A	891.60
Nicholson, James	on Whiskey Run	house & lot	26 x 26	stone	2	4	12	2 A	500.00
	Stevenson, James	kitchen				[?]	4		
		[?]				1	9		
[son of Richard and brother of Mary,		cellar							
the wife of James McElwain]		barn 1	55 x 20	wood				287 A	3387.60
		barn 2	62 x 22	wood	2	10	72		
		tract						287 A	3387.60
Stewart, James,	Three Square Hollow	house & lot	22 x 20	wood	1	2	12	2 A	100.50
heirs of	Road	cellar		wood					
Carnahan, James	Barr, Robert	stable		old				118 A	944.00
[a neighbor of James McElwain]		tract						118 A	944.00

LAND WARRANTS ISSUED TO JAMES MCELWAIN
AND TO ANDREW, ROBERT, AND WILLIAM MCELWAIN, 1786

At the time the warrants were issued the properties lay in
Newton Township. They became part of Mifflin township in 1797.

SURVEYS OF THE PLANTATIONS OF JAMES MCELWAIN
AND OF ANDREW, ROBERT, AND WILLIAM MCELWAIN

THE WILLS OF ANDREW MCELWAIN
AND JAMES MCELWAIN

The signature portions are reproduced. The signature of Andrew is largely obscured by repairs, but the lower portion of his first name can be seen immediately to the right of the word "published". That of James is somewhat damaged but legible; he signed "Jas." Tomson's name appears as Thompson in most records and in this book. Note his use of the old-fashioned long or medial "s", which looks somewhat like an "f" with the lower loop reversed.

MERCER COUNTY

The area that later became Mercer County, along with that which now makes up all or part of twenty two other western Pennsylvania Counties was opened to settlement upon the extinction of the Indian title by a treaty signed on October 21, 1784 at Fort Stanwix (now Rome), New York. The year before, in anticipation of this, the Legislature had enacted a law setting aside certain lands, which included Mercer County as "donation lands" for the benefit of soldiers who had served in the Revolution, and who were issued certificates to be redeemed later in payment for their services. These certificates became greatly depreciated in value, and this act was an attempt to do justice to the claims of these men. The certificates were to be redeemed at face value in payment for the donation lands.

Before 1788 most of the northwestern part of Pennsylvania was included in Westmoreland County. In that year Allegheny County was erected by joining portions of Westmoreland and Washington Counties. This new county ran all the way north to Lake Erie, and from a portion of it Mercer County was created in 1800. Included in the original boundaries was the area it now occupies plus the northern part of what became Lawrence County in 1849.

Settlement of Mercer County began in 1796. Although there is some doubt as to who was the first settler, Matthias Zahniser was certainly among the earliest, as he arrived in April 1796. Other early settlers included Adam Carnahan and Ruth McElwain who came about 1797 according to the *Mercer County History*, and possibly Thomas McCracken, father of Joshua who was the grandfather of Mary McCracken, the wife of John T. McElwain.

John S. McElwain and Hannah Thompson came to Mercer County about 1806, according to the Mercer County History. John had married Hannah Thompson on March 16, 1805 at the Middle Spring Church in Cumberland County, and apparently moved west shortly thereafter. The couple settled on a farm in French Creek township in the northeastern corner of the county.

MERCER COUNTY IN 1873

[from *Combination Atlas of the County of Mercer and the State of Pennsylvania*,
Philadelphia, G. M. Hopkins & Co., 1873

French Creek township was created in 1805 from Sandy Creek; at that time it included what
later became Deer Creek, New Vernon, and Mill Creek townships. Mill Creek was created from
French Creek in 1849, Deer Creek and New Vernon, in 1851. The townships remain today the same
as in 1873, except for Pymatuning from which has been detached South Pymatuning and Clark.

THE BOROUGH OF NEW LEBANON, PENNSYLVANIA

[from *Combination Atlas of the County of
Mercer and the State of Pennsylvania*
Philadelphia, G. M. Hopkins & Co., 1873]

The plan of the Borough of New Lebanon shows
eight properties of John McElwain. Six lay just
south of Centre Street.   Of these, lots 69 and
70 were between Main and Crawford, and lots 155
156, 157, and 158 were between Main and Venango
Streets.   Two additional lots, 92 and 93, were
on Franklin Street, east of Crawford Street.
There the name is given as J. M. Elwain.

The town of New Lebanon has disappeared.
The site now has on it a few scattered houses,
but there is no sign of the Public Squares or of
any commercial buildings.

The map is reproduced in the original size
and the scale is therefore corrrect,

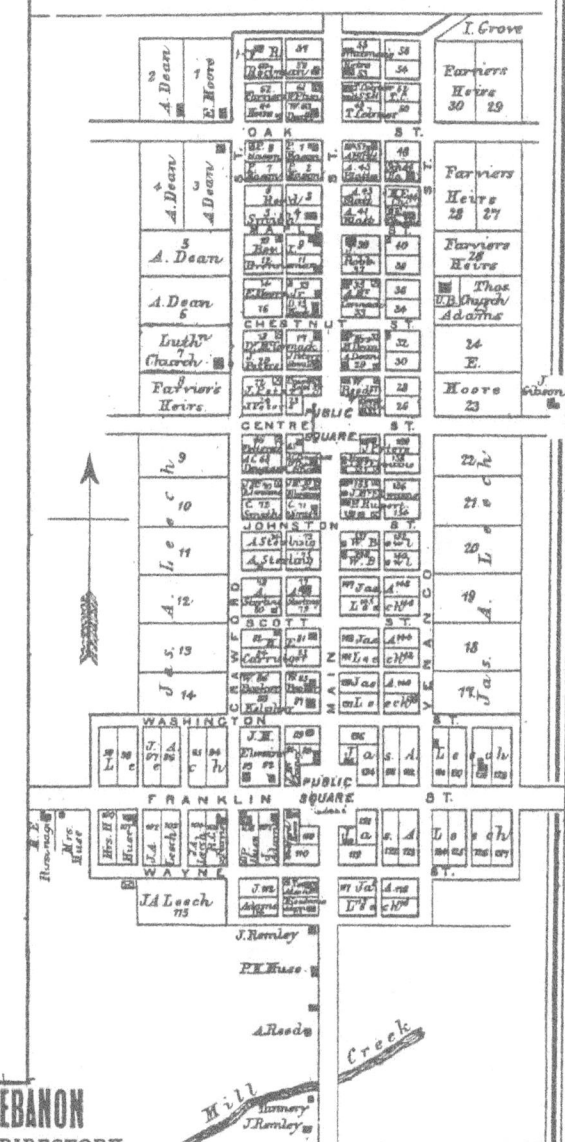

Plan of
Part of the Borough of
NEW LEBANON.
Scale: 400 ft. to the inch.

NEW LEBANON
BUSINESS DIRECTORY.

JOHN McELWAIN,
Dealer in Dry Goods, Groceries, Hardware,
Drugs, Hats, Caps, Shoes, Boots, Flour, &c.
Main st.

JOHN PETERS,
Proprietor Union Hotel,
Main st.

J. GROVE,
Farmer,
New Lebanon.

SANDY LAKE BOROUGH, MERCER COUNTY, PENNSYLVANIA

[from *Combination Atlas* of the County of Mercer and
the State of Pennsylvania, Philadelphia, G. M.
Hopkins, 1873]

The McElwain livery stable was located along
Main Street, between College and Lacock Streets. The
property is shown as that of "J. McElwain", since
James (#245000000) was still living at the time. The
advertisement in the Business Directory names M. M.
(Montgomery Murdoch) McElwain (#245300000), the son
of James, as the proprietor. The spelling of the
name was changed to McElwaine at some time prior to
1880, when it so appears in the census.

This reproduction is the same size as the original and therefore the scale of the map is correct.

SANDY LAKE
Business Directory.

J. L. Cross,
Undertaker and Dealer in all kinds Furniture
Chairs, Chamber and Parlor Sets, Coffins, &c.
Cor. Main and Maple sts.

J. F. Brown,
Residence, Lynch Road.

N. Amon,
Farmer,
Residence, Main st.

Henry Nizon,
Residence, Main st.

S. Newkirk,
Residence, cor. Main and Lake sts.

D. C. Reed,
Residence, Wood st.

J. F. Johnston,
Merchant Tailor,
Main st.

Ballet & Zahniser,
Dealers in Hardware, Stoves, Tinware, Tools,
Doors and Sash, and all kinds of Agricultural
Implements,
Main st.

H. S. Blatt Co.
Dealer in Hardware, Iron, Glass, Housefur-
nishing Goods and all kinds of Carriage
Goods, &c.
Main st.

J. P. Cummings,
Justice of the Peace,
Office, Main st.
Sandy Lake.

J. W. Peck,
Agent J. and F. R. R.

W. W. West,
Sandy Lake Iron Works,
Works, West of Main st.

E. M. Latham,
Planing Mill,
Lynch Road.

H. S. Blatt & Co.
Carriage Works,
Main st.

J. B. Maxwell,
Contractor and Builder,
Main st.

I. D. Powell,
Contractor and Builder,
Wood st.

Vitalis Park,
Dealer in Drugs, Medicines, Chemical, Dye
Stuffs, Combs, Brushes and Fancy Goods,
Main st.

Kirk & Simcox,
Dealers in Dry Goods, Groceries, Boot, Shoes
Queensware, &c.
N. E. cor. Main and Lake sts.

Wm. Carmichael,
Dealer in Dry Goods, Groceries, Queensware,
Boots, Shoes, &c.
Main st.

J. J. Snider,
Dealer in Groceries, Boots and Shoes, and
general assortment of Goods,
Main st.

J. A. McCormack & Co.
Dealers in Dry Goods, Groceries, Hats, Caps,
Boots, Shoes, &c.
Main st., Sandy Lake, and General Store at
Clark's Mills.

John Cook,
Dealer in Boots and Shoes, Clothing, Groceries,
Tobacco, Cigars, &c.
Main above College st.

A. Niles,
Manufacturer of Gloves and Mittens,
Cor. Main and Mill sts.

R. Adams,
Gardner and Dealer in Lumber,
Forest Gardens,
Main st.

Alto House,
Cor. Main and College sts.
Wm. Googs, Proprietor.

Byers & Foster,
Livery, Sale, Exchange Stables,
College st.
Rear Alto House, Sandy Lake. Offices, Alto
House, Sandy Lake, and Lake Hotel, Stoneboro.

M. M. McElwain,
Livery, Sale and Exchange Stables,
Near Main st.
Sandy Lake.

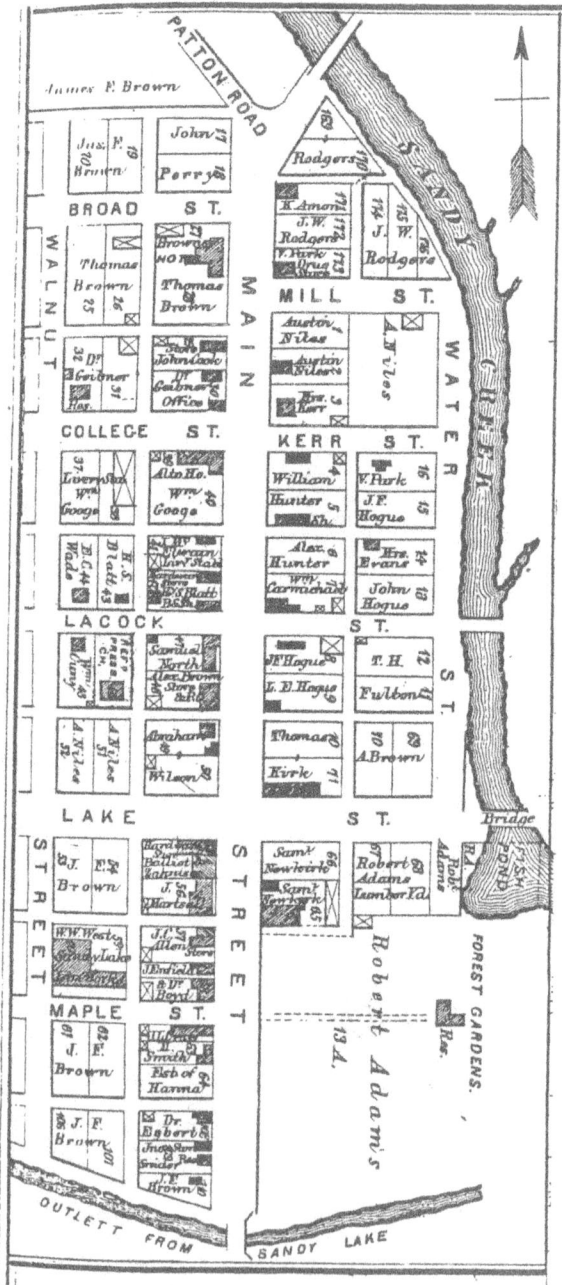

Sub-Plan of
SANDY LAKE.
Scale: 200 ft to one inch

SOUTHWESTERN PENNSYLVANIA

Southwestern Pennsylvania was settled early thanks to its accessibility by two roads constructed during the French and Indian War. Braddock's Road, built in 1755 as a part of the campaign to capture Fort Duquesne by the ill-fated general for whom it was named, ran from Ft. Cumberland, Maryland to Fort Duquesne (Pittsburgh). A second road, built a few years later by General John Forbes ran from Harrisburg through Cumberland County to Bedford, directly through Westmoreland County, and on to Pittsburgh in Allegheny County. Both roads were much used in the settlement of western Pennsylvania, but it was Forbes Road that tempted Cumberland County people to seek opportunites in the west.

Three of the children of Andrew and Mary Mickey McElwain are known to have moved westward. Robert (#900000000) and William (#a00000000) were in Westmoreland County by 1799, and Ruth (#700000000) and her husband George McIlvaine went to Washington County about 1785.

Westmoreland County was a pre-Revolutionary county, having been created in 1773 from Bedford County. Population growth in the area was sufficiently great that in 1781 both Washington and Fayette Counties were detached from Westmoreland. Population figures for 1790 and afterwards show the continued growth.

County	1790	1800	1810	1820	1860	1990
Westmoreland	16,018	22,726	26,392	30,540	53,736	370,221
Washington	23,866	28,298	36,289	40,038	46,805	204,584
Greene		8,605	12,544	15,554	24,343	39,550
Fayette	13,325	20,159	24,714	27,285	39,909	145,351
Allegheny	10,309	15,087	25,317	34,921	178,831	1,336,449

After the capture of Ft. Duquesne from the French, the place was renamed Ft. Pitt; settlement began in the adjoining areas about 1760 and the town which grew up was incorporated as Pittsburgh in 1794. Settlement around what was to become the town of Washington began in 1769, and the town, which later became part of Washington County, was laid out in 1781. In that portion of Westmoreland County which remains so named settlement began about 1782; Greensburg, the county seat was incorporated in 1798. Comparing these dates with the migration dates of Robert, William, and Ruth show that they did not move into an unsettled area; they would best be described as early settlers and not as pioneers.

OHIO

The Land Ordinance of 1785 gave the United States government possession of all the land in what is now Ohio,

70

and the Northwest Ordinance provided for the subsequent
admission of portions of that area as states. Congress
authorized the United States Treasury to sell parcels of land
to the highest bidder, but with little results. The task was
then turned over to a private concern, the Ohio Company,
which was more successful and brought about the first
settlement in Ohio, at Marrietta in 1788. Cincinnati was
founded in the same year by people from New Jersey, and
Chillocothe in 1796 by Virginians.

So rapidly did the population increase that the native
inhabitants became sufficiently alarmed to cause them to form
a confederation to drive out the whites. After they had
achieved some initial successes, the Indians were finally
defeated on August 20, 1794 by General Anthony Wayne at the
Battle of Fallen Timbers, on the Maumee River a few miles
southwest of the present location of Toledo. In the
following year the Treaty of Greenville formally ended the
Indian wars and, accelerating growth began.

In the year 1800 the population of Ohio was 42,000.
Three years later, on November 1, 1803, Ohio was admitted as
the seventeenth state. The population grew to 230,760 by
1810, and in 1820 Ohio's population of 581,434 made it the
fifth-ranking state in population.

Settlement by several third-generation McElwain and
related families occurred in Greene, Wayne, and Licking
Counties. James McElwain (4b0000000) moved from Cumberland
County, Pennsylvania to Greene County about 1834, and Greer
McIlvaine (7b0000000), from Washington County, Pennsylvania
to Licking County about 1831. Their settlements were
facilitated by the construction of the National Road which
was gradually extended from Cumberland, Maryland through
Washington, Pennsylvania to Wheeling, West Virginia (1818),
Zanesville (1826), Columbus (1833), and Springfield (1838).
The route to Wayne County, a considerably shorter trip, was
along the Great Trail which ran from Pittsburgh through Wayne
County to Detroit.

WESTWARD THE COURSE OF EMPIRE

Over the nineteenth century McElwain families gradually
spread westward. As with the early McElwain settlers, the
later ones usually moved to well-settled areas. The chart on
page 70 summarizes some of these migrations Moves to nearby
areas, Mercer Co. to Crawford or Venango Counties, for
example, have been omitted.

MIGRATION PATTERNS OF THE FIRST FOUR GENERATIONS

Serial #	Year	Name	From	To
000000000	1745c	Andrew McElwain & Mary Mickey	Sussex Co., DE	Cumberland Co., PA
700000000	1787c	Ruth McElwain & George McIlvaine	Cumberland Co., PA	Washington Co., PA
900000000	1799<	Robert McElwain & Elizabeth McGlaughlin	Cumberland Co., PA	Westmoreland Co., PA
a00000000	1799<	William McElwain & Lydia Curren (?)	Cumberland Co., PA	Westmoreland Co., PA
230000000	1802	Ruth McElwain and Adam Carnahan	Cumberland Co., PA	Mercer Co., PA
220000000	1806	John S. McElwain & Hannah Thompson	Cumberland Co., PA	Mercer Co., PA
7b0000000	1831	Greer McIlvaine & Martha Browne	Washington Co., PA	Licking Co., OH
4b0000000	1834c	James McElwain & Alice Carson	Cumberland Co., PA	Greene Co., OH
750000000	1839<	John McElwain & Margaret Smith	Washington Co., PA	Wayne Co., OH
240000000	1840<	Richard McElwain and Rosanna Thompson	Cumberland Co., PA	Mercer Co., PA
a10000000	1850<	Elizabeth McElwain & John Love	Westmoreland Co., PA	Jefferson Co., PA
242000000	1840<	Andrew T. McElwain & (Nancy Wheatley)	Mercer Co., PA	Iowa City, IA
783000000	1844-57	George W. McIlvaine & (Jane Robb)	Washington Co., PA	Tuscarawas Co., OH
4a3000000	1846<	Andrew McElwain & (Mary -----)	Cumberland Co., PA	Greene Co., OH
221000000	1850<	James McElwain & (Nancy Nicholson)	Mercer Co., PA	Wyandotte Co., OH
237000000	1850-55	Adam Carnahan & Mary Jane -----)	Mercer Co., PA	Portage Co., OH
754000000	1851c	Ruth McIlvaine & George Waltenberg	Wayne Co., OH	Sauk Co., WI
755000000	1854-59	Mary Jane McIlvaine & Alexander Dunlap	Wayne Co., OH	Sauk Co., WI
784000000	1855-57	John D. McIlvaine & Charlotte Wilson	Washington Co., PA	Tuscarawas Co., OH
4a4000000	1856c	William B. McElwain & Mary Jane Mapps	Cumberland Co., PA	Knox Co., IL
421000000	1866c	Isabel McElwain & James B. Ervin	Cumberland Co., PA	Allegheny Co., PA
4a5000000	1865c	James McElwain & (Eliza Bechtel)	Cumberland Co., PA	Johnson Co., KS
4ab000000	1877<	Robert H. McElwain & (Martha Adamson)	Cumberland Co., PA	Rice Co., KS
4ac000000	1879	Thomas S. McElwain & Mary Nickey	Cumberland Co., PA	Crawford Co., KS
4a9000000	1893<	Lacy McElwain & John Ramp	Cumberland Co., PA	Johnson Co., KS
237200000	1886c	Carlos Carnahan & (Rosetta Williams)	Portage Co., OH	Cassia Co., ID
4a4300000	1887-90	Nancy McElwain & Benjamin Corbin	Knox Co., IL	Kansas
245500000	1890<	Albert & Florence McElwain	Mercer Co., PA	Marion Co., IN
237100000	1899<	Vicnelia Carnahan & Francis Wilson	Portage Co., OH	Noble Co., OK
4a9500000	1899<	Harvey Ramp & Anna Earnshaw	Johnson Co., KS	Hemphill Co., TX

Names of wives who lived in the area to which the husband moved are enclosed in parenthesis. A question mark in parenthesis after the name of a wife means the area of her origin is uncertain.

CHAPTER V

THE MCELWAIN INSTITUTE

The McElwain Institute provided to the residents of Mercer County educational facilities beyond the elementary level for many years. It was named for John McElwain (#226000000), the major contributor to the foundation of the institution.

The strong and lasting influence upon the Mercer County area of the McElwain Institute appears in an article from a Greenville, Pennsylvania newspaper of August 22, 1930 which describes the seventh annual reunion which had taken place two days before. More than two hundred persons attended, some from as far away as Boston and Buffalo. The writer concluded that "memories of the days spent at McElwain holds the students in a grip which calls them to the old grounds every third Wednesday of August."

Beyond the academic program, the Institute provided for the community a varied program of dramatic, musical, and athletic activities. Even the graduation programs, as described by a newspaper of the time, were community events, attracting large crowds.

[This article from a newpaper, name and date unknown, is here condensed and slightly altered.]

The commencement at McElwain Institute passed off very successfully. The rostrum and the chandeliers had been handsomely decorated, and the stage was made fragrant by a great variety of blooming plants. The chapel, which has a seating capacity of over 400, was well filled. At the appointed hour Profs. Lamb and Dodd, accompanied by the class of '86 passed, up the aisle. Miss Anna McCracken came first on the program and read an essay entitled, "Heroes Uncrowned." C. M. Grove next delivered an oration, "Education a Physical Necessity," in an easy eloquent manner. Next Miss Hattie McClelland read an essay, "Pictures in Words," in which she merited much praise both as a reader and a writer. In presenting the diplomas Prof. Lamb addressed the class in a touching and effective manner. Prof. McMullen and W. W. Moore, Esq. made a few terse remarks, while W. A. McCormick, Esq. and Prof. Montgomery of Allegheny College made short but able addresses. The vocal music furnished by the McClintock sisters was highly enjoyed and appreciated by all.

The Ciceronian literary society gave an entertainment at night. The people began to pour in early in the evening until the chapel became so crowded it became necessary to stop selling tickets. The Institute Glee Club open the exercises by singing "Jesus, Lover of My Soul," and Rev. R. A. Buzza followed in prayer. The salutatory "Character, the Culture" was given by Miss Mary Nelson; an oration, "Eight Hours of Labor for a Day's Work" by Mr. R. V. Canon; a recitation, "Archy Dean," by Miss Nellie McQuiston; an essay, "The Hand of God in History," by Miss Lizzy McMurray, and a declamation, "The Old Surgeon's Story," by Mr. W. A. Thompson.

Next came a pantomime, "Bluebeard." Then Miss McClintock sang "Coming through the Rye," and was called back. Mr. J. R. Burrows then delivered the valedictory address, "Just Beyond." To conclude, Miss Montgomery was encored on the song, "Better Bide a Wee."

The history of McElwain Institute is told by the two contemporary writings to be found on the following pages. A few Institute publications have survived, having been passed down for generations

and coming finally to rest in my collection. Programs for a
graduation, a dramatic performance, and a music recital are
illustrated by the foxed and crumbling pages which are reproduced
after the histories.

HISTORY OF MCELWAIN INSTITUTE

[author unknown]

McElwain Institute, situated in the borough of New Lebanon, Mercer County, was established in the Spring of
1880 under the name of New Lebanon Institute. The citizens of New Lebanon and vicinity, feeling a need of a
greater facility of learning for the youth of this and neighboring counties, subscribed $25,000 [$2,500 ?] for the
purchase of the land and erection of such a building as would serve as an Academic School. A fine site was
selected and the erection began at once and was completed in January 1881, but it was not dedicated till February
1881 by Prof. W. G. Williams, then of Allegheny College. Its entire cost was $6,166 and to provide for its
indebtedness $4,650 was then and there subscribed. It was then decided the building should be dedicated by the
name of McElwain Institute in honor of John McElwain, of New Lebanon, whose most generous donation, being $2,000,
went for its future support and success. It was their aim to build up a first class Academy between the Common
school and the College, which was certainly needed in such a locality.

About 100 books were at once donated to the library by several men who were friends of the Institution; such
as Hon. James McConnell, Milledgeville; Hon. S. B. Dick, Meadville; Prof. A. J. Palm, then of Mercer, who
afterward became Supt. of Mercer Co.; and many others. More were added in later years until the library became
quite a storehouse of Universal Knowledge.

At its dedication the directors, who were A. C. Grove, S. S. Overenoyer, John McElwain, James Lindsay, New
Lebanon; W. E. McDowell, Sandy Lake; James C. Brown, Greenville; A. J. Palmer, Mercer; B. N. Carnahan, Oil City;
and James McConnell, Milledgeville; met and elected the following corps of teachers: Prin. Erving L. Richardson,
A.M. of Conn., J. T. Carnahan, J. W. Lackey, Prof. A. S. M. Hopkins and wife. The two latter to take charge of
the Music Department both vocal and instrumental.

The first term began August 23, 1881 and during the entire year they had an attendance of 118 students in all
three departments--Grammar School, Academic, and Music. At the end of that school year a new faculty was elected
which was: W. H. Dodds, A.B., Prin., with assistants J. N. Martin, Mary Cousins, and Nellie F. Ordell. By this
time the attendance increased till during the Fall Term alone there were 105 in attendance and during the entire
year there were 192. Prof. Dodds remained just one year when Prof. S. H. Sheakley was elected to succeed him and
it was under his principalship that the first graduation exercise was held, in the spring term of 1884. This class
had four members--Harry Heydrick, Leon Grove, J. W. Rider, now of the Rider Hotel, Cambridge, and Ella McCormack.

In the fall of 1885 George H. Lamb with a corps of very able assistants took control of the Institute and had
the largest attendance that at that time was on record of McElwain Institute, graduating the following spring, four
more: W. B. Blatt, John N. Dunn, Moses B. Griffith, and Nettie C. Grove. Prof. Lamb remained two years and had
three graduates the spring of 1886. He was elected to teach the third year, but resigned in favor of Moses B.
Griffith, of the class of '80.

On account of financial affairs and so frequent changes in Principals the success of the Institute seemed to
be on the decline. But [the Principalship] was next given to W. E. Canon, a former student of McElwain, but then
a recent graduate of Edinboro State Normal, who, by the aid of Prof. Campbell, our district attorney in Mercer
County at the present time, and James McCracken, now Esq. in Mercer, etc., he built the school up till it was once
more in a fair way to success. Prof. Canon stayed two years when he, like his predecessors, felt strong enough
financially to step up higher, so he entered a Medical School and by great perseverance became a doctor but died
shortly after his graduation.

During the next six years a number of Principals had charge, among them being C. N. Moore, now pastor of the Presbyterian Church in Slippery Rock, Prof. Irvine W. E. Coonser, then a recent graduate of McElwain, but by the start he got there he "while his companions slept was toiling upward in the night." After staying here only a short term he entered the Seminary at Schirs Grove [?] and came out in a few years of patient toil and endeavor, a Lutheran minister, and is now pastor of the First Lutheran Church in San Jose, Cal., with a salary of about $2,000 a year. He, as well as many others, owes his standing in life wholly to the start he got at McElvain. Among others who might be mentioned as using McElwain as a first stepping stone are: Dr. J. C. Covley, Sandy Lake; Rev. J. C. Such, Ill.; Rev. J. D. McCaughtry, also of Ill.; Rev. J. C. Borland, New Castle; Dr. Leon V. Grove, Anandale, Pa.; Leech Grove, Esq., Ellwood City; Rev. J. Riveous, Burrows; Dr. D. B. Biggs, Pittsburgh; Rev. John Nelson; Dr. Frank F. Urey, Wampum; Dr. C. L. Moore, Burg Hill, Ohio; Jno. N. Dunn, Esq., Pittsburgh; Moses B. Griffith, Principal of School in Indiana; J. W. Rider, Cambridge; W. B. Blatt, Pittsburgh; Fred Hogue, Esq., Cleveland, Ohio; Chas. H. Donnell, one of Venango County's greatest educators; Dr. F. F. McClellan, Utica; Dr. Chas. Snyder, Polk; Dr. W. A. Womer, Sharon; Dr. Josie L. DeFrance, who is now located in St. Louis. All of these and more owe their standing to the education that they received at McElwain Institute.

Many of these were farmer's children living in the vicinity who could board at home or bring their board from home and by paying $8.50 tuition and by buying their books which most of them did with the money they earned during vacations, they received a good education. Had they been forced either to go to Meadville or Grove City, or stay at home they would simply have had to give up and remain farmer men and women, all their lives toiling early and late to keep the wolf from the door, but by the knowledge they received at McElwain they were put upon a basis where they could gradually climb the ladder of fame till now McElwain has representatives in many states in the United States in professional work, and Maggie Nelson is doing a grand work among the heathen in China.

In 1895 Prof. J. C. Fruit was elected Principal and with his great perseverance and determination to succeed in whatever he undertakes, built the school from a complete standstill to the largest attendance in its history. The first week of his first term he had seven students, six of whom remained with him till they graduated, four of whom were in the banner class of '98 when there graduated the largest number that had at that time ever left that Institute, being 13 graduates in the different courses. During the first year he had an attendance of 170 and the next year it increased to 317. There were 180 in the spring term alone, and the next spring, 1898, there were 150 in attendance. During his stay he graduated 28, nearly all of whom are now engaged in education work. About one hundred of his students are teachers and are found in many counties in this State and in other states. Some are teaching in the country schools, while others, either by good management or luck, have become graded teachers, and still others have become principals.

Altho but one of his students have as yet become professional people, yet some of them are climbing that way as fast as financial affairs will allow them. Among these might be mentioned those in College and Universities. Jesse Fanna, who is now attending North Dakota State University, and C. B. Livingston, Drew [?] Seminary, N. J. The former of whom has lately written that he would like to thank Prof. Fruit for the encouragement he gave him at McElwain Institute, fully realizing that to be his first stepping stone to something higher. Also C. F. Wheeler, who is now Treasurer of [?] Trust Co. Bank in New Castle and is working his way upward in the business, all due to his start at McElwain. And many more might also be worthily mentioned but time does not permit.

After Prof. Fruit left McElwain it seemed to take a backward movement, but the interest created could not die out all at once so it kept smoldering away under the management of different principals among whom were Prof. Steele and wife, Prof. Conner, Prof. Smathers, and others, some of whom remained only a term or two, just till they could get a better position or a little help on their way to something higher. At the present time it is idle, but is undergoing repairs getting ready for another noble man to present himself, which reminds us that

> The old Institute bell is silent   And when we see its massive wall
> Hushed is now its iron tongue   Whenever we enter the town
> But the spirit it awakened   May we not forget Jim Fruit
> Still is living, ever young.   Who gave it its last coat of brown

THE PASSING OF THE VILLAGE ACADEMY

By Earle D. Bruner

No longer does the bell of the Village Academy send forth its call to youth of town and country-side. No more do the long lines of buggies and surreys wend their way to Chapel Hall during the Commencement Week.   Gone are the merry faces that once were seen on the campus.   Hushed is the hearty laughter that once resounded through the halls. The Village Academy has passed away.

This institution came into existence during the second generation of the pioneer of the sod.   It has had a glorious past, has a present of decay, and no future save when one finds a dust-covered catalog in an old attic, or some biographer seeks the history of the great. The modern High School brings to the door of all youth the opportunity which during the past century was denied save to the children of the wealthy, or to the ones who had enough ambition to make the sacrifice necessary in order to secure some measure of higher education.   It is better now that these   opportunities come to every American Citizen, but we who must see all from the viewpoint of middle age may be excused for harking back and spending an occasional hour in the period of red flannel, Kentucky Jeans, and the bootjack.

The incentive to write this article was stimulated (I dare not say inspired) by a reunion of some five hundred former students of my old village academy.   Once again the old bell in the chapel rang, but the fact that it was also a toll for many who had passed away dulled the note of gladness.   Laughter again resounded through the halls but the merriment had a subdued note that comes from burdens and cares.   We view the scenes of youth and talk with those whom we once knew, but if we seek for the ardor of youth, we seek in vain.

In this article I shall deal not in masked phrases and implied hints, but in names and places, dates and data as these events occurred insofar as memory serves after forty years.

McElwain Institute was founded during the latter part of the nineteenth century and named in honor of a pioneer.   It flourished for a decade or more and among the instructors of this period was a Dr. Samuel Dodds, the father of the president of Princeton. Hard times then fell on this little institution and the panic of 1893 almost destroyed it.

During the summer of 1895, a young graduate of Grove City College, James S. Fruit (always Professor Fruit to us) was elected principal and set himself the task of rebuilding McElwain Institute.   In August, 1895, he called a meeting in the Chapel Hall and the entire village and country side turned out. Addresses were made by Dr. Isaac C. Ketler, President of Grove City College, and Judge Miller, of the Mercer County Courts.

Dr. Ketler gave an address so forceful that we lads in our early teens sensed that we were in the presence of greatness.   Time has changed our measuring stick for humanity, but time has not changed our estimate of the greatness of Dr. Ketler, the wisdom of Judge Miller, or the kindness of Professor Fruit.

When school opened in September, eight boys and three girls were present.   Among that group of country boys were Dr. A. A. Borland, head of the Department of Animal Husbandry at State College, Pa.;   Dr. William A. Womer, a noted pathologist of New Castle, Pa.; Fred Wheeler, a banker; Thomas Lindsey, a successful lumberman; Dr. Vance Thompson and Dr. Clare Thompson of Franklin; Dr. Don Wheeler, head of the Pulpit Oratory at Princeton Theological Seminary; Exie Grove (now Mrs. Lindsey); Mabel Dunn (a cousin of Harold Dodds); and Kathryn Reagle.

Professor Fruit helped the janitor build the fires and sweep the building in the morning.   He taught special students from seven-thirty until nine o'clock when we all assembled for chapel.   After chapel he taught steadily until noon.   He taught from one until five, helped us with our literary on Friday nights and coached our dramas on Monday and Wednesday evening.   I don't know what he did with the remainder of the time but we didn't have thirty hour weeks so it didn't matter.

The dramas were the spice of school life.   How well we remember "Past Redemption."   Billy Womer was Captain

Bragg, Tom Lindsey was John Maynard, Exie Grove was Kitty Koram, Len Crouser was Stubbs, the negro comedian, Julia Burnett was Charity Goodall, Professor was the hero, and on account of my ruddy face and liberal girth, I was selected as Daley, the bartender. Dr. Womer still kids me because of my awkwardness; I knocked down part of the bar fixtures. Let me say in self-defense that during the next two years I improved in dramatic grace to such a degree that I was given the role of Simon Slade in "Ten Nights in a Bar-room." I fear that this early training is responsible for the fact that, being absolutely dry and anti-liquor, in any group I am taken for one who is ready to have a drink. The winter enrollment was forty. The hard work of Professor Fruit was beginning to tell. The attendance for the spring term was about seventy-five. Among the students were a number of fairly good baseball players. Professor played first base and coached the team. While several years younger than the majority of the boys, I tried my best to make the team. I was large for my age and fairly strong, but too awkward. I believe that I trained twice as much as any other player, but just couldn't make the grade even as a substitute.

We won several local games and finally our most vicious and deadly rival, Fredonia Institute agreed to play us. I never shall forget the day of that game. John S. Runniger, a professional, agreed to pitch for us. We had worked ourselves up to such a pitch that had any fair-minded person even hinted that there was a chance that we might be defeated, he would have been branded as a traitor and an enemy.

The day we left for Fredonia every one turned out to back up the team. Local pride was at its height. There were a few surreys, many more buggies, several bicycles all flying McElwain colors, and the big hack containing the heroic players with their white uniforms and the letters M C I boldly across the chest. We had practiced our yells and from time to time we stopped to give:

Kalli ki lick ki lick ki lix
Kalli ki lick ki lick ki lix
McElwain in Ninety-Six
McElwain in Ninety-Six

No Persian ever crossed the Hellespont with more determination than we entered Fredonia that day so many years ago. Could I have worn that uniform even as a substitute on the bench, my cup would have been running over. "The worldly hope men set their hearts upon turns ashes." O woeful day: O wounded pride. Oh deep humiliation: Our catcher could not hold the terrific speed of John S. Runniger, Professor Fruit was hit a blow on the nose by a ground ball, and disaster stalked our steps at every turn.

I can still hear those derisive laughs when our catcher would muff the third strike while the ball rolled to the backstop, and the batter reached first base. Inning after inning of humiliation while George Maxwell held our side scoreless. Final result was: Fredonia - 12. McElwain - 0. Oh, the long journey home! Fifteen miles of driving and reflection. We had a consolation and indignation meeting in Milt Byham's Hotel late that night and reviewed the game play by play and in the end had deceived ourselves into believing that the umpire had robbed us instead of facing the fact that we were a group of raw, untrained country boys who never even had a look-in with a skilled and well-trained team.

I did not attend McElwain during the fall and winter terms of the following year. Having reached the mature age of sixteen years, I taught in a country school of some forty-eight pupils. My school was over in time to enter McElwain for the spring term. What a change. There were one hundred and fifty students and a faculty of seven. Anna Dunn, a cousin of Harold Dodds, was the head of the music department; Cora Glenn taught vocal music while Prof. S. I. (Sam) Conner was the instructor in elocution and oratory. All day long one might hear the drum of the piano, the agonizing notes of the ones taking voice culture, or down in Sam Connor's studio the "Legend of the Organbuilder," "The Seminole's Defiance," "Cataline's Reply to Cicero," or "The Death-bed of Benedict Arnold."

I still can see Sam's graceful little hands as he taught us to say, "Vipers which creep where man disdains to climb and having wound their loathsome track to the top of this huge, mouldering monument, Rome, hang hissing at the nobler men below." There was defiance in every pose, gesture, and face expression as he quoted:

"He dare not touch a hair of Cataline," or

"And e'er yet the song was ended
He who bore the Coffins head,
With the air of one forgiven,
Gently sank beside it dead."

One morning in Chapel Professor Fruit announced that a rising young actor, Joe Ketler, was to coach our play, "From Sumpter to Appommatox." This was great news. To think that we were about to meet a real actor was enough to excite any country boy, but to meet one as noted as Joe Ketler was happiness supreme. Milt Byham had been in Franklin the preceding fall and had seen Joe in a leading role at the Franklin Opera House. In Milt's opinion Joe Ketler was Edwin Booth, E. H. Southern, and Joe Jefferson all rolled into one. Never did the actor have a more active press agent. We who gathered daily at the hotel at noon hour listened while Milt orated on the greatness of Joe and described each detail of his roles. Then Milt would say, "One week from next Monday, Joe will be here," and finally the great day arrived.

When the hack which met the train at Sandy Lake, four miles distant and carried the mail arrived that day the streets were lined with people. Farmers had left their work to come to town. All students and townsmen were present. Milt was doing the honors of the occasion and Joe climbed out of the hack amid cheers and shouting. The day was to come when the name of Joe Ketler was to blaze forth for weeks on Broadway and in every city in the United States, but in no place did he ever receive a more sincere tribute or finer reception than the day he came to Milt Byham's Hotel, and remained to coach our play. And let me say that Joe lived up to every detail of Milt's description. We country boys learned the great kindness of the man and it was to me the beginning of a friendship that grows stronger every year. The week that I do not see Joe Ketler seems lacking.

But there was a deep scar on our souls. Those awful laughs that still rang in our ears when we thought of the Fredonia ball game. We needed no servant paid to tell us constantly to "Remember the Fredonia." We felt both resentful and revengeful.

In even the warm days of early spring we were on the ball field. Again I trained double the amount of any other player, but when the team was selected I was not even a substitute on the bench. The proud letters M C I did not grace my chest. Our team rounded into shape and defeated Sandy Lake, Cochranton, and tied Polk. The usual village teams were unequal to us and we were so elated that we feared that Fredonia would become frightened and cancel their game with us as it was to be the last of the season, and to be played during commencement week.

Of course there was only one result. Jim George and Fred Bonnet each got a hit; that was all. Final scores: Fredonia - 6. McElwain - 0. Think of the dastardly deed Fredonia had committed. They had shamelessly actually played a man who was not a student. But what could you expect of such a rival.

Because I dwell so much on matters outside the classroom does not mean that it was all play and no work. Professor Fruit's school was a workshop, not a playhouse. You were expected to have your lessons and to be called to his office was an ordeal. I know. During the following year the school continued to grow and reached its zenith in the spring of 1898. There were almost two hundred students.

In the catalogs of that year it is noted that the school has a high moral standard. In proof of this fact we find that a rather colorful music student was expelled for singing "Casey would waltz with the strawberry blonde, and the band played on; She would waltz with the one she adored, and the band played on."

I did not attend school after 1898. Professor Fruit secured another position after three years at McElwain. He served two terms as Mercer County Superintendent of Schools, and has been prominent in Pittsburgh educational activities for the past thirty years. The High school began to develop and to reach all classes so that the purpose of which the Village Academy existed was gradually assumed by it. Among the able instructors who followed during the next decade are found the names of Blaine Smather, Harold McClelland, C. C. Crawford, and M. L. McBride. The need of the school became less from year to year and it closed permanently as a school in 1912.

[The Bruner essay has been reduced in length by the excision of some material concerning the baseball team.]

PROGRAM FOR A MUSICAL RECITAL AT THE MCELWAIN INSTITUTE

The selections illustrate musical tastes of the time. Modern music lovers will be familiar with the Mendelsohn selection, but "Les Dames De Seville" by Schubert seems to have disappeared from the repertoire. The De Koven warhorse "Oh Promise Me" and "Home Sweet Home" are the only other pieces that have survived. There are no McElwain relatives among the musicians.

The reproduction is 80% of actual size of the original, which is very badly foxed and is crumbling at the edges.

RECITAL
MUSIC :: DEPARTMENT
McElwain Institute,
WEDNESDAY EVENING,
FEBRUARY 17, 1897.

PROGRAMME.

Midsummer Night's Dream..........Mendelssohn.
Misses Bonnie Jewel and Sadie McKnight.
Fifth Nocturne.......................Leybach.
Miss Vinnie Nelson.
Ben Hur Chariot Race...................Paull.
Miss Florence Noel.
Harbinger of Spring.....................Devrient.
Kern Cooper.
Mandolin Duette ....
J. S. Fruit and Miss Stephenson.
Evening Reverie.........................Rosen.
Miss Elizabeth Bodine.
Rose.... ....Goerdeler.
Miss Effie Frame.
Vocal Solo, "Oh Promise Me".........DeKoven.
Miss Margaret Nelson.
Twittering of Birds........................Billema.
Miss Sadie McKnight
Storm on Lake Platten....................Mihaly.
Miss Clyde Blatt.
By Moonlight...........................Zannoni.
Miss Lily Reynolds.
Husarenritt.............................Spindler.
Miss Nora Pittinger.
Vocal Solo ....Selected.
Prof. J. S. Fruit.
Warblings at Eve.......................Richards.
Misses Mattie Reynolds and Grace Womer.
Sonatina................................Lange.
Miss Mary Bruner.
La Cascade ....Bendel.
Miss Bonnie Jewell.
At Twilight ....Waddington.
Clare Thompson.
Showers of Blossoms.................. Spindler.
Miss Mattie Reynolds.
Home Sweet Home (var.)...............Slack.
Miss Grace Womer.
Les Dames De Seville.................Schubert.
Misses Clyde Blatt and Vinnie Nelson.
Mandolin Duette.............................
J. S. Fruit and Miss Stephenson.

PROGRAM FOR A PUBLIC "ENTERTAINMENT" AT THE MCELWAIN INSTITUTE

A participant in the "Entertainment" was Mary Florence (Mamie) McElwain (#226310000), who was also a member of the organizing committee. She was then age seventeen. Maud McElwain (#226210000) had a part in the play. "Ten Nights" must have been popular as it was performed again eight or nine years later with Earle Bruner, the author of the memoir on the McElwain Institute, in the part of Simon Slade. (The reproduction is about 70% of actual size.)

ENTERTAINMENT
IN THE
ACADEMY CHAPEL,
NEW LEBANON, PA.,
ON THE
Evening of June 16th, 1887,
AT 8:00 O'CLOCK.

COMMITTEE:
D. B. BEGGS.
MAMIE McELWAIN.
A. E. VOORHIES.

N. B.—Fall Term Begins Tuesday, August 16th, 1887.

PROGRAMME:

MUSIC. PRAYER. MUSIC.

Salutatory—"School Days,"...Mary Burrows, New Lebanon.
Oration—"The Reign of Terror,"..J. A. McCrone,
...........Hubbard, Ohio.

MUSIC.

Recitation—"Only the Brakeman,"..Mamie McElwain,
...........New Vernon.
Declamation—"Uncle Reuben's Baptism,"..D. B. Beggs,
...........Sandy Lake.

MUSIC.

DRAMA—"TEN NIGHTS IN A BAR-ROOM."

CAST OF CHARACTERS:

SAMPLE SWITCHEL,	J. F. Boyd.
SIMON SLADE,	W. N. Houser.
JOE MORGAN,	J. R. Burrows.
FRANK SLADE,	F. D. Voorhies.
HARVEY GREEN,	J. C. Dalby.
MR. ROMAINE,	R. S. Jewell.
WILLIE HAMMOND,	J. O. Anderson.
MRS. SLADE,	Mary Nelson.
MRS. MORGAN,	Maud McElwain.
MARY MORGAN,	Nettie Unangst.
MEHITABLE CARTWRIGHT,	Nellie McQuiston.

JUDD LYMEN, EDGAR VOORHIES,
NED HARGRAVE, MEADE BURROWS, } Patrons of the Bar.
TOM PETERS, WM. DAVIS,

PROGRAMME OF INCIDENTS.

ACT I.—Exterior view of "Sickle and Sheaf." Interview between Mr. Romaine and the Yankee. Sample's idea of moderate drinking. Return of the landlord. SCENE 2—Interior of "Sickle and Sheaf." Ex-miller and happy landlord. The young 'squire. The landlord's wife. "We shall never again be so happy as we were at the old mill." Poor old Joe Morgan, the inebriate. Little Mary in search of her father. Departure of the inebriate and his child. Quarrel between Green and Willie Hammond. Timely arrival of the Yankee.

ACT II.—The Yankee and the philanthropist. Slade's progress in tavern-keeping. The landlord's enterprising son, Frank. Quarrel between the landlord and the drunken customer. The bottle and the fatal blow. Arrival of little Mary. "Father! Father! they have killed me!"

ACT III.—The Yankee and the gambler. Sample's definition of the word "gentleman." The treat. The Yankee's desire for Green's happiness. SCENE 2—The drunkard's home. The patient wife by the side of her suffering child. Joe Morgan's promise. Mary's anxiety for her father's good. Frightful delirium of the poor inebriate. "Come here, dear father! this is little Mary's room! nothing can hurt you here!" Affecting tableau.

ACT IV.—The "Sickle and the Sheaf." The landlord and his son. Mrs. Slade's account of the interview with Mary. Sample and the young 'squire on a time. The Yankee's story about Uncle Josh and the poor-house. The fight and death of Willie Hammond. SCENE 2—Escape of Green. The arrest. SCENE 3—Joe Morgan's wretched home. The wife and mother watching by her suffering ones. Little Mary's advice to her father. Despair of the inebriate. The child's dream. The promise. "I'll never drink another drop of liquor as long as I live." The dying child. Death of little Mary.

ACT V.—The meeting of Sample and Mr. Romaine, after an absence of five years. Sample a teetotaler. His quaint description of matters and things that have transpired in Cedarville. SCENE 2—Appearance of Simon Slade. Wonderful transformation of the once happy miller. Frank's progress in dram-drinking. The quarrel between father and son. Death of Simon Slade. "Frank Slade, you have murdered your father." SCENE 3—The happy home of Mr. Morgan. Arrival of Mr. Romaine. The resolution. The wife's joy. Sample and his new suit.

"A drunkard now no longer—that is o'er!
Free, disenthralled, I stand a man once more!"

EPILOGUE AND HAPPY TERMINATION.

MUSIC.

TWO GRADUATION PROGRAMS
FROM MCELWAIN INSTITUTE

The graduation program for 1909, to the right, indicates that the Institute had amended its name to McElwain Collegiate Institute.   The reproduction is 80% of the size of the original.

The three-page program for 1897 is enclosed by two sheets of parchment-like paper, and is held together at the top by a blue and gold cord.   The size of the original is 5" by 8 1/4".   The cover displays in gold print a shield enclosing the class year, "97".   The second and third pages are reproduced here; the first page, an announcement and invitation has been omitted.

Graduating Exercises
McELWAIN COLLEGIATE INSTITUTE

Thursday Evening, June 24, 1909, at 8 o'clock.

Programme.

Invocation.

Solo—"If I Could Call the Years Back"..............*..Abt
Mrs. Hallie Walker-MacTyre.

Reading .... Mable Byham '10

History............................ John N. Gallagher '10

Music..Selected

Prophecy ....Richard A. Ebbert '10

Pessimist.............................Florence O. Rupert '10

Music—Piano Duet

Oration—"The Thorny Pathway"...Grace C. Mook '09

Solo—"Hast Thou E'er Seen the Land" ....
..................................Thomas (from Mignon)
Mrs. Hallie Walker-MacTyre.

Oration—"True and False Ambition"..................
.... James Addison DeFrance, Jr. '09

Solo—"Spanish Boat Song"............ ....North
Mrs. Hallie Walker-MacTyre.

Presentation of Diplomas......................Rev. S. Fidler

PROGRAMME

CLASSROLL

SABBATH, JUNE 27, 1897, 8 P M.
Baccalaureate Sermon,   Rev. Dr. Ferguson
West Minster College, New Wilmington. Pa.

MONDAY, JUNE 28 8 P. M.
Principal's Reception

TUESDAY, JUNE 28, 8 P M.
Declamation Contest

WEDNESDAY, JUNE 30, 2 00 P M.
Class Day Exercises

WEDNESDAY, JUNE 30, 8 P M.
Commencement Lecture

LITERARY COURSE
W. E. McCaughtry
Oretta McQuiston
Blanche M. Robb
E. V. Thompson
C. F. Wheeler

MUSIC COURSE
Mattie Belle Reynolds
M. Bellgrace Womer

BUSINESS COURSE
Benj. H. Mook
Pearl B. Moore
Sam'l E. Opitz
Geo. M. McKnight
C. F. Wheeler

CLASS ORGANIZATION
President, C. F. Wheeler
Secretary, Blanche M. Robb
Treasurer, Sam'l E. Opitz

CHAPTER VI

THE CHURCHES OF CUMBERLAND COUNTY

THE BIG SPRING PRESBYTERIAN CHURCH

According to Swope's *History of the Big Spring Presbyterian Church* there was a Presbyterian congregation in the neighborhood of Big Spring not later than the spring of 1737. On June 22 of that year this group petitioned the Presbytery for permission to employ Rev. Thomas Craighead as pastor. Because there was an objection by the congregation of Upper Pennsboro to the creation of a new church so near to an existing one, the matter was, after some negotiation, postponed for a year. A second reason for the postponement was that Craighead (apparently appropriately named) was in trouble with church authorities for suspending his own wife from "church privelege" becauses of her failure to live in peace in the same house with her daughter-in-law. The installation finally occurred in October of 1738. It was none too soon, as in late April of 1739, Mr. Craighead, who was well advanced in years, "having preached until quite exhausted, waved his hand being unable to pronounce the benediction and exclaimed: 'Farewell! Farewell!' and sank down and died in the pulpit."

A number of temporary and permanent pastors were engaged over the next few decades until March 21, 1786 when a call was extended to the Rev. Samuel Wilson, and a subscription was made to provide the funds to pay the proposed annual salary of one hundred and fifty pounds. The lists of the petitioners and the subscribers are extant, and each includes many names found in the pages of this book, but none of the McElwains.

Wilson assumed his duties on June 20, 1787. Some time in the next two years he made, or caused to be made, a census of his flock. Swope says the date was about 1789, but objections have been raised that it was in fact earlier. In the appendix to my book *Genealogical Data Abstracted from History of Big Spring Presbyterian Church* (Heritage Books, 1992) the problem is considered in some detail and, based on what little other information was available, it seems that March and April of 1788 is a more probable date. Additional information is needed to sustain that conclusion, and birth dates in the Genealogy derived from the membership list are based on the year 1789. Because so many birth dates are unrecorded for persons born in the eighteenth century, this list, which provides ages for most members, has been of great use to family historians, providing at least the approximate year of birth.

Wilson divided his parish into districts and set an elder

over each district. The district over which Robert Lusk was an elder was that in which the McElwains were located. Lusk owned a farm adjacent to that of the McElwains, and, as is set forth in the biographical sketch of Andrew McElwain, the son of the original Andrew, he purchased a portion of the McElwain farm in 1799.

The names and ages of persons appearing in the Genealogy are here listed in the order in which they appear in the original list; there is no notation made as to what persons constitute a separate family, but the order of the names, here transcribed as in the original list, makes it simple enough to determine. It is not possible to determine, however, whether families had separate residences. Church members who were "in full communion" (whatever that may mean) were identified by an asterisk.

James McElwain *	37
Mary McElwain	12
John McElwain	10
Ruth McElwain	7
Andrew McElwain *	33
Elizabeth McElwain *	30
Mary McElwain	8
Robert McElwain	7
Jane McElwain	5
Mary McElwain	70
Robert McElwain	22
Elizabeth McElwain	20

James' lack of a wife in this list is one of the pieces of evidence that was used in determining that the wife who appears in his will was a second wife, and that Mary Nicholson, his first wife, died before this time. Among others in the list are Richard and Mary Nicholson, the parents of Mary.

Another membership list was prepared in 1808. Unlike the original this list provided only the name of the head of the family and the number of persons in the family, making it much less useful for the historian. James and Andrew are both listed with four family members each.

The first church building was erected in 1737 or 1738. It was a log structure, but there is no description of it in existence. The present structure was built in 1790. As described in Swope,

The two back pews along the south wall in every tier from east to west wall were raised above the floor; the one next the wall about sixteen inches. The one in front of it about eight inches. The same was true of the elevation of the back pews in the tiers on the east and west of the pulpit. Every pew in the church had its price on it in shillings and pence, varying from sixty shillings, the highest to twenty shillings the lowest. The raised pews at the back walls were about eight shillings higher than those before them. The church was heated by three stoves placed in the three aisles leading from the front doors.   The pulpit was placed high against the north wall and was reached by a flight of steps on each side.   The pews had high straight backs."

Pewholders in 1790 included Andrew McElwain, who shared pew 75 with John Bell, and Robert McElwain, who shared pew 81 with Nellie Stewart.

The Big Spring Presbyterian Church

[from Swope, Gilbert, *History of the Big Spring Presbyterian Church*, 1898]

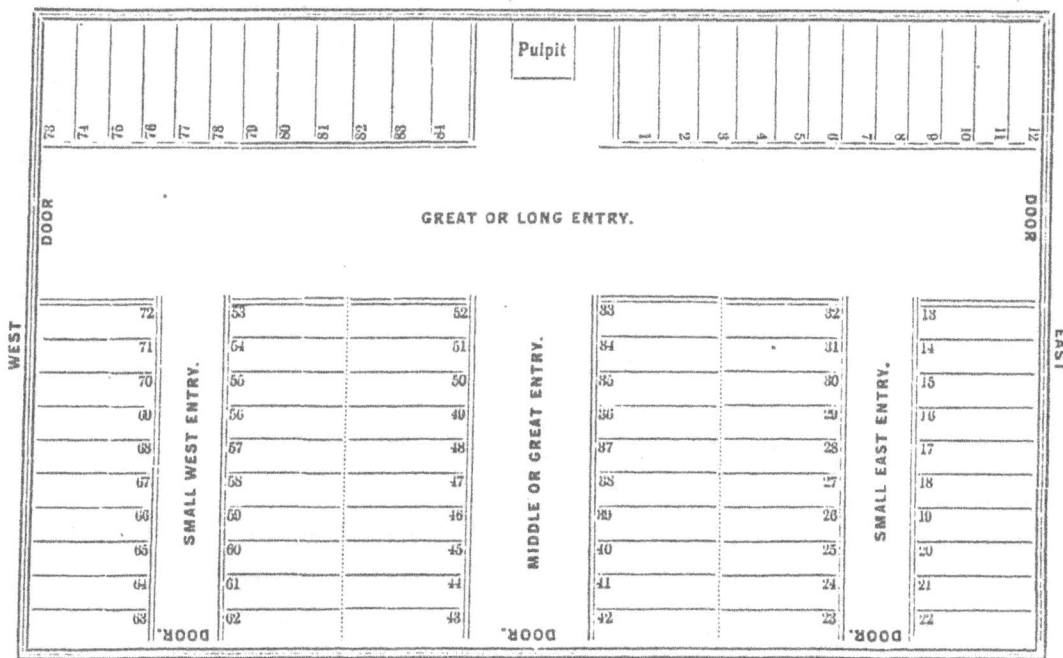

South.   GROUND PLOT OF THE CHURCH AS IT WAS IN 1790.

By 1832 it seemed necessary either to build a new church or to remodel the old. Although the sum of three thousand dollars was allocated for a new building, no action was taken, and in 1840 it was decided to remodel the old structure. It was a rather drastic remodeling: the pulpit was to be placed at the east end of the building and the remainder of the interior adjusted accordingly. The final cost came to two thousand three hundred and thirty nine dollars and thirty-five cents, and the work was completed in late 1841.

At the time of this remodelling the original stone masonry was "rough coated". The coating began to fall off in a few years, and another coating was applied in 1881. Apparently this too was unsatisfactory, for in 1894 the coating was removed to reveal once more the old stone work which is what the visitor of today sees.

The church owned glebe land of slightly over eighty nine acres, obtained by a warrant from the Land Office of the Province on March 2, 1744, and patented on September 23, 1794. The matter of laying out a town on the glebe land was agitated for some time, until, in 1790 sixty lots of sixty by one hundred feet were layed off for a town to be called Newville. The lots were to be disposed of by a lottery at six dollars a ticket. In the end some of the lots were sold in this fashion and others were sold in the normal fashion. The lots were deeded in limited fee, subject to a quit rent ranging from $1.07 to $1.33 per year. These quit rents were gradually abolished, and were eliminated by about 1884. A William McElwain purchased one of the lots; this was probably the youngest of the four sons of Andrew and Mary McElwain.

Adjacent to the Big Spring Church is a large grave yard. The earliest grave is dated 1776, but there are few others from the eighteenth century. Many of the early graves were probably unmarked, others had markers of wood or soft stone which have decayed, and still others simply have sunk into the earth. Swope notes that most of the ground is occupied by graves, though it does not appear so because of the absence of markers.

The earliest McElwain grave, that of Andrew (#450000000) is from 1840. Many of the main actors in this volume died in the first part of the century, and, despite the fragility of markers, it does seem strange that of the early family members--Andrew and his wife Mary Mickey, James and his two wives, James' daughter Margaret, Andrew, his two wives, and the three of his children who died in those years-- none have a grave marker at Big Spring cemetery. This at least suggests that a family cemetery existed on the McElwain farm. The custom of setting a small plot of land aside for family burials was quite common in the early days. Jeremy Zeamer, who collected a large number of grave inscriptions in the first decade of the twentieth century, visited seventy-

three cemeteries, of which twenty four were small family
cemeteries located on farms.   There is no evidence to sustain
such an hypothesis, and, even should it be found to be correct,
the chances are great that the cemetery has long since
disappeared. but the idea is an interesting one to keep in the
back of one's mind.

The Big Spring Presbyterian Church stands in Newville and not
in the community of Big Spring, which is situated about three
miles directly south of Newville.

THE MIDDLE SPRING PRESBYTERIAN CHURCH

The date of the founding of the Middle Spring Presbyterian
Church is a vexed question in Belle Swope's history of that
institution, but she determined that it was before 1740.   The date
of the construction of the first church building certainly bears
out that conclusion since Mrs. Swope quotes an unidentified old
Carlisle newspaper actually setting it in 1738.

"In 1738 the Presbyterians living in the vicinity of Middle
Spring met to devise a plan for building a church, and the result
of of the consultation was the erection of a log building about
thirty-five feet square, at the gate of the old graveyard, near
the bank of the stream." In 1765 this structure was replaced by a
similar one, with dimensions of forty-eight feet on each side.
The second building was probably still rather primitive, but it
was noted as having a pulpit of walnut of extremely fine
workmanship. A third building, this one of stone, fifty-eight by
sixty-eight feet was constructed about the year 1781; it had
forty-six seats on the main floor, and thirty in a gallery. The
present building was erected in 1847. It has since been repaired,
remodeled, and enlarged a number of times.

The cost of the original old stone church of 1781 was raised
by the subscriptions of one hundred and thirty person.
subscribing.   One of these was an Andrew Thompson, quite likely
the father of Hannah and Rosanna, who married James and Richard
McElwain.

Andrew Thompson is also mentioned in a Treasurer's report for
1783 as contributing one pound, 2 shillings, and six pence to the
church, and in 1784, two pounds, seventeen shillings, and 6 pence.

The Middle Spring Church has three older grave yards, called
the Upper, the Lower, and Hanna's, and a fourth, dating from 1890,
called simply the Cemetery. The earliest of these, the Lower
Graveyard, is surrounded by a massive stone wall built before
1805. The oldest slab is dated 1770, but most of the older
graves, and even those of a later date, are now unmarked. In this

cemetery the grave of Andrew Thompson might be expected to be found, but if it is there the stone has disappeared. The Upper Graveyard is located at the rear of the church, and is also surrounded by a stone wall. There is a stone here bearing that date 1798, but most are from much later.

The Hanna Cemetery is located four miles or so north of the church, near the town of Newburgh. This cemetery was opened some time early in the nineteenth century. The oldest stone here is dated 1815. This is the only one of the cemeteries with McElwain graves. Buried there are William Bell McElwain (4a0000000), his two wives, and a daughter, Ellen.

The authority of the state was not great in the remote, sparsely populated areas in the middle of the eighteenth century, and some of the functions which are usually handled by local governments were assumed by the churches, particularly the settlement of disputes, and discipline for minor breeches of the peace. The minutes of the Session Book of the Middle Spring Church are extant for at least the years 1742 to 1748 and give rare insight into the private lives of people of the times. Few of the parishioners appear in the minutes since they did nothing particularly good or bad. The people who do appear were either saints or sinners—those who were on trial and those who were sitting in judgement of them. We must read the record with forgiveness for the sinners as well as for the saints.

One interesting incident fom the Session records is related in the biographical sketch of George McElwain. Several others are included here. The actors in these little dramas are not McElwain relatives, but they were friends and neighbors of some of the persons to be found in the Genealogy. The incidents are selected to show handling of four several sorts of problems: disputes, insobriety, sexual irregularity, and (probably worst of all) religious deviationism.

[extracts from the Minute Book of the Session of the Middle Spring Presbyterian Church]

May 2, 1743 Charles Cummins inform'd the session that Willⁿ McCall Junr. was the worse for liquor at Saml. Culbertson's Wedding as appeared in that he was not capable to govern himself as usual & that sitting on a bench at the end of the house he fell back over. David Herron appointed to cite Willⁿ McCall to appear Friday come a week also to cite Thomas McComb for evidence.

May 13, 1743 Willⁿ McCall junr appear'd and (Thomas McComb not being present) from what he acknowledg'd himself he was too merry jocose & loose in his conduct and that he drank more than he should have done. The session agree that he be rebuk'd for his loose and intemperate conduct & behavior unbecoming one professing Christianity to which he submitted.

Sept. 5, 1743   Agnas Pattan enter'd a complaint against Daniel Smith for hurting her Character by reporting that she had a handkerchiefe of his which he lost at Middle Spring Meeting House.   Daniel Smith denies that he had possitively reported such a thing but only had sent word to her to see whether it was her own handkerchief she had got.   It appears from George Hamilton's Evidence that said Daniel had said in Company that he heard that Angas Pattan had got the Handkerchiefe, (refering to the one he had lost) from Daniel Kidd & upon Martha Hamilton's expressing her Wonder that She would take it reply'd that the Devil wou'd be as ready to catch at her as another.   [Some other evidence is presented and then a judgement is made.] ..the session judge that there is no Ground of suspicion that Agnas Pattan has Daniel Smith's Handkerchiefe & that Daniel acted very wrong in speaking to others in the manner he did.

June 22, 1744   The session apprehend it is necessary, in order to promote a good under-standing between Andrew Murphey & Robt. McComb, that some proper measures be taken to remove the main cause of their uneasiness; & to that purpose advise, that William Younge and Thomas Edmiston meet with them and settle [property] Lines between them, and that they draw up Articles of Agreement between them; and that Robt. McComb have what rails Andrew Murphey may have split on McComb's side of the Line that shall be fixed & that McComb shall split an equal number of Rails to said Murphey, on his side of the line.

April 19, 1745   Elizabeth Neil came to the session, professing her Desire to give satis-faction to the church for her offense in the sin of fornication. But not finding, upon examin-ation, sufficient evidence of a suitably penitent sense of the Evil of her sin, the session defer her public satisfaction, for some time longer.
   James Finley appear'd, confessed he was guilty of fornication with Elizabeth Neil, and was bro't (with considerable reluctance) to own the child she has born; but not giving suitable evidence of penitence, his admission to give satisfaction to the church is further defer'd.

James Poag appear's & acknowledg'd that being at home one Sabbath Day he heard a gun go off twice quickly, and said he wou'd go see who it was.   Having gone a little way he saw an indian, who had just killed a Fawn & dressed it; the Indian coming toward the house with him, to get some victuals, having, he said, eat nothing that morning, he saw a deer and shot it. Said Poag stod by the Indian untill he skinn'd the deer; when he had done, he told said Poag, he might take it in if he wou'd, for he would take no more with him; upon which, said Poag & Willm Kieth, who had then come to them, took it up, & carry'd it in.   When he had given the Indian his Breakfast said Indian ask'd if he had any Meal, he said he had & gave him some; then the Indian ask'd for Butter, & he gave the Indian some but he denies that he gave these things as a Reward for the Venison, inasmuch as they had made no bargain about it.
   The session judge that James Poag do acknowledge his Breach of Sabbath in this Matter, & be rebuk'd before the session, for his sin.

Dec. 28--1748   The committee of the session of Middle Spring met at James Wallace's according to Appointment. Begun with Prayr.
   The committee proceeded to enquire, as appointed, in to the matter of scandale reported concerning Hannah Wallace; which shou'd have fallen out, when she was returning from Shippensbourgh, in Septr. last.
   James Paxton being call'd, solemnly declar'd that he was at Shippensburgh at the time above refer'd to; was frequently in committee with Hannah Wallace that Day, & came out of town in company with her; that he observ'd nothing amiss with her untill after they pass'd by Andrew McCluir's, when having her some distance behind in company with Charles Morrow & Francis McCall; said McCall came up, & the Depont. having ask'd where Hannah Wallace was, he reply'd she had fallen, & lost her shoe; that upon said McCall's going back he coud'nt find her; that after some time, the Depont. & said McCall found her sleeping on a log, & Charles Morrow on another at some yards distance, their horses being hitch'd hard by. The Depont. further adds

that having heard it was reported that John Carnachan shou'd have seen said Hannah & said
Morrow in an unseemly posture together, he spoke to said Carnachan about it, who told him he
was willing to take his oath he saw no such thing. Upon further Enquiry, the Depont. says that
when they found said Wallace, she was very sick; & that they drank some kind of punch made of
Liquor & sweeten'd with mollasses at Andw. McChir's, which he suppos'd made her sick; and
further observ'd that when she awoke she spoke sensibly enough.

    Mary Paxton being call'd solemnly declar'd that it was true that Hannah Wallace & herself
moved once or twice across the floor to a fiddle; that she did'nt observe said Wallace any way
mov'd with drink till after they drank the punch above mention'd that she did'nt see said
Wallace when she was found & set on horse back, nor overtake her untill they were almost home,
when she observ'd said Hannah was very sick.

[The minutes break off at this point.]

CHAPTER VII

THE MCILVAINE FAMILY OF GRIMET, SCOTLAND

The McIlvaine family of Ayrshire, Scotland held the title of
Laird of Grimet and the estates of Grimet and Attiquin from the
middle ages, and later added the estate of Thomaston to their
possessions through marriage. The male line ended in the mid-
eighteenth century and the title Laird of Grimet lapsed. The word
"laird" (related to English "lord") means a landed proprietor; it
is not a title of mobility. The family seems most of the time to
be followers of the Kennedy family, which held the title of Earl
of Cassilis, although on occasion they seem to have been enemies.

This book provides only a brief sketch of the family in
Scotland. For those interested in more detail there is in
Ordway's, *The House of Grimet* an extensive introduction by Jean
Moore and Andrew G. McIlvaine (#776733000) combining Scottish and
McIlvaine history in an interesting and reasonably coherent
manner, considering the confused state of the sources. Much of
this material can also be found in Frank McElvain's *Complete
History of McIlvaine-McElvain Family Line* available on microfilm
through the Family History Library. The material in Frank's book,
however, is not organized into a coherent whole; it is made up
documents, extracts from histories, correspondence with family
members, all connected by comments of Frank. From this work are
taken the following descriptions of the several McIlvaine castles.

[adapted from McElvain, Frank, The Complete History.., pp. 20-24]

Grimet, the original castle of the McIlvaines, was built of stone with moat and tower, and
was as nearly impregnable as possible to make it in those days. It was situated on the exposed
border about two miles northwest of Dalmellington, in sight of Keirs castle, the home of the
Shaws, with whom the McIlvaines had much in common, intermarrying frequently in succeeding
generations. Nearby is the River Doon, made famous by Robert Burns.
Grimet Castle is no more. The outline of its walls are covered with soil and moss, and
the thick stones of its walls, which once formed a barrier to protect Wallace and the Bruces,
have been converted into a commodious farmhouse, with its rectangle of dairies, storehouses,
barns, and piggeries. A depression shows where the old moat ran around the castle and many of
the original outlines are distinguishable. Grimet has many evidences of former magnificence.
The heavy paneled staircase was transferred intact from the castle to the present farmhouse and
would be worth a fortune to relic hunters. A stone cap over the doorway of the creamery, an
ell of the main building, contains the hewn stone figures of the two covered cups which are the
lower half of the family coat of arms, engraved on the castle perhaps 600 years ago.
Attiquin, named perhaps from a Gaelic word meaning rowan tree house, for the two rows of
rowan [mountain ash] trees leading to it, was located about ten miles from Grimet in the
direction of the town of Maybole. It, too, has been rebuilt into a farmhouse. Thomaston,
acquired prior to 1600 by the marriage of John McIlvaine to Ann Corry, became the home
thereafter of the laird and his family. It is a substantial stone castle, with its thick walls
well preserved, but in 1920 the roof had fallen in. The walls were nearly four feet thick, of
cut stone, with an ornamental cornice around the eaves. The tower is gone but the three large
dungeons below remain. In each of those dungeons, is a narrow vertical slit, about three feet

long, and beveled wider inside, so that the defending archers could shoot arrows from their crossbows. The old moat is filled with the accumulations of years, and the drawbridge and portcullis are gone. The houses stands in a thick wood, within sight of Ailsa Craig in th Firth of Clyde.

Before the fifteenth century, although there is considerable material reputed to relate to the family, it is not certain that the persons concerned are really ancestors of the proven line. Things become more certain during the life of Nigel McYlveyne (the name thus spelled is a delight, rather like one from a medieval romance), who lived from about 1395 to about 1465. From Nigel a direct line can be traced through the many generations to those family members who emigrated to America. Ordway has traced ten families directly to this succession. There are numerous other families who are probably descended from the McIlvaines, but whose descent it has not been possible to establish.

The McIlvaines were probably neither better nor worse than their fellows, but the period from the sixteenth and seventeenth century was one of conflict, and the family was in the midst of it. There are a great number of existing documents which mention the family--wills, records of the courts and of the Kings Council, church records, and history books. A few incidents must serve to give a picture, however fragmentary, of life in those times. Since particularly notorious and heroic incidents are the most interesting, several of those have been selected

[adapted from McElvain, Frank, The Complete History..]

In 1528 Alan McIlvaine, along with Gilbert, Earl of Cassilis and others, was cited for several murders. The accused were all pardoned by King James V for previous good services.

Edward Seymour, Duke of Somerset (brother of Jane, and therefore a brother-in-law of Henry VIII), invaded Scotland with a large English army, equipped with both muskets and artillery. The Scots met him, with their army of spearmen and archers, at the Battle of Fawside (or Pinckie), on September 10, 1547, and were crushingly defeated. Among the battle deaths was Gilbert McIlvaine, Laird of Grimet, who was a colonel of cavalry.

John, Earl of Cassilis, Patrick McIlvaine, John Corrie, Hew Kennedy, and others were accused in 1602 of the ambush and murder of Gilbert Kennedy, Laird of Bargany (a cousin of the Earl). The group was let off after admitting guilt and promising to keep the peace in the future. Some time earlier Gilbert had kidnapped and held for fifteen days several people, including John McIlvaine, so the guilt was not all on one side.

In 1613 John McIlvaine, several of the Corries, and others attacked the Earl of Cassilis, "with swords, gentillatis, plaitsleeves, buffilcoitis" and drove him into his castle. When the Earl ordered John to go to the tolbooth [city jail], John defied him, making matters worse. The Lords of the Kings Council found him guilty of "very great insolence and Misbehavioure" and committed him to the Tolbooth of Edinburgh, "there to remain at his own expense till further order." That same year John made a complaint that "while reposing himself in a sober manner within the Kaitchepoole of Maybole, he was there attacked and shamefully treated by Johnne Kenedy of Blairquhan and others" and that he had escaped only "by the providence of God and his awne bettir defense."

RELATED AMERICAN FAMILIES

There are several supposed origins of the name McIlvaine, but most do not sound convincing. Obviously, the name is based upon the name of a particular ancestor, as the "Mc" implies. Thus the people bearing the name are probably mostly of the same descent. This distinguishes the name from the many surnames which could have been adopted by unrelated families in various parts of the world. Typical of such names are those based on occupations (Baker, Farmer, Clark, Bishop, Chancellor), places of residence (Somerset, Welch, Rivers, Hill), and personal characteristics (Brown, Black, Short, Strong). It is unlikely that two randomly selected persons named Farmer are related, but two McElwains (however spelled) are very probably cousins, though most likely very distant ones.

The family tree on the following page traces the lineage down to the immediate ancestors of those persons who emigrated to the colonies. The spelling of the surname varies considerably, following that used by Frank McElvain. Many of the dates are vague and some are doubtful. For most of the tree only the main line is followed; there were many more children, but they are mostly lost in obscurity. The younger sons, from a genealogical point of view are important, since it is from them that many branches of the family derive. In Scotland there was not so strong a line of demarcation between the classes as in England. Many of the families of the nobility and the gentry (the McIlvaines) intermarried, and many their descendents declined (or rose) into the middle class—and perhaps not a few into the lower classes.

The stupendous collection of McIlvaine-McElvain-McElwain-McIlwain, etc. family members assembled by William Ordway, numbering over 22,000, are probably related, with some exceptions. The ten families in Chapters 1 through 10 certainly are. Thus every person in the genealogy in this book (which is the family of Chapter 3 in Ordway) is related to every person in those initial ten chapters—perhaps 15,000 cousins are there listed. That beats even Sir Joseph Porter, K. C. B. (of *Pinafore*) who had cousins "whom he reckoned up by dozens"—a paltry few by our standards.

This section provides some guide to families related to the family of Andrew McElwain and Mary Mickey. The information here is taken from *The House of Grimet*, by William Ordway. The families enumerated in the following section are distinguished by the use of the chapter numbers in Ordway's work for those known to be related, or for those families whose relationship has not been established, by the use of the letters A through G. The number in parenthesis is the total number of persons listed by Ordway for that family.

THE MCILVAINE FAMILY OF SCOTLAND

```
                        NIGEL MACYLVEYNE
                         (A 1395-1465)
                               !
                               !
                        GILBERT MCILVAINE
                         (A 1460-1537)
                         = ----- Kennedy
                               !
                               !
                         ALAN MCILVENE
                         (L 1529-1547)
                        = Marian Ferguson
                               !
                               !
                        GILBERT MCILVENE
                          (1510c-1547)
                         = Janet Corry
                               !
                               !
                        PATRICK MCILVANE
                          (L 1547-1612)
                        = Isobel Kennedy
                               !
                               !
                        JOHNNE MCKELVANE
                         (A 1613-1632)
                          = Anne Corry
                               !
                               !----------------------------!
                               !                            !
                        JOHN MCILVANE               Gilbert
                         (L 1637-1669)              [8, 9, 10]
                         = Juliann Schaw
              McIlvaine                !
     !------------------!--------------!------------------!
     !                  !              !                  !
  QUENTIN            Juliann         John            Alexander
 (L 1669-1699)    = Andrew Rogers = Anne Cunningham   = --- McAdam
  Marian Blair                     [4, 5, 6, 7]         !
     !                      !------------!--------------!
     !                      !            !              !
   JOHN                  Andrew        David           Mary
 (L 1699-1739)          (1669-1726)     !           = Robert Mickey
     !                = Martha Mickey    !              !
     !                    [1]            !              !
   JOHN                              Joseph           Mary
  (b. 1699)                           [2]             [3]
```

Names of the Lairds of Grimet are capitalized.
A = known to be alive these years   L = Laird of Grimet these years
Numbers in brackets correspond to families in the text and to chapters in *The House of Grimet*
  and pages 92-94 of this book.

Families descended from the McIlvaines of Grimet

1 Andrew McIlvaine and Martha Mickey (2,547)
        This family is represented in the genealogy by the large number of persons descended
from Ruth McElwain and George McIlvaine, and numbered in the 700000000 series.   Some of
the history of the family is narrated in Chapter III of this book.   As was there
explained, the original immigrant, Andrew McIlvaine, came to what is now Delaware in
1719.   One of Andrew's sons, George McElwain, moved to Cumberland County, Pennsylvania,
where some of his descendents still live. George and Ruth McIlvaine moved to Washington
County, Pennsylvania, as did Greer, George's brother.

2 Joseph McIlvaine and Anna Rogerson   (118)
        Joseph died in Scotland, but his son William (1722-1770) came to America in 1745.
He lived in Bristol, Pennsylvania, where he was a shipping merchant.   He retired to his
estate, "Fair View", and lived as a country gentleman until his death in 1767.
        William's eldest son, Joseph (1749-1787), was an officer in the Revolution, holding
the rank of lieutenant-colonel and being responsible for such important tasks as seizing
property of loyalists and collecting clothing for families of the men in the Pennsylvania
forces.   His son Joseph (1768-1826) moved to New Jersey, where he served, under an
appointment from President Jefferson, as United States Attorney for the District of New
Jersey.   In 1823 he entered the United States Senate where he served until his death.
Senator Joseph McIlvaine, in turn, had several prominent sons.   Bowes Reed McIlvaine
(1795-1866) graduated from the College of New Jersey (now Princeton) in 1812 and had a
notable career in the army during the War of 1812.   He then engaged in business in
Cadiz, Spain, and later in New York, where he was engaged in the New York Sugar
Refining Company and other businesses.   He later was interested in the Pacific Mail
Steamship Company.   A second son, Bloomfield, was also a graduate of the College of
New Jersey.   He was admitted to the bar in Philadelphia and became prominent in poli-
ical and social affairs.   He served as Vice Provost of the Law Academy of Philadelphia,
as secretary of the group promoting the presidency of John Quincy Adams, and as an
Assistant Marshal of the parade which in 1824 welcomed the Marquis de Lafayette to the
city. His career was cut short by his premature death at age 29 in 1826.   A third son,
Charles Pettit, after graduating from the College of New Jersey, went on to study
theology, and was ordained in the Episcopal Church.   While still young he served
twice as chaplain to the United States Senate.   From 1825 to 1828 he served as chaplain
and professor of ethics at the United States Military Academy at West Point.   In 1831
he was appointed a professor of theology at the University of the City of New York, and,
in the same year, was elected Bishop of Ohio. At the time the affairs of Kenyon College
were in disarray, so he assumed the presidency of that institution and restored its
fortunes.   After 1830 the Bishop made numerous voyages to England. During the Civil
War he was appointed by President Lincoln to the commission to negotiate with England to
settle the Trent Affair, which had brought Great Britain to the verge of war with the
United States.   He also served as a member of a group sent to Europe to negotiate with
the prime minister of Russia to provide relief to persecuted Protestants in the Baltic
countries.
        William's second son, William (1750-1806), was, like his brother, an officer in the
Revolutionary Army. He later was a judge of the Court of Common Pleas in New Jersey.
William also had a daughter, Mary (1752-1818). She married General Joseph Bloomfield, who
served as Governor of New Jersey from 1801-1812, and later as a Member of Congress.
        In subsequent generations the family produced many other persons prominent in
business, law, the arts, religion, and in both the army and the navy.   Nevertheless, in
searching for information for his book, William Ordway was not able to locate any members
of the family, and his genealogy for the family ends at the year 1900.

4 James McIlvaine and Mary Tyson   (34)
        James McIlvaine was born in Ayrshire, Scotland in 1688 and came to America before
1720. He spent his life in Craven County, North Carolina.
        The history of this family is scant both in the number of known descendents and in
time, which reaches only to the mid-nineteenth century.   However, the line is known to
have continued well into the twentieth century through the marriage of Gatsey Moody, a
great-great-granddaughter of James, to Andrew Jackson McIlwain, who was a member of the
family of Andrew and Margaret McIlvain of Alabama. (See "C" below)
        What is known is that James became a man of influence in his community. He was a
member of the House of Burgesses in 1736 and a Justice of the Peace as well as Chairman
of a Peace Commission 1739. His granddaughter Mary Macilwean (the spelling varies greatly
in this family) married Richard Caswell, Jr., who became governor of North Carolina.

5 Moses McIlvain and Margaret Martin   (499)
        Moses was born in Adams County, Pennsylvania in 1713 and died there in 1782.   Many
of his descendents continued to live there for many years, while others moved to Ohio,
Michigan, and Illinois. This is another family which Mr. Ordway was not able to contact.
The genealogy has only a few entries for the period after World War II.

6 Robert McIlvaine and Mary Duffield   (1,728)
        Robert (1715-1770) and Mary were both born in Antrim County, Ireland.   They are
thought to have married in Virginia about 1740. They lived in Sadsbury township, Chester
County, Pennsylvania for most of their married lives, and died there.
        Like most families, this one sent its sons and daughters westward.   Many family
members contributed information to Ordway, from a widely scattered area--Pennsylvania,
North Carolina, Illinois, Missouri, Kansas, Colorado, Texas, Nevada, and California.

7 Moses McIlvain and Agnes Miller (2,573)
        Moses father Robert was born at Grimet, Scotland, and was taken by his parents to
County Antrim, Ireland. He came to America between 1712 and 1718, landing at Newcastle,
Delaware. He owned a farm in Hunterdon County, New Jersey until 1723 when he sold it and
migrated to South Carolina.   In 1738 he moved north to Lancaster County, Pennsylvania
where he lived until his death in 1760.
        Moses, the only known son of Robert, was born in South Carolina in 1723 and died in
Lancaster County, Pennsylvania in 1761.   He and Agnes had nine children, four of whom
have known descendents and four more of whom are known to have married.   The family grew
and spread out widely.   Living descendents are to be found in North Carolina, New Jersey,
Ohio, Illinois, Missouri, Kansas, Colorado, Arizona, California, and Oregon.

8 Gilbert McIlwain and Jane Graham (328)
        Gilbert McIlwain (1716-1777) was born in Belfast, Ireland and came to America in
1733.   For many years most of the family continued to live in Kentucky, although one
grandson moved to Westmoreland County, Pennsylvania.   Later, of course, it spread more
widely. There are descendents living today in Missouri and California.

9 James McIlvaine and Jane Heany   (581)
        James McIlvaine (1703-1764) and Jane Heany (d. 1764) were both born in Ireland. They
married about 1725 and came to America about 1740, bringing with them their four children.
They settled in the Philadelphia area, where most of the family lives today. Members of
the family entered the lumber business in both Ridley and Philadelphia.   The lumber yard
in Philadelphia stood on its original site for fifty years, and the business continued, in
a place not more than three miles from the original site, at least until 1948 when a book
by William Barton Nash, *Philadelphia Hardwood; the Story of the McIlvaines of
Philadelphia* was published.

10 The McIlvains of Virginia (336)

When Richard McIlvain of Derry County, Ireland died leaving a widow and nine children, it was not possible for his son Archibald to continue his education for the bar. With the consent of his mother, Jane Mary Graham, Archibald went to Virginia where he found a position with a mercantile firm. In the course of his life he became a prominent and very wealthy merchant. He was a trustee of Hampton-Sydney College, thus beginning an association which tied the family to that institution for more than a century. Many of the men of the early generations of the family attended Hampton-Sydney. Richard McIlwaine (1834-1913), the son of Archibald, was appointed President of the college in 1883, and dedicate much of his life to expanding the enrollment, increasing the endowment, and building modern facilities.

Families not proven to be descended from the McIlvaines of Grimet

A   Daniel McIlvaine and Mary Smith (149)

Daniel's parents moved to Ireland where they were murdered by their Catholic neighbors; only Daniel, who was a small baby at the time and was overlooked by the murderers, survived. He immigrated to America about 1726 at age 19, and eventually settled in Wyndham, New Hampshire. Some branches of the family later changed their name to McAlvin.

B   John McIlvain and Sarah Bell (1,719)

John and Sarah remained in Scotland, but a son, John (b. 1798), who spelled his name Malvin, came to Stroudsburg, Pennsylvania. The name later appears as Malven and Malvern. This family is very interested in family history; more than fifty copies of The House of Grimet--one-seventh of the total printed--were purchased by descendents of this family.

C   James and Elinor McElvain (295)

James came to America in 1718 and settled in an area that is now Warren, Massachusetts. His great-great grandson, William Howe McElvain began a shoe manufacturing business, which, as the McElvain Shoe Company, grew to a very large size. William was known as one of the pioneers in industrial efficiency.

D   Patrick McElvain and Mary Campbell (201)

Patrick left England in 1771 to escape conscription into the British army. He settled in Lancaster County, Pennsylvania

E   Alexander and Frances McElvain (536)

Alexander, a commoner, eloped with and married Frances, daughter of Lord Rouden of Liverpool, England. She was disinherited. In 1790, some time after Alexander died, Frances came to America, bringing, at her own expense, her children, an aunt and uncle, and seven servants. They settled in Maryland, where they remained until about 1800, when the entire family moved to Kentucky, where many of their descendents remain to this day.

F   James McIlvain and Katy Scott (520)

Several of the children of this couple immigrated to South Carolina in 1798, settling at Lone Cane Creek. In 1811 (or 1814), some of them moved west, some to Indiana and others to Illinois. Later some went on to Oregon.

G   Andrew J. McIlvain and Margaret Douglas (2,163)

Andrew (1750-1829) first settled in Pennsylvania, before moving on to South Carolina. In 1818 the family moved to Alabama, and there many of them live at the present time. Many from this family also live in neighboring Mississippi. Later some of this McIlvain family moved to the states of California and Washington.

CHAPTER 8

SOURCES

It is not possible to show the source of each piece of information in a compilation covering the lives of over 4,000 persons. The list of sources which follows should, however, provide some indication of where a particular bit might have come from.

The McElwain Family Histories

The McElwain Family Histories is a name I have given to five short accounts of the family of James (#200000000) which I received from various sources just before and after World War II. These histories were compiled at various times, but at least four of them seem to be related, each building upon the one that had gone before. The fifth was a form designed to collect recent information, but also listing family members back to the beginnings in America.

Lacking any basis other than partial records and family tradition, all versions were both incomplete and, particularly concerning the early years, incorrect. All begin with James McElwain, his father Andrew, the original settler of Cumberland County, being unknown to them. James' life is also much confused: he is said to have been born in 1729 in Ireland, to have come to America in 1751 or 1752, to have married a Bell, and to have had four children. In beginning my serious research six years ago this incorrect information caused me a great deal of difficulty. I ignored all references to Andrew McElwain and to his son James simply because the dates did not fit into the pattern I had had in my mind for nearly fifty years.

Information on the later members of this branch of the family is generally correct and is the source for some of the data in this book.

The following summary provides a guide to these histories so that anyone who possesses one or more of them can compare them with the more recent, and, I trust, more reliable, information in this book.

A   "History of the McElwain Family Down to the Present
       Generation' (1 page)
The concluding sentence, "We the undersigned are descendents of John, the son of John and Hannah, shows that the "present generation" is that of the children of John T. and Mary McElwain, born between 1844 and 1862, although none of them are named, and the signatures are not on the copy I received. The most recent date given is 1848, but the document must have been written much

later, probably in the late nineteenth century when the children of John were mature.

B   "McElwain History" (2 pp.)
This version states that it was completed on September 17, 1904. It has only a small amount of information in addition to that in the first version.

C   "History of the McElwain Family Down to the Present
        Generation" (2 pp.)
The most recent date in this version is July 15, 1929. It adds information on the children of John and Mary McElwain.

D   "Record of the McElwain Family as Furnished Oct. 30, 1933
        by Mrs. Annabelle (McElwain) Hannah" (1860-1938) (2 pp.)
Mrs. Hannah added the names of the spouses of the children of John T. and Mary McElwain E. McElwain family

E   "McElwain Family History" [with a worksheet for adding in-
        formation] (3 pp.)
This is by far the most complete of the five histories. It includes only birth, marriage, and death dates, omitting the narrative information found in the other four. It appears that the person who compiled this version was engaged in bringing the history of the family up to date. It is not signed, but a good guess would be that it was Forrest C. McElwain (#226410000). Forrest had published a brief summary of the information in the first four histories in *Genealogy* magazine of April 20, 1912 when he was thirty five years of age. At the time the questionnaire was circulated he was in his sixties and probably had more time to spend on genealogy, as many of us do.

Both the *Genealogy* article and this history continue the erroneous information on James, and neither mention Andrew. However, Forrest evidently continued his research and did unearth the truth. A genealogical chart he compiled later, a copy of which I recently received from his grandson Arden Emery, has the correct information. Ah, that I had had the chart when I started!

Torrence and Allied Families by Robert M. Torrence (1938)

Robert Torrence compiled an extensive genealogy of his family, and because his grandmother was Gertrude McIlvaine he included a chapter on her family. The fifty two pages devoted to the McIlvaines includes material from Scotland, but is mostly concerned with American genealogy. Gertrude was descended from Andrew McIlvaine (d. 1726) of Cool Spring, Delaware. The material includes many persons of only remote relationship to his family, and one of these, unfortunately, was the Andrew McElwain (Torrence spells it McIlvaine) who is the progenitor of the family which is the subject of this book.

In going over the numerous persons named Andrew McElwain (by whatever spelling) in early Pennsylvania, Torrence confused our Andrew with Andrew, the son of George McElwain. The result was that numerous genealogies exist today in which this error is embedded. Torrence was an experience genealogist and he should not have made this mistake. Andrew McElwain, the subject of this book, died in 1770 leaving ten children. Andrew the son of George was very young when his father died, as Torrence noted in remarking that money was left for his education. Investigation would have revealed that George's son was born about 1740; had he died in 1770 with ten children he would have accomplished a splendid (though not impossible) feat of generation. In Chapter III will be found a biographical material on George which should clear up any lingering doubts in the minds of persons who might have adopted this error from older family histories.

Torrence also managed to add another error which has spread into many genealogies. He shows that Andrew and Mary Mickey McElwain had a son named Thomas. Somehow this non-existent Thomas became confused with a Thomas who was killed in the Revolution, and a remark to that effect also appears in older genealogies. To confute this error it is necessary only to read the will of Andrew, written five years before the Battle of Lexington-Concord, in which there is no mention of a son Thomas.

The Complete History of the McElvain-McIlvaine Family, by Frank McElvain.

Frank McElvain was born in 1865. He spent his life in newspaper work, as a typesetter, reporter, sports editor, editor, publisher, and owner, mostly in Illinois but also as far afield as California. He had two hobbies, genealogy and soldiering. The latter he indulged by many years of service in the National Guard with the 5th Illinois Infantry and later the 1st Illinois Cavalry. He served in 1916 on the Mexican border in the Pancho Villa affair, although age fifty at the time. At the outbreak of war with Germany in 1917 he reported to the adjutant general for recruiting duty, but somehow managed to get transferred to the Sixth Illinois Infantry, where he was promoted to the rank of Captain. His unit took part in the St. Mihiel and Meuse-Argonne offensives. When his unit returned to the United States, he transferred to an embarkation depot, where he served until October 1919. There is on a microfilm at the Salt Lake City Family History library a copy of a letter from Frank, headed from the "Western Front", replying to an inquiry from a woman back on the home front. Even in the midst of battle he was still a genealogist.

Frank gathered an immense amount of material on every family with a surname in any way similar to his own. He seems never to have got through researching, and in 1946, apparently despairing of publishing it in finished form, he sent his work, only partially organized to the Family History Library of the Church of Jesus Christ of the Latter Day Saints. It is now available on microfilm in Salt Lake City or at any local Family History Library.

There is a great deal of valuable material in this gigantic compendium. Many pages are taken up by the McYlveyne family in Scotland, from which most, if not all, of the American families are descended. The American section includes considerable material on the family of Andrew and Mary Mickey McElwain. He did pick up the two errors of Robert Torrence concerning the parentage of Andrew and the fictitious son Thomas, and through this managed to spread the Torrence errors even more widely. Anyone at all interested in family history will find it interesting to look through the microfilm.

The House of Grimet, A Family Genealogy, with an Introduction by
   Jean Moore and Andrew G. McIlvaine, by William O. Ordway. 1993.
   Second edition, 1994.

Bill Ordway, who is descended from George McIlvaine and Ruth McElwain (700000000), and thus belongs not only to this family, but to that of Andrew McIlvaine of Cool Spring, Delaware, has accomplished in this stupendous work the task of gathering into one volume the genealogies of fifteen major branches of the families descended, or probably descended, from the McYlveyne (or McIlvaine) family of Ayrshire, Scotland. There are well over 20,000 individuals listed. Chapter 3 deals with the family of Andrew and Mary Mickey McElwain and occupies fifty-nine pages. The Delaware McIlvaine family, including that descended from Ruth and George McIlvaine appears in Chapter 1.

Mr. Ordway's book is concerned primarily with genealogy, but also contains brief biographical information and a great number of pictures. Because I worked closely with Bill on Chapter 3 of his book, the material in his book and in the Genealogy of this one is essentially the same, except that a considerable volume of material discovered since his publication date has been added.

The number of copies of *The House of Grimet* is about 350 so anyone without a personal copy or a near or distant cousin who has one will find it difficult of access. However, there is a copy in the Family History Library at Salt Lake City. In addition I have placed copies in three locations: The Cumberland County Historical Society, Carlisle, PA; The Newville Historical Society, Newville, PA., and the Buhl-Henderson Library (The Mercer County Genealogical Society) in Sharon, PA.

Mr. Ordway's book is purged of the errors found in earlier publications. I am sure he feels that it is still imperfect, but it is as perfect as the raw material and the hazards of publishing will allow. I have therefore created an honorary position for

him as Dean of McIlvaine-McElwain Research.   The position carries
no stipend, but it carries my unlimited respect for the work he
has done.

The Family History Libary of the Church of Jesus Christ of the
   Latter Day Saints

     The Family History Library resides in Salt Lake City, Utah,
and in hundreds of branch Family History Libraries located in
connection with churches throughout the United States.

     The Mormon Church, as it is commonly called, has assembled
the largest collection of genealogical material ever assembled, or
likely to be assembled, at any time in history or any place in the
world. It is a truly astonishing accomplishment. The same church
that sends out those nice looking, polite young persons to try to
convert us, has sent out reinforced battalions throughout the
nation and the world to collect genealogical information, and they
have applied the same indefatigable diligence to the one task as
to the other.

     For what purpose all this information has been collected is
an interesting question. Some of the competing religions seem to
think it is to steal away some of their members--not the living,
breathing, and contributing members, but those long since, it is
presumed, to have been taken up into some celestial paradise. A
few years ago there was an item in the press which related the
struggle which arose between the irrepressible Mormon collectors
of data and the Church of England. That august Church, which
numbers among its members the royalty and the nobility of the
United Kingdom, concluded that the Mormons were collecting names
of its members with the purpose of baptising them posthumously as
Latter Day Saints and thereby, somehow, translating them from the
supposed splendor of the Anglican heaven into the unknown, and
certainly less aristocratic, heaven of the Mormon Church, where
there will certainly be no sherry before dinner. The Anglicans at
first forbade the Mormons access to their churches and records,
and, when this restriction was precluded by the courts, prohibited
the use of photographic equipment. As they, or any sensible
person, should have forseen, the Mormon data collectors, nothing
daunted, simply attacked the records with paper and pencil. What
eventually will come of this titanic theological struggle is
difficult to conjecture, but no doubt it will rank in
ecclasiastical history as equal to some of the celebrated
controversies of the primitive church.

     Whatever the purpose of the Mormon Church, nefarious or
otherwise, it has generously made all of these resources freely
available to everyone. The gentle folk who man the Family History
libraries are both helpful and knowledgeable; probably they are
the sometime cheerful young proselytizers grown older.

A visit to the main library in Salt Lake City is fascinating: three stories of books and microforms, dozens of attendents eager to help, and hundreds of patrons crowding the place through the whole day, and sometimes into the night, diligently perusing the material and laboriously recording their findings in notebooks.

The material is varied beyond imagination. On the shelves are printed books--family genealogies, local histories, and all sorts of other things. In cabinets are the microfilms--wills, deeds, court records, county documents, church registers, and even more genealogies, histories. And it will all be available forever (by that time there will be a considerable accumulation), since duplicate records are, we are told, safely stored deep underground in a location outside the city.

The International Genealogical Index (usually called the IGI) is a catalog of individuals arranged by nation and, withing the United States, by state. Material is now being computerized and each branch libary has computers available for using this material.

Microforms of much of the material in the main library either exist in, or can, for a small fee, be sent to the branch libraries. The location of the branches can be found by consulting the local telephone directory.

The Zahniser Foundation

The Zahniser family has an organization dedicated, among other things, to the preservation of its family history. To achieve this purpose they have created a computer file of every descendent of the original immigrant, Matthias Zahniser. These are available both in print and computer formats from the Foundation by addressing J. Stuart Zahniser, 3961 Tulip Tree Drive, Erie, PA 16137.

In 1906 the Foundation published *The Zahnisers, A history of the family in America*. The volume has been reprinted since with supplements, and presently, Fall 1995, a new edition is being considered. The Foundation is constantly seeking additions to its mailing list; persons who are members of either of the two branches of the Zahniser family which are related to the McElwains may be placed on the list by writing Helen Harrison, 7119 East State Street, Sharon, PA 16146.

The Foundation also helps to maintain cemeteries in which family members are buried and sponsers an annual picnic and family reunion in August.

Local histories

During the nineteenth century, particularly in the last three decades, there was a great interest in the writing of local histories--those of states, counties, cities, and churches. Many of these have in the past few decades been reprinted or placed on microfilm, and are available in libraries and historical societies. Some of those which may be of interest to users of this book are listed here.

Allegheny County   Cushing, Thomas.   A Genealogical and Biographical History of Allegheny County,
                        Pennsylvania (excerpts from History of Allegheny County by Thomas Cushing,
                        et al).   Chicago, 1889.   Reprinted 1975 by the Genealogical Publishing
                        Company, Baltimore, MD.
                     History of Allegheny County, Pennsylvania. Chicago, Illinois, A. Warner & Co.,
                        1889, (2 vols.)

Crawford County   History of Crawford County, Pennsylvania.   Chicago, Warner, Beers & Co, 1885,
                        (2 vols.)

Cumberland County   McElwain, Wilbur J.   Cumberland County, Pennsylvania, Cemetery Records,
                        Collected by Jeremy Zeamer. Bowie, MD, Heritage Books, Inc., 1994.
                     McElwain, Wilbur J.   United States Direct Tax of 1798, Tax Lists for Cumberland
                        County, Pennsylvania. Bowie, MD, Heritage Books, Inc., 1994.
                     Swope, Belle McKinney Hays.   History of The Middle Spring Presbyterian Church,
                        Middle Spring, Pa., 1738-1900. Newville, Pa., Times Steam Printing House,
                        1900.
                     Swope, Gilbert Ernest. History of the Big Spring Presbyterian Church, Newville,
                        PA,   1737-1898.   Newville, PA, Times Steam Printing House, 1898.
                        [Genealogical extracts from this and the previous book compiled by Wilbur
                        J. McElwain were published by Heritage Books, Inc., Bowie, MD in 1993.]

Franklin County   McCauley, J. H. Historical Sketch of Franklin County, Pennsylvania.   Chambers-
                        burg, Pennsylvania, D. F. Pursel, 1878.

Jefferson County   McKnight, W. J.   A Pioneer History of Jefferson County, Pennsylvania.   Phila-
                        J. B. Lippencott Company, 1898.

Mercer County   History of Mercer County, Pennsylvania, with Illustrations Descriptive of its
                        Scenery. Philadelphia, L. H. Everts & Co., 1877.
                     Atlas of the County of Mercer and of the State of Pennsylvania.   Philadelphia,
                        Edward Busch, 1873
                        [These two books were reprinted in a single volume, probably in the 1970s.]

Washington County   Creigh, Alfred.   History of Washington County, from its first settlement to the
                        Present Day. Harrisburg, PA, B. Singerley, 1871
                     Crumrine, Boyd, ed.   History of Washington County, Pennsylvania, with Biograph-
                        Biographical Sketches. Philadelphia, L. H. Everts & Co., 1882

Westmoreland County Boucher, John N.   Old and New Westmoreland. American Historical Society, 1918.
                        3 vols.

THE DECENNIAL CENSUS OF THE UNITED STATES

The Federal government has taken a census of population every ten years since 1790. Copies of the original documents have been placed on microfilm and are available for use by the public at the National Archives in Washington, D. C. and at twelve branch offices of the National Archives. Each census is made available seventy years after it was taken; thus, at the present time, 1920 is the most recent which can be consulted. The 1890 census was almost completely destroyed by fire in 1921; that portion which survived occupies only three microfilm rolls covering small portions of Alabama, the District of Columbia, and Georgia

The censuses from 1790 to 1840 list only the name of the head of the family and the number of additional persons by age groups and by sex. Thus, although these early reports can be useful in establishing the location of a family, they provide little information on individuals in that family. Most of these censuses have been provided with indexes published by private organizations.

Beginning with the 1850 census all persons are listed. Those for 1850, 1860, and 1870 also have been indexed by private organizations.

The censuses for 1880 and thereafter have been indexed by the National Archives itself. Indexes for the censuses from 1880 to 1920, which are on a separate series of microfilms, are based upon a coded system, called Soundex, designed to place under one heading all surnames with similar sounds but varying spellings. Each letter of the alphabet, except the vowels, h, w, and y, is assigned a code number from one to six. The name is coded by combining the first letter of the surname with a three digit numeric designation for the subsequent significant letters, zeroes being added at the end if the number of letters is insufficient to complete the three. Thus, for example, M245 places such variants as McElwain, McElwaine, and McIlwain in the same group, and M241 does the same for McIlvaine, McIlvain, and McElvain. Within the group the individuals are arranged alphabetically by the given name of the head of the family. There are, of course, many quite dissimilar names within the group, including in M245 such names as Musselman and even Mussolini. The Soundex entry usually provides the essential information about the names, ages, and sometimes other data; its purpose, however, is to lead the user to the full census record which is on another film.

Census records are often available at libraries and historical societies, but the great number of films makes it impossible for such organizations to acquire films beyond those of local interest. The 1880 census and Soundex, for example, are on 1,454 and 2,367 rolls respectively, and would cost somewhere near $100,000.

The most satisfactory census is that for 1900, which gives the month and year of birth of each individual, while those for the

other 1850 and later censuses give only the age. This bit of
additional information is the reason that there are so many entries
in the genealogy with the month and year of birth, but lacking the
day. Those births recorded with only a year followed by "c" (for
"about") usually have been computed by deducting the age from the
year of the census, a not wholly satisfactory method, but one which
is far better than the complete lack of dates which appear in some
family entries.

In certain years other information was recorded. Much of
this has been included in the genealogy, including the value of
real and personal property, the street address, and the occupation
of the individual, including, in addition to employment, "keeping
house" and "at school." One young fellow even had his occupation
listed as "loafer", probably the only instance of humor ever to
creep into a census.

INDIVIDUAL CONTRIBUTIONS

In the course of assembling this volume I have corresponded
with a great number of cousins, some of whom I had previously known
long ago. By sending out letters to persons whose name and
residence suggested that they might be family members I was able to
establish contact with many more. Still more entered the circle by
various sorts of happenstances. The list which follows contains, I
hope, everyone who provided information either in copious or sparse
amounts, according to their individual knowledge.

I first must mention a select group to whom I am particularly
indebted because of the volume of material they have provided.

William L. Ordway (#755616000), whose name has appeared
frequently in this book, provided vast amounts of information in
his book, by a voluminous correspondence, a number of telephone
conversations, and one personal meeting. Most of the information
on the family of George and Ruth McIlvaine (#700000000) came from
Chapter 1 of *The House of Grimet*.

To Carol Zapolnik of Pentwater, Michigan I owe much of the
information on the family of Richard McElwain (#240000000). In
addition I have by letter discussed with her various genealogical
problems concerning Andrew and Mary Mickey, as well as difficulties
with several related families, particularly those of Bell and
Thompson.

George Johnston (#421235100) of Tavernier Florida, in addition
to providing information on the family of Isabel McKee McElwain and
James Bard Erwin, has also given me much help in dealing with the
confusions that were once such a problem concerning Andrew McElwain
and Mary Mickey.

Janet Lynn Edmiston Womer (#226465100) of New Wilmington, PA
gave me a great deal of help with the entire line descended from

Laura Belle McElwain and David W. McQuiston.

Glenn Miller, Sr. of Carlisle, Pennsylvania, who is not of the McElwain family, but is an enthusiast for history, national, local, and family, has generously provided documents which he has turned up in his research at the Cumberland County Court House and the Cumberland County Historical Society.

Stuart Zahniser of Erie, Pennsylvania provided listings of all descendents in the two branches of the McElwain family who are also descended from Zahnisers.

First cousins, with most of whom I had long been out of touch, were very helpful with family information.

Dorothy McElwain Hill, Clarksburg, WV (#226324100)
Richard A. McElwain, Century, WV (#226324300)
Donald M. Porter, Washington, PA (#226326100)
Betty Jeanne Porter Katich, Midland, PA (226326200)
Marilyn L. Porter Kovach, (#226326300)
Celia Jane Porter Tilley, Clearwater, FL (#226326400)
Doris Ann McElwain Law, Clarks Mills, PA (#226327100)
Children of Robert Orion McElwain (#226324200)
    Sally Jo McElwain Blake, Coolville, OH (#226324210)
    Penelope Sue McElwain Pruitt, Moses Lake, WA (#226324220)
    Polly Ann McElwain Bordelon, Parkersburg, WV (#226324240)

And finally, distant cousins who were willing to provide information to a stranger claiming to be a long-lost cousin.

Louise McElwain Boatman, Littleton, CO (#4ac820000)
Glenn Frank Carnahan, Arco, ID (#237234000)
Marjorie Anne McElwain Clum, Greenville, OH (#221875200)
Douglas Jon Crawford, Columbus, OH (#221333313)
Gordon Cooper Cross, Las Vegas, NV (#4a9513000)
Arden McElwain Emery, Wilmington, DE (#226411300)
Raymen Forrest Emery, Battle Creek, MI (#226411100)
William Reaney Emery, Pittsburgh, PA (#226411200)
David B. and Cheryl Cress Gray, Clarksdale, AZ (#242711200)
Clyde S. Hill, Elwood City, PA (#238825100)
William J. and Florence McElwain, Sandy Lake, PA (#226223000)
Marion Holm McElwain Lyons, Boulder, CO (4a4562000)
David Allen McElwain, Denver, CO (#4a5563100)
Donald Ray McElwain, Vestal, NY (#221872200)
Andrew McElwaine, Pittsburgh, PA (#245572100)
Myron M. (Bud) McElwaine, Monterey, CA (#245341000)
Naldene Rose Carnahan Penrod, Heyburn, ID (#237235000)
John and Al'Louise Suthers Ramp, Canadian, TX, (#4a9551000)
Rita Richards, Springfield, OH (4b5121000)
Janet Louise McMurray Stewart, Watertown, NY (#225314300)
Beverly Jean McElwain Verner, Nampa, ID (#4a4574000)
Val and Maryamber Shaw Villa, Van Nuys, CA (#426162100)
Irving Weber, Iowa City, IA (#242311000)
Jeanne Lea McElwain Zahm, Hallowell, KS (#4ac711000)

ILLUSTRATIONS FROM *HISTORY OF MERCER COUNTY, PENNSYLVANIA*

The Fairfield Presbyterian Church is located in New Vernon township on Deer Creek Road, two-tenths of a mile north of Georgetown Road. The church cemetery contains the graves of numerous McElwains, including John S. and Hannah, and John T. and Mary.

The portrait is that of John Thompson McElwain (#226000000). Of the numerous prominent men whose portraits appear in the *History*, he is one of the few who is clean-shaven.

The residence of James Madison Carnahan (#235000000) is located in Mill Creek township about a mile south and slightly east of New Lebanon.

FAIRFIELD PRESBYTERIAN CHURCH, NEW VERNON, MERCER CO., PA.
ELDERS { JAMES A. LEECH. J. W. STEWART. GEN. J. M. CARNAHAN. JOHN & DAVID McELWAIN, PRINCIPAL SUBSCRIBERS TO THE PICTURE

John McElwain

RES. OF GEN. J. M. CARNAHAN, MILL CREEK TP, MERCER CO., PA.

Serial # and Name	Birth	Marriage	Death
000000000 MCELWAIN			
Andrew McElwain			1770 Aug Cumberland Co. PA
Mary Mickey	1719c	Robert Mickey &	1789>
		Mary McIlvaine	

See the History, pages 1-6, for information on this family.

1 Elizabeth	*1751<	1770<	
2 James	*1752 May Cumberland Co. PA		1816 Nov Cumberland Co. PA
3 Prudence	*		
4 Andrew	*1756 Mar Cumberland Co. PA	1779>	1820 Apr Cumberland Co. PA
5 Mary	*	1794 Jul 29 Newville PA	
6 Hannah	*1761		1794
7 Ruth	*		
8 Eleanor	*1762c Cumberland Co. PA	1783	
9 Robert	*1766 Oct Cumberland Co. PA	1789 Oct 7	
a William	*1767c Cumberland Co. PA		

100000000 NICHOLSON			
Elizabeth McElwain	1751<	1770<	
William Nicholson			

See the History, page 7, for a discussion of genealogical problems concerning Elizabeth.

200000000 MCELWAIN			
James McElwain	1752 May Cumberland Co. PA		1816 Nov Cumberland Co. PA
s Mary Nicholson		Richard Nicholson &	1789<
		Mary -----	
t Margaret -----			1823 Sep Cumberland Co. PA

See the History for information on this family (pages 8-13), and the Nicholson family (pages 33-34).

1 Mary	s*1776 Feb 1 Cumberland Co. PA		1859 Aug 19
2 John S.	s*1779 Oct Cumberland Co. PA	1805 Mar 21 Middle Spring PA	1845 Nov 14 Mercer Co. PA
3 Ruth	s*1781 Jan 21 Cumberland Co. PA	1802 Feb 25 Cumberland Co. PA	1853 Jun 23 Mercer Co. PA
4 Richard	s*1784 Jul Cumberland Co. PA		
5 Margaret	t 1789> Cumberland Co. PA	never married	1828 Oct Cumberland Co. PA

210000000 STEEL			
Mary McElwain	1776 Feb 1 Cumberland Co. PA		1859 Aug 19
Robert Steel	1766		1836 Aug 17 Cumberland Co. PA

Mary is mentioned in the will (written 1812) of her father James.   Because the date of her birth as estimated from the 1789 census of the Big Spring Church is close to that found on a gravestone in the Carlisle cemetery, it has been assumed that this Mary McElwain and her husband are buried there. See the History section, pages 13-14, for further information concerning Mary and her family.

Serial # and Name	Birth	Marriage	Death

220000000 MCELWAIN

John S. McElwain	1779 Oct Cumberland Co. PA	1805 Mar 21 Middle Spring PA	1845 Nov 14 Mercer Co. PA
Hannah Thompson	1786	PA Andrew Thompson &	1829 May 4 Mercer Co. PA
		Elizabeth Bell	

See the History, pages 14-16, for information on this family.

1 James	* 1805 Dec 16 Cumberland Co. PA		1851 Aug 2 Crawford Co. OH
2 Elizabeth Bell	* 1807 Nov 6 Mercer Co. PA		
3 Eliza	* 1811 Feb 16 Mercer Co. PA		
4 Margaret	* 1813 Aug 17 Mercer Co. PA	1854> Mercer Co	PA 1875 Feb 12 Mercer Co. PA
5 Ruth C.	* 1815 Oct 2 Mercer Co. PA		
6 John Thompson	* 1817 Dec 3 Mercer Co. PA	1843 Oct 24	PA 1883 Jan 29 Mercer Co. PA
7 Hannah	* 1820 Aug 31 Mercer Co. PA		
8 Allen	* 1825 Jan 1 Mercer Co. PA	1852c	1900 Apr 21 Crawford Co. PA
9 Cynthia	* 1828 Feb 12 Mercer Co. PA		1904 Mercer Co. PA
a Andrew T.	1809 May 6 Mercer Co. PA		1809 Nov 30 Mercer Co. PA
b Mary Jane	1823 Aug 4 Mercer Co. PA		1823 Sep 3 Mercer Co. PA

221000000 MCELWAIN

James McElwain	1805 Dec 16 Cumberland Co. PA		1851 Aug 2 Crawford Co OH
Nancy Judith Nicholson	1807 Sep 4		1864 Aug 16

In 1850 James was a farmer with $550 in property living in Antrim twp., Wyandotte County, OH.   The statement in various McElwain histories that he moved to Iowa and died young is evidently not correct.

1 Henry			
2 Ira C.	1829 Jan 20		1852 May 13
3 Hannah A.	* 1832c		
4 Margaret A.	* 1833c		1878
5 William H.	1835c		
6 John S.	1836 Jul 25		1854 Dec 20
7 Ruth Ellen	* 1838c	1856 Aug 17 Wyandotte Co. OH	
8 Andrew Thomas	* 1840 Jan 7 Greenville PA	1865	1891 Apr 20 Lafayette OH
9 Eliza B.	* 1841c		Delphos OH
a Robert G.	1842		1882 i. Delphos OH
b Lucy A.	* 1845c	OH	
c Mary Jane	1847 Aug 11		1865 Feb 28
d James P.	1851 Sep 11		1852 Aug 18

Henry went west and was never heard from.   Ira appears in the 1850 census as a laborer.   William went to llinois; he was a laborer.   Robert served in Co. E, 34th Ohio Volunteer Infantry in the Civil War; more than 1,000 persons attended his funeral as "a last tribute of Respect to one who had braved death in war and individual wounds and loss of health that the Nation might live." (from a Bucyrus, OH newspaper of the time)

221300000 MCELVAIN

Hannah A. McElwain	1832c		
John McElvain			

Both Hannah and John are buried in White's Cemetery, Crawford Co., OH.

1 Adarene			died at age 3
2 Alice E.	* 1855 Dec	OH	
3 Wilbert E.	* 1857 Oct	OH 1879 Jul 16 Crawford Co. OH	

Serial # and Name	Birth	Marriage	Death

221320000   MCMANUS

| Alice E. McElvain | !1855 Dec | OH! | ! |
| John McManus | !1856 Jun | NY! | !1919c |

This family's residence in 1900 was Bath twp., Allegheny Co., PA; in 1910 it was in Columbus, OH.

1 Cora	*!1887 May	OH!	!
2 Carl L.	*!1889 Feb	OH!	!
3 Maggie M.	*!1890 Mar	OH!	!
4 Estella	*!1892 Sep	OH!	!1968
5 Eva	*!1895 Nov	OH!	!

221321000   CRAIG

| Cora McManus | !1887 May | OH! | ! |
| Rolla Craig | !1886c | OH! | ! |

In 1920 this family lived on Boop Road, Allegheny County, Ohio.

1 Lloyd	!1908c	OH!	!
2 Alice	!1910c	OH!	!
3 Grethel	!1912c	OH!	!
4 Raymond	!1913c	OH!	!
5 Robert	!1915c	OH!	!
6 Irene	!1917c	OH!	!
7 Dale	!1919	OH!	!

221322000   MCMANUS

| Carl L. McManus | !1889 Feb | OH! | ! |
| Edna Aldrich | !1896c | OH! | ! |

The McManus family lived in Auglaize County, Ohio in 1920.

| 1 Lenore | !1917c | OH! | ! |

221323000   HEDGES

| Maggie M. McManus | !1890 Mar | OH! | ! |
| Owen H. Hedges | !1889c | OH! | ! |

Maggie and Owen, with their two children, lived in Allen County, Ohio in 1920.

| 1 Leroy E | !1913c | ! | ! |
| 2 Ralph L. | !1919 | ! | ! |

221324000   HALL

| Estella McManus | !1892 Sep | OH! | ! |
| Ester Hall | !1890c | OH! | ! |

The Hall family resided on Church Street, Lafayette, Allen Co., OH in 1920.

1 Nevelda	*!1914	OH!	!
2 Beulah	*!1918	OH!	!
3 Eleanor	*!1920	!	!
4 Ruth Odetta	!1923	!	!1941

221324100   BASIL

Nevelda Hall	!1914	OH!	!
John Basil	!	!	!
	!	!	!
1 Deloris Jean	!	!	!

Serial # and Name	Birth	Marriage	Death

221324200   BINKLEY

Beulah Hall	1918c	OH	
Joseph Binkley			
1 Suzanne			
2 [son]			

221324300   CRAWFORD

Eleanor Hall	1920		
Arthur Crawford	1915		1969
1 Gary Arthur	*1937		
2 Jacqueline	*		

221324310 CRAWFORD

| Gary Arthur Crawford | 1937 Dec 12 Lima | OH 1954 Mar 15 Lima   OH | |
| Judith Kay Griffin | 1938 Jul 6 Lima | OH Bernard Griffin & Mary Bishop | |

David retired as an Air Force Captain; he is now a civil engineer. Daniel is a system engineer for On-Line Library Center in Columbus. Douglas studied Commercial Design and has a B. F. A from Ohio State University.

1 Debra Kay	*1954 Dec 27 Lima	OH 1972 Jun 16 Lima OH	
2 David James	1956 Dec 30 Dayton	OH	
3 Daniel Joseph	1958 Feb 14 Columbus	OH	
4 Douglas Jon	1959 Oct 24 Columbus	OH	
5 Glen Alan	*1962 Jun 25 Lima	OH	
6 Scott Jeffrey	*1963 Sep 1 Lima	OH	

221324312   WRIGHT / POWELL

Debra Kay Crawford	1954 Dec 27 Lima	OH 1972 Jun 16 Lima OH	
s Frank Wright			
t Dennis Powell	1955 Apr 22 Lima	OH	

Debra is continuing her education in the health care field.   She and Frank were divorced Feb. 7, 1973.

1 Heather Dawn	s 197? Aug Lima	OH	
2 Amanda Jo	t 1976 Jan 1 Lima	OH	
3 Jodi Denise	t 1980 Mar 4 Lima	OH	

221324315   CRAWFORD

| Glenn Alan Crawford | 1962 Jun 25 Lima | OH | |
| Traci Lynn Moon | | | |

Glenn has been a police officer in the Lima, Ohio area for ten years.

221324316   CRAWFORD

Scott Jeffrey Crawford	1963 Sep 1 Lima	OH	
Jennifer Miller	1974 Jan 21 Lima	OH	
1 Brooke Anne	1995 Jul 3 Lima	OH	

221324320   MUSTO

Jacqueline Crawford			
Richard Musto			
1 Christina	1962		
2 Vincent	1964		
3 Ann	1971		
4 Regina	1972		

Serial # and Name	Birth		Marriage		Death	

221325000   ANDREWS

| Eva McManus | 1895 Nov | OH | | | | |
| Harold Andrews | 1892c | OH | | | | |

  Eva and Harold lived in Allen County, Ohio in 1920.

221330000   MCELVAIN

| Wilbert E. McElvain | 1857 Oct | OH | 1879 Jul 16 Crawford Co. OH | | | |
| Sophia D. Davis | 1858 Feb | OH | | | | |

  Wilbert, Sophia, and Delia (under the pseudonym of "Birdie") lived in Liberty twp., Crawford County, PA
  in 1880, They lived in Lima, OH in 1900, 1910, and 1920; their address in 1900 was 954 So. Elizabeth St.
  Wilbert is in the 1880 census as William and in that for 1920 as Wilbur.

| 1 Delia | *1880c | OH | | Toledo | OH | 1943 |
| 2 Emmet | 1882 Oct 8 | OH | | | | |

  Emmitt lived with his parents in 1900, but not in 1910. In 1920 he was again living with them.

221331000   CORNFELT

| Delia McElvain | | | | Toledo | OH | 1943 |
| ----- Cornfelt | | | | | | |

  Delia did not live with her parents at the time of the 1900 census, suggesting that she may have been married.

221400000   HARVEY

Margaret A. McElwain	1833c				1878	
Robert Harvey	1815				1871 Aug 6	
1 Frank	1861 Jul 27		never married			
2 Mary Isabel	1862 Aug 6				1864 May 27	
3 Minnie	1867 Aug 21		never married			

221700000   HUDSON

| Ruth Ellen McElwain | 1838c | | 1856 Aug 17 Wyandotte Co. OH | | | |
| David M. C. Hudson | | | | | | |

  This couple moved to Nebraska.

| 1 Minnie | | | | | | |

221800000   MCELWAIN

| Andrew Thomas McElwain | 1840 Jan 7 Greenville | PA | 1865 | | 1891 Apr 20 Lafayette | OH |
| Catherine C. Halliwell | 1846 Dec 16 | OH | | | 1915 Jan 19 i. Lafayette OH | |

  Andrew was a Sergeant in the 101st Volunteer Infantry of Ohio in the Civil War and later a United Brethren
  minister. The family moved to a farm near Lafayette, OH in 1880.   In 1900 Catherine, Carrie, and Ottie
  were living in Jackson twp., Allen County, Ohio.

1 [son]	1866 Sep 22				1866 Sep 22	
2 [daughter]	1866 Sep 22				1866 Sep 22	
3 Ernest Eugene	*1868 Jan 21	OH	1890 Feb 15		1931 Jun 19	
4 Bertha Artemisia	*1869 Aug 7	OH	1887 Aug 21		1942 Nov 22	
5 [daughter]	1871 Feb 22				1872	OH
6 Grace Viorqua	*1875 Mar 1	OH			1966 May 13	
7 Minor Leroy	*1878 Jan 16	OH			1949	
8 Carrie Biantha	*1884 Apr 21	OH			1968 Jan 27	
9 Ottie Ethel	*1886 Sep 1	OH	1904 Aug 6 Allen Co. OH			

Serial # and Name	Birth	Marriage	Death

221830000 MCELWAIN

Ernest Eugene McElwain	¦1868 Jan 21	OH¦1890 Feb 15	¦1931 Jun 19
Ora Ellen Jennings	¦1868 Sep 14	OH¦	¦1936 Jul 13

Ernest graduated from Beaverdam High School (1890) and Ohio Northern University.   He taught school for sixteen years and then farmed.   In 1900 the family lived in Jackson twp., Allen County, OH.

1 Edgar Marshall	*¦1890 Sep 15	OH¦1917 May 20	¦
2 Ralph Andrew	¦1897 Apr 13	¦	¦1898 Jul 24
3 Carl Willard	¦1899 Aug 4	OH¦never married	¦1928 May 8

Ralph was killed by bees. Carl was a graduate of Ohio State University, and taught vocational agriculture.

221831000   MCELWAIN

Edgar Marshall McElwain	¦1890 Sep 15	OH¦1917 May 20	¦
Lola Olive Cotner	¦1895 May 4	¦	¦
	¦	¦	¦
1 Maxine Edna	*¦1918 Jan 7	¦1936 Jul 12	¦
2 Eleanor Grace	*¦1920 Mar 7	¦1940 Jan 17	¦
3 Margaret Joan	¦1928 May 20	¦	¦1928 May 20
4 Jean Ellen	*¦1931 Mar 7	¦1950 Sep 24	¦

221831100   HOLMAN

Maxine Edna McElwain	¦1918 Jan 7	¦1936 Jul 12	¦
Ronald Leroy Holman	¦1914 Aug 12	¦	¦
	¦	¦	¦
1 Arthur Leroy	*¦1942 Jun 26	¦	¦
2 Robert Wayne	*¦1947 Mar 11	¦	¦

221831110   HOLMAN

Arthur Leroy Holman	¦1942 Jun 26	¦	¦
Linda Ellen Gratz	¦	¦	¦
	¦	¦	¦
1 Kira Ellen	¦1969 Dec 22	¦	¦
2 Krista Elaine	¦1972 Apr 21	¦	¦
3 Kathryn Elizabeth	¦1975 Feb 28	¦	¦

221831120   HOLMAN

Robert Wayne Holman	¦1947 Mar 11	¦	¦
Rita Louise Staley	¦	¦	¦
	¦	¦	¦
1 Cale Matthew	¦1972 May 14	¦	¦
2 Ronald Wayne	¦1974 Jul 2	¦	¦
3 Colleen Louise	¦1976 Jun 20	¦	¦

221831200   FISHER

Eleanor Grace McElwain	¦1920 Apr 7	¦1940 Jan 17	¦
Basil Westa Fisher	¦1918 Dec 8	¦	¦
	¦	¦	¦
1 Frederick Eugene	¦1941 Apr 2	¦	¦
2 Janet Ann	¦1943 Aug 13	¦	¦
3 Sandra Sue	¦1948 Apr 25	¦	¦
4 Dortha Kay	¦1951 May 29	¦	¦

Serial # and Name	Birth	Marriage	Death

221831400   SCHMIDT

	Birth	Marriage	Death
Jean Ellen McElwain	1931 Mar 7	1950 Sep 24	
Thomas Loren Schmidt	1929 Dec 4		
1 David Thomas	1952 May 10		
2 Carol Ann	1954 Feb 18		
3 Susan Jean	1955 Sep 26		
4 Lynn Louise	1957 Nov 8		

221840000   PATTERSON

	Birth	Marriage	Death
Bertha Artemisia McElwain	1869 Aug 7	OH 1887 Aug 21	1942 Nov 22
John N. Patterson	1863 Dec 4		
1 Harry Leicester	* 1889 Apr 14		
2 Leo May	1894 Apr 27		1902 Apr 16

221841000   PATTERSON

	Birth	Marriage	Death
Harry Leicester Patterson	1889 Apr 14		
Edith Shinerberry	1892 Aug 12		
1 Ilo May	* 1914 May 13	1946 Jun 22	
2 Chester LaVerne	* 1916 Mar 28	1938 Oct	1966 Aug 22
3 Gilda Mary	* 1917 Oct 2		

221841100   FELDNER

	Birth	Marriage	Death
Ilo May Patterson	1914 May 13	1946 Jun 22	
Frederick Feldner	1915 Mar 6		
1 Joyce Ann	1947 Jul 22		
2 Nancy Sue	1949 Dec 8		

221841200   PATTERSON

	Birth	Marriage	Death
Chester LaVerne Patterson	1916 Mar 28	1938 Oct	1966 Aug 22
Margaret Louise Herr			
1 Elizabeth Louise	1940 Nov 3		
2 John	1941 Jun 12		
3 Frederick	1942 Aug		

221841300   LEHMAN

	Birth	Marriage	Death
Gilda Mary Patterson	1917 Oct 2		
Theodore Lehman			
1 Rebecca Joe			

221860000   BOYD

	Birth	Marriage	Death
Grace Viorqua McElwain	1875 Mar 1	OH	1966 May 13
John Boyd			
1 Gladys Elwain	* 1897 Aug 3		
2 Russell Garner	* 1906 Mar 17		1959 Jul 19
3 Raymond DeWitt	* 1915 Aug 25	1936 Sep 28	

Serial # and Name	Birth	Marriage	Death
221861000 WEAVER			
Gladys Elwain Boyd	1897 Aug 3		
Dale Weaver			
1 Helen	*1918 Jan 2		
2 Ruth			
3 Beryl			
4 Bernice			
221861100 MOTOR			
Helen Weaver	1918 Jan 2		
----- Motor			
1 [daughter]			
221862000 BOYD			
Russell Garner Boyd	1906 Mar 17		1959 Jul 19
Mary Arnold			
1 Joan	*1930 Dec 30	1966	
2 Donald			
3 Linda Lou	1941		
221862100 LININGER			
Joan Boyd	1930 Dec 30	1966	
Howard Lininger			
221863000 BOYD			
Raymond DeWitt Boyd	1915 Aug 25	1936 Sep 28	
Gladys Maxine Guthrie	1918 Aug 19		
1 Meredith Ann	1937 Apr 3		
2 Barbra			
221870000 MCELWAIN			
Minor Leroy McElwain	1878 Jan 16	OH	1949
Lunda Mae Clark	1879 Mar 20		1970
1 Daisy Marie	*1898 Aug 19	1919 Nov	
2 Lester Leroy	*1900 Mar 18 Lafayette OH	1922 Aug 12 Beaverdam [?] OH	1985 Apr 28 Lima OH
3 Audrey Fay	*1901 Nov 9		
4 Ralph Gerald	*1904 Aug 3		1962 Nov 13
5 Richard Clair	*1907 Jan 20	1926 May 8	
221871000 HELSER			
Daisy Marie McElwain	1898 Aug 19	1919 Nov	
Howard Helser			

Serial # and Name	Birth	Marriage	Death

221872000 MCELWAIN

Lester Leroy McElwain	:1900 Mar 18 Lafayette	OH:1922 Aug 12 Beaverdam	OH:1985 Apr 28 Lima OH
Lula Maxine Fowler	:1904 Mar 26 Tiffin	OH:	:1991 Aug 26 Fremont OH
	:	:	:
1 Robert Morris	*:1923 Oct 12 Lima	OH:1950 Oct 7 Vermillion AB:	
2 Donald Ray	*:1927 Apr 28 Lima	OH:1951 Jul Fairview Park OH:	
3 Janet Lou	*:1928 Apr 21 Lima	OH:1951 Sep 16 Lima OH:	

221872100 MCELWAIN

Robert Morris McElwain	:1923 Oct 12 Lima	OH:1950 Oct 7 Vermillion AB:	
Jean Irene Corley	:1927 May 30 Vermillion	AB:	:

This family was living in Calgary, Canada in 1994

1 Cathie Jean	*:1951 Nov 18	:1973 Nov 9 Edmonton AB:	
2 Lester Corley	*:1952 Oct 25	:1979 May 12 Edmonton AB:	
3 Dean Robert	*:1956 Jun 11	:1986 Aug 23 Edmonton AB:	

221872110 O'KANE

Cathie Jean McElwain	:1951 Nov 18	:1973 Nov 9 Edmonton AB:	
Gerald O'Kane	:1948 Mar 15	:	:
	:	:	:
1 Patrick Gabriel	:1979 Oct 9	:	:

221872120 MCELWAIN

Lester Corley McElwain	:1952 Oct 25	:1979 May 12 Edmonton AB:	
Edith Makowecki	:1956 Mar 3	:	:
	:	:	:
1 Sean Andrew	:1983 Jan 11	:	:
2 Caley Jean	:1985 Jan 27	:	:

221872130 MCELWAIN

Dean Robert McElwain	:1956 Jun 11	:1986 Aug 23 Edmonton AB:	
Jill Atkinson	:1965 Feb 5	:	:
	:	:	:
1 Corley	: Edmonton AB:		:
2 Amy	: Edmonton AB:		:
3 Evangeline	: Edmonton AB:		:

221872200 MCELWAIN

Donald Ray McElwain	:1927 Apr 28 Lima	OH:1951 Jul 21 Fairview Park OH:	
Dittie Jo Mayer	:1927 Jul 19 Lafayette	IN:	:
	:	:	:
1 Charles Robert	*:1954 Dec 5 Cleveland	OH:1979 Jun 23 Binghamton NY:	
2 Molly Jo	*:1957 May 9 Cleveland	OH:1979 Nov 23 Binghamton NY:	
3 Andrew Walter	*:1966 May 12 Binghamton	NY:1988 Aug 20 Columbus OH:	

221872210 MCELWAIN

Charles Robert McElwain	:1954 Dec 5 Cleveland	OH:1979 Jun 23 Binghamton NY:	
Cheryl Lynn Reinhart	:1957 Jun 9 Binghamton	NY:	:

Serial # and Name	Birth	Marriage	Death
221872220 CLARK			
Molly Jo McElwain	1957 May 9 Cleveland OH	1979 Nov 23 Binghamton NY	
Benjamin Franklin Clark	1953 Jun 3 IL		
1 Ryan Douglas	1988 Jan 15 Corpus Christi TX		
2 Jason Walter	1991 Jul 15 Corpus Christi TX		
221872230 MCELWAIN			
Andrew Walter McElwain	1966 May 12 Binghamton NY	1988 Aug 20 Columbus OH	
Tina Renee Jenkins	1966 Sep 21		
1 Kiersten Alyssa	1995 Jun 12 Columbus OH		
221872300 BUCKLAD			
Janet Lou McElwain	1928 Apr 21 Lima OH	1951 Sep 16 Lima OH	
Carl Francis Bucklad	1929 Mar 16 Cleveland OH		
1 Mark Steven	1956 Mar 15		
2 Matthew Alan	*1958 Jun 12		
221872320 BUCKLAD			
Matthew Alan Bucklad	1958 Jun 12		
Mary -----			
1 Carley Marie			
2 Katy Elizabeth			
3 Jeremy Allen			
221873000 STEARN			
Audrey Fay McElwain	1901 Nov 9		
Milton Stearn			
1 William Robert	1930 Feb 1		
2 Donald Leroy	1934 Sep 24		
221874000 MCELWAIN			
Ralph Gerald McElwain	1904 Aug 3		1962 Nov 13
Marion Lyle			
1 Herbert Lyle	*1930 Mar 15	1950 Sep 3	
2 Rebecca Joan	*1932 Jul 25	1953 Dec 31	
3 Doris Jean	*1935 Sep 24		
4 Carolyn Joyce	*1937 Dec 31		
221874100 MCELWAIN			
Herbert Lyle McElwain	1930 Mar 15	1950 Sep 3	
Elizabeth Dirmeyer			
221874200 HOOKER			
Rebecca Joan McElwain	1932 Jul 25	1953 Dec 31	
Dewey A. Hooker			

Serial # and Name	Birth	Marriage	Death
221874300 SMITH			
Doris Jean McElwain	1935 Sep 24		
Richard Smith			
1 Steven			
221874400 ZIMMERMAN			
Carolyn Joyce McElwain	1937 Dec 31		
Eugene Zimmerman			
221875000 MCELWAIN			
Richard Clair McElwain	1907 Jan 20	1926 May 8	1987 Aug
Ethel Hefner			
Ethel was living in Lafayette, OH at the time of her marriage.			
1 [son]	1926 Nov		1926 Nov
2 Marjorie Anne	*1928 Nov 16		
3 Alan Clair	*1942 Apr 20		
221875200 CLUM			
Marjorie Anne McElwain	1928 Nov 16	1949 April 8	
Gerald Clum			
1 Sara Beth	1950 Feb 15		
2 Scott Charles	1951 Sep 29		
3 Spencer Ray	1953 Jul 30		
4 Amy Claire	1955 Apr 21		
5 Brian Curtis	1955 Oct 25		
221875300 MCELWAIN			
Alan Clair McElwain	1942 Apr 20		
Judy Malinas			
1 Andrew William	1966 May 13		
2 Adam Clair	1969 Dec 30		
3 Kathryn Louise	1971 Jan 29		
4 Peter Alan	1978 Aug 5		
5 Ann Marie	1978 Aug 5		
221880000 CLARK			
Carrie Biantha McElwain	1884 Apr 21	OH	1968 Jan 27
Richard Clark			1946 Apr 16
1 Mary Lucinda	*1918 Mar 30		
2 Naomi Grace	*1921 Sep 19		
221881000 SPRAGUE			
Mary Lucinda Clark	1918 Mar 30		
Donald Sprague			
1 Donald Norbert	*1949 Sep 30		
2 Allen	*1955 May 3		

Serial # and Name	Birth	Marriage	Death
221881100 SPRAGUE			
Donald Norbert Sprague	1949 Sep 30		
Shirley Tropah			
1 Matthew Donald			
2 Timothy Joseph			
221881200 SPRAGUE			
Allen Sprague	1955 May 3		
Melody Glenn			
221882000 LIEBER			
Naomi Grace Clark	1921 Sep 19		
Richard Paul Lieber			
1 Roger Lee	1941 Nov 22		
2 Dennis Lynn	*1949 Aug 9		1972 Oct 2
221882200 LIEBER			
Dennis Lynn Lieber	1949 Aug 9		1972 Oct 2
Cathline Johnson			
1 Daniel			
221890000 DRIVER			
Ottie Ethel McElwain	1886 Sep 1	OH 1904 Aug 6 Allen Co.	OH
David Henry Driver	1881 Mar 26	OH	
The Driver family was living at 352 E. High St., Defiance, OH in 1920.			
1 [son]	1905 Feb 28		1905 Feb 28
2 Treva Alma	*1906 Sep 6 Lafayette	OH 1928	1976
3 Avery M.	*1908 Jun 15 Lima	OH 1931 Jun	
4 Wava Marie	*1908 Jun 15 Lima	OH 1928	
5 Rollie C.	1911 May 29	OH	
6 Arlene	*1914 Oct 8		
7 Ruby Ethel	*1920 Mar 3	1939	
221892000 CARYER			
Treva Alma Driver	1906 Sep 6 Lafayette	OH 1928	1976
Robert Caryer	1905 Sep 2		
1 [daughter 1]	1928 Nov 26		1928 Nov 26
2 [daughter 2]	1928 Nov 26		1928 Nov 26
3 Ruth	*1930 Jul 18		
4 Robert	*1932 Dec 3		
5 Phyllis	*1936 Jun 29		
6 Bernice	*1938 Jan 11		
7 Carol Catherine	1943 Dec 23		

Serial # and Name	Birth	Marriage	Death
221892300 ESCHBACH			
Ruth Caryer	1930 Jul 18		
Harold Eschbach			
1 Ronald Dean	1950 Aug 5		
2 Linda Mae	1953 Mar 26		
3 Larry Lynn	1955 Jan 30		
4 Marianne	1957 Jan 26		
221892400 CARYER			
Robert Caryer	1932 Dec 3		
Sharon Zeller			
1 Carl James	1955 May 12		
221892500 DIX			
Phyllis Caryer	1936 Jun 29		
Roger Dix	1932 Mar 17		
1 Roger Lee	1953 Feb 24		
2 Debra Jean	1955 May 6		
3 Lonetta Ray	1956 May 9		
221892600 SPEISER			
Bernice Caryer	1938 Jan 11		
Lloyd Speiser			
221893000 DRIVER			
Avery M. Driver	1908 Jun 15 Lima	OH 1931 Jun	
Ida Swigert			
1 Nancy Sue	1932 Mar 7		
2 Rollie S.	1936		
3 Russell E.	1938		
4 Judith Ann	1940		
221894000 LAYMAN			
Wava Marie Driver	1908 Jun 15 Lima	OH 1928	
Virgil C. Layman			
1 David	1929 May 11		
2 John	1930 Oct 17		
3 Paul	1932 Aug 19		
4 Ralph	1938 Sep 22		
5 Floyd	1940 Jul		

Serial # and Name	Birth	Marriage	Death
221896000 FETTER			
Arlene Driver	1914 Oct 8		
Paul Fetter			
1 Barbara Gaye	1945 Dec 1		
2 Beverly Grace	1945 Dec 1		
3 Mary			
4 Shirley	1949 Oct 29		
5 Sharon	1956 Sep 17		
221897000 SMITH			
Ruby Ethel Driver	1920 Mar 3	1939	
Chester R. Smith			
1 Charlotte L.	1940 Mar 11		
2 Elizabeth L.	1942 Apr 4		
3 Diane Ellen	1944 Apr 18		
4 Ray Wesley	1946		
5 Cameron	1947		
6 Byron	1949 Dec		
7 Marsha	1950 May		
8 Teresa	1952 Jan		
9 Virginia	1953		
221900000 MCDONNELL			
Eliza B. McElwain	1841c		Delphos OH
George McDonnell			
Eliza and George had no children.			
221b00000 MEIKSEL			
Lucy A. McElwain	1845c	OH	
----- Meiksel			
222000000 JOBS			
Elizabeth Bell McElwain	1807 Nov 6 Mercer Co. PA		
----- Jobs			
223000000 GIBSON			
Eliza McElwain	1811 Feb 16 Mercer Co. PA		
James Gibson			
224000000 DILLEY			
Margaret McElwain	1813 Aug 17 Mercer Co. PA	1854> Mercer Co PA	1875 Feb 12 Mercer Co. PA
Mathias Dilley	1798 Nov 1		1880 Jun 16
Mathias' marriage to Margaret was his third.			

Serial # and Name	Birth	Marriage	Death

225000000 MILNER

Ruth C. McElwain	1815 Oct 2 Mercer Co. PA		1895 May 5 Mercer Co. PA
Levi Milner	1818c OH		

Levi and Ruth are listed in the 1850 census for Mercer County, he as a farmer with property value of $500; in 1860, also in Mercer Co., he owned real property of $1600 and personal of $320. He was known as Lev.

1 Hester Jane	1844c PA		
2 Hannah Mariah	1848c PA		
3 Mary Melvina	*1849 Nov 9 Erie PA	1873	1920 Sep 20 Venango Co. PA
4 Eugene W.	1852 Sep PA		
5 Elmer	1855 PA		
6 Levi	*1856 Aug PA		
7 Charles	*1857 Feb PA		

In 1900 and 1910 Eugene was living alone in Venango County, PA.

225300000 VOGAN

Mary Melvina Milner	1849 Nov 9 Erie PA	1873	1920 Sep 20 Venango Co. PA
Thompson James Vogan	1850	Washington Vogan &	1898 Nov 21 Mercer Co. PA
		Sarah Porter	

Thompson was a farmer.   He and his daughter Ruth died of typhoid fever contracted at an ice cream social. In 1920 Mary, Judson, and Vesta were living together in Sandy Lake twp., Mercer County, Pennsylvania.   In the census for that year, between the names of the two children, there is listed another person, born on February 1880. The name is undecipherable. Sarah Porter Vogan also lived with them.

1 Judson Clyde	*1875 Jun 25 Mercer Co. PA	1900 Feb 21 Jamestown NY	1947 Feb 26 Venango Co. PA
2 Ruth Pearl	1881 Mercer Co. PA		1898 Oct 11 Mercer Co. PA
3 Vesta Viola	*1884 Dec 2 PA		1954 Jan 3
4 [child}			died in infancy
5 [child]			died in infancy

225310000 VOGAN

Judson Clyde Vogan	1875 Jun 25 Mercer Co. PA	1900 Feb 21 Jamestown NY	1947 Feb 26 Mercer Co. PA
Nancy Queen Butterfield	1880 Feb 14 Karns City PA	John Floyd Butterfield &	1975 May 16 Franklin PA
		Catherine E. Cornelius	

Judson was a farmer, a telegraph operator, and a carpenter.

1 Mary Lucille	*1900 Dec 26 Mercer Co. PA	1919 Nov 26 Franklin PA	1992 Dec 26 Utica PA
2 Paul Eugene	1902 Jun c Mercer Co. PA		lived only a few hours
3 Anna Bernice	*1904 Apr 2 Mercer Co. PA	1927 Sep 22	1984 Nov 3 Meadville PA
4 Cecile Elizabeth	*1905 Dec 14 Franklin PA	1927 Mar 5 Franklin PA	1976 Feb 10 Franklin PA
5 Hazel Anita	1907 Jun c Mercer Co. PA		died at six weeks
6 Thomas Floyd	*1909 Jul 15 Raymilton. PA	1940 Jul 15 Sheakleyville PA	1979 Mar 31 Buffalo NY

Hazel died of whooping cough.

225311000 GILLILAND

Mary Lucille Vogan	1900 Dec 26 Mercer Co. PA	1919 Nov 26 Franklin PA	1992 Dec 26 Utica PA
Oren Boyd Gilliland	1890 Oct 14 Franklin PA	Rankin Gilliland &	1960 Jun 8 Pittsburgh PA
		Alletta Law	

Oren was a farmer; he served in the 108th Field Artillery Battalion in World War I.   Mary gave private piano lessons.

1 Alletta Ruth	*1921 Mar 23 Venango Co. PA	1948 May 14 Utica PA	
2 Judson Rankin	*1922 Aug 28 Utica PA	1946 May 24	1994 Nov 25 Meadville PA

Serial # and Name	Birth	Marriage	Death

225311100   NETZLER

Alletta Ruth Gilliland	1921 Mar 23 Venango Co. PA	1948 May 14 Utica PA	
Robert Edward Netzler		----- Netzler & ----- Bickel	
Robert was a machinist.			
1 Soni Sue	*1956 Oct 10 Franklin PA	1977 Nov 19	
2 Jeneen Dawn	*1960 Aug 13 Franklin PA	1980 Mar 22	

225311110   DUTKO

Soni Sue Netzler	1956 Oct 10 Franklin PA	1977 Nov 19	
Michael Francis Dutko			

225311120   GAHR

Jeneen Dawn Netzler	1960 Aug 13 Franklin PA	1980 Mar 22	
Francis Gene Gahr			
1 Joshua Gene	1981 Aug 1 Venango Co. PA		
2 Jeremy Robert	1983 Mar 7 Venango Co. PA		
3 Jacob Lee	1986 Mar 17 Venango Co. PA		

225311200   GILLILAND

Judson Rankin Gilliland	1922 Aug 28 Venango Co. PA	1946 May 24	1994 Nov 25 Meadville PA
Lois Virginia Kimes	1924 Nov 23	----- Kimes & Janet -----	1995 Oct 5 Stoneboro PA
Judson served in the United States Navy in World War II. He was a member of the the Sandy Lake Borough			
Council for many years and was active in Boy Scout work.			
1 Oren Kim	*1947 Oct 5 Grove City PA	1975 May 24	
2 Cheryl Gay	*1952 Dec 27 Grove City PA	1976 Jun 19	

225311210   GILLILAND

Oren Kim Gilliland	1947 Oct 5 Grove City PA	1975 May 24	
Sharon Brook			
1 Brooke Nichole	1979	PA	
2 Megan Elizabeth	1983	PA	

225311220   GUYTON

Cheryl Gay Gilliland	1952 Dec 27 Grove City PA	1976 Jun 19	
John Guyton			
1 Lisa Michelle	1981 Jan	PA	
2 Gregory Kyle	1984 Jul 15	PA	

225313000   CHATLEY

Anna Bernice Vogan	1904 Apr 2 Mercer Co. PA	1927 Sep 2	1984 Nov 3 Meadville PA
Wallace Jerome Chatley	1900 Mercer Co. PA	Errett Martin Chatley &	1988 Jul 17 Meadville PA
		Belle -----	
1 Errett Clyde			died age 1
2 Leon			died age 2
3 Herbert Dale	*1930 Sep 11		
4 Shirley Dianne			died age 6 weeks
5 Marian Delores	*1941 Dec 11 Meadville PA	1961 Jan 21 Meadville PA	

Serial # and Name	Birth	Marriage	Death

225313300   CHATLEY

Herbert Dale Chatley	1930 Sep 11		
Dorothy Gearhart			

Herbert served in the United States Naval Air Force

1 Edward R.			
2 Linda			
3 Donald Paul	#	1993 Jun 5	
4 Nancy Lee	#1964 Nov 26 Baltimore	MD 1986 Jul 11	

225313330   CHATLEY

Donald Paul Chatley		1993 Jun 5	
Debbie Strait			

225313340   RICHARDS

Nancy Lee Chatley	1964 Nov 26 Baltimore	MD 1986 Jul 11	
Harry Richards			
1 Michael Wilson	1987	PA	
2 Andrew James	1991 Dec	PA	
3 Jamie Ellen	1993 Mar 29	PA	

225313500   PHILLIPS

Marian Delores Chatley	1941 Dec 11 Meadville	PA 1961 Jan 21 Meadville PA	
Warren Phillips	1939 Nov 22 Arborville	WV Roland John Phillips &	
		Violet Belle Halterman	

Marian and Warren were divorced in 1987. Warren worked as a toolmaker.

1 David Michael	#1963 Jul 26 Denver	CO 1984 Oct 13 Conneaut PA	
2 Gloria Diane	#1965 Dec 9 Meadville	PA 1983 Jun 18	
3 Kenneth Eugene	1967 Mar 12 Meadville	PA	both boys died in infancy
4 Kevin John	1969 Nov 18 Meadville	PA	and are buried in New
			Lebanon, PA

225313540   PHILLIPS

David Michael Phillips	1963 Jul 26 Denver	CO 1984 Oct 13 Conneaut Lake PA	
Melissa Jean Weber			

David and Melissa have two children.

225313510   BUCHANAN

Gloria Diane Phillips	1965 Dec 9 Meadville	PA 1983 Jun 18	
Daniel Joseph Buchanan			
1 Amy Sue	1984 Apr 28		
2 -----			

225314000   MCMURRAY

Cecile Elizabeth Vogan	1905 Dec 14 Franklin	PA 1927 Mar 5 Franklin PA 1976 Feb 13 Franklin PA	
John Stewart McMurray	1902 Sep 28 Mercer	PA Stewart Archibald McMurray & 1965 Nov 22 Franklin PA	
		Maude Runninger	

John owned a convalescent home and Cecile was a practical nurse.

1 John Stewart, Jr.	#1927 Oct 6 Venango Co.	PA 1961 Apr 8 Knox PA 1979 Oct 2 Franklin PA	
2 Paul William	#1929 Jul 29 Mercer Co.	PA 1950 Feb 14 Venango Co. PA	
3 Janet Louise	#1931 Aug 27 Venango Co.	PA 1954 Apr 15 Theresa NY	
4 Margaret Elizabeth	#1934 Aug 29 Venango Co.	PA 1952 Aug 22 North Sandy PA 1983 Jul 18 Buffalo NY

124

Serial # and Name	Birth	Marriage	Death

225314100 MCMURRAY

John Stewart McMurray, Jr.	1927 Oct 6 Venango Co. PA	1961 Apr 8 Knox PA	1979 Oct 2 Franklin PA
Marlene Fay Henry	1935 Jul 22 Knox PA	Wilbur B. Henry &	
		Grace Louella Garris	

John served in the United States Army in World War II. He held a B.S. from Tri-State College and worked as a mechanical engineer.   Marlene was a secretary at Knox Glass, Inc, and now is secretary for The Salvation Army in Franklin, Pennsylvania.

| 1 Mark Stewart | 1965 Dec 31 Franklin   PA | | |
| 2 James Wilbur | *1968 Jun 18 Franklin   PA | 1991 Jan 26 | |

Mark graduated from Pennsylvania State University in a program which gave him both a B.S. in mechanical engineering from Pennylvania State and a B.S. in physics from Slippery Rock State University.   He also holds a Master's degree in Mechanical Engineering from Pennsylvania State University. He is employed as a mechanical engineer in the racing division of Champion Spark Plug, Toledo, OH.

225314120 MCMURRAY

James Wilbur McMurray	1968 Jun 18 Franklin PA	1991 Jan 26 Franklin PA	
Jacqueline K. Martin	1968 Jul 14 PA	John R. Martin & ----- -----	

James works as a network operator and Jacqueline as a day care group supervisor.

225314200 MCMURRAY

Paul William McMurray	1929 Jul 29 Mercer Co. PA	1950 Feb 14 Venango Co. PA	
s Barbara Jean Smoyer	1932 Jan 19 PA	Frank Smoyer & Winifred ----	
t Dorothy Lynn Lovers	1940 Feb 23 Franklin PA		
		Scott Thomas Lovers &	
		Opal Lucille Frantz	

Paul is an automobile technician for the Ford garage in Spring Valley, PA.   Dorothy is a supervisor at a day care center. They are divorced.

1 Terry Wayne	s*1951 Jun 27 Franklin PA	1972	
2 Steven Craig	s 1954 Jan 8 Franklin PA		
3 Rodney Eugene	s*1958 May 1 Franklin PA	1992 Feb 28 Mercer PA	
4 Paula Lynne	t 1976 Feb 1 Franklin PA		
5 Jeffrey Lee	t 1960 Sep 16 Franklin PA		

Jeffrey is Dorothy's son by a previous marriage.   Steven was formerly a member of the United States Army Band; he now gives private music lessons and plays in a band.

225314210 MCMURRAY

Terry Wayne McMurray	1951 Jun 27 Franklin PA	1972	
s Amy Phillips			
t Louanne Neeley	1955 Jul 29	1976 Oct 1 Franklin PA	
		Eugene Charles Neeley &	
		Donna Ruth Mattern	
u Melissa Grill		1990 Dec 15 Franklin PA	
		Guy Anthony Grill &	
		Margie Jane Shawgo	

Terry, formerly a shop foreman at Cadillac Garage, Greenville, Pennsylvania, is a corrections officer with the Sheriff's Department of Venango County at Franklin, PA.   He was divorced from Amy in December 1975 and from Louanne in 1985. Louanne had a previous marriage.

| 1 Ryan Patrick | 1982 Aug 28 | | |

Ryan was adopted.

Serial # and Name	Birth	Marriage	Death

225314230   MCMURRAY

Rodney Eugene McMurray	1958 Mar 1 Franklin PA	1992 Feb 28 Mercer PA	
Cynthia Louise Krison		John Delmar Krison &	
		Helen Lou Morrow	

Rodney works as a machinist. Cynthia from a previous marriage had a child, Billy Parker, born about 1981.

1 Cassie Elissa	1992 Jul 20 Venango Co. PA		

225314300   STEWART

Janet Louise McMurray	1931 Aug 27 Venango Co. PA	1954 Apr 15 Theresa NY	
Charles Arthur Stewart	1927 Aug 24 Watertown NY	Clarence Arthur Stewart &	
		Edith Margaret Smith	

Janet has a B.A. from Grove City College, and an M. Ed. from St. Lawrence University.   She was an English teacher in the Watertown School District, Watertown, NY.   Charles received a B. A. from St. Lawrence University; he was a district manager for Kemper Insurance.   During the Korean War he served with the United States Army in the Far East Network, Okinawa.

1 Karen Ann	*1955 Mar 7 Watertown NY	1977 Aug 6 Watertown NY	
2 Cynthia Sue	*1957 May 17 Watertown NY	1979 Jul 14 Watertown NY	
3 Kevin Charles	1960 Jan 1 Watertown NY		

Kevin received a B. A. from St. Lawrence University (1982), and a M. S. (Technical Writing) from Rensselaer Polytechnic Institute (1984).   He has worked for Pratt & Whitney, East Hartford, CT, Simmonds Precision Engineering, Vergennes, VT, and KeyCorp, Albany NY. He is currently an independent contract writer.

225314310   SCHEER

Karen Ann Stewart	1955 Mar 7 Watertown NY	1977 Aug 6 Watertown NY	
Mark Walter Scheer	1954 Sep 1 Binghamton NY	Walter Jacob Scheer &	
		Arlene Combellack	

Mark holds a B.S. and an M.B.A. from Clarkson College;   he is Director, Supplier Relations for AMP Inc. of Harrisburg, PA.   Karen hold a B.A. from St. Lawrence University, and an M.S. (Education) from Colgate University; she teaches English at Red Land High School, West Shore District, west of Harrisburg, PA.

1 Christopher James	1980 Jun 27 Rome NY		
2 Lindsey Diane	1983 Jun 29 Rome NY		

225314320   GENTER / BRUNETT

Cynthia Sue Stewart	1957 May 17 Watertown NY	1979 Jul 14 Watertown NY	
s Gregory James Genter	1956 Oct 23	Charles Roy Genter &	
		Elaine Adams	
t Timothy Edward Brunett	1963 May 3 MI	1989 Mar 4 Riverview MI	
		Michael Thomas Brunett &	
		Deanne Yvonne Johnson	

Cynthia has a B. A. from Russell Sage College, and has worked as a bank teller.   Gregory has a B.S. from Buffalo State University, has worked as a foreman for Great Lakes Steel, and is now a salesman for NALCO. He and Cynthia were divorced in 1987.   Timothy is an engineer, designing fire prevention equipment for Tri-Star, Plymouth, Michigan

1 Shaun Stewart Genter	1981 Sep 1 Dearborn MI		
2 Mitchell Arthur Brunett	1989 Sep 20 Dearborn MI		

Serial # and Name	Birth	Marriage	Death

225314400   BLOOMQUIST

Margaret Elizabeth McMurray	1934 Aug 29 Venango Co. PA	1952 Aug 22 North Sandy PA	1983 Jul 18 Buffalo NY
Robert Leslie Bloomquist	1932 Mar 27 Jamestown NY	Melvin Bloomquist &	
		Ruby Wheelock	

Margaret attended Hornell (NY) Business School and was an EEG technician. Robert was employed by the Buffalo Evening News.

1 Robert Leslie	#|1954 Mar 20 No. Hornell NY	1976 Aug 14 Kenmore NY	
2 Jean Elizabeth	#|1955 Apr 28 No. Hornell NY	1980 Nov 1 Buffalo NY	
3 Gary Stewart	1960 May 23 Buffalo NY		1960 Jul 1 Buffalo NY
4 Michael Ray	1964 May 14 Buffalo NY		

225314410   BLOOMQUIST

Robert Leslie Bloomquist	1954 Mar 20 No. Hornell NY	1976 Aug 14 Kenmore NY	
Nancy M. Raiff		Robert Raiff & ----- -----	

Nancy works as an inhalation therapist.

1 Shannon Marie	1985 Apr 6 Cleveland OH		
2 Valentina	1986 Apr 6 Roumania		

Valentina was adopted; she arrived in the United States June 6, 1993.

225314420   JUEN / WOLF

Jean Elizabeth Bloomquist	1955 Apr 28 No. Hornell NY	1980 Nov 1 Buffalo NY	
s Douglas Richard Juen	Oct 10		
t Michael Wolf		1991 Feb 16	

Michael had two children from his first marriage, Christopher (b. 1976 Nov 5) and Jennie (b. 1979 Oct 9).

1 Darcy Marie Juen	1982 Dec 15 Buffalo NY		1982 Dec 16 Buffalo NY
2 Richard Douglas Juen	1984 Oct 9 Buffalo NY		

225316000   VOGAN

Thomas Floyd Vogan	1909 Jul 15 Raymilton PA	1940 Jul 15 Sheakleyville PA	1979 Mar 31 Buffalo NY
s Mildred Elizabeth Bickel	1906 Dec 12 Oil City PA	Samuel Bickel & Mary Gorton	1949 Jul 12 Venango Co. PA
t Mildred Beers Bickel		1957 May 30 Greenville PA	
u Edna Mae Wilson		1961 Oct 21 Titusville PA	

Mildred Beers Bickel had another child, Ray Bickel, born about 1927.

1 Daryl Gene	s#|1941 Aug 29 Venango Co. PA	1962 Jan 7	
2 Samuel Judson	s#|1943 Feb 2 Franklin PA		1978 Jan 7 Erie PA
3 Carl Alvin	s#| Jan		

225316100   VOGAN

Daryl Gene Vogan	1941 Aug 29 Venango Co. PA	1962 Jan 7	
Mary Rosalind Farnoff			

Daryl served in Vietnam with the United States Army.

225316200   VOGAN

Samuel Judson Vogan	1943 Feb 2 Franklin PA		1978 Erie PA
----- -----			
1 Kathy	#|1966c		
2 Peggy	#|1967c		
3 Timmy	1969c		

Serial # and Name	Birth	Marriage	Death

225316210 KING

| Kathy Vogan | 1966c | | |
| Fred King | | | |

225316220 CORTRIGHT

| Peggy Vogan | 1967c | | |
| Michael Cortright | | | |

225316300 VOGAN

| Carl Alvin Vogan | Jan | | |
| ----- ----- | | | 1995 |

225330000 SHANNON

Vesta Viola Vogan	1884 Dec 2 Mercer Co. PA		1954 Jan 3 Venango Co. PA
William Earl Shannon	1884 Nov 24 Venango Co. PA	William Robert Shannon &	1961 Nov 7 Venango Co. PA
		Mary Ann Sikes	
1 William Russell	*1906 Apr 28 Venango Co. PA	1932 Jan 13 Ripley NY	
2 Judson Clyde	*1908 Sep 2 Venango Co. PA		1990 Mar 24 i. Utica PA

225331000 SHANNON

William Russell Shannon	1906 Apr 28 Venango Co. PA	1932 Jan 13 Ripley PA	
Mary Mildred Hurd	1912 Feb 13 Venango Co. PA	John Clarence Hurd &	
		Mary Gertrude Carnahan	
1 Kenneth Leroy	*1933 Jan 27 Venango Co. PA		
2 Barbara Jean	*1937 Jan 15 Crawford Co. PA		1959 Jun 17

225331100 SHANNON

| Kenneth Leroy Shannon | 1933 Jan 27 Venango Co. PA | | |
| Leona Kagy | | | |

225331200 SPRAGUE

| Barbara Jean Shannon | 1937 Jan 15 Crawford Co. PA | | |
| Frank E. Sprague | | | |

The Spragues had no children.

225332000 SHANNON

Judson Clyde Shannon	1908 Sep 2 Venango Co. PA		1990 Mar 24 i. Utica PA
s Eleanor Polansky			
t Catherine Eleanor Shannon	1908 May 15		1959 Jun 17 i. Utica PA

Judson and Eleanor adopted the three children.

1 Bette			
2 Raymond			
3 Martha			

128

Serial # and Name	Birth	Marriage	Death

225600000 MILNER

Levi Milner	¦1856 Aug PA¦		¦
Mary -----	¦1865 Aug PA¦		¦

Levi and Mary, with these six children, were living in Venango Co., PA in 1900.

1 Floyd	*¦1886 Oct PA¦		¦
2 Vance	¦1888 Oct PA¦		¦
3 Grace	¦1891 Jul PA¦		¦
4 Bertha	¦1893 May PA¦		¦
5 Pearl	¦1894 Apr PA¦		¦
6 Helen	¦1896 Oct PA¦		¦

Vance was living alone in Venango County in 1910

225610000 MILNER

Floyd Milner	¦1886 Oct PA¦		¦
Emma -----	¦1891c PA¦		¦

This family was living in Venango County in 1910 and 1920. Leroy was not listed in the 1910 census;   John was not listed in that for 1920.

1 John A.	¦1907c PA¦		¦
2 Leroy	¦1909c PA¦		¦

225700000 MILNER

Charles Milner	¦1857 Feb PA¦		¦
Alice J. Rollya	¦1864 Jun PA¦		¦

This family appears in the 1900, 1910, and 1920 censuses for Venango County, PA, in 1900 in Jackson twp.

1 Clarence	¦1888 Apr PA¦		¦
2 Clyde	*¦1889 Mar PA¦		¦
3 James	*¦1890 Dec PA¦		¦

In 1920 Clarence was living in Venango County, PA, unmarried.

225720000 MILNER

Clyde Milner	¦1889 Mar PA¦		¦
Ruth A. Rollya	¦1888c	PA¦Silas F. Rollya & ----- -----¦	

Clyde and Ruth were living with her father in Franklin twp., Venango Co., in 1920.

225730000 MILNER

James Milner	¦1890 Dec PA¦		¦
Daisy C. -----	¦1896c PA¦		¦

This family was living in Armstrong Co., PA in 1920.

1 Geraldine E.	¦1919 PA¦		¦

Serial # and Name	Birth	Marriage	Death

226000000 MCELWAIN

John Thompson McElwain	!1817 Dec 3 Mercer Co. PA	!1843 Oct 24 Mercer Co. PA	!1883 Jan 29 Mercer Co. PA
Mary McCracken	!1820 Oct 6	! Joshua McCracken &	!1894 Apr 15 Mercer Co. PA
	!	! Mary Zahniser	!

See the History for information on the family of John Thompson McElwain (pages 16-19), the McCracken family (pages 42-43), and the Zahniser family (pages 39-43).

1 Cyrus	#!1844 Sep 7 Mercer Co. PA	!1885 Sep 24 Mercer Co. PA	!1893 Nov 11 Mercer Co. PA
2 David	#!1845 Nov 24 Mercer Co. PA	!1869 Jul 8 PA	!1912 May 26 Mercer Co. PA
3 Alexander	#!1847 Feb 11	!1868 Feb	!1896 Aug 3 New Vernon PA
4 Harvey	#!1848 Aug 9 Mercer Co. PA	!1876 Apr 5	!1907 Nov 16 New Vernon PA
5 Watson	!1850 Jul 24 Mercer Co. PA	!never married	!1891 Jul 3 PA
6 Mary Therese	!1852 Aug 11	!	!1929 Jul 15 PA
7 Emma A.	#!1855 Jan 13 Mercer Co. PA	!	!1886 Feb 10 Mercer Co. PA
8 Adam T.	#!1856 Sep 7 Mercer Co. PA	!1883	!1928 Dec 14 New Lebanon PA
9 William Penrose	#!1858 May 26 Mercer Co. PA	!	! Seattle WA
a Anna Bell	#!1860 Jan 14	!1883 Mar 6 Sandy Lake PA	!1935
b Malinda F.	#!1862 Aug 4 Mercer Co. PA	!1881 May 18	! Franklin PA

Watson's occupation according to the 1870 census was clerk in a store. He never married, and, to judge by the comments in his father's will, was something of a scapegrace.

226100000 MCELWAIN

Cyrus McElwain	!1844 Sep 7 Mercer Co. PA	!1885 Sep 24 Mercer Co. PA	!1893 Nov 11 Mercer Co. PA
Phoebe Price	!1854 Dec PA	!	!1916 Jan 3 PA

Cyrus was enrolled in Company E of the 83rd Regiment of Pennsylvania Infantry Volunteers on February 23, 1864. He was severely wounded in the right arm at the Battle of Hatcher's Run, Virginia (February 5-6, 1865), and was mustered out May 19, 1865. His injury seriously reduced his ability to work at farming, and he later received a disability pension, which was continued to his wife after his death.

1 Florence G.	!1889 Apr 18	!	!1915 PA

Florence is said to have married a man named Bishop, but her grave stone in the Mt. Hope Cemetery bears the name of McElwain.

226200000 MCELWAIN

David McElwain	!1845 Nov 24 Mercer Co. PA	!1869 Jul 8 PA	!1912 May 26 Mercer Co. PA
Elizabeth E. Ross	!1850 Oct PA	!	!1937 New Vernon PA

David was educated in the common schools. He entered the mercantile business in 1870, and carried a stock of about $3,000. He was postmaster at New Vernon from 1876 to 1888. David was listed as a farmer in the 1870 census for Mercer County, PA. He also appears in the 1880, 1900, and 1910 censuses for New Vernon twp.

1 Maud	#!1870 Apr Mercer Co. PA	!1889 Sep 23	!
2 John Clair	#!1872 Feb 24 PA	!1895 Oct 23	!1957 May 1

226210000 ROSS

Maud McElwain	!1870 Apr Mercer Co. PA	!1889 Sep 23 PA	!
Clement Valindingham Ross	!1867 Sep 7	! John Ross &	!
	!	! Elizabeth Stright	!

The Ross family, with four children, was living with Maud's parents in 1900. Maud lived in New Vernon, PA around 1906.

1 David S.	!1891	!	!1892
2 Lela E.	#!1892 Jun PA	!	!
3 Franklin Clair	#!1895 Jan 3 New Vernon PA	!1919 Sep 3 Derry PA	!1956 Jan 17 Philadelphia PA
4 Harold C.	!1898 Mar PA	!	!1905 i. Mercer Co. PA
5 Hortense	!1899 Sep PA	!	!1901 i. Mercer Co. PA
6 William	!1909 PA	!	!1911

Serial # and Name	Birth	Marriage	Death
226212000 KYLE			
Lela E. Ross	¦1892 Jun	PA¦	¦
----- Kyle	¦	¦	¦
	¦	¦	¦
1 Clement	¦	¦	¦
226213000 ROSS			
Franklin Clair Ross	¦1895 Jan 3 New Vernon	PA¦1919 Sep 3 Derry	PA¦1956 Jan 17 Philadelphia PA
Carrie Elizabeth Bennett	¦	¦ Harvey Bennett & ----- -----¦	

Clair earned an A.B. from Grove City College, and an L.L.B. from Columbia University.   He worked while at Columbia with Harlan Fiske Stone, later a justice of the United States Supreme Court.   He served as Deputy Attorney General of Pennsylvania in 1935; State Treasurer, 1937-1940; Auditor General, 1940; and Judge of the Superior Court, 1944-1956. He also was a member of many boards and commissions, including the Pennsylvania Historical Commission. During World War I Clair served in the United States Army. An article on his life appears in the National Cyclopedia, p. 630.

Serial # and Name	Birth	Marriage	Death
1 Marilyn Grace	*¦	¦	¦
2 Carita Beryl	*¦	¦	¦
226213100 LOUTZENHISER			
Marilyn Grace Ross	¦	¦	¦
Theodore Raymond	¦	¦	¦
Loutzenhiser	¦	¦	¦
226213200 CUSTER			
Carita Beryl Ross	¦	¦	¦
James Scott Custer	¦	¦	¦
226220000 MCELWAIN			
John Clair McElwain	¦1872 Feb 24	PA¦1895 Oct 23	¦1957 May 6
Margaret Mae Livingston	¦1875 Sep 15	PA¦	¦1975 Mar 1

John and Margaret lived in New Vernon twp., Mercer Co., PA in 1900, 1910, and 1920.

Serial # and Name	Birth	Marriage	Death
1 Harry D.	*¦1905 Apr 18	PA¦1925 Oct 27	¦1939 Aug 22 i. Mercer Co. PA
2 Kathryn E.	*¦1910 Dec 23	PA¦1934 Oct 3	¦1981 Oct 17 i. Washington DC
3 William John	*¦1918 Jun 19	PA¦1944	¦
226221000 MCELWAIN			
Harry D. McElwain	¦1905 Apr 18	PA¦1925 Oct 27	¦1939 Aug 22 i. Mercer Co. PA
Mary Miles	¦	¦	¦
	¦	¦	¦
1 Beva Jean	*¦1926	¦	¦
226221100 LEWIS			
Beva Jean McElwain	¦1926	¦	¦
H. K. Lewis	¦	¦	¦
226222000 MCCARTNEY / TALBOTT			
Kathryn E. McElwain	¦1910 Dec 23	PA¦1934 Oct 3	¦1981 Oct 17 i. Washington DC
s Albert McCartney	¦		¦1974 Mar 18
t William Talbott	¦1909 May 10	¦1946 Sep 14	¦1971 Mar 29 i. Washington DC

Kathryn and Albert were divorced August 2, 1940.

Serial # and Name	Birth	Marriage	Death
1 Mary Margaret McCartney	*¦1935 Oct 11	¦1955 Jul 1	¦
2 Patricia Ann Talbott	*¦1952 Aug 22	¦	¦

Serial # and Name		Birth		Marriage		Death

226222100 SEARS / DARCY / YATES

Mary Margaret McCartney	!1935 Oct 11	!1955 Jul 1	!
s Curtis J. Sears	!1934	!	!
t Lewis Darcy	!1907 Aug 22	!1964 May 27	!1972 Mar 18
u Edward A. Yates	!1923 Apr 22	!1976 Aug 6	!

Margaret and Curtis were divorced September 26, 1958.

226222200 BUTLER / OLIVER

Patricia Ann Talbott	!1952 Aug 22	!	!
s James Butler	!	!	!
t David Oliver	!	!1984 Jun	!

Patricia and James were divorced.

| 1 William E. Butler | !1978 Jul 27 | ! | ! |
| 2 Joshua Butler | !1981 Nov 1 | ! | ! |

226223000 MCELWAIN

| William John McElwain | !1918 Jun 19 | PA!1944 | ! |
| Florence Noble | !1918 Jun 29 | PA! | ! |

William served in the United States Air Force, 1940-1965. After his retirement he was employed as a store-keeper for the Science Department of the University of Illinois.   He and Florence later moved to Mercer County, where he has since lived.   He and Florence spend winters in Florida.

| 1 Beverly Kay | *!1947 Nov 15 | !1969 | ! |
| 2 Robert Douglas | *!1951 Sep 9 | !1974 | ! |

226223100 MCHALE

| Beverly Kay McElwain | !1947 | !1969 | ! |
| Joseph R. McHale | !1942 | ! | ! |

The McHales live in McDonald, OH.

| 1 Kevin Joseph | !1972 Jul 28 | ! | ! |
| 2 Kari Janelle | !1974 Nov 25 | ! | ! |

Kevin graduated from Akron University, majoring in chemistry; he is employed in that field with the DuPont Corporation in Newark, DE.   Kari is a student at a Bible college in Springfield, MO and plans to major in Christian education, intending to work with young people.

226223200 MCELWAIN

| Robert Douglas McElwain | !1951 Sep 9 | !1974 | ! |
| Lorraine Bartell | !1951 Nov 7 | ! | ! |

Robert and Lorraine live near Thomasboro, IL, and both teach in Rantoul, IL.   They both graduated from the University of Illinois; Robert went on to get a master's degree.   Emily is a good musician, playing the flute, piano, and piccolo; she is also an excellent swimmer and a straight "A" student.

| 1 Emily Marie | !1981 Nov 17 | ! | ! |

226300000 MCELWAIN

Alexander McElwain	!1847 Feb 11	!1868 Feb	!1896 Aug 3 New Vernon PA
Catherine Jewell	!1837 Jul 19	! Ralph Jewell &	!1909 Aug 19 PA
	!	! Margaret -----	!

This family lived in New Vernon twp., Mercer Co., PA in 1870 and 1880. In 1900 Catherine was living in the household of James Moore, her son-in-law.   Catherine was a twin.

| 1 Mary Florence | *!1869 Nov 5 Mercer Co. PA!1888 Sep 12 | ! | Chicago IL |
| 2 Edward Lenore | *!1874 Jun 11 Mercer Co. PA!1893 Apr 19 Jamestown NY!1933 | Mercer Co. PA |

Serial # and Name	Birth	Marriage	Death

226310000   MOORE

Mary Florence McElwain	:1869 Nov. 5 Mercer Co.	PA:1888 Sep 12	:1945<	Chicago	IL
James Reed Moore	:1867 Jun	PA: James Moore & Zilpha Hill	:		

Mary was known all of her life as Mamie.   She attended the McElwain Institute, where she participated in dramatic activities.   A program in which she participated both as an organizer and a speaker is reproduced on page 79.   The family was living at 622 Liberty St., Franklin PA in 1900.   They were separated some time before 1910.   In the 1930s Mamie lived in Chicago in the home of her daughter Edna Kavanaugh.   In her later life she was a member of the Moody Bible Institute in Chicago.   The house of James' father was a station on the underground railroad.

1 Edna Florence	*:1889 Sep 5	:	:1946>	Chicago	IL

226311000   MCCLIMANS / KAVANAUGH

Edna Florence Moore	:1889 Sep 5	:	:1946>	Chicago	IL
s ----- McClimans	:	PA:	:		
t William Kavanaugh	:1890c	IL:1920<	:1950>		

In 1920 William was an Employment Agent for Standard Oil in Chicago.   He operated the Northwestern Parking Garage from before 1930 until his retirement.   He and Edna kept homing pigeons on the roof of the multi-storied garage, and trained them to return to the loft from long distances.   They separated during the early 1940's, and Edna was living alone in Chicago in 1946.

1 Frederick McClimans	*:1908c	IL:	:

226311100   MCCLIMANS

Frederick McClimans	:1908c	IL:	:1945<
Leona -----	:	:	:

Fred was employed as a steward on the Milwaukee Railroad's "Hiawatha".

226320000   MCELWAIN

Edward Lenore McElwain	:1874 Jun 11 Mercer Co.	PA:1893 Apr 19 Jamestown	NY:1933	Mercer Co.	PA
s Nettie Maud Montgomery	:1876 Mar 18	: Joseph Montgomery &	:1909 May 29 Sharpsville	PA	
	:	: Sarah Drake	:		
t Ella May Ledger	:1877	:	:1934		

This family lived in Mercer Co., PA in 1900.

1 Montgomery Leroy	s :1894 Apr 12 Mercer Co.	PA:	:1904 Nov 10 Mercer Co.	PA		
2 Floyd Miller	s :1895 May 29 Mercer Co.	PA:	:1898 Mar 24 Mercer Co.	PA		
3 Wilbur Jay	s*:1898 Apr 13 Mercer Co.	PA:1920 May 4 Chicago	IL:1984 Feb 26 Port Richey	FL		
4 Orion Roosevelt	s*!:1900 May 17 Mercer Co.	PA:1920 Apr 21 Chicago	IL:1961 Mar 3 Clarksburg	WV		
5 Izora	s :1902 Jul 26 Mercer Co.	PA:never married	:1985 Aug 25 Harrisburg	PA		
6 Linda Louise	s*!:1904 Apr 20 Sharpsville	PA:1920 Aug 24	:1985 Jul 19 Midland	PA		
7 Joseph Edward	s*!:1906 July 1 Sharon	PA:1935 Nov 28	:1965 Jan 31 Youngstown	OH		

Serial # and Name	Birth	Marriage	Death

226323000 MCELWAIN

	Birth	Marriage	Death
Wilbur Jay McElwain	1898 Apr 13 Mercer Co. PA	1920 May 4 Chicago IL	1984 Feb 26 Port Richey FL
s Adelaide Carberry	1898 Feb 27 Chicago IL	Walter Carberry &	1960 Jan Chicago IL
		Alice Eaton	
t Roena Bashaw	Jul 30		

Wilbur served the the Medical Corps of the United States Army during World War I. In 1920 he was employed as a chemist at a steel mill in Chicago, and lived with his cousin Edna and her husband William Kavanaugh. After spending several years in Clarksburg, WV operating a commercial window cleaning company with his brother Orion and his father-in-law, Walter Carberry, he returned to Chicago and operated a parking lot owned by the Northwestern Parking Garage near downtown Chicago. During World War II he was employed in the accounting department of the Dupont Corporation in Chicago, where he remained until his retirement in 1963. He and Roena then moved to the area around New Port Richey, FL, where he lived until his death. Adelaide lived with her family on a Canadian wheat farm at some time in her youth. She died of amyotrophic lateral sclerosis.

1 Wilbur Jay	s*1923 Feb 8 Chicago IL	1949 Dec 17 Chicago IL	
2 Donald James	s*1929 Aug 10 Clarksburg WV	Chicago IL	

226323100 MCELWAIN

	Birth	Marriage	Death
Wilbur Jay McElwain	1923 Feb 8 Chicago IL	1949 Dec 17 Chicago IL	
Eve Otto	1925 Nov 24 Chicago IL	Arthur Otto &	
		Geneva Carlson	

Wilbur holds degrees of B. S., Northwestern University, 1950; M. A., University of Miami, 1958; Ed. D., Florida Atlantic University, 1976, all in English. He was employed by the Dade County, Florida public schools adult education divison from 1952-1960, and by Miami-Dade Community College from 1960 to 1986. He served at the South Campus as Associate Dean for adult, military, and non-credit programs for twenty years. During World War II he spent three and a half years in the Army, two years as a private in the anti-aircraft artillery, and, returning to the United States after a year in the South Pacific, he received a commission as a lieutenant of field artillery. He served for a year (1945-1946) as a liason officer with the Philippine Army, at Ormoc, Leyte with the 132nd Infantry Division and on Luzon with the Second Infantry Division at Luna, Luzon, Army, assisting in training and demobilization. After his retirement he devoted his life entirely to pleasure--travel, reading, gardening, and compiling genealogical and historical books. Eve, after dedicating 1953 to 1972 to raising her children, worked for fourteen years as a medical transciber for South Miami Hospital. In their nine years in Washington they have made more than 200 trips into the Cascades, have walked over 1,000 miles on Forest Service roads, and have come to know and love the streams, waterfalls, and lakes; the wildflowers of each season, and the endless beauty of the place.

1 Alison Eaton	*1953 Jul 30 Miami FL	1979 Jul 27 Seattle WA	
2 Adrienne Muriel	*1954 Oct 27 Dade Co. FL	1988 Dec 23	
3 Jaye Ellen	*1956 Jun 16 Miami FL	1991 Aug 10 Tacoma WA	
4 Peter Leigh	*1962 Dec 6 Miami FL	1993 Jul 19 Key West FL	

226323110 ERICKSON

	Birth	Marriage	Death
Alison Eaton McElwain	1953 Jul 30 Miami FL	1979 Jul 27 Seattle WA	
George Thomas Erickson	1945 Oct 14 King Co. WA	Emil Ericsson &	
		Alice Erickson	

Alison has a B. A. from Florida Atlantic University, and an M. A. (Economics) from the University of Washington. She has been employed for several years as an Economist for King County, WA. Tom operates a home remodeling company. Their hobby is sailing Puget Sound on their thirty-two foot sailboat.

1 Andrew Jay	1987 Jan 11 King Co. WA		
2 Lissa Aylene	1989 Sep 4 King Co. WA		

Serial # and Name	Birth	Marriage	Death

226323120   STEINER

Adrienne Muriel McElwain	!1954 Oct 27 Miami	FL!1988 Dec 23	!
David Denison Steiner	!1953 Oct 13 Berkeley	CA! Peter Steiner &	!
	!	! Ruth Riggs	!

Both Adrienne and David hold the Ph. D. in Economics, Adrienne from Duke University, and David from the University of Michigan.   Adrienne has held faculty positions at Louisiana State University and the University of New Hampshire, and is (1996) teaching part-time at Rosary College in River Forest, IL.   David is a partner in a brokerage firm, in charge of research and computers.

1 Annie Riggs	!1990 Oct 10 Chicago	IL!	!
2 Alexander Eun	!1995 Apr 15	KO!	!

Alexander was adopted.

226323130   SPENCER

Jaye Ellen McElwain	!1956 Jun 16 Miami	FL!1991 Aug 10 Tacoma	WA!
Terrence Richard Spencer	!1951 Oct 19	! Richard Spencer	WA!
	!	! Phyllis Shaw	!

Jaye has a B. S. degree in medical technology from the University of Washington and is employed (1995) in the laboratory of Group Health, a large HMO.   Terry has a Ph. D. from University of the Pacific and works as a psychologist for Tacoma area school systems.

1 Elisabeth Shaw	!1992 Jun 9 Tacoma	WA!	!
2 Ian Douglas	!1994 Jul 23 Tacoma	WA!	!

226323140   MCELWAIN

Peter Leigh McElwain	!1962 Dec 6 Miami	FL!1993 Jul 17 Key West	FL!
Jo Ann Miller	!1968 Jun 11 Miami	FL! Richard Miller &	!
	!	! Beth Marshall	!
1 James Alexander	!1995 Feb 2 Miami	FL!	!

Peter has a B. S. B. A. from the University of Florida, and an M. P. A. from Nova Southeastern University. He assumed the position of Assistant Director of the Bass Museum (Miami Beach) in the summer of 1996.   Ann has an M. B. A. from Nova Southeastern University and is employed in the Education department of that institution.

226323200   MCELWAIN

Donald James McElwain	!1929 Aug 10 Clarksburg	WV! Chicago	IL!
Ruth -----	!	!	!

For many years Don has been employed as a printer by the R. R. Donnelly and Sons Company.   He and Ruth live in Northfield, Illinois.

226324000   MCELWAIN

Orion Roosevelt McElwain	!1900 May 17 Mercer Co.	PA!1920 Apr 21 Chicago	IL!1961 Mar 3 Clarksburg WV
Martha Luella Field	!1899 Jun 9 Chicago	IL!	!1991 Jun 2 Clarksburg WV

In 1920 Orion was a mechanic for Standard Oil in Chicago, IL.   He later moved to Clarksburg, WV, where he operated a commercial window cleaning company with his brother Wilbur.   He was active in his church, Christian Endeavor, and the Gideons International, serving in various positions of leadership.

1 Dorothy Mae	#!1921 Jul 6 Chicago	IL!1939 Sep 17	!
2 Robert Orion	#!1923 Jul 28 Clarksburg	WV!	!1988 Sep 23 Gonzalez LA
3 Richard Allen	#!1927 May 3 Clarksburg	WV!1955 Feb 12 Clarksburg	WV!
4 Thomas Field	#!1933 Apr 24 Clarksburg	WV!1952 Oct 03	!1985 Jan 15 Clarksburg WV

Serial # and Name	Birth	Marriage	Death

226324100 HILL

Dorothy Mae McElwain	1921 Jul 6 Chicago	IL 1939 Sep 17	
Paul Eugene Hill	1920 Apr 4 Clarksburg	WV Thomas Hill &	
		Beulah Bartlett	

Paul worked for Union Carbide Corp. for 42 years, retiring about 1982. Dorothy and he, during most of their married life, operated a mimeographing and direct mailing service. They have both been active in church work and with Gideon International.

1 Paul Orion	* 1940 May 6 Clarksburg	WV 1961 Jan 13	
2 Robert Aaron	* 1942 Nov 5 Clarksburg	WV 1965 Aug 15	
3 Allen Edward	* 1947 Aug 23 Clarksburg	WV 1970 Jul 11 Fairmont	WV
4 Timothy Eugene	* 1952 Oct 22 Clarksburg	WV 1980 Jul 18 Parkersburg	WV

226324110 HILL

Paul Orion Hill	1940 May 6 Clarksburg	WV 1961 Jan 13	
s Ellen Jane Wilt	1942 Mar 5 Clarksburg	WV	
t JoAnn Lance	1941 Oct 19 Barbour Co.	WV 1986 Oct 20	
1 Ann Michelle	s* 1963 Feb 5 San Antonio	TX 1994 Jun 4 Clarksburg	WV
2 Melinda Kay	s* 1965 Jun 23 Clarksburg	WV 1991 Jul 12 Clarksburg	WV
3 Melissa Rene	s* 1965 Jun 23 Clarksburg	WV 1991 Nov 16 Clarksburg	WV

226324111 CAMPBELL

Ann Michelle Hill	1963 Feb 5 San Antonio	TX 1994 Jun 4 Clarksburg	WV
Ronald Lee Campbell	1961 Jun 15 Clarksburg	WV Bennie L. Campbell &	
		Loverne Wilfong	
1 Adam Paul Hill	1988 Jul 6 Clarksburg	WV	
2 Meagan Elizabeth Campbell	1994 Dec 30 Clarksburg	WV	

226324112 TALKINGTON

Melinda Kay Hill	1965 Jun 23 Clarksburg	WV 1991 Jul 12 Clarksburg	WV
Mark Edward Talkington	1970 Oct 24 Clarksburg	WV Clifford Talkington &	
		Diane Cork	
1 Alexa Jane	1991 Aug 19		
2 Mark Edward II	1993 Aug 15		

226324113 HITT

Melissa Rene Hill	1965 Jun 23 Clarksburg	WV 1991 Nov 16 Clarksburg	WV
Ronald Mark Hitt	1961 Jun 8 Clarksburg	WV	
1 Harlee Rene	1994 Jul 4 Clarksburg	WV	
2 Hunter Cole	1996 Jul 17 Clarksburg	WV	

226324120 HILL

Robert Aaron Hill	1942 Nov 5 Clarksburg	WV 1965 Aug 15	
Catherine Marie Wienmann	1943 Apr 30 Detroit	MI	
1 Deborah Ann	* 1966 Aug 13 Detroit	MI 1989 May 27 Jacksonville FL	
2 David Allen	1969 Apr 29 Detroit	MI	
3 Darin Aaron	1970 Mar 27 Detroit	MI	

David graduated from Florida State University with a degree in Psychology in 1996.

Serial # and Name	Birth	Marriage	Death

226324121   NORMAN

Deborah Ann Hill	1966 Aug 13 Detroit MI	1989 May 27 Jacksonville FL	
John E. Norman	1965 Aug 25 Tallahassee FL		
1 Brandon Aaron	1994 Jun 16 Tallahassee FL		

226324130   HILL

Allen Edward Hill	1947 Aug 23 Clarksburg WV	1970 Jul 11 Fairmont WV	
Carolyn Rosa Stevens	1949 Aug 5 Fairmont WV	Gerald Stevens &	
		Beulah Smith	
1 Michael Edward	1972 Jul 4 Clarksburg WV		
2 Erin Alexis	1975 Jun 2 Fairmont WV		
3 Seth Andrew	1977 Feb 8 Fairmont WV		
4 Emily Melinda	1980 Jan 23 Fairmont WV		
5 Olivia Rebecca	1982 Sep 11 Clarksburg WV		

Michael was an exchange student in Denmark, 1990-1991. He is presently a Law student at Tulane University, and will be an exchange student to Cambridge University (England) in the summer of 1996. Erin was an exchange student in Sweden in 1993-1994; she is (1996) a second-year student in Architecture at Louisiana State University.

226324140   HILL

Timothy Eugene Hill	1952 Oct 22 Clarksburg WV	1980 Jul 18 Parkersburg WV	
Julie Sue Turner	1958 Nov 6 Parkersburg WV	Darrell Turner &	
		Lona Burge	
1 Meredith Ashley	1983 Mar 16 Clarksburg WV		
2 Thaddeus Joel	1985 Sep 22 Clarksburg WV		
3 Jacob Kelly	1991 May 06 Clarksburg WV		

226324200   MCELWAIN

Robert Orion McElwain	1923 Jul 28 Clarksburg WV		1988 Sep 3 Gonzalez LA
s Elizabeth Silverhorn	1919 May 11 Clarksburg WV		1968 Jul 24 Parkersburg WV
Feathers			
t Dorothy Mae Huff	1928 Jun 3 MS	1979c	1986 Jan Baton Rouge LA
1 Sally Jo	s* 1952 Oct 31 Clarksburg WV		
2 Penelope Sue	s* 1955 Jan 29 Clarksburg WV		
3 Joseph Robert	s* 1958 Jul 11 Parkersburg WV	1978 Nov 25 Ft. Sill OK	
4 Polly Ann	s* 1962 Jul 2 Parkersburg WV	1981 May 24	
5 Michael Guy	? 1966 Nov 1 Clarksburg WV		1966 Nov 19

226324210   MCDONALD / BLAKE

Sally Jo McElwain	1952 Oct 31 Clarksburg WV	1970 Nov 10	
s Lloyd Emerson McDonald,	1951 Mar 6 Parkersburg WV		
Jr.			
t Steven Lee Blake	1958 Jul 15 WY	1983 Dec 12	

Sally and Lloyd were divorced on October 26, 1982.

1 Amanda Kaye McDonald	* 1972 Aug 20 Parkersburg WV		
2 Lloyd Robert McDonald	* 1973 Jun 6 Parkersburg WV		

226324211   MCDONALD

Amanda Kaye McDonald	1972 Aug 20 Parkersburg, WV		
1 Keith Allen McLeod, Jr.	1995 Aug 7		

Serial # and Name	Birth	Marriage	Death

226324212   MCDONALD

Lloyd Robert McDonald	1973 Jun 6 Parkersburg WV	1995 Nov 3	
Lisa Michelle Cunigan	1972 Oct 30		

226324220   DEEM / ASBERRY / PRUITT

Penelope Sue McElwain	1955 Jan 29 Clarksburg WV		
s Mark Deem			
t Dennis Asberry	1959 Aug 20		
u Hubert Royce Pruitt			
1 Patricia Lynn <u>Deem</u>	#1971 Jun 6 Parkersburg WV		
2 Amy Elaine <u>Asberry</u>	1979 Feb 13		

Patricia was adopted by Dennis Asberry.

226324221   ELISAR

Patricia Lynn Deem	1971 Jun 06 Parkersburg WV		
Kyle Elisar			
1 Zachary Michael			

226324230   MCELWAIN

Joseph Robert McElwain	1958 Jul 11	1978 Nov 25 Ft. Sill OK	
Rhonda Delane Staley	1961 May 17		
1 Joseph Robert, Jr.	1981 Mar 03		
2 Jacob Orion	1986 Aug 18		

226324240   BORDELON / GRIGGS

Polly Ann McElwain	1962 Jul 02 Parkersburg WV	1981 May 24	
s John Wayne Bordelon	1958 Oct 18 Cottonport LA		
t Ronnie Richard Griggs		1984 Jul 03	
u John Wayne Bordelon	1958 Oct 18 Cottonport LA	1985 Jan 5	
Polly and John are divorced.			
1 Shantel Marie <u>Bordelon</u>	1982 Feb 16 Baton Rouge LA		
2 Samantha Marie <u>Bordelon</u>	1988 Aug 26 Baton Rouge LA		

226324300   MCELWAIN

Richard Allen McElwain	1927 May 3 Clarksburg WV	1955 Feb 12 Clarksburg WV	
Hazel E. Perrine	1928 Jul 7 Filbert WV	Richard Perrine &	
		May Cogar	
1 Richard Allen, II	#1955 Dec 22 Clarksburg WV	1976 Jan 10 Clarksburg WV	
2 Carol Diane	#1958 Oct 20 Clarksburg WV	1976 Feb 7 Clarksburg WV	
3 Thomas Edward	#1964 Jan 30 Clarksburg WV	1990 Jun 23 Pampa TX	

226324310   MCELWAIN

Richard Allen McElwain II	1955 Dec 22 Clarksburg WV	1976 Jan 10 Clarksburg WV	
Judith Kay Bennington	1955 May 8 Buckhannon WV		
Richard and Judith were divorced in 1995.			
1 Richard Allen III	1977 Feb 2 Clarksburg WV		
2 Jennifer Nichole	1981 Jun 16 Clarksburg WV		

138

Serial # and Name	Birth	Marriage	Death

226324320 THORNHILL / SNYDER

Carol Diane McElwain	1958 Oct 20 Clarksburg WV	1976 Feb 7 Clarksburg WV	
s David L. Thornhill	1955 Mar 4 Clarksburg WV		
t Greg Snyder	1964 Feb 26	1993 Nov 6	
1 David Nicholas Thornhill	1981 Apr 13 Clarksburg WV		
2 James Wesley Snyder	1995 Mar 23		

226324330 MCELWAIN

Thomas Edward McElwain	1964 Jan 30 Clarksburg WV	1990 Jun 23 Pampa TX	
Kelly Lee Tucker	1959 Apr 3 Pampa TX		
1 Thomas Evan	1992 Jul 13 Pampa TX		

226324400 MCELWAIN

Thomas Field McElwain	1933 Apr 24 Clarksburg WV	1952 Oct 03	1985 Jan 15 Clarksburg WV
Marjorie Lyon	1934 Jan 29		
1 Terry Lynn	*1954 Oct 5		

226324410 DRAIN

Terry Lynn McElwain	1954 Oct 15		
Robin Dale Drain	1956		
1 Nathaniel Scott	1982 Sep 20		
2 Jason Matthew	1984 Apr 02		
3 Thomas Dale	1985 Feb 02		
4 Racheal Dawn	1991 Sep 24		

226326000 PORTER

Linda Louise McElwain	1904 Apr 20 Sharpsville PA	1920 Aug 24	1985 Jul 19 Midland PA
James Lawrence Porter	1900 May 14 W. Bridgewater PA	James Porter &	1988 Apr 29 E. Liverpool OH
		Olive Fisher	

In 1920 Linda lived in Utica, Venango Co., PA with her great aunt Anna B. Hanna (226a00000).

1 Donald Moore	*1921 Jun 27 Midland PA	1948 Sep 11 Beaver PA	
2 Betty Jeanne	*1924 Jun 9 Midland PA	1950 Aug 23 Bridgewater PA	
3 Marilyn Louise	*1927 Apr 21 Midland PA	1962 Jun 30	
4 Celia Jane	*1934 Aug 2 Midland PA	1953 Dec 8	
5 Patricia Ann	*1937 Dec 2 Midland PA	1960 Aug 27 Pittsburgh PA	

226326100 PORTER

Donald Moore Porter	1921 Jun 27 Midland PA	1948 Sep 11 Beaver PA	
Esther M. Erwin	1920 Jan 14 Beaver PA	Earl Erwin &	
		Edith Hartenbach	
1 Drew Erwin	1951 Aug 21 Beaver PA		
2 Mark Wayne	1954 Aug 22 Beaver PA		
3 Nancy Ann	1957 Sep 4 Shreveport LA		

226326200 KATICH

Betty Jeanne Porter	1924 Jun 9 Midland PA	1950 Aug 23 Bridgewater PA	
Nick Katich	1923 Aug 31 Midland PA	Sava (Samuel) Katich &	1985 Sep 17 Midland PA
		Martha Cacic	
1 Brent	*1954 Apr 27 E. Liverpool OH	1974 Mar 25 McKean PA	
2 Luann	1957 Nov 21 E. Liverpool OH		

Serial # and Name	Birth	Marriage	Death

226326210   KATICH

Brent Katich	1954 Apr 27 E. Liverpool OH	1974 Mar 25 McKean PA	
Karen Lynn Turchich	1953 Mar 4 Rochester PA		

226326300   KOVACH

Marilyn Louise Porter	1927 Apr 21 Midland PA	1962 Jun 30 Winchester PA	
Louis Andrew Kovach	1923 Dec 7 Glouster OH	Andrew Kovach &	1995 Dec 26 Rochester PA
		Rose Molnar	

226326400   TILLEY

Celia Jane Porter	1934 Aug 2 Midland PA	1953 Dec 8	
Neil William Tilley	1934 Oct 30 Midland PA	Richard Tilley &	
		Anna Welsh	
1 Jane Ann	*1960 Apr 1 E. Liverpool OH	1982 Dec 4	
2 Jason Lloyd	1966 Jun 19 Port Jervis NY		

226326410   GRAYSON

Jane Ann Tilley	1960 Apr 1 E. Liverpool OH	1982 Dec 4	
Tom Grayson	1955 Jul 10 San Jose CA		
1 Jacob John	1990 Sep 28 St. Charles MO		

226326500   TADAJSKI

Patricia Ann Porter	1937 Dec 2 Midland PA	1960 Aug 27	
Bernard John Tadajski	1933 Oct 20 Pittsburgh PA	Stanley Tadajski &	
		Mary Karolski	
1 Christine	*1965 Jul 30 Pittsburgh PA	1995 Oct 7 Pittsburgh PA	

226326510   VILLAMAGNA

Christine Tadajski	1965 Jul 30 Pittsburgh PA	1995 Oct 7 Pittsburgh PA	
Robert Villamagna			

226327000   MCELWAIN

Joseph Edward McElwain	1906 July 1 Sharon PA	1935 Nov 28	1965 Jan 31 Youngstown OH
Bertha Lucille Pearson	1913 May 19 Jackson Cntr. PA		

Joseph worked as a machinist for Cooper Bessemer, Grove City, PA

1 Doris Ann	*1937 Feb 16 Jackson Cntr. PA	1956 Feb 24	

226327100   LAW

Doris Ann McElwain	1937 Feb 16 Jackson Cntr. PA	1956 Feb 24	
Albert William Law	1937 Mar 29 Titusville PA	Albert Law &	
		Gladys Anderson	

Doris has served as New Vernon township secretary.   Albert was employed as Supervisor at Trinity
Industries, a railroad car builder; he has served as a Supervisor of New Vernon township.

1 William Edward	*1956 Sep 15 Grove City PA	1975 Sep 6	
2 David Alan	*1958 Apr 26 Grove City PA	1977 Nov 12	
3 Robert Laverne	*1959 Oct 16 Grove City PA	1985 Feb 14	

140

Serial # and Name	Birth	Marriage	Death

226327110   LAW

William Edward Law	1956 Sep 15 Grove City PA	1975 Sep 6	
Linda Ann Keep	1954 Oct 12 Mercer Co. PA	Richard Keep &	
		Mary Cheverine	

William has worked as a welder and a carpet installer. He and Linda are divorced.

1 Christopher Shane	1972 Dec 9 Greenville PA		
2 Valorie Alison	1979 Jan 10 Greenville PA		

Christopher Mowery was born of Linda's first marriage and was adopted by William.

226327120   LAW

David Alan Law	1958 Apr 26 Grove City PA	1977 Nov 12	
Lucinda Jean Carey	1959 Jan 26 Mercer Co. PA	Charles Carey &	
		Eileen Griffin	

David is employed as a line inspector for Coinco, Cochrantown, PA, and Linda as a line inspector for Werner Ladder Co., Greenville, PA.

1 Decinda Marie	1981 Jun 30 Greenville PA		
2 Alan Dashton	1984 Jul 21 Greenville PA		

226327130   LAW

Robert Laverne Law	1959 Oct 16 Grove City PA	1985 Feb 14	
Gale Wanda Freeman	1958 Feb 11 Allegheny Co PA	Clarence Freeman	
		Alice Hayes	

Robert is owner of Law's Floor Coverings.

1 Anthony John Gesmond	1974 Oct 22 Allegheny Co. PA		
2 Jessica Renee Law	1986 Jul 18 Greenville PA		

Gale was formerly Mrs. Gale Gesmond; Anthony, a child from a previous marriage, elected to keep his birth name.

226400000   MCELWAIN

Harvey McElwain	1848 Aug 9 Mercer Co. PA	1876 Apr 5	1907 Nov 16 New Vernon PA
Sarah Jane Russell	1856 Nov 8 New Vernon PA	Joseph R. Russell & Jane ---	1920 Jan 11 New Vernon PA

Harvey and Sarah lived in New Vernon township, Mercer Co., PA. He was listed as a teamster in the 1870 census.

1 Forrest Chetwynd	*1877 Jan 29 Franklin Co. PA	1903 Nov 18	1956 Dec 24
2 Nellie T. McElwain	1879 Oct 17 PA		1898 Nov 18
3 Ethel Lorena	*1880 Jul 5 PA	1907 Jul 2	1952 Oct 19
4 Elsie Alberta	1882 Jul 14		1902 Apr 26
5 Howard Russell	1886 Dec 9	never married	1909 Oct 30
6 Laura Belle	*1888 Dec 18 New Vernon PA	1911 Apr 20	1964 Apr 29
7 Roscoe H.	1897 Jul		1920 PA

226410000   MCELWAIN

Forrest Chetwynd McElwain	1877 Jan 29 Franklin Co. PA	1903 Nov 18	1956 Dec 24
Bessie Coffey	1877 Feb 2		1944 Apr 7

Forrest settled in Washington County, PA, where, for most of his working life, he was employed as a foreman for pumping and drilling activities by South West Penn Oil Company.   An active Mason, once a week he was off to the Lodge dressed in his uniform, sword and all.   He achieved the 32nd Degree and was a member of the Knights Templar. He also did genealogical research on the McElwain family.   Chet was known for driving black Plymouth sedans--always at about thirty miles an hour. Despite the fact that his duties took him into muddy and dusty back roads, his car always seemed immaculately clean. He continued to drive until his final illness and never had a significant accident.

1 Elsie Alberta	*1904 Sep 1 Washington Co. PA	1930 Jul 1 Washington PA	1984 Jul 28
2 Martha Grace	*1908 Jan 20	1961 Mar 7	1985 Aug 18

Serial # and Name	Birth	Marriage	Death

226411000 EMERY

Elsie Alberta McElvain :1904 Sep 1 Washington Co. PA:1930 Jul 1 Washington PA:1984 Jul 28
Raymen Graham Emery :1898 Jan 17 nr Eighty Four PA: :1976 May 7

Elsie graduated from Pennsylvania College for Women (now Chatham College), and taught school for several years at Tridelphia, WV. She was interested in art and music, and was a trained soprano who, for many years, sang for the First Presbyterian Church of Washington, PA. Raymen graduated from Washington and Jefferson College, and earned the M. D. degree from the University of Pennsylvania. After interning at McGee and Mercy Hospitals in Pittsburgh, he began practice in Washington, PA in 1927. Specializing in obstetrics and gynecology, he practiced actively for 44 years, until suffering a stroke in 1971. He was a member of the Rotary Club and an elder of the First Presbyterian Church.

1 Raymen Forrest *:1931 Apr 27 Washington PA:1959 Aug 10 :
2 William Reaney *:1937 Jul 7 Washington PA:1964 Jun 13 :
3 Arden McElvain *:1938 Dec 22 Washington PA:1961 Jun 24 :

226411100 EMERY

Raymen Forrest Emery :1931 Apr 27 Washington PA:1959 Aug 10 :
Mary Janis Rutherford :1936 Mar 13 Muncie IN: :

Ray studied at Carnegie Institute of Technology (now Carnegie-Mellon University), earning a B. S. and an M. S. in Mechanical Engineering. He served two years in the United States Army Signal Corps. He is a Registered Professional Engineer and worked for 31 years for the Bendix Corp. and Eaton Corp. After his retirement he has performed consulting work. He has served as a board member and officer of the Battle Creek Symphony Orchestra, and has also been active in Community Access Television and the Rotary Club of Marshall, MI. He is a member and officer of St. Mark Lutheran Church of Battle Creek, and sings in the choir. Jan is a graduate of Purdue University. She is a trained soprano and she sings with the St. Marks choir. She is now very active in volunteer work, has served twelve years on the Battle Creek Lakeview School Board, and is also active with the League of Women Voters, the American Association of University Women and the Battle Creek Symphony Orchestra.

1 Raymen Lewis *:1959 May 10 South Bend IN:1984 Aug 4 :
2 Alice Anne *:1961 Aug 19 South Bend IN:1984 Aug 18 :
3 Robert William *:1965 Jan 4 South Bend IN:1989 Jun 10 :
4 John Lawrence :1967 Jul 8 Baltimore MD: :

John graduated in Mechanical Engineering from Valparaiso University. He is employed (1996) by Sunstrand Corp. in Denver Colorada, and lives in neighboring Westminster.

226411110 EMERY

Raymen Lewis Emery :1959 May 10 South Bend IN:1984 Aug 4 :
Tammy Kiesevetter :1961 Oct 6 : :

Ray attended Purdue University. He farms 500 acres in Henry County, IN, marketing soybeans, corn, and hogs and cattle. Tammy is a graduate of Ball State University, and holds a degree in fine art.

1 Amanda Rae :1990 Apr 11 New Castle IN: :
2 Jessica Ann :1993 Aug 3 New Castle IN: :

226411120 GOODMAN

Alice Anne Emery :1961 Aug 19 South Bend IN:1984 Aug 18 :
Timothy Paul Goodman :1961 Oct 29 : :

The Goodmans live (1996) in Lausanne, Switzerland. Alice graduated from Albion College and earned a Master's Degree in Human Genetics from the University of Michigan. Until the arrival of her children she worked in cancer research in Lausanne. Tim holds a Ph. D. from the University of Michigan, and is employed in fusion research by the Swiss government university in Lausanne.

1 Jeanne Louise :1993 Mar 31 Lausanne SZ: :
2 Silas Michael :1996 May 26 Lausanne SZ: :

142

Serial # and Name	Birth	Marriage	Death

226411130 EMERY
Robert William Emery 1965 Jan 4 South Bend IN 1989 Jun 10
Kandice K. Murray 1956 Feb 24

Bob holds the D. V. M degree from Michigan State University School of Veterinary Medicine.   He lives and practices in Battle Creek, where he is a partner in a large mixed-practice clinic.   Kandy is a registered Nurse, working at Bronson Methodist Hospital in Kalamazoo, Michigan.

1 Jacob Estes 1991 Oct 25 Kalamazoo MI
2 Daniel Eric 1993 Jul 25 Kalamazoo MI

226411200 EMERY
William Reaney Emery 1937 Jul 7 1964 Jun 13
Leddie Claire Hartner 1941 Feb 28

William ("Bill") graduated from Bucknell University in Mechanical Engineering in 1961.   He has been a Duquesne Light Company employee for thirty-five years as a Heating, Ventilating, and Air Conditioning Engineer.   He has held positions at the Shippingport Experimental Nuclear Power Station, Reed and Colfax Coal Power Stations, Marketing Services Department, and is presently located at the Beaver Valley Nuclear Plants at Shippingsport, PA. Leddie Claire graduated from the University of Pittsburgh with a B. S. and an M. S. in Education.   She is employed by the Mt. Lebanon School District as an elementary reading specialist.

1 William George *1966 Aug 17 1990 Jun 23
2 Janis Marie 1968 May 14
3 Jill Elizabeth 1970 May 20

Janis graduated from Bucknell University in 1991 with a degree in Mechanical Engineering and Business. She has been employed by Anderson Consultants and has been placed on projects in Washington, D. C., England, and Germany.   She is presently employed by Bellcable Media in London, England.   Jill graduated from Bucknell University with a B. A. in Dramatic Arts, and attended AMDA on Broadway, New York City for a year. She is presently employed by an advertising company, and performs in plays when opportunities arise.

226411210 EMERY
William George Emery 1966 Aug 17 1990 Jun 23
Pamela Cortinovis 1954 Oct 12

William ("Bill") graduated from Bucknell University in 1989 with a degree in Social Studies, and has been employed as a Federal Corrections Officer for the Lewisburg Federal Penitentiary, a teacher in a Federal program, and is now a teacher for the Williamsport School District, Williamsport, PA.   Pamela graduated from Pennsylvania State University with a master's degree in special education; she is employed by the Williamsport School District.

226411300 EMERY
Arden McElwain Emery 1938 Dec 22 1961 Jun 24
Mary Lou Wilcox 1938 Mar 18

Arden ("Ardie") graduated from Lehigh University in Mechanical Engineering in 1961, and earned an M. B. A. at night at the University of Delaware (1970). He has been a DuPont employee for over 33 years in Wilmington, DE.   Mary Lou graduated from Centenary College for Women in 1958, and has held secretarial jobs at RCA, Bethlehem Steel, and school districts in Bethlehem, PA and Wilmington, DE.

1 David Arden *1964 Aug 8 1989 Aug 19
2 Linda Graham 1968 Apr 16

Linda graduated from Lehigh University in 1990 with a degree in Finance/Marketing. After working in sales for three years in Detroit, she earned an M. B. A. from the Fuqua School of Business (Duke University) in 1996. She will take a position at GTE in July, 1996.

Serial # and Name	Birth	Marriage	Death

226411310   EMERY

David Arden Emery	1964 Aug 8	1989 Aug 19	
Karen Lynne Maynard	1966 Sep 2		

David ("Dave") graduated from Lehigh University in 1986 with a degree in Mechanical Engineering.   He is a sales engineer for Torrington Bearing Co. and currently lives in Doylestown, PA.   Karen earned a Master's degree in Social Work (Cedar Crest College and Rutgers University), and is a psychotherapist working with regional hospitals.

1 Michael Dymock	1993 Apr 22		

226412000   CLELAND

Martha Grace McElwain	1908 Jan 20	1961 Mar 7	1985 Aug 18
James J. Cleland	1892		1970

Grace (the name she always used) graduated from Wooster College (Ohio), and was for many years the executive secretary for Drakenfeld Glass Company in Washington, Pennsylvania.   After the death of her mother, she remained home and kept house for her father.   During those years the two of them did considerable work on McElwain genealogy.   She did not learn to drive until after the death of her father, when she purchased a 1957 Rambler and learned to drive well enough to get around.   She retired from work upon marrying Jim Cleland, an old friend who had lost his wife a few years earlier.   They travelled extensively during the nine years of their marriage.   James held various positions with the State of Pennsylvania.

226430000   STEPPE

Ethel Lorena McElwain	1880 Jul 5	PA 1907 Jul 2	1952 Oct 19
Joseph Steppe			
1 Laura Belle	* 1912 May 7		

226431000   STEFFAN / RHODES

Laura Belle Steppe	1912 May 7		
s ----- Steffan			
t ----- Rhodes			
1 Thomas Steffan	1935 Jan 22		

226460000   MCQUISTON

Laura Belle McElwain	1888 Dec 18 New Vernon	PA 1911 Apr 20	1964 Apr 29
David William McQuiston	1881 Mar 24 Deer Cr. twp.	PA William M. McQuiston &	1966 Jul 8
		Susan E. Gailey	
1 Rita Margaret	* 1912 Feb 3 Sandy Lake	PA 1929 Sep 3	1952 Mar 19
2 Robert J.	* 1913 Sep 24 Sandy Lake	PA 1939 Dec 28 Sandy Lake	PA 1993 Oct 13
3 Paul B.	1916 Aug 22		1917 Mar 18
4 Marion Rose	1919 Jan 5		1987 Apr 11 Mercer PA
5 Dorothy Mae	* 1920 Nov 16 Sandy Lake	PA 1940 Jul 27 Mercer	PA
6 Carl David	* 1923 Feb 23 Sandy Lake	PA 1947 Apr 26	

226461000   MINNIS

Rita Margaret McQuiston	1912 Feb 3 Sandy Lake	PA 1929 Sep 3	1952 Mar 19
Paul Wayne Minnis	1907 Apr	Elmer E. Minnis &	1952 Mar 19
		Rebecca M. Roberts	
1 Marilyn Jean	* 1931 Jan 3	1953 Aug 15	
2 Paul Ramon	* 1933 Sep 28	1957 Jun 21	
3 Kay Ann	* 1939 Sep 13	1958 Apr 26	

144

Serial # and Name	Birth	Marriage	Death
226461100 HUTCHINSON			
Marilyn Jean Minnis	:1931 Jan 3	:1953 Aug 15	:
Lawrence Frederick	:1922 Apr 14	:	:
Hutchinson	:	:	:
	:	:	:
1 Pamela Ann	*:1954 Jun 23	:1976 Aug 7	:
2 Robin Kay	*:1958 Feb 28	:1982 Feb 20	:
3 Lawrence Frederick II	:1959 Jun 15	:	:
4 Mark David	:1959 Jun 15	:	:
5 Diane Elizabeth	*:1961 Apr 4	:1979 Sep 1	:
226461110 HEILMAN			
Pamela Ann Hutchinson	:1954 Jun 23	:1976 Aug 7	:
Stephen Thomas Heilman	:1952 Oct 8	:	:
	:	:	:
1 Sarah Elizabeth	:1983 Sep 15	:	:
2 Rachel Ann	:1986 Feb 18	:	:
226461120 WIDYOLAR			
Robin Kay Hutchinson	:1958 Feb 28	:1982 Feb 20	:
Keith Kirati Widyolar	:1960 Feb 8	:	:
	:	:	:
1 Bennett Kuang Tai	:1987 Nov 19	:	:
2 Delaney McQuiston	:1989 Jun 6	:	:
226461150 SIMMONS / BAYLOR			
Diane Elizabeth Hutchinson	:1961 Apr 4	:1979 Sep 1	:
s Douglas Herbert Simmons	:1958 Dec 24	:	:
t David Leslie Baylor	:1967 Feb 11	:1990 Oct 11	:
	:	:	:
1 Bryonite Elizabeth Simmons	:1980 Aug 25	:	:
2 Jonathan Michael Baylor	:1989 Nov 26	:	:
3 Sharon Marie Baylor	:1991 Mar 11	:	:
4 Rebecca Jean Baylor	:1991 Mar 11	:	:
226461200 MINNIS			
Paul Ramon Minnis	:1933 Sep 28	:1957 Jun 21	:
s Carole Schmitz	:	:	:
t Nancy E. Jernigan	:	:	:
Paul was divorced from both wives.		:	:
1 Maureen Lee	s*:1958 Nov 2	:1980 Apr 5	:
2 Rita Lynn	s*:1960 Jul 18	:1988 Jun 18	:
226461210 SINGLETON			
Maureen Lee Minnis	:1958 Nov 2	:1980 Apr 5	:
Robert Jerome Singleton	:1954 Mar 16	:	:
	:	:	:
1 Robert Jerome	:1980 Nov 24	:	:
2 Ramon Asa	:1984 May 2	:	:

Serial # and Name	Birth	Marriage	Death

226461220   DWYER

Rita Lynn Minnis	1960 Jul 18	1988 Jun 18	
Joseph Charles Dwyer	1951 Dec 18		
1 Rachel Ann	1989 Nov 1		

226461300   BORDONARO / BROWN

Kay Ann Minnis	1939 Sep 13	1958 Apr 26	
s Cosmo Charles Bordonaro			
t Robert Wilson Brown	1940 Jul 9	1963 Jul 27	
Kay and Cosmo were divorced.			
1 Sharon Lynn Bordonaro	*1958 Oct 29		
2 Mary Ann Bordonaro	*1960 May 9	1990 Sep 22	
3 Kimberly Jean Brown	1965 Jul 13		
4 Wayne Hall Brown	*1969 Dec 30	1991 Mar 23	
Wayne was adopted.			

226461310   TAYLOR / LYNCH

Sharon Lynn Bordonaro	1958 Oct 29		
s Bryan Taylor			
s William Lynch		1985 Sep 1	
1 Michael Joseph Taylor	1984 Oct 24		
2 Matthew Lynch	1988 Mar 4		

226461320   BOUDIETTE

Mary Ann Bordonaro	1960 May 9	1990 Sep 22	
Carey Boudiette			

226461340   BROWN

Wayne Hall Brown	1969 Dec 30	1991 Mar 23	
April Michelle Reddin	1973 Apr 13		

226462000   MCQUISTON

Robert J. McQuiston	1913 Sep 24 Sandy Lake PA	1939 Dec 28 Sandy Lake PA	1993 Oct 13 Sandy Lake PA
s Edith Mae Hays	1920 Mar 18		1964 Sep 28
t Wilma Leone Johnson	1929 Mar 31	1966 Jun 18	
Andrews			
1 Fred Eugene	s*1941 Aug 15	1959 Mar	
2 Carol Jane	s*1943 Jul 26	1961 Oct 6	
3 Tom Albert	s*1946 Jun 2		
4 Glen Lee	s 1952 Aug 22		

146

Serial # and Name	Birth	Marriage	Death
226462100 MCQUISTON			
Fred Eugene McQuiston	1941 Aug 15	1959 Mar	
s Nancy Seibold			
t Kay Jones			
u Karen Tidd			
v Delores Jean Fedak		1971	
Fred was divorced from his first three wives.			
1 Patty Jean	s* 1962 Nov 9	1983 Jul 22	
2 Susan Kay	t 1966 Jul		
3 Bonnie Jane	u* 1969 Mar		
4 David Jon	v 1973 Jun 18		
226462110 ALLEN			
Patty Jean McQuiston	1962 Nov 9	1983 Jul 22	
David Allen	1960 Jun 8		
226462130 JAMES			
Bonnie Jane McQuiston	1969 Mar		
----- James			
1 Brandon	1986 Apr 28		
226462200 BOYLES / GILLILAND			
Carol Jane McQuiston	1943 Jul 26	1961 Oct 6	
s John T. Boyles			
t Edward Gilliand	1938 May 9	1977 Jun 11	
1 John Robert Boyles	1962 Aug 8		
2 George Richard Boyles	* 1963 Jul 19		
226462210 BOYLES			
George Richard Boyles	1963 Jul 19		
s Cathy Collins			
t Diane Pearl -----	1964 Jan 23	1985 Sep 1	
1 Jessica Renea	s 1981 Nov 18		
226462300 MCQUISTON			
Tom Albert McQuiston	1946 Jun 2		
s Bobbie -----			
t Juanita Irene Frances Smith	1951 Jul 3	1980 Apr 15	
1 Thomas Robert	s 1966 Jun 27		
2 Paula Jean	s 1970 Jan 17		

Serial # and Name	Birth	Marriage	Death

226465000   EDMISTON

Dorothy Mae McQuiston	!1920 Nov 16 Sandy Lake	PA!1940 Jul 27 Mercer PA!	
Chester Leroy Edmiston	!1919 Aug 30 New Castle	PA!	!1993 Jun 15
	!	!	!
1 Janet Lynn	*!1941 Jun 21 New Castle	PA!1961 Aug 1 New Wilmington PA!	
2 Evelyn Mae	*!1943 Feb 6 New Castle	PA!1965 Jun 12 New Wilmington PA!	
3 Sue Ellen	!1944 Jun 19 New Castle	PA!	!1955 Jun 14 New Castle PA
4 Elizabeth Ann	*!1947 Mar 11 New Castle	PA!1968 Mar 25 Winchester VA!	
5 William David	*!1950 Jul 8 New Castle	PA!1975 Jul 25 New Wilmington PA!	
6 Robert Carl	*!1951 Sep 27 New Castle	PA!1971 Oct 18 New Wilmington PA!	
7 Patricia Joan	*!1955 May 6 New Castle	PA!1975 Oct 18 Beaver PA!	
8 John Howard	*!1956 Sep 21 New Castle	PA!1980 Sep 7 Red Bank PA!	
9 Richard Bruce	*!1959 Mar 24 New Castle	PA!1981 Mar 28 W. Pittsburgh PA!	
a Dale Ann	*!1961 Aug 4 New Castle	PA!1980 Mar 3 Salt Lake City UT!	
b Marilyn Jean	*!1967 Feb 22 New Castle	PA!1985 Jun 29 New Castle PA!	

226465100   WOMER

Janet Lynn Edmiston	!1941 Jun 21 New Castle	PA!1961 Aug 1 New Wilmington PA!	
David Edward Womer	!1940 Aug 28 Ellwood City	PA!	!
	!	!	!
1 Leanna Beth	*!1962 Sep 6 New Castle	PA!1982 Aug 28 New Wilmington PA!	
2 Brandon Paul	*!1964 Sep 6 New Castle	PA!1989 Sep 30	!
3 Heidi Sue	!1968 Aug 29 New Castle	PA!	!

226465110   GRANEY

Leanna Beth Womer	!1962 Sep 6 New Castle	PA!1982 Aug 28 New Wilmington PA!	
Richard Edward Graney	!1962 Feb 13	!	!
	!	!	!
1 David Thomas	!1989 Aug 12	!	!
2 Julianna Mae	!1993 Oct 30	!	!

226465120   WOMER

Brandon Paul Womer	!1964 Sep 6 New Castle	PA!1989 Sep 30	!
Beatrice Lorinda Berringer	!1964 Dec 18	!	!
	!	!	!
1 Mara Renee	!1992 Sep 20	!	!

226465200   MACDONALD

Evelyn Mae Edmiston	!1943 Feb 6 New Castle	PA!1965 Jun 12 New Wilmington PA!	
David Neil MacDonald	!1943 Feb 18 Perryopolis	PA!	!
	!	!	!
1 Randall David	*!1967 Jun 20 Pittsburgh	PA!1991 Apr 25	!
2 Lane Ellen	*!1970 Jan 31 Pittsburgh	PA!1989 Nov 22	!
3 Shay Douglas	!1976 Jun 14 Charleroi	PA!	!

226465210   MCDONALD

Randall David McDonald	!1967 Jun 20 Pittsburgh	PA!1991 Apr 25	!
Patricia Ann Allen	!	!	!
	!	!	!
1 English Brenna	!1992 Mar 19	!	!
2 Kane Erik	!1994 Apr 12	!	!

148

Serial # and Name	Birth	Marriage	Death
226465220 WALKER / MOQUIN			
Lane Ellen MacDonald	1970 Jan 31 Pittsburgh PA	1989 Nov 22	
s Jason William Walker	1969 Nov 8		
t Jeffrey Thomas Moquin		1994 Sep 6	
Lane and Jason were divorced July 11, 1993.			
1 Austin David	1994 Jan 4		
226465400 JOHNSTON			
Elizabeth Ann Edmiston	1947 Mar 11 New Castle PA	1968 Mar 25 Winchester VA	
Darrell Edward Johnston	1947 Apr 20 New Castle PA		
1 Samantha Lynn	*1968 Dec 3 New Castle PA		
2 Adam Darrell	1972 Jan 17 New Castle PA		
3 Todd Robert	1975 Aug 23 New Castle PA		
4 Janna Maureen	1978 Mar 30 New Castle PA		
226465410 FARRELL			
Samantha Lynn Johnston	1968 Dec 3 New Castle PA	1995 Jul 22	
Cullen Farrell			
226465500 EDMISTON			
William David Edmiston	1950 Jul 8 New Castle PA	1975 Jul 25 New Wilmington PA	
Elizabeth Mary Guarnieri	1953 Mar 22 New Castle PA		
1 Sarah Elizabeth	1976 Jun 11 New Castle PA		
2 Abigail Lynne	1977 Oct 28 New Castle PA		
3 Jenny Marie	1979 Aug 7 New Castle PA		
4 Suanne Elaine	1983 Nov 2 New Castle PA		
226465600 EDMISTON			
Robert Carl Edmiston	1951 Sep 27 New Castle PA	1971 Oct 18 New Wilmington PA	
Donna Joann Gerber	1953 May 6 Grove City PA		
1 Kimberly Lynn	1974 Apr 20 Grove City PA		
2 Corrin Jo	1977 Aug 10 New Castle PA		
3 Joshua Robert	1982 Mar 27 New Castle PA		
226465700 SCORUPAN			
Patricia Joan Edmiston	1955 May 6 New Castle PA	1975 Oct 18 Beaver PA	
Donald William Scorupan	1954 Mar 6 Rochester PA		
1 Colton William	1977 Feb 23 New Castle PA		
2 Hayvn Michael	1979 May 31 Rochester PA		
226465800 EDMISTON			
John Howard Edmiston	1956 Sep 21 New Castle PA	1980 Sep 7 Red Bank PA	
Kathleen Jane Fiscus	1962 Jun 27		
1 Logan John	1981 Oct 1 Greenville PA		
2 Sandra May	1983 May 15 Greenville PA		

Serial # and Name	Birth	Marriage	Death

226465900   EDMISTON

	Birth	Marriage	Death
Richard Bruce Edmiston	1959 Mar 24 New Castle PA	1981 Mar 28 W. Pittsburgh PA	
Michele Ann Lenhart	1961 Apr 8 New Castle PA		
1 Benjamin Richard	1984 Dec 25 New Castle PA		
2 Matthew Michael	1986 Aug 18 New Castle PA		

226465a00   GILLILAND

	Birth	Marriage	Death
Dale Ann Edmiston	1961 Aug 4 New Castle PA	1980 Mar 3 Salt Lake City UT	
Ronald James Gilliland	1960 Jan 22		
1 Zachary Samuel	1981 Sep 8 Salt Lake City UT		
2 Jesse Brione	1986 Jan 17 Sumpter SC		

226465b00   GLENN / FISHER

	Birth	Marriage	Death
Marilyn Jean Edmiston	1967 Feb 22 New Castle PA	1985 Jun 29 New Castle PA	
s Douglas Edward Glenn	1964 May 18		
t Greg Fisher		1989 Oct	

Marilyn and Douglas were divorced.

	Birth	Marriage	Death
1 Caleb Joseph Fisher	1990 Apr 11		
2 Nathaniel Jude Fisher	1991 Dec 8		

226466000   MCQUISTON

	Birth	Marriage	Death
Carl David McQuiston	1923 Feb 23 Sandy Lake PA	1947 Apr 26	
Margaret Edith Klasen	1924 Mar 29		1996 June 17

Carl operates the family farm.

	Birth	Marriage	Death
1 Kathie Jean	*1950 Jan 15	1970 May 16	
2 Kevin Paul	1955 Nov 2		

226466100   VANDERVORT

	Birth	Marriage	Death
Kathie Jean McQuiston	1950 Jan 15	1970 May 16	
Paul Tim Vandervort	1948 May 16		
1 Bonnie Lee	1971 Aug 15		
2 Patty Ann	1975 Dec 20		
3 Scott David	1978 Jan 1		

226700000   FINDLEY

	Birth	Marriage	Death
Emma A. McElwain	1855 Jan 13 Mercer Co. PA		1886 Feb 10 Mercer Co. PA
William Findley			

226800000   MCELWAIN

	Birth	Marriage	Death
Adam T. McElwain	1856 Sep 7 Mercer Co. PA	1883	1928 Dec 14 New Lebanon PA
Mary Farrah	1858 Mar 2 New Lebanon PA		1939 Jan 26 New Lebanon PA

This family lived in Mill Creek twp., Mercer Co. PA in 1900. In 1920 Adam, Mary, and Vance lived in Mercer
Co. The 1880 census states that Adam was employed in teaching music.

	Birth	Marriage	Death
1 Lee Penrose	*1885 Nov PA		1918 Jan Seattle WA
2 Vance	*1887 Jul PA		

Serial # and Name	Birth	Marriage	Death

226810000 MCELWAIN

Lee Penrose McElwain	¦1885 Nov PA¦		¦1918 Jan Seattle WA
Lenna Claire Prouty	¦	¦	¦

Lee earned an MA in English from the University of Washington. He later practiced law in Seattle. He died during the influenza epidemic which occurred at the end of World War I.

1 Maxine McElwain	¦	¦	¦

226820000 MCELWAIN

Vance McElwain	¦1887 Jul PA¦		¦
----- -----	¦	¦	¦

Vance lived with his parents in Mercer County, PA in 1920; he was then unmarried.

1 [daughter]	¦	¦	¦

226900000 MCELWAIN

William Penrose McElwain	¦1858 May 26 Mercer Co. PA¦		¦ Seattle WA
Mabel Canney	¦1877c	NY¦ Albert J. Canney &	¦
		Agnes A. -----	

William earned a A. M. from Allegheny College in 1888, and moved to Seattle in 1889, just after the great fire.   There he served one term (1893-1894) in the State Legislature as representative for the Forty-first District. Thereafter he practiced law and was active in politics.   He travelled extensively; photographs exist showing him at the Taj Mahal, and striding the deck of an ocean liner in the company of William H. Taft.   In 1910 he lived with his wife in the home of her parents in Seattle, and in 1910 he and Mable lived at 3529 Densmore, Seattle, WA.

226a00000 HANNA

Anna Bell McElwain	¦1860 Jan 14	¦1883 Mar 6	¦1935
Charles M. Hanna	¦	¦	¦

226b00000 MILLER

Malinda F. McElwain	¦1862 Aug 4 Mercer Co. PA¦1881 May 18		¦1944 Franklin PA
George S. Miller	¦1853	¦	¦1900 May 29 Franklin PA
Malinda, George, and Jay lived in Franklin, PA in 1900			
1 Clyde McElwain	*¦1884 Jul	¦	¦1960 Feb 18 Venango Co. PA
2 Jay George	*¦1891 May 19 Jackson Center PA¦		¦

226b10000 MILLER

Clyde McElwain Miller	¦1884 Jul 27 Jackson Cntr. PA¦		¦1960 Feb 18 Venango Co. PA
s Ida -----	¦1885c PA¦		¦
t Mary Elizabeth McNamara	¦1901 Sep 9	¦1944 Nov 28	¦

Clyde and Ida lived in Oil City, PA in 1920. No children were listed in the census for that year.   Clyde and Mary had no children.

226b20000 MILLER

Jay George Miller	¦1891 May 19 Jackson Center PA¦		¦
----- -----	¦	¦	¦
	¦	¦	¦
1 Jay E.	¦	¦	¦

227000000 BERRY

Hannah McElwain	¦1820 Aug 31 Mercer Co. PA¦		¦
----- Berry	¦	¦	¦

Serial # and Name	Birth	Marriage	Death

228000000 MCELWAIN

Allen McElwain	1825 Jan 1 Mercer Co. PA	1852c	1900 Apr 21 Crawford Co. PA
Sarah Peterson	1826c PA		1900 Crawford Co. PA

In 1860 Allen and Sarah were living in Greenwood twp., Crawford Co., PA. The 1870 census for Greenwood twp. shows Allen with $3,000 in real and $835 in personal property. Sarah was a widow at the time of her marriage to Allen; she had two children, Cyrus (b. 1851c) and Catherine (b. 1852c) Peterson by her first marriage.

1 Frank	1853c PA		
2 Ella	1859c PA		
3 John	*1860 Dec PA		
4 Laura	1863c PA		
5 Martha	1867 PA		

228300000 MCELWAIN

John McElwain	1860 Dec PA		
Matilda -----	1861 Nov PA		

John and Matilda lived in Fairfield twp., Crawford Co., PA in 1900, and in Crawford Co in 1910. No children were listed in either census.

229000000 THOMPSON

Cynthia McElwain	1828 Feb 12 Mercer Co. PA		1904 Mercer Co. PA
Benjamin A. Thompson	1823 PA		1898 PA

The Thompson family lived in Mercer County in 1860 (Sandy Lake twp) and 1870.

1 Henry A.	1846 Nov 10 PA		1852 Jul 4 PA
2 Addison E.	*1849 Mar PA		PA
3 Augustus M.	1851 PA		1852 Jun 22 PA
4 Marietta	1854c PA		PA
5 James	*1856 PA		PA
6 Emma L.	1859 Aug 6 PA		1860 Feb 7 PA

The 1870 census for Mercer County lists Addison as a farm laborer, Marietta as teaching school, and James as attending school.

229200000 THOMPSON

Addison E. Thompson	1849 Mar PA		
Emma -----	1849 Sep OH		

This family lived in New Vernon, Pennsylvania in 1900.

1 Vance E.	1878 Mar PA		

22950000 THOMPSON

James T. Thompson	1857 Jan PA		
Anna M. -----	1859 Apr PA		

The birth date for James from the 1920 census are sufficiently close to suggest that this may be the son of Benjamin and Cynthia Thompson, but there is no certainty that he is. This family lived in Lackawannock twp., Mercer Co., PA in 1900.

1 Bessie	1882 May PA		
2 Harry	1888 Feb PA		
3 Albert	1897 Jul PA		

Serial # and Name	Birth	Marriage	Death

230000000   CARNAHAN

Ruth McElwain	1781 Jan 21 Cumberland Co. PA	1802 Feb 25 Cumberland Co. PA	1853 Jun 23 Mercer Co PA
Adam Carnahan	1777 Nov 17 Cumberland Co. PA	James Carnahan & ----- -----	1853 Aug 25 Mercer Co PA

Adam was a soldier in the War of 1812.   In the 1850 census the two were living in Mill Creek twp., Mercer Co., PA; Adam was listed as a farmer. See the History section, pages 19-20, for further information.

1 [daughter]	1802 Jul 18 New Lebanon PA		
2 Margaret	*1804 Feb 6 New Lebanon PA		
3 Nancy	*1806 Jan 18 New Lebanon PA		
4 Maria	*1808 Jul 5 New Lebanon PA		
5 James Madison	*1810 Feb 3 Mercer Co PA	1837	1901 Sep 12 Mercer Co PA
6 Elizabeth	*1813 Apr 16 Mercer Co PA		1888 Jan 2
7 Adam, Jr.	*1816 Oct 12 New Lebanon PA	1850<	
8 Ruth	*1818 Dec 28 New Lebanon PA	1841 Mercer Co PA	1894
9 John	*1821 Apr 15 Mercer Co. PA		
a William	*1823 Jul 19 New Lebanon PA		

232000000   WALKER

Margaret Carnahan	1804 Feb 6 New Lebanon PA		
Wilkes Walker			

233000000   HANNAH

Nancy Carnahan	1806 Jan 18 New Lebanon PA		
John Hannah	1804 PA		

In 1850, 1860, and 1870 this family lived in Mill Creek twp., Mercer Co., PA. John was a farmer at each of those times.   In 1860 their farm was valued at $1,500 and personal property at $590; in 1870 these values were $4,000 and $1,000.

1 James C	*1826c PA		
2 Adam C.	1829c		
3 John, Jr.	*1832c		
4 Ruth	1834c		
5 Jane	1836c		
6 Andrew J.	*1838c PA		
7 Arthur	1840c		
8 Lavinia	1842c		
9 William	1845c		
a Oliver W.	1847c		

Adam C. is listed as a farm laborer living with his parents in the 1870 census.

233100000   HANNAH

James C. Hannah	1826c PA		
Maria -----	1847c IL		

This family resided in Cherrytree twp., Venango Co. PA in 1870, and in Cornplanter twp., Venango Co., PA in 1880. In 1870 James was a teamster with $300 in personal property.

1 Alice	1863c PA		
2 Mary B.	1865c IL		
3 Evalina	1868c PA		
4 Elizabeth C.	1868c PA		
5 Charles	1871c PA		
6 Dora B.	1873c PA		
7 Hervey B.	1876c PA		
8 Nancy	1879c PA		
9 Bessie	1880c PA		

153

Serial # and Name	Birth	Marriage	Death
233300000 HANNAH			
John Hannah, Jr.	1832c		
Elvia [?] -----	1839c		

John, Elvia, and Blanche lived in West Fallowfield twp., Crawford Co., PA in 1860.

1 Blanch	1859c		
233600000 HANNAH			
Andrew J. Hannah	1838c	PA	
Mary -----	1842c	PA	

This family was lived in Elk twp., Clarion Co., PA in 1880.

1 Ella M.	1863c	PA	
2 Olive B.	1865c	PA	
3 Minnie L.	1872c	PA	
4 Maud R.	1876c	PA	
234000000 WALKER / RHODES			
Maria Carnahan	1808 Jul 5 New Lebanon	PA	
s ----- Walker			
t ----- Rhodes		1853<	
235000000 CARNAHAN			
James Madison Carnahan	1810 Feb 3 Mercer Co	PA 1837	1901 Sep 12 Mercer Co PA
s Mary Jane McElwain	1808 Oct 13 Cumberland Co. PA	Richard McElwain & Rosanna Thompson	1846 Apr 4 Mercer Co. PA
t Mary Wilson			1853<
u Permelia Coulson	1817 Nov 26		1888 Jan 2

James was President of the Mercer County Agricultural Society in 1877. The 1850 census for Mill Creek twp., Mercer Co., PA gives his real property as $2500; in that for 1860 his real property was $4,800 and personal property $1,200; and in that for 1870 he had real property of $10,000 and personal property of $15,000. He was listed as a farmer in all three censuses. There is some confusion over his first wife. McElwain family records state that she was Mary Nicholson McElwain, daughter of Richard and Rosanna McElwain. The Venango County history gives her name as Mary McElwayne, daughter of Thompson and Margaret (Lindsey) McElwayne. Both records were contemporary and were written by close family members. However, no record has been found of a Thompson McElwayne

1 Buchanan Hanna	s* 1839 May 2 Mercer Co	PA 1863 Oct 3 Boulder CO	1916>
2 Mary Jane	s* 1841		
3 Lacey G.	s* 1842c		
4 Rosanna	s 1846 Mar 7		1846 Apr 4 Mercer Co. PA
5 Melvina	t* 1849c		
6 Ruth Ann	? 1850 May 27		1851 Oct 10
7 Elmira	u* 1852c		
8 James T.	u* 1854c		
9 John Milton	u* 1856c		
a Otis O.	u* 1857		1936
b Idoletta	u 1859 Mar 14		1888 Jan 2
c Cassius Shields	u* 1860 Aug	PA	

154

Serial # and Name	Birth	Marriage	Death
235100000 CARNAHAN			
Buchanan Hanna Carnahan	1839 May 2 Mercer Co PA	1863 Oct 3 Boulder CO	1916>
Melinda Coulson	1837c	Maxwell Coulson &	
		Permelia -----	

Buchanan operated the Carnahan Moving and Storage Co. until 1916. He served as a member of the water board and the city council, and was elected Mayor of Oil City in 1908. Melinda was his step-sister. There is an account of his life and of the Carnahan family in the *History of Venango County, Pennsylvania.*

1 Nettie G.	*!1864 Jul 8 Venango Co. PA		
2 James M.	*!1866 Jul 25 Venango Co. PA		1910 Jan 8
3 Howard	*!1873 Oct 3 Venango Co. PA		
4 William	*!1876 Feb 2 Venango Co. PA		

235110000 SHOOK / ACKLEY			
Nettie G. Carnahan	1864 Jul 8 Venango Co. PA		
s Oliver Shook			1900<
t Newton Ackley			

In 1900 Nettie was living, under the name of Shook, with her father.

235120000 CARNAHAN			
James M. Carnahan	1866 Jul 25 Venango Co. PA		1910 Jan 8
s Lucy Sloper			
t Susie Runkle			

235130000 CARNAHAN			
Howard Carnahan	1873 Oct 3 Venango Co. PA		
Minnie Paul			

Howard was living unmarried with his father in 1900.

1 Marion			
2 Christopher Paul			

235140000 CARNAHAN			
William Carnahan	1876 Feb 2 Venango Co. PA		
Cora Bannon			

235200000 BAILEY			
Mary Jane Carnahan	1841		
Caleb Bailey			

Mary was living unmarried with her father in 1860.

1 Oscar			
2 James			

235300000 SPONSLER			
Lacey G. Carnahan	1842c		
Andrew Sponsler			

Lacey was living unmarried with her father in 1860.

235500000 SMITH			
Melvina Carnahan	1849c		
Joseph Smith			

Serial # and Name	Birth	Marriage	Death

235700000 CHRISTIE

Elmira Carnahan	1852c	PA	
Charles Christie	1848c	OH	
1 David	1876c	PA	
2 Daisy	1879	PA	

   Elmira and Charles, with David and Daisy, lived in Sandy Lake twp. Mercer Co., PA, in 1880.

235800000 CARNAHAN

James T. Carnahan	1854c		
Kate Bird			

   James was a farm laborer in 1870 and was living with his father.

235900000 CARNAHAN

John Milton Carnahan	1856c		
Lucy Gilmore			

   In the 1870 census John was listed as Milton; he was a farm laborer living with his parents.

235a00000 CARNAHAN

Otis O. Carnahan	1857		1936
Florence Simcox			

   Otis was living with his parents and attending school in 1870.

235c00000 CARNAHAN

Cassius Shields Carnahan	1860 Aug	PA	
Florence Mook	1861 Oct	PA	

   This family lived in Oil City, PA in 1900 and 1920; their address in 1920 was 13 Graffe Street.

1 Samuel I.	1885 Oct	PA	
2 Florence I.	1887 Jan	PA	
3 Lewis Clare	1888 May	PA	
4 Mary M.	*1894 Mar	PA	
5 Leo D.	1900 Mar	PA	

235c40000 NEUBAUER

Mary M. Carnahan	1894 Mar	PA	
----- Neubauer			

   In 1920 Mary and the children were living, under the name of Neubauer, in the home of her parents.

1 Ardelle	1915c	PA	
2 Robert	1918	PA	

236000000 THOMPSON / GRIDLEY

Elizabeth Carnahan	1813 Apr 16 Mercer Co	PA	1888 Jan 2
s Adam Thompson	1812c	PA	
t Samuel Gridley (Rev.)			

   Adam and Elizabeth lived in Salem twp., Mercer Co., PA in 1850; he was a farmer.

Serial # and Name	Birth	Marriage	Death

237000000   CARNAHAN

Adam Carnahan, Jr.	1816 Oct 12 New Lebanon PA	1850<	
s Elizabeth Moore			
t Mary Jane -----		PA	

Adam and Mary Jane lived in Mill Creek twp., Mercer Co., PA in 1850; they later moved to Mantua, OH, and to
Marshall, KS.   Her family name appears in some records as Converse, but this is not unanimously accepted.

1 Vicnelia	t*1855 Jun Mantua	OH1871 Feb 28	1901 Dec	OK
2 Carlos	t*1858 Jun 11 Mantua	OH1886 Mar 23 Albion	ID1936 Feb 12 Malta	ID

237100000   WILSON

Vicnelia Carnahan	1855 Jun Mantua	OH1871 Feb 28	1901 Dec	OK
Francis Marion Wilson	1850 Apr	IN		

Vicnelia and Francis lived in Noble Co., OK in 1900.

1 Lula	#1880 Sep	KS	

237110000   GRANT

Lula Wilson	1880 Sep	KS	
----- Grant			

Lula and her son were living with her parents in Noble County, OK in 1900. Her husband was not present.

1 Howard	1899 Dec	OK	

237200000   CARNAHAN

Carlos Carnahan	1858 Jun 11 Mantua	OH1886 Mar 23	1936 Feb 12 Malta	ID
Rosetta Jane Williams	1868 Jun 7 Montpelier	ID Robert Hanna Williams &	1940 Aug 30 Malta	ID
		Sarah Ann Cottrell		

Carlos, Rosetta, and the three children lived in Cassia Co., ID in 1900.   Rosetta lived in Cassia Co., ID
in 1920. This couple was divorced May 9, 1925.

1 Lafayette Adam	#1886 Oct 14 Malta	ID1922 Oct 26 Park City	UT1948 Feb 19 Malta	ID
2 Orvil William	#1888 Apr 21 Malta	ID1914 Dec	1924 Nov 18 Ogden	UT
3 Marion Carlos	#1892 Apr 22 Malta	ID1927 Aug 13 Soda Springs	ID1976 Jan 26 Burley	ID

237210000   CARNAHAN

Lafayette Adam Carnahan	1886 Oct 14 Malta	ID	1948 Feb 19 Malta	ID
s Ora Delphine Stokes	1890 Dec 27 Albion	ID William S. Stokes &	1913 May 8 Walla Walla	WA
		Esther Jane Barton		
t Helen Agnes Deason	1880 Jan 28 Park City	UT1922 Oct 26 Park City	UT1980 Aug 23 Twin Falls	ID
	1888 Jan 28 Park City	UT William Francis Deason &		
		Elizabeth Lockman		

Lafayette (Lafe) lived as a boarder and worked as a laborer in 1910, residing in Malta, ID.

1 Cleo Clinton	*s1913 Sep 12 Walla Walla WA		1984 May 20
2 Rita	*t1923 Nov 5 Malta ID		
3 Roma Jean	*t1928 Apr 8 Alma ID		
4 Lafayette Ernest	*t1931 Sep 20 Malta ID		

237211000   CARNAHAN

Cleo Clinton Carnahan	1913 Sep 12 Walla Walla WA		1984 May 23
Helen Summers			

In 1920 Cleo was living with his grandmother Rosetta Carnahan in Cassia Co., ID.

Serial # and Name	Birth	Marriage	Death
237212000 ----- / DIXON			
Rita Carnahan	:1923 Nov 5 Malta ID:		:
s ----- -----	:	:	:
t David Dixon	:	:	:
237213000 ----- / WALTON			
Roma Jean Carnahan	:1928 Apr 8 Alma ID:		:
s ----- -----	:	:	:
t Darwin Walton	:	:	:
237214000 CARNAHAN			
Lafayette Earnest	:1931 Sep 20 Malta ID:		:
Carnahan	:	:	:
Janice White	:	:	:
237220000 CARNAHAN			
Orvil William Carnahan	:1888 Apr 21 Malta ID:	1914 Dec	:1924 Nov 18 Ogden UT
Martha Ann Burton	:1890 Oct 2 Kaysville UT:	James Robert Burton &	:1961 Mar 31 Ogden UT
	:	Mary Jane Lithgol	:
1 Lola Venice	:1917 Jan 13 Malta ID:		:1921 Logan UT
2 Carlos Burton	*:1918 Mar 28 Malta ID:		:1984 Mar 1
3 Wanda Mary	*:1919 Mar 4 Ogden UT:		:
4 Orvil Leon	*:1920 Dec 26 Ogden UT:		:
237222000 CARNAHAN			
Carlos Burton	:1918 Mar 28 Malta ID:		:1984 Mar 1
Audrey Stafford	:	:divorced	:
237223000 MASTEN			
Wanda Mary Carnahan	:1919 Mar 4 Ogden UT:		:
Frank Masten	:	:	:
237224000 CARNAHAN			
Orvil Leon Carnahan	:1920 Dec 26 Ogden UT:		:
Lucille Hadley	:	:	:
237230000			
Marion Carlos Carnahan	:1892 Apr 22 Malta ID:	1927 Aug 13 Soda Springs ID	:1976 Jan 22 Burley ID
Leola Pearl Putnam	:1902 Jul 2 Garden City UT:	Frank Nathaniel Israel	:1982 Jun 13 Burley ID
	:	Putnam & Lucy Hildt	:

    In 1920 Marion Carlos (called Carlos in the census) was living with his mother Rosetta in Cassia Co., ID.

1 Carlos Blaine	*:1928 May 11 Malta ID:	1961 Apr 14 Logan UT:	
2 Orville Darrell	*:1929 Dec 25 Elba ID:	1951 Dec 14 Mesa AZ:	
3 Merna Carlyn	*:1931 Mar 23 Malta ID:	1949 Dec 1 Salt Lake Ci. UT:	
4 Glenn Frank	*:1933 Mar 24 Malta ID:	1957 Jun 26 Logan UT:	
5 Naldene Rose	*:1935 Feb 20 Malta ID:	1962 Dec 14 Logan UT:	
6 Rulan Marion	*:1937 Apr 28 Auburn WY:		: 1993 Jul 13 Murray UT

158

Serial # and Name	Birth	Marriage	Death
237231000 CARNAHAN			
Carlos Blaine Carnahan	1928 May 11 Malta ID	1961 Apr 14 Logan UT	
Ruby Joyce Tanner			
1 Paul Carlos			
2 Kyle			
3 Brenda			
4 Lynn			
5 Kathleen			
6 Rosemarie			
7 Annette			
8 Crystal			
237232000 CARNAHAN			
Orville Darrell Carnahan	1929 Dec 25 Elba ID	1951 Dec 14 Mesa AZ	
Colleen Arrott			
1 Karen	*1955 Jun 27 El Paso TX	1987 Jun 5 Salt Lake City UT	
2 Jeannie	*1956 Jul 31 Logan UT	1991 Apr 13 Salt Lake City UT	
3 Orville Darrell, Jr.	*1959 Oct 13 Twin Falls ID	1988 Apr 15 Mesa AZ	
4 Carla	*1961 Jun 20 Twin Falls ID	1981 Dec 19 Salt Lake City UT	
237232100 EVANS			
Karen Carnahan	1955 Jun 27 El Paso TX	1987 Jun 5 Salt Lake City UT	
Kevin Hyde Evans	1956 Feb 2 Rexburg ID		
1 Morgan Carnahan	1989 Jun 14 Pirmasens, GR		
2 Anora Amanda	1991 Jan 28 Pirmasens, GR		
237232200 ALLEN			
Jeannie Carnahan	1956 Jul 31 Logan UT	1991 Apr 13 Salt Lake City UT	
Michael Scott Allen	1952 Apr 7 Salt Lake City UT		
237232300 CARNAHAN			
Orville Darrell Carnahan, Jr.	1959 Oct 13 Twin Falls ID	1988 Apr 15 Mesa AZ	
Margori Lee Magnusson	1960 Dec 6		
1 Clara Priscilla	1990 Oct 13 Phoenix AZ		
2 Margorie Lee	1993 Dec 2 Phoenix AZ		
237232400 NELSON			
Carla Carnahan	1961 Jun 20 Twin Falls ID	1981 Dec 19 Salt Lake City UT	
James Randy Nelson	1952 Mar 10 Logan UT		
1 Candice	1984 Jun 15 Salt Lake City UT		
2 Shannon	1986 Apr 7 Salt Lake City UT		
3 Gillian	1987 Sep 21 Salt Lake City UT		

Serial # and Name	Birth	Marriage	Death

237233000   SMITH

	Birth	Marriage	Death
Merna Carlyn Carnahan	1931 Mar 23 Malta ID		
William Samuel Smith	1930 Sep 27 Yost UT		
1 Connie Leola	1950 Oct 10 Burley ID		
2 Elizabeth Evelyn	1951 Nov 5 Brigham City UT		
3 Thomas William	1953 Feb 7 Burley ID		
4 Denise Ann	1955 Jul 3 Heber City UT		
5 Cheryl Lynne	1958 Feb 1 Ogden UT		
6 Sandra Dee	1962 Jul 19 Murray UT		
7 Robert Samuel	1966 Jan 8 Murray UT		

237234000   CARNAHAN

	Birth	Marriage	Death
Glenn Frank Carnahan	1933 Mar 24 Malta ID	1957 Jun 26 Logan UT	
Janis Lloyd	1938 Dec 21 Elba ID		
1 Tamara	*1958 Apr 23 Logan UT		
2 Carl Jeffrey	*1959 Nov 27 Logan UT	1994 Jul 1 El Tigre VZ	
3 Clayton Patrick	*1961 Aug 28 Logan UT	1989 Jun 17 Arco ID	
4 Curtis Gregory	*1963 Aug 9 Logan UT	1982 Jul 17 Rexburgh ID	

237234100   DONATI

	Birth	Marriage	Death
Tamara Carnahan	1958 Apr 23 Logan UT		
Benedict William			
Donati, II			
1 Benedict William, III	1987 Nov 8 Colorado Spr. CO		

237234200   CARNAHAN

	Birth	Marriage	Death
Carl Jeffrey Carnahan	1959 Nov 27 Logan UT	1994 Jul 1 El Tigre VZ	
Vilma Mercedes Quijada	1960 Jun 21 VZ		
1 Nicholas Andrew	1995 Mar 23 Arco ID		

237234300   CARNAHAN

	Birth	Marriage	Death
Clayton Patrick Carnahan	1961 Aug 28 Logan UT	1989 Jun 17 Arco ID	
Brenda Lee Thomas	1969 Oct 7 Arco ID		
1 Tyson Alexander	1989 Feb 16 Arco ID		
2 Amber Lee	1990 Jul 31 Idaho Falls ID		

237234400   CARNAHAN

	Birth	Marriage	Death
Curtis Gregory Carnahan	1963 Aug 9 Logan UT	1982 Jul 17 Rexburg ID	
s Laurel Hunsaker			
t Anna Bertha Vela	1962 Jul 24	1986 Sep 20	
1 Cory Glenn	s 1982 Dec 10 Rexburg ID		
2 Evan Vela	s 1984 Mar 4 Portland OR		
3 Christine Dawn	t 1987 Jul 8 Rexburg ID		
4 Caitlin Marie	t 1990 Jan 6 Rexburg ID		

Serial # and Name	Birth	Marriage	Death
237235000 PENROD			
Naldene Rose Carnahan	1935 Feb 20 Malta	ID 1962 Dec 14 Logan UT	
Lawrence Owen Penrod	1929 Aug 14 Park City	UT Owen Keller Penrod &	
		Reva Arona Berry	
1 Rosemarie	1963 Nov 18 Burley	ID	
2 Nelda Ann	# 1965 Feb 6 Burley	ID 1984 May 11	
3 Laurie Jane	# 1967 Feb 25 Rupert	ID 1992 Oct 23	
4 Pamela Kay	# 1971 May 26 Burley	ID 1992 Aug 8	
5 Eileen Amber	# 1973 Jul 31 Burley	ID 1995 Sep 9	
237235200 DAVIS			
Nelda Ann Penrod	1965 Feb 6 Burley	ID 1984 May 11	
Scott Duane Davis			
237235300 TERRY			
Laurie Jane Penrod	1967 Feb 25 Rupert	ID 1992 Oct 23	
Harold Wilmer Terry			
237235400 MILLER			
Pamela Kay Penrod	1971 May 26 Burley	ID 1992 Aug 8	
Shane David Miller			
237235500 HARDY			
Eileen Amber Penrod	1973 Jul 31 Burley	ID 1995 Sep 9	
Travis Leslie Hardy			
237236000 CARNAHAN			
Rulan Marion Carnahan	1937 Apr 28 Auburn	WY	1993 Jul 13 Murray UT
s Verna Lorna Bangerter			
t Sandra Rodriguez			
1 Steve s			
2 David s			
3 Teresa s			
4 Debbie s			
5 Christopher Neil t	1983 Mar 10		

Serial # and Name	Birth	Marriage	Death

238000000   ZAHNISER

Ruth Carnahan	1818 Dec 28 New Lebanon PA	1841 Mercer Co. PA	1894
William Zahniser	1811 Feb 6 Mercer Co. PA	Michael Zahniser &	1877 Nov 19
		Mary Mourer	

William received a common school education and supplemented it with much private study.   He had a remarkable memory and was a close student of history. For many years he taught school in winter and farmed in the summer.   When the couple were married they settled on a farm three miles north of the old Zahniser homestead, where they lived for the rest of his life..

1 Thompson	*|1842 Mercer Co PA	1872	1924	
2 Michael Carnahan	*|1844 Mercer Co PA	1874	1923	
3 Fidelia	1846 Sep 1 Mercer Co PA		1876 Apr 21 Mercer Co. PA	
4 Mary Elizabeth	*|1849 Jul 21 Mercer Co PA	1871	1941 Jan 23 Mercer Co. PA	
5 Margaret	*|1851 Sep Mercer Co. PA	1878	1933	
6 William Plummer	*|1854 Mar Mercer Co PA	1878		
7 Ruth Emma	1856 May 19 Mercer Co PA		1856 Oct 30 Mercer Co. PA	
8 Ira Condit	*|1858 Mercer Co PA	1880		
9 Philip Kearney	1862 Dec 27 Mercer Co PA		1863 Feb 23	

Fidelia was a teacher in the common schools.

238100000   ZAHNISER

Thompson Zahniser	1842 Mercer Co PA	1873 Jun 12	1924
Alma Young	1857c PA		1921

Thompson enlisted in the 57th Regiment, Pennsylvania Volunteers, where he served until the end of the war. He was a sergeant, and was wounded once in battle.   After the war he engaged in the lumber business. Thompson and Alma lived in Perry twp., Mercer Co., PA in 1880; in 1920 Alma lived with the Southworths.

1 Cora Mabel	*|1874 May 28 Mercer Co. PA	1903 Oct 8 Riceville	PA	1949 Nov 18 Titusville PA
2 Ruth Ella	1878 Aug 6 Mercer Co. PA		1878 Aug 17 Mercer Co. PA	
3 William Matthew	1879 Jun 27 Mercer Co. PA		1879 Jul 16	
4 Queene Alice	*|1880 PA	1898	Titusville PA	
5 Clover	1883 Feb 2 Mercer Co. PA		1883 Nov 11	
6 Roscoe Conkling	*|1885	1906	1994	
7 Ruth Delia	*|	1908		

238110000   SOUTHWORTH

Cora Mabel Zahniser	1874 May 28 Mercer Co. PA	1903 Oct 8 Riceville PA	1949 Nov 18 Titusville PA
Lee C. Southworth	1869 Jun 18 nr. Riceville PA	Clark Southworth &	1937 Jun 29 Titusville PA
		Catherine McGee	

The Southworths lived on Murray Street in Hydetown, Crawford Co., PA in 1920.

1 Archie Clark	1905 Apr 26 Hydetown PA		1905 Hydetown PA	
2 Frances Eleanor	*|1907 Jun 10 Hydetown PA	1931 Jun 6 Titusville PA	1994 Oct 7 Mt. Pleasant MI	
3 Lettie Camilla	*|1910 Aug 22 Hydetown PA	1934 Oct 27 Titusville PA	1981 Davison MI	

238112000   HESCH

Frances Eleanor Southworth	1907 Apr 26 Hydetown PA	1931 Jun 6 Titusville PA	1994 Oct 7 Mt. Pleasant MI
Russell Jacob Hesch	1908 Jul 1 Welland ON	Frank Charles Hesch &	1954 Feb 16 Mt. Pleasant MI
		Lora Elizabeth Briggs	

Frances was a graduate of Clarion State Teachers College.   She worked as a teacher, and, for eighteen years, was employed in the registrar's office of Central Michigan University.

1 Barbara Jane	*|1934 May 20 Titusville PA	1956 Nov 24 Mt. Pleasant MI	
2 Russell Joseph	*|1937 Mar 11 Titusville PA	1958 Aug 23 Mt. Pleasant MI	
3 John Thomas	*|1941 Aug 24 Titusville PA	1963 Oct 19 Flint MI	

162

238112100   SCHNOES
  Barbara Jane Hesch   :1934 May 20 Titusville   PA:1956 Nov 24 Mt. Pleasant MI:
  Paul Joseph Schnoes   :1934 Apr 21 Pittsburgh   PA: Sebastian Joseph Schnoes & :
                          :   :   Henrietta C. Schertler   :
1 Paul Joseph   *:1957 Sep 23   :   :
2 James Thomas   :1959 Aug 4   :   :
3 Karen Jane   *::1961 Jun 18   :   :
4 Mark Joseph   :1963 Feb 27   :   :
5 Diane Marie   *::1965 Dec 4   :   :

238112110   SCHNOES
  Paul Joseph Schnoes   :1957 Sep 23   :   :
  Mindy -----   :   :   :
                          :   :   :
1 Paul Vincent   :1990 Aug 2   :   :

238112120   KRANZ
  Karen Jane Schnoes   :1961 Jan 18   :   :
  Mark Kranz   :19-- Feb 8   :   :
                          :   :   :
1 Rebecca Michelle   :1990 Feb 6   :   :

228112130   COTE
  Diane Marie Schnoes   :1967 Mar 9   :1992 Sep 5 St. Ignatius   MT:
  Michael A. Cote   :1965 Dec 4   :   :

238112200   HESCH
  Russell Joseph Hesch   :1937 Mar 11 Titusville   PA:1958 Aug 23 Mt. Pleasant MI:
  Catherine Ann Gross   :1936 Dec 30 Rosebush   MI: :
      Russell has an A. B. from Central Michigan University, an M. S. (Chemistry) from the University of Missouri
      at Rolla, and an M. T. S. (Scriptures) from St.John's Seminary.   He served in the United States Army for
      twenty-one years, attaining the rank of lieutenant colonel. He also taught at the secondary and university
      level. They lived in Redford, MI.
1 David Gerard   *:1960 Dec 10 Tripler Hosp. HI:1984 Jan 21 Cheyenne   WY:
2 Patrick Gerard   *:1963 Feb 18 Ft. McClelland AL:1984 Aug 18 Leslie   MI:
3 Richard Gerard   :1964 Jul 31 Ft. Wood   MO: :1985 Apr 22 Redford   MI
4 Carolyn Ann   *:1969 Mar 4 West Point   NY:1992 Sep 26 Birmingham   MI:

238112210   HESCH
  David Gerard Hesch   :1960 Dec 10 Tripler Hosp. HI:1984 Jan 21 Cheyenne   WY:
  Robyn Davis   :1961 Sep 7   NE: :
                          :   :   :
1 Faith Marie   :1993 Apr 28   CO: :1993 Apr 28   CO
      Faith was born in the Pruder Valley Hospital.

238112220   HESCH
  Patrick Gerard Hesch   :1963 Feb 18 Ft. McClelland AL:1984 Aug 18 Leslie   MI:
  Christine Carol Cornwell :1962 Jul 3   : David Cornwell &   :
                          :   : Kathryn Beach   :
1 Stephanie Carol   :1986 Sep 12 Garden City MI: :
2 Janelle Katherine   :1989 Feb 24 Lansing   MI: :
3 Jacob Gerard Hesch   :1991 Sep 1 Lansing   MI: :

Serial # and Name	Birth	Marriage	Death

238112240 WESTMORELAND

	Birth	Marriage	Death
Carolyn Ann Hesch	1969 Mar 4 West Point NY	1992 Sep 26 Birmingham MI	
Adam Ross Westmoreland	1967 Jul 19 New York NY		
1 Austin Reed	1992 Jul 19 Southfield MI		
2 Dakota Bennett	1994 May 25 Southfield MI		

238112300 HESCH

	Birth	Marriage	Death
John Thomas Hesch	1941 Aug 24 Titusville PA	1963 Oct 19 Flint MI	
Mary Jane Mikolaizik	1941 Nov 18 Flint MI		
1 Susan Jane	*1966 Jul 25 Flint MI	1989 Aug 19 Rochester MI	
2 Jean Ann	*1969 Mar 29 Flint MI	1994	
3 Janice Lynn	1975 May 21 Flint MI		
4 Lora Jane	1980 Dec 15 Flint MI		

238112310 WHALEN

	Birth	Marriage	Death
Susan Jane Hesch	1966 Jul 25 Flint MI	1989 Aug 19 Rochester MI	
Kirk James Whalen	19-- Jun 11		
1 Kaitlyn Jane	1993 Jun 23 FL		

23811232 HERTIA

	Birth	Marriage	Death
Jean Ann Hesch	1969 May 29 Flint MI		
Timothy Hertia			

238113000 REYNOLDS

	Birth	Marriage	Death
Lettie Camilla Southworth	1910 Aug 22 Hydetown PA	1934 Oct 27 Titusville PA	1981 Davison MI
Joseph J. Reynolds	1906 Mar 14	Loris Reynolds &	1974 Flint MI
		Mary Enright	
1 Camilla Bernadette	*1941 Feb 18 Flint MI	1963 Flint MI	

238113100 HEROD

	Birth	Marriage	Death
Camilla Bernadette	1941 Feb 18 Flint MI	1963 Flint MI	
Southworth			
Donald M. Herod			

Camilla attended Central Michigan University, and is employed by Genessee County Community Health in the Record/Billing Department

	Birth	Marriage	Death
1 Camilla	*1966	1986 Ann Arbor MI	
2 Donald Michael	*1967 Sep 2 Flint MI	1991 East Lansing MI	
3 Catherine	*1971 Flint MI	1994 Jun 11 Williamston MI	

238113110 D'ADDIO

	Birth	Marriage	Death
Camilla Herod	1966	1986 Ann Arbor MI	
Daniel F. D'Addio			

Camilla has a B. A. (English) from the University of Bridgeport, and is a graduate student at Wayne State University in the M. L. I. S program in Archive Administration.

	Birth	Marriage	Death
1 Francesca Camilla	1988 Jan 29		

Serial # and Name	Birth	Marriage	Death

238113120   HEROD

| Donald Michael Herod | 1967 Sep 2 Flint | MI 1991   East Lansing MI | |
| Heather J. Martin | | | |

Donald is a graduate of Michigan State University (B.S in Electrical Engineering/Computer Science).   He is a software developer for Coopers Lybrand.

238113130   FILLWOCK

| Catherine Herod | 1971   Flint | MI 1994 Jun 11 Williamston   MI | |
| Patrick L. Fillwock | | Lewis Fillwock & ----- ----- | |

Catherine is a graduate of Michigan State University (B.S. Electrical Engineering) and is a manufacturing engineer for Delco Electronics.

238140000   AMES

| Queene Alice Zahniser | 1880 | PA 1898 | | Titusville   PA |
| Fred W. Ames, Jr. | 1874c | PA | |

In 1920 the Ames family lived at 502 S. Franklin, Titusville, PA

1 Warren P.	1904	PA	1904	PA
2 Marjory A.	* 1905	PA 1928	1968	Sharon	PA
3 Lucille	* 1907	PA 1930	
4 Arlene	* 1909	PA 1947	

238142000   RUPERT

| Marjory A. Ames | 1905 | PA 1928 | 1968 | Sharon | PA |
| Ernest Victor Rupert | | | |

Ernest was a minister.

1 Queene			infancy death
2 Alice Marion	* 1934 Jun 20 New Hartford	NY 1960 Mar 19 Farrell	PA 1989
3 David Fred Ames	* 1936 Feb 1 Jamestown	NY 1958 Apr 12 Pughtown	WV
4 Mildred Arlene	* 1937 Sep 3 Jamestown	NY 1959 Aug 21 Farrell	PA
5 Marjory Almaretta	* 1940 Oct 15 Gowanda	NY 1964 Apr 4 Farrell	PA
6 Mark Zahniser	* 1943 Sep 2 Dunkirk	NY 1968 Mar 23 Cleveland	OH

238142200   EMAD

Alice Marion Rupert	1934 Jun 20 New Hartford	NY 1960 Mar 19 Farrell	PA 1989 Dec 21 Holland Patent NY
Jamal Emad			
1 Linda Shorhreh	1964 Apr 19 New Hartford NY		
2 Paul Reza	1965 Dec 3 New Hartford NY		
3 Jeffrey Sharif	1968 Sep 16 New Hartford NY		

238142300   RUPERT

David Fred Ames Rupert	1936 Feb 1 Jamestown	NY 1958 Apr 12 Pughtown	WV
s Joyce Carol Hudak			
t Dolores Jean Mizicko		1974 Aug 3 Brookfield	OH

Dolores had three children, Norman, Michael, and Lucille by a previous marriage.

1 Evelyn Joyce	s* 1959 Mar 8 Sharon	PA 1980 May 17 Nashua	NH
2 Susan Renee	s* 1960 Oct 30 Sharon	PA 1984 Aug 25	
3 David Fred Ames, Jr.	s 1962 Sep 25 Sharon	PA	

Serial # and Name	Birth	Marriage	Death
238142310 FARIA			
Evelyn Joyce Rupert	1959 Mar 8 Sharon PA	1980 May 17 Nashua NH	
Walter John Faria			
1 Benjamin Hollis			
2 Tyler John			
238142320 MORGAN			
Susan Renee Rupert	1960 Oct 30 Sharon PA	1984 Aug 25	
James Anthony Morgan			
238142400 SUMMERHILL			
Mildred Arlene Rupert	1937 Sep 3 Jamestown NY	1959 Aug 21 Farrell PA	
George A. Summerhill, Jr.	1937 Apr 13		
1 Craig Alan	1961 Jul 6 Pittsburgh PA		
2 George A.	1964 Jul 18 Chillicothe OH		
3 Bradley P., III	1969 Nov 18 Decatur IL		
238142500 BURKE			
Marjory Almaretta Rupert	1940 Oct 15 Gowanda NY	1964 Apr 4 Farrell PA	
Roger Joseph Burke			
1 Roger Ames	1977 Mar 24 New Hartford NY		
2 Karen Elizabeth	1978 Jul 28 New Hartford NY		
238142600 RUPERT			
Mark Zahniser Rupert	1943 Sep 2 Dunkirk NY	1968 Mar 23 Cleveland OH	
Sandra Nicol			
1 Stacey Nicol			
238143000 WRIGHT			
Lucille Ames	1907	PA 1930	
Willard W. Wright			
238144000 BEST			
Arlene Ames	1909	PA 1947	
Harold A. Best			
238160000 ZAHNISER			
Roscoe Conkling Zahniser	1885	1906	1944
Clara Boeber			
In 1906 Roscoe was a machinist living in Chicago, Illinois.			
1 Frederick Boeber	* 1907	1941	
238161000 ZAHNISER			
Frederick Boeber Zahniser	1907	1941	
Carol Ham			
1 William Frederick	1946		

Serial # and Name	Birth	Marriage	Death
238170000 HIBBARD / DAVIS			
Ruth Delia Zahniser		1908	
s Carl J. Hibbard			
t Herschel J. Davis		1938	
1 Jafola <u>Hibbard</u>	*1908	1934	
2 Roscoe Carl <u>Hibbard</u>	*1910		
238171000 STEWART			
Jafola Hibbard	1908	1934	
Charles LeRoy Stewart			
238172000 HIBBARD			
Roscoe Carl Hibbard	1910		
Hazel Abel			
1 Wallace Carl	1936		
2 Gerald Abel	1942		
3 David Allen	1950		

238200000 ZAHNISER

Michael Carnahan Zahniser	1844 Mercer Co PA	1874	1923
Sarah Emma Young	1856 Apr PA		

Michael served in Company F, 57th Pennsylvania Volunteers in the Civil War.   After the war he was in the lumber business. Michael and Sarah (Emma S.) lived in Mercer, PA in 1900.

1 Eleanor G.	*1880 Aug	1900	1948 Austin MN

238210000 DASCOMB

Eleanor G. Zahniser	1880 Aug	1900	1948 Austin MN
Arthur S. Dascomb			

At the time the 1900 census was taken Eleanor was still living with her parents.   Arthur was a Congregationalist minister. About 1906 the family resided in Austin, Minnesota.

1 Edmund Brooke	1902		1934 i. Mercer Co. PA

Edmund served as a Lieutenant in the United States Navy.

238400000 MCCULLOUGH

Mary Elizabeth Zahniser	1849 Jul 21 Mercer Co PA	1871	1941 Jan 23 Mercer Co. PA
John B. McCullough	1842 Feb 26		1894 Apr 20

The McCulloughs lived in Cool Spring twp., Mercer Co., PA in 1880. Mary lived with her son Paxton in 1920. *The Zahnisers* gives 1896 as the year of John's death.

1 William Zahniser	1873 May 17		1952 Oct 29 Lincoln NE
2 Leonard D.	1875	PA	1877
3 Paxton Kerr	1876	PA	1937
4 Bessie Ida	*1880 May 17	PA 1899	1941 Franklin PA
5 Jessie Ira	*1880 May 17	PA 1916	1950 Dec 19
6 Michael Plummer	*1887	PA 1912	1982

In 1900 William was a servant in the home of William A. Esser in Lancaster County, Nebraska, and later was a mechanic there; in 1920 he was living with his brother Paxton.   Paxton lived on District Road (place not known), PA in 1920.

Serial # and Name	Birth	Marriage	Death
238440000 VOGAN			
Bessie Ida McCullough	:1880 May 17	PA:1899	:1941 Franklin PA
Harry Benton Vogan	:1877 Mar	PA:	:1944 Franklin PA

The Vogans lived at 312 Liberty, Franklin, PA in 1900;   in 1910 and 1920 they lived in Oil City   (15 W. 8th St. in 1920).

Serial # and Name	Birth	Marriage	Death
1 Jessie Raymond	*:1900	PA:1936	:
2 Harry Roscoe	:1909	PA:	:1941
3 Mary Elizabeth	*:1915	PA:1940	:
238441000 VOGAN			
Jessie Raymond Vogan	:1900	PA:1936	:
Hazel D. Hepler	:	:	:
	:	:	:
1 Jessie Raymond, Jr.	:1937	:	:
2 Patricia Ann	:1940	:	:
3 Sandra Joy	:1942	:	:
4 Gloria Faith	:1946	:	:
238443000 FRANCISCO			
Mary Elizabeth Vogan	:1915	PA:1940	:
Lee Francisco	:	:	:
	:	:	:
1 Marlene Faye	*:1942	:1960	:
2 Mary Lee	*:1945	:1966	:
3 Brad Emery	*:1948	:1971	:
238443100 LESHER			
Marlene Faye Francisco	:1942	:1960	:
Albert D. Lesher	:	:	:
	:	:	:
1 Jeffrey Duane	*:1961	:1986	:
2 Lisa Elaine	*:1964	:1989	:
3 Jason Douglas	:1968	:	:
238443110 LESHER			
Jeffrey Duane Lesher	:1961	:1986	:
Bobbie Jean Gregory	:	:	:
238443120 DEEMER			
Lisa Elaine Lesher	:1964	:1989	:
James Deemer	:	:	:
238443200 RILEY			
Mary Lee Francisco	:1945	:1966	:
John J. Riley, Jr.	:	:	:
	:	:	:
1 Angela Marie	:	:	:
2 Andrew Jay	:1970	:	:
3 Michael Sean	:1974	:	:
4 Matthew Lee	:1976	:	:

168

Serial # and Name	Birth	Marriage	Death
238443300 FRANCISCO			
Brad Emery Francisco	1948	197!	
Kathleen Spencer			
1 Amy Elicia	1973		
2 Kerry Elizabeth	1976		
3 Laura Jane	1976		
238450000 MCCULLOUGH			
Jessie Ira McCullough	1880 May 17	PA!1916	1950 Dec 19
Clara Maxwell			
1 John Ira	*!1917	1941	
238451000 MCCULLOUGH			
John Ira McCullough	1917	1941	
Mildred Hindman			
1 Patricia Ann	1941		
238460000 MCCULLOUGH			
Michael Plummer	1887	PA!1912	1982
McCullough			
Mary Kathryn Elizabeth	1886 Nov 30		1941 Jan 17
Wilson			
1 Thomas P.	*!1919	1945	
2 Paul Wilson	*!1921	1948	1980
3 Harold Elliot	*!1925	1963	1980
238461000 MCCULLOUGH			
Thomas P. McCullough	1919	1945	
Helen Foster			
1 Joyce Kathryn	*!1950		
2 Carl Plummer	1955		
3 Karen Lynn	*!1957	1980	
4 William Thomas	1960		
238461100 REMALEY			
Joyce Kathryn McCullough	1950	1977	
Terrance Remaley			
1 Kelly Marie	1986		
238461300 STEWART			
Karen Lynn McCullough	1957	1980	
Jonathan Stewart			
1 Kathryn Elizabeth	1988		

169

Serial # and Name	Birth	Marriage	Death
238462000 MCCULLOUGH			
Paul Wilson McCullough	1921	1948	1980
Shirley Gibson			
1 Audrey Marie	*1953	1977	
2 Paul Wilson, Jr.	*1956	1983	
3 Nancy Lou	*1958	1981	
4 Linda Mae	*1961	1981	
238462100 REHN			
Audrey Marie McCullough	1953	1977	
Bruce Rehn			
Bruce is a dentist.			
238462200 MCCULLOUGH			
Paul Wilson	1956	1983	
McCullough, Jr.			
Trina Hardesty			
1 Jared Paul	1985		
238462300 NORRIS			
Nancy Lou McCullough	1958	1981	
Douglas Norris			
1 Adam Douglas	1986		1986
2 Tyler Douglas	1987		
238462400 SEALAND			
Linda Mae McCullough	1961	1981	
David Sealand			
1 Amanda Mae	1986		
238463000 MCCULLOUGH			
Harold Elliot McCullough	1925	1963	1980
Sarah George			
1 John Mark	1965		
2 David Harold	1968		
238500000 CANON			
Margaret Zahniser	1851 Sep Mercer Co. PA	1878	1933
John C. Canon	1848 Jun PA		1911
This family resided in Lake twp., Mercer Co., PA in 1900.			
1 Claude Ira	1879 Jan PA		1907
2 Carrie Irene	*1879 Jan PA	1901	
3 Jessie E.	*1882 Jun PA	1910	
4 Mabel E.	*1885 Apr PA	1922	
5 Raymie Elizabeth	*1887 Mar PA	1913	1963 New Wilmington PA
6 Ruth Zahniser	*1888 Dec PA	1921	
Claude was a medical student about 1906.			

Serial # and Name	Birth	Marriage	Death
238520000 RHODES			
Carrie Irene Canon	1879 Jan	PA 1901	
Otis M. Rhodes			
1 William Lawrence	* 1901	1922	1935
2 Claude O.	* 1904	1927	
3 Clara May	* 1906	1941	
238521000 RHODES			
William Lawrence Rhodes	1901	1922	1935
Angie Todd			
1 William Lawrence, Jr.	1926		
238522000 RHODES			
Claude O. Rhodes	1904	1927	
Thelma Ross			
1 Doris Elaine	1933		
238523000 EDWARDS			
Clara May Rhodes	1906	1941	
Lowell S. Edwards			
1 Jerry	1943		
238530000 BORLAND			
Jessie E. Canon	1882 Jun	PA 1910	1976
Andrew A. Borland	1879c	PA Adam Borland &	
		Sarah -----	

Jesse attended Sandy Lake Institute, and taught in Mercer Co. and Radium, CO.   Andrew was head of the
Department of Dairy Husbandry at the Pennsylvania State University from 1920 to 1948.   The Borlands lived
at 304 Atherton St., State College, PA in 1920. Andrew attended the McElwain Institute (See p. 75).

1 Gerald Canon	* 1911	PA 1937	
2 Margaret Eleanor	* 1914	PA	
238531000 BORLAND			
Gerald Canon Borland	1911	PA 1937	
Alice Marshall			

Gerald had a B.S. from Pennsylvania State University and an M.S. from the University of Arizona.   He
taught at Pembroke State University (NC), and was a geologist for New York State Gas and Oil.

1 Andrew Charles	* 1941	1978	
2 Margaret Jane	* 1944		
3 Kermit Marshall	* 1948		
238531100 BORLAND			
Andrew Charles Borland	1941	1978	
Darlene Mega			

This family was living in Seattle, WA in 1994.

1 Anthony Mega			
2 Gina Mega			

Serial # and Name	Birth	Marriage	Death
238531200 GILLEN			
Margaret Jane Borland	¦1944	¦	¦
John Gillen	¦	¦	¦
This family was living in Danbury, CT in 1994			
1 April	¦1980	¦	¦
238531300 BORLAND			
Kermit Marshall Borland	¦1948	¦	¦
Isabel Alvarez	¦	¦	¦
This family was living in Shrewsbury, MA in 1994			
1 Neil Carlos	¦1987	¦	¦
238532000 HARTZELL			
Margaret Eleanor Borland	¦1914	PA¦	¦
William Hartzell	¦	¦	¦

Margaret had a B. S. from Pennsylvania State University; before her marriage she worked for the Farm Security Administration and the United Nations Relief and Rehabilitation agency in Germany. Margaret and William were living in Redlands, CA in 1994.

Serial # and Name	Birth	Marriage	Death
1 Diana Sue	¦1949	¦	¦
2 William Tisdale	*¦1951	¦1983	¦
3 Walter Andrew	*¦1953	¦1982	¦
238532200 HARTZELL			
William Tisdale Hartzell	¦1951	¦1983	¦
Shanta Kelly	¦	¦	¦
William and Shanta were living in Kaneohe, HI in 1994.			
238532300 HARTZELL			
Walter Andrew Hartzell	¦1953	¦1983	¦
Deborah Carr	¦	¦	¦
This family lived in Redlands, CA in 1994.			
1 Kathrine Andrea	¦1982	¦	¦
2 Jacob William	¦1986	¦	¦
238540000 FOSTER			
Mabel E. Canon	¦1885 Apr	PA¦1922	¦
Charles E. Foster	¦	¦	¦
	¦	¦	¦
1 Margaret Ellen	¦1923	¦	¦
2 Phyllis Jane	*¦1926 Oct 20 Bradford	PA¦1945 Sep 5 Bradford	PA¦
3 Gene Allen	¦1935	¦	¦
238542000 CARPENTER			
Phyllis Jane Foster	¦1926 Oct 20 Bradford	PA¦1945 Sep 5 Bradford	PA¦
Reynold L. Carpenter	¦1925 May 11 Ellington	NY¦	¦
	¦	¦	¦
1 Carolyn Ann	*¦1947 Feb 10 Bradford	PA¦1968 Oct 12	¦
2 Janet M.	*¦1949 Jun 8 Bradford	PA¦1969 Mar 29 Bradford	PA¦
3 David R.	*¦1961 Sep 22 Bradford	PA¦1988 Oct 8 Kane	PA¦
238542100 MACKEY			
Carolyn Ann Carpenter	¦1947 Feb 10 Bradford	PA¦1968 Oct 12	¦
Gary L. Mackey	¦1944 Feb 15	¦	¦

Serial # and Name	Birth	Marriage	Death
238542200 ZURAT			
Janet M. Carpenter	¦1949 Jun 8 Bradford	PA¦1969 Mar 29 Bradford PA¦	
Michael A. Zurat	¦1948 Feb 28	¦	
238542300 CARPENTER			
David R. Carpenter	¦1961 Sep 22 Bradford	PA¦1988 Oct 8 Kane PA¦	
Elizabeth A. Fleeger	¦	¦	
238550000 COX			
Raymie Elizabeth Canon	¦1887 Mar	PA¦1913	¦1963 New Wilmington PA
Pearson Cox	¦1886	PA¦	¦1968
The Cox family lived in Mercer Co., PA in 1920.			
1 Mable Louise	*¦1917	PA¦1937	¦
2 Roscoe Calvin	*¦1923	¦1946	¦
3 Catheryn Rebecca	*¦1926	¦1946	¦
4 Pearson Wayne	¦1930	¦	¦
238551000 HOPPER			
Mable Louise Cox	¦1917	PA¦1937	¦
Walter C. Hopper	¦	¦	¦
	¦	¦	¦
1 Norman Maynard	¦1939	¦	¦
2 Arthur Leroy	¦1940	¦	¦
3 Susan Winona	¦1944	¦	¦
4 Carol Ruth	¦1947	¦	¦
238552000 COX			
Roscoe Calvin Cox	¦1923	¦1946	¦
Joan Woods	¦	¦	¦
	¦	¦	¦
1 Ronald Eugene	¦1947	¦	¦
2 Eleanor	¦1949	¦	¦
238553000 MOOSE			
Catheryn Rebecca Cox	¦1926	¦1946	¦
Richard Moose	¦	¦	¦
	¦	¦	¦
1 Gerald	¦1948	¦	¦
2 John	¦1951	¦	¦
238560000 SLATER			
Ruth Zahniser Canon	¦1888 Dec	PA¦1921	¦
H. Clay Slater	¦	¦	¦
	¦	¦	¦
1 Lois Patricia	¦1922	¦	¦infancy death
2 Richard Watson	*¦1923	¦	¦
3 John Canon	*¦1925 Nov 22	¦1952 Aug 29	¦

Serial # and Name	Birth	Marriage	Death
238562000 SLATER			
Richard Watson Slater	1923		
----- -----			
1 Bruce Richard	*｜1952 Feb 28	1976 Jun 18	
2 Lena Jane	1954 Mar 19		
3 Gary Alan	1958 Mar 1		
238562100 SLATER			
Bruce Richard Slater	1952 Feb 28	1976 Jun 18	
Susan Gale Antonacci			
1 Richard Bruce	1982 Jan 19		
2 Jennifer Susan	1982 Jan 19		
238563000 SLATER			
John Canon Slater	1925 Nov 22	1952 Aug 29	
Julie E. Zimmer			
1 Douglas D.	1953 Aug 20		
2 John Clinton	1957 Apr 26		
238600000 ZAHNISER			
William Plummer Zahniser	1854 Mar Mercer Co PA	1878	
Charlotte Slater	1858 Jan PA		

William and Charlotte lived in Perry twp., Mercer Co., PA in 1900; no children were listed in the census. For most of his life William was in the mercantile business.

238800000 ZAHNISER			
Ira Condit Zahniser	1858 Mercer Co PA	1880	
Elizabeth Stright			
1 Edna V.	*｜1882	1901	
2 Mary Jane	*｜1885	PA｜1907	
3 J. Wilbur	*｜1886	1921	
238810000 PATTON			
Edna V. Zahniser	1882	PA｜1901	
Charles V. Patton	1875c	PA	

In 1906 Charles was a telegraph operator in Conneaut Lake, Mercer County, Pennsylvania. The family lived in Butler Co., PA in 1910.

1 Rita Imelda	*｜1903	OH｜1928	
2 Mary Elizabeth	*｜1905	PA｜1944	
238811000 KERR			
Rita Imelda Patton	1903	1928	
Harold A. Kerr			
1 William Agnew, II	1934		

174

Serial # and Name	Birth	Marriage	Death
238812000 TRIMPEY			
Mary Elizabeth Patton	|1905	|1944	
Paul E. Trimpey					
Paul was a minister.			
238820000 HILL			
Mary Jane Zahniser	|1885	PA|1907	
Clyde Samuel Hill	|1884c	PA|	
In 1920 the Hills lived at 214 Fountain Ave., Ellwood City, PA			
1 James Hulbert	*|1910	PA|1935	
2 Jeane Isabelle	*|1912	PA|1936	
3 Mary Dorothea	*|1918	PA|1942	
4 Sara Elizabeth	*	1920			
5 Clyde Samuel, Jr.	*|1927		|1985
238821000 HILL			
James Hulbert Hill	*|1910	PA|1935	
Lois G. Gibson					
James was a personnel manager.			
1 Susan Rae		1941			
2 James R.					
238822000 SCANLON			
Jeane Isabelle Hill	|1912	PA|1936	
W. E. Scanlon					
W. E. operated an automobile service station.			
1 Mary Jane		1939			
238823000 ARKET			
Mary Dorothea Hill	|1918	PA|1942	
W. F. Arket					
1 William McCormick		1944			
2 James Ray		1948			
3 Baule					
4 Bob					
Baule and Bob are twins.			
238824000 JOHNS			
Sara Elizabeth Hill		1920			
Jay Johns					
1 Betsy Ann		1952			
2 Lynn		1955			
3 Leslie		1955			
4 Jay		1962			
Lynn and Leslie are twins.			

Serial # and Name	Birth	Marriage	Death
238825000 HILL			
Clyde Samuel Hill, Jr.	¦1927	¦1952	¦1985
Patricia Jacobs	¦1929	¦	¦
	¦	¦	¦
1 Clyde Samuel, III	*¦1953	¦	¦
2 Lori	*¦1955	¦	¦
3 Jodi	*¦1963	¦	¦
238825100 HILL			
Clyde Samuel Hill, III	¦1953	¦	¦
Laurie Sberna	¦	¦	¦
	¦	¦	¦
1 Samuel P.	¦1991	¦	¦
238825200 DENT			
Lori Hill	¦1955	¦	¦
Philip Dent	¦	¦	¦
	¦	¦	¦
1 Philip M.	¦	¦	¦
238825300 WEISZ			
Jodi Hill	¦1963	¦	¦
Robert Weisz	¦1963	¦	¦
	¦	¦	¦
1 Kara	¦1994	¦	¦
2 Rachel	¦	¦	¦
238830000 ZAHNISER			
J. Wilbur Zahniser	¦1886	¦1921	¦
s Ethel Smith	¦	¦	¦
t Helen Faye Riddle	¦	¦1937	¦
239000000 CARNAHAN			
John Carnahan	¦1821 Apr 15 Mercer Co. PA¦		¦
Sarah Ann -----	¦	¦	¦

In 1850 and 1860 John was a tailor; in 1860 he owned real estate worth $700 and personal propery of $200. In the census listings the name of his wife is given as Cecelia Jane.

1 Winfield	¦1846	¦	¦
2 Adolphus	¦1848c	¦	¦
3 Charles B.	¦1852c	PA¦	¦
4 John	*¦1857c	PA¦	¦
239400000 CARNAHAN			
John A. Carnahan	¦1858 Apr	PA¦	¦
Belle -----	¦1858 Aug	PA¦	¦

In 1900 this family lived at 98 Pine Street, Meadville, Pennsylvania. The identification of this family as that of John, son of John and Sarah Carnahan, is uncertain.

1 George	¦1883 Sep	PA¦	¦

176

Serial # and Name	Birth	Marriage	Death

23a000000 CARNAHAN

William Carnahan |1823 Jul 19 New Lebanon PA| |1880>

Mary L. Dilley |1822c   Mercer Co. PA| |

In 1850 William was a tailor, living with his family in Mill Creek twp, Mercer Co., PA. In 1860 the family was living in Hartford twp., Trumbull Co., OH.

1 Lafayette Kerr   *|1846 Apr 5   PA| |1924 May 18 Philips Co. KS

2 Hugh |1848 | |1848 Nov 2 i. Mercer Co. PA

3 Mary |1849c   PA| |1860 May 11 Hartford   OH

4 John M.   *|1852 Nov   OH| |1924>

5 Myrtle |1871c | |

23a100000 CARNAHAN

Lafayette Kerr Carnahan |1846 Apr 5   PA| |1924 May 18 Philips Co. KS

Cynthia A. ----- |1847 Oct   KY| |

23a400000 CARNAHAN

John M. Carnahan |1852 Nov   OH| |1924>

Eleanor ----- | | |

240000000 MCELWAIN

Richard McElwain |1784 Jul   Cumberland Co. PA| |

Rosanna Thompson |1785c   Cumberland Co. PA| Andrew Thompson |1860>

   | | Elizabeth Bell |

See the History section for information on Richard's family (pages 20-22), the Thompson family (pages 34-37), and the Bell family (pages 37-38).

1 Mary Nicholson |1808 Oct 13 Cumberland Co. PA|1837 |

2 Andrew Thompson *|1811 Jun 18 Cumberland Co. PA|1840 Jun 1 Iowa City IA|1876 Sep 5 Iowa City IA

3 Elizabeth Bell |1813 Mar   Cumberland Co. PA| |

4 Martha Jane |1816 Mar 18 Cumberland Co. PA| |

5 James   *|1819 Mar 12 Cumberland Co. PA| PA|1885 Mar 3 Sandy Lake PA

6 Margery Ellen *|1822 Sep 4 Cumberland Co. PA|1843c |

7 Ruth Rosanna *|1825 Nov 13 Cumberland Co. PA|1844 Sep 3 Mercer   PA|1900 May 27 Meadville PA

Mary Nicholson McElwain's family will be found under that of her husband James M. Carnahan (#235000000).

242000000 MCELWAIN

Andrew Thompson McElwain |1811 Jun 18 Cumberland Co. PA|1840 Jun 1 Iowa City IA|1876 Sep 5 Iowa City IA

Nancy A. Wheatley |1818 Jul   Jackson Co OH| |1893 Sep 24 Iowa City IA

Andrew was a farmer in 1850 (real property $150, personal, none), and a constable in 1860 (real property $250, personal $50). The family resided in Iowa City at both those times.

1 John Roop |1841 Apr 20 Iowa City IA| |1852 Aug 16   IA

2 Rosanna *|1843 Mar 1 Iowa City IA|1862 Nov 28 Iowa City IA|1904

3 Agnes Matilda *|1845 Mar 20 Iowa City IA|1869 |1916 Oct 29 Iowa City IA

4 James Thompson |1847   IA| |1895

5 Sarah Parrot *|1855   Iowa City IA| |1923 Jan 1 Phoenix AZ

6 Jennie |1857   Iowa City IA| |1864   Iowa City IA

7 Jesse Bowen *|1860 Oct 8 Iowa City IA|1892 May 2 Iowa City IA|1938 Jan 26 Long Beach CA

John drowned in the Iowa River.

Serial # and Name	Birth	Marriage	Death

242200000 MCCULLOUGH

Rosanna McElvain　　　　1843 Mar 1 Iowa City　　　IA 1862 Nov 28 Iowa City　　IA 1904

Henry B. McCullough　　1838 Aug 28 Tuscarawas Co. OH Samuel McCullough &　　1902 Oct 24
　　　　　　　　　　　　　　　　　　　　　　　Sarah -----

　　The McCulloughs lived in River Junction, Fremont twp., Johnson Co., IA in 1880, and in Fremont twp. in 1900.

1 William L.　　　　　*1864 Oct　　　　　　IA

2 Agnes　　　　　　　1869c　　　　　　　　IA

3 Ora Belle　　　　　1874c　　　　　　　　IA

4 Jessie　　　　　　　1877c　　　　　　　　IA

242210000 MCCULLOUGH

William L. McCullough　1864 Oct　　　　　IA

Ellen -----　　　　　　1867 Dec

　　In 1900 the McCulloughs lived in Hawarden, Sioux Co., IA

1 John R.　　　　　　1893 Oct　　　　　IA

242300000 BURGE

Agnes Matilda McElvain　1845 Mar 20 Iowa City　IA 1869　　　　　　　1916 Oct 29 Iowa City　IA

James William Burge　　1848 Oct 24　　　　IA　　　　　　　　　　1915 Apr 04 Davenport　IA

　　The Burge residence in 1900 was on West 4th Street, West Liberty, IA.

1 Grace Valentine　　　*1875 Feb 14 Iowa City　IA 1895 May 15 Iowa City　IA 1963 May 08 Omaha　NE

2 Oka Dot　　　　　　　　　　　　　　　　　　　　　　　　infancy death

3 Daisy Inez　　　　　1877　　　　　　　　　　　　　　　　1878

4 Charles Raymond　　　1881 Mar 22　　　　　　Los Angeles CA　　　Los Angeles CA

5 Vannie G.　　　　　　1884 Oct 20　　　　IA 1928　　　　　　1930 Feb 15

6 Marjorie Lou　　　　1890 Sep 1　　　　　IA　　　　　　　　1916 May 1 Chicago　IL

242310000 WEBER

Grace Valentine Burge　1875 Feb 14 Iowa City　IA 1895 May 15 Iowa City　IA 1963 May 8 Omaha　NE

Edward H. Weber　　　1868 Jul 9　　　　　　　　　　　　1951 May 3

　　In 1900 the Webers lived at 927 Iowa Ave., Iowa City, IA.

1 Irving Burge　　　　*1900 Dec 19 Iowa City　IA 1926 Feb 19

242311000 WEBER

Irving Burge Weber　　1900 Dec 19 Iowa City　IA 1926 Feb 19

Martha Thoren Whiteside 1902 Aug 16

　　Irving received the B. A. from Iowa University in 1922. He was President of Quality Chekd Dairy Product
　　Association for 25 years. He has written eight books and numerous articles on local history, and an elem-
　　entary school was named for him in 1994.

1 Willis Edward　　　　*1931 Jan 4　　　　　1956 Feb 4

242311100 WEBER

Willis Edward Weber　　1931 Jan 4　　　　　1956 Feb 4

Lou Ann Hopkins　　　1934 May 5

1 Michiko Winona　　　*1959 Jun 14 Fukouka　JP 1977 Aug 1 Rapid City　SD

2 John Philip　　　　1960 Sep 9 Fukouka　JP

3 Ingrid Margaret　　*1963 Aug 9 Minot　ND

4 Ann Nicole (Ott Lynne) 1969 Dec 30 Riverside　CA

　　Michiko and John were born at Itazuki Air Force Base, Ingrid at Minot AFB, and Ann at March AFB.

Serial # and Name	Birth	Marriage	Death

242311110   SANDUSKY / FRIESEK

Michiko Winona Weber	1959 Jun 14 Fukouka	JP 1977 Aug 1 Rapid City SD	
s Leslie Sandusky			
t Vern Friesek			
1 Danielle Marie <u>Sandusky</u>	1977 Aug 24 Rapid City SD		

242311130   KNOK

Ingrid Margaret Weber	1963 Aug 09 Minot ND		
Gregory Knok			

242500000   CLARK

Sarah Parrot McElwain	1855 Iowa City IA		1923 Jan 1 Phoenix AZ
William Clark			

242700000   MCELWAIN

Jesse Bowen McElwain	1860 Oct 8 Iowa City IA	1892 May 2 Iowa City IA	1938 Jan 26 Long Beach CA
Mary Matilda Shoop	1869 Aug 2 Columbus Jct. IA	John Shoop &	1956 Oct 2 Long Beach CA
		Margaret Clark	

Jesse and Mary (Mollie) lived in 1900 in Columbus Junction, IA.

1 Jessie Marie	*1893 Dec 31 Columbus Jct. IA	1914 Jun 24 Mesa AZ	1983 May 25 Phoenix AZ
2 Leola	*1895 Dec 15 Columbus Jct. IA	1919 Apr 18 Phoenix AZ	198-
3 Andrew Thompson	*1897 Dec 20 Columbus Jct. IA	1921 Jan 31 Mesa AZ	1920? Apr 17 Long Beach CA
4 Adam Norbert	*1899 Oct 28 Columbus Jct. IA	1929 Nov 30	
5 Urva Cleda	*1901 Aug 5 Columbus Jct. IA	1919 Oct 15	1989 Jan 18 Long Beach CA
6 Forest John	*1903 Sep 17 Columbus Jct. IA	19-- Jun 28	1984 Long Beach CA
7 Mary Hazel	*1905 Mar 22 Columbus Jct. IA	1927 Jul 1	
8 Robert N.	*1907 Mar 10 Columbus Jct. IA	1930 Nov 10	1937 Jul 19 FL
9 Ruth	*1909 Apr 11 Columbus Jct. IA	1927 Oct 28	1943 Feb 24 Long Beach CA
a Jeanette E.	*1911 Oct 8 Mesa AZ	1930 Apr 21	
b Katherine	1914 Jan 16 Mesa AZ		1917 Feb 3 Mesa AZ

242710000   GARRETT

Jessie Marie McElwain	1893 Dec 31 Columbus Jct. IA	1914 Jun 24 Mesa AZ	1983 May 25 Phoenix AZ
Eugene Thrall Garrett	1893 Nov 10 New Harmony IN	Andrew J. Garrett &	1954 Jul 10 Phoenix AZ
		Louise C. Cleavelin	

In 1920 the Garretts lived in Phoenix, AZ, at 749 E. Peirce St. Eugene was a Certified Public Accountant.

1 Dorothea Jean	*1916 Aug 12 Phoenix AZ	1938 Oct 15 Phoenix AZ	
2 Eugene Thrall, Jr.	*1919 Mar 20 Phoenix AZ	1942 Oct 24 Phoenix AZ	

242711000   CRESS

Dorothea Jean Garrett	1916 Aug 12 Phoenix AZ	1938 Oct 15 Phoenix AZ	
Leighton Edward Cress	1911 Jul 7 Council Grove KS	Loren W. Cress &	1992 Jan 16 Phoenix AZ
		Clarice Leighton	

Leighton was a businessman.

1 Leighton Edward, Jr.	*1942 Jan 18 Phoenix AZ		
2 Cheryl Elizabeth	*1951 Jun 6 Phoenix AZ	1974 Oct 4	

242711100   CRESS

Leighton Edward Cress, Jr.	1942 Jan 18 Phoenix AZ		
Carol Welch			

Serial # and Name	Birth	Marriage	Death

242711200   GRAY

| Cheryl Elizabeth Cress | 1951 Jun 6 Phoenix | AZ:1974 Oct 4 | |
| David Barry Gray | | | |

242712000   GARRETT

| Eugene Thrall Garrett, Jr. | 1919 Mar 20 Phoenix | AZ:1942 Oct 4 Phoenix | AZ: |
| Katherine Mary Newhall | | | |

242720000   REEVES / IVERSON

Leola McElwain	1895 Dec 15 Columbus Jct. IA:1919 Apr 18 Phoenix		AZ:
s Harry Reeves			
t Irvin J. Iverson			
1 Betty Lee Reeves	#:1920 Apr 25	1937 Oct 23	

242721000   SPITZER

Betty Lee Reeves	1920 Apr 25	1937 Oct 23	
Raymond Spitzer			
1 Raymond E.	1939 Aug 26		
2 Sherrion Lee	1941 Sep 27		

242730000   MCELWAIN

Andrew Thompson McElwain	1897 Dec 20 Columbus Jct. IA:1921 Jan 31 Mesa	AZ:	Apr 17 Long Beach CA
Mae Eunice Neal			
1 Mary Louise	1921 Dec 30		
2 Beverly Jane	1923 Jun 11		

242740000   MCELWAIN

Adam Norbert McElwain	1899 Oct 28 Columbus Jct. IA:1929 Nov 30		
Emily Maxwell			
1 Clark Wallace	1938 Jul 22		
2 Bonnie Lynn	1941 Jun 30		

242750000   TERRY

Urva Cleda McElwain	1901 Aug 5 Columbus Jct. IA:1919 Oct 15		1989 Jan 18 Long Beach CA
George C. Terry			
1 Robert C.	1920 Feb 3		

242760000   MCELWAIN

Forest John McElwain	1903 Sep 17 Columbus Jct. IA:19-- Jun 28		
s Carol Virginia Fisher			
t Mary Violet Nicholas		1941 Jan 4	
1 Virginia Rae	s :1930 Jan 4		
2 Mary Arline	t :194- Aug 17		

Serial # and Name	Birth	Marriage	Death

242770000 HAUSER

Mary Hazel McElwain	1905 Mar 22 Columbus Jct. IA	1927 Jul 1	
Roger Hauser			
1 Wilton A.	1929 Dec 28		
2 Roger, Jr	1931 Nov 25		

242780000 MCELWAIN

Robert N. McElwain	1907 Mar 10 Columbus Jct. IA	1930 Nov 10	1937 Jul 19
Doris Zonke			
1 J. B. Robert	1931 May 3		
2 Herman Lee	1933 Jun 1		

242790000 ROST / MITCHELL

Ruth McElwain	1909 Apr 11 Columbus Jct. IA	1927 Oct 28	1943 Feb 24 Long Beach CA
s Earl A. Rost			
t Vernon R. Mitchell		1936 Sep 10	
1 Richard J. <u>Rost</u>	1928 Oct 6		
2 Robert J. <u>Mitchell</u>	193- Jun 25		

2427a0000 LUNDQUIST

Jeanette E. McElwain	1911 Oct 8 Mesa AZ	1930 Apr 21	
Eddie H. Lundquist			
1 Donnie E.	193- Oct 28		
2 Gary D.	193- Jun 6		

245000000 MCELWAIN

James McElwain	1819 Mar 12 Cumberland Co.PA		PA 1885 Mar 3 Sandy Lake PA
Penelope Jane Long	1822 Sep 4 PA		PA 1898 Jun 6 Sandy Lake PA

This family lived in Mill Creek twp., Mercer Co., PA in 1850.   James was a teamster (real estate $290, personal property $293).   In 1860 they lived in Sandy Creek twp, and James was a constable (real estate $0 personal property $400), and in 1870, still in Sandy Creek twp., he was a laborer (real estate $400, personal property $400). He operated a livery stable in Sandy Lake from some time after 1870.

1 Samuel	1848 PA		
2 Buchanan	1850 PA		1900c?
3 Montgomery Murdoch	* 1852 PA		1920c
4 Sarah Ella	* 1854 PA	1881 Apr 29	1926 Apr 2 Harrisville PA
5 Albert	* 1856 Sandy Lake PA		1920c Indianapolis IN
6 William	1857 PA		
7 Cass B.	1859 Sandy Lake PA		
8 Eugene	* 1860 Dec PA		
9 Carrie	* 1868c PA		

Serial # and Name	Birth	Marriage	Death
245300000 MCELWAINE			
Montgomery Murdoch	¦1852	PA¦	¦1896-97c
McElwaine	¦	¦	¦
Evaline Turner	¦1854c	PA¦	¦

In 1870 Montgomery was a laborer living unmarried with his parents.   The McElwains lived in Duke Center, McKean Co., PA in 1880. and later moved to Indiana.   The family business, the McElwaine-Richards Company, manufactured the first enameled cast iron bathtubs. He also was in the oil field service business, which evolved into the Central Supply Company.

1 Claude M.	*¦1873 Jan 21 Sandy Lake PA¦		¦1940-41c
2 Edward L.	¦1875 Jun 12 Sandy Lake PA¦		¦
3 Jay B.	*¦1887 Nov 9 Bradford PA¦		¦1945 Sep 3 Seattle WA
4 Myron Murdoch	*¦1890 May 20	¦1911	¦1951 Oct 20

Edward is believed to have moved to British Columbia.

245310000 MCELWAINE			
Claude M. McElwaine	¦1873 Jan 21 Sandy Lake PA¦		¦1940-41c
s Helen F. -----	¦1875 Aug	IN¦	¦1910c
t Marie -----	¦	¦	¦

Claude and Helen lived at 3019 No. Illinois St., Indianapolis, IN in 1900.

1 Montgomery Monroe	s*¦1900 May Indianapolis IN¦1927		¦1977
2 Jack	t ¦	¦	¦
3 [child]	t ¦	¦	¦
4 [child]	t ¦	¦	¦
5 [child]	t ¦	¦	¦

245311000 MCELWAINE			
Montgomery Monroe	¦1900 May Indianapolis IN¦1927		¦1977
McElwaine	¦	¦	¦
Helen Scoby	¦1899c	¦	¦1991

Montgomery lived in 1920 in Seattle, Washington in the home of his uncle Myron McElwaine. He attended the University of Washington for two years, and worked at the Seattle Plumbing Supply Company, the family business of his uncle Myron, until 1934.   He worked at several sales positions until 1943. During World War II he served in the Army Transport Service on tug boats in Alaska and the South Pacific, attaining the rank of Major. After the war he worked as a real estate salesman for John Scott Realty Company, Bellevue, Washington until his retirement in 1965. Montgomery and Helen had no children.

245330000 MCELWAINE	¦		
Jay B. McElwaine	¦1887 Nov 9	PA¦	¦1945 Sep 3 Seattle WA
s Mary -----	¦	¦	¦1970c
t Jennie -----	¦	¦	¦
u Jennie -----	¦	¦	¦
v Una M. -----	¦	¦1941c	¦

Jay and Mary were divorced; Mary later married a member of the Katz theater family and lived in New York in relative splendor. Jay and Jennie were married twice and were finally divorced in about 1934; they lived at 658 E. 12th Street, Indianapolis, Indiana in 1920. In World War I Jay served with a hospital unit in Europe. Before and after the war he was employed by Crane and Co. in Indianapolis.   In the late 1920s he lived in Florida, engaging in land speculation. He moved to Seattle in 1932, where he joined his brother Myron in the Seattle Plumbing Supply Co.

Serial # and Name	Birth	Marriage	Death
245340000 MCELWAINE			
Myron Murdoch McElwaine	1890 May 20	1911	1951 Oct 20
Irene Austin	1891 Oct 28	Alec Austin &	1986 Mar 15
		Josephine McBean	

Myron moved to Seattle in 1906; he lived there with his family at 1711 32nd S., Seattle, Washington in 1920.   Also living with this family was Josephine Austin, age 53, Irene's mother.   She was born in Scotland into the McBean family, which is regarded by many as a member of the same clan as the McIlvaines. Myron was part owner of the Seattle Plumbing Supply Co. from 1919 until his death.   He was quite prominent in business and social life in Seattle, and was a member of the Ranier Club and the Seattle Golf Club.   At the time of his death Myron was recognized as the top executive in the plumbing supply industry in the Pacific Northwest.   He lived at 403 West Prospect Street in Seattle.

1 Mary Elizabeth	#1913 Dec Seattle WA	1932	1948 Jan Lake Stevens WA
2 Myron Monroe	#1917 Aug Seattle WA	1939 Aug	

245341000 WALTON			
Mary Elizabeth McElwaine	1913 Dec Seattle WA	1932	1948 Jan Lake Stevens WA
Lawrence C. Walton			

Lawrence operated the Walton Lumber Co. in Everett, WA.

1 Lawrence C., Jr.			
2 Judith	#		

245341100 ROMO			
Judith Walton			
----- Romo			

245342000 MCELWAINE			
Myron Monroe McElwaine	1917 Aug Seattle WA	1939 Aug	
s Ellen Stewart			
t Kathleen Carrigan		1946 Mar	
u Myrtle Ward		1968 Nov	

Myron ("Bud") was employed by the Seattle Plumbing Co. from 1936 to 1952, except for the years 1942 to 1945 when he served with the United States Navy.   He moved to Pebble Beach, CA in 1952.   From 1953 to 1956 he was the owner of West Coast Distributing Co. of Monterey, CA, and from 1958 to 1965 he was a partner in Birr Wilson & Co. of San Francisco, a company dealing in stocks and bonds.   Thereafter he was concerned with the Bemax Corporation of San Francisco as an import-export agent for Mining--Heavy Construction Industries.   He retired to Monterey, CA in 1988.   He was divorced from Ellen in 1942, and from Kathleen in 1956.

1 Mary Sheila	s 1940 May Seattle WA		
2 Margaret Ellen	s 1941 Nov Seattle WA		

245400000 SMITH			
Sarah Ella McElwain	1854	PA1881 Apr 29	1926 Feb 4 Harrisville PA
William A. Smith			

In 1880 Sarah was living with her parents and working as a school teacher.

Serial # and Name	Birth	Marriage	Death

245500000 MCELWAINE

Albert G. McElwaine	:1856 Feb Sandy Lake PA:		:1920c Indianapolis IN
Florence -----	:1857 Dec PA:		:

     Albert and Flora lived in Sandy Lake twp., Mercer Co., PA in 1880, in Indianapolis, IN, at 3320 North Capitol Ave. in 1900, and at 3162 Kenwood Ave in 1920.   The surname is spelled with a final "e" in the censuses of 1900 and 1920.   Albert operated the family livery stable in Sandy Lake until his father's death.   He then joined his brother Montgomery in operating oil well servicing and equipment companies in Pennsylvania, Ohio, and Indiana, until the collapse of the business about 1898 left him destitute. Thereafter he supported his family by working at odd jobs.

1 Frank L.	:1879 Mar Sandy Lake PA:		:
2 Harry E.	:1880 May Sandy Lake PA:		:
3 Grace L.	*:1884 Dec PA:		: Los Angeles CA
4 Fred G.	:1887 Dec PA:		:
5 Hazel	*:1890 Nov Indianapolis IN:		:1990c Los Angeles CA
6 Floyd	:1893 Sep Indianapolis IN:		: Los Angeles CA
7 Donald	*:1899 Feb Indianapolis IN:		:1958 Los Angeles CA

     Floyd moved to California in the 1930s.

245530000 YOUNG

Grace L. McElwaine	:1884 Dec	:	: Los Angeles CA
----- Young	:	:	:

     Grace lived with her parents in 1920, under the name of Young.   She was widowed or divorced shortly after the birth of Martha, and did not remarry.   She moved to California in the 1930s.

1 Martha	:1917	:	:

245550000 PRATHER

Hazel McElwaine	:1890 Nov IN:		:1990c Los Angeles CA
Frank Prather	:	:	:

     The Prathers moved to California in the 1930s.

245570000 MCELWAINE

Donald McElwaine	:1899 Feb Indianapolis IN:	:1918	:1958 Los Angeles CA
Ina Estelle Fowler	:1898 Indianapolis IN:	Franklin Fowler &	:1957 Los Angeles CA
	:	Lulubelle Tice	

     Donald was a reporter for an Indianapolis newspaper before moving to New York in 1920 to become editor of Fox Studios newsreel division. He met Buck Jones, a very popular cowboy actor of the time, and accompanied him in 1928 to Los Angeles where he became President of Buck Jones film company.   When that company went bankrupt in 1929, Donald was hired by Louis B. Mayer as a mid-level executive of Metro-Goldwyn-Mayer, and there spent the remainder of his career.

1 Donna	:1919		:1936 Los Angeles CA
2 Robert Marshall	*:1923 May 19 New York NY:		:
3 Donald, Jr.	:1932 Los Angeles CA:		:1978 Oxnard CA
4 Guy	:1936 Los Angeles CA:		:

     Donna died in a drowning accident.   Guy's career has been in the motion picture industry. He was Chairman of the Board of Columbia Pictures, and President of Warner Brothers, and is now (1996) Vice-Chairman of International Creative Management.

245572000 MCELWAINE

Robert Marshall McElwaine	1923 May 19 New York NY		
Sandra C. -----	1935 Nov 22 New York NY		

After spending 1942 to 1945 in the Navy and Air Force, Robert worked for several years as a press agent for MGM Studios, and as an independent press agent, with Errol Flynn as one of his clients. From 1950 to 1952 he worked for Samuel Goldwyn Studios, and then in various film and creative ventures, including assignments with Danny Kaye. He was Director of Public Relations for Mercedes-Benz of North America from 1963 to 1968. The last twenty years of his career was as President of the American International Automobile Dealers Association. In 1996 he was retired and living in rural Virginia.

1 Andrew	#1960 Nov 9 New York NY		

245572100 MCELWAINE

Andrew McElwaine	1960 Nov 9 New York NY		
Barbara Lieber	1958 Aug 30 Neenah WI		

Andrew worked as Congressional aide to Senator John Heinz (PA) from 1984 to 1989, and then for four years as a lobbyist in Washington for various environmental causes. Since 1993 he has been Environmental Director for the Heinz Endowment, Pittsburgh, Pennsylvania. He is a Ph. D. student at Carnegia Mellon University.

1 Robert John	1991 Jul 24 Arlington VA		
2 Mark Lieber	1994 Sep 2 Pittsburgh PA		

245800000 MCELWAIN

Eugene McElwain	1860 Dec PA		
----- -----			

The 1900 census lists Eugene (L. E.) as living with the three boys, but no relationship is stated and no wife is listed. It has been assumed these are his sons. The address was 215 South Ave., Bradford, PA.

1 Brad	1884 Mar PA		
2 Robert	1890 Nov PA		
3 Lawrence	1894 Jan PA		

245900000 BLACK

Carrie McElwain	1868c PA		
Will Black			

246000000 CARNAHAN

Margery Ellen McElwain	1822 Sep 4 Cumberland Co.PA	1843c	
Adam Carnahan	1810 Jan 3		1866 Feb 27

Adam lived in Mill Creek twp., Mercer Co., PA in 1860, with his wife, the six children, and his mother-in-law, Rosanna (real estate $2400, personal property $700).   In 1870 Ellen (Margery) lived in French Creek twp. of Venango Co, PA, with her five youngest children (real estate, $4000; personal property, $700).

1 Elizabeth	1844c		
2 Rosanna	1847c		
3 Margaret Ellen	1849c Mercer Co. PA		
4 LeRoy	1853c Mercer Co. PA		
5 William	1856c Mercer Co. PA		
6 Melissa	1858c Mercer Co. PA		
7 James M.	1863c PA		

185

Serial # and Name	Birth	Marriage	Death

247000000 DAVIS

Ruth Rosanna McElwain	1825 Nov 13 Cumberland Co. PA	1844 Sep 3 Mercer PA	1900 May 27 Meadville PA
David Davis	1820 PA		1862 Dec 13 Fredericksburg VA

The family of Ruth and David lived in New Lebanon, PA in 1860 (real estate value $300). David was killed at the Battle of Fredericksburg while serving in Company G, 145th Regiment. In that battle three other soldiers of Co. G died, and four later died of wounds. Company G also fought and sustained casualties at Chancellorsville (May 1863), Gettysburg (July 1863), Tolopotamy (May 1864), Spottsylvania Court House (May 1864), Petersburg (July 1864), and Cold Harbor (July 1864). Of the 171 men listed on the company roster, 53 were killed, died of wounds, or died of disease. Nine of the men were among the 12,000 Union soldiers done to death by the atrocious conditions deliberately maintained at Andersonville Prison.   In 1870 Ruth and the three younger children lived in Greensville, PA.

1 Mary Jane	*!1848 Nov 4 OH	1870 Sep 8 Meadville PA	1908 Dec 10 Meadville PA
2 [infant]	1850		
3 Lucinda B.	*!1854 May 23 Mercer Co PA		1914 May 6 Meadville PA
4 Andrew Thompson	*!1855 Sep 9 Mercer Co PA	1874 Dec 16 Leechs Corner PA	1923 Jun 29 Scottdale PA
5 Emma	*!1859 Jan 25 Mercer Co PA		1922 Jan Lawton OK
6 Cora Olive	*!1862 Jun 7 Mercer Co PA		1915 May 31 Meadville PA

247100000 TOWNLEY

Mary Jane Davis	1848 Nov 4 OH	1870 Sep 8 Meadville PA	1908 Dec 10 Meadville PA
Thomas Jefferson Townley	1839 Sep 11 Richmond PA	John B. Townley & Priscilla McKinley	1903 Apr 25 Meadville PA

Both in 1880 and 1900 the Townleys lived in Meadville, Crawford Co., PA, but in the interval they had moved from 519 to 865 Arch Street. Mary Jane's birth year may be 1847.

1 John Brown	*!1875 Apr 17 Meadville PA	1901 Apr 11 PA	1943 May 15 Pittsburgh PA
2 [child]	1881 Jan 18 Meadville PA		
3 Nina Ruth	1882 Aug 24 Meadville PA	never married	1976 Sep 11 Frankfort IL

Nina taught school in Pittsburgh, PA.

247110000 TOWNLEY

John Brown Townley	1875 Apr 17 Meadville PA	1901 Apr 11 PA	1943 May 15 Pittsburgh PA
Nellie Emma Jeffrey	1875 Allegheny Co. PA	William W. Jeffrey & Margaret Guy	1943 Apr 2 Pittsburgh PA

John was political editor of the *Pittsburgh Press*. This couple had no children.

247300000 ADAMS

Lucinda B. Davis	1853 May 27 Mercer Co PA	1884 Sep	1914 May 7 Meadville PA
William Adams			

Lucinda's occupation in 1870, when she was 18 and living with her mother, was that of a milliner.

1 Ethel C.	1885 Oct 13 Meadville PA		

247400000 DAVIS

Andrew Thompson Davis	1855 Sep 9 Mercer Co PA	1874 Dec 16 Leechs Corner PA	1923 Jun 29 Scottdale PA
s Mary Elizabeth Kee	1856 Crawford Co. WV	John Kee & Emily Minnis	1883 Aug 23 Crawford Co. PA
t Mary Elizabeth Newbold	1862 Jun 6 Crawford Co. PA	1885 Jun 3 E. Fallowfield PA	1916 Feb 22 Crawford Co. PA

Andrew and his first wife lived in East Fallowfield twp., Crawford Co., PA in 1880; in 1910 he and his second wife lived in Crawford Co. In 1920 Andrew was living with his son Donald in Allegheny County, PA.

1 Bessie Jeanette	s*!1876 Jul 31 Meadville PA	1901 Oct 1 Meadville PA	1929 Mar 22 Grand Rapids MI
2 Robert John	s*!1878 Jul 27 Meadville PA	1912 Jun 18 Denver CO	1923 Jan 26 Boise ID
3 Donald Page	t*!1888 Jul 6 Atlantic PA	1910 Jun 28 Hartstown PA	1978 Feb 5 Harrisburg PA

Serial # and Name	Birth	Marriage	Death

247410000   JUDY

Bessie Jeanette Davis	1876 Jul 31 Meadville	PA 1901 Oct 1 Meadville	PA 1929 Mar 22 Grand Rapids MI
Charles Burton Judy, Jr.	1879 Apr 18 Mercer	PA Mathias Judy &	1977 Jul 3 Grand Rapids MI
		Amanda Slater	
1 LaVesta Laverne	* 1902 Aug 23 Freedom	PA 1942 Sep 4 Grand Rapids	MI 1968 May 19 Grand Rapids MI
2 Ella Mae	* 1906 Dec 5 Allegan	MI 1927 Jun 14 Allegan	MI 1992 Aug 18 Ellsworth MI
3 Benjamin Ivan	* 1908 Sep 10 Lowell	MI 1932 May 4	1992 Jun 1 Grand Rapids MI
4 Robert John	* 1910 Oct 24 Grand Rapids	MI 1936 Jun 20 Grand Rapids	MI 1980 Oct 7 Grand Rapids MI
5 Charles Burton	* 1912 Dec 1 Grand Rapids	MI 1936 Mar 18 Grand Rapids	MI 1974 Jun 6 Grand Rapids MI
6 Bessie	1915 Dec 2 Grand Rapids	MI	1915 Dec 3 Grand Rapids MI

247411000   MONTROY

LaVesta Laverne Judy	1902 Aug 23 Freedom	PA 1942 Sep 4 Grand Rapids	MI 1968 May 19 Grand Rapids MI
Lawrence H. Montroy	1894 Apr 13 Saginaw	MI William Montroy &	1981 Sep FL
		Mary Bennett	

247412000   WYNSMA

Ella Mae Judy	1906 Dec 5 Allegan	MI 1927 Jun 14 Grand Rapids	MI 1992 Aug 18 Ellsworth MI
Thomas M. Wynsma	1897 Oct 15	NL Niles Wynsma & Eve Hoeksema	1986 Apr 27 Ellsworth MI
Theunis anglicized his name to Thomas.			
1 Thomas M., Jr.	* 1929 Jan 22 Grand Rapids	MI 1953 Aug 21 Ellsworth	MI
2 [daughter]	1931 Nov 29 Central Lake	MI	1931 Nov 29 Central Lake MI
3 Miles Burton	* 1935 May 24 Central Lake	MI 1956 Jun 8 Grand Rapids	MI
4 Ralph William	* 1937 Sep 24 Ellsworth	MI 1961 May 19 Central Lake	MI
5 Betty Lou	* 1950 Mar 23 Charlevoix	MI 1984 Mar 17 Ellsworth	MI

247412100   WYNSMA

Thomas M. Wynsma, Jr.	1929 Jan 22 Grand Rapids	MI 1953 Aug 21 Ellsworth	MI
Flora Veenstra	1930 Apr 8 Ellsworth	MI	
1 Timothy Jay	* 1955 Mar 30 Charlevoix	MI 1982 Aug 7	
2 Dee Ann Elayne	* 1957 Nov 24 Charlevoix	MI 1980 Aug 22	
3 Steven Paul	* 1961 Jan 8 Charlevoix	MI 1984 Jul 21	
4 Kevin John	1962 Sep 18 Charlevoix	MI	

247412110   WYNSMA

Timothy Jay Wynsma	1955 Mar 30	MI 1982 Aug 7	
Sue Marcus	1956 Sep 14 Chicago	IL	
1 Philip Marcus	1985 Mar 5 Champaign Co.	IL	
2 Benjamin Joel	1987 Feb 11 Champaign Co.	IL	
3 Jonathan Luke	1991 Feb 8 Urbana	IL	1991 Feb 8 Urbana IL

247412120   MATTHEWS

Dee Ann Elayne Wynsma	1957 Nov 24	MI 1980 Aug 22 Ellsworth	MI
Dale LeRoy Themm Matthews	1954 Jun 25	PR	

247412130   WYNSMA

Steven Paul Wynsma	1961 Jan 8	MI 1984 Jul 21	CA
Linda Berkompas	1963 Nov 20 Arcadia	CA	

Serial # and Name	Birth	Marriage	Death

247412300   WYNSMA

	Birth	Marriage	Death
Miles Burton Wynsma	:1935 May 24 Central Lake MI:	1956 Jun 8 Grand Rapids MI:	
Carol Jean Simpson	:1936 May 3 Grand Rapids MI:		:
	:	:	:
1 Roger Allen	*:1958 Feb 5 Grand Rapids MI:	1979 Jun 30 Grand Rapids MI:	
2 Ronald Burton	*:1959 Jul 3 Grand Rapids MI:	1980 Apr 11 Grand Rapids MI:	
3 Rick Alan	#:1963 Apr 22 Grand Rapids MI:	1988 May 7 Grand Rapids MI:	

247412310   WYNSMA

	Birth	Marriage	Death
Roger Allen Wynsma	:1958 Feb 5 Grand Rapids MI:	1979 Jun 30 Grand Rapids MI:	
Lisa Lynn Flint	:1961 Apr 28 Grand Rapids MI:		:
	:	:	:
1 Mark Adam	:1987 Jan 12 Inchon KO:		:
2 Thomas Victor	:1988 Sep 26 Grand Rapids MI:		:
Mark was adopted.			

247412320   WYNSMA

	Birth	Marriage	Death
Ronald Burton Wynsma	:1959 Jul 3 Grand Rapids MI:	1980 Apr 11 Grand Rapids MI:	
Marcia Postma	:1960 Oct 3 Grand Rapids MI:		:
	:	:	:
1 Wendy Marie	:1981 Aug 28 Grand Rapids MI:		:
2 Rachel Lynn	:1984 Aug 9 Grand Rapids MI:		:
3 Kristin Kay	:1989 Mar 26 Grand Rapids MI:		:

247412330   WYNSMA

	Birth	Marriage	Death
Rick Alan Wynsma	:1963 Apr 22 Grand Rapids MI:	1988 May 7 Grand Rapids MI:	
Shari Lee McConnell	:1964 Jun 4 Royal Oak MI:	David McConnell &	:
	:	Marlene Beryl Smith	:
1 Brianne Nichole	:1992 Aug 7 Grand Rapids MI:		:
2 Brandon Richard	:1994 Jun 9 Grand Rapids MI:		:

247412400   WYNSMA

	Birth	Marriage	Death
Ralph William Wynsma	:1937 Sep 24 Ellsworth MI:	1961 May 19 Central Lake MI:	
Donna Gail Klooster	:1942 Apr 16 Ellsworth MI:		:
	:	:	:
1 Sherri Lynn	*:1963 Jul 2 Bellaire MI:	1985 Aug 3 Ellsworth MI:	
2 Debra Sue	*:1965 Dec 15 Charlevoix MI:	1990 Sep 29 Ellsworth MI:	
3 Kathy Jo	*:1969 Jul 6 Charlevoix MI:	1993 Jul 31 :	

247412410   MILLER

	Birth	Marriage	Death
Sherri Lynn Wynsma	:1963 Jul 2 Bellaire MI:	1985 Aug 3 Ellsworth MI:	
James Aaron Miller, Jr.	:1955 Jul 24 Grosse Point MI:		:
	:	:	:
1 James Aaron, III	:1989 Dec 8 Grosse Point MI:		:
2 Joel Alexander	:1991 Jul 26 Grosse Point MI:		:
3 Abigail Marie	:1994 May 14 Grosse Point MI:		:

247412420   BATTERBEE

	Birth	Marriage	Death
Debra Sue Wynsma	:1965 Dec 15 Charlevoix MI:	1990 Sep 29 Ellsworth MI:	
Michael Arnold Batterbee	:1965 Mar 7 Lansing MI:	Michael A. Batterbee &	:
	:	Margaret Nachazel	:
1 Ashley Marie	:1992 May 20 Lansing MI:		:
2 Katherine Paige	:1994 Aug 28 Lansing MI:		:

Serial # and Name	Birth	Marriage	Death

247412430 MAIN

Kathy Jo Wynsma	1969 Jul 6 Charlevoix MI	1993 Jul 31 Ellsworth MI	
Stephen Michael Main	1969 Jul 18 Sturgis MI		

247412500 RING / SWOVELAND

Betty Lou Wynsma	1950 Mar 23 Charlevoix MI	1984 Mar 17 Ellsworth MI	
s Ernest Harvey Ring, Jr.	1931 Jul 24 New Haven CT		1987 Feb 15 Goshen IN
t Devon Ray Swoveland	1946 Aug 9 Goshen IN	1990 Jul 28 Goshen IN	

247413000 JUDY

Benjamin Ivan Judy	1908 Sep 10 Lowell MI	1932 May 4 Elkhart IN	1992 Jun 1 Grand Rapids MI
s Alma Rita Gezlov	1911 Dec 1 Cedar Rapids MI		1980 Mar Jefferson IN
t Nettie Esther Clark	1912 Jul 29 Grand Rapids MI	1950 Dec 11 Angola IN	
Pierson		Joseph Clark & Grace Allen	

Nettie was married first to Mr. Pierson.

1 Mary Ellen	s* 1934 May 4 Grand Rapids MI	1951 Jan 1	
2 Mary Elizabeth	t* 1952 Jul 6 Grand Rapids MI	1974 Jun 15	

Mary Ellen was adopted by Casey and Gertrude Maring, March 14, 1939.

247413100 VOS

Mary Ellen Judy	1934 May 4 Grand Rapids MI	1951 Jan 1	
Wayne Vos			
1 Traci	* 1952 Oct 7 Grand Rapids MI		
2 Scott	1953 Grand Rapids MI		
3 Martin	1955 Grand Rapids MI		
4 Jason	1959 Dec 17 CA		

Scott may have been born in 1954, and Martin in 1956.

247413110 RENGO / STEWART

Traci Vos	1952 Oct 7 Grand Rapids MI		
s Phil Rengo			
t Douglas Stewart			
1 Trevor Stewart			

247413200 PERRIN

Mary Elizabeth Judy	1952 Jul 6 Grand Rapids MI	1974 Jun 15 Grand Rapids MI	
Thomas Wesley Perrin	1951 Dec 31 Grand Rapids MI	Wesley Perrin & Doris Bailey	

247414000 JUDY

Robert John Judy	1910 Oct 10 Grand Rapids MI	1936 Jun 20 Grand Rapids MI	1980 Oct 17 Grand Rapids MI
Ethel Janet Dosenberry	1911 Mar 8 Ada MI	Harvey Dosenberry &	1989 Dec 14 Grand Rapids MI
		Margaret Tumbell	
1 Janet Elaine	* 1941 Aug 5 Grand Rapids MI	1963 Aug 23 Grand Rapids MI	
2 Mary Ethel	* 1944 Jan 3 Grand Rapids MI	1967 Jul 29 Grand Rapids MI	1994 Aug 30 Greenville MI

Serial # and Name	Birth	Marriage	Death
247414100 MATHEWS			
Janet Elaine Judy	1941 Aug 5 Grand Rapids MI	1963 Aug 23 Grand Rapids MI	
Victor Monroe	1942 Sep 2 Seattle WA	Victor Matthews &	
Matthews, Sr.		Bonnie Reem	
1 Julie Marie	*1966 Apr 12 Pullman WA	1986 May 25 Belmont MI	
2 Victor Monroe, Jr.	*1969 Nov 16 Edmonton AB	1992 Sep 5 Comstock MI	
247414110 LEHMAN / LYONS			
Julie Marie Matthews	1966 Apr 12 Pullman WA	1986 May 25 Belmont MI	
s Jeffrey Andrew Lehman			
t John Lee Lyons	1961 Dec 15 Big Rapids MI	1987 Nov 21 Stanwood MI	
1 Nicholas Lee Lyons	1989 Dec 12 Grand Rapids MI		
2 Ashley Marie Lyons	1991 Aug 2 Grand Rapids MI		
3 Jacob Lee Lyons	1995 May 31 Grand Rapids MI		
247414120 MATTHEWS			
Victor Monroe	1969 Nov 16 Edmonton AB	1992 Sep 5 Comstock MI	
Matthews, Jr.			
Wanda Lee Mountain	1973 Aug 28 St. Paul MN		
1 Kryslyn Saige	1994 Feb 10 Grand Rapids MI		
2 Victor Monroe	1995 Nov 10 Grand Rapids MI		
247414200 SEAVER			
Mary Ethel Judy	1944 Jan 3 Grand Rapids MI	1967 Jul 29 MI	1994 Aug 30 Greenville MI
Thomas Martin Seaver	1940 Feb 10 Montague MI	Clare Seaver &	
		Viola Hepworth	
1 Jeffrey Alan	*1970 May 18 Greenville MI		
2 Jodi Lynn	*1972 May 26 Greenville MI		
247414210 SEAVER			
Jeffrey Alan Seaver	1970 May 18 Greenville MI	1991 Apr 13 East Lansing MI	
Catherine Michelle	1969 Apr 7 Lansing MI		
Weinert			
1 Jordan Lemuel	1992 Apr 6 Grand Rapids MI		
2 Marah Eleanor	1994 Jul 6 Grand Rapids MI		
247414220 LEWIS			
Jodi Lynn Seaver	1972 May 26 Greenville MI	1994 Dec 17 Allendale MI	
Jamie Scott Lewis	1970 Apr 3 Grand Rapids MI		
247415000 JUDY			
Charles Burton Judy	1912 Dec 1 Grand Rapids MI	1936 Mar 18 Grand Rapids MI	1974 Jun 6 Grand Rapids MI
Edith Caroline Norris	1918 Feb 14 Grand Rapids MI	Charles Norris &	
		Mary Bull	
1 Carol Sue	*1941 Nov 28 Grand Rapids MI	1963 Jul 13 Grand Rapids MI	

190

Serial # and Name	Birth	Marriage	Death

247415100 ZAPOLNIK
  Carol Sue Judy |1941 Nov 28 Grand Rapids MI|1963 Jul 13 Grand Rapids MI|
  Daniel James Zapolnik |1935 Dec 5 Grand Rapids MI| Antoni Zapolnik & |
                          | | Anna Strekowski |

Carol is presently (1996) working as a resident aide at a home for the aged in Hart, Michigan.   Dan has
worked as a service man with a propane gas company in Hart, Michigan.   He recently resigned from the Oceana
County Health Board after fifteen years of service.

1 Gerald Lee   *|1961 Jan 3 Grand Rapids MI|1984 Apr 28 Livonia   MI|
2 Theresa Lynn |1964 Mar 29 Grand Rapids MI| |
3 Charyl Marie   *|1965 Jun 22 Grand Rapids MI|1988 Oct 1 Hart   MI|
4 Judy Rae |1969 Jun 25 Grand Rapids MI| |

Theresa received an Associate in Arts Degree in Early Childhood Development from West Shore Community
College; she is employed as a secretary at a printing company in Grand Rapids. Judy is a registered Nurses
Aide, working in nursing homes.

247415110 ZAPOLNIK
  Gerald Lee Zapolnik |1961 Jan 3 Grand Rapids MI|1984 Apr 28 Lavonia   MI|
s Linda Marie Burbo |1959 Jan 8   MI| |
t Sharon Elizabeth Muck |1960 May 13 Toledo   OH|1991 Sep 28 Maumee   OH|
                           | | David Edward Muck & |
                           | | Norma Ruth Shephard |

Gerald has an A. A. in Emergency Medical System Services and Management from Davenport College,   an EMT
certificate from Grand Valley College, and a B. B. A. from Madonna College.   He is employed as support
service manager for Huron Valley Ambulance, Washtenaw, MI, and been has President of the Michigan Association of Emergency Medical Technicians.   He also teaches classes in emergency management, and is certified
in life support by the American College of Emergency Physicians and by the American Heart Association.
Sharon is a registered Pharmacist.

1 Sara Elizabeth   t |1994 Nov 3 Ann Arbor   MI| |

247415130 BARTOCCI
  Charyl Marie Zapolnik |1965 Jun 22 Grand Rapids MI|1988 Oct 1 Hart   MI|
  Paul Louis Bartocci |1967   Dover   DE| John Bartocci & |
                           | | Esther Schultz |

Cheryl has a B. S. in Elementary Education from Western Michigan University; she teaches at Our Lady of
Peace Catholic School in North Augusta, SC.   Paul also attended Western Michigan, where he earned a degree
in paper Engineering; he is an engineer with Kimberly Clark Corp. in Beech Island, SC.   In 1994 and 1995
Paul worked at the Masters Golf Tournament in Augusta, GA. They are expecting their first child in October
1996.

247420000 DAVIS
  Robert John Davis, Sr. |1878 Jul 27 Meadville   PA|1912 Jun 18 Denver   CO|1923 Jan 26 Boise   ID
  Lulu A. Fee |1885c   Wheeling   WV| ---- Fee & Mary V. ----- |
    Robert attended Whitman College. He served in the armed forces during World War I, and was a brakeman on
    the Union Pacific Railroad in Idaho
1 Mary Virginia |1913   ID| |
2 Betty Lou   *|1915 Sep 2   ID| Boise   ID|1985 Nov 23 Boise   ID
3 Robert John, Jr. |1919 Sep 19   ID| |1945<
    Robert, Jr. was killed in the Pacific Theater in World War II.

Serial # and Name	Birth		Marriage		Death		

247422000   MAW

Betty Lou Davis	:1915 Sep 2	:	Boise	ID:1985 Nov 23 Boise	ID
Johnson Ebert Maw	:	:		:1980 Sep 18 Boise	ID
	:	:		:	
1 John Davis	*:1954 Sep 24 Boise	ID:1978 May 6 Boise	ID:	

247422100   MAW

John Davis Maw	:1954 Sep 24 Boise	ID:1978 May 6 Boise	ID:
Sharon Loretta Connell	:1953 Nov 3 Stratford	CN:	:
	:	:	:
1 Loretta Louis	:1975 Jun 28 Okinawa	JP:	:
2 John Connell	:1977 May 9 Mountain Home ID:		:
3 Elizabeth Mary	:1981 Jun 20 Bridgeport	CT:	:

247430000   DAVIS

| Donald Page Davis | :1888 Jul 6 Atlantic | PA:1910 Jun 28 Hartstown | PA:1978 Feb 5 Harrisburg | PA |
| Mildred B. Peters | :1890 Jan 28 | : | :1959 Nov 25 Harrisburg | PA |

Donald held a B. A. (1920), an M. A. (1930), and a Ph. D. (1935) from the University of Pittsburgh.   He taught and served as a principal in several Pennsylvania counties, was Superintendent of Schools in Arnold, PA (1925-1936), and Director of the Bureau of Administration and Finance with the Pennsylvania Department of Public Instruction (1936-1940).   He served with the U. S. Office of Education, Washington, D. C. (1942-1954) and as a field representative in Denver, CO until 1958.

| 1 Dorothea Lovenia | *:1921 May 10 E. McKeesport PA:1940 Feb 3 Harrisburg | PA: |

247431000   STRICKER

| Dorothea Lovenia Davis | :1921 May 10 E. McKeesport PA:1940 Feb 3 Harrisburg | PA: |
| Charles Andrew Stricker | :1920 Jan 22 Harrisburg | PA: | :1993 Apr 11 Harrisburg | PA |

Charles retired as Vice President of B. & L. E. Railroad.

1 Bonita Lee	*:1942 Dec 26 Harrisburg	PA:1962	Harrisburg	PA:
2 Carol Jean	*:1945 Jun 9 Harrisburg	PA:1966 Feb 19 Elizabethtown PA:
3 Althea Grace	*:1951 Feb 9 Harrisburg	PA:1979 May 19	PA:

247431100   DEMARCO /BOLAS

Bonita Lee Stricker	:1942 Dec 26 Harrisburg	PA:1962	Harrisburg	PA:
s Bruce Lee DeMarco	:1941	:	:1966	Steelton	PA
t Donald M. Bolas	:1942 May 8	:1968 Jun 28	:
	:	:	:
1 Eric Lee DeMarco	:1963 Apr 20 Allentown	PA:	:
2 David Justin Bolas	:1974 Mar 2 Lancaster	CA:	:

247431200   DOST

Carol Jean Stricker	:1945 Jun 9 Harrisburg	PA:1966 Feb 19 Elizabethtown PA:
Lawrence Edward Dost	:1943 Sep 22	:	:
	:	:	:
1 Lawrence Adam	:1972 Mar 16 Harrisburg	PA:	:
2 Lisa Jane	:1974 Mar 15 Harrisburg	PA:	:

247431300   SASSAMAN

Althea Grace Stricker	:1951 Feb 9 Harrisburg	PA:1979 May 19	PA:
Stephen Harry Sassaman	:1951 Feb 26	PA:	:
	:	:	:
1 Avary Gale	:1991 Jul 8	PA:	:

Serial # and Name	Birth	Marriage	Death

247500000 BEMIS

Emma Davis	!1859 Jan 25 Mercer Co PA!		!1922 Jan Lawton OK
John C. Bemis	!1852 Jun 19 MA!		!

In 1880 and 1900 the Bemis family lived in Meadville, PA; in 1880 their address was 495 Pine St.

1 Harry C.	!1879 Dec Meadville PA!		!
2 Marion E.	*!1881 Sep 24 PA!		!
3 Helen T.	!1893 Aug PA!		!

247520000 DOUGLAS

Marion E. Bemis	!1881 Dec PA!		!
Charles E. Douglas	!	!	!

In 1922 Marion and Charles lived in Lawton, OK.

247600000 OXLEY

Cora Olive Davis	!1862 Jun 7 Mercer Co PA!		!1915 May 31 Meadville PA
John H. Oxley	!1850 Nov 16 EN!		!1917 Aug 18 Meadville PA

Cora and John and their two children lived in Meadville, PA in 1910.

1 Ray D.	!1896 PA	!	!1918 May 26 Meadville PA
2 Edna A.	!1899c PA!		!

Ray, an innocent bystander, was killed in a shooting.

300000000

Prudence McElwain	!	!	!
Robert McLean	!	!	!

400000000 MCELWAIN

Andrew McElwain	!1756 Mar Cumberland Co. PA!1778		!1820 Apr Cumberland Co. PA
s Elizabeth Shannon	!1759	! Robert Shannon & Jean -----!1790<	
	!	!	!
t Margaret Bell	! Belltown PA!1790 Aug 26		!

See the History section for information on Andrew's family (pages 22-27), and the Shannon family (pages 43-44).

1 Mary Jane	s*!1779 Dec 5 Cumberland Co. PA!1802 Feb 4 Newville PA!1823 Mar 29		
2 Robert	s*!1781 Apr 7 Cumberland Co. PA!1808 Apr 12 Newville PA!1853 Jan 18 Cumberlnd Co. PA		
3 Jane	s*!1782 Nov 17 Cumberland Co. PA!1807 May 29 Newville PA!1835 Jan 6		
4 Benjamin	s !1784	!	!
5 Andrew	s*!1785 May 1 Cumberland Co. PA!1819 Apr 15 Cumberland Co. PA!1840 Aug 21		
6 Thomas	s !1787 May 13	!never married	!1855 Sep 21
7 Elizabeth	s*!1789 Jul 15	!1816 Jan 11 Cumberland Co. PA!1826 Dec 18	
8 Sarah	t !1791 Jun 23	!	!1791 Dec
9 Sarah	t*!1793 Jan 29	!	!
a William Bell	t*!1794 Jul 1 Cumberland Co. PA!1816 Dec 12 Cumberland Co. PA!1874 Aug 8 Cumberlnd Co. PA		
b James	t*!1796 Oct 29 Cumberland Co. PA!		!1884 Feb 25
c John	t !1798 Apr 23	!	!1828 Apr 8
d Stewart	t !1805 Mar 3	!	!1805 Sep 16

In 1850 Thomas lived in the household of Joseph Officer, Mifflin twp., Cumberland Co., PA

Serial # and Name	Birth	Marriage	Death
410000000 RICHARDS			
Mary Jane McElvain	1779 Dec 5 Cumberland Co. PA	1802 Feb 4 Newville PA	1823 Mar 29
James Richards			
1 Elizabeth			
2 Margaret			
3 Robert	*1810c	PA	
4 James, Jr.			
5 Mary			
6 Sarah			
7 Thomas			
8 Alexander	1808c		
9 Andrew	1810c	PA	
a Richard			

Andrew, Elizabeth, and Alexander lived together in West Pennsboro twp., Cumberland Co., PA in 1850. Also in the household was Sarah, age 24, seemingly too young to be a sister; she may be the wife of Alexander. This surname appears as Ritchey in some records. The three census records found (1850 and 1860 for Robert, and 1850 for Andrew) all spell the name Richards.

413000000 RICHARDS			
Robert Richards	1810c		
Susan -----	1806c	PA	

In 1850 Robert was a farmer, in 1860, a medicine vendor. The family lived in Carlisle.

1 James	1835c		
2 Thomas	1837c	PA	
3 Lydia	1841c	PA	

Lydia was living with her parents in 1860 and working as a music teacher.

420000000			
Robert McElwain	1781 Apr 7 Cumberland Co. PA	1808 Apr 12 Newville PA	1853 Jan 18 Cumberlnd Co. PA
Jane Shannon	1790	James Shannon & Isabel McKee	1869 May 12

Robert and Jane lived in Mifflin twp, Cumberland Co., PA in 1850. Robert was a farmer.

1 Isabel McKee	*1809 Feb 7 Cumberland Co. PA	1831 Nov 30 Cumberland Co. PA	1888 Jan 6
2 Elizabeth Ann	1811 Feb 13 Cumberland Co. PA		
3 Mary	1813 Aug 30 Cumberland Co. PA		1868 Mar 27
4 Andrew	*1820 Jan 7 Cumberland Co. PA	1844 Jan 25 Cumberland Co. PA	
5 Sara Jane	*1822 Jan 5 Cumberland Co. PA	1865	
6 Margaret Elinor	*1825 Apr 2 Cumberland Co. PA	1845 Sep 4 Newville PA	
7 Liberty McKinney	1828 Jan 5 Cumberland Co. PA	never married	1914 Aug 13
8 James Shannon	*1830 Aug 2 Cumberland Co. PA	1857 Dec 29 Newville PA	
9 Robert McCachran	1833 Jun 18 Cumberland Co. PA		1833 Oct 1
a [daughter]	1816 Jan 11		1816 Mar 27
b [son]	1817 Mar 12		1817 May 10
c [daughter]	1818 Nov 8		1818 Nov 8

Liberty in 1850 was living in the household of John Criswell, with two of John's brothers, Andrew and Robert, and an Elizabeth McIlwain. She moved to Iowa and in 1870 she was living with her brother James, in Shell Rock; there she was listed as having no occupation.

Serial # and Name	Birth	Marriage	Death

421000000 ERWIN

Isabel McKee McElvain :1809 Feb 27 Cumberland Co. PA:1831 Nov 30 Cumberland Co. PA:1888 Jan 6

James Bard Erwin :1810 Apr 30 Franklin PA: James Irvin & Olivia Bard :1883 Oct 20 Sewickley PA

Isabel appears in the 1850 census in the household of her parents who were living in Cumberland Co. The purpose of her being there is not known. She is found in 1880 living with her husband in Pittsburgh, PA. The spelling of the name was changed to Erwin.

1 James Bard, Jr.	*:1832 Nov 20	:1859 Jul 4	:1902 Jan 22 Zelienople PA
2 Robert McElvain	*:1834 Jan 6 Cumberland Co. PA:1863 Oct 13		:1902 Jun 4 Sewickley PA
3 John Richard	:1838 Jul 28	:	:1842 Mar 27
4 Jane Mary	*:1840 Apr 21	:	:1922 Jan 3
5 Katherine McFarland	:1842 Aug 27	:	:1916 Jul 18
6 Thomas McElvain	*:1844 Oct 12	:1869 Jan	:1910 Mar 30
7 Sarah Belle	*:1852 Jul 16	:1880 Sep 7	:1935
8 [child]	:1846 Mar 6	:	:
9 Joseph McFarland	:1847 Apr 8	:	:1863 Aug 16
a [twin 1]	:1850 Jan 1	:	:1850 Jan 2
b [twin 2]	:1850 Jan 1	:	:1850 Jan 2

421100000 ERWIN

James Bard Erwin, Jr. :1832 Nov 20 :1859 Jul 4 :1902 Jan 22 Zelienople PA

Elizabeth Deborah Grady :1832 Jun IN: David Grady & ----- ----- :1909 Jul 4

In 1880 the Erwins were living at 38 Mulberry St., Pittsburgh, PA. In 1900 they lived in Zelienople, PA with their son Charles

1 Ellen Whalley	*:1860 Apr 6	PA:1889 Mar 30	:
2 Minnie Bell	*:1862 Aug 24	PA:1890 Apr 4	:
3 Robert McElvain	:1865 Feb 5	:	:1865 Feb 5
4 Charles Shannon	*:1865 Oct 27	PA:1889 Oct 8	:
5 Henry Bard	:1868 Mar	PA:	:
6 Jane Emily	*:1871c	PA:	:
7 Elizabeth Maria	*:1873 Oct 27	PA:1893 Oct 21	:

In 1900 Harry lived with his brother Charles in Zelienople, PA.

421110000 GEISSEHEINER

Ellen Whalley Erwin	:1860 Apr 6	PA:1889 Mar 30	:
Charles Augustus	:	:	:
Geisseheiner	:	:	

421120000 PRICHARD

Minnie Bell Erwin	:1862 Aug 24	:1890 Apr 4	:
John Prichard	:	:	:

421140000 ERWIN

Charles Shannon Erwin :1865 Oct 27 :1889 Oct 8 :

Alice Wenzel :1869 Oct : :

This family lived on Newcastle Street, Zelienopole, Pennsylvania in 1900.

1 Rachel E.	:1893 Jun	PA:	:
2 Wenzel W.	:1898 Mar	PA:	

421160000 SMITH

Jane Emily Erwin	:1871c	:	:
Samuel E. Bowers	:	:	:

Serial # and Name	Birth	Marriage	Death

421170000 SMITH / BOYD

Elizabeth Maria Erwin	:1873 Oct 27	PA:1893 Oct 21	:
s John L. Smith	:1851 Feb	PA:	:
t Hiram Elmer Boyd	:	:1903 Jun 7	:

Elizabeth and John, with two children lived at 215 Christian St. in Steelton, Pennsylvania in 1900.

1 Ethel Smith	:1886 Aug	PA:	:
2 Eva Boyd	:1899 Oct	PA:	:

421200000 ERWIN

Robert McElvain Erwin	:1834 Jan 6 Cumberland Co.	PA:1863 Oct 13	:1902 Jun 4 Sewickley PA
s Ann Ecca Tracy	:1840 Mar 17 Sewickley	PA: Bruce Tracy & ----- -----	:1891 Aug 4 Seattle WA
t Martha Louise Little	:1840 Jan 5	PA:1892 Jun 20	:

Robert worked in Sewickley as a carpenter (1855-1866), a coal dealer (1866-1882), and thereafter as the owner of a livery business, which by 1889 had the most extensive stables in the city. Robert and Ann lived on Broad St, Sewickley in 1880. He was living with Louisa (Martha) in 1900 also on Broad St.

1 John Dickson	s :1865 Feb 8	:	:1865 Feb 8
2 Katherine Bruce	s*:1866 Apr 29 Sewickley	PA:1888 Oct 18 Sewickley	PA:1915 Jul 18 CA
3 Annie May	s*:1868 Dec 9 Sewickley	PA:1889 Mar 7 Sewickley	PA:1942 Dec 9 Brookville PA
4 William Kingsley	s :1870 Sep 9	:never married	:1897 Mar 29 Sewickley PA
5 Robert McElvain, Jr.	s*:1874 Jul 30	PA:1898 Jun 1 Sewickley	PA:1857 Jan 18 St.Petersburg FL
6 Walter Tracy	s :1876 Jun 5 Sewickley	PA:	:1877 Nov 3 Sewickley PA
7 Edward Eaton Brennan	s :1879 Feb 15	:never married	:1930) CA
8 June Tracy	s*:1884 Jun 12	:1903 Mar 11 Sewickley	PA:1908 May 25 Leetonia OH

421220000 WHITE

Katherine Bruce Erwin	:1866 Apr 29 Sewickley	PA:1888 Oct 18 Sewickley	PA:1915 Jul 18 CA
William H. White	:	: J. W. F. White &	:
	:	: Mary Thorn	:
1 William Harbaugh	:	:	: Seattle WA
2 Kathryn	:	:	:
3 Esther	:	:	:
4 Emma	:	:	:

421230000 CUNNINGHAM

Annie May Erwin	:1868 Dec 9 Sewickley	PA:1889 Mar 7 Sewickley	PA:1942 Dec 9 Brookville PA
Samuel Roberts Cunningham	:1867 Feb 9 Allegheny Co. PA: William Cunningham &	:1944 Jun 9 McKee's Rock PA
	:	: Eliza J. McIntosh	:

In 1900 the Cunningham's home was on Centennial Ave., Sewickley, PA

1 Annie May	*:1890 Jan 22 Sewickley	PA:1912 May 23 Lisbon	OH:1967 May 29 Sewickley PA
2 Mary Ellen	*:1891 Jul 25 Sewickley	PA:1916 Aug 8 Leetonia	OH:1964 Jan 17 Bellevue PA
3 Samuel Roberts, Jr.	*:1893 Aug 26 Sewickley	PA:	:1962 May 20 Philadelphia PA
4 Bruce Tracy	*:1894 Nov 16 Sewickley	PA:1917 Jul 28 Youngstown	OH:1929 Nov 2 Norwalk OH
5 Katherine Erwin	*:1898 Nov 30 Sewickley	PA:1920 Apr 17	:1983 Aug 18 Mineral Ridge OH
6 Sarah Lawson	*:1900 Jun 1 Sewickley	PA:1926 Sep 15 Bellevue	PA:1990 Mar 11 Brookville PA
7 June Erwin	*:1901 Nov 19 Sewickley	PA:	:1982 Dec 8 Zelianopole PA
8 George Oliver	*:1903 Jun 24 Leetonia	OH: Bellevue	PA:1967 Dec 9 Oil City PA

196

Serial # and Name	Birth	Marriage	Death

421231000 DEEMER

Annie May Cunningham	1890 Jan 22 Sewickley PA	1912 May 23 Lisbon	OH 1967 May 29 Sewickley PA
Lester Earl Deemer			1961 Dec 28 Bellevue PA

The Deemers lived at 5703 Callowhill, Pittsburgh, Pennsylvania in 1920.

1 Betty Ann			
2 Robert Ervin			

421232000 MCLAUGHLIN

Mary Ellen Cunningham	1891 Jul 25 Sewickley PA	1916 Aug 8 Leetonia	OH 1964 Jan 17 Bellevue PA
Frank Parnell McLaughlin	1891 Jul 28 Sewickley PA		1968 Jun 24 Bellevue PA

The McLaughlin family lived at 219 Laurel Ave., Bellevue, PA in 1920.

1 Frank Parnell, Jr.	1917c PA		1930c Bellevue PA
2 Eleanor Ann	1920 Jun 6 Bellevue PA		

421233000 CUNNINGHAM

Samuel Roberts	1893 Aug 26 Sewickley PA		1962 May 20 Philadelphia PA
Cunningham, Jr.			
s Dorothy Lucille Blizard			1933 Apr 18 Coraoplis PA
t Laura Yost		1937 Jun 9	
1 Dorothy Ellen	s* 1925 Dec 9	OH	
2 Mary Jane	s* 1928 Apr 12 Salem	OH	
3 Barbara Ann	s* 1930 Jan 12		
4 Lois May	t* 1944 Jul 1		

421233100 SHEPARD

Dorothy Ellen Cunningham	1925 Dec 9	OH	
----- Shepard			

421233200 CLARK

Mary Jane Cunningham	1928 Apr 12 Salem	OH	
Richard Lee Clark			
1 Richard Lee, Jr.	1949 Aug 26 Salem	OH	
2 Judith Lee	1952 Nov 7 Salem	OH	

421233300 GIBSON

Barbara Ann Cunningham	1930 Jan 12		
----- Gibson			

421233400 MCCARTNEY

Lois May Cunningham	1944 Jul 1		
James McCartney			

421234000 CUNNINGHAM

Bruce Tracy Cunningham	1894 Nov 16 Sewickley PA	1917 Jul 28 Youngstown	OH 1929 Nov 2 Norwalk OH
Gladys Marie Wake	1897c OH		1960 Oct 25

Bruce, Gladys, and Gladys May lived in Youngstown, Ohio in 1920.

1 Gladys May	* 1918	OH 1937 Mar 6	
2 Bruce Tracy	* 1920 Aug 4	1944 Mar 25	
3 June Ervin	*		

Serial # and Name	Birth	Marriage	Death
421234100 CULLEN			
Gladys May Cunningham	1918	1937 Mar 6	
Joseph F. Cullen			
1 Thomas Bruce			
2 Robert Dean			
3 Michael William			
4 Caroline			
421234200 CUNNINGHAM			
Bruce Tracy Cunningham	1920 Aug 4	1944 Mar 25	
Marjorie Ellis			
1 Miriam Ruth	1945 Feb 14		
2 Bruce Tracy, III	1947 Dec 16 Van Wert OH		
421234300 ULLMAN			
June Erwin Cunningham			
Myron Edward Ullman, Jr.	Youngstown OH		
1 Myron Edward, III	Canfield OH		
2 Carl Tracy	Canfield OH		
3 Christine Ann	Canfield OH		
4 Curtis Alan	Canfield OH		
5 Gregory Ernst	Canfield OH		
6 Gretchen	Canfield OH		
421235000 JOHNSTON			
Katherine Erwin Cunningham	1898 Nov 30 Sewickley PA	1920 Apr 17	1983 Aug 18 Mineral Ridge OH
John Raymond Johnston	1891 Aug 23 E. Liverpool OH		1938 Apr 14 Youngstown OH
Katherine and John were divorced October 24, 1924.			
1 George Oliver Cunningham*	1920 Sep 5 Leetonia OH	1948	
421235100 JOHNSTON			
George Oliver	1920 Sep 5 Leetonia OH	1948	
Cunningham Johnston			
s Helene Boulley Duparc	1924 Jul 14 Paris FR		
t Paula Etta Greenblatt	1924 Mar 22 New York NY	1981 Apr 30	

George attended Allegheny College and Harvard Business School.   From 1943 to 1946 he served as a naval
officer.   From 1946 to 1950 he was an idealistic union organizer.   He spent 1950 to 1957 in Sweden and
there earned a graduate degree from Uppsala University.   He resided in Europe (France, Switzerland,
Denmark, Sweden, England, and Belgium) as Controller and Marketing Mangager for a large corporation.   He
then worked as a fund raiser until his retirement in 1977. In his retirement he has resided in Key Largo,
FL,, spending summers on the island of Lesbos, Greece. Paula (Peggy) was married first to David Gleicher.

1 Julian Ross	s*	1949 Jun 26 Chambersburg PA	1977c
2 Bruce Erik	s*	1952 Jun 26 Uppsala SW	
421235110 JOHNSTON			
Julian Ross Johnston	1949 Jun 26 Chambersburg PA	1977c	
Susanna Francesca Maier	1949 Jul 2 Londen EN	Alan John Maier &	
		Anne Winifred Bulley	
1 Samuel Barnaby	1989 Nov 4 London EN		
2 Felix George Alan	1992 Dec London EN		

Serial # and Name	Birth	Marriage	Death

421235120 JOHNSTON

Bruce Erik Johnston	1952 Jun 26 Uppsala SW		
Linda Lee Mucke	1957 Oct 16 New Britain CT	Ernest Berthold Mucke &	
		Dorothy Mary Shiller	
1 Sophy Mabel Cunningham	1993 Mar 25 Chester CT		
2 Ian Gregory	1995 May 5 Chester CT		

421236000 MEANS

Sarah Lawson Cunningham	1900 Jun 1 Sewickley PA	1926 Sep 15 Bellevue PA	1990 Mar 11 Brookville PA
Lawrence Allen Means			
1 Sarah Katherine			
2 Thomas Allen			

421237000 BUNDY

June Erwin Cunningham	1901 Nov 19 Sewickley PA		1982 Dec 8 Zelianople PA
Raymond Bundy	1904 Jan 8 Columbiana Co. OH		1982 Sep 18 Zelianople PA
1 June Erwin	1930 Mar 13		

421238000 CUNNINGHAM

George Oliver Cunningham	1903 Jun 24 Leetonia OH		1967 Dec 9 Oil City PA
s Hilda Wright			
t Matilda Sendek			
1 George, III s			

421250000 ERWIN

Robert McElwain Erwin, Jr.	1874 Jul 30 PA	1898 Jun 1 Sewickley PA	1957 Jan 18 St.Petersburg FL
s Florence Bevington	1877 Mar OH		1951 May 23 St.Petersburg FL
t Edith Hogue		St. Petersburg FL	1968 Dec 23 St.Petersburg FL

In 1900 Robert and Florence lived on Broad St., Sewickley, PA.; in 1910 they lived in Sewickley.   There were no children by either marriage.   Robert was Pittsburgh's first painless dentist.

421280000 MCKEEFREY

June Tracy Erwin	1884 Jun 12	1903 Mar 11 Sewickley PA	1908 May 25 Leetonia OH
Neil McKeefrey			
1 Jane Erwin	1904 Apr 1		

421400000 SWAYZE / STURGES

Jane Mary Erwin	1840 Apr 21 PA	1872 Mar 3	1922 Jan 3
s Jason Clark Swayze			1877 Mar 23 Topeka KS
t Phineas M. Sturges	1816 Mar PA	1880c	1901 Jul 10 Topeka KS

Jane was a school teacher in 1870, living in Pittsburgh, PA with her parents.   In 1880 Phineas and Jane lived with the two children on Van Buren St. in Topeka, KS.   In 1900 they all still lived in Topeka; Phineas was a physician, Jane a school teacher, Horace a newspaper reporter, and Jason a druggist. In 1880 Mary A. McElwain, listed as an aunt, was also living with them.

1 Horace George Swayze	1875 Oct KS		
2 Jason Clark Swayze	1876 Dec KS		

Serial # and Name	Birth	Marriage	Death

421600000   ERWIN

Thomas McElwain Erwin	:1844 Oct 12	:1869 Jan	:1910 Mar 20
s Jennie Calhoun Neemes	:1846 Jul	:	:1879< Apr 27
t Alice L. Jenkins	:1858 Feb 19	:1880 Apr 16	:

Thomas and Alice lived in 1880 at 140 Bidwell, Allegheny, PA; and in 1900, on Thorn St., Sewickley.

1 Mary Belle	s*:1869 Sep	PA:1891 Mar 26	:
2 Lucille Wilson	s*:1871 Aug 7	:1901 Apr 16	:
3 Scott Ward	s*:1874 Mar 21	:1901 Dec 31	:
4 Frank H.	t*:1886 Nov	PA:	:
5 Clyde	t :1891 Jan	PA:	:

421610000   VENNING

Mary Belle Erwin	:1869 Sep	PA:1891 Mar 26	:
Jesse C. Venning	:1865 Nov	OH:	:

The Venning's residence in 1900 and 1910 was in Sewickley, at the earlier date on Thorn St.   In 1920 they were living at 4251 Center St., Pittsburgh, PA

1 Margaret Hamilton	*:1892 May	PA:	:
2 Jesse Neemes	:1894 Jun 5	PA:	:
3 Richard E.	:1906c	PA:	:

421611000   MCMASTER

Margaret Hamilton Venning	:1892 May	PA:	:
Robert B. McMaster, Jr.	:1892c	PA:	:

The McMasters in 1920 lived at 4251 Center St., Pittsburgh, PA in the home of the Vennings.

1 Mary E.	:1918c	PA:	:

421620000   WHITE

Lucille Wilson Erwin	:1871 Aug 7	:1901 Apr 16	:
John Wesley White	:	:	:
	:	:	:
1 John Wesley, Jr.	:1904 Dec 22	:	:

421630000   ERWIN

Scott Ward Erwin	:1874 Mar 21	:1901 Dec 31	:
Katherine Graeff	:	:	:

Scott was living with his parents in 1900.

1 Catherine Poe	:1902 Nov 22	:	:
2 Richard Bard	:1904 Mar 19	:	:

421640000   ERWIN

Frank H. Erwin	:1886 Nov	PA:	:
Kathryn -----	:1889c	PA:	:

Frank and Kathryn and their two children lived at 325 Frederick Street, Sewickley, PA in 1920.

1 William T.	:1915c	PA:	:
2 Alice	:1917c	PA:	:

421700000   MCKNIGHT

Sarah Belle Erwin	:1852	:1880 Sep 7	:1935
Levi A. McKnight	:1846 Jun 1	:	:1916 Sep 26

Sarah worked as a clerk and lived with her parents in Pittsburgh, PA in 1870.

Serial # and Name	Birth	Marriage	Death

424000000 MCELWAIN

Andrew McElwain	1820 Jan 7 Cumberland Co. PA	1844 Jan 25 Cumberland Co.PA	
s Sarah Ann McElwain	1817c		1876<
t Mary Jane Richards	1817c	PA: Andrew Richards & ----- ----	1876<

The entry for this family has been compiled from several sources.   Ordway lists a marriage for Andrew and Sarah Ann and names Robert and Anna as their children.   From the 1876 will of William Bell McElwain it is established that these two children were named McElwain, and that Sarah Ann was then deceased.   The census for 1850 lists Andrew as married to Mary, and includes Robert and Anna.   The 1860 census lists Andrew and Mary Jane, with the five children then living.   From this I have surmized that Sarah's death was before 1850, that Mary Jane Richards had recently married him, and that their first child was Agnes, born in 1852. This family has been confused in many records with that of Andrew McElwain (#4a3000000), the brother of Sarah Ann. Living with the family in 1860 was Andrew Richards, gentleman, the father of Mary Ann.

1 Robert Shannon	s*1845 Feb	PA	1903
2 Anna Belle	s*1847c	PA	
3 Thomas Challen	t 1854c	PA	1919c
4 Mary Ella	t 1856 Oct		
5 Lillie Alice	t*1859c	1879 Jan 25 Green Co. OH	
6 Agnes	t 1852		1859c

Agnes is mentioned only in DAR records.   Mary was living alone in Chambersburg, PA in 1900.

424100000 MCELWAIN

Robert Shannon McElwain	1845 Feb	PA 1869 Jan 21	1903
Alta May Lindsey	1847 Feb 24	John F. Lindsey &	
		Rachel W. Davidson	

The McElwains lived in Chambersburg, PA in 1880 and 1900, at 38 W. Queen St. in the later year.

1 Florence Woodburn	1870 Mar 22		
2 Mary Belle	1874 May 14		
3 William Thomas	1877 Dec 22		
4 Lindsey L.	1880 Apr 21		1937 Chambersburg PA

Mary was living unmarried with her parents in 1900.

424200000 RALSTON

| Anna Belle McElwain | 1847c | PA | |
| Andrew Ralston | 1844 Jan 25 | | |

Anna and Andrew had four children.

424500000 CLEMONS

| Lillie Alice McElwain | 1859c | 1879 Jan 25 Green Co.   OH | |
| John C. Clemons | | | |

425000000 WEIST

Sara Jane McElwain	1822 Jan 5 Cumberland Co. PA	1845	
Leonard Weist			
1 Catherine Jane	*1870	Cumberland Co. PA	1961
2 Mary L.	*	Cumberland Co. PA	

Serial # and Name		Birth		Marriage		Death	

425100000 MCCRAE

| Catherine Jane Weist | 1870 | Cumberland Co. PA | | 1961 | |
| William Henry McCrea | 1856 | | John McCrae & Barbara Snyder | 1931 | |

1 Sara McElwain	*1900 Jan 24 Newville	PA 1927 Nov 23	1978	Carlisle	PA
2 Barbara Snyder	1901 Jul 2	1921 May 21	
3 Elizabeth Norcross	1903 Apr 12		1986 Nov 17
4 Margaret Ballantyne	*1905 Mar 24		
5 John	*1907 Feb 25		1970 Jul 3
6 William Henry, Jr.	*1909 Jul 8		1976 Sep 1
7 Katherine Jane	*1909 Jul 8	1939 Jun 24	

425110000 CHAPMAN / JONES

Sara McElwain McCrea	1900 Jan 24 Newville	PA 1927 Nov 23	1978	Carlisle	PA
s Alfred Chapman			1962
t Joseph H. Jones			
1 Alfred McCrae <u>Chapman</u>			

425140000 OLINGER

| Margaret Ballantyne McCrea | 1905 Mar 24 | | |
| Henri Caesar Olinger | | | |

425150000 MCCRAE

| John McCrea | 1907 Feb 25 | | 1970 Jul 3 |
| Rebecca Slichter | | | |

425160000 MCCRAE

| William Henry McCrea, Jr. | 1909 Jul 8 | | 1976 Sep 1 |
| Mary Kathryn Herb | | | |

425170000 MORRIS

| Katherine Jane McCrea | 1909 Jul 8 | 1939 Jun 24 | |
| John E. Morris, Jr. | | | |

425200000 CELLAR

Mary L. Weist		Cumberland Co. PA	
Calvin M. Cellar			
1 Catherine	*		

425210000 MCCRAE

| Catherine Cellar | | | |
| William H. McCrae | | | |

Serial # and Name	Birth	Marriage	Death

426000000   MCCOY

Margaret Elinor McElwain	1825 Apr 2 Cumberland Co. PA	1845 Sep 4 Newville PA	
Daniel McCoy	1820c Cumberland Co. PA		
1 Albert Shannon	*1846 Aug 15 Newville PA	1869 Mar 9 Mechanicsburg PA	1909 Apr 5 Mechanicsburg PA
2 Mary M.	*1848 Jan 13 PA	1874c PA	1904 Mar 26 PA
3 Robert W.	1849c Cumb. Co. (?) PA		
4 Alice	1851c Cumberland Co. PA		
5 Anna	1853c Cumberland Co. PA		
6 John	1855c Cumberland Co. PA		
7 Stewart	1858c Cumberland Co. PA		

426100000   MCCOY

Albert Shannon McCoy	1846 Aug 15 Newville PA	1869 Mar 9 Mechanicsburg PA	1909 Apr 5 Mechanicsburg PA
Ezemiah Jane Ruth	1848 Sep 17 Mechanicsburg PA	William R. Ruth &	1916 Aug 3 Mechanicsburg PA
		Elizabeth Conner	

Albert's name appears also as William Albert Shannon McCoy.   He served in the Civil War as a private in Co. B, 12th Regt., Pennsylvania Volunteer Cavalry, September 20, 1864 until June 2, 1865, enlisting at Harrisburg, and being discharged at Winchester, VA.

1 Louella D.	*1871 Mar Mechanicsburg PA		1916 Aug>
2 Maurice C.	1874 Mechanicsburg PA		1890 Mechanicsburg PA
3 Bertrand S.	1875c Mechanicsburg PA		1916 Aug>
4 Harry E.	1878 Mechanicsburg PA		1921 Mechanicsburg PA
5 Raymond W.	*1880c Mechanicsburg PA		1916 Aug>
6 William Daniel	*1883 Oct 17 Mechanicsburg PA	1903c	1959 Oct 5 Pittsburgh PA
7 Carrie Bell	1888 Feb 6 Mechanicsburg PA		1919 Nov 16 Mechanicsburg PA

426110000   STICKEL

Louella D. McCoy	1871 Mar Mechanicsburg PA		1916>
Daniel Stickel	1852 Oct PA		

Louella and Daniel, with Percy and two children from Daniel's first marriage (Bruce, age 21 and Mabel, age 19), lived at 660 Boas St., Harrisburgh, PA in 1900.   In 1910 they lived in Harrisburg with all four of their children.

1 Percy L.	1899 Jun PA		
2 Mildred V.	1902c PA		
3 Edward E.	1907c PA		
4 William A.	1909c PA		

426150000   MCCOY

Raymond W. McCoy	1880c Mechanicsburg PA		1916 Aug>
Minerva Urber	1883c PA	----- Urber & Sarah E. -----	

In 1920 this family lived at 3908 Fourth Ave in an unspecified town in Blair County, PA. With them lived Minerva's mother Sarah E. Urber.

1 Margaret E.	1912c PA		
2 Rachel W.	1913c PA		

Serial # and Name	Birth	Marriage	Death

426160000 MCCOY

William Daniel McCoy	1883 Oct 17 Mechanicsburg PA	1903c	1959 Oct 5 Pittsburgh PA
Florence Catherine Kerr	1877 Nov 19 Carlisle PA	James Kerr & Rebecca Martin	1957 May 13 Pittsburgh PA

William graduated from the University of Pittsburgh and Harvard University, and was employed in education for 41 years, the last 30 of which he was a statistician for the Pittsburgh schools. He served as President of the Pennsylvania State Education Association in 1943. Florence attended a girl's finishing school in Carlisle; she taught high school mathematics during World War I.

1 William Kerr	*1904 Dec 10 Juniata PA	1924	
2 Amber Regina	*1908 June 9 Altoona PA	1927 Dec 22 Pittsburgh PA	
3 Miriam Rebecca	*1912 Apr 28 Pittsburgh PA		1986 Jan 16 Pittsburgh PA

426161000 MCCOY

William Kerr McCoy	1904 Dec 10 Juniata PA	1924	
s Anne Elizabeth Barrett	1906 Sep 30 Ligonier PA	Michael Francis Barrett &	1988 Oct 30
		Mary Jane Harrold	
t Maryellen Morton Moore	1908 Philadelphia PA	1940 Sep 7	
		Henry Moore & Ida Morton	

William earned an Electrical Engineering degree at the University of Pittsburgh. He was employed by AT&T and Gulf Oil. In 1942 he became Gulf Oil's representative for the petroleum industry as a "Dollar-a-Year Man" as Director of Facility Security (sabotage prevention) until 1945. He then returned to Gulf Oil and served as Director of Marketing Equipment for 11 years in Ohio, Texas, and Oklahoma. William and Maryellen are retired and living in LaJolla, California. Ann was a physician.

1 William Barrett	s*1931 Aug 24 Pittsburgh PA	1956 Jul 1 Pittsburgh PA	
2 Michael Moore	t*1944 May 23 Washington DC		

426161100 MCCOY

William Barrett McCoy	1931 Aug 24 Pittsburgh PA	1956 Jul 1 Pittsburgh PA	
Barbara Ruth Martin	1934 Mar 5 Brooklyn NY	Harry Martin & Sylvia Weiner	

William graduated from the University of Pittsburgh with an Electrical Engineering degree. He was employed by IBM. Barbara was a school teacher, who was from New Paltz, NY.

1 Susan Lynn	*1957 Sep 7 Poughkeepsie NY	1980 Jun 15 New Paltz NY	

426161110 FANELLI

Susan Lynn McCoy	1957 Sep 7 Poughkeepsie NY	1980 Jun 15 New Paltz NY	
Salvatore A. Fanelli	1956 Feb 25 Utica NY	Anthony R. Fanelli &	
		Marie Elizabeth King	

Susan and Salvatore both graduated from Clarkson University, she in Chemistry, he in Mechanical Engineering. Susan is an analytical chemist, working in environmental matters. She is an avid horsewoman and competes in riding competitions. Salvatore has been employed since 1982 by FN Manufacturing (a subsidiary of Fabrique Nationale, Herstal, Belgium), where he is North American Technical Sales Manager. He collects interesting and not-so-common rifles, shotguns, and pistols, shoots competitive match rifle, and is an amateur auto mechanic.

1 Staci Ann	1986 Feb 26 Columbia SC		

Staci shoots with her father, and, like her mother, rides in horse competition.

Serial # and Name	Birth	Marriage	Death

426161120   AGINS / MOORE

Michael Moore McCoy	1944 May 23 Washington DC		
s Sherman Leonard Agins	1929 Jun 19 Brooklyn NY		
		Irving Agins & Celia Saltzer	
t F. Richard Moore		1988 Sep 2 NY	

Michael has a B. S. (Mathematics) from Carnegie Institute, and an M. B. A.   Michael retains her maiden name in business. The family has moved from New York City to Rochester, New York, where Michael is employed in an advertising firm. Sherman does free lance work in advertising.

1 Bret McCoy Agins	1979 Jan 25		

426162000   SHAW

Amber Regina McCoy	1908 June 9 Altoona PA	1927 Dec 22 Pittsburgh PA	
James Albert Shaw	1904 Sep 14 Wilkinsburg PA	Albert Baker Shaw &	1979 Jan 21 Encino CA
		Florence E. Schofield	

Amber attended the University of Pittsburgh, majoring in foreign languages, and graduated from California State University--Los Angeles with a B.A. in Elementary Education.   She taught elementary school for 15 years.   After her retirement she did volunteer community service work, including teaching English to foreign students.   Jim Shaw attended West Point and the University of Pittsburgh; he was a civil engineer, and was employed by the United States Army Corps of Engineers, Alcoa, and the County of Los Angeles, from which he retired as Director of Architectural Specifications.

1 Maryamber Florence	*1929 Feb 21 Pittsburgh PA	1947	
2 Shirley Jane	*1930 Mar 1 Johnstown PA		1994 Jul 1 Encino CA
3 Ruth Ellen	1931 Dec 5 Pittsburgh PA		
4 James Albert, Jr.	1941 May 25 Pittsburgh PA		1941 May 25 Pittsburgh PA
5 Jacqueline Lee	1943 Oct 30 Pittsburgh PA		1966 Jan Los Angeles CA

Ruth graduated from UCLA and earned the M.S. from California State University--Los Angeles.   She worked as a physical education and science teacher and an administrator in the Los Angeles city school system, retiring in 1991.   She was active in badminton and softball, and was a licensed pilot of light aircraft. Jacqueline held a BA from UCLA and taught high school in Los Angeles; she was killed in a traffic accident.

426162100   REDMAN / HOPPERSTAD / VILLA

Maryamber Florence Shaw	1929 Feb 21 Pittsburgh PA	1947	
s Wallace Redman			
t Robert Donald Hopperstad	1920 Dec 1 Ridgeway IA	1951 Dec 22 Las Vegas NV	1967 Oct 16 Encino CA
		Edward Hopperstad &	
		Ella Brekke	
u Angelo Sanchez Villa		1968 Jun 22	

Maryamber has a B.A. and an M.A. from the University of California--Los Angeles.   She taught history at Los Angeles Valley College, 1966-1989, retiring as Professor of History.   Angelo's family is from old Castile, Spain. He has an A. B. and an M. A. from the University of Southern California, and a graduate degree from Harvard University.   He was Chairman of Foreign Languages, and later Dean of Academic Affairs at Los Angeles Valley College.

1 Donald Robert Hopperstad	*1953 Sep 18 Los Angeles CA	1987 Apr 25 Los Angeles CA	

Donald changed his named to Villa when his mother married Angelo Villa.

Serial # and Name	Birth	Marriage	Death

426162110 VILLA

Donald Robert Villa	1953 Sep 18 Los Angeles CA	1987 Apr 25 Los Angeles CA	
Julie Ann Passarelli	1951 Aug 1 Los Angeles CA	Francis Passerelli &	
		Carmel Gentile	

Donald is the son of Robert Hopperstad and Maryamber Shaw. He attended the University of Oregon and graduated from the University of California, Santa Barbara.   He did graduate work in Asian Studies at the University of California, Berkeley, and, while a student, he visited Nepal, to which country he later returned for two years as a member of the Peace Corps, installing village water systems. He then became a plumbing contractor in Berkeley.

1 Francesca Carmel	1990 Feb 6 Berkeley CA		

426162200 VENTO

Shirley Jane Shaw	1930 Mar 1 Johnstown PA	1950 Oct CA	1994 Jul 1 CA
Joseph Nicholas Vento	1927 Apr 25 Pittsburgh PA		1992 Feb 18 PA

After graduating from high school in Wilkinsburg, PA, Shirley completed a Medical Secretary course.   She moved to California and worked at the University of Southern California School of Medicine.   After her marriage she returned to Pennsylvania where she did volunteer work with foster children and with the police department and other agencies. She also worked with her husband in their large Pittsburgh area steak house, "The Ranch." She returned to California in 1979 and became a teaching assistant in Special Education, and attended Los Angeles Valley (community) College.

1 Joseph Albert	*1950 Sep 21 Pittsburgh PA	1972 Dec 24 Jeanette PA	
2 David Allen	*1952 Jun 11 Pittsburgh PA	1971 Aug 7	

426162210 VENTO

Joseph Albert Vento	1950 Sep 21 Pittsburgh PA	1972 Dec 24 Jeanette PA	
s Charlene Marie Carlson	1950 Nov 26 Greensburg PA	Charles C. Carlson &	
		Thelma Solberg	
t Barbara Szokoly Colella	1952 Feb 19 PA	1986 Aug 16 Jeanette PA	
1 Christi Lynn	s 1974 Oct 7 Pittsburgh PA		
2 Diane Marie	s PA		
3 Jason Szokoly			
4 Angela Szokoly			

Jason and Angela are Barbara's children from a previous marriage.

426162220 VENTO

David Allen Vento	1952 Jun 11 Pittsburgh PA	1971 Aug 7	
s Mary Catherine Hanz		Jack Hanz & Sally -----	
t Cynthia Mary Tina Ciummo	1954 Jan 7 Pittsburgh PA	1977 Pittsburgh PA	
1 David Allen, Jr.	s 1972 Feb 20 PA		
2 Matthew David	t 1983 Apr 15 Pittsburgh PA		
3 Valerie Ann	t 1986 Aug 10 Pittsburgh PA		

David, Jr. graduated from the University of California (Riverside).

426163000 BECKEMAN

Miriam Rebecca McCoy	1912 Apr 28 Pittsburgh PA	1937 Nov 24 Pittsburgh PA	1986 Jan 16 Pittsburgh PA
Eric Byrman Beckeman	1910 Feb 26 Pittsburgh PA		1981 Nov 30 Pittsburgh PA

426200000 MCCURDY

Mary M. McCoy	1848 Jan 13 PA	1874c PA	1904 Mar 26 Altoona PA
William M. McCurdy			

206

Serial # and Name	Birth	Marriage	Death

428000000 MCELWAIN

| James Shannon McElwain | 1830 Aug 2 Cumberland Co. PA | 1857 Dec 29 Newville   PA | |
| Malinda Rhoads | 1832c | PA | |

James and Malinda lived in Shell Rock, IA. in 1870 (personal property $635).

1 Robert H.	*1858 Oct	PA	
2 Charles R.	*1862c	PA	
3 Sarah	1864c	PA	
4 Lilly B.	1868c	PA	

Robert, Charles, and Sarah were attending school in 1870.

428100000 MCELWAIN

| Robert H. McElwain | 1858 Oct | PA | |
| Elizabeth ----- | 1871 Jul | IA | |

In 1900 the McElwains lived in Lake twp, Humboldt Co., IA; in 1920, at 114 S. Adams Ave., Mason City, IA

| 1 Marjorie | 1902c | IA | |

428200000 MCELWAIN

| Charles R. McElwain | 1862c | PA | |
| Lulu E. ----- | 1869 Apr | IA | |

Charles and Lula lived in Hartley twp., O'Brien Co., IA in 1900.

430000000 STEWART

| Jane McElwain | 1782 Nov 17 Cumberland Co. PA | 1807 May 29 Newville   PA | 1835 Jan 6 |
| James Stewart | | | |

1 Elizabeth	1808 Cumberland Co. PA		
2 Samuel	*1819c Cumberland Co. PA		
3 Thomas	Cumberland Co. PA		
4 Lucy	Cumberland Co. PA		
5 John	*1811c Cumberland Co. PA		
6 Eleanor	Cumberland Co. PA		
7 Andrew	Cumberland Co. PA		
8 Robert	Cumberland Co. PA		
9 Mary Jane	Cumberland Co. PA		

432000000 STEWART

| Samuel Stewart | 1819c Cumberland Co. PA | | |
| Margaretta ----- | 1825c | PA | |

Samuel and Margaretta lived in Mifflin twp. Cumberland Co., PA in 1860.   He was a farmer with real estate of $2,600 and personal property of $900.

| 1 Eliza J. | 1856c | PA | |
| 2 William McD. | 1858c | PA | |

Serial # and Name	Birth	Marriage	Death

435000000   STEWART

| John Stewart | 1811c   Cumberland Co. PA | | |
| Rebecca ----- | 1816c   PA | | |

John and Rebecca, with their nine children lived in Mifflin twp., Cumberland Co., PA in 1850 and 1860.   He was a farmer. (1860 real estate $3,780 and personal property $1000.)

1 Jane A.	1841 Apr 24 Cumberland Co. PA		
2 Susan E.	1842 Aug 7 Cumberland Co. PA		
3 John M.	1844 Aug 10 Cumberland Co. PA		
4 Mary E.	1846 May 26 Cumberland Co. PA		
5 Caroline R.	1848 Jun 11 Cumberland Co. PA		
6 Margaret L.	1849c Cumberland Co. PA		
7 Laura C.	1851c Cumberland Co. PA		
8 Clara B.	1855c Cumberland Co. PA		
9 Evaline A.	1858c Cumberland Co. PA		

450000000   MCELWAIN

| Andrew McElwain | 1785 Apr 19 Cumberland Co. PA | 1819 Apr 15 Cumberland Co.PA | 1840 Aug 21 |
| Mary McKinney | 1798 Jul 16 | | 1868 Oct 27 |

This couple had no children. Mary lived with her brother Thomas in 1850, in Newton twp., Cumberland Co., PA.

470000000   CRISWELL

Elizabeth McElwain	1789 Jul 15	1816 Jan 11 Cumberland Co. PA	1826 Dec 18
Robert Criswell			
1 Jane			
2 Elizabeth	1820c Cumberland Co. PA		
3 Robert	1822c Cumberland Co. PA		
4 John	*1823c PA		
5 Andrew McElwain	*1825c Cumberland Co. PA		

The first four children were baptised January 18, 1825 at the United Presbyterian Church, Newville. Andrew and Robert lived with John in Green twp., Franklin Co., PA in 1850.   John was a C. (coal ?) Merchant (real estate $3,500), and Robert a farmer (real estate $11,000).   Robert still lived with John in 1860 as a "gentleman" (real estate $11,000, personal property $300).

474000000   CRISWELL

| John Criswell | 1823c   PA | | |
| Susan ----- | 1834c   OH | | |

John in 1850 was a farmer (real estate $3,000) maintaining a household in Green twp., Franklin Co., PA in which lived his brothers Andrew and Robert, his cousin Liberty McElwain, Elizabeth McIlvain (age 30), and John H----, age 14. In 1860 John and Susan lived in Green twp. with his brother Andrew still a boarder.

1 Henry C.	1853c PA		
2 Julia K.	1856c PA		
3 Robert W.	1857c PA		
4 Andrew	1859c PA		

475000000   CRISWELL

| Andrew McElwain Criswell | 1825c   Cumberland Co. PA | | |
| Louisa ----- | 1832c   PA | | |

Andrew, then still a bachelor, lived with his brother John in Green twp., Franklin Co., PA in 1850.   In 1880 he and Louisa and their children lived in Guilford twp., Franklin Co., PA.

1 Robert	1869c PA		
2 Henrietta	1872c PA		
3 John R.	1874c PA		

Serial # and Name	Birth	Marriage	Death
490000000 WILSON			
Sarah McElwain	1793 Jan 29		
Andrew Wilson			
1 Cyrus			
2 Margaretta			
4a0000000 MCELWAIN			
William Bell McElwain	1794 Jul 1 Cumberland Co. PA	1816 Dec 12 Cumberland Co. PA	1874 Aug 8 Cumberland Co. PA
s Susanna Failor	1797 Mar 4 Cumberland Co. PA	Andrew Failor &	1839 May 2 Cumberland Co. PA
		Elizabeth Unangst	
t Elizabeth Carr	1809 Oct	PA 1846?	1853 May 26 Cumberland Co. PA

William and Elizabeth lived in Hopewell twp., Cumberland Co., PA in 1850. In 1860 William was living with Ellen, Elizabeth, Thomas, and Rebecca in Mifflin twp. (1860 real estate $3000, personal property $300.)

1 Sarah Ann	s* 1817c	1844 Jan 25	1876<
2 Margaret J.	s* 1819c	PA 1843 Dec 12	1876<
3 Andrew	s* 1821 Mar 22 Cumberland Co. PA		1897 Mar 4 Xenia OH
4 William Bell, Jr.	s* 1825 May 4 Cumberland Co. PA	1847 Nov 17 Springfield OH	1886 Feb 10 Knox Co. IL
5 James	s* 1827 Mar 5	PA 1853 Feb 3 Springfield OH	1901 Aug 25 Kansas City MO
6 Susan	s 1830 May 11 Newville PA		1876>
7 Mary	s* 1832c		KS
8 Ellen	s 1833 Feb 6	PA	1860 Dec 23 Cumberland Co. PA
9 Lacy Ralston	s* 1835 Apr 19 Newburg PA	1857 Dec 24 Newville PA	1893 Mar 12 Johnson Co. KS
a Elizabeth A.	s* 1839	PA	
b Robert Henderson	t* 1847 May 31 Cumberland Co. PA	1877 Apr 11 Pleasant Grove KS	1904 Jun 20 Rice Co. KS
c Thomas Simpson	t* 1849 Jan 26 Cumberland Co. PA	1878 Jul 11 Chambersburg PA	1909 Dec 23 Crawford Co. KS
d Rebecca A.	t* 1851 Mar 7 Allegheny City PA	1879 Sep 25 Butler Co. KS	1912 Oct 28 Randolph Co. MO
e Eliza	t		

Sarah is shown in some records as the wife of Andrew McElwain (#424000000); see remarks in the entry for Andrew on page 200. Ellen was living in Cumberland Co., PA in the home of John Shulenbarger in 1850. Susan was a domestic in the home of Jacob Coover in 1860.

4a2000000 ZELLERS			
Margaret J. McElwain	1818c	1843 Dec 12	1876<
John Zellers	1819c		
1 Daniel F.			
2 John W.			
3 James A.			
4 Mary F.	*		
4a2400000 FREEBURG			
Mary F. Zellers			
----- Freeburg			

Serial # and Name	Birth	Marriage	Death

4a3000000   MCELWAIN

Andrew McElwain	1821 Mar 22 Cumberland Co. PA		1897 Mar 4 Xenia OH
s Mary -----			
t Catherine Dorey Bower	1828	MD 1852 Aug 17 Greene Co. OH	1892

In 1860 this family lived in Xenia, Greene County, OH.   Andrew owned real estate of $1200, and personal property of $800. They lived in Greene County in 1880. Andrew was a carpenter.

1 Mary E.	s 1846c	OH	
2 Andrew	t* 1855c	OH	
3 Dennis	t* 1857 Mar	OH	
4 Alice	t 1859	OH	
5 Laverna Kate	t* 1862 Apr	OH 1884	OH
6 Laura B.	t 1864 Sep	OH	
7 Etta G.	t 1868 May	OH	

Laura and Etta were living together at 109 E. Church St., Xenia, OH in 1900. In 1920 Etta was living with Frank and Laverna Wolf.

4a3200000   MCELWAIN

Andrew McElwain	1855c	OH	
Elizabeth -----	1860 May	OH	

The McElwain family lived at 713 W. Maine, Xenia, OH in 1900.

1 Frank	1883 May	OH	
2 Gertrude	1885 Feb	OH	
3 Andrew	1889 Dec	OH	
4 Ruth	1892 Sep	OH	

Frank lived in 1910 in the household of James Parker in Morral, OH.

4a3300000   MCELWAIN

Dennis McElwain	1857 Mar	OH	
Rosetta Beal	1861 Apr	OH ----- Beal & Amanda -----	

Dennis lived with his parents in 1880 and worked as a carpenter.   In 1900 the family lived in Cedarville, Greene County, OH. In 1910 Dennis, Rosetta, and Burton lived in Greene County, OH.

1 Fred B.	* 1883 Sep	OH	
2 Burton D.	* 1893 May	OH	

4a3310000   MCELWAIN

Fred B. McElwain	1883 Sep	OH	
Ethel -----	1883c	OH	

This family resided in Washington Court House, OH in 1910.

1 Eugene	1909	OH	

4a3320000   MCELWAIN

Burton D. McElwain	1893 May	OH	
Edna L. -----	1896c	OH	

This family lived on Hopping Road, Cedarville Village, Greene Co., OH in 1920.

1 Eleanor J.	1919	OH	

Serial # and Name	¦ Birth	¦ Marriage	¦ Death

4a3500000 WOLF

| Laverna Kate McElwain | ¦1862 Apr | OH¦1884 | OH¦ |
| Frank Wolf | ¦1858 Jul | OH¦ | ¦ |

The Wolf family lived in Xenia, OH in 1900, 1910, and 1920. In 1920 their address was 103 Chestnut St.

1 Margaret	*¦1884 Nov	OH¦	¦
2 Charles Raymond	*¦1886 Aug	OH¦	¦
3 Frank A.	*¦1890 Jun	OH¦	¦
4 Laura K.	¦1892 Oct	OH¦	¦
5 Laverna Louise	¦1895 Feb	OH¦	¦

4a3510000 MCCALMONT

| Margaret Wolf | ¦1884 Nov | OH¦ | ¦ |
| ----- McCalmont | ¦ | ¦ | ¦ |

4a3520000 WOLF

| Charles Raymond Wolf | ¦1886 Aug | OH¦ | ¦ |
| Bessie ----- | ¦1894c | OH¦ | ¦ |

Charles was listed as Raymond in the 1920 census. He and his family then lived in Greene Co., OH.

| 1 William | ¦1916c | OH¦ | ¦ |
| 2 Catherine | ¦1917c | OH¦ | ¦ |

4a3530000 WOLF

| Frank A. Wolf | ¦1890 Jun | OH¦ | ¦ |
| Helen S. ----- | ¦1898c | OH¦ | ¦ |

Frank and Helen, with their two children, lived in Greene County, OH in 1920.

| 1 Frank J. | ¦1917c | OH¦ | ¦ |
| 2 Robert E. | ¦1918c | OH¦ | ¦ |

4a4000000 MCELWAIN

William Bell McElwain Jr.	¦1825 May 4 Cumberland Co. PA¦1847 Nov 17 Springfield	OH¦1886 Feb 10 Knox Co.	IL
Mary Jane Mapps	¦1829 Aug 20 Cumberland Co. PA¦ John Mapps &	¦1908 Apr 14 York	NE
	¦	¦ Elizabeth Highland	¦

William volunteered for service in the Union Army in August, 1862.   The privations of military life seriously undermined his health, which was never very good afterward.

1 Edward Harrison	*¦1855 Feb 6 Springfield	OH¦1879 Sep 25 Knox Co.	IL¦1926 Feb 21 Galesburg	IL
2 William Wright	¦1857 Dec 18	IL¦	¦1860 May 20 i. Knox Co. IL
3 Nancy Owen	*¦1859 Apr 30	IL¦1882 Mar 23 Knox Co.	IL¦1923 Nov 3 Denver	CO
4 John Wilson	¦1861 Aug 6	IL¦	¦1875 Dec 3	IL
5 William Henry	*¦1863 May 9 Appleton	IL¦1887 Aug 30 Appleton	IL¦1940 Mar 30 Denver	CO
6 Mary Jane	¦1866 Apr 15	IL¦	¦1873 May 2
7 Albert Barnes	¦1871 May 27	IL¦	¦1872 Mar 2 i. nr. Gilson IL

4a4100000 MCELWAIN

| Edward Harrison McElwain | ¦1855 Feb 6 Springfield | OH¦1879 Sep 25 Knox Co. | IL¦1926 Feb 21 Galesburg | IL |
| Laura Belle Lacey | ¦1859 Dec 21 | ¦ | ¦1933 Nov 15 |

Edward and Laura lived at 327 E. Main St, Knoxville, IL in 1920.

| 1 Jennie | ¦1880 Oct 3 Knox Co. | IL¦never married | ¦1945 Oct 14 Knoxville | IL |
| 2 Ortie Lacy | *¦1885 Nov 23 Knox Co. | IL¦1916 Oct 11 Abingdon | IL¦1952 Mar 6 Knox Co. | IL |

Jennie had a Master's degree from the University of Illinois, and attended summer school at Columbia University.

211

Serial # and Name	Birth	Marriage	Death
4a4120000 MCELWAIN			
Ortie Lacy McElwain	:1885 Nov 23 Knox Co.	IL:1916 Oct 11 Abingdon	IL:1952 Mar 6 Knox Co. IL
Lilly Irene Walker	:1896 May 10	: Harry Hampton Walker &	:1989 Dec 7 Abingdon IL
	:	: Edith Minor	:
1 Keith Edward	*:1919 Oct 2 Abingdon	IL:1940 Jun 15 Knoxville IL:	
2 Helen Edith	*:1921 Dec 15 Knox Co.	IL:1945 Nov 24 Knox Co. IL:	
3 Jeannette Viola	:1926 Dec 31	:never married	:1943 May 24
4 Laura June	*:1931 Jun 5 Knox Co.	IL:1952 Jun 12 Knox Co. IL:	
4a4121000 MCELWAIN			
Keith Edward McElwain	:1919 Oct 2 Abingdon	IL:1940 Jun 15 Knoxville IL:	
Inez Marie Johnson	:1916 Oct 12 Knox Co.	IL: David Johnson &	:
	:	: Nellie Nelson	:
1 Margaret Ann	*:1943 Dec 4 Galesburg	IL:1968 Dec 29 Abingdon IL:	
2 John Edward	*:1946 Sep 6 Galesburg	IL:1966 Galesburg IL:	
3 Edith Irene	*:1950 Dec 18 Galesburg	IL:1967 Galesburg IL:	
4a4121100 WILSON			
Margaret Ann McElwain	:1943 Dec 4 Galesburg	IL:1968 Dec 29 Abingdon IL:	
Charles Wilson (Dr.)	:1944 Dec 29 Harve de Grace MD: Thomas Wilson &	:	
	:	: Dorothy Jean Adams	:
1 Julie Marie	:1973 Mar 1 Salt Lake City UT:		
2 Morgan Lee	:1975 Jun 17 Salt Lake City UT:		
4a4121200 MCELWAIN			
John Edward McElwain	:1946 Sep 6 Galesburg	IL:1966 Galesburg IL:	
s Sherry Holtz	:1947 May 26	:	:
t Judith Mary Glowacki	:1947 Jan 11 Peoria	IL:1976 Oct 22 Toulon IL:	
	:	: Henry Glowaki &	:
	:	: Laverna Dunphy	:
1 Adam Keith	t :1979 Dec 24 Peoria	IL:	:
2 Eric Henry	t :1981 Sep 24 Peoria	IL:	:
4a4121300 WILLIAMS / HARRISON			
Edith Irene McElwain	:1950 Dec 18 Galesburg	IL:1967 Galesburg IL:	
s Lyle Williams	:1948 Feb 16	:	:
t Rodger Paul Harrison	:1944 Mar 4 Salt Lake City	UT:1975 Sep 21 Salt Lake City UT:	
	:	: Ross Steele Harrison &	:
	:	: Hanna Elizabeth Mueller	:
1 Jill Marie Harrison	:1979 Oct 17 New Albany	IN:	:
2 Paul Edward Harrison	:1984 Jun 20 Annapolis	MD:	:
4a4122000 CLARK			
Helen Edith McElwain	:1921 Dec 15 Knox Co.	IL:1945 Nov 24 Knox Co. IL:	
Howard Raymond Clark	:1919 Sep 9 Clinton	IL: Emory R. Clark &	:
	:	: Esther Artie Randle	:
1 Steven Lee	:1947 Jan 12 Canton	IL:	:
2 James Allen	*:1948 Nov 13 Canton	IL:	:
3 Neil Kent	*:1953 Mar 14 Canton	IL:1975 Dec 30 Deerfield Bch. FL:	

212

Serial # and Name	Birth	Marriage	Death
4a4122200 CLARK			
James Allen Clark	1948 Nov 13 Canton IL		
(single parent)			
1 Greyser James	1987 Nov 14 Peru, So. America		
Greyser was adopted in 1990.			
4a4122300 CLARK			
Neil Kent Clark	1953 Mar 14 Canton IL	1975 Dec 30 Deerfield Bch. FL	
Karen Dawn Strock	1955 Apr 28 Key West FL	Arthur V. Strock &	
		Frances Eaton	
1 Elliott Neal	1984 Mar 8 Newberry SC		
4a4124000 CANSLER			
Laura June McElwain	1931 Jun 5 Knox Co. IL	1952 Jun 12 Knox Co. IL	
Loman D. Cansler	1924 Sep 6 Dallas Co. MO	Pruitt Herschell Cansler &	
		Nettie Opal Broyles	
1 Philip Trent	*1953 Nov 3 Kansas City MO	1975	
2 Joel Ethan	*1954 Nov 19 Kansas City MO	1977 Jan 1 Jefferson City MO	
3 Myra Annette	*1956 Aug 21 Kansas City MO	1981 Mar 18 Copenhagen DN	
4a4124100 CANSLER			
Philip Trent Cansler	1953 Nov 3 Kansas City MO	1975	
Jeaninne Ann Zielke	1954 Jul 29 Wichita KS	Donald Dean Zielke &	
		Doris Ann Jones	
4a4124200 CANSLER			
Joel Ethan Cansler	1954 Nov 19 Kansas City MO	1977 Jan 1 Jefferson City MO	
Debra Sue Bell	1954 Dec 12 Jefferson City MO	Virdie David Bell &	
		Gladys Elizabeth Adams	
1 Grant Carlton	1980 Mar 10 Kansas City MO		
2 Amber Corcelles	1982 Dec 10 Kansas City MO		
4a4124300 KIPP			
Myra Annette Cansler	1956 Aug 21 Kansas City MO	1981 Mar 18 Copenhagen DN	
Bruce Eric Kipp	1950 Nov 29 Detroit MI	Robert Kipp & Marian Geiga	
Robert Kipp's birth name was Robert Kelley.			
1 Erin Leigh Kipp	1976 Apr 18		
2 Mackenzie Devon Cansler-Kipp	1983 Jun 2 Manhattan KS		
3 Zachary Adam Cansler-Kipp	1990 Jan 18 Garmisch GR		

Erin is Bruce's daughter by his first marriage.

Serial # and Name	Birth	Marriage	Death

4a4300000   CORBIN

Nancy Owen McElwain	:1859 Apr 30	IL:1882 Mar 23 Knox Co.	IL:1923 Nov 3 Denver	CO
Benjamin Corbin	:1859 Feb	OH:	:1904 Joplin	MO

In 1900 the Corbin family lived in Melford twp., Barton County, MO.   In 1920 Nancy was living with the family of her daughter Mary.

1 Laverna	:1883 Jul	IL:	:
2 George E.	:1885 Jun	IL:	:
3 Ora B.	:1887 Feb	KS:	:
4 Mary E.	*:1890 Mar	KS:	:
5 Eva L.	:1891 Oct	KS:	:
6 Nellie F.	:1896 Jan	KS:	:
7 Ralph H.	:1897 Oct	KS:	:

4a4340000   MATTHEIS

Mary E. Corbin	:1890 Mar	KS:	:
Edward P. Mettheis	:1888c	MO:	:

The Mattheis family lived at 1016 Champa Street, Denver, Colorado in 1920.

1 Nadene	:1917c	CO:	:
2 Arvid	:1919c	CO:	:

4a4500000   MCELWAIN

William Henry McElwain	:1863 May 9 Appleton	IL:1887 Aug 30 Appleton	IL:1940 Mar 30 Denver	CO
Ella Nora Burkholder	:1870 May 15 Newburg	PA: William Henry Burkholder &	:1942 Mar 7 Denver	CO
	:	: Mary Elizabeth Ramp	:	

William was a rancher.   He owned until 1916 the North Park Ranch in Colorado.   After a search for a new ranch over much of the western United States, he bought the 15,000 acre Churn Ranch in Cherry County, Nebraska. Because rail cars were not obtainable, he and his sons drove a large herd of cattle 160 miles to the new ranch, through North Platte, across the North Platte River, to Tryon, Mullen and, finally, to the ranch. William had planned to have his son Harley take over the ranching operations, but Harley's death in the Battle of St. Mihiel caused him gradually to lose interest in ranching, and, in 1934 he sold the Churn Ranch to Chris Abbott, who developed the Abbott Land and Cattle Co. into one of the largest operations in the region.   A description of the cattle drive, written by Wren (William Wren) as a memorial to Harley, is printed in William Ordway's work *The House of Grimet.*

1 Otto Galen	*:1888 Aug 27 Appleton	IL:1911 May 24 York NE	:1943 Jul 19 Welby	CO
2 Lloyd Delford	*:1891 Apr 8 Appleton	IL:1913 Jul 21	:1976 Feb 14	
3 Percy	*:1893 Apr 11 Appleton	IL:1917 Jul 17 Golden	CO:1983 May 13 Arvada	CO
4 Harley	:1895 Aug 14 Appleton	IL:	:1918 Sep 12 St. Mihiel	FR
5 Winifred Frances	*:1897 Aug 30 Appleton	IL:1921 Jul 16 Denver	CO:1979 Nov 5 Lincoln	NE
6 William Wren	*:1899 Dec 5 Appleton	IL:1922 Oct Fullerton	NE:1987 Mar 9 Denver	CO
7 Mark	*:1906 Jun 8 York	NE:	:1989 Oct Brighton	CO
8 Mabel	:1906 Jun 8 York	NE:	:1952 Oct 12 Wheatridge	CO

Harley registered for the World War I draft while working on a cattle drive to move the family herd from Colorado to Nebraska.   He entered the army, was trained at Ft. Riley, KS, and served in the 89th Division, 355th Regiment. He was killed September 12, 1918 in the battle of St. Mihiel.

4a4510000   MCELWAIN

Otto Galen McElwain	:1888 Aug 27 Appleton	IL:1911 May 24 York	NE:1943 Jul 19 Welby	CO
Cleo Shipley	:1891 Dec 13 York	NE: F. T. J. Shipley &	:1983 May 26 Denver	CO
	:	: ------ -----	:	

1 Lilly	:1912 Apr 7 Central City	NE:	:1912 Apr 7 Central City	NE
2 Katherine Ella	*:1914 Sep 4 Central City	NE:1931 Dec 16	:1988 May 14 Denver	CO
3 Mabel Janice	*:1918 Apr 7 Central City	NE:1937 Dec 16 Denver	CO:	
4 Gale K.	:1926 Oct 7 Denver	CO:	:1929 Feb 3 Wheatridge	CO

Serial # and Name	Birth	Marriage	Death
4a4512000 MATTINGLY			
Katherine Ella McElwain	1914 Sep 4 Central City NE	1931 Dec 16	1988 May 14 Denver CO
Joseph A. Mattingly			
1 Richard	1932 Aug 3		
2 Galen Wayne	*1934 Nov 22		
3 Evelyn Mae	*1936 May 22		
4 Nancy Belle	*1938 May 17		
5 Lawrence Logan	*1941 May 19		
6 Cleo Marie	*1943 Jun 9	1959	
7 Leonard LaDean	*1944 Oct 5		
4a4512200 MATTINGLY			
Galen Wayne Mattingly	1934 Nov 22		
Myrna Ann Dunn			
1 Kenneth Wayne	1959 Sep 14		
2 Scott Allen	1960 Sep 24		
3 Robert James	1964 Aug 4		
4 Patrick Galen	1969 Jan 12		
4a4512300 JONES			
Evelyn Mae Mattingly	1936 May 22		
Harold Joseph Jones			
1 Russell Lee	1959 Aug 24		
2 Gail Laureen	1963 Mar 14		
3 Sharon LeAnn	1965 Sep 20		
4 Connie Lynn	1967 Apr 17		
4a4512400 PACHELLO			
Nancy Belle Mattingly	1938 May 17		
Donald Michael Pachello			
1 Terri Marie	1961 Dec 28		
2 Jerry Joseph	1963 Sep 11		
3 Greg James	1968 Jun 14		
4a4512500 MATTINGLY			
Lawrence Logan Mattingly	1941 May 19		
s Shannon Elaine Reed			
t Helen -----			
1 Tawnya Rae	s 1966 Mar 17		
2 Joseph Michael	t 19xx Nov 25		

Serial # and Name	Birth	Marriage	Death
4a4512600 NORDSTROM			
Cleo Marie Mattingly	1943 Jun 9	1959	
Carl Andrew Nordstrom			
1 Clinton Andrew	1961 Jun 25		
2 Chris Alden	1965 May 28		
3 Curt Allen	1968 Aug 22		
4 Cally Arlen	1971 Jul 4		
4a4512700 MATTINGLY			
Leonard LaDean Mattingly	1944 Oct 5		
s Donna Jean -----			
t Terri -----			
1 Douglas Lee s			
2 Kir-Lee t			
4a4513000 KNOPF			
Mabel Janice McElwain	1918 Apr 7 Central City NE	1937 Dec 16 Denver CO	
Edward Knopf			
1 Cheryl Lyn	*1946 Nov 1 Denver CO		
4a4513100 DAVIS			
Cheryl Lyn Knopf	1946 Nov 1 Denver CO		
Leslie Ray Davis		Leslie Davis & Cheryl -----	
1 Timothy Ray	1971 Feb 22 Denver CO		
4a4520000 MCELWAIN			
Lloyd Delford McElwain	1891 Apr 8 Appleton IL	1913 Jul 21	1976 Feb 14
Josephine Pauline Thordell	1892 Jun 16 Grand Island NE		1933 Denver CO
1 Vernelle C.	*1920 Jul 1 Kansas City MO	1941 Oct 19	
4a4521000 CARPENTER			
Vernelle C. McElwain	1920 Jul 1 Kansas City MO	1941 Oct 19	
Noel V. Carpenter	1916 Jan 5 Albia IA	Clyde Earl Carpenter &	
		Nora Marie Thomas	
1 Michael Alan	*1946 May 9 Denver CO		
2 Gary Lee	*1950 Apr 22 Denver CO		
4a4521100 CARPENTER			
Michael Alan Carpenter	1946 May 9 Denver CO		
Kathy McCumber		Max McCumber &	
		Bernadine -----	
1 Michaela Katharine	1972 Feb 13 Denver CO		
2 Chandra	1974 Nov 8 Denver CO		
3 Micah Vincent	1977 Nov 17 Denver CO		

Serial # and Name	Birth	Marriage	Death

4a4521200 CARPENTER

Gary Lee Carpenter	1950 Apr 22 Denver	CO	
Michelle Marie Hughes		Michael J. Hughes &	
		Lois -----	
1 Gary Noel	1981 Oct 18		

4a4530000 MCELWAIN

Percy McElwain	1893 Apr 11 Appleton	IL 1917 Jul 17 Golden	CO 1983 May 13 Arvada CO
Marie Frances McReynolds	1894 Nov 3 Saybrook	IL John Rumsey Means &	1985 May 12 Arvada CO
		Florence C. Lewis	

Marie was born to John & Florence Means. After her mother's death, when Marie was 3 1/2, she was adopted
by William E. McReynolds and Sarah Stranger, and her name was changed to Marie Frances McReynolds.

1 Eileen Ruth	* 1918 Jul 1 Merriman	NE 1941 Jun 6	
2 Lucille Eunice	* 1922 Jun 19 Central City	NE 1942 Jul 3 Broomfield CO	
3 Doris Anne	* 1929 Jan 31 Archer	NE 1949 Apr 10 Morgan CO	
4 Marva Lee	* 1934 May 31 Archer	NE 1953 Aug 24	

4a4531000 ETHERIDGE

Eileen Ruth McElwain	1918 Jul 1 Merriman	NE 1941 Jun 6	
Ellis F. Etheridge	1920 Jul 30		
1 David Ellis	* 1942 Sep 11 Denver	CO 1964 Aug Denver CO	
2 Janet Lynn	* 1947 Feb 2 Tacoma	CO	
3 Ross Lane	1951 Sep 17 Denver	CO	1951 Sep 17 Denver CO

4a4531100 ETHERIDGE

David Ellis Etheridge	1942 Sep 11 Denver	CO 1964 Aug Denver CO	
Cheryl Wolf	1943 Feb 22 Denver	CO Wendell Wolf & CO	
		Wilma Hopkins	
1 Scott David	1968 Nov 9 Potsdam	NY	
2 Suzanna Lynn	1970 Oct 23 Potsdam	NY	

4a4531200 JORDAN / ----- / DILLON

Janet Lynn Etheridge	1947 Feb 2 Denver	CO	
s Larry Jordan	Denver	CO	
t ----- -----			
u Harry Dillon	Puyallup	WA	
1 Janet Lynn <u>Dillon</u>	1984 Nov 10 Tacoma	WA	

4a4532000 TYLER

Lucille Eunice McElwain	1922 Jun 19 Central City	NE 1942 Jul 3 Broomfield CO	
Donald Wayne Tyler	1921 Nov 9 Central City	NE Leslie Lloyd Tyler &	
		Jessie May Hanks	

Donald was a lieutenant in the Air Force in World War II; he flew forty-two missions in B-24 bombers. On
his second mission, because the plane was overloaded with bombs, the fuel supply was almost exhausted when
they reach the target. By dropping everything possible into the Pacific Ocean, the crew was able to return
to their base, landing just as one of the engines quit from lack of fuel. All of the crew survived not
only this mission, but the war as well.

1 Kathleen Marie	* 1946 May 22 Denver	CO 1966 Apr 10 Central City NE	
2 Daniel Elwain	* 1949 Jan 31 Central City	NE 1971 Jun 26 Central City NE	
3 Brian Wayne	* 1954 Feb 23 Central City	NE 1975 Jan 4 La Jolla CA	
4 Joyce Elaine	1958 Feb 4 Central City	NE	1958 Feb 5 Central City NE

Serial # and Name	Birth	Marriage	Death

4a4532100   TROTTER

Kathleen Marie Tyler	1946 May 22 Denver CO	1966 Apr 10 Central City NE	
Richard Donald Trotter	1932 Jun 9 Fullerton NE	Dean Trotter &	1992 Jul 28
		Ethel Masters	

Kathleen attended Wesleyan University and the University of Nebraska, graduating in 1968.   She was appointed manager of Storm Mountain Retreat in the Black Hills, and later became Executive Director of Camps and Conferences of the United Methodist Church of South Dakota, replacing her husband.   Richard was an ordained minister, and held a Ph. D. in counselling.   He became head minister of Canyon Lake United Methodist Church in Rapid City, SD.   He was President of the Board of Education of Rapid City when, in 1980, he suffered a heart attack.   Kathleen became director of the Collins Retreat Center near Portland, OR, and later head of the camping program of the Northern Indiana Conference of the Methodist Church in Marion, IN. Richard later served as regional director of the AYUSA (A Year in the USA) student exchange program, preached on an interim basis, conducted divorce seminars, and was active in community theater.

1 Terri Marie	1968 Mar 7 Seward NE		
2 Nancy Lee	1970 Feb 20 Scottsbluff NE		
3 Laurel Lynn	1971 Sep 28 Miller SD		

In 1987 Terri was a student at Northwestern University.

4a4532200   TYLER

Daniel Elwain Tyler	1949 Jan 31 Central City NE	1971 Jun 26 Central City NE	
Vickie Barbara Moody	1948 Oct 12 Sydney AU	Louis Moody &	
		Constance Barham	

Daniel enlisted in the United States Army in late 1968, qualified as a helicopter pilot and was appointed a Warrant Officer on January 25, 1970. He was assigned to the First Cavalry Division in Vietnam. His unit led the assault into Cambodia and he saw action frequently in the next few months. He received the Distinguished Flying Cross, the Bronze Star with Oak Leaf Cluster, forty awards of the Air Medal, the Army Commendation Medal with Oak Leaf Cluster, and the Purple Heart.   He was appointed Aircraft Commander of UH-1H "Huey" helicopters, and commissioned a Second Lieutenant during his tour in Vietnam.   After his release from active duty, he and his wife moved to Australia where he took a law degree.

1 Michael Wayne	1975 Sep 10 Sydney AU		
2 Brett Daniel	1977 Apr 19 Sydney AU		
3 Karli Lee	1979 May 9 Sydney AU		

4a4532300   TYLER

Brian Wayne Tyler	1954 Feb 23 Central City NE	1975 Jan 4 La Jolla CA	
Sharon Grace Hackett	1954 Jul 14 San Diego CA	Donal Hackett & Merrie -----	

Brian and Sharon graduated from Westminster College in 1976.   Brian taught Aviation Science at his alma mater for two years while Sharon earned a Master's Degree in Special Education.   She has taught handicapped children in Utah and North Hollywood, CA. In 1991 Brian was a DC 10 co-pilot for United Airlines.

1 Nathan Brian	1984 Sep 13 Pasadena CA		
2 Jennifer Lynn	1989 Oct 5 Sylmar CA		
3 Philip Wayne	1991 Oct 23 Pasadena CA		

4a4533000   SOUTHWORTH

Doris Anne McElwain	1929 Jan 31 Archer NE	1949 Apr 10 Morgan CO	
Dean LaVerne Southworth	1923 Mar 13 Danbury NE	Elijah Southworth &	
		Thelma Puelz	
1 Linda Loree	*1951 Apr 15 Denver CO	1973 Sep 8 Wheatridge CO	
2 Duane LaVerne	*1952 Aug 19 Denver CO	1971 Nov 12 Greeley CO	
3 Donna Leanne	*1962 Aug 17 Denver CO	1984 Aug 4 Arvada CO	

218

Serial # and Name	Birth	Marriage	Death
4a4533100 KAUFMANN			
Linda Loree Southworth	1951 Apr 15 Denver	CO 1973 Sep 8 Wheatridge CO	
Marc Allen Kaufmann	1945 Aug 12 Denver	CO Benjamin Kaufmann &	
		Leone Diner	
1 Michael Benjamin	1981 Nov 5 Denver	CO	
2 Timothy	1987 Sep 22 Denver	CO	
4a4533200 SOUTHWORTH			
Duane LaVerne Southworth	1952 Aug 19 Denver	CO 1971 Nov 12 Greeley CO	
s Diane Elizabeth Marshall	1955 Apr 5	Robert Marshall &	
		Elizabeth Weist	
t Dorothy Dalene Groves	1957 Apr 27	1986 Apr 7 Hulett NY	
		Glenn Groves & Frances Shaw	
1 Jessica Elizabeth s	1973 May 17 Englewood	CO	
2 Joy Melissa s	1978 May 23 Laramie	WY	
3 Julia Ann s	1980 Jan 23 Sheridan	WY	
4 Terry John t	1987 Mar 14 Gillette	WY	
5 Dean t	1990 Jul 24 Gillette	WY	
4a4533300 BELL			
Donna Leanne Southworth	1962 Aug 17 Denver	CO 1984 Aug 4 Arvada CO	
David Patrick Bell	1960 Oct 15 Denver	CO	
1 Nicole Marie	1989 Nov 1 Denver	CO	
4a4534000 MAY			
Marva Lee McElwain	1934 May 31 Archer	NE 1953 Aug 24	
Donald Boyd May	1931 Feb 17 Ft. Collins	CO Boyd May & Violet Steiner	
1 Laurinda Lea *	1956 May 19 Denver	CO 1977 Mar 26 Eastlake CO	
2 Carolyn Jean *	1957 Nov 26 Denver	CO 1981 Dec 19 Eastlake CO	
3 Gregory Donald	1959 Jul 29 Denver	CO	
4 Douglas	1961 Jan 1 Denver	CO	
4a4534100 FONAY			
Laurinda Lea May	1956 May 19 Denver	CO 1977 Mar 26 Eastlake CO	
Gary William Fonay	1954 Oct 15 Denver	CO Milton William Fonay &	
		----- -----	
1 Kyle William	1981 Jul 6 Hobbs	NM	
2 Shelley Jean	1985 Sep 14 Hobbs	NM	
4a4534200 CARDINELLI / BROWN			
Carolyn Jean May	1957 Nov 26 Denver	CO 1981 Dec 19 Eastlake CO	
s Donald Anthony Cardinelli	1955 Jul 3 Salida	CO Angelo Cardenelli &	
		Donna Sniff	
t Terry Joe Brown	1952 Jun 9 Liberal	KS 1988 Aug 27 Liberal KS	
		Joseph Brown & Dorothy Fraim	
1 Thomas Anthony Cardinelli	1984 May 5 Lamar	CO	
2 Courtney Marie Brown	1989 Aug 20 Liberal	KS	

Serial # and Name	Birth	Marriage	Death

4a4550000 HENDERSON

Winifred Frances McElwain	1897 Aug 30 Appleton	IL	1921 Jul 16 Denver	CO	1979 Nov 5 Lincoln	NE
Clyde Patterson Henderson	1898 Apr 29 Buena Vista	PA	Henry Ebenezer Henderson &		1984 Jan 17 Lincoln	NE
			Nan Eliza Rankin		
1 Robert Edward	*1922 May 18 Loveland	CO	1944 Jul 16 Ann Arbor	MI	
2 Lois Arlene	1925 Nov 20 Denver	CO		
3 Cynthia Jane	*1934 Dec 10 Lincoln	NE	1956 Jun 8 Lincoln	NE	

4a4551000 HENDERSON

Robert Edward Henderson	1922 May 18 Loveland	CO	1944 Jul 16 Ann Arbor	MI	
Marilouise Miles	1923 Aug 30 Lincoln	NE	Clarence G. Miles &	
			Elsie C. Zics	
1 Jo Anne	*1945 Jan 18 Ann Arbor	MI	1966 Sep 10 Lincoln	NE	
2 Miles Rankin	*1949 Jul 17 Lincoln	NE	1980 Jul 27 Jacksonville	FL	
3 Nancy Elizabeth	*1951 Aug 13 Lincoln	NE	1977 Oct 24 Miami	FL	
4 Mary Adele	1955 Jan 15 Lincoln	NE		

4a4551100 EINSPAHR

Jo Anne Henderson	1945 Jan 18 Ann Arbor	MI	1966 Sep 10 Lincoln	NE	
Ronald Kent Einspahr	1942 Jun 7 Imperial	NE		
1 Matthew Warren	1969 Jul 21 Omaha	NE		
2 Clayton Gregory	1971 Jul 9 Brookings	SD		

4a4551200 HENDERSON

Miles Rankin Henderson	1949 Jul 17 Lincoln	NE	1980 Jul 27 Jacksonville	FL	
Patricia Ann Garrett	1956 Apr 13 LaGrange	KY	John T. Garrett &	
			Irena Sinlock	
1 Garrett Robert	1988 Sep 4 Minneapolis	MN		
2 Blake	1990 Oct 7 Louisville	KY		

4a4551300 CASKEY

Nancy Elizabeth Henderson	1951 Aug 13 Lincoln	NE	1977 Oct 24 Miami	FL	
Wayne Joseph Caskey	1952 Apr 6 Madison	NJ	Lott Ellsworth Caskey &	
			Angela La Porta	
1 Lott Edward	1979 Nov 20 Miami	FL		
2 Elizabeth Lauren	1985 Jun 6 Orlando	FL		

4a4553000 BURT / KUESPERT

Cynthia Jane Henderson	1934 Dec 10 Lincoln	NE	1956 Jun 8 Lincoln	NE	
s Warren Brooker Burt	1934 May 16 New York	NY	Conamore V. Burt (Dr.) &	
			Mazie G. Brooker	
t Don Raymond Kuespert			1983 Jan 2 Wilmington	DE	
1 David Henderson Burt	*1958 Feb 7 Charlottesville	VA	1983 May 29 Wilmington	DE	
2 John Warren Burt	1960 Oct 6 Wilmington	DE		

4a4553100 BURT

David Henderson Burt	1958 Feb 7 Charlottesville	VA	1983 May 29 Wilmington	DE	
Audrey Whiteside	1960 Aug 10 Wilmington	DE	George Morris Whiteside III	
			& Donna Wilson	
1 Evan Whiteside	1989 Nov 12 Wilmington	DE		
2 [child]	1991 Jun			

Serial # and Name	Birth	Marriage	Death
4a4560000 MCELWAIN			
William Wren McElwain	1899 Dec 5 Appleton IL	1922 Oct Fullerton NE	1987 Mar 9 Denver CO
Ona Belle Minor	1905 Jul 4 Fullerton NE	Will Minor &	1987 Jul
		Edith Fitzgerald	
1 Eleanor Edith	*1925 Feb 27	1946 Jun 6 Denver CO	
2 William Harley	*1928 Feb 27	1950 Dec 30	
3 Randall Robert	*1933 Oct 21	1951 Sep 27	1990 Jan 30
4a4561000 LOCK			
Eleanor Edith McElwain	1925 Feb 27	1946 Jun 6 Denver CO	
Donald J. Lock	1915 Jan Marquette NE	Elmer Lock & Minnie -----	
1 Stephen Kent	*1948 Nov 13 Central City NE	1972 Jun 10 Bartlett NE	
2 William Donald	1951 Jan 4 Central City NE		
3 Lloyd Leslie	1957 Feb 12 Central City NE		
4a4561100 LOCK			
Stephen Kent Lock	1948 Nov 13 Central City NE	1972 Jun 10 Bartlett NE	
Dianna Lichtenberg	1949 Nov 15 Spalding NE	Raymond Lichtenbert &	
		Florence Rasselder	
1 Andrew John	1983 Dec 11 Neenah WI		
2 Sara Rae	1987 Jun 24 Neenah WI		
4a4562000 MCELWAIN			
William Harley McElwain	1928 Feb 27	1950 Dec 30	
Sarah Marion Holm	1932 May 28		
William was an oil company executive. His career is outlined in *Who's Who in the West* (1974-75).			
1 Mary Katherine	*1951 Aug 29		
2 Martin William	*1953 Oct 8		
3 Donna Marie	1955 Jan 20		
4a4562100 MALM			
Mary Katherine McElwain	1951 Aug 29		
Gerald Malm	1948 Mar 3		
1 Meredith	1971 Feb 6		
2 Heather	1974 Feb 28		
3 Joshua	1982 Oct 10		
454562200 MCELWAIN			
Martin William McElwain	1953 Oct 8		
Debra -----			
1 Melody			
2 Alyssa			
4a4563000 MCELWAIN			
Randall Robert McElwain	1933 Oct 21	1951 Sep 27	1990 Jan 30
Mary Ann Jacobs	1933 Oct 11		
1 Lorna Diane	*1954 Mar 20		
2 David Allen	1955 Dec 9	divorced	
3 Shelly Kay	*1959 Jul 6		

Serial # and Name	Birth	Marriage	Death
4a4563100 STEGALL			
Lorna Diane McElwain	1954 Mar 20		
William Stegall	1942 Aug 9		
4a4563300 CASE			
Shelly Kay McElwain	1959 Jul 6	divorced	
Ron Case			
4a4570000 MCELWAIN			
Mark McElwain	1906 Jun 8 York NE		1989 Oct Brighton CO
Ruby Giles	1914 Jul 4 Denver CO		
1 Mary Ellen	*1930 Sep 5 Denver CO		
2 LeRoy Edward	*1933 Aug 6	1953 Nov 29	
3 Jo Ann	1934 Dec 18 Brighton CO		1949 Jul 27 Brighton CO
4 Beverly Jean	*1941 Jul 14	1962 Aug 3	
Jo Ann died of polio.			
4a4571000 SEWELL			
Mary Ellen McElwain	1930 Sep 5 Denver CO		
Clair D. Sewell	1929 Sep 17 Eckley CO		
1 Jo Ann Clare	*1952 Aug 8		
2 Janet Gail	*1955 Feb 3 Denver CO		
3 Judy Lynn	*1956 Mar 8 Denver CO		
4a4571100 CAMPBELL			
Jo Ann Clare Sewell	1952 Aug 8		
Darrel Lee Campbell	1951 Jun 22		
1 Kelly Ann	1977 Jun 21 Denver CO		
2 Ryan Lee	1979 Oct 6 Denver CO		
3 Kari Lynn	1983 Jul 16 Denver CO		
4a4571200 SAGE			
Janet Gail Sewell	1955 Feb 3 Denver CO		
David Carleton Sage			
1 Lindsay Gail	1983 May 4		
2 Jeffrey Carlton	1987 Jun 21		
4a4571300 SCHNEIDMILLER			
Judy Lynn Sewell	1956 Mar 8 Denver CO		
John Schneidmiller	1954 Dec 7		
1 Kurtis	1978 Aug 2		
2 Joie Marie	1982 Jun 17		

222

Serial # and Name	Birth	Marriage	Death
4a4572000 MCELWAIN			
LeRoy Edward McElwain	1933 Aug 6	1953 Nov 29	
Barbara Nell	1935 Mar 24		
Ormsby-Bristol			
1 Kammy Lee	*1962 Mar 10		
2 Blake Edward	*1966 Nov 21	1988 Apr 23	
4a4572100 MORRISON			
Kammy Lee McElwain	1962 Mar 10		
----- Morrison			
1 Jamieson Cory	1985 Feb 15		
4a4572200 MCELWAIN			
Blake Edward McElwain	1966 Nov 21	1988 Apr 23	
Sheri Heuschkel	1968 Apr 23		
1 Justin Lee	1992 Jun 9		
4a4574000 VERNER			
Beverly Jean McElwain	1941 Jul 14	1962 Aug 3	
Reese Vernor	1941 Dec 5		
1 Reese Allan	*1964 Dec 4 Phoenix AZ	1989 Aug 8 San Diego CA	
2 Tracey Ann	*1966 Oct 20 Phoenix AZ	1898 Jul 8 Nampa ID	
3 Holly Andrea	*1970 Apr 6 Caldwell ID	1991 Dec 20 San Diego CA	
4 Christopher Mark	1975 May 11 Nampa ID		
4a4574100 VERNER			
Reese Allan Verner	1964 Dec 4 Phoenix AZ	1989 Aug 8 San Diego CA	
Robin Marie Moore	1964 May 8 San Bernardino CA	Robert Moore &	
		Cathy -----	

Reese and Robin graduated from Point Loma Nazarene College, and Reese from Albany Medical College in May
1993.

1 Jordan Reese	1991 Aug 22 Loma Linda CA		
2 Riley Allen	1992 Nov 4 Nampa ID		
4a4574200 COOK			
Tracey Ann Verner	1966 Oct 20 Phoenix AZ	1898 Jul 8 Nampa ID	
Carey Williamson Cook	1965 Nov 17 Kansas City MO	Franklin Cook &	
		Mary Lou Williamson	

Tracy and Carey graduated from Point Loma Nazarene College in 1989.   In 1994 Tracey was a high school
biology teacher in Homedale, ID. She received her teaching credentials from Northwest Nazarene College.

1 Samuel Verner	1992 Apr 7 Nampa ID		
4a4574300 STRAWN			
Holly Andrea Verner	1970 Apr 6 Caldwell ID	1991 Dec 20 San Diego CA	
Brent Allen Strawn	1970 Jul 20 Kankakee IL	David A. Strawn &	
		Sharon Jensen	

Holly and Brent both graduated from Nazarene College in 1992. In 1993, Brent was attending Princeton Theological Seminary, and Holly was Assistant Graduate Admissions Director at Princeton University.

Serial # and Name	Birth	Marriage	Death

4a5000000 MCELWAIN

James McElwain	:1827 Mar 5	PA:1853 Feb 3 Springfield	OH:1901 Aug 25 Kansas City MO
Eliza Jane Bechtle	:1834 May 27 nr. Springfield OH: Henry Bechtle &		:1926 Mar 29 Lenaxa KS
	:	: Betsey -----	:

In 1870 James was a farmer with $2800 in real and $800 in personal property.   He and his family lived in Oxford twp., Johnson Co., KS. In 1900 James and Eliza were living alone in Olathe, KS.   James died from injuries suffered in a fall from a fruit tree.

1 Ann Cecelia	#:1853 Dec	OH:	:1926>
2 Mary A.	#:1856c	OH:	:1915>
3 Alice B.	:1857 Oct 28	IL:	:1892 Jun 6 Johnson Co. KS
4 Jessie Ellen	#:1862 Oct 7 Knox Co.	IL:1883 Jan 11	:1965 Feb 20
5 Lillie Hannah	#:1865c	IL:	:
6 James H.	#:1867 Feb 4	KS:1896 May 17 Olathe	KS:1896 Jun 25 Hemphill Co. TX

4a5100000 PENNOCK

Ann Cecelia McElwain	:1853 Dec	OH:	:1926>
Nathaniel Pennock	:1857c	IN:	:

This couple lived with two children in Oxford twp., Johnson Co., KS in 1880.   In 1900 Celica with the four younger children lived in Olathe twp. in the same county. In 1910 "Celia", Della, Florence, and Lois lived in Baldwin City, Douglas County, Kansas. The three young women were unmarried.

1 William	:1878c	KS:	:
2 Gertrude L.	:1879 Oct	KS:	:
3 Della B.	:1885 Apr	KS:	:
4 Florence E.	:1887 Jul	KS:	:
5 Lois	:1892 Jul	KS:	:

4a5200000 AULT

Mary A. McElwain	:1856c	IL:	:1915>
----- Ault	:	:	:

4a5400000 BROWN

Jessie Ellen McElwain	:1862 Oct 7 Knox Co.	IL:1883 Jan 11	:1965 Feb 20 i. Johnson Co. KS
George Washington Brown	:1856 Jul 31 Guthrie Co.	IA:	:

In 1900 this family lived in Oxford twp., Johnson Co., KS, and in 1910 in Lenaxa, KS.

1 George Edward	:1885 Mar 23	KS:	:
2 Oliver William	:1887 Aug	KS:	:1913 Liverpool EN
3 James Lester	:1890 Aug	KS:	:1961
4 David	:	:	:died at age one month
5 Jessie LaVerne	#:1895 Jun 10	KS:	:

George graduated from Baker University and the Boston Theological Seminary; he became a prominent minister in Brooklyn, New York.   Oliver was a graduate of Baker University, and taught in Egerton High School.   He died of a brain tumor while vacationing in Europe.   James graduated from Baker University; he became a realtor and served as president of the Johnson County Real Estate Board.

4a5450000 DART

Jessie LaVerne Brown	:1895 Jun 10	KS:	:
Harry Dart	:	:	:

Jessie graduated from Baker University and attended Radcliff College. The Darts lived in Elmira NY in 1963.

4a5500000 RAINES

Lillie Hannah McElwain	:1865c	IL:	:
D. W. Raines	:	:	:

This couple lived in Spokane, Washington in 1926.

Serial # and Name	Birth	Marriage	Death

4a5600000 MCELWAIN

| James H. McElwain | :1867 Feb 4 | KS:1896 May 17 Olathe | KS:1896 Jun 25 Hemphill Co. TX |
| Florence McKissick | : | : | : |

James was a prominent stockman in Hemphill Co., TX during the last decade of the nineteenth century.   He married Florence, who had taught school locally. James died of typhoid fever only a month later.

4a7000000 BRECKINRIDGE

| Mary McElwain | :1832c | : | :   KS |
| H. Breckinridge | : | : | : |

In 1850 Mary, then age 18, was living with the family of Samuel Gilmore in Newville, PA.

| 1 Ruby | *: | : | : |

4a7100000 ENSIGN

| Ruby Breckinridge | : | : | : |
| ----- Ensign | : | : | : |

4a9000000 RAMP

Lacy Ralston McElwain	:1835 Apr 19 Newburg	PA:1857 Dec 24 Newville	PA:1893 Mar 12 Johnson Co. KS
John Ramp	:1829 Sep 8 Newburg	PA: Jacob Ramp, Sr. &	:1901 Aug 25 Kansas City MO
	:	: Eve Failor	:
1 Ella E.	*:1858 Dec 2 Cumberland Co. PA:		MO:
2 Jacob Rupley	:1860 Jul 2	PA:	:1861 Feb 15 Cumberland Co. PA
3 Laura Belle	*:1862 Sep 12 Newburg	PA:1888 Apr 11 Glenn	KS:1965 Apr 10 McCune KS
4 Ida Mae	*:1867 Sep 21	PA:	:
5 Harvey McElwain	*:1870 Jun 9 Newville	PA:1894 Sep 6 Johnson Co. KS:1957 Aug 8 Canadian TX
6 Andrew Mervin	*:1874 May 17 Cumberland Co. PA:1898 Dec 28		:1912 Dalhart TX

4a9100000 CHOWNING

| Ella E. Ramp | :1858 Dec 2 Cumberland Co. PA: | | MO: |
| Robert Chowning | :1857c | MO: | : |

The Chownings lived in Lathrop twp., Clinton Co., Missouri in 1880.

1 Anna Belle	*:1880c	MO:	Seminole OK:
2 Harry	:	:	Wichita KS:
3 Eva	:	:	:

4a9110000 HUNT

| Anna Belle Chowning | :1880c | MO: | Seminole   OK: |
| ----- Hunt | : | : | : |

4a9300000 MASON

| Laura Belle Ramp | :1862 Sep 12 Newburg | PA:1888 Apr 11 Glenn | KS:1965 Apr 10 McCune   KS |
| Frank E. Mason | :1865 Sep | KS: ----- Mason & Ellen E. -----:1963 Jan 25 McCune   KS |

The Masons lived in McCune, Crawford Co., Kansas in 1900, and were also in Crawford Co., in 1920.

| 1 Ruby Mae | *:1892c | KS: | :1951 |

4a9310000 RUST

| Ruby Mae Mason | :1892c | KS: | :1951 |
| Ralph G. Rust | :1890c | KS: | : |

The Rust family lived at 716 Thornton, Parsons, Kansas in 1920.

| 1 Ralph Mason | *:1917c | KS: | : |
| 2 Paul L. | :1919c | : | : |

Serial # and Name	Birth	Marriage	Death
4a9311000 RUST			
Ralph Mason Rust	:1917c	KS:	:
Arlene -----	:	:	:
Ralph was an M. D.			
1 David	:	:	:
2 Robert	:	:	:
4a9400000 MCCALL / FORRESTER			
Ida Mae Ramp	:1867 Sep 21	PA:	:
s ------ McCall (Dr.)	:	:	:
t ----- Forrester	:	:	:
4a9500000 RAMP			
Harvey McElwain Ramp	:1870 Jun 9 Newville	PA:1894 Sep 6 Johnson Co. KS:1957 Aug 8 Canadian TX	
s Letty Cornatzer	:	:	:1895 Jul 20 Johnson Co. KS
t Anna Jane Earnshaw	:1875 Sep 8	PA:1896 Dec 10 Johnson Co. KS:1919 Nov 4 Canadian TX	
	:	: William Earnshaw &	:
	:	: Joanna Sherman	:
u Annie Byrd Spaulding	:	:	:
Harvey and Anna Jane, with John, William, and Velma, lived in Hemphill Co., TX in 1910.			
1 Letta Cornatzer	s*:1895 Jun 7	:1918 Aug 12 Johnson Co. KS:1957 Sep 20 Wichita KS	
2 John Clifford	t :1899 Sep 22 Hemphill Co. TX:	:1916 Dec 30 Hemphill Co. TX	
3 William Earnshaw	t*:1902 Jun 22 Hemphill Co. TX:1923 May 16 Follett TX:1971 Mar 30 Canadian TX		
4 Velma Lacy	t*:1908 Jul 27 Hemphill Co. TX:	:	
5 Harvey Leroy	t*:1913 Feb 13 Oklahoma City OK:1936 Nov 15 Taloga OK:1992 Dec 2 Canadian TX		
4a9510000 CROSS			
Letta Cornatzer Ramp	:1895 Jun 7	:1918 Aug 12 Johnson Co. KS:1957 Sep 20 Wichita KS	
John Milton Cross	:1895 Mar 1 Goddard	KS: Edmund D. Cross & :1981 Nov 25 Kotzebue AK	
	:	: Mittie Reece	:
1 Letty Jean	:1922 Sep 11 Wichita	KS:	:1984 Jun 8 Wichita KS
2 Emily Alice	*:1925 Mar 25 Wichita	KS:	:
3 Gordon Cooper	*:1927 Dec 7 Wichita	KS:1959 Jan 24 New Orleans LA:	
4a9512000 PARKS			
Emily Alice Cross	:1925 Mar 25 Wichita	KS:	:
Robert Parks	:	:	:
1 Frank Gary	*:1950 Sep 4	:1992 Nov 22	:
2 Carol Anne	:1953 Sep 16	:	:
3 Fredrick Andrew	*:1955 Feb 15	:	:
4a9512100 PARKS			
Frank Gary Parks	:1950 Sep 4	:1992 Nov 22	:
Martha Lyons	:1951 Aug 27	:	:
4a9512200 PARKS			
Fredrick Andrew	:1955 Feb 15	:	:
Lynn Friedel	:	:	:
1 Michael Allen	:1991 Nov 4	:	:
2 Shannon Nicole	:1994 Aug 3	:	:

Serial # and Name	Birth	Marriage	Death
4a9513000 CROSS			
Gordon Cooper Cross	1927 Dec 7 Wichita KS	1959 Jan 24 New Orleans LA	
Mary Lou Sanchez Detagle	1932 May 31 Mexico City MX		
y Lozano			
1 Alan Ray	*1960 Nov 22 Fairbanks AK	1990 Jun 9	
2 Linda May	*1962 Jul 22 Fairbanks AK	1990 Apr 28 Acapulco MX	
4a9513100 CROSS			
Alan Ray Cross	1960 Nov 22 Fairbanks AK	1990 Jun 9 Laguna Niguel CA	
Wendy Louise Martineau	1958 Dec 14 Los Angeles CA	Arthur Ernest Martineau &	
		Suzanne Elizabeth Montgomery	
1 Caitlin Noel	1992 Jan 9 Los Angeles CA		
4a9513200 GLANDON			
Linda May Cross	1962 Jul 22 Fairbanks AK	1990 Apr 28 Acapulco MX	
William Clarence Glandon	1961 Jul 29 Spokane WA	Frederic Ralph Glandon &	
		Shirley Jean Dahlgren	
1 Alexandra Nicole	1993 Nov 24 Seattle WA		
2 Nicholas Cooper	1995 Sep 7 Seattle WA		
4a9530000 RAMP			
William Earnshaw Ramp	1902 Jun 22 Hemphill Co. TX	1923 May 16 Follett TX	1971 Mar 30 Canadian TX
Amelia Marilla Cook	1901 May 15 Hamilton TX	Leslie Benjamin Cook &	
		----- Keller	
1 Peggy Joan	*1932 Apr 29 Hemphill TX	1951 Jul 1 Canadian TX	1989 Aug 27 Hemphill TX
4a9531000 WALKER			
Peggy Joan Ramp	1932 Apr 29 Hemphill TX	1951 Jul 1 Canadian TX	1989 Aug 27 Hemphill TX
Glenn William Walker	1930 Jun 27 Durham OK	----- Warner & Verona Keller	
1 William Patrick	*1955 May 24 Canadian TX	1979 Jun 2 Canadian TX	
2 Anna Jane	*1957 Oct 28 Canadian TX	1981 May 23 Hemphill Co. TX	
4a9531100 WALKER			
William Patrick Walker	1955 May 24 Canadian TX	1979 Jun 2 Canadian TX	
Gwendolyn Lee Walser			
4a9531200 BROWN			
Anna Jane Walker	1957 Oct 28 Canadian TX	1981 May 23 Hemphill Co. TX	
Donald R. Brown, Jr.		Donald R. Brown, Sr. &	
		----- -----	
1 Emily Amelia	1987 Dec 26 Dallas TX		
4a9540000 MILLER			
Velma Lacy Ramp	1908 Jul 27 Hemphill Co. TX	Hemphill Co. TX	
Virgil Miller			

Serial # and Name	Birth	Marriage	Death

4a9550000 RAMP

Harvey Leroy Ramp	!1913 Feb 13 Oklahoma City OK!	1936 Nov 15 Taloga OK!	1992 Dec 2 Canadian TX
s Sarah Elizabeth McMeans	!1916 Dec 17 Shamrock TX!	Paul Edwin McMeans & !	1969 Feb 22 Canadian TX
	!	Jewell Madeline Crim !	
t Harriet Austin Longhofer	!	!1971 Canadian TX!	
	!	!	!
1 John Dale	s*!1938 Jul 18 Pampa TX!	1962 Jun 10 Arnett OK!	
2 James Harvey	s*!1943 Mar 13 Canadian TX!	1969 Mar 2 Canadian TX!	

4a9551000 RAMP

John Dale Ramp	!1938 Jul 18 Pampa TX!	1962 Jun 10 Arnett OK!	
Al'Louise Suthers	!1940 Jun 26 Shattuck OK!	William Howard Suthers & !	
	!	Gwendoline Lenoir Robinson!	
1 Susan Lynn	!1963 Oct 5 Canadian TX!	!	
2 Karlyn Beth	!1966 Jul 21 Canadian TX!	!	

4a9552000 RAMP

James Harvey Ramp	!1943 Mar 13 Canadian TX!	1969 Mar 2 Canadian TX!	
Bobbie Jo Bunch	!1949 Oct 4 Premont TX!	Joe Bob Bunch & Neva King !	
	!	!	!
1 Cindy Nell	!1972 Nov 22 Canadian TX!	!	
2 Vicki Jo	!1975 Aug 20 Canadian TX!	!	
3 Jake William	!1979 Oct 24 Canadian TX!	!	

4a9600000 RAMP

Andrew Mervin Ramp	!1874 May 17 Cumberland Co. PA!	1898 Dec 28 !	1912 Dalhart TX
Cora Protsman	!1878c May MO!	!	1955c Lubbock TX
	!	!	!
1 Ruby Fern	*!1904c Dalhart TX!	!	1985 Brashear TX
2 Harvey Robert	*!1908 Nov 11 Dalhart TX!	1934 Feb 22 Dallas TX!	1990 Jan 3 Lubbock TX

4a9610000 BURKETT

Ruby Fern Ramp	! Dalhart TX!	!	1985 Brashear TX
M. M. Burkett, Sr.	!	!	!

4a9620000 RAMP

Harvey Robert Ramp	!1908 Nov 11 Dalhart TX!	1934 Feb 22 Dallas TX!	1990 Jan 3 Lubbock TX
Rhetta Wilmoth	!	!	!

4aa000000 BUTT

Elizabeth A. McElwain	!1839 PA!	!	
John W. Butt	!	!	!
	!	!	!
1 John	!	!	!

4ab000000 MCELWAIN

Robert Henderson McElwain	!1847 May 31 Cumberland Co.PA !	1877 Apr 11 Pleasant Grove KS!	1904 Jun 20 Rice Co. KS
Martha Jane Adamson	!1854 Dec 1	!	1922 Jun 6 Rice Co. KS
Martha was living in Hutchinson, KS in 1920, with Rock and Martha L.			
1 Thomas Ralph	*!1878 Jun 10 Frederick KS!	!	1937 Sep Hutchinson KS
2 Rock S.	*!1885 May 18 Frederick KS!	!	1938 Jan
3 Martha L.	*!1890 Jan 10 KS!	!	
4 Mary	*!1890 Jan 10 KS!	!	

Serial # and Name	Birth	Marriage	Death

4ab100000   MCELWAIN

Thomas Ralph McElwain	1878 Jun 10 Frederick KS		1937 Sep 25/28? Hutchinson KS
Nancy -----	1878c IN		

Thomas served in the Spanish American War. The family lived on 6th Street West, Hutchinson, KS in 1920.

1 Fay Etta	1912c MO		

4ab200000   MCELWAIN

Rock S. McElwain	1885 May 18 Frederick KS		1938 Jan 5 Hutchinson KS
----- -----			

Rock was living unmarried with his mother in 1920. He and his family lived in Lyons, KS until 1930 when he
moved to Hutchinson. He worked as a meat cutter.

1 Robert			
2 Roy			
3 Mildred Louise			

4ab300000   FRANKLIN

Martha L. McElwain	1890 Jan 10 KS		
Ray A. Franklin			

4ab400000   HOLLOWAY

Mary McElwain	1890 Jan 10 KS		
George C. Holloway			

4ac000000   MCELWAIN

Thomas Simpson McElwain	1849 Jan 26 Cumberland Co. PA	1878 Jul 11 Chambersburg PA	1909 Dec 23 Crawford Co. KS
Mary Martha Nickey	1848 Jan 11 Cumberland Co. PA	George Nickey &	1936 Jan 24 Crawford Co. KS
		Elizabeth Springer	

Thomas and Mary, with all of their living children, resided in Crawford Co., KS in 1900.   Thomas was a
farmer. Mattie (Mary) died from burns suffered when her dress caught fire from a stove.

1 Ellen May	1879 May 4 Butler Co. KS		1896 Jun 24 Crawford Co. KS
2 Elmer Edward	*1880 Dec 17 Butler Co. KS	1905 Dec 24 Crawford Co. KS	1974 Dec 23 Girard KS
3 George Roscoe	1882 Dec 18 Butler Co. KS	never married	1923 Aug 17 Miami Co. KS
4 John Kerr	1884 Nov 14 Butler Co. KS	never married	1959 Jun 29 Crawford Co. KS
5 Thomas Earl	1887 Jan 22 Butler Co. KS	never married	1963 Aug 10 Bourbon Co. KS
6 Charles Ross	*1889 Mar 31 Butler Co KS	1915 Dec 29 Crawford Co KS	1953 Dec Denver CO
7 Louie Robert	*1892 Mar 13 Butler Co. KS	1914 Feb 18 Crawford Co. KS	1957 May 31 Crawford Co. KS
8 Shirley Vivian	*1894 Apr 24 Butler Co. KS	1916 Apr 23 Crawford Co. KS	1964 Nov 9 Girard KS

In 1920 John, Earl, George, and their mother Martha lived together in Crawford Co., KS.   John was a farmer
and never married.   Thomas, also a farmer and a bachelor, served in the Army in World War I, George died
in the Oswatomie State Hospital after a lengthy mental illness

4ac200000   MCELWAIN

Elmer Edward McElwain	1880 Dec 17 Butler Co. KS	1903 Nov 1 Crawford Co. KS	1974 Dec 23 Girard KS
s Bessie M. Nicholson	1885c	Sam Nickelson & ----- -----	1904 Jun 26 Crawford Co. KS
t Rosa May Pefley	1885 May 2 Labette Co. KS	1905 Dec 24 Crawford Co. KS	1974 Jun 12 Girard KS
		George Pefley & Mary -----	

Elmer, Rosa, and Francis lived in Crawford Co., KS in 1920.

1 Forest Glen	t 1907 Feb 13		1907 Mar 24
2 Francis Marion	t*1908 Sep 1 Crawford Co. KS	1930 Oct 2 McCune KS	

Serial # and Name	Birth	Marriage	Death

4ac220000 MCELWAIN

Francis Marion McElwain	1908 Sep 1 Crawford Co. KS	1930 Oct 2 McCune KS	1995 Sep 2 Crawford Co. KS
Cleo Patricia Neal	1913 Jul 31 Brumley MO	Arthur W. Neal &	
		Anna W. Hickman	

Francis was a farmer. He retired in 1975.

1 William Ray	*1931 May 28 McCune KS	1953 Oct 10 McCune KS	1960 Sep 29 Girard KS
2 Anna Mae	*1934 Dec 2 Crawford Co. KS	1953 Jun 13 McCune KS	
3 Marian P.	*1935 Dec 28 Crawford Co. KS	1956 Aug 23 McCune KS	
4 Mervin LeRoy	*1938 Jul 8 Crawford Co. KS	1957 Dec 23 Girard KS	
5 Carol Marie	*1948 Sep 28 Pittsburg KS	1967 Nov 23 McCune KS	

4ac221000 MCELWAIN

William Ray McElwain	1931 May 28 McCune KS	1953 Oct 10 McCune KS	1960 Sep 29 Girard KS
Helen Carlene Johnson	1935 Sep 18 McCune KS	Carl Thomas Johnson &	
		Florence Ninetta Rogers	

William served for two years in the United States Army, thirteen months of that time in Germany.   He died from an accident at his workplace.   Helen later married in Seattle, WA, Arthur W. Neal. Jr., brother of Cleo Neal McElwain (#4ac220000).

1 Deborah Rae	*1957 Jul 27 Girard KS		
2 William E.	1960 Dec 8 Pittsburg KS		

4ac221100 -----

Deborah Rae McElwain	1957 Jul 27 Girard KS		
----- -----			
1 Freddie			

4ac222000 SLAPER

Anna Mae McElwain	1934 Dec 2 Crawford Co. KS	1953 Jun 13 McCune KS	
Frank Milton Slaper	1928 Jun 13 MO	Frank Slaper &	
		Stephannia Licci	

The Slapers were living in Pittsburg, Kansas in 1990.

1 Larry	1954 Sep 15 Pittsburg KS		
2 Lonnie	*1955 Sep 20 Pittsburg KS	1982 Jul 3 Rochester NY	
3 Lynette	*1958 Feb 3 Wichita KS	1985 Nov 9 Kansas City KS	
4 Lloyd	1967 Jun 22 Hutchinson KS		

4ac222200 SLAPER

Lonnie Slaper	1955 Sep 20 Pittsburg KS	1982 Jul 3 Rochester NY	
Constance Dawn Eselgroth			
1 Jessica Constance	1987 Sep 25		
2 Frank Thomas	1990 Jul 17		

4ac222300 SCHMIDT

Lynette Slaper	1958 Feb 3 Wichita KS	1985 Nov 9 Kansas City KS	
Daniel Schmidt			

230

Serial # and Name	Birth	Marriage	Death

4ac223000   WHIRLEY / HAWLEY

Marian P. McElwain |1935 Dec 28 Crawford Co. KS|1956 Aug 23 McCune   KS|

s Bernard L. Whirley |1933 Sep 29 McPherson   KS| Fred W. Whirley & |1992 Mar   DeSoto   KS
| | Pauline Huber |

t William C. Hawley | | |

Marian and Bernard were divorced. She graduated from McPherson College.

1 Douglas L. <u>Whirley</u>   *|1957 Mar 5 McPherson   KS|1976 Jun 25 Wyandotte Co. KS|
2 Carmella Kay <u>Whirley</u> |1960 Aug 30 Kansas City   KS| |1970 Jan   Kansas City KS
3 Bradley Lynn <u>Whirley</u> *|1962 Jan 20 Paolo   KS|1987 Aug 15 Kansas City   MO|

4ac223100   WHIRLEY

Douglas L. Whirley |1957 Mar 5 McPherson   KS|1976 Jun 25 Wyandotte Co. KS|
s Cheryl Lynn Jackson | | Forrest Jackson & ---- ----|
t Yvonne ----- | | |
u Margaret ----- | | |

Douglas and Cheryl were divorced.

1 Crystal   s |

4ac223300   WHIRLEY

Bradley Lynn Whirley |1962 Jan 20 Paolo   KS|1987 Aug 15 Kansas City   MO|
Candace Elaine Henderson | | John R. Henderson & ---- ---|

Candace was previously married and has a son Jordan Whirley (not adopted by Bradley) from that marriage.

1 Alexandria Michelle |1988 Jan 1

4ac224000   MCELWAIN

Mervin LeRoy McElwain |1938 Jul 8 Crawford Co. KS|1957 Dec 23 Girard   KS|
Patricia Joan Neil |1938 Jun 16 Crawford Co. KS| Earnest Neil & |
| | Georgene Opal Shipman |

This family lived in Girard, Kansas in 1990. Mervin was the manager of the furniture department of Sauer's Department Store.

1 Jeffrey Joe |1962 Aug 18 Crawford Co. KS|
2 Jan LeRoy |1965 Jul 11 Crawford Co. KS|
3 Lisa Diane   *|1967 Aug 18 |1989 Aug 20 Crawford Co. KS|
4 Lori Lee   *|1970 Jun 8 |1989 Oct 20 Crawford Co. KS|

4ac224300   LENATI

Lisa Diane McElwain |1967 Aug 18 Pittsburg   KS|1989 Aug 20 Girard   KS|
Frank Lenati | | |

1 Jonathan S. |1990 Aug 8 Wichita   KS|

4ac224400   SHULER

Lori Lee McElwain |1970 Jun 8 Girard   KS|1989 Oct 20 Pittsburg   KS|
Don Shuler | | |

1 Christian Lee |1990 Sep 25 Gravitt   AR|

Serial # and Name	Birth	Marriage	Death

4ac225000 BEST

	Birth	Marriage	Death
Carol Marie McElwain	1948 Sep 28 Pittsburg KS	1967 Nov 23 McCune KS	
Terry Best	1946 Dec 1 Cherokee Co. KS		
1 Darren Michael	1969 Feb 7 Crawford Co. KS		
2 Kevin Randall	1971 Jul 26 Crawford Co. KS		
3 Teresa Lea	1976 Jan 27 Crawford Co. KS		

4ac600000 MCELWAIN

	Birth	Marriage	Death
Charles Ross McElwain	1889 Mar 31 Butler Co KS	1915 Dec 29 Crawford Co KS	1953 Dec Denver CO
Daisy Ora Carter	1890 Sep 16	John W. Carter & ----- -----	1961 Jul 4 Colorado Spr. CO

Charles, Daisy, and Mary lived in Rice County, KS in 1920.   Charles was a doctor of veterinary medicine.
He served briefly in the Army in World War I.

	Birth	Marriage	Death
1 John Paul		Walnut KS	
2 Mary Charlotte	#1919c	Walnut KS	
3 Marvin Glenister			
4 Harold Carter			
5 Daisy Ruth	#		
6 Pauline Esther	#		

4ac620000 JOHNSON

	Birth	Marriage	Death
Mary Charlotte McElwain	1919c	Walnut KS	
----- Johnson			

4ac650000 SLIKE

	Birth	Marriage	Death
Daisy Ruth McElwain			
----- Slike			

4ac660000 LYMAN

	Birth	Marriage	Death
Pauline Esther McElwain			
Richard "Dick" Lyman			

This family was living in Evanston, Illinois in 1979-80.   Richard worked for the Rock Island Railroad, and
Pauline for the Illinois Bell Telephone Co.

	Birth	Marriage	Death
1 Ann			
2 John			

4ac700000 MCELWAIN

	Birth	Marriage	Death
Louie Robert McElwain	1892 Mar 13 Butler Co. KS	1914 Feb 18 Crawford Co. KS	1957 May 31 Crawford Co. KS
Inez Ann Smith	1892 Apr 21 Crawford Co. KS	Columbus Washington Smith &	1988 Jun 5 Columbus KS
		Dora Bell Mann	

This family lived in Crawford Co., KS in 1920. Louie farmed in the McCune area; he retired in 1952.

	Birth	Marriage	Death
1 Lawrence Edward	#1916 May 6 Crawford Co. KS	1939 Oct 29 McCune KS	1994 May 12 Columbus KS
2 Charles Wesley	#1918 Jun 10 Crawford Co. KS	1948 Jun 10 Lyons KS	
3 L. J. Simpson	1921 May 28 Crawford Co. KS		1928 May 5 Crawford Co. KS
4 Herbert Lee	#1928 Nov 9 Crawford Co. KS	1950 Jun 11 Baxter Springs KS	
5 Roy Eugene	#1930 Dec 27 Crawford Co. KS	1959 Oct 10 Kansas City MO	
6 James Arthur	1932 Oct 16 Crawford Co. KS		1936 Jan 14 Crawford Co. KS

James died of scarlet fever.

Serial # and Name	Birth	Marriage	Death

4ac710000 MCELWAIN

Lawrence Edward McElwain	1916 May 6 Crawford Co. KS	1939 Oct 29 McCune	KS	1994 May 12 Columbus	KS
Valeta Inone Hamilton	1918 Sep 1 Crawford Co. KS	Edward Daniel Hamilton &			
		Emma Grace Ross			

Lawrence served in the United States Army in World War II. He managed and later owned a grocery store in Columbus, Kansas. Valeta graduated from Parson's Junior College, and taught school in 1938-1939.

1 Jeanna Lea	#1941 Jul 11 Columbus	KS1959 Dec 19 Columbus	KS
2 Phyllis Kay	#1944 Apr 26 Columbus	KS1966 Aug 25 Kansas City	MO
3 Sandra Jo	#1949 Aug 21 Columbus	KS1972 Apr 15 Wea	KS

4ac711000 ZAHM

Jeanna Lea McElwain	1941 Jul 11 Columbus	KS1959 Dec 19 Columbus	KS
Clark Linn Zahm	1942 Feb 20 Cherokee Co. KS	John William Zahm &	
		Mary Marie Wiseman	

Jeanna, after graduating from high school, worked for a short time and then retired to raise her family. She returned to work in 1980, first for the Cherokee County Appraiser's Office, and then in 1989 at the Columbus State Bank. She was promoted in 1990 to supervisor of the bookeeping department. Clark worked for Swift and Company from 1960 to 1963, when he and Jeanna moved to Columbus to take over part of the Zahm farming operations. In 1990 the operation was sold and Clark has since worked for several local companies. He was employed in 1996 with Cash Grain of Pittsburg, Kansas.

1 Lawrence William	#1960 Dec 17 Kansas City	KS1983 Jul 9 Columbus	KS
2 Susan Linn	#1962 Jul 30 Kansas City	KS1989 May 20 Columbus	KS
3 Michael Alan	#1966 Apr 11 Columbus	KS1992 Dec 19 Columbus	KS
4 Philip Edward	#1968 Mar 20 Columbus	KS1996 Feb 29 Columbus	KS

4ac711100 ZAHM

| Lawrence William Zahm | 1960 Dec 17 Kansas City | KS1983 Jul 9 Columbus | KS |
| Cindy Jean Roark | 1961 Oct 29 Columbus | KS Bill Roark & Linda Goben | |

Larry graduated from Pittsburg State University (Kansas) with a B. S. in Mechanical Design and Drafting Technology. After working for several firms, he joined General Steel Fabricators in Joplin, Missouri, where he is a sales estimator. Cindy is employed as Director of Administration and Community Relations for Class Ltd. in Columbus, KS.

1 Nicholas Lawrence	1986 Jun 23 Joplin	MO	
2 Curtis Paul	1987 Oct 19 Joplin	MO	
3 Jacob Ryan	1989 Sep 28 Joplin	MO	

4ac711200 WILLIAMS

Susan Linn Zahm	1962 Jul 30 Kansas City	KS1989 May 20 Columbus	KS
Brett Stephen Williams	1958 Jun 1	Charles Wesley Williams &	
		Joan Robertson	

Susan graduated from Pittsburg State University (Kansas). After their marriage this couple moved to Bullhead City, Arizona, where Susan worked for a local newspaper, and then to Phoenix where she managed an Alphagrapics franchise. Brett worked in sales for Rainbo Bread and Holsum Bakery. Susan and Brett were divorced in 1995.

| 1 Lauren Jeanna | 1990 Apr 20 Phoenix | AZ | |
| 2 Addison Grace | 1991 Nov 12 Glendale | AZ | |

Serial # and Name	Birth	Marriage	Death

4ac711300   ZAHM

Michael Alan Zahm	:1966 Apr 11 Columbus KS:	1992 Dec 19 Columbus KS:	
Michelle Susan Parsons	:1969 Dec 12 Columbus KS:	Ernest Freeman Parsons & :	
		Joyce Charlene Handshy :	

Michael graduated from Pittsburg State University with a degree in Plastics Engineering.   In September 1994 he was employed in Pittsburg by Polytron in their plastics department. Michelle graduated from Kansas University with a degree in Medical Records Administration.   She works in a physician's office in Joplin, Missouri.

1 Jonathan Q. Counsil Zahm :		:	:

Jonathon is the son of Nancy A. Counsil and Michael.   After he was proven to be Michael's son he came to live with his father, who was awarded custody on February 24, 1992. He changed his name to Zahm.

4ac711400   ZAHM

Philip Edward Zahm	:1968 Mar 20 Columbus KS:	1996 Feb 29 Columbus KS:	
Brandi Renee Thompson	:	:	:

Brandi has a son, Joshua Thompson, by a previous marriage.

Taylor Renee	:1995 Aug 10	:	:

4ac712000   SMITH

Phyllis Kay McElwain	:1944 Apr 26 Columbus KS:	1966 Kansas City MO:	
Rodney Martin Smith	:1944 Jan 26 Clark Co. MO:	Leroy Smith & Kathleen Horn :	

Rodney served in the United States Army in Vietnam.   He graduated from college at Kirkville, MO.   He has since owned and operated a feed and grain business in Wyaconda, Missouri, and has been on the local school board for eighteen years, serving as president six or eight times.   He declined to run again in 1994.

1 Scott Martin	*:1969 Aug 25 Columbus KS:	1995 Jul 15 Kahoka MO:	
2 Stacy Lynne	*:1972 Jul 18 Jefferson City MO:		:
3 Leslie Kathleen	:1978 Dec 3 Keokuk IA:		:

4ac712100   SMITH

Scott Martin Smith	:1969 Aug 25 Columbus KS:	1995 Jul 15 Kahoka MO:	
Rachel Jeanne Knight	:1973 Jul 9	:	:
	:	:	:
1 Grace Alice	:1994 Dec	:	:

4ac712200   SMITH

Stacey Lynne Smith	:1972 Jul 18 Jefferson City MO:		:
	:	:	:
1 Paige Kathleen	:1995 Nov 6 Iowa City IA:		:1995 Nov 6 Iowa City IA

4ac713000   KOBETS

Sandra Jo McElwain	:1949 Aug 21 Columbus KS:	1972 Apr 15 Wea KS:	
Thomas Harvey Kobets	:1947 Feb 20 Kansas City KS:	Godfrey Kobets & :	
	:	Deloris Gardner :	

Sandra and Thomas are divorced.

1 Brian Godfrey	:1973 Apr 12 Kansas City MO:		:
2 Rebecca Ann	:1974 Jun 28 Kansas City MO:		:
3 Mary Elizabeth	:1975 Jun 5 Kansas City MO:		:
4 Teresa Christine	:1978 Jan 12 Kansas City MO:		:

Serial # and Name	Birth	Marriage	Death

4ac720000 MCELWAIN

Charles Wesley McElwain	1918 Jun 10 Crawford Co. KS	1948 Jun 10 Lyons KS	
Marguerite Moore	1919 Jul 29		
1 Wesley Joe	*1954 May 28 Topeka KS	1974 Aug 10 Ft. Morgan CO	
2 Kathy Lynn	*1957 Oct 4 Ft. Morgan CO	1975 Oct 18 Ft. Morgan CO	

4ac721000 MCELWAIN

Wesley Joe McElwain	1954 May 28 Topeka KS	1974 Aug 10 Ft. Morgan CO	
Nancy Rangel	1956 Feb 22 Greeley CO		
Joe and Nancy are divorced.			
1 Tyson Matthew	1979 Aug 18 Greeley CO		
2 Andrew Craig	1982 Nov 27 Greeley CO		
3 Steven W.	1986 Feb 3 Greeley CO		
4 Brandon J.	1987 Sep 25 Greeley CO		

4ac722000 LENHARDT

Kathy Lynn McElwain	1957 Oct 4 Ft. Morgan CO	1975 Oct 18 Ft. Morgan CO	
Lance Hugh Lenhardt	1957 Feb 7		
1 Rhiannon R.	1980 May 10		

4ac740000 MCELWAIN

Herbert Lee McElwain	1928 Nov 9 Crawford Co. KS	1950 Jun 11 Baxter Springs KS	
s Charlene June Albertson	1930 Jun		
t Pauline (Wheeler) Johnson		1961 Aug 6 Kansas City MO	
Herbert and Charlene were divorced.			
1 Connie Jean	s*1953 Oct 14		

4ac741000 SCAMMON

Connie Jean McElwain	1953 Oct 14		
Jed Scammon			

4ac750000 MCELWAIN

Roy Eugene McElwain	1930 Dec 27 Crawford Co. KS	1959 Oct 10 Kansas City MO	
Kathryn Annabell Drury	1925 Dec 28 Pawhauska OK		
Roy and Kathryn lived in Overland Park, Kansas until about 1985; they retired to the Lake of the Ozarks			
area in Missouri.			
1 Gary Ray	*1963 Jul 27 Kansas City MO	1990 Sep 22 Overland Park KS	

4ac751000 MCELWAIN

Gary Ray McElwain	1963 Jul 27 Kansas City MO	1990 Sep 22 Overland Park KS	
Janette Renee Bisang			
1 Luke Spencer	1994 Jun 1		

Serial # and Name	Birth	Marriage	Death

4ac800000   MCELWAIN

Shirley Vivian McElwain	1894 Apr 24 Butler Co. KS	1916 Apr 23 Crawford Co. KS	1964 Nov 9 Girard	KS
Emma Josephine Smith	1898 Apr 21 Crawford Co. KS	Columbus Washington Smith	1992 Dec 27 Girard	KS
		Dora Belle Mann	

The McElwains lived in Crawford Co., KS in 1920. Shirley was a farmer in the Girard, Kansas area.

1 Martha Belle	*	1917 Jun 17 Crawford Co. KS	1941 Dec 11 Girard KS	
2 Malinda "Millie" Louise	*	1919 Mar 31	1941 Apr 23 Crawford Co. KS	
3 Luella Virginia	*	1921 Jan 11	1941 Aug 17 Crawford Co. KS	
4 Lillian Grace	*	1923 Jun 27	1945 Jul 16 Crawford Co. KS	

4ac810000   BALDWIN

| Martha Belle McElwain | 1917 Jun 17 Crawford Co. KS | 1941 Dec 11 Girard   KS | |
| John Lloyd Baldwin | 1916 Oct 1 Crawford Co. KS | | |

John was in the Air Force in World War II.

| 1 Shirley Joanne | *|1948 May 18 Parsons   KS | 1970 Aug 30 Farlington   KS | |
| 2 Eleanor Mae | *|1951 Mar 15 Parsons   KS | 1971 Dec 6 Girard   KS | |

4ac811000   DAVENPORT

| Shirley Joanne Baldwin | 1948 May 18 Parsons   KS | 1970 Aug 30 Farlington   KS | |
| Harold Dwayne Davenport | 1934 Oct 19 | | |

| 1 Michael Charles | 1972 Mar 19 Ft. Scott   KS | | |
| 1 Gabriel Joseph | 1977 Nov 29 Ft. Scott   KS | | |

4ac812000   BLAZIC

| Eleanor Mae Baldwin | 1951 Mar 15 Parsons   KS | 1971 Dec 6 Girard   KS | |
| Gerald Lee Blazic | 1948 Nov 12 | | |

Eleanor and Gerald are divorced.

1 Amy Lynn	1973 May 30 Ft. Scott KS		
2 Jonathan Rudy	1976 Apr 15 Ft. Scott KS		
3 Adam Lee	1979 Jun 16 Ft. Scott KS		

4ac820000   BOATMAN

Malinda "Millie" Louise McElwain	1919 Mar 31	1941 Apr 23 Crawford Co. KS	
Alvin Taylor Boatman	1916 Aug 12 Crawford Co. KS	Earl Clarence Boatman &	1971 Jul 30 i. Crawford Co. KS
		Lota Estella Taylor	
1 Patricia Louise	*|1943 Mar 8 Girard KS	1963 Nov 16	
2 Kathryn Kay	*|1944 Aug 16 Girard KS	1964 Sep 5	
3 Janice Rae	*|1950 Oct 4 Girard KS	1969 Aug 23	

4ac821000   WUTKE

| Patricia Louise Boatman | 1943 Mar 8 Girard   KS | 1963 Nov 16 | |
| Ronald Dean Wutke | | | |

4ac822000   PICCINELLI

| Kathryn Kay Boatman | 1944 Aug 16 Girard   KS | 1964 Sep 5 | |
| Robert James Piccinelli | | | |

4ac823000   MCCRACKEN

| Janice Rae Boatman | 1950 Oct 4 Girard   KS | 1969 Aug 23 | |
| Roger Earl McCracken | | | |

Janice and Roger were divorced in 1983.

Serial # and Name	Birth	Marriage	Death

4ac830000 MURPHY

Luella Virginia McElvain	1921 Jan 11	1941 Aug 17 Crawford Co. KS	
Lawrence Murphy	1917 May 21 Girard KS		
1 Marvin Lawrence	*1942 Nov 8 Girard KS	1966 Sep 15 Crawford Co. KS	
2 Betty Virginia	*1944 Jun 30 Girard KS	1962 Jul 4 Crawford Co. KS	
3 Calvin Lynn	*1950 Jan 22 Girard KS	1971 Aug 14 Girard KS	
4 Carol Diane	*1952 Jan 1 Girard KS	1971 May 2 Girard KS	
5 Donald Dean	*1954 Jan 27 Girard KS	1971 Apr 23	
6 Richard Allen	*1959 Jan 18 Girard KS	1978 Oct 21 Farlington KS	

4ac831000 MURPHY

Marvin Lawrence Murphy	1942 Nov 8 Girard KS	1966 Sep 15 Crawford Co. KS	
Helen Louise Foster			
1 Kenneth Marvin	1971 Mar 16		
2 Karen LeAnn	1972 Nov 25		

4ac832000 GATES

Betty Virginia Murphy	1944 Jun 30 Girard KS	1962 Jul 4 Crawford Co. KS	
Charles Arthur Gates			
1 Robert Charles	1965 Apr 1 Wichita KS		1991 Girard KS
2 Connie Jean	*1968 Feb 18	1987 Jun 20	

Robert died, after several years in a coma, from injuries received in an automobile accident.

4ac832200 KARHOFF

| Connie Jean Gates | 1968 Feb 18 | 1987 Jun 20 | |
| Mark Joseph Karhoff | | | |

Connie and Mark were divorced in 1989.

4ac833000 MURPHY

Calvin Lynn Murphy	1950 Jan 22 Girard KS	1971 Aug 14 Girard KS	
Cathy Sue Akers			
1 Michael David	1975 May 27		
2 Mandy Lynn	1979 Sep 27		

4ac834000 YOHO

Carol Diane Murphy	1952 Jan 1 Girard KS	1971 May 2 Girard KS	
Charles LeRoy Yoho			
1 Jennifer Dawn	1974 Oct 17		
2 Carol Beth	1977 Feb 16		

4ac835000 MURPHY

Donald Dean Murphy	1954 Jan 27 Girard KS	1971 Apr 23	
s Judith Ann Mitchell			
t Mary K. Grotheer		1978 Nov 22 Pittsburg KS	

Donald is divorced from both Judith and Mary.

1 Joseph Dean	s 1971 May 31		
2 Jesse Allen	s 1975 Jul 16		
3 Mathew Dean	t 1979 Aug 20		

Serial # and Name	Birth	Marriage	Death

4ac836000   MURPHY

Richard Allen Murphy	1959 Jan 18 Girard KS	1978 Oct 21 Farlington KS	
Ramona Rae Boggs			
1 Scott Richard	1981 Aug 3		
2 Lisa Rae	1984 Feb 19		
3 Lori Lynn	1988 Mar 9		

4ac840000   ROSE

Lillian Grace McElwain	1923 Jun 27	1945 Jul 16 Crawford Co. KS	
Roy Lee Rose	1920 Mar 5 Crawford Co. KS		

Roy was a mechanic. He served three and a half years in the Army in World War II, sixteen months overseas.

1 Jerry Lee	*1946 Jun 7 Girard KS	1966 Aug 21 Parsons KS	
2 Judy Anneira	*1947 Aug 23 Girard KS	1963 Jul 12 Parsons KS	
3 Nancy Darlene	*1950 Mar 3 Parsons KS	1969 Feb 14 Parsons KS	
4 Charles Leroy	*1952 May 13 Parsons KS	1975 Aug 9 Parsons KS	

4ac841000   ROSE

Jerry Lee Rose	1946 Jun 7 Girard KS	1966 Aug 21 Parsons KS	
Malinda Dale Mullen	1947 Feb 24		

This family lived in Tulsa, Oklahoma in the 1980s

1 Jeffrey Lee	1975 Dec 14 Tulsa OK		
2 Richard Allen	1978 Nov 24		

Jeffrey is adopted; he is one-half Pawnee Indian.

4ac842000   JANSSEN

Judy Anneira Rose	1947 Aug 23 Girard KS	1963 Jul 12 Parsons KS	
Leo Dale Janssen	1942 May 24		
1 Robin Dale	1964 Jul 7		
2 Tracey Lee	1966 Jul 3		

4ac843000   SONKA

Nancy Darlene Rose	1950 Mar 3 Parsons KS	1969 Feb 14 Parsons KS	
Daniel Craig Sonka	1952 May 22		
1 Travis Darin	1974 Jun 23		
2 Chenney Rebecca	1979 May 19		

4ac844000   ROSE

Charles Leroy Rose	1952 May 13 Parsons KS	1975 Aug 9 Parsons KS	
Susan Nan Ruthrauff	1957 Mar 1		
1 Dustin Charles	1976 Feb 9		1976 Feb 9
2 Sonny Todd	1977 Aug 15		
3 Casey Lee	1980 May 14		

Serial # and Name	Birth	Marriage	Death

4ad000000 FRYER

	Birth	Marriage	Death
Rebecca A. McElwain	:1851 Mar 7 Allegheny City PA	:1879 Sep 25 Butler Co. KS	:1912 Oct 28 Randolph Co. MO
William A. Fryer	:1846 Jan 7 Adams Co. IL	: John Fryer & Lucinda Whitley	:1923 Apr 5 Randolph Co. MO
William was a farmer.			
1 Lucy	*:1880 Jul 7	KS:	:1912 Oct 28 Cairo MO
2 Frank Mervin	*:1882 Jul 24 Butler Co.	KS:1908 Nov 17 Dodge City KS	:1958 Mar 3 Cairo MO
3 Jessie	*:1885 Apr 8	KS:1923>	:1971 Aug 3 Moberly MO
4 Harry	*:1887 Apr	KS:1914> Oct 31 Linneus MO	:1959 Jul 31 Brookfield MO
5 Opal	:	:	:died as a child

4ad100000 VINCENT

	Birth	Marriage	Death
Lucy Fryer	:1880 Jul 7	KS:	:1912 Oct 28 Cairo MO
Charles Vincent	:	: Ezekiel G. Vincent &	:1964 Sep 4 Moberly MO
	:	: Elizabeth -----	:

4ad200000 FRYER

	Birth	Marriage	Death
Frank Mervin Fryer	:1882 Jul 24 Butler Co.	KS:1908 Nov 17 Dodge City KS	:1958 Mar 3 Cairo MO
Eliza Ann Keith	:1892 Feb 13 Jackson Co.	MO: William John Keith	:1952 Dec 16 Cairo MO
	:	: Josephine Moler	:
1 Zona Hazel	*:1908 Aug 11 Wichita	KS:	:1986 Feb 10 Winterset IA
2 Virgil Dale	:1911 Feb 21 Dodge City	KS:	:1911 Oct 11
3 Velma Ruth	*:1915 Sep 23 Cairo	MO:1933 Apr 29 Cairo MO:
4 Juanita Faye	*:1918 Nov 8 Cairo	MO:1940 Oct 5 so. of Rucker MO:
5 Alberta May	*:1928 Feb 2 Cairo	MO:1950 Jul 30 Cairo MO:

4ad210000 RANKIN

	Birth	Marriage	Death
Zona Hazel Fryer	:1908 Aug 11 Wichita	KS:	:1986 Feb 10 Winterset IA
Frank Rankin	:	:	:

4ad230000 DOWDING

	Birth	Marriage	Death
Velma Ruth Fryer	:1915 Sep 23 Cairo	MO:1933 Apr 29 MO:
Willard Paul Dowding, Jr.	:1915 Feb 15 Sedalia	MO: Willard Paul Dowding &	:
	:	: Viola Prudence Hayden	:
1 Ruth Ann	:1942 Aug 24 Kansas City	MO:	:
2 Jenny Kay	*:1945 Feb 11 Kansas City	MO:1965 Aug 7 Cairo MO:

4ad232000 LEE / RICHTER / BAKER

	Birth	Marriage	Death
Jenny Kay Dowding	:1945 Feb 11 Kansas City	MO:1965 Aug 7 Cairo MO:
s Charles Lee	:1944 Nov 30 Springdale	AR:	:
t Vincent Richter	:1941 Jul 31 Kansas City	MO:1977 Nov 11 Columbia MO:1979 Jan 6 Columbia MO
u Charles Baker	:	:	:
	:	:	:
1 Gina Michelle Lee	:1969 Oct 31 Fayetteville	NC:	:
2 Kristen Kay Lee	:1970 Nov 20	AK:	:

Serial # and Name	Birth	Marriage	Death

4ad240000   BUCKLER

Juanita Faye Fryer	:1918 Nov 8 Cairo	MO:1940 Oct 5 so. of Rucker MO:	
Durward Preston Buckler	:1919 Jun 24 Higbee	MO: Clarence Maurice Buckler & :	
	:	: Roxie Noel	:

After the children were grown Juanita worked for State Farm Insurance Co. in Columbia, MO.   Durward was employed by the state prison, near which they built a new home.   They love to fish in the big lake they have.

1 Melvin Douglas	*:1943 Mar 21 Cairo	MO:1966 Jan 18 Norwich	CT:
2 Darrell Wayne	*:1946 Dec 27 Cairo	MO:1965 Aug 13 Moberly	MO:
3 Terry Lynn	*:1950 Jun 20 Clark	MO:1984 Oct 20 Clark	MO:

4ad241000   BUCKLER

Melvin Douglas Buckler	:1943 Mar 21 Cairo	MO:1966 Jan 18 Norwich	CT:
Marylin Lucille Gottesfeld	:1946 Dec 12 Norwich	CT: Meyer Gottesfeld &	:
	:	: Ann Consentino	:

Douglas served in the U. S. Navy from 1961 to 1969.   He went on ten patrols on the submarine "Edison", and spent over two years underwater, once without surfacing for 87 days.

1 Pamela Dawn	:1968 May 7 Charlestown	SC:	:

4ad242000   BUCKLER

Darrell Wayne Buckler	:1946 Dec 27 Cairo	MO:1965 Aug 13 Moberly	MO:
Connie Jean Brandow	:1947 Apr 20 Clark	MO: William Brandow &	:
	:	: Stella Strouvelle	:
1 Toni Lanatte	:1973 Jun 27 Columbia	MO:	:1973 Jun 27 Columbia MO
2 Timothy Wayne	:1979 Apr 11 Columbia	MO:	:

4ad243000   BUCKLER

Terry Lynn Buckler	:1950 Jun 20 Clark	MO:1984 Oct 20 Clark	MO:
Marsha Faye (Brooks)	:	: Herman Curry Brooks &	MO:
Dobson	:	: Agnes -----	:

Terry was a "Green Beret" in the U. S. Army, and the youngest of the Santa Raiders seeking to rescue the POW's.   For this service he received the Silver Star.

1 Hana Kalani	:1989 Apr 18 Kansas City	MO:	:
2 Aaron Dobson	:1978 Aug 4	:	:

Aaron was born of Marsha's first marriage.

4ad250000   SMITH

Alberta May Fryer	:1928 Feb 2 Cairo	MO:1950 Jul 30 Cairo	MO:
Rodney Douglas Smith	:1928 Apr 27 Freeman	MO: Liggon William Smith	:
	:	: Clara Angeline DeField	:
1 Lynda Fay	*:1951 Apr 27 Ft. Gordon	GA:1975 Sep 6 Columbia	MO:
2 Gail Ann	*:1952 May 30 Atlanta	GA:	:
3 Rodney Dale	*:1954 May 27 Columbia	MO:1987 Feb 21 Oak Ridge	TN:
4 Carol May	:1963 May 4 Columbia	MO:	:1979 Aug 30
5 Sharol Kay	*:1963 May 4 Columbia	MO:1985 Jul 13 Columbia	MO:
6 Leslie Renee	:1965 Jul 23 Columbia	MO:	:
7 Amy Jo	:1967 Jan 29 Columbia	MO:	:

Serial # and Name		Birth		Marriage		Death

4ad251000   BAUMGARTNER

| Lynda Fay Smith | :1951 Apr 27 Ft. Gordon | GA:1975 Sep 6 Columbia | MO: |
| Howard Steven Baumgartner: | Jan 29 Columbia | MO: | : |

Lynda graduated from Missouri State University, Springfield, with a B. S. degree in Education.   She taught school in Columbia until the birth of her second child.   Howard has a B. S. in Education from the University of Missouri.

1 Michael Paul	:1976 Jul 29 Columbia	MO:	:
2 Rebekah Clare	:1979 Aug 20 Columbia	MO:	:
3 Steven Douglas	:1981 Apr 12 Columbia	MO:	:

4ad252000   STRAMPHER / BOYEA

Gail Ann Smith	:1952 May 30 Atlanta	GA:	:
s Cecil William Strampher :		:	:
t Douglas Paul Boyea, Jr. :1950 Mar 15		:1976 Jul 3 Casper	WY:

Gail has a B. S. in Education from a South Dakota state college, and taught in the adult education program in Casper, WY. Douglas is a geologist with a B. S. from the University of New Mexico.   He worked locating uranium and, later, oil.

| 1 Keith Boyea | :1980 Jul | WY: | : |
| 2 Luke Boyea | :1983 May 27 Garland | TX: | : |

4ad253000   SMITH

Rodney Dale Smith	:1954 May 27 Columbia	MO:1987 Feb 21 Oak Ridge	TN:
Patricia Ann McManus	:1961 Oct 31 Dallas	TX: Ronald P. McManus &	:
	:	: Mary Lou -----	:
1 Ryan Douglas	:1990 May 17	:	:

4ad255000   NUCKOLLS

Sharol Kay Smith	:1963 May 4 Columbia	MO:1985 Jul 13 Columbia	MO:
Desmond Nuckolls, III	:1960 Sep 9 West Covina	CA: Desmond Nuckolls, II	:
	:	: Joyce Janet Weber	:

Sharol is a representative for the Syntex Pharmacetical Co., calling on physicians, and Desmond represents Proctor and Gamble Co., calling on dentists.

1 Desmond, IV	:1986 Jul 1 Dallas Co.	TX:	:
2 Lauren Carol	:1988 Jul 21 Grapevine	TX:	:
3 Drew Tyler	:1990 Jun 1 Grapevine	TX:	:

4ad300000   BARNETT

| Jessie Fryer | :1885 Apr 8 | KS:1923> | :1971 Aug 3 Moberly | MO |
| Clay Barnett | : | : | : | |

4ad400000   FRYAR

Harry Fryer	:1887 Apr	KS:1914 Oct 31 Linneus	MO:1959 Jul 31 Brookfield	MO
Bess Lucille Baker	:1893 Jul 18 College Mound MO: Francis Lloyd Baker &	:1979 Mar 29 Brookfield	MO
	:	: Laura -----	:	
1 Thelma Marguerite	#:1915 Jun 6 Brookfield	MO:	:	
2 Kenneth Wayne	:1916 Jun 12 Brookfield	MO:	:1916 Oct 10	
3 Ruth Helen	:1919	:	:1919	

4ad410000   MARK

| Thelma Marguerite Fryer | :1915 Jun 6 Brookfield | MO: | : | |
| Russell Mark | : | : | : | Stormlake   IA |

Serial # and Name	Birth	Marriage	Death

4b0000000   MCELWAIN

James McElwain	1796 Oct 29 Cumberland Co. PA		1884 Feb 25 i. Cable OH
Alice Carson	1801 Dec 27 PA		1878 Jan 6 i. Cable OH

This family lived in Greene County, OH, in 1850 in Sugar Creek, and in 1860 in Xenia.

1 Jane	1823 Mar 18 Cumberland Co. PA		
2 Margaret Bell	#1824 Nov 20 Cumberland Co. PA	1850 Dec 12 Greene Co. OH	
3 Andrew McKinney	#1827 Apr 11 Cumberland Co. PA	1850 Jan 13 Greene Co. OH	
4 William Stewart	1829 Dec 30 Cumberland Co. PA		
5 James R.	#1832 Jun 15 PA	1893 Apr 17 Champaign Co. OH	1898 Dec 30 i. Cable OH
6 Isaac W.	#1835 Feb OH	1861 Jan 31 Greene Co. OH	1911
7 Ellen			
8 James S.			

In 1860, according to one census record, Andrew, James, and Isaac lived in Xenia, OH in the home of their married sister Margaret; all three are listed as laborers. They are also listed in that same census, along with William, in the home of their parents; all four were stated to be working as stone cutters.   Also living in the home of James and Alice were Mary B. (age 7) and Emily (age 3) McElwain, both born in Ohio. No relationship is given for these two children.   It is possible that they are the daughters of Andrew. See the entry below for Andrew.

4b2000000   RINKER

Margaret Bell McElwain	1824 Nov 20 Cumberland Co. PA	1850 Dec 12 Greene Co. OH	
George Washington Rinker	1819c OH		

Xenia, OH was the home of this family in 1860.   George was then a teamster.   Living with them was John McElwain Rinker, born in Pennsylvania about 1845; his relationship is not made clear by the census.

1 Alice M.	1852c OH		
2 James A.	1855c OH		
3 William H.	1857c OH		

4b3000000   MCELWAIN

Andrew McKinney McElwain	1827 Apr 11 Cumberland Co. PA	1850 Jan 13 Greene Co. OH	
Emma -----	1854c MO		

Andrew was a bachelor living with his parents in Greene County, Ohio at the time of the 1860 census.   In the 1880 census, from which this entry is taken, he was living with Emma in Champaign County, Ohio.   See the entry for Andrew's father, James (#4b0000000) concerning possible daughters of Andrew and Emma.

4b5000000   MCELWAIN

James R. McElwain	1832 Jun 15 PA	1893 Apr 17 Champaign Co OH	1898 Dec 30 Cable OH
Laura Ann Bodey	1862 Oct 30 Millerstown OH	Andrew Bodey & Clarissa ----	1948 Aug 8 St. Paris OH

Laura married four times: (1) Robbins, (2) Jones, (3) McElwain, and (4) Kline.   She had sons William C. Robbins and Edward Kline, and may have had a son from her second marriage.   In 1900 she was living with her sons James and William in Wayne twp., Champaign County, Ohio.

1 James Roger, Sr.	#1895 Feb 6 Cable OH	1925 Aug 4 Urbana OH	1984 Mar 13 New Carlisle OH

4b5100000   MCELWAIN

James Roger McElwain, Sr.	1895 Feb 6 Cable OH	1925 Aug 4 Urbana OH	1984 Mar 13 New Carlisle OH
Elizabeth Lucille Miller	1909 Nov 18 Urbana OH	Henry Lincoln Miller &	1983 Nov 16 New Carlisle OH
		Laura Almeda Buckles	

James served in France and Germany as a Private in the United States Army in World War I.

1 Thomas Jackson	#1926 Oct 9 Urbana OH	1948 Jun 5 Springfield OH	
2 James Roger, Jr.	#1928 Feb 28 Springfield OH	1948 Jun 4 Springfield OH	1990 Feb 23 New Carlisle OH

Serial # and Name	Birth	Marriage	Death

4b5110000 MCELWAIN

Thomas Jackson McElwain	1926 Oct 9 Urbana OH	1948 Jun 5 Springfield OH	
Effie Louise Gifford	1925 Jan 4 Jackson OH	Ben M. Gifford &	
		Vorlie Poynter	

Effie had a daughter, Marilyn Lou Gifford, prior to this marriage.

1 John Thomas	1948 Dec 9 Clark Co. OH		
2 Jerry Lee	*1958 Dec 9 Springfield OH	1983 Jan 21	

4b5112000 MCELWAIN

Jerry Lee McElwain	1958 Dec 9	1983 Jan 21	
s Brenda Gayle Nichols	1960 Oct 20 Springfield OH	Charles Norman Nichols &	1987 Jan 13 i. New Carlisle OH
		Ethel Marie Mapes	
t ----- -----			

Brenda died of an aortic aneurysm.

1 Lori Sheree	s 1983 Aug 8		
2 Christopher James	s 1986 Dec 27		

4b5120000 MCELWAIN

James Roger McElwain, Jr.	1928 Feb 28 Springfield OH	1948 Jun 4 Springfield OH	1990 Feb 23 New Carlisle OH
Doris Ellen Cline	1928 Dec 27 Jonesboro AR	John Cline & Myrtle Sheets	

James worked at many things during his life, the longest periods being in construction and cross-country truck driving. He and Doris operated an auto salvage business while he worked in construction. For a time he was a deputy sheriff, and when younger he had tried professional boxing and car racing.

1 Rita Lucille	*1949 Oct 14	1967 Dec 2 Lawrenceville OH	
2 James Roger, III	*1951 Aug 12	1969 Aug 22 Dayton OH	

4b5121000 HUBBARD / THOMPSON / RICHARDS

Rita Lucille McElwain	1949 Oct 14 Springfield OH	1967 Dec 2 Lawrenceville OH	
a William Henry Hubbard	1949 May 21 Portsmouth OH	Albert Hubbard & Anna Mae Copas	
b Douglas DeWayne Thompson	1951 Jan 23 Springfield OH	not married	
		Ewel Thompson & Tarcie Goode	
c Timothy Wayne Richards	1942 Sep 10 Springfield OH	1986 Oct 24 Jellico TN	
		Wayne Richards & Ruth Callison	

Douglas is the biological father of the two children. Rita was divorced from William Sept. 16, 1968. They remarried Feb. 14, 1970 in Springfield, OH and were divorced a second time Oct. 2, 1986.   Rita collects dolls, books, and postcards. Timothy is a crane operator for Navistar, where he has been for over 33 years.

1 Brian Todd Hubbard	*1969 Jun 26 Springfield OH		
2 William Wyatt Hubbard	*1970 Sep 10 Springfield OH		

4b5121100 HUBBARD

Brian Todd Hubbard	1969 Jun 26 Springfield OH		
Jane Maria Hubbard	1962 Jul 30 Columbus OH	Paul Hubbard & Nancy Lipari	

Brian and Jane are not related, nor are they married.   Brian works at Meijer as order writer for frozen foods. Jane has a degree from Columbus State Community College, and is a Medical Laboratory Technician.

1 Christopher Ryan	1994 May 13 Columbus OH		

4b5121200 HUBBARD

William Wyatt Hubbard	1970 Sep 10 Springfield OH		
Billi Vanessa Jenkins	1977 May 18 Springfield OH	Jerry Allen & Terri Jenkins	

Wyatt is employed as a tool maker at Pentaflex. Billi had a previous marriage to a Beal.

1 Alyssa Alexandria Jenkins	1996 May 6 Springfield OH		

Serial # and Name	Birth	Marriage	Death

4b5122000 MCELWAIN

James Roger McElwain, III	1951 Aug 12 Springfield OH	1969 Aug 22 Dayton OH	
s Patricia Lea McMillen	1951 Jun 13 Fairborn OH	Charles McMillen & Maxie Hamilton	
t Laura Lynn Wild	1960 Sep 2 Springfield OH	1990 Oct 20 Jellico TN	
		James Wild & Ruthann Dillon	

James and Patricia were divorced in 1985. James has been a tool maker at Navistar for twenty years. Laura
had prior marriages to Jim Gilmore and Robert Miller.

1 Monica Lea	s*	1970 Apr 22 Xenia OH	1993 Dec 31	
2 James Roger, IV	s	1973 Dec 3 Xenia OH		
3 Melanie Jean	s*	1975 Jun 4 Springfield OH		

James, IV is majoring in sociology and criminology at Ohio University in Athens, Ohio.

4b5122100 DOWTY

| Monica Lea McElwain | 1970 Apr 22 Xenia   OH | 1993 Dec 31 | |
| Gary Joe Dowty | 1957 Dec 27 Troy   NY | Raymond Dowty & Betty Thorpe | |

Monica has a degree in English Literature from Wright State University. She and Gary are separated.

4b5122300 HAFFNER

| Melanie Jean McElwain | 1975 Jun 4 Springfield OH | | |
| Robert Michael Haffner Jr. | 1975 Apr 24 Springfield OH | Robert M. Haffner, Sr. & Carol S. Rodgers | |

Melanie works in the therapy department at Dr. Daubenspeck. Robert lives separately; he supports his son.

| 1 Robert Michael, III | 1994 Dec 14 Springfield OH | | |

4b6000000 MCELWAIN

| Isaac W. McElwain | 1835 Feb   OH | 1861 Jan 31 Greene Co.   OH | 1911 |
| Rebecca Hook | 1838 Mar   OH | | 1905 |

In 1880 Isaac and Rebecca were living in Ridge, Van Wert Co., OH and in 1900 at 136 Kepler, Pleasant, OH.
In 1880 Nancy, Minnie, and Pearl were living with them; in 1880 only Pearl still lived with the parents.
No sons appear in either census. In 1910 Isaac lived with Pearl in Van Wert, OH.

1 Nancy Elizabeth	*	1866	1887>	
2 James C.	1870 Aug 3 Van Wert Co. OH		
3 Minnie E.	1875 Jan 24 Van Wert Co. OH		
4 Stewart			
5 Andrew			
6 Pearl D.	1880 Mar OH		

4b6100000 NICODEMUS

| Nancy Elizabeth McElwain | 1866 | 1887> | |
| Edgar Nicodemus | 1861 | | |

500000000 NICHOLSON

| Mary McElwain | | 1794 Jul 29 Newville   PA | |
| John Nicholson | | | |

600000000 MCKIM

Hannah McElwain	1761		1794
James McKim			
1 James			
2 Ruth	*|		

620000000 HARLAN

| Ruth McKim | | | |
| ----- Harlan | | | |

Serial # and Name	Birth		Marriage		Death	

700000000   MCILVAINE

Ruth McElwain						
George McIlvaine	!1754	Cumberland Co. PA!	John McIlvaine & Mary Greer !			

See the History for information on this family (pp. 37-38), and the McIlvaine family (pp. 45-56).

1 Mary	*!1780	Cumberland Co. PA!			!1836	Washington Co. PA
2 Catherine	*!1782 Jun 6	Cumberland Co. PA!	1804		!1873 Aug 12	
3 Elizabeth	*!1784 Sep 13	Cumberland Co. PA!	1803 Mar 22		!1835 Jun 9	
4 Ruth	*!1786	Cumberland Co. PA!	1817 Jun 19		!1850>	
5 John	*!1788 Nov 7	Washington Co. PA!		Washington Co. PA!	1880 May 5 Wayne Co.	OH
6 Andrew	!1791	Washington Co. PA!				
7 George, Jr.	*!1793	Washington Co. PA!				
8 Robert	*!1795	Washington Co. PA!			!1864 Nov 5	
9 Greer	!1797	Washington Co. PA!			!1801<	
a Eleanor	!1799	Washington Co. PA!			!1805<	
b Greer	*!1801 Jan 10	Washington Co. PA!	1831 Mar 6		!1871 Nov 16	
c Eleanor	*!1805	Washington Co. PA!				

The first Greer and Eleanor both died in infancy, and the next two children were given the same names.

710000000   CROUCH

Mary McIlvaine	!1780	Cumberland Co. PA!			!1836	Washington Co. PA
John Crouch	!1774				!1849	

This couple had six children; nothing further is known of them.

720000000   RAMSEY

Catherine McIlvaine	!1782 Jun 6	Cumberland Co. PA!	1804	!1873 Aug 12	
Josiah Ramsey	!1783			!1835	

Josiah was a physician.   In 1850 Catherine lived in South Straban township, Washington Co. PA; in her home lived her sons William and Josiah, Catherine A. Dill, age 11 (probably her grandchild, daughter of Mary Jane), and William Wibley (unidentified). Her home was valued at $1540.

1 Mary	!1808			!1811	
2 Ruth	*!1810	PA!			
3 William	!1812 Jan 16	Washington Co. PA!	never married	!1880 Jun 30	
4 Katherine	*!1814c				
5 Mary Jane	*!1816	Washington Co. PA!			
6 George	*!1820 Apr 19	Washington Co. PA!		!1902 Apr 13	
7 Eleanor	*!1823c	Washington Co. PA!			
8 Maria	!1825	Washington Co. PA!		!1829	
9 Josiah A.	*!1828 Mar 31	Washington Co. PA!		!1873 Jan 8	
a Martha	*!	Washington Co. PA!			
b Elizabeth	*!				
c Charlotte	*!				

722000000   NESBIT

Ruth Ramsey	!1810	PA!	
John Nesbit	!1797	PA!	

John and Mary with the three children listed lived in 1850 in South Straban township, Washington Co., PA. Their home was valued at $5760.   Ordway suggests that the great age difference in the children indicates that this was a second marriage for John.

1 James	!1831c	PA!	
2 Mary	!1836c	PA!	
3 Maria Jane	*!1849 Dec	PA!	

Serial # and Name	Birth	Marriage	Death
722300000 WILSON			
Maria Jane Nesbit	:1849 Dec	PA:	:
Samuel Wilson	:1850 Dec	PA:	:
The Wilson family lived in South Strabane township, Washington Co., PA in 1900.			
1 John	:1882 Jul	PA:	:
2 William	:1885 Jun	PA:	:
3 Arthur	:1886 Jul	PA:	:
4 Bernard	:1889 May	PA:	:
724000000 CHAMBERS			
Katherine Ramsey	:1814c	PA:	:
John Chambers	:1813c	:	:
Katherine and John, with Martha, Josiah, John, and Nancy lived in Canonsburg, Washington Co., PA in 1850.			
John was a merchant, and owned real estate valued at $1500.			
1 Martha	*:1835c	:	:
2 Dora	*:	:	:
3 Josiah	*:1839c	PA:	:
4 William B.	:	:	:
5 John	:1842c	PA:	:
6 Nancy	*:1844c	PA:	:
724100000 KADY			
Martha Chambers	:1835c	:	:
----- Kady	:	:	:
724200000 GALBRAITH			
Dora Chambers	:	:	:
----- Galbraith	:	:	:
724300000 CHAMBERS			
Josiah Chambers	:1839c	PA:	:
Mary -----	:1850c	PA:	:
Josiah and Mary, with these children (except Martha), lived in Chartiers twp., Washington Co., PA in 1880.			
1 John M.	:1870c	PA:	:
2 Margaret M.	*:1872c	PA:	:
3 William	:1873c	PA:	:
4 Catherine	*:1876c	PA:	:
5 Elizabeth	:1878c	PA:	:
6 Dora	*:1880c	PA:	:
7 Martha	:	:	:
Elizabeth was living unmarried with her sister, Catherine Warrick, in Washington Co., PA in 1910.			
724320000 SOWERS			
Margaret M. Chambers	:1872c	:	:
----- Sowers	:	:	:
724340000 WARRICK			
Catherine C. Chambers	:1877c	PA:	:
John W. Warrick	:1862c	PA:	:
Catherine (Katherine in the census) and John lived with their two children in Washington Co. PA in 1910.			
1 George R.	:1900c	:	:
2 John W., Jr.	:1904c	:	:

Serial # and Name	Birth	Marriage	Death

724360000   RETZELL

Dora Chambers	1882c	PA	
----- Retzell			

724600000   MCCLOY

Nancy Chambers	1834c		
----- McCloy			

725000000   DILL

Mary Jane Ramsey	1816	Washington Co. PA	
John Dill			

The 1850 census lists Catherine A. Dill as an occupant of the household of Catherine Ramsey, Mary Jane's mother. Catherine is listed here as it is probable that she was the child of Mary Jane and John.

1 Catherine A.	1839c	PA	

726000000   RAMSEY

George Ramsey	1820 Apr 19	Washington Co. PA	1902 Apr 13
Annie -----			

George was a physician.

727000000   MARTIN

Eleanor Ramsey	1823c	Washington Co. PA	
James Martin	1818c	PA	

The couple and their first four children lived in North Straban twp., Washington Co., PA in 1850.

1 Samuel	*1843c	PA	
2 Josiah	*1844c	PA	
3 Mary Catherine	*1846c	PA	
4 Margaret	*1848c	PA	
5 Rose	*		
6 Sadie	*		
7 William	*		
8 James	*		
9 Lulu	*		

727100000   MARTIN

Samuel Martin	1843c		
Elizabeth Wilson			

727200000   MARTIN

Josiah Martin	1846c	PA	
Mary Law	1849c	PA	

727300000   CRAIG

Mary Catherine Martin	1848c	PA	
Joseph Craig	1844c	PA	

This family lived in Raccoon twp., Beaver Co., PA in 1880.

1 Ella M.	1869c	PA	
2 Alvin B.	1871c	PA	
3 James H.	1873c	PA	
4 Margaret D.	1875c	PA	
5 Ramsy	1877c	PA	

Serial # and Name	Birth	Marriage	Death
727400000 CROOKS			
Margaret Martin	1849c		
T. M. Crooks			
727500000 FINNEY			
Rose Martin			
----- Finney			
727600000 SAWHILL			
Sadie Martin	1845c	PA	
John Sawhill	1836c	PA	

Ordway shows Sadie Martin as marrying John Sawhill, but nothing further is known of her.   The only entries in the Pennsylvania censuses of 1870 and 1880 for a Sawhill family are those for John and Jane B. Sawhill.   Sadie is not a standard nickname for Jane, but not all children are given standard nicknames. The deciding factor in placing this information here was the name of the youngest Sawhill child--Sadie M. There is, however, no proof that those census entries pertain to Sadie, the daughter of James and Eleanor Martin, and that conclusion should be viewed with caution.   In both years the couple lived in Buffalo twp., Washington Co., PA. John was a farmer; in 1870 his real estate was worth $22,850, and his personal property, $2,036.

1 Mary Jane	1865c	PA	
2 William S. (or L.)	1866c	PA	
3 Elizabeth Jane	1869c	PA	
4 Elmer C.	1871c	PA	
5 Oscar H.	1871c	PA	
6 John M.	1875c	PA	
7 Ina M.	1878c	PA	
8 Sadie M.	1879c	PA	
727700000 MARTIN			
William Martin			
Margaret Finney			
727800000 MARTIN			
James Martin			
Geneva Craig			
727900000 WILEY			
Lulu Martin			
Frank Wiley			
729000000			
Josiah A. Ramsey	1828 Mar 31 Washington Co. PA		1873 Jan 8
s Mary West			
t Emeline E. -----			

Josiah was a physician.

72a000000 FOSTER			
Martha Ramsey		Washington Co. PA	
Alexander Foster			
1 Martha	*		
2 Josiah			
3 Alexander			

Serial # and Name	Birth	Marriage	Death
72a100000 FARRINGTON			
Martha Foster			
----- Farrington			
72b000000 FOSTER			
Elizabeth Ramsey			
John Foster			
72c000000 DINSMORE			
Charlotte Ramsey			
William Dinsmore			
1 Katie	#		
2 Robert A.	#		
3 Josiah G.	#		
4 Androse T.	#		
5 William	#		
6 May	#		
7 Florence Hope	#		
8 Frank A.	#		
72c100000 JACKSON			
Katie Dinsmore			
Samuel Jackson			
72c200000 DINSMORE			
Robert A. Dinsmore			
Jennie Armstrong			
1 Ward		Washington Co. PA	
2 Chester		Washington Co. PA	
3 Lloyd	# 1889c	Washington Co. PA	
4 Robie		Washington Co. PA	
5 Lottie		Washington Co. PA	
72c230000 DINSMORE			
Lloyd Dinsmore	1889c	Washington Co. PA	
Adeline J. -----	1890c	PA	
This family lived in Washington Co., PA in 1920.			
1 Bettie	1919	PA	
72c300000 DINSMORE			
Josiah G. Dinsmore			
Sue Whiteman			
1 William B.	#	Washington Co. PA	
2 Odessa B.	#	Washington Co. PA	
72c310000 DINSMORE			
William B. Dinsmore		Washington Co. PA	
Mabel Lemon			

Serial # and Name	Birth	Marriage	Death
72c320000 FLEMING			
Odessa B. Dinsmore		Washington Co. PA	
----- Fleming			
72c400000 DINSMORE			
Androse T. Dinsmore			
Martha Moore			
1 Delsa L.	#	Washington Co. PA	
2 Lenore L.		Washington Co. PA	
3 Aletha H.		Washington Co. PA	
4 Lester R.		Washington Co. PA	
72c410000 SHOCKLEY			
Delsa L. Dinsmore			
Charles Shockley			
72c500000 DINSMORE			
William Dinsmore			
Delia Grimes			
72c600000 KILGORE			
May Dinsmore			
William Kilgore			
72c700000 KIGER			
Florence Hope Dinsmore			
Belle Kiger			
1 Florence		Washington Co. PA	
2 Maybelle		Washington Co. PA	
3 Harvey		Washington Co. PA	
72c800000 DINSMORE			
Frank A. Dinsmore			
Mame Gray			
1 William B.			
2 Gray			

Serial # and Name	Birth	Marriage	Death
730000000 CROUCH			
Elizabeth McIlvaine	1784 Sep 13 Cumberland Co.PA	1803 Mar 22	1835 Jun 9
William Crouch	1772 Dec Washington Co.PA		1853 Oct 20
1 George	*1804 Jan 2 Washington Co.PA		1891 Nov 27
2 Robert	*1807 Jun 11 Washington Co.PA		1880 Dec
3 John	*1809 Jan 27 Washington Co.PA		1875 Feb 7
4 William	1811 Jan 24 Washington Co.PA		1819 Aug 28
5 Ruth	1813 Jan 14 Washington Co.PA		1837 Mar 28
6 Eliza	1814 Nov 27 Washington Co.PA		1854 Oct 10
7 Joseph R.	*1816 Nov 8 Washington Co.PA		1882 Oct
8 Watson	1818 Sep 28 Washington Co.PA		1893 Apr 13
9 Mary	1820 Nov 20 Washington Co.PA		1844 Jul 28
a Isaiah	1823 Jan 15 Washington Co.PA		1853 Jul 26
b Daniel	*1827 Nov 10 Washington Co.PA		1880 Dec 25
c William	*1828 Aug 18 Washington Co.PA		

Watson was living unmarried in the home of James Crawford of No. Straban twp., Washington Co., PA in 1850.
William (Sr.) and his son Daniel, both unmarried, were living in No. Straban twp. in 1850.   The families
of George, Robert, John, and Joseph have been connected with this family through census records only.

731000000 CROUCH			
George Crouch	1804 Jan 2 Washington Co. PA		1891 Nov 27
----- -----			

In 1850 George was living with his seven children in Nottingham twp., Washington Co., PA. He was a farmer.

1 William H.	*1829c PA		
2 Elizabeth	1832c PA		
3 John	*1834c PA		
4 Mary	1836c PA		
5 Rachel C	1840c PA		
6 Ellen H.	1842c PA		
7 Anne S.	1846c PA		

In 1850 William was a carpenter, and John, a laborer.

731100000 CROUCH			
William H. Crouch	1829c PA		
Hannah -----	1828c PA		

This family lived in East Bethleham, Washington Co., PA in 1880.

1 Florence	1866c PA		
2 Annie	1866c PA		
3 William	1870c PA		

731300000 CROUCH			
John Crouch	1834c PA		
Isabel -----	1835c PA		

This entry was compiled through census records only and is therefore hypothetical.   In 1860 and 1870 this
family lived in South Strabane twp., Washington Co., PA. Harmon does not appear in the 1870 census.

1 Harmon	1856c PA		
2 Robert C.	1858c PA		
3 Alphonso	1861c PA		
4 William H.	1864c PA		
5 Laura Bell	1866c PA		
6 Josiah B.	1868c PA		
7 Anna May	1870 PA		

Serial # and Name	Birth	Marriage	Death

732000000   CROUCH

| Robert Crouch | 1807 Jun 11 Washington Co. PA | | 1880 Dec |
| Anne ----- | 1807c   PA | | |

The Crouchs lived with these children in North Straban twp., Washington Co., PA in 1850.   Robert was a
farmer with real property of $3600.   In 1860 and 1870 the couple were living in North Straban; they owned
real property worth $5000 in 1860, and $14,000 in real property and $500 in personal property in 1870.

1 Nancy L.	1831c PA		
2 John	#1833c PA		
3 Eleanor	1847c PA		

732200000   CROUCH

| John Crouch | 1833c   PA | | 1875 Feb 7 |
| Martha ----- | 1837c   PA | | |

John and Martha lived in North Straban township, Washington County, PA in 1860. He was a farmer.   In 1870
they lived with these four children in Nottingham twp., Washington County, PA.

1 Linn [?]	1863c PA		
2 Robert	1865c PA		
3 Harriet	1867c PA		
4 James B.	1869 PA		

733000000   CROUCH

| John Crouch | 1809 Jan 27 Washington Co. PA | | 1875 Feb 7 |
| Mary ----- | 1814c   PA | | |

This Crouch family lived in 1850 in Carroll twp., Washington Co., PA.   John was a farmer (real property
$4510).   In 1860 they lived in Somerset township, and in 1870, in Bentleyville, PA.   In 1860 John's real
property was worth $9720 and his personal property $1800.

1 Alexander	#1837 May PA		
2 Elizabeth A.	1840c PA		
3 Andrew	1843c PA		

Elizabeth and Andrew, both unmarried, lived with their parents in 1870.

733100000   CROUCH

| Alexander Crouch | 1837 May   PA | | |
| Sarah P. ----- | 1847 Jun   IN | | |

Alexander, Sarah, and their unmarried daughter Mary lived in Pittsburgh, PA in 1900.

| 1 Mary M. | 1869 Mar   PA | | |

737000000   CROUCH

| Joseph R. Crouch | 1816 Nov 8 Washington Co. PA | | 1882 Oct |
| Frances B. ----- | 1822c   PA | | |

Joseph and Frances lived in Peters twp., Washington Co., PA in 1850; in 1860 they lived with their two sons
in Wayne township, Washington Co., PA, and owned real estate worth $500 and personal property of $300.
They and their sons lived in Wayne twp. in 1870, with real estate of $2800 and personal property of $2000.
In 1880 they lived in Dayton, PA.

| 1 Wallace Hunter | #1860 May   PA | | |
| 2 Daniel Ogden | #1857c   PA | | |

737100000   CROUCH

| Wallace Hunter Crouch | 1860 May   PA | | |
| Mary M. ----- | 1864 Aug   PA | | |

Wallace lived, unmarried, with his parents in 1880.   He and Mary lived at 354 Main Street, Greenville,
Mercer County, PA in 1900.   The year of birth of Wallace in the 1900 census does not agree with the
calculated year from two earlier censuses (in which he was listed with his parents) by five years.

252

Serial # and Name	Birth	Marriage	Death

737200000   CROUCH

| Daniel Ogden Crouch | 1857c | PA | |
| Margie C. ----- | 1854c | PA | |

In 1880 Daniel and Margie lived with his parents in Dayton, PA. In 1910 they and their six younger children lived in Armstrong County, PA.

1 Greta V.	*1877c	PA	
2 Frances [?]	1879	PA	
3 Frank, Jr.	1885c	PA	
4 Fern D.	1885c	PA	
5 Laura C.	1888c	PA	
6 Joseph R.	1891c	PA	
7 George P.	1894c	PA	
8 Ruth D.	1897c	PA	

737210000   SHRECCGART

| Greta V. Crouch | 1877c | PA | |
| Albert Shreccgart | 1880c | PA | |

Greta and Albert lived with Greta's parents in 1910 in Washington County, PA.

73b000000   CROUCH

Daniel O. Crouch	*1829c*	*PA*	*1880 Dec 25*
Harriet Hartshorn	*1835c*	*PA ----- Hartshorn &*	
		Sophinia -----	

The identity of Daniel as the son of William Crouch is not certain. In 1870 and 1880 the family was living in Curwinsville, Clearfield County, PA.   In 1870 Daniel's occupation was that of a physician; he had real property worth $4000 and personal property worth $1500.

1 Elizabeth	*1861c*	*PA*	
2 Harriet	*1867c*	*PA*	
3 Joseph M.	*1869c*	*PA*	
4 John M.	*1872c*	*PA*	

73c000000   CROUCH

| William Crouch | 1828 Aug 18 Washington Co. PA | | |
| Ellen Conley | 1838c | PA | |

William and Ellen, with these four children, lived in Baldwin twp., Allegheny Co., PA in 1880.

1 Cooley Samuel	1861c	PA	died age 26
2 Mary E.	1865c	PA	
3 George	1869c	PA	
4 Nancy	1872c	PA	died age 8

740000000   STRINGER

Ruth McIlvaine	1786	Cumberland Co. PA 1817 Jun 19	1850>
Robert Stringer	1798	Washington Co. PA Joseph Office Stringer &	1850>
		Mary Dawson	

1 George	*1818	Washington Co. PA	
2 James	*1821	Washington Co. PA 1849	
3 John	*1826	Washington Co. PA	
4 Ruth	1831	Washington Co. PA	
5 Robert		Washington Co. PA	

George, a farmer (real property $500), lived with Jerome Grable in Fallowfield township, Washington Co., PA in 1870.

Serial # and Name	Birth	Marriage	Death

741000000 STRINGER

| George Stringer | 1818 | PA | |
| Diannah ----- | | | |

In 1870 George was living unmarried in the household of Jerome Grable of Fallowfield twp., Washington Co., Pennsylvania.

742000000 STRINGER

| James Stringer | 1821 | Washington Co. PA 1849 | |
| Mary J. Teeters | 1831c | PA | |

James and Mary lived in Somerset township, Washington County, PA in 1850. In 1870 they lived with their children in Fallowfield twp., Washington Co., PA.

| 1 Albert Melville | *1852 May | PA | 1927 |
| 2 Franklin Elmer | *1865 Sep 19 | | 1937 Jan 10 |

742100000 STRINGER

| Albert Melville Stringer | 1852 May | PA | 1927 |
| Sarah Ann Sphar | 1859 Jul | PA Jacob Sphar & Rosanna ----- | |

In 1900 this couple, with their children Blanche and Nelson, lived in Pike Run township, Washington County, PA in the home of Sarah's parents

1 Blanche	*1884 Oct	PA	
2 Frances	*		
3 Nelson Devey	*1899 Jan 19	PA	1962 Jan 9

742110000 SMILEY

Blanche Stringer	1884 Oct	PA	
John Smiley			
1 Joella	*		
2 Irene	*		
3 Rex			

742111000 WILLIAMS

Joella Smiley			
Ray Williams			
1 Marian Rae	*		

742111100 MARCOZZI

Marian Rae Williams			
Ernest Marcozzi			
1 Joellen	*		
2 Raymond Paul			

742111110 WALTER

Joellen Marcozzi			
Paul Walter			
1 Cara			
2 Alyssa			

Serial # and Name	Birth	Marriage	Death

742112000   MARCH

Irene Smiley			
George March			
1 Rex Smiley			

742120000   SMILEY

Frances Stringer			
----- Smiley			
1 Georgia	*		
2 Ruth	*		

742121000 SCHULTISE / SMILEY

Georgia Smiley			
s Edwin Schultise			
t John Smiley			

742122000   CHRIST

Ruth Smiley			
Joseph Christ			
1 Clifford	*		

742122100   CHRIST

Clifford Christ			
----- -----			
1 Leslie			
2 Jason			

742130000   STRINGER

Nelson Dewey Stringer	1899 Jan 19		1962 Jan 9
Clara Bradson			
1 Jacqueline Kay	*	MI	
2 Thomas	*		1985

742131000   JACOBS / RUZIKA

Jacqueline Kay Stringer		MI	
s ----- Jacobs			
t ----- Ruzika			

742132000   STRINGER

Thomas Stringer			1985
----- -----			
1 Thomas Dwayne			
2 Timothy			
3 Theodore			
4 Tracy			

Serial # and Name	Birth	Marriage	Death
742200000 STRINGER			
Franklin Elmer Stringer	1865 Sep 19		1937 Jan 10
Florence Estelle Wells	1868 Jun 30		1921 May
1 Clara Josephine	1892 Jun 5		1965
2 Mary Alice	*1895 Jun 18		1967 May
3 Freda Belle	1898 Jul 24		
4 Florence	*1900 Dec 31		1990 Mar
5 Harry Elmer	*1903 Jul 30		1979
6 Martha Ruth	*1906 Mar 28		
7 Frank Vernon	*1908 Jul 20		1970 Mar 9
8 Charles Boyd	*1911 Feb 4		1989 Mar 9
742220000 FERGUSON			
Mary Alice Stringer	1895 Jun 18		1967 May
Rolla Ferguson			
1 Zelda Lorena	*1918 Apr 12		1986 May 7
2 Robert Franklin	1921 Jan 13		1973 Jan 28
3 Sevilla	*1928 Dec 6		
742221000 WIGGINS			
Zelda Lorena Ferguson	1918 Apr 12		1986 May 7
Virgil Wiggins			
1 Lynne	*1945 Aug 1		
2 Todd	*1949 Jan 26		
742221100 SMAROFF			
Lynne Wiggins	1945 Aug 1		
a John Smaroff			
b Keith Dunham			
1 John Smaroff	*1968		
2 Sherri Smaroff	*1970		
742221110 SMAROFF			
John Smaroff	1968		
Lori -----			
1 Jennifer	1986		
2 Lisa	1988		
742221120 BERRDINE			
Sherri Smaroff	1970		
James Berrdine			

256

Serial # and Name		Birth	Marriage	Death
742221200 WIGGINS				
Todd Wiggins		1949 Jan 26		
s Patricia Kennemond				
t Cynda -----				
1 Shane	s	1984		
2 Kevin	t	1990		
742223000 ADAMS				
Sevilla Ferguson		1928 Dec 6		
Ray Adams				
1 Ray Charles	*	1949 Jul 11		
2 Jeffrey Lee		1951 Apr 13		
742223100 ADAMS				
Ray Charles Adams		1949 Jul 11		
Joann Rackley				
1 Ryan Lee		1974 Mar 11		
742240000 WELLINGTON				
Florence Stringer		1900 Dec 31		1990 Mar
Richard Wellington				
742250000 STRINGER				
Harry Elmer Stringer		1903 Jul 30		1979
s ----- -----				
t Julia -----				
1 Harry	s			
2 Patty	t			

Harry was missing in action in the Korean War.

742260000 RENNIE				
Martha Ruth Stringer		1906 Mar 20		
Joseph Rennie				
742270000 STRINGER				
Frank Vernon Stringer		1908 Jul 20		1970 Mar 9
Mildred Mattis		1912 Apr 15		1968 Jul 12
1 Ray	*	1934		
742271000 STRINGER				
Ray Stringer		1934		
Virginia -----				
1 Barry	*			

Serial # and Name	Birth	Marriage	Death
742271100 STRINGER			
Barry Stringer			
----- -----			
1 Justin			
742280000 STRINGER			
Charles Boyd Stringer	1911 Feb 4		1989 Mar 9
Florence Ermlich			
743000000 STRINGER			
John Stringer	1826 Washington Co. PA		
Kate Stewart			
1 Emma J.	#1855 Nov 12 Washington PA		1924 Feb 27
743100000 CAPRITZ / TYNAN			
Emma J. Stringer	1855 Nov 12 Washington PA		1924 Feb 27
s John F. Capritz	1850	FR	1880 Aug Pittsburgh PA
t Thomas Tynan	1851 Mar	EN 1881 Aug 21	
1 John Capritz	#1874 Mar 17		1947 Mar 13
2 [son] Capritz			1880<
3 Gertrude Capritz	#1878 Nov	PA	
4 Harry George Capritz	#1880 Jan 7 Pittsburgh PA 1907 Jun 6		1960 Oct 22 Pittsburgh PA
5 Thomas, Jr. Tynan	1886 Aug		
6 Ida Tynan	1888 Aug 8		
743110000 CAPRITZ			
John Capritz	1874 Mar 17	PA	1947 Mar 13
Catherine Irwin	1874 Sep	CN	

John and Catherine lived at 4611 Friendship St., Pittsburgh, PA in 1900.

Serial # and Name	Birth	Marriage	Death
743130000 LOCKHART			
Gertrude Capritz	1878 Nov	PA	
John B. Lockhart	1879 May	PA	

In 1900 Gertrude, John, and Emma lived at 4064 Woolslayer Alley, Pittsburgh, PA.

Serial # and Name	Birth	Marriage	Death
1 Emma C.	#1899 Jan	PA	
743131000 DASH			
Emma C. Lockhart	1899 Jan	PA	
William Dash			
743140000 CAPRITZ			
Harry George Capritz	1880 Jan 7 Pittsburgh PA 1907 Jun 6		1960 Oct 22 Pittsburgh PA
Alice Cecilia Coleman	1882 May 29 Pittsburgh PA Henry Coleman & Anna King		1974 Jul 14 Pittsburgh PA
1 Anna Catherine	#1908 Mar 23 Pittsburgh PA		
2 John Henry	#1910 Aug 8		1975 Apr 14
3 Alice Emma	#1912 Jul 20 Pittsburgh PA 1935 Feb 17 Dormont PA		
4 Rose Marie	#1922 Aug 11		
5 Gertrude Agnes	#1924 Apr 18 Pittsburgh PA 1946 Jan 26 Pittsburgh PA		

Serial # and Name	Birth	Marriage	Death

743141000   MOORE / PIGONI

Anna Catherine Capritz	1908 Mar 23 Pittsburgh PA		
s Henry George Moore	1903 Aug 8 Pittsburgh PA	Alexander Moore &	
		Bridget Gorham	
t Charles George Pigoni		Joseph Pigoni &	1983 May 30
		Philippina -----	
1 Patricia Irene Moore	*1926 Jun 5		
2 Harriet Ann Moore	*1928 Mar 11 Pittsburgh PA	1947 Jun 2	
3 Joan Josephine Moore	*1930 Sep 30 Pittsburgh PA	1952 Sep 13 Pittsburgh PA	
4 Charles George, Jr. Pigoni	*1934 Jul 8 Pittsburgh PA	1955 Sep 17 Pittsburgh PA	

743141100   SMITHYMAN

Patricia Irene Moore	1926 Jun 5		
John Leo Smithyman		John Leo Smithyman &	
		Catherine Ford	
1 Patricia Jean	*1948 Mar 14 Pittsburgh PA	1979 Jul 11	
2 John	*1949 Feb 21		
3 Daniel Raymond	*1951 Jun 21		
4 Michael Joseph	*1953 Jun 27 Pittsburgh PA		

743141110   ZITO

Patricia Jean Smithyman	1948 Mar 14 Pittsburgh PA	1979 Jul 11	
John Joseph Zito	1940 Nov 25 Cleveland OH	John Ross Zito &	
		Ruth Joan -----	

Patricia graduated from St. John's College, Cleveland, OH.

1 Matthew	1980 Feb 19 Lake Co. OH		
2 Lisa	1981 Oct 15 Lake Co. OH		

743141120   SMITHYMAN

John Smithyman	1949 Feb 21		
Diane DiBardeleben			

John graduated from St. Vincent's College and received his Master's Degree from Tennessee State University.

1 Owen	1985 Dec 3		
2 Austin	1987 Jun 18		
3 Drew	1987 Jun 18		

743141130   SMITHYMAN

Daniel Raymond Smithyman	1951 Jun 21		
Elizabeth Dinning		Richard Dinning & Nancy ----	

Daniel was a teaching Tennis Professional.

1 Christal	1972 Oct 3		
2 Tracy	1975 Sep 22		
3 Jesse [male]	1985 Jun 10		

743141140   SMITHYMAN

Michael Joseph Smithyman	1953 Jun 27		
Christine Sopira	1953 Jul 22	----- Sopira & Mary -----	
1 Jennifer	1980 Mar 20		

259

Serial # and Name	Birth	Marriage	Death
743141200 HOWARTH			
Harriet Ann Moore	1928 Mar 11 Pittsburgh PA	1947 Jun 2	MI
John M. Howarth	1926 Apr 20		
1 Jacqueline A.	* 1953 Oct 26 MI		
2 Karla M.	* 1955 Dec 1 AK		
3 Philip J.	1959 May 26 FL		
743141210 SHELDON			
Jacqueline A. Howarth	1953 Oct 26 MI		
Robert Sheldon			
Jacqueline graduated from Slippery Rock State College, PA.			
1 Gregory J.	1982 Dec 2		
2 Michael R.	1985 May 4		
743141220 HENWOOD			
Karla M. Howarth	1955 Dec 1 AK		
Jerry Henwood	1949 Aug 21		
1 Jessica B.	1984 Aug 10		
2 David P.	1985 Nov 20		
3 Daniel J.	1988 May 24		
743141300 UNICO			
Joan Josephine Moore	1930 Sep 30 Pittsburgh PA	1952 Sep 13 Pittsburgh PA	
Daniel Vincent Unico	1927 Feb 4 Pittsburgh PA		
1 Kenneth Anthony	* 1953 Jul 18 Pittsburgh PA	1985 Oct 12	
2 Mark Daniel	* 1954 Sep 12 Pittsburgh PA	1990 Dec	
3 Renee Ann	* 1958 May 4 Pittsburgh PA		
4 Lisa Marie	* 1963 Mar 10 Pittsburgh PA	1984 Jul 11	
743141310 UNICO			
Kenneth Anthony Unico	1953 Jul 18 Pittsburgh PA	1985 Oct 12	
Sheila Marie Dicroce	1959 Oct 4 Pittsburgh PA	Alexander Dicroce &	
		Theresa Ann Moran	
Kenneth graduated from Duquesne University, and was a tennis champion and a former coach at Duquesne.			
1 Shannon Theresa	1987 Apr 17 Mt. Lebanon PA		
2 Christopher Vincent	1989 Nov 4 Mt. Lebanon PA		
743141320 UNICO			
Mark Daniel Unico	1954 Sep 12	1990 Dec	
Mark graduated from the University of Pittsburgh.			
743141330 CHABAN / EATON			
Renee Ann Unico	1958 May 4 Pittsburgh PA		
s Larry Chaban			
t Mark Eaton			
Renee graduated from Chatham College, Pittsburgh, PA.			

Serial # and Name	Birth	Marriage	Death
743141340 -----			
Lisa Marie Unico	1963 Mar 10 Pittsburgh PA	1984 Jul 11	
----- -----			
743141400 PIGONI			
Charles George Pigoni, Jr.	1934 Jul 8 Pittsburgh PA	1955 Sep 17 Pittsburgh PA	
Rose Exrott			
1 Sharon	*1956 Jul 4		
2 Stephen	*1958 Sep 14		
3 Donna	*1963 Aug 30	1988 Sep 10	
743141410 ROBERTSON			
Sharon Pigoni	1956 Jul 4		
David Robertson			
1 Christopher	1990 Mar 23		
743141420 PIGONI			
Stephen Pigoni	1958 Sep 14		
Ann Vozar			
743141430 KURPIK			
Donna Pigoni	1963 Aug 30	1988 Sep 10	
Russell Kurpik	1958 Sep 15		
743142000 CAPRITZ			
John Henry Capritz	1910 Aug 8		1975 Apr 14
Tensie -----			
743143000 SIAS			
Alice Emma Capritz	1912 Jul 20 Pittsburgh PA	1935 Feb 17 Dormont PA	
John Dando Sias	1911 Aug 26	James Sias & Anna Lester	
1 Gayle Alice	*1936 Jun 7 Pittsburgh PA	1957 Jan 26 Castle Shannon PA	
2 John Dando, Jr.	*1938 Dec 31 Pittsburgh PA		HI
3 Joan Delane	*1938 Dec 31 Pittsburgh PA		
4 David Lester	1941 Nov 2 Pittsburgh PA	never married	1962
743143100 SEFZIK			
Gayle Alice Sias	1936 Jun 7 Pittsburgh PA	1957 Jan 26 Castle Shannon PA	
Gustave William	1933 Feb 28 PA	Gustave William Sefzik &	
Sefzik, Jr.		Ethel -----	
1 Susan Ann	*1957 Dec 30 Pittsburgh PA	1981 May 30 Cecil PA	
2 Linda Lou	*1959 Jul 19 Pittsburgh PA	1980 Oct 4 Cecil PA	
3 Tracy Lee	*1960 Jun 13 Pittsburgh PA	1979 Mar 17 Washington PA	
4 Diane	*1965 Aug 9		
5 David Lester	1966 Sep 11 Mt. Lebanon PA		

Serial # and Name	Birth	Marriage	Death

743143110   GODFREY

Susan Ann Sefzik	1957 Dec 30 Pittsburgh PA	1981 May 30 Cecil PA	
Richard Godfrey	1957 Jun 6	Richard Godfrey &	
		Gloria Scanny	

Susan graduated from Pennsylvania State University.

1 Matthew Richard	1982 Jul 8 Pittsburgh PA		
2 Nicholas	1986 Mar 13 Pittsburgh PA		
3 Evan Michael	1991 Oct 20		

743143120   KOLLJESKI

Linda Lou Sefzik	1959 Jul 19 Pittsburgh PA	1980 Oct 4 Cecil PA	
George Kolljeski	1957 Mar 26	George Kolljeski &	
		Gladys Scanny	
1 Brandon Edward	1982 Dec 25 Mt. Lebanon PA		
2 Allyson Elizabeth	1987 Feb 2 Mt. Lebanon PA		

743143130   RODGERS

Tracy Lee Sefzik	1960 Jun 13 Pittsburgh PA	1979 Mar 17 Washington PA	
Donald Tracy Rodgers	1959	Donald Rogers & ----- -----	
1 Leah	1979 Aug 7 Pueblo CO		

743143140   MORGAN

Diane Sefzik	1965 Aug 9		
Dale Morgan			

743143200   SIAS

John Dando Sias, Jr.	1938 Dec 31 Pittsburgh PA		HI
Janice Mederios	19-- Jan 31 Hilo HI	John Mederios & ----- -----	

John graduated from Clarion College (PA), received his master's degree from the University of West Virginia, and his Ph. D. from Pennsylvania State University.

1 Melia Kathleen	1974 Mar 5		
2 James Russell	1974 Mar 5		

743143300   TERRELL

Joan Delane Sias	1938 Dec 31 Pittsburgh PA		
William Terrell		William Terrell &	
		Sarah Ann -----	
1 William	1957 Sep 8		
2 Richard	*1959 Apr 30		
3 John	*1961 Apr 21	1987 Sep 19	
4 Joseph M.	*1962 Jul 17		
5 Pamela	*1963 Oct 22		

743143320   TERRELL

Richard Terrell	1959 Apr 30		
Deanna DeFelice			

743143330   TERRELL

John Terrell	1961 Apr 21	1987 Sep 19	
Diana Sabila			

Serial # and Name	Birth	Marriage	Death
743143340 TERRELL			
Joseph M. Terrell	1962 Jul 17		
Shannon Tilger			
743143350 DEL BIANCO			
Pamela Terrell	1963 Oct 22		
Daniel Del Bianco			
1 Ashley Danielle	1988 Nov 20		
743144000 HUNT			
Rose Marie Capritz	1922 Aug 11		
Ray Edward Hunt		John Hunt & ------ ------	
1 Kathleen	*1942 Sep 15		
2 Karen Ann	*1952 Jun 12		
3 Beverly Rea	*1954 Jan 5		
4 Barbara Ann	*1955 Dec 18		
743144100 MILLER			
Kathleen Hunt	1942 Sep 15		
Regis Miller		Regis Miller & ------ ------	
1 Michael	1959 Nov 17		
2 Mark	*1960 Nov 26		
3 Marcie	*1964 Aug 23		
743144120 MILLER			
Mark Miller	1960 Nov 26		
Ruthann Tuggle			
743144130 BILESIMO			
Marcie Miller	1964 Aug 23		
David Bilesimo			
1 Toni Ann	1989 Oct 22		
2 Michael Allen	1991 Mar 17		
743144200 KOZA			
Karen Ann Hunt	1952 Jun 12		
Casmir Koza			
1 Michael	1982 Feb 4		
2 Katie	1984		
743144300 COPE			
Beverly Rea Hunt	1954 Jan 5		
William Cope			
1 Brian	1972 Jun 14		
2 Brandy	1975 Jan 7		
3 Barry	1976 Jun 3		

Serial # and Name	Birth	Marriage	Death
743144400 LAWLER			
Barbara Ann Hunt	1955 Dec 18		
Joseph Lawler			
1 Nichole	1979 Apr 8		
2 Jolene	1982 Aug 5		
3 Geri	1984		
743145000 HETRICK			
Gertrude Agnes Capritz	1924 Apr 18 Pittsburgh PA	1946 Jan 26 Pittsburgh PA	
William Hetrick	1901 Sep 1 Dayton PA	Sharp Hetrick & Maude Baume	1983 May 17
1 Lucinda Ann	#:1948 Aug 3	1968 Jul 6	
743145100 HILTY			
Lucinda Ann Hetrick	1948 Aug 3	1968 Jul 6	
Eugene Arthur Hilty			
1 William Arthur	1972 Jun 12		
2 Jennifer Lynn	1974 Sep 7		

750000000 MCILVAINE

John McIlvaine	1788 Nov 7 Washington Co. PA	Washington Co. PA	1880 May 5 Wayne Co. OH
s Margaret Smith			1839 Wayne Co. OH
t Annis Martin	1817c	PA	

John was born in the log cabin built by his father.   He brought his wife and two small children by horseback from Washington Co., PA, on rough and indistinct roads, across mountains and rivers, and through dense forests, a distance of over 120 miles to Wayne Co., OH, where they settled on a quarter section of land at Jackson, Canaan twp. John was a staunch Democrat and an admirer of Andrew Jackson.   He became an influential man in the community; he was a Presbyterian and donated land for a church and a cemetary.   His first home was a log cabin, and he later built another cabin, and finally a frame house.   John, Ann (Annis), and the six younger children lived in Canaan twp., Wayne Co., OH in 1850.   With them lived Lydia A. Martin, whose relationship is not given. Separate census entries in 1850 give Pennsylvania as the birth state of both George and Smith; if these entries are correct, it would make the migration date later than other records show.

1 Margaret	s :1814< Wayne Co. OH		1830< Wayne Co. OH
2 George B.	s #:1815 Jun 5 Wayne Co. OH	1842 Dec 1 Wayne Co. OH	1888 Mar 15 Wayne Co. OH
3 Smith	s #:1820		186x
4 Ruth	s #:1822 Aug 7 Wayne Co. OH	1848 Jan 13 Wayne Co. OH	1883 Sep 8 Tomah WI
5 Mary Jane	s #:1825 Sep 9 OH	1854 Sep 18 Wayne Co. OH	1893 Sep 3 Rock Springs WI
6 Andrew Jackson	s #:1829 Sep 9 OH		1873 Dec 7
7 Eleanor	s #:1831 OH		
8 John	s #:1835 OH		
9 James Greer	s #:1835 May 7 OH	1868 Oct 7	1913 Jan 9
a Maria	t #: OH		

Serial # and Name		Birth		Marriage		Death	

752000000 MCILVAINE

George B. McIlvaine		1815 Jun 5 Wayne Co.	OH	1842 Dec 1 Wayne Co.	OH	1888 Mar 15 Wayne Co.	OH
s Lucinda Aiken		1822 Jan 17	PA	George Aiken & Hannah Davis		1861 Feb 6 Wayne Co.	OH
t Sarah Ann Baker		1831 Jan 1		1863 Nov 11 Wayne Co.	OH	1901 Jul 4	
				David Baker &			
				Melinda Cockrell			

In 1850 George, Lucinda, and the three oldest children lived in Canaan twp., Wayne Co., OH. George later bought the homestead which his father had settled, and there farmed until his death.

1 John Jay	s	1844 Jul 18	OH			1863 Aug 24	
2 Margaret Jane	s	1846 Sep 23	OH			1925 May	
3 Hannah Eleanor	s#	1849 Feb 6	OH	1875 Oct 21 Wayne Co.	OH	1927	
4 George Andrew	s#	1851 Feb 8 Wayne Co.	OH	1875 Sep 30 Wayne Co.	OH	1938 Apr 12 i. Wayne Co. OH	
5 Daniel Webster	s#	1853 Apr 6 Jackson	OH	1876 Mar 23		1938 Jul 19	
6 Mary Alice	s	1855 Sep 16				1886 Jun 30	
7 James Buchanan	s	1857 Sep 22				1862 Aug 21	
8 Sarah Catherine	s	1860 Dec 25				1862 Jul 1	
9 David Ellsworth	t#	1866 May 26		1896 Jun 23		1946 Oct 17	
a Arthur Franklin	t#	1868 May 5 Wayne Co.	OH			1889 Dec 30	

John was in Company K, 16th Regiment, Ohio Volunteer Infantry in the Civil War; he was killed in Louisiana. Margaret lived, single, with her brother Daniel in Wayne Co., OH in 1920.

752300000 COCKRELL

| Hannah Eleanor McIlvaine | 1849 Feb 6 | | 1875 Oct 21 Wayne Co. | OH | 1927 | |
| John F. Cockrell | 1852 Feb 2 | | | | 1881 Jan 1 | |

The Cockrell family lived in Canaan twp., Wayne Co., OH in 1880. Hannah was living with the family of Ada and LeRoy in 1900, still in Canaan twp.

| 1 Ada G. | # | 1877 Oct 1 | | 1895 Oct 10 | | 1957 Apr 9 |

752310000 SMITH

| Ada G. Cockrell | 1877 Oct 1 | | 1895 Oct 10 | | 1957 Apr 9 |
| LeRoy C. Smith | 1874 Jul 15 | | | | 1957 Nov 18 |

Ada and LeRoy lived in Canaan twp., Wayne Co., OH in 1900.

752400000 MCILVAINE

| George Andrew McIlvaine | 1851 Feb 8 Wayne Co. | OH | 1875 Sep 30 Wayne Co. | OH | 1938 Apr 12 i. Wayne Co. OH |
| Anna Marsh | 1855 May 14 | OH | Benjamin Marsh & ----- ----- | | 1948 Jul   i. Wayne Co. OH |

George was born in the second log cabin built by his grandfather, was reared on the family farm, and assisted his father in completing the clearing of the place. He was educated in the home schools of Canaan township, and attended Canaan Academy. He farmed a rented farm until the death of his father, at which time he built a small house on 26 acres of the original homestead and worked there in truck and general farming. He was a Presbyterian and a Democrat.

1 Roy Emmett	#	1876 Aug 19	OH			1951 Feb 11 i. Wayne Co. OH
2 Earle		1883	OH			1899
3 Benjamin M.	#	1884 Sep 1 Creston	OH	1913 Creston	OH	1966 Nov 16 Wooster OH
4 Ross C.	#	1889 Aug 25	OH	1914		1985 i. Wayne Co. OH
5 Dean Alton	#	1894 Dec 30	OH			1980 Dec 8

Serial # and Name	Birth	Marriage	Death

752410000   MCILVAINE

Roy Emmett McIlvaine	1876 Aug 19	OH	1951 Feb 11 i. Wayne Co. OH
Alma Venora Neal	1880 Feb 29		1962 Feb 17 i. Wayne Co. OH
1 Helen M.	#1902 Oct 7 West Salem	OH 1921 Jun 2 Wooster	OH 1988 Jul 6 i. Wooster OH
2 Neal George	1904 Mar 1 West Salem	OH	1917
3 Meredith	#1906 Aug 28 West Salem	OH 1929	1977 Magadore OH
4 James M.	1909 Apr 26 Pleasant Home	OH	1920 i. Wayne Co. OH
5 Iris P.	#1914 Apr 9 Wooster	OH 1936 Feb 7 Wooster	OH
6 Frances Elevan	1916 Feb 18 Wooster	OH	1920 Wooster OH
7 Perry E.	#1920 Nov 28 Wooster	OH	CA

752411000   KEEN

Helen M. McIlvaine	1902 Oct 7 West Salem	OH 1921 Jun 2 Wooster	OH 1988 Jul 6 i. Wooster OH
George Calvin Keen	1885 Jun 2	Charles Kean & Anna Wolfe	1974 Dec 4 i. Wooster OH

The Army changed the spelling of George's name to Keen and the family has continued that spelling.

1 Earl Maynard	#1924 Jul 16 Wooster	OH 1943 Apr 25	
2 George Calvin	#1929 Dec 19 Wooster	OH 1956 Feb 12	

752411100   KEEN

Earl Maynard Keen	1924 Jul 16 Wooster	OH 1943 Apr 25	
Mary Jean Shearer			
1 David Earl	1948 Jan 2		
2 Robert George	1953 Apr 17		1989 Nov
3 Janet Sue	#1954 May 17	1974 Oct	
4 Jeffry Allen	1967 May 7		

David, Robert, and Jeffry were adopted.

752411130   BYLER

Janet Sue Keen	1954 May 17	1974 Oct	
Hal Byler			
1 Benjamin			
2 Peter John			

752411200   KEEN

George Calvin Keen	1929 Dec 19 Wooster	OH 1956 Feb 12	
Alice Katherine Zook			
1 Cynthia Alice	#1957 May 29	1980 Mar 1	
2 Thomas George	1958 Oct 3		
3 Gary Paul	1960 Dec 27		

752411210   BRICKER

Cynthia Alice Keen	1957 May 29	1980 Mar 1	
David W. Bricker			
1 Matthew David	1982 Oct 31		
2 Daniel Calvin	1985 May 23		

Serial # and Name	Birth	Marriage	Death
752413000 PEARCH			
Meredith McIlvaine	1906 Aug 28 West Salem OH	1929	1977 Magadore OH
Franklin David Pearch	1892 Oct 15	David D. Pearch &	i. Port Charlotte FL
		Mary Alice Wade	
1 Edith Ann	*1932 Nov 1 Akron OH	1956 Oct 21 Akron OH	
2 David Neal	*1936 May 2 Akron OH	1956 Oct 10 Cuyahoga Falls OH	
752413100 BOWMAN			
Edith Ann Pearch	1932 Nov 1 Akron OH	1956 Oct 21 Akron OH	
David Adrian Bowman, Jr.	1932 Jan 24 Akron OH	David Bowman & Esther Lewis	
1 Douglas Brian	*1959 Sep 12 Akron OH	1992 Jun 12 Akron OH	
2 Cheryl Lynn	*1961 Nov 1 Akron OH	198- Oct 5	
3 Denise Ann	1963 Mar 30 Akron OH		
752413110 BOWMAN			
Douglas Brian Bowman	1959 Sep 12 Akron OH	1992 Jun 12 Akron OH	
Donna Anne Iannotti	1959 Sep 21 Long Island NY	Pasquale Gared Iannotti &	
		Deanna Joan Kost	
752413120 FORNEY			
Cheryl Lynn Bowman	1961 Nov 1 Akron OH	198- Oct 5	
Edward J. Forney	1961 Dec 5		
1 Sara A.	1991 Mar 1 Martinsburg WV		
752413200 PEARCH			
David Neal Pearch	1936 May 2 Akron OH	1956 Oct 10 Cuyahoga Falls OH	
s Lois Carol Shadley	1936 May 7 Akron OH	Russell Park Shadley &	
		Margaret Irene Foxhall	
t Francine Aumack			
1 Steven Dale	s*1959 Mar 3 Akron OH		
2 Dan Scott	s 1961 Sep 5 Akron OH		
3 Karen Sue	s*1963 Dec 21 Akron OH	1985 Nov 9	
752413210 PEARCH			
Steven Dale Pearch	1959 Mar 3 Akron OH		
Dora McCullick			
1 Brianna Leigh	1991 Nov 29 Mesa AZ		
752413230 LEONARD			
Karen Sue Pearch	1963 Dec 21 Akron OH	1985 Nov 9	
Robert John Leonard			
1 Robert John	1987 Nov 3 Phoenix AZ		
2 Victoria	1989 May 11 Phoenix AZ		
3 Rebecca	1991 May Phoenix AZ		

Serial # and Name	Birth	Marriage	Death

752415000 BELL

Iris P. McIlvaine	:1914 Apr 9 Wooster	OH:1936 Feb 7 Wooster	OH:
Walter William Bell	:1912 Nov 24 Wooster	OH: William Foster Bell &	:1978 Jan 20 i. Tacoma WA
	:	: Florence Melissa Cotter	:
1 Joyce Pauline	*:1937 Jan 15 Canton	OH:	:
2 Florence Elma	*:1938 Oct 26 Fredericksburg	OH:	:
3 William Walter	:1955 Jan 18 Tacoma	WA:	:

752415100 GERBER

Joyce Pauline Bell	:1937 Jan 15 Canton	OH:	:
Caleb J. Gerber	:	:	:

752415200 CRAVEN

Florence Elma Bell	:1938 Oct 26 Fredericksburg	OH:	:
Francis Sanderson Craven	:	:	:

752417000 MCILVAINE

Perry E. McIlvaine	:1920 Nov 28 Wooster	OH:	CA:
Jean -----	:	:	:
	:	:	:
1 Michael	:1957	CA:	:
2 Patricia	:1957	CA:	:

752430000 MCILVAINE

Benjamin M. McIlvaine	:1884 Sep 1 Creston	OH:1913 Creston	OH:1966 Nov 16 Wooster OH
Candace Amy Tuttle	:1884 Dec 23 Creston	OH:	:1929 Dec 21 Wooster OH

Ben served as Wayne County Treasurer from 1936 until 1961 and as President of the Ohio Association of County Treasurers.   In his early years he had been a bookkeeper for the Moniter Sad Iron Company in Big Prairie, office manager for the Buckeye Aluminum Co. in Wooster, and a deputy in both the Wayne Co. Recorder's Office and the Treasurer's Office.   He was a member of the Independent Order of Odd Fellows, and was treasurer for the organization for many years.   He was also a deacon, an elder, the treasurer, and the Sunday School Superintendant for the First Reformed (now Trinity United Methodist) Church in Wooster.

1 Elinor Narcine	*:1916 Dec 10 Wooster	OH:1939 Aug 14 Wooster	OH:

752431000 TAYLOR

Elinor Narcine McIlvaine	:1916 Dec 10 Wooster	OH:1939 Aug 14 Wooster	OH:
James Nelson Taylor	:1913 Jun 21 Massilon	OH: Joseph Taylor & Amy Curnick	:1984 Oct 19 i. Wooster OH
	:	:	:
1 Lynn Stanley	*:1940 Sep 18 Wooster	OH:1963 Apr 13 Wooster	OH:
2 Theodore Merle	:1944 Apr 6 Wooster	OH:	:
3 James Benjamin	:1950 Apr 10 Wooster	OH:	:

752431100 TAYLOR

Lynn Stanley Taylor	:1940 Sep 18 Wooster	OH:1963 Apr 13 Wooster	OH:
Judith K. Kinney	:1940 Apr 17 Wooster	OH:	:
	:	:	:
1 Rebecca Lynn	:1966 Sep 29 Wooster	OH:	:

Serial # and Name	Birth	Marriage	Death
752440000 MCILVAINE			
Ross C. McIlvaine	1889 Aug 25	1914	1985 i. Wayne Co. OH
s Helen McIntire	1890		1925 i. Wayne Co. OH
t Catherine Rose Weaver			
1 Earl Eugene	s# 1915 Jul 19 Wayne Co.	OH 1943 Sep 25 New York	NY 1976 Apr 7 Dover OH
2 Rex Gibson	s# 1917 Wadsworth	OH	Wadsworth OH
752441000 MCILVAINE			
Earl Eugene McIlvaine	1915 Jul 19 Wayne Co.	OH 1943 Sep 25 New York	NY 1976 Apr 7 Dover OH
Caroline Elmira Clawson	1920 Apr 30 Youngstown	OH James Winfred Clawson &	
		Hazel D. Brownlee	
1 James Ross	# 1944 Jul 22 Youngstown	OH 1967 Jun 24 Independence OH	
2 Karen Barbara	1947 Apr 12 Wadsworth	OH	
3 William Andrew	# 1948 Nov 20 Dover	OH 1975 Aug 2 Dover OH	
4 Stephen Brownlee	# 1953 Feb 28 Dover	OH 1977 Jun 4	
752441100 MCILVAINE			
James Ross McIlvaine	1944 Jul 22 Youngstown	OH 1967 Jun 24 Independence OH	
Carol Beth Boyer	1945 Aug 29	Robert Boyer & ----- -----	

James graduated from Muskingum College in 1966 and, with honors, from Ohio State College of Law in 1969.

1 Andrew S.	1971 Jun 10 Akron	OH	
2 Katherine Erin	1975 Sep 17 Akron	OH	
752441300 MCILVAINE			
William Andrew McIlvaine	1948 Nov 20 Dover	OH 1975 Aug 2 Dover OH	
Deborah Jeanne Bentley	1950 Jul 12 Akron	OH Orville Franklin Bentley &	
		Jean Elizabeth Chamberlain	
1 Karen Jeanne	1976 Feb 18 Akron	OH	
2 Timothy Earl	1978 Aug 21 Youngstown	OH	
3 Jonathan Franklin	1980 Dec 29 Youngstown	OH	
4 Patrick William	1983 Jun 12 Medina	OH	
752441400 MCILVAINE			
Stephen Brownlee	1953 Feb 28 Dover	OH 1977 Jun 4	
McIlvaine			
Sara Sue Aubihl	1954 Oct 9	George Allen Aubihl &	
		Ruby Jane Jentes	
1 Jacob Ross Alexander	1982 Apr 21 Wadsworth	OH	
2 Alexander Jentes	1986 Feb 2 Wadsworth	OH	
752442000 MCILVAINE			
Rex Gibson McIlvaine	1917 Wadsworth	OH	Wadsworth OH
Betty Veronica McDermott			
1 John Haldane	# 1945 May 12 Camp LeJeune	NC	
2 Lynne M.	# 1946 Sep 17 Wadsworth	OH 1969 Aug 2 Wadsworth OH	
3 Michael Terry	# 1949 Feb 20 Wadsworth	OH 1973 Aug 4 Devon PA	
4 Jean	# 1953 Aug 20 Wadsworth	OH	
5 Donald	# 1958 Jan 12 Wadsworth	OH	

Serial # and Name	Birth	Marriage	Death
752442100 MCILVAINE			
John Haldane McIlvaine	1945 May 12 Camp LeJeune NC		
Sandra Moser			
1 John Tyler	1978 Feb 4 Cincinatti OH		
752442200 SMITH			
Lynne M. McIlvaine	1946 Sep 17 Wadsworth OH	1969 Aug 2 Wadsworth OH	
Douglas Smith	1946 Jan 28 Ontario CN	Bruce Smith & Lois Sexsmite	
1 Scott Douglas	1971 Oct 16 Ravenna OH		
2 Kristen McIlvaine	1974 Feb 19 Ravenna OH		
752442300 MCILVAINE			
Michael Terry McIlvaine	1949 Feb 20 Wadsworth OH	1973 Aug 4 Devon PA	
Joyce Lydia Martin	1949 Jul 1 Allentown PA	Robert Welles Martin & Jeanette Simon Hoffner	
1 Keith Welles	1975 Jul 28 Bryn Mawr PA		
752442400 CRABTREE			
Jean McIlvaine	1953 Aug 20 Wadsworth OH		
Butch Crabtree			
752442500 MCILVAINE			
Donald McIlvaine	1958 Jan 12 Wadsworth OH		
Kim -----			
752450000 MCILVAINE			
Dean Alton McIlvaine	1894 Dec 30		1980 Dec 8
s Olive Knepper			
t Mildred Hemming			
1 Wayne ?			
752500000 MCILVAINE			
Daniel Webster McIlvaine	1853 Apr 6 Jackson OH	1876 Mar 23	1938 Jul 19
Hattie Houghton	1855 Mar OH	Franklin Houghton & ----- -----	1943 Mar 25

Daniel and Hattie with their two children lived in Jackson City, Wayne Co., OH in 1880.   In 1900 they lived, with the four children, on Main Street in Creston, OH.   They lived alone in Wayne Co. in 1910 and 1920.

1 Cloyd Almont	#1877 Feb 22 OH		1948
2 Laverne	#1879 Dec 12 OH		1939
3 Robert Bruce	#1881 Jan 23 Jackson OH		1962 Aug 12
4 Mary	#1887 OH		
752510000 MCILVAINE			
Cloyd Almont McIlvaine	1877 Feb 22 OH		1948
----- -----			
1 Carmen			

Serial # and Name	Birth	Marriage	Death
752520000 EWING			
Laverne McIlvaine	1879 Dec 12		1939
Edgar Ewing	1880		1918
1 Sumner	1904 Dec 24		1966 Jun 10
2 Edgar Clair	1906		1976
3 Cloyd E.	1908		
4 Charles E.			
752530000 MCILVAINE			
Robert Bruce McIlvaine	1881 Jan 23 Jackson OH		1962 Aug 12
Martha Alice Wells	1878 Aug 26 OH		
This family lived in Creston, OH in 1910, and at 91 Greenwood Ave., Mansfield, OH in 1920.			
1 Clarence Bruce	*1903 Feb 12 Jackson OH		1979 Mar 31
2 Lew W.	1905 May OH		
3 Robert Bruce, Jr.	1917c Wayne Co. OH		
752531000 MCILVAINE			
Clarence Bruce McIlvaine	1903 Feb 12 Jackson OH		1979 Mar 31
Anna Grace Bowers			
1 Alice Jean	*1923 Aug 10 Mansfield OH		
2 James William	*1925 Jan 19 Wadsworth OH	1946 Dec 27 Wadsworth OH	
3 Lois Irene	*1929 Aug 15 Wadsworth OH		
752531100 PENNINGTON			
Alice Jean McIlvaine	1923 Aug 10 Mansfield OH		
Paul Pennington			
752531200 MCILVAINE			
James William McIlvaine	1925 Jan 19 Wadsworth OH	1946 Dec 27 Wadsworth OH	
Janice E. Knecht	1927 Mar 31 Lodi OH	George Henry Knecht &	
		Emma Lucinda Curtis	
1 James Bruce	*1947 Sep 20 Philadelphia PA		
2 Mark George	1949 Aug 12 Philadelphia PA		
3 Sandra Lee	*1952 Apr 26 Wadsworth OH	1985 Feb 23 San Diego CA	
4 Luanne	*1954 Dec 11 Canton OH	1976 May 29 Canton OH	
5 Brian Andrew	1962 Jan 26 Canton OH		
752531210 MCILVAINE			
James Bruce McIlvaine	1947 Sep 20 Philadelphia PA		
Kay Morgan			
752531230 KAUSTINEN			
Sandra Lee McIlvaine	1952 Apr 26 Wadsworth OH	1985 Feb 23 San Diego CA	
Brad William Kaustinen	1954 Mar 21 Baldwin Park CA	Tauno Alex Kaustinen &	
		Jean Catherine Mitchell	
1 Kaitlyn Beth	1986 Apr 1 San Diego CA		
2 Kelsey Leanne	1988 Mar 23 San Diego CA		

Serial # and Name	Birth	Marriage	Death
752531240 PYLE			
Luanne McIlvaine	1954 Dec 11 Canton	OH 1976 May 29 Canton OH	
Charles David Pyle	1949 Aug 11 Canton	OH Harold Pyle & Anna Indorf	
1 Charles David	1978 Jul 16 Canton	OH	
2 Lindsey Ann	1982 Dec 22 Canton	OH	
752531300 BUIS			
Lois Irene McIlvaine	1929 Aug 15 Wadsworth	OH	
Robert Buis			
752540000 BROOMALL			
Mary McIlvaine	1887	OH	
Jesse Broomall	1882c	OH	

Mary and Jesse lived with their children in Creston, OH in 1910.

1 Norris Mark	#1907 Sep 24	OH	
2 Dorothy Laverne	#1909 Mar 31	OH	
752541000 BROOMALL			
Norris Mark Broomall	1907 Sep 24		
Lois Carpenter			
752542000 HALL			
Dorothy Laverne Broomall	1909 Mar 31		
Glen Hall			
752900000 MCILVAINE			
David Ellsworth McIlvaine	1866 May 26	1896 Jun 23	1946 Oct 17
Clara Belle Irvin	1869 Nov 25	George Irvin & -----	1957 Feb 15

David was educated at Ada Normal and spent two years at the University of Wooster. After a year of teaching he turned to farming, and raising stock and poultry. He served one year as township assessor and three years as trustee, as well as other small offices. In 1906 he was elected county commissioner, and he was re-elected in 1908. David was a Democrat and a Presbyterian. Clara was a member of the Dunkard Church. They resided in Creston, OH. The 1900 census record is listed under Elsworth D. McIlvaine.

1 Donald Irvin	#1897 Apr 29	1929 Aug 10	1965 Dec 31
2 Ruth Eleanor	#1899 Jun 17	1924 Aug 17	
3 Mary Kathleen	#1901 Mar 17	1923 Aug 30	
4 Wallace Jay	#1902 Sep 15	1925 Oct 18	
5 Doris Isabel	1904 Aug 23		
6 Flora Gail	#1906 Sep 22	1927 Mar 6	1931 Apr 15
7 Susan Grace	#1906 Sep 22	1938 Jun 18	1960 Jan 23
8 George Ellsworth	#1910 May 19	1933 Aug 28	1964 May 9

In 1920 all of the children except Donald and Mary lived with their parents in Wayne Co., OH.

752910000 MCILVAINE			
Donald Irvin McIlvaine	1897 Apr 29	1929 Aug 10	1965 Dec 31
Ruth Garnet Sovash	1904 Sep 14		1990 May 16
1 Dale Irvin	#1932 Dec 14	1956 Apr 1	
2 Joe Donald	#1937 Oct 7	1958 May 2	

Serial # and Name	Birth	Marriage	Death
752911000 MCILVAINE			
Dale Irvin McIlvaine	1932 Dec 14	1956 Apr 1	
Louise Drysdale	1936 Mar 27		
1 Dean William	*1957 Sep 4 Wadsworth OH		
2 Susan Ruth	*1961 May 21 Medina OH	1985 Dec 22 Orrville OH	
752911100 MCILVAINE			
Dean William McIlvaine	1957 Sep 4 Wadsworth OH		
Luanne Moffett	1954c		1991 Feb 3
1 Danielle Rae	1983 Oct 15 Wooster OH		
2 Ian Moffett	1986 Nov 23 Wooster OH		
752911200 HAYES			
Susan Ruth McIlvaine	1961 May 21 Medina OH	1985 Dec 22 Orrville OH	
George Ambrose Hayes, III			
1 Mark McIlvaine	1991 Feb 3		
752912000 MCILVAINE			
Joe Donald McIlvaine	1937 Oct 7	1958 May 2	
s Janice Ann Brubaker	1938 Aug 4		
t Carol Markley		1965 Dec 4	
u Pat Stephen		1977 Feb 25	
1 Brian Matthew	s*1958 Oct 23 Wooster OH		
2 Gregg Allen	s*1959 Dec 26 Wooster OH	1983 Sep 10 Wooster OH	

Five children of Mrs. Pat Stevens were also members of this family: Terri, Marie, Lisa, Patsy, and Todd.

Serial # and Name	Birth	Marriage	Death
752912100 MCILVAINE			
Brian Matthew McIlvaine	1958 Oct 23 Wooster OH		
Leona -----			
752912200 MCILVAINE			
Gregg Allen McIlvaine	1959 Dec 26 Wooster OH	1983 Sep 10 Wooster OH	
Christine Carol Ege	1960 Sep 3 Cleveland OH	Harry Walter Ege &	
		Gisela Irmgard Klopper	
1 Sarah Ruth	1987 Nov 13 Wooster OH		
2 Ellen Christine	1989 Aug 28 Wooster OH		
752920000 LINTER			
Ruth Eleanor McIlvaine	1899 Jun 17	1924 Aug 27	
Nellis Devitt Linter			
752930000 GILLERON			
Mary Kathleen McIlvaine	1901 Mar 17	1923 Aug 30	
George E. Gilleron			

Serial # and Name	Birth	Marriage	Death
752940000 MCILVAINE			
Wallace Jay McIlvaine	1902 Sep 15	1925 Oct 18	
Emma Curry	1905 Oct 5		
1 David Eugene	*1930 Dec 2	1951 Sep 8	
2 Mary Jane	*1938 Jun 30	1960 Dec 17	
3 Doris Irene	*1940 May 17	1962 Jun 23	
752941000 MCILVAINE			
David Eugene McIlvaine	1930 Dec 2	1951 Sep 8	
Dorothy Ambro			
1 Ronald James	1952 Nov 29		
2 Sheril Anne	1954 Nov 27		
3 Carl Allen	1963 Nov 5		
752942000 MAYHER			
Mary Jane McIlvaine	1938 Jun 30	1960 Dec 17	
Mike Mayher			
752943000 CASSILLY			
Doris Irene McIlvaine	1940 May 17	1962 Jun 23	
Thomas C. Cassilly			
752960000 ALLEN			
Flora Gail McIlvaine	1906 Sep 22	1927 Mar 6	1931 Apr 15
Floyd Nathaniel Allen	1891 Dec 11		1964 Feb 8
1 Richard George	*1928 Jan 28	1950 Jan 7	
2 Donald Wesley	*1929 Feb 17	1950 Oct 21	
3 Charles William	*1930 Oct 10	1954 Jun 11	
752961000 ALLEN			
Richard George Allen	1928 Jan 28	1950 Jan 7	
Jacqueline Collins	1932 Jan 1		
1 Andrew Richard	1950 Dec 11		
2 Daniel Floyd	1952 Aug 11		
3 Lee Jonathan	1954 Oct 16		
4 Scott Dale	1957 Feb 3		
5 Benjamin David	1959 Nov 4		
6 Jacqueline	1962 Feb 23		1966 Aug 15
7 George Harold	1967 Nov 3		
752962000 ALLEN			
Donald Wesley Allen	1929 Feb 17	1950 Oct 21	
Norma Detwiler	1931 Mar 18		
1 Cynthia Gail	1953 Sep 8		
2 Patricia Jo	1955 ? 26		
3 Donald Joseph	1957 Sep 15		
4 Susan Rae	1967 Oct		

Serial # and Name	Birth	Marriage	Death

752963000 ALLEN

Charles William Allen	1930 Oct 10	1954 Jun 11	
Sally Jane Kratzer	1934 Oct 16 Lodi	OH	

Charles received a B. S. degree from Ashland College. He is a veteran of the Korean War, and was a school teacher, coach, and athletic director.   In 1991 he was working as a real estate salesman and an antique dealer.   Sally has a Master's Degree in Education from Akron University, and has taught school for more than twenty years.

1 Steven Robert	*1955 Oct 18		
2 Jon Brian	*1959 Jun 20		
3 Michael James		Medina OH	
4 Jill Lynn	1963 Jan 18		

Michael has a B. S. in Education from North Carolina State University, and in 1991 was a graduate student at Old Dominion University. Jill has a B. S. from Ohio State University, and a Master's degree from Kent State University.   In 1991 she was working as a high school teacher and women's athletic director in Shaker Heights,

752963100 ALLEN

Steven Robert Allen	1955 Oct 18		
Rose -----			

Steven in 1991 was an architect in Thurmont, Maryland.

1 Ross Charles	19xx Apr 29		

752963200 ALLEN

Jon Brian Allen	1959 Jun 20		
----- -----			

In 1991 Jon was owner and operator of the Pike Station in Creston, Ohio.

1 John Marty	1983 Mar 17		

752970000 KELLER

Susan Grace McIlvaine	1906 Sep 22	1938 Jun 18	1960 Jan 23
Matthew E. Keller	1908 Dec 31		
1 Jane Elizabeth	*1947 Mar 24	1968 Oct 11	
2 Matthew David	1949 Sep 11		

752971000 WELIVER

Jane Elizabeth Keller	1947 Mar 24	1968 Oct 11	
David Weliver			
1 Matthew	1969 Aug 21		

752980000 MCILVAINE

George Ellsworth McIlvaine	1910 May 19	1933 Aug 28	1964 May 9
s Lois Aldorf			
t Harriet Patterson Hatfield	1959 Mar 20		
1 Joan Alice	s*1936 Apr 9	1957 Dec 28	
2 David Ellsworth, II	s*1937 Sep 2	1960 Sep 2	

Serial # and Name	Birth	Marriage	Death
752981000 SIMPSON			
Joan Alice McIlvaine	1936 Apr 9	1957 Dec 28	
Robert W. Simpson	1938 May 20		
1 Terri Lynn	1958 Oct 29		
2 Robert Scott	1959 Oct 11		
3 Sarah Jean	1962 Aug 19		
4 Mitchell Nolan	1963 Jul 24		
5 Beth Ann	1964 Sep 18		
752982000 MCILVAINE			
David Ellsworth	1937 Sep 2	1960 Sep 2	
McIlvaine, II			
Nancy Randolph	1939 Nov 24 Angola IN	Paul Armel Randolph &	
		Helen June Mortorff	
1 David Ellsworth III	1961 Dec 29		
2 Michael Griffith	1963 Sep 15		
752a00000 MCILVAINE			
Arthur Franklin McIlvaine	1868 May 5 Wayne Co. OH		1889 Dec 30
----- -----			
1 John H.			1909
753000000 MCILVAINE			
Smith McIlvaine	1820	PA	186x
Margaret McIlvaine	1823c	PA	

Smith, Margaret, Gilbert, Cynthia, and Anderson lived in Canaan twp., Wayne Co. OH in 1850.

1 Marquis			
2 Lawrence			
3 Gilbert	1846c	OH	
4 Cynthia	1847c	OH	
5 Anderson L.	1848c	OH	

In the 1900 census for Wayne County, Ohio there is listed a Marcus McElvaine, born October 1845 in Ohio. Living in his household is Laurence, a brother (born Dec 1850, Ohio) and a sister Josephine (born Jun 1864, Ohio). It is uncertain whether these are members of this family.

754000000 WALTENBERG			
Ruth McIlvaine	1822 Aug 7 Wayne Co. OH	1848 Jan 13 Wayne Co. OH	1883 Sep 8 Tomah WI
George Henry Waltenberg	1827 Oct 29 Wayne Co. OH	Jacob Waltenberg & xx	1903 Feb 14 Baltimore MD
		Catherine -----	

George served in the 19th Wisconsin Regiment in the Civil War.

1 Mary Jane	*1848 Dec 30 Akron OH	1873 Sep 30	1926 Feb 27 Elkhorn WI
2 John Andrew	1850 Sep 18		1903>1911
3 Rebecca Frances	*1852 Oct 28 Reedsburg WI	1877 Nov 9 Tomah WI	1911 Oct 18
4 George James	*1854 Dec 27 Reedsburg WI	1889 Oct 15	1924 Sep 22 Coburn WI
5 Breck Henry	*1857 Jun 27 Reedsburg WI	1887	1931 Mar 4 Buckley WA
6 Orminda Ruth	*1859 Nov 16 Sauk Co. WI	1880 Sep 26	1918 Apr 11 Baltimore MD
7 Menzo Romaine	*1862 May 7 Sauk Co. WI	1886 Nov 3	1946 Aug 24 Roselle NH

Serial # and Name	Birth	Marriage	Death

754100000 HENDERSON

Mary Jane Waltenberg	!1848 Dec 30 Akron OH!	1873 Sep 30	!1926 Feb 27 Elkhorn WI
John Herrit Henderson	!1845 Mentor OH!	Samuel Wirt Henderson &	!1893 Elkhorn WI
	!	Rebecca Hicks	!
1 Emmett Eugene	*!1874 Mar 10 Norway Ridge WI!	1912 Oct 12 Ellensburg WA!	1966 Apr 7 Ellensburg WA
2 Cora Rebecca	!1876 Tomah WI!	never married	!
3 Breck Andrew	!1881 Tomah WI!	never married	!
4 John Henry	!1884 Tomah WI!	married, no children	!

754110000 HENDERSON

Emmett Eugene Henderson	!1874 Mar 10 Norway Ridge WI!	1912 Oct 12 Ellensburg WA!	1966 Apr 7 Ellensburg WA
Leila Marshel	!1885 Mentor OH!	Jefferson D. Marshel &	!1971 Puyallup WA
	!	Linda E. McCoy	!
1 Eugene Marshel	*!1913 Apr 19 Ellensburg WA!	1943 Feb 10 Centralia WA!	
2 John Breck	*!1915 Apr 24 Ellensburg WA!	1945 Jan 6 New Orleans LA!	
3 Jane	*!1924 Aug 30 Ellensburg WA!	1944 Mar 24	!

754111000 HENDERSON

Eugene Marshel Henderson	!1913 Apr 19 Ellensburg WA!	1943 Feb 10 Centralia WA!	
Charlotte Loretz Osterle	!1918 Feb 26 Minneapolis MN!	William F. Oesterle &	!
	!	Charlotte L. Bost	!
1 William Robert	*!1946 Dec 1 Aberdeen WA!		!
2 Edward Lee	*!1948 Mar 5 Ellensburg WA!		!
3 Gregory Eugene	*!1950 Jun 22 Ellensburg WA!		!

754111100 HENDERSON

William Robert Henderson	!1946 Dec 1 Aberdeen WA!		!
s Beth Ann Scott	!		!
t Linda Lou Moye	!		!
	!		!
1 Cassandra Rene	s !1973 Nov 19		!
2 Stephanie Jo	t !1980 Apr 27		!

754111200 HENDERSON

Edward Lee Henderson	!1948 Mar 5 Ellensburg WA!		!
Patricia Ann Snyder	!		!
	!		!
1 Aaron Marshel	!1979 Jun 28		!
2 Marcus Lee	!1983 Mar 10		!

754111300 HENDERSON

Gregory Eugene Henderson	!1950 Jun 22 Ellensburg WA!		!
Leslie Jacinta Potter	!		!
	!		!
1 Katie Eugenia	!1981 Sep 1		!
2 Laura Ann	!1988 Jun 30		!

Serial # and Name	Birth	Marriage	Death

754112000   HENDERSON

John Breck Henderson	1915 Apr 24 Ellensburg WA	1945 Jan 6 New Orleans LA	
Rosemary Wenger			
1 Breck Wenger	* 1948 Ellensburg WA		
2 John Marshel	* 1950 Baton Rouge LA		
3 Michael Emmet	* 1952 Baton Rouge LA		
4 Louise Elizabeth	1962 Mar 15 Baton Rouge LA		

754112100   HENDERSON

Breck Wenger Henderson	1948 Ellensburg WA		
Mary Simmons			
1 Lauren Michelle	1976		
2 Shelly	1983		

754112200   HENDERSON

John Marshel Henderson	1950 Baton Rouge LA		
Joy Brandon Simmons			
1 Marshel Andrew	1974		1981
2 Michael Eugene	1976		
3 Carrie Louise	1983		
4 Callie Rose	1986		

754112300   HENDERSON

Michael Emmet Henderson	1952 Baton Rouge LA		
Rachel Ann Frasure			
1 Kezia Catherine			
2 Haley			

754113000   HANKS

Jane Henderson	1924 Aug 30 Ellensburg WA	1944 Mar 24	
Philip Donald Hanks	1924	John Hanks & ----- -----	
1 Richard Philip	* 1947		
2 Alan Eugene	* 1949		
3 Bryan Donald	1952		

754113100   HANKS

Richard Philip Hanks	1947		
Jody Lynn Johnson			
1 Melissa Dawn	1973		
2 John Cameron	1975		

Serial # and Name	Birth	Marriage	Death
754113200 HANKS			
Alan Eugene Hanks	1949		
Becky Way			
1 Tracy Jane	1970		
2 Philip			
3 Tammy Kay	1972		
754300000 KING			
Rebecca Frances Waltenberg	1852 Oct 28 Reedsburg WI	1877 Nov 9 Tomah WI	1911 Oct 18
John Nelson King			
1 Ruth	*	WI	
2 Margaret Dick	* 1886c	WI	
754310000 JAMES			
Ruth King		WI	
J. E. James			
754320000 JEWETT			
Margaret Dick King	1886c	WI	
Kent Jewett	1891c	WI	
The Jewett family lived in Monroe County, WI in 1920.			
1 John A.	1912c	WI	
754400000 WALTENBERG			
George James Waltenberg	1854 Dec 27 Ableman WI	1889 Oct 15	1924 Sep 22 Coburn WI
Julia Graff	1863 Nov	WI	
In 1900 the Waltenbergs lived in Colburn Town, Adams County, Wisconsin with Edna, James, and Stella, In 1900 they lived in Adams County, Wisconsin; James was still living with them			
1 Edna R.	* 1892 Mar	WI	
2 James E.	1893 Dec	WI	
3 Pearl			
4 Stella V.	1898 Jul	WI	infancy death 1900>
754410000 MCGREGOR			
Edna R. Waltenberg	1892 Mar	WI	
----- McGregor			
754500000 WALTENBERG			
Breck Henry Waltenberg	1857 Jun 27 Reedsburg WI	1887	1931 Mar 4 Buckley WA
Alice M. Wise	1856c	WI	
Breck and Alice were living in Buckley, WA with Lulu and her husband in 1910. His age was given as 62 in the census taken that year. Fred was also living with Lulu at that time.			
1 Lulu E.	* 1877c	WI	
2 Fred	1881c	WI never married	
754510000 MORGAN			
Lulu Waltenberg	1877c	WI	
Frank Morgan	1866c	WA	
Lulu and Frank lived on Pearl St, Buckley, WA in 1910. In their household also lived his brother John, her parents Breck and Alice Waltenberg, and her brother Fred.			

Serial # and Name	Birth	Marriage	Death

754600000 HICKS

Orminda Ruth Waltenberg	1859 Nov 16 Sauk Co.	WI 1880 Sep 26	1918 Apr 11 Baltimore MD
John Frederick Hicks			
1 Jessie A.	1881 Jul 24		1889 Feb 3
2 Ruth	1885 Aug 16		1886 Jan

754700000 WALTENBERG

Menzo Romaine Waltenberg	1862 May 17 Sauk Co.	WI 1886 Nov 3	1946 Aug 24 Roselle NH
Margaret Gibbs Denton	1869 Jul 24 Baltimore	MD William Denton &	1939 Nov 10 Washington DC
		Margaret Gibbs Mitchell	
1 Miriam Denton	* 1888 Feb 8 Tomah	WI 1913 Jun 14 Washington	DC 1975 Dec 16 Arlington VA
2 Romaine George	* 1889 Sep 18 Tomah	WI 1918 Aug 1	1980 Oct 5 Onancock VA

754710000 DAHM

Miriam Denton Waltenberg	1888 Feb 8 Tomah	WI 1913 Jun 14 Washington	DC 1975 Dec 16 Arlington VA
Paul Emil Dahm			
1 Margaret Miriam	1914 Sep 18 Chicago	IL	
2 George Paul	* 1920 Nov 21 Washington	DC 1943 Apr 10	

754712000 DAHM

George Paul Dahm	1920 Nov 21 Washington	DC 1943 Apr 10	
Mary Jo Allen	1921 Aug 1		
1 Julie Sharon	* 1944 Feb 9	1966 Apr 9	
2 Geoffrey Allen	1945 Sep 29		1948 Sep 23
3 Deidre	* 1951 Jun 19	1973 Dec 22	

754712100 LIEN

Julie Sharon Dahm	1944 Feb 9	1966 Apr 9	
Egil Lien	1940 Jan 15		
1 Matthew Allen	1967 Dec 27		
2 Justin Tyler	1976 Feb 27		
3 Megin Elizabeth	1976 Feb 27		

754712300 WARRINGTON / BEARD

Deidre Dahm	1951 Jun 19	1973 Dec 22	
s Ross Warrington			
t William J. Beard		1983 Jul 9	
1 Bethany Allen Warrington	1975 Jun 20		
2 Lucas Emerson Warrington	1976 Nov 9		

754720000 WALTENBERG

Romaine George Waltenberg	1889 Sep 18 Tomah	WI 1918 Aug 1	1980 Oct 5 Onancock VA
Thelma P. Smith	1898 Apr 2		
1 Elizabeth Smith	* 1918 Nov 15	1941 Feb 1	

Serial # and Name	Birth	Marriage	Death

754721000 COLLINS

	Birth	Marriage	Death
Elizabeth Smith Waltenberg	1898 Nov 15	1941 Feb 1	
Ralph Aloysius Collins, Jr.			
1 Ralph Aloysius, III	1943 Jul 23		
2 Walter William	1944 Oct 20		
3 James Ronald	1945 Oct 7		
4 Vickie Rose	1950 Jun		

755000000 DUNLAP

	Birth	Marriage	Death
Mary Jane McIlvaine	1825 Sep 9	1854 Sep 18 Wayne Co.	OH 1893 Sep 3 Rock Springs WI
Alexander Dunlap	1816 May 12		1872 May 8 Rock Springs WI
1 James Crosby	* 1855 Aug 25		Tomah WI
2 Ida Isabel	* 1857 Mar 29		
3 John McIlvaine	* 1859 Apr 2 Ableman	WI 1882 Jan 20	1953 Sep Dayton WA
4 Harriet Janette	* 1861 Feb 6 Ableman	WI	1943 May 16
5 Wallace Lafayette	* 1863 Dec 8 Ableman	WI 1891 Jan 28 Dayton	WA 1937 Dec 6 Dayton WA
6 Mary Estelle	* 1864 Aug 11 Ableman	WI Ableman	WI 1947 Oct 13 Hood River OR
7 Laura	* 1868 Aug 28 Ableman	WI Sauk Co.	WI 1958 Feb 13 Rock Springs WY

755100000 DUNLAP

	Birth	Marriage	Death
James Crosby Dunlap	1855 Aug 25		Tomah WI
Cella -----			
1 Raymond		never married	i. Tomah WI

755200000 FLICKNER

	Birth	Marriage	Death
Ida Isabel Dunlap	1857 Mar 29		
----- Flickner			
1 Claud			
2 [daughter 1]			
3 [daughter 2]			

755300000 DUNLAP

	Birth	Marriage	Death
John McIlvaine Dunlap	1859 Apr 2 Ableman	WI 1882 Jan 20	1953 Sep Dayton WA
Pearl E. Prater	1864 Gainesville	GA	1948 Dec Dayton WA
1 Oliver C.	1887 Dec 29	never married	1943 Mar 16
2 Mary Ina	* 1891 Apr 23 Dayton	WA 1913 Jun 15 Dayton	WA 1985 Dec 1 Belmont CA
3 Earl Alexander	* 1895 Oct 8 Dayton	WA 1922 Jun 5	1964 Nov 16 Dayton WA

Oliver served in the 41st Division of the United States Army in World War I.

755320000 FALL

	Birth	Marriage	Death
Mary Ina Dunlap	1891 Apr 23 Dayton	WA 1913 Jun 15 Dayton	WA 1985 Dec 1 Belmont CA
Francis Elbert Fall	1884 Jan 28	John M. Fall &	1968 Jul San Mateo CA
		Frances Price	
1 Frances M.	* 1914 May 6 Dayton	WA 1953 Dec 7	
2 Mack Dunlap	* 1916 May 10 Dayton	WA 1942 Oct 2	1984 May 22

Serial # and Name	Birth	Marriage	Death
755321000 WILKENS			
Frances M. Fall	1914 May 6 Dayton	WA 1953 Dec 7	
Kenneth I. Wilkens			
755322000 FALL			
Mack Dunlap Fall	1916 May 10 Dayton	WA 1942 Oct 2	1984 May 22
Mary Frances Timmons	1924 May 12 Stillwater	OK Francis F. Timmons &	1982 May 22 Phoenix AZ
		Edith Christenson	
1 Robert A.	* 1943 Jul 16 Riverside	CA	
2 Ann C.	* 1951 Feb 1 Moses Lake	WA	
755322100 FALL			
Robert A. Fall	1943 Jul 16 Riverside	CA	
Carolyn Crews			
755322200 STONE			
Ann C. Fall	1951 Feb 1 Moses Lake	WA	
Jerry Stone			
755330000 DUNLAP			
Earl Alexander Dunlap	1895 Oct 8 Dayton	WA 1922 Jun 5	1964 Nov 16 Dayton WA
Lois Ann McCroskey	1891 Feb 27 Palouse	WA Samuel Mayo McCroskey &	
		Margaret Ann Cochran	
1 Richard Earl	* 1924 Jul 18 Dayton	WA	1985 Oct 6 St. Louis MO
755331000 DUNLAP			
Richard Earl Dunlap	1924 Jul 18 Dayton	WA	1985 Oct 6 St. Louis MO
Patricia Ann Dingle			
1 Mark	195? Mar 26		
2 William Earl	* 1952 Apr 22 Lawton	OK 1974 Dec 20 Columbia	MO
3 Richard	1953 Jul 21		
4 Virginia Ann	1957 Sep 26		

William, Richard, and Virginia were adopted by Patricia's second husband and their name was changed to Dalton.

Serial # and Name	Birth	Marriage	Death
755331200 DUNLAP			
William Earl Dunlap	1952 Apr 22 Lawton	OK 1974 Dec 20 Columbia	MO
Margaret Lynn Baker	1953 Oct 6 San Angelo	TX George L. Baker &	
		Ora Marie Miller	
1 Joshua Dale	1976 Jul 2 Columbia	MO	
2 Joanna Marie	1981 Dec 14 Tucson	AZ	
755400000 SPAULDING			
Harriet Janette Dunlap	1861 Feb 6 Ableman	WI	1943 May 16 i. N. Freedom WI
Albert Ross Spaulding	1852 Oct 19 Lake Delton	WI Oliver W. Spaulding &	1927 Nov 1 i. N. Freedom WI
		Ruth E. Pike	
1 Ross	1880		i. N. Freedom WI
2 Roy M.	* 1884 Sep 25	1906 Sep 11	1936 Feb 4
3 Flossye Irene	* 1889 Apr 10 North Freedom WI		1972 Jun 23 Wisconsin Dells WI
4 Bernice Hazel	* 1896 Jun 15	1924 Jun 23	
5 Ruth Marie	* 1903 Apr 21 Baraboo	WI 1924 Sep 20 North Freedom WI	1965 Dec 16 Chicago IL

Serial # and Name	Birth	Marriage	Death
755420000 SPAULDING			
Roy M. Spaulding	1884 Sep 25	1906 Sep 11	1936 Feb 4 i. N. Freedom WI
Flossye S. Douglas	1888 May 1		1971 i. N. Freedom WI
1 Lenore R.	1908 Jul 26		1909 Apr 14 i. N. Freedom WI
2 Eunice H.	*1911 Jan 25	1936 Oct 17	
3 Albert D.	1912 Mar 20		1922 Apr 22 i. N. Freedom WI
4 Golden	*1913 Oct 16	1946 Apr 9	
5 Viva B.	*1917 Feb 21	1944? May 29	
6 Raymond B.	*1920 Aug 7	1945 Sep 26	
755422000 JAMES / PAFF			
Eunice H. Spaulding	1911 Jan 25	1936 Oct 17	
s Charles B. James	1907 Jul 11		1954 Oct 1
t Russell D. Paff	1913 Mar 11	1963 Oct 9	1974 Jun 9 i. Reedsport WI
1 Phyllis L. James	*1937 Nov 30	1957 Mar 9	
755422100 POTTER / COOPER / BAUMGARTNER			
Phyllis L. James	1937 Nov 30	1957 Mar 9	
s Claude Potter	1935 Sep 23		1970 Nov 30 i. Geneva City WI
t William Cooper		1971 Jun 26	
u Francis Baumgartner		1974 Jun 1	
1 Laurie F. Potter	*1958 Apr 24	1979 May 19	
2 Laverne G. Potter	*1960 Jul 22	1977 Jun 14	
3 Leon J. Potter	*1961 Dec 5	1984 Mar 24	
4 LeRoy C. Potter	1964 May 17		
5 Landry C. Potter	1969 Dec 28		
755422110 BOTTLEMY			
Laurie F. Potter	1958 Apr 24	1979 May 19	
Greg Bottlemy			
1 Nicklass J.	1981 Mar 24		
2 Bryan M.	1982 Oct 19		
755422120 POTTER			
Laverne G. Potter	1960 Jul 22	1977 Jun 14	
Denise G. Koch			
1 DeBlaine	1977 Oct 15		
2 Brandie	1982 Dec 29		
3 Eric	1984 Jan 31		

DeBlaine was adopted June 16, 1986.

Serial # and Name	Birth	Marriage	Death
755422130 POTTER			
Leon J. Potter	1961 Dec 5	1984 Mar 24	
Ruby -----			
1 Crystal	1984 Oct 13		

283

Serial # and Name	Birth	Marriage	Death
755424000 BARTON			
Golden Spaulding	1913 Oct 16	1946 Apr 9	
Edward Barton			
755425000 WILCOX / DWARS			
Viva B. Spaulding	1917 Feb 21	1944? May 24	
s Lyle Wilcox	1914 May 29		
t Milo Dwars		1972 Mar 26	
755426000 SPAULDING			
Raymond B. Spaulding	1920 Aug 7	1945 Sep 26	
Marcella Holty			
755430000 PHILLIPS			
Flossye Irene Spaulding	1889 Apr 10 North Freedom WI		1972 Jun 23 Wisconsin Dells WI
Burt J. Phillips	1888 Jan 29 Centerville SD		1954 Nov 8
1 Dorothy Mae	# 1915 Sep 4		
2 Harriet Ann	# 1919 Feb 28 Milwaukee WI	1943 Jun 19 Wauwatoso WI	
755431000 HAAGENSEN			
Dorothy Mae Phillips	1915 Sep 4		
Kenneth W. Haagensen			
1 Mark	#		
2 Kenneth	#		
3 Karen			
755431100 HAAGENSEN			
Mark Haagensen			
Margaret Armstrong			
755431200 HAAGENSEN			
Kenneth Haagensen			
Cindy Weiss			
1 Rebecca			
2 Carrie			
3 Michael			
755432000 GISSAL			
Harriet Ann Phillips	1919 Feb 28 Milwaukee WI	1943 Jun 19 Wauwatoso WI	
Fred Wilmer Gissal (Dr.)	1917 Aug 17 Lannon WI	Frederick E. Gissal &	
		Rose Miller	
1 Jeffrey Joseph	# 1944 Apr 6 Milwaukee WI	1965 Apr 24 Rockford IL	
2 Cindy Ann	# 1948 Jul 10 Baraboo WI	1986 Sep 64 Wisconsin Dells WI	
3 Mary Lee	1950 Mar 15 Baraboo WI		
4 Frederick William	# 1952 May 20 Baraboo WI	1980 Jun 21 Wisconsin Dells WI	
5 Judy Lynn	# 1956 Dec 10 Portage WI	1981 Aug 15 Wisconsin Dells WI	
6 Wendy Jane	1959 Dec 1 Portage WI		

Serial # and Name	Birth	Marriage	Death
755432100 GISSAL			
Jeffrey Joseph Gissal	1944 Apr 6 Milwaukee	WI 1965 Apr 24 Rockford IL	
Ann Marie Gallota	1943 Apr 2 Rockford	IL Jasper J. Gallota &	
		Kathryn Lentine	
1 Jeff Joseph	1966 Jan 11		
2 Marci Ann	1967 May 25		
3 Tina Marie	1969 Sep 7		
4 Stephanie Lynn	1971 Nov 23		
5 Alex William	1975 Aug 13		
755432200 HORNSTEIN			
Cindy Ann Gissal	1948 Jul 10 Baraboo	WI 1986 Sep 6 Wisconsin Dells WI	
Paul Jay Hornstein	1946 Sep 25 Suffix	NJ Bertram Hornstein &	
		Gladys Dworkowitz	
1 Philip Bryan	1989 Jan 20 Hazelcrest	IL	
755432400 GISSAL			
Frederick William Gissal	1952 May 20 Baraboo	WI 1980 Jun 21 Wisconsin Dells WI	
Christine Anne Reifstock	1957 Aug 5 Portage	WI Paul F. Reifstock &	
		Orpha Marie Derksen	
1 Jessie Lynn	1982 Oct 3 Lacrosse	WI	
2 Matthew Ryan	1984 Apr 6 Rockford	IL	
3 Adam William	1985 Sep 20 Rockford	IL	
755432500 ANDERSON			
Judy Lynn Gissal	1956 Dec 10 Portage	WI 1981 Aug 15 Wisconsin Dells WI	
Richard John Anderson	1957 Aug 5 Portage	WI John Phileson Anderson &	
		Joan Nelson	
1 Sara Nicole	1986 Jun 26 Renton	WA	
2 Ross	1989 Feb 12 Renton	WA	
755440000 VOLL			
Bernice Hazel Spaulding	1896 Jun 15	1924 Jun 23	
S. Leonard Voll	18xx Oct 22		1963 Jul 11
1 Noreen	*1925 Aug 5		
2 Gerry Worden	*1931 Apr 23	1955 May 30	
755441000 WADOLNY			
Noreen Voll	1925 Aug 5		
Donald Wadolny			
1 Donette	*1954 Mar 26	1978 Sep 16	
2 Lynette	*1957 Apr 9		
755441100 LAMBRECHTS			
Donette Wadolny	1954 Mar 26	1978 Sep 16	
John Lambrechts			
1 Benjamin	1983 Feb 13		

285

Serial # and Name	Birth	Marriage	Death
755441200 JATZAK			
Lynette Wadolny	#:1957 Apr 9		
Kenneth Jatzak			
755442000 VOLL			
Gerry Worden Voll	:1931 Apr 23	:1955 May 30	
s Barbara Weigand			
t Linda Spilker			
1 James	s :1958 May 14		
2 Cheryl	s#:1960 Jan 24		
3 Nancy	s :1963 Feb 18		
4 Sarah	t :		
755442200 VACEL			
Cheryl Voll	:1960 Jan 24		
John Vacel			
755450000 COOKE			
Ruth Marie Spaulding	:1903 Apr 21 Baraboo WI	:1924 Sep 20 North Freedom WI	:1965 Dec 16 Chicago IL
Donald Cyril Cooke	:1904 Jun 12 Lime Ridge WI	John Fletcher Cooke &	:1988 Dec 17 Platteville WI
		Louise M. Gregg	
1 Jeanette Ruth	#:1929 Jan 7 Joliet IL	:1950 Aug 26 Chicago IL	
2 Lois Marie	#:1937 Aug 1 Chicago IL	:1959 Sep 5 Quantico VA	
755451000 GIELOW			
Jeanette Ruth Cooke	:1929 Jan 7 Joliet IL	:1950 Aug 26 Chicago IL	
Howard L. Gielow	:1924 Dec 24 Chicago IL	Edward Richard Gielow &	
		Eleanor Laver	
1 Diane Lynn	#:1953 Mar 23 Urbana IL	:1974 Jan 26 No. Hollywood CA	
2 Tad Alan	#:1957 Jun 17 Urbana IL	:1984 Feb 4 Camarillo CA	
755451100 LEVINSON			
Diane Lynn Gielow	:1953 Mar 23 Urbana IL	:1974 Jan 26 No. Hollywood CA	
Lawrence Michael Levinson	:1951 Dec 17 Los Angeles CA	Jack Levinson &	
		Jacqueline Susman	
1 Eric Michelle	:1976 Dec 23		
2 Carly Leah	:1979 Dec 11		
3 Brian Matthew	:1982 Oct 27		
755451200 GIELOW			
Tad Alan Gielow	:1957 Jun 17 Urbana IL	:1984 Feb 4 Camarillo CA	
Judy Marie Ray	:1960 Aug 14 Sacramento CA	Jerry Ray & Judy M. Robidoux	

Judy was adopted by Gustavo P. and Aberdeen Louise (Robidoux) Valenzuela.

1 Aberdeen Jenae	:1987 Nov 7 Los Angeles CA		

Serial # and Name		Birth		Marriage		Death	

755452000   WETZEL

Lois Marie Cooke		1937 Aug 1 Chicago	IL	1959 Sep 5 Quantico	VA		
Richard Alan Wetzel		1937 Dec 31 Berrien Co.	MI	Lester K. Wetzel &			
				Helen S. Menser			

Lois is a graduate of St. Luke's School of Nursing.   Richard received B. S., M. S., and Ph. D. degrees from Illinois Institute of Technology.   He was (1988) Professor of Civil Engineering at the University of Wisconsin, Platteville.   He served three years as a Lieutenant in the Marine Corps.

1 Glen Alan	#	1960 Nov 18 Oceanside	CA	1986 Oct 4 Greenville	OH		
2 Nathan Richard	#	1963 Sep 23 Chicago	IL	1987 Jul 25 Lindstrom	MN		
3 Ruth Helen		1968 Feb 6 Melrose Park	IL				

755452100   WETZEL

Glen Alan Wetzel		1960 Nov 18 Oceanside	CA	1986 Oct 4 Greenville	OH		
Mary Caroline Skinker		1958 Jan 13 Springfield	IL	William Garrett Skinker &			
				Mary Parks Bugg			

755452200   WETZEL

Nathan Richard Wetzel		1963 Sep 23 Chicago	IL	1987 Jul 25 Lindstrom	MN		
Wendy Sue Anderson		1968 Jan 13 Chisago City	MN	Lloyd E. Anderson &			
				Lois M. Swanson			

755500000   DUNLAP

Wallace Lafayette Dunlap		1863 Dec 8 Ableman	WI	1891 Jan 28 Dayton	WA	1937 Dec 6 Dayton	WA
Anna Estelle Gholson		1871 Feb 2 Umatilla	OR	Huston D. Gholson &		1944 Dec 17 Dayton	WA
				Isabelle Goodman			
1 Ina Grace	#	1892 Jan 18 Dayton	WA	1910 Nov 2 Dayton	WA	1985 Nov 27 Tacoma	WA
2 Bonnie Laura	#	1893 Nov 26 Dayton	WA	1914 Mar 15 Dayton	OH	1979 May 24 Portland	OR
3 Wallace Elwood	#	1906 Dec 26 Dayton	WA	Seattle	WA	1966 Mar 30 Seattle	WA
4 Elden Wayne	#	1908 Apr 3 Dayton	WA	1933 Sep 23 Dayton	WA	1988 Apr 12 Dayton	WA
5 Estella Irene	#	1910 Oct 18 Dayton	WA	1936 Oct 3 Pomeroy	WA		

755510000   ROYSE

Ina Grace Dunlap		1892 Jan 18 Dayton	WA	1910 Nov 2 Dayton	WA	1985 Nov 27 Tacoma	WA
Martin Jefferson Royse		1890 Oct 14 Dayton	WA	Frank B. Royse &		1957 Mar 4 Tacoma	WA
				Martha E. Rose			

Ina was educated in a one room school.   She rode horse-back to and from the school, and to music lessons. She and Martin moved to Tacoma in 1918.   There they grew and canned all of their vegetables and fruits, and spent weekends clamming, swimming, fishing, or hiking. Martin worked as a carpenter at Ft. Lewis, WA until he was paralyzed in a fall, a condition in which he remained until his death.   Ina lived alone in her home at age 91 1/2.

1 Bernita Madeline	#	1911 Aug 26 Dayton	WA	1935 Aug 23 Tacoma	WA		
2 Lucille Isabel	#	1913 Jan 17 Dayton	WA	1936 Jan 28 Fairbanks	AK		
3 Wallace Dunlap	#	1920 Oct 19 Tacoma	WA	1942 Dec 25 Yonkers	NY	1988 Jul 14 Tacoma	WA
4 Betty Jean		1925 Nov 4					

755511000   GORDON

Bernita Madeline Royse		1911 Aug 26 Dayton	WA	1935 Aug 23 Tacoma	WA		
Donald Paul Gordon		1916 Jun 14 Tacoma	WA	Joseph J. Gordon &			
				Minnie Archer			
1 Donna Lee	#	1938 May 2 Tacoma	WA	1957 Jan 10 Tacoma	WA		
2 Patricia Diane		1940 Jun 5 Tacoma	WA				

Patricia graduated in 1961 as a Registered Nurse, attended classes at the University of Washington, and earned a B. S. N. at the Univ. of Utah.   She worked seventeen years as a surgical nurse, and four years on an open heart team. Thereafter she nursed at a treatment center for children with behavioral problems.

Serial # and Name	Birth	Marriage	Death

755511100 ALESHIRE / WHITT

Donna Lee Gordon	!1938 May 2 Tacoma	WA!1957 Jan 10 Tacoma	WA!
s Gary Lee Aleshire	!1934 Jul 18 Tacoma	WA! Warren S. Aleshire &	!
	!	! Rayetta Scrandrett	!
t ----- Whitt (Rev.)	!	!	!
	!	!	!
1 Loree Linn	s#!1957 Jul 15 Tacoma	WA!1981 Apr 11 Tacoma	WA!
2 Linda Lee	s !1959 Jan 7	!	!
3 Gary Lee, Jr.	s !1960 Mar 4 Tacoma	WA!	!
4 Gordon Stephen	s !1961 Dec 12 Tacoma	WA!	!

Linda won a four-year scholarship to Washington State University. While at Lincoln High School and WSU she was sent to Germany as an exchange student. She majored in French and German, graduating Magna Cum Laude in 1991. She graduated from the American School of International Management in Phoenix, AZ in December 1982. She was then employed by the Continental Bank of Chicago. Gary graduated from Tacoma Community College in 1983, and is employed as a fireman and paramedic. Gordon was employed in 1984 by Belknap Industries in Kent, WA. He completed two years of carpenter training at Tacoma Bates Vocational School.

755511110 WERNER

Loree Linn Aleshire	!1957 Jul 15 Tacoma	WA!1981 Apr 11 Tacoma	WA!
Frederick Andreas Werner	!	!	!

Loree won a four-year scholarship to the University of Puget Sound, which she attended for two years before transferring to Western Washington University, from which she graduated with a B. A. in Special Education. She lives and teaches in Tacoma.

755512000 LAING

Lucille Isabel Royse	!1913 Jan 17 Dayton	WA!1936 Jan 28 Fairbanks	AK!
Edward Everett Laing	!1911 Dec 4 Tacoma	WA! Charles E. Laing &	!
	!	! Mary E. Maxwell	!

The Laings have lived in Alaska, Oregon, Idaho, Washington, Virginia, and Ohio. Ed is a graduate of Washington State University and was an electrical engineer at Coulee Dam and St. Joseph Dam. He studied nuclear power at the University of Virginia, and worked at the first nuclear power station in Virginia. Lucille worked during the years that her husband was in the service, but otherwise has been a housewife taking care of their two adopted children. They retired about 1972 and built a house in Vancouver, WA.

1 Larry Everett	#!1947 May 30 Spokane	WA!1970 Jul 25	!
2 Susan	#!1950 Feb 23 Soap Lake	WA!	!

755512100 LAING

Larry Everett Laing	!1947 May 30 Spokane	WA!1970 Jul 25	!
Judith Ann Vornheder	!1948 Feb 23 Hamilton	OH! Howard Humphrey Vornheder & !	
	!	! Helen Marie Sharkey	!

755512200 GAUDREAU

Susan Laing	!1950 Feb 23 Soap Lake	WA!	!
James Arnott Gaudreau	!	!	!

755513000 ROYSE

Wallace Dunlap Royse	!1920 Oct 19 Tacoma	WA!1942 Dec 25 Yonkers	NY!1988 Jul 14 Tacoma WA
Kathrine Yatchyshyn	!1923 Mar 1 New York	NY! Zachary Yatchyshyn &	!
	!	! Rose Hrymolowska	!
1 Rose Mary	#!1944 Feb 21 New York	NY!1965 Dec 15 Tacoma	WA!
2 Barbara Jean	#!1946 Oct 1 New York	NY!1977 Aug 6 Chambers	WA!
3 Judith Ann	#!1947 Oct 21 Tacoma	WA!1978 Jun 10 Yelm	WA!

Serial # and Name	Birth	Marriage	Death

755513100   ARNOLD

	Birth	Marriage	Death
Rose Mary Royse	:1944 Feb 21 New York	NY:1965 Dec 15 Tacoma	WA:
Thomas Eugene Paul Arnold	:1942 Jul 16 Tacoma	WA: Thomas P. Arnold &	:
	:	: Ruby M. Davis	:
1 Tamara Rose	:1968 Dec 5 Tacoma	WA:	:

755513200   CHURCH

Barbara Jean Royse	:1946 Oct 1 New York	NY:1977 Aug 6 Chambers	WA:
James Matthew Church	:1949 Oct 12 Tacoma	WA: Fred Monroe Church &	:
	:	: Gloria J. Buchanan	:
1 Zachary Wallace	:1979 Jul 21 Tacoma	WA:	:

755513300   FRIEDHOFF

Judith Ann Royse	:1947 Oct 21 Tacoma	WA:1978 Jun 10 Yelm	WA:
Francis William Friedhoff	:1952 May 23 Augsburg	GR: Leo P. Friedhoff &	:
	:	: Mildred A. Clark	:
1 Kalan Ina	:1983 Jun 12 Tacoma	WA:	:
2 Deidre Lee	:1986 Feb 3 Tacoma	WA:	:

755520000   BOWMAN

Bonnie Laura Dunlap	:1893 Nov 26 Dayton	WA:1914 Mar 15 Dayton	OH:1979 May 24 Portland OR
Edward Roy Bowman	:1890 Oct 6	: Charles B. Bowman &	:1981 Feb Seattle WA
	:	: Jane Anna -----	:
1 Dorothy Jean	*:1916 Apr 3 Dayton	WA:1939 Aug 21 Grangeville	ID:

755521000   NELSON

Dorothy Jean Bowman	:1916 Apr 3 Dayton	WA:1939 Aug 21 Grangeville	ID:
Guy Buford Nelson	:1911 Oct 20 Pomeroy	WA: John A. Nelson &	:
	:	: Sylvia M. Crumpacker	:
1 Laura Lee	:1945 Apr 13 Portland	OR:	:
2 Barbara Lou	*:1950 Sep 20 Portland	OR:1972 Aug 19 Portland	OR:

755521200   HOVEY

Barbara Lou Nelson	:1950 Sep 20 Portland	OR:1972 Aug 19 Portland	OR:
Craig Warren Hovey	:1950 Oct 17 Seattle	WA: Warren G. Hovey &	:
	:	: Delores M. Dressen	:
1 Erin Kathleen	:1978 May 10 Portland	OR:	:

755530000   DUNLAP

Wallace Elwood Dunlap	:1906 Dec 26 Dayton	WA: Seattle	WA:1966 Mar 30 Seattle WA
Nelda -----	:	:	: Seattle WA

755540000   DUNLAP

Elden Wayne Dunlap	:1908 Apr 3 Dayton	WA:1933 Sep 23 Dayton	WA:1988 Apr 12 Dayton WA
Gladys Emma Abraham	:1913 Sep 1 Dayton	WA: Thomas C. Abraham &	:
	:	: Delia M. Trescott	:
1 Jerry Wayne	*:1934 Oct 2	:1960 Oct 8	:
2 Duane Charles	*:1938 Mar 30 Dayton	WA:1961 Nov 29 Seattle	WA:
3 Nancy Gayle	*:1952 Feb 4 Dayton	WA:1976 Jun 5	:

Serial # and Name	Birth	Marriage	Death
755541000 DUNLAP			
Jerry Wayne Dunlap	!1934 Oct 2	!1960 Oct 8	!
Joannie L. Lyman	!1936 Jul 24 Dayton	WA! William C. Lyman &	!
	!	! Sarah A. Woodward	!
1 Jory Patrick	!1964 Mar 26 Spokane	WA!	!
755542000 DUNLAP			
Duane Charles Dunlap	!1938 Mar 30 Dayton	WA!1961 Nov 29 Seattle	WA!
Susan Ann Larson	!1942 Jul 4 Mayville	ND! Loren W. Larson &	!
	!	! Lucille F. Rice	!
1 Heidi Lynn	!1963 Jun 24 Ft. Eustis	VA!	!
2 Christopher Loren	!1965 Apr 3 Seattle	WA!	!
3 Ian Charles	!1972 Sep 8 Walla Walla	WA!	!
755543000 PAYNE			
Nancy Gayle Dunlap	!1952 Feb 4 Dayton	WA!1976 Jun 5	!
David Wallace Payne	!1952 May 2 Dayton	WA! Wallace Milton Payne &	!
	!	! Myra Jane Summerfield	!
	!	!	!
1 Emalee Suzanne	!1977 May 9 Walla Walla	WA!	!
2 Roxanne	!1979 Oct 3 Walla Walla	WA!	!1979 Oct 3 Walla Walla WA
3 Matt David	!1980 Aug 26 Walla Walla	WA!	!
4 Todd David	!1981 Dec 16 Walla Walla	WA!	!
755550000 DORR			
Estella Irene Dunlap	!1910 Oct 18 Dayton	WA!1936 Oct 3 Pomeroy	WA!
Frederick Fortson Dorr	!1901 Sep 22 Dayton	WA! George Boardman Fortson	!1968 Mar 21 i. Dayton WA
	!	! Maude Sherborne	!
755600000 ORDWAY			
Mary Estelle Dunlap	!1864 Aug 11 Ableman	WI! Ableman	WI!1947 Oct 13 Hood River OR
Robert William Ordway	!1853 Dec 13	WI!	!1920 Oct 27 Hood River OR
	!	!	!
1 Earl	*!1888 Nov 1 Burns	KS!1910 May 1 Silverton	OR!1974 Oct 8 Hood River OR
2 Alta Fern	*!1889 Jan 9	!	!1976 May 11 Vancouver WA
3 Edith	*!1890 Dec 1 Burns	KS!1913 Jan 1	!1982 Dec 31 Seattle WA
4 Glen	*!1892 Burns	KS! Hood River	OR! Hood River OR
5 Floy	*!1895 Burns	KS!	!1974 Hood River OR
6 Edna Lucille	!1905 May 11 Hood River	OR!	!infancy death i. Hood Riv. OR
755610000 ORDWAY			
Earl Ordway	!1888 Nov 1 Burns	KS!1910 May 1 Silverton	OR!1974 Oct 8 Hood River OR
Pearl Evedna Blaylock	!1888 May 16 Grass Valley	OR! William A. Blaylock &	!1979 Nov 3 Hood River OR
	!	! Josephine L. Prevost	!
1 Lloyd Arthur	*!1912 Jul 15 Hood River	OR!1941 Aug 27 Dufer	OR!1976 Mar 20 The Dalles OR
2 Malcolm Earl	*!1914 Nov 8 Hood River	OR!1949 Jan 15 San Francisco CA!
3 Doris Irene	*!1916 Sep 10 Hood River	OR!1949 Sep 16 Bellingham	WA!
4 Arlo Blaylock	*!1918 Aug 23 Hood River	OR!1938 Aug 15 Hood River	OR!1968 Hobbs NM
5 Robert Wayne	*!1923 Apr 19 Hood River	OR!1955 May 15 LaGrande	OR!1965 Nov 1
6 William Leslie	*!1923 Apr 19 Hood River	OR!1945 Jul 8 Elkhart	IN!
7 Kenneth Raymond	!1926 Feb 4 Hood River	OR!	!1926 Feb 23 Hood River OR

Serial # and Name	Birth	Marriage	Death

755611000 ORDWAY

Lloyd Arthur Ordway	!1912 Jul 15 Hood River	OR!1941 Aug 27 Dufer	OR!1976 Mar 20 The Dalles OR
Gladys Irene Perkins	!1922 Aug 1 Edison	NE! Gayle Reynolds Perkins & !	
	!	! Nellie Viola Bishop !	

Lloyd attended Oregon Normal School (now Western Oregon College); he worked for the Union Pacific Railroad all his life.

1 Gayle Arthur	*!1942 Jun 11 The Dalles	OR!1963 Sep 3 The Dalles OR!	
2 Russell Edwin	*!1943 Aug 7 The Dalles	OR!196x The Dalles OR!	
3 Janice Terrell	*!1946 Jul 15 The Dalles	OR!1965 Jul 15 Coeur D'Alene ID!	
4 Gary Lynn	*!1947 Aug 18 The Dalles	OR!1965 Feb !	
5 Susan Carol	!1953 Feb 23 The Dalles	OR!	!1973 Apr 14 Chemult OR
6 Raymond Keith	*!1954 Nov 9 Hood River	OR!1973 Apr 14 The Dalles OR!	
7 Danny Joe	*!1957 Feb 5 The Dalles	OR!1982 Aug 29 Mosier OR!	

Susan was attending college in Los Angeles, and while she was on the way home to The Dalles, OR to attend her younger brother's wedding she was killed in a tragic automobile accident.

755611100 ORDWAY

Gayle Arthur Ordway	!1942 Jun 11 The Dalles	OR!1963 Sep 3 The Dalles OR!	
Anita Ruth Anthony	!1942 Jun 9 The Dalles	OR! James Eble Anthony & !	
	!	! Violete May Oades !	

Gayle joined the U. S. Navy after graduating from high school, and served for twenty years.   After his retirement from the service he worked installing telephone systems.

1 Gayle Anthony	!1966 Jan 14 Charleston	SC!	!
2 Heather LeAnn	*!1968 Dec 15 Portsmouth	VA!1990 Jul 14 Astoria OR!	
3 James Russell	*!1971 Aug 3 Charleston	SC!1992 May 23 Beaverton OR!	

755611120 ALLEN

Heather LeAnn Ordway	!1968 Dec 15 Portsmouth	VA!1990 Jul 14 Astoria OR!	
Michael Ray Allen	!1968 Apr 30 Astoria	OR! Curtis J. Allen & !	
	!	! Hazel Diane Palmorse !	
1 Dominic Michael	!1992 Jul 23 Beaverton	OR!	!
2 Hayden Ray	!1995 Apr 5 Tualatin	OR!	!

755611130 ORDWAY

James Russell Ordway	!1971 Aug 3 Charleston	SC!1992 May 23 Beaverton OR!	
Hyon Jung Kim	!1971 Aug 6 Seoul	KO! Hak Gun Kim & !	
	!	! Young Ok Lee !	
1 Sebastian James	!1992 Sep 17 Portland	OR!	!
2 Christian Russell	!1995 Sep 14 Tualatin	OR!	!

The Korean name of Sebastian is Sang Jun, and that of Christian is Sang Min.

755611200 ORDWAY

Russell Edwin Ordway	!1943 Aug 7 The Dalles	OR!196- The Dalles OR!	
Georgia Jean Davis	!1943 Jan 27 The Dalles	OR! George Milton Davis & !	
	!	! Eva Mae Anderson !	
1 Todd Owen	*!1964 Feb 2 Portland	OR!1983 Sep 7 The Dalles OR!	
2 Laura Ann	*!1968 Feb 23 Portland	OR!1988 May 27 Portland OR!	
3 Linda Marie	*!1968 Feb 23 Portland	OR!1990 Apr 14 The Dalles OR!	

Serial # and Name	Birth	Marriage	Death
755611210 ORDWAY			
Todd Owen Ordway	1964 Feb 2 Portland	OR 1983 Sep 7 The Dalles	OR
s Michelle Marie Dell	1964 Feb 7	Ervin John Dell &	
		Patsy Ann Holloway	
t Barbara Grace Brown	1958 May 5	1988 Sep 25 Vancouver	WA
		James R. Brown &	
		Catherine Ann Keho	
1 Bryan Michael	s 1984 Oct 26 Portland	OR	
2 Robert James	t 1989 Apr 10 Portland	OR	
755611220 WAMBOLD			
Laura Ann Ordway	1968 Feb 23 Portland	OR 1988 May 27 Portland	OR
Michael Alan Wambold		Larry L. Wambold &	
		Judy L. Rudarmel	
1 Shauna Lynn	1989 Oct 9 Portland	OR	
755611230 HANSON			
Linda Marie Ordway	1968 Feb 23 Portland	OR 1990 Apr 14 The Dalles	OR
Daniel LeRoy Hanson	1966 Apr 10 Goldendale	WA Clarence Lister Hanson &	
		Deanna Lee Andrew	
1 Jessica Lynn _Ordway_	1985 Nov 10 Portland	OR	
2 Jeremy Russell _Ordway_	1989 Jun 6 Portland	OR	
3 Julie Marie _Hanson_	1991 May 28 Portland	OR	

Jessica and Jeremy are Linda's children prior to her marriage to Daniel.

Serial # and Name	Birth	Marriage	Death
755611300 KENNEY			
Janice Terrell Ordway	1946 Jul 15 The Dalles	OR 1965 Jul 15 Coeur D'Alene ID	
John Henry Kenney, II		John H. Kenney, Jr. &	
		----- -----	
1 Jon Michael	* 1970 Aug 26 Ft. Lewis	WA 1987 Nov 14 Hermiston	OR
755611310 KENNEY			
Jon Michael Kenney	1970 Aug 26 Ft. Lewis	WA 1987 Nov 14 Hermiston	OR
Sue Ann Johnson			
1 Justin Michael	1988 Aug 6 The Dalles	OR	
2 Brittany Dale	1991 May The Dalles	OR	
755611400 ORDWAY			
Gary Lynn Ordway	1947 Aug 18 The Dalles	OR 1965 Feb	
s Billie Jean Kortge	1947 Oct 19 The Dalles	OR William O. Kortge &	
		Virginia -----	
t Linda Jo Hollenbeak	1947 Apr 25 Tillamook	OR 1970 Dec 26 Twin Falls	ID
		James William Hollenbeak &	
		Ruth Louise Snow	
1 Ingrid Jo	s* 1965 Sep 8 Corvallis	OR	
755611410 DAVIS			
Ingrid Jo Ordway	1965 Sep 8 Corvallis	OR	
Greg Davis			
1 Tyler William	1990 Feb Portland	OR	
2 Alea Joe	1992 Dec 28 Portland	OR	

Serial # and Name	Birth	Marriage	Death

755611600   ORDWAY

Raymond Keith Ordway	1954 Nov 9 Hood River OR	1973 Apr 14 The Dalles OR	
Debra Ruth Hurn	1950 Sep 21 Sunnyside WA	Charles Carroll Hurn &	
		Ruth Louise Snow	
1 Kristal Ruth	1969 Mar 15 Shelton WA		
2 Katrina Sue	1974 Apr 28 The Dalles OR		
3 Kamala Cassandra	1979 Aug 2 The Dalles OR		

755611700   ORDWAY

Danny Joe Ordway	1957 Feb 5 The Dalles OR	1982 Aug 29 Mosier OR	
Rebecca Classen	1958 Apr 16 Portland OR	Bart Fred Classen &	
		Esther Rosalee Friesen	
1 Kyle Jo	1982 Dec 25 The Dalles OR		

755612000   ORDWAY

Malcolm Earl Ordway	1914 Nov 8 Hood River OR	1949 Jan 15 San Francisco CA	
Helen Margaret Stevenot	1913 Jul 1 Carson Hill CA	Ferdinand Gabriel Stevenot	
		Adeline Julia DeLuca	

Malcolm served in the United States Navy from December 1941 until August 1945.   He served on a troop transport which was involved in the landings in the South Pacific up to and including Iwo Jima.   At Iwo Jima he was re-united with his younger brother who was Captain of an LST.   Malcolm received his Bachelor's degree from the University of Oregon, and his Master's degree from San Francisco State University.   He was both a teacher and a school principal for many years in central California.

1 John Malcolm	*1950 Jun 27 San Francisco CA	1977 Jul 23 Gilroy CA	
2 Stephen Blaylock	1951 Dec 5 San Francisco CA		
3 Mark Edward	*1952 Dec 16 San Francisco CA	1982 Oct 13 San Jose CA	

755612100   ORDWAY

John Malcolm Ordway	1950 Jun 27 San Francisco CA	1977 Jul 23 Gilroy CA	
Maryjo Goodnight	1953 Jun 3 Washington DC	Randall Eugene Goodnight &	
		Jacqueline Carlisle	

John received his law degree from Stanford University, and has a career in the Diplomatic Corps.

1 Christopher William	1979 Aug 21 Nurnberg GR		
Stevenot			
2 Julie Marie	1981 Feb 29 Concord CA		

755612300   ORDWAY

Mark Edward Ordway	1952 Dec 16 San Francisco CA	1982 Oct 13 San Jose CA	
Fran Noreen Evansek	1952 Apr 7 Greensburg PA	Raymond Paul Evansek &	
		Carmela Frances Scarcella	
1 Scott Jeremy	1984 Mar 29 Santa Cruz CA		
2 Carey	1985 Oct 9 Santa Cruz CA		

755613000   WOODLEY / BROOKS

Doris Irene Ordway	1916 Sep 10 Hood River OR	1949 Sep 16 Bellingham WA	
s James Robert Woodley	1902 Oct 28 London EN	Robert Woodley & Mary -----	1963 Aug 31 The Dalles OR
t Paul Philip Brooks	1920 Apr 23 Mosier OR	1964 Dec 24 The Dalles OR	
		Charles Brooks &	
		Etta Mae Lewis	

Irene received a Bachelor's degree in Education from Western Washington University, and taught school for many years in Oregon and Washington.

1 Priscilla Ruth Woodley	1951 Nov 21 Prosser WA		

Serial # and Name	Birth	Marriage	Death	

755614000 ORDWAY

	Birth	Marriage	Death	
Arlo Blaylock Ordway	1918 Aug 23 Hood River OR	1938 Aug 15 Hood River OR	1968 Hobbs NM	
Marguerite Florence Clark	1919 May 16 Hood River OR	Bliss Lucius Clark &	19-- i. Hood River OR	
		Florence Brown		

Arlo received his Bachelor's degree in Finance from the University of Oregon.   He was manager of a bank in Oregon, and later was involved with a group of banks in New Mexico.   In World War II he received a commission in the Coast Guard from the Coast Guard Academy, New London, CT, and served aboard ships in the North Atlantic run and later in the Pacific Theater, where he was Captain of an LST and participated in the landings at Iwo Jima.

	Birth	Marriage	Death	
1 Earl Clark	#1942 Nov 26 Corvallis OR	1962 Sep 9 Detroit MI		
2 Jean Ann	#1947 Mar 4 Hood River OR	1962 Jun 12 NM		

755614100 ORDWAY

	Birth	Marriage	Death	
Earl Clark Ordway	1942 Nov 26 Corvallis OR	1962 Sep 9 Detroit MI		
s Helen Ann Thomas	1940 Mar 13 McMinnville OR	James Lief Thomas &		
		Helen Sarah Walter		
t Jan Newman	1940 Dec 2 Charleston SC	1973 May 26 Charleston SC		
		Clarence Judson Newman &		
		Jeanette Arnot		
1 Sondra Estelle	s 1965 Apr 3 Moses Lake WA			

755614200 COPE / DOBKOWSKI

	Birth	Marriage	Death	
Jean Ann Ordway	1947 Mar 4 Hood River OR	1962 Jun 12 NM		
s Kenneth Arthur Cope	1940 Dec 2 Medford MA	Clarence Homer Cope &		
		Dorothea Marianne Johnson		
t Marc Edward Dobkowski	1954 Nov 20 Newark NJ	1980 Aug 92 Anchorage AK		
		Lionel Francis Dobkowski &		
		Eileen Hughes		
1 Wendy Louellen Cope	1967 Nov 29 Anchorage AK			
2 Joshua Francis Dobkowski	1983 Jan 4 AK			

755615000 ORDWAY

	Birth	Marriage	Death	
Robert Wayne Ordway	1923 Apr 19 Hood River OR	1955 May 15 LaGrande OR	1965 Nov 1 Spokane WA	
Rose Catherine Kucera	1926 Mar 17 American Falls ID	Joseph Kucera & ----- -----		
1 Stanley Allen	#1954 Oct 17 Pendleton OR	1974 Dec 31 Coeur D'Alene ID		
2 Linda Marie	#1956 Jul 23 Pocatello ID	1976 Aug 7		
3 Duane Lee	1958 Oct 4 Pocatello ID			

755615100 ORDWAY

	Birth	Marriage	Death	
Stanley Allen Ordway	1954 Oct 17 Pendleton OR	1974 Dec 31 Coeur D'Alene ID		
s Diane Applington	1958 May 29 Renton WA	James Nathan Applington &		
		Audrey Mask		
t Cheryl Diane Coffield	1962 Oct 1 Spokane WA	1979 Sep 29 Spokane WA	1980 Mar 31 Spokane WA	
		Bates Le Roy Coffield &		
		Erma Evelyn Werban		
u Joan Marie Baird	1957 Jan 18 Spokane WA	1980 Nov 29 Spokane WA		
		Glenn Corvin Baird &		
		Helen Joann Hoffman		
1 Jennifer Marie	s 1975 Dec 7 Spokane WA			
2 Nicholas Noel	t 1980 Mar 6 Spokane WA			
3 Jolie Lynn	u 1981 Jul 2 Spokane WA			

Serial # and Name	Birth	Marriage	Death

755615200 MCKAY

Linda Marie Ordway	1956 Jul 23 Pocatello	ID 1976 Aug 7	
David Alan McKay	1955 Sep 27	Donald McKay & Carol Golob	

755616000 ORDWAY

William Leslie Ordway	1923 Apr 19 Hood River	OR 1945 Jul 8 Elkhart IN	
s Mary Elizabeth Smith	1924 Mar 25 Elkhart	IN Ira J. Smith &	
		Angeline Matilda Wachtel	
t Virginia Lee Helmick	1937 Mar 26 Steamboat Spr. CO 1957 Oct 5 Las Vegas NV		
		Thomas Galloway Helmick &	
		Nora Eileen Whitt	

William compiled and printed the monumental volume *The House of Grimet, a family Genealogy* (first edition, 1993; revised edition, 1994),   a history of every family in the United States which is, or might be, descended from the Ayrshire family of McYlveyne (McIlvaine), Lairds of Grimet, including this McElwain family.   He has also compiled other family histories and is presently working on the Dunlap family, a portion of which appears in this book under the number 755000000.   His retirementnt has been spent living in The Dalles, Oregon.   During World War II he held a commission as an ensign in the United States Navy.

1 Angeline Estelle	s 1948 Mar 2 Elkhart IN		
2 Amy Lee	s 1950 Sep 1 Elkhart IN		
3 Lori Kay	t# 1959 Jan 8 Pasadena CA 1994 Dec 30 Las Vegas NV		
4 Lois Jean	t# 1961 Mar 25 Anaheim CA 1984 Aug 19 Garden Grove CA		
5 David Glen	t 1962 Dec 21 Anaheim CA		
6 Jennifer Lee	t# 1965 Apr 2 Anaheim CA 1988 Dec 16 Hesperia CA		
7 Bryon Alan	t 1973 Jun 4 Mission Hills CA		

755616300 PECK

Lori Kay Ordway	1959 Jan 8 Pasadena	CA 1994 Dec 30 Las Vegas NV	
Paul John Peck	1949 Jun 2 Burbank	CA Milo Peck & ----- -----	
1 Alysse Amber	1995 Apr 12 Lancaster	CA	

755616400 AHMED

Lois Jean Ordway	1961 Mar 25 Anaheim	CA 1984 Aug 19 Garden Grove CA	
Rashed Mohamed Ahmed	1958 Apr 29 Hyderabad	IN Mohamed A. Ahmed &	
		Sara Banu	
1 Arshad	1988 Jan 24 Riverside	CA	1988 Jan 24 Riverside CA
2 Ayoub Afzal	1989 Sep 19 Riverside	CA	
3 Aliyah Yasmeen	1993 Jul 28 Riverside	CA	

755616600 FERGUSON

Jennifer Lee Ordway	1965 Apr 2 Anaheim	CA 1988 Dec 16 Hesperia CA	
Otis Ferguson			
1 Morgan Brianna	1993 Nov 18 Loma Linda	CA	

755620000 STEWART

Alta Fern Ordway	1889 Jan 9		1976 May 11 Vancouver WA
William Thompson Stewart		William Stewart &	1966 Apr 6 Vancouver WA
		Jane -----	
1 Russell William	# 1914 Sep 24 Vancouver	WA 1941 Dec 24 Vancouver WA 1982 Oct 14 Vancouver WA
2 Mary Frances	# 1916 Mar 27 Vancouver	WA 1937 Jun 1	1991

Serial # and Name	Birth	Marriage	Death

755621000   STEWART

Russell William Stewart	:1914 Sep 24 Vancouver	WA:1941 Dec 24 Vancouver	WA:1982 Oct 14 Vancouver WA
Jane Kathryn Petri	:1923 Feb 17 Portland	OR: Jacob Petri &	:
	:	: Hazel Grace Beavers	:
1 Kathy Ann	*:1942 Nov 19 Vancouver	WA:	:
2 William Francis	:1947 Apr 1 Vancouver	WA:	:
3 Janelle Kay	*:1952 Aug 13 Vancouver	WA:1972 Apr 20 Vancouver	WA:

755621100   LOVELADY

Kathy Ann Stewart	:1942 Nov 19 Vancouver	WA:	:
Harold Lovelady	:	:	:

755621300   TAYLOR

Janelle Kay Stewart	:1952 Aug 13 Vancouver	WA:1972 Apr 20 Vancouver	WA:
Raymond Earl Taylor	:1949 Apr 11 Walla Walla	WA: Earl Howard Taylor &	:
	:	: Phyllis May York	:
1 Cody Lawrence	:1977 Jul 2 Vancouver	WA:	:
2 Casey William	:1979 Sep 27 Vancouver	WA:	:

755622000   KAUFMAN

Mary Frances Stewart	:1916 Mar 27 Vancouver	WA:1937 Jun 1	:1991
Peter Arthur Kaufman	:	: Peter Kaufman & ----- ----- :	
1 Carolyn Lucille	*:1942 Jul 19 Vancouver	WA:1966 Jun 30 Vancouver	WA:
2 Dale Stewart	*:1946 Apr 13 Vancouver	WA:1965 Jun 30 Vancouver	WA:

755622100   KAMPSULA

Carolyn Lucille Kaufman	:1942 Jul 19 Vancouver	WA:1966 Jun 30 Vancouver	WA:
Bruno Benjamin Kampsula	:1924 Apr 22 New York Mills NY: Andrew Kampsula &	:
	:	: Ida Marie Yaskinen	:
1 Jennifer Sue	:1972 Nov 21 Vancouver	WA:	:

755622200   KAUFMANN

Dale Stewart Kaufman	:1946 Apr 13 Vancouver	WA:1965 Apr 30 Ridgefield	WA:
Georgia Carol	:1946 Nov 13 Portland	OR: Glenn Ulysses Sickenberger &:
Sickenberger	:	: Thelma -----	:
	:	:	:
1 Kyle Kevan	:1967 Oct 12 Portland	OR:	:
2 Troy Dale	:1969 Oct 7 Portland	OR:	:
3 Andrea Janine	:1972 Jun 29 Portland	OR:	:

755630000   SURRELL

Edith Ordway	:1890 Dec 1 Burns	KS:1913 Jan 1	:1982 Dec 31 Seattle WA
John Surrell	:1890 Aug 13 Cle Elum	WA:	:1963 Oct 13 Albany OR
	:	:	:
1 Mildred Geraldine	*:1915 Jul 11 Hood River	OR:	:1973 Jul 7 Seattle WA
2 John, Jr.	:1924 Mar 7 Hood River	OR:	:

Serial # and Name	Birth	Marriage	Death

755631000   TIMMONS / SCHICK

Mildred Geraldine Surrell	1915 Jul 11 Hood River OR		1973 Jul 7 Seattle WA
s Floyd A. Timmons			
t Raymond Wallace Schick			
		James Franklin Schick &	
		Annie Johns	
1 Kenneth Lee <u>Schick</u>	1953 Jul 23 Seattle WA		

755640000   ORDWAY

Glen Ordway	1892 Burns KS	Hood River OR	Hood River OR
Mary Hannigsmann	1896c MN		
1 Lillian	* 1914c OR		

755641000   DEAVILLE

Lillian Ordway	1914 OR		
John T. Deaville			Hood River OR

755650000   MOONEY

Floy Ordway	1895 Burns KS		1974 Hood River OR
Clinton Mooney			

755700000   HINDES

Laura Dunlap	1868 Aug 28 Ableman WI	Sauk Co. WI	1958 Feb 13 Rock Springs WI
John William Hindes	1868 Sauk Co. WI		1942 May Sauk Co. WI
1 Hubert John	* CA		1985 Aug 9 CA
2 Lawrence	* 1903 Aug 24	Ableman	WI 1990 May 24 Houston TX
3 Marguerite Estelle	* Ableman WI		1954c
4 Mary Fern	* 1892 Oct 1 Rock Springs WI 1923 Aug 15 Rock Springs WI		
5 Hazel M.	* 1895 Mar 7 Ableman WI 1921 Oct 22		1975 Nov 1 Oregon WI
6 John			i. Sauk Co. WI
7 Laurena			

755710000   HINDES

Hubert John Hindes			1985 Aug 9 CA
Sylvia -----			
1 Harriet	*		
2 Margie	*		

755711000   ANDERSON

Harriet Hindes			
----- Anderson			

755712000   ANDERSON

Margie Hindes			
----- Anderson			

755720000   HINDES

Lawrence Hindes	1903 Aug 24	Ableman	WI 1990 May 24 Houston TX
Bernice Kennedy			

Serial # and Name	Birth	Marriage	Death

755730000   WILLARD

	Birth	Marriage	Death
Marguerite Estelle Hindes	Ableman WI		1954c
Gerald W. Willard	Mankato MN	Charles K. Willard &	
		----- -----	
1 Michael			
2 Margie	#		1987 Nov 5

755732000   KLUG

	Birth	Marriage	Death
Margie Willard			1987 Nov 5
----- Klug			

755740000   STOECKMANN

	Birth	Marriage	Death
Mary Fern Hindes	1892 Oct 1 Rock Springs WI	1923 Aug 15 Rock Springs WI	
Otto Stoeckmann	1894 May 11	Theodore Stoeckmann &	1962 Sep 2 Baraboo WI
		Bertha Eschenbach	
1 George	#1924 Sep 22 Merrimac WI		
2 Marguerite Estelle	#1926 May 17 Merrimac WI	1950 Dec 30	
3 James Otto	#1928 Mar 10 Baraboo WI	1951 Nov 17	1970 Nov 20 Baraboo WI
4 Janice Fern	#1930 Aug 11 Baraboo WI	1951 Oct 20 Baraboo WI	1986 Mar 19

755741000   STOECKMANN

	Birth	Marriage	Death
George Stoeckmann	1924 Sep 22 Merimac WI		
Lois Zurheide			

755742000   KOPP

	Birth	Marriage	Death
Marguerite Estelle	1926 May 17 Merrimac WI	1950 Dec 30	
Stoeckmann			
Luvern Van Doren Kopp	1925 Sep 23		

Marguerite obtained her B.S. degree from the University of Wisconsin, Madison in January 1949.   After she raised her family she returned to school and earned an M. A. from Cardinal Stritch College.   She was a teacher for many years, first in Sharon and then in Sheboygan, WI.   Luvern was in the infantry in World War II and participated in the Normany invasion.   He graduated from the University of Wisconsin, Platteville in 1949 with a degree in history, and obtained his Master's degree from the University of Wisconsin, Madison in 1953.

	Birth	Marriage	Death
1 Mary Marguerite	1952 Mar 31 Sheboygan WI		
2 James Luvern	1953 Jun 2 Sheboygan WI		
3 Kathryn Ann	#1954 Dec 8 Milwaukee WI	1986 Aug 2 Boulder CO	
4 Susan Ellen	#1961 Jul 1 Sheboygan WI	1991 Oct 5 Sheboygan WI	

Mary obtained her B. S. degree in Geography in 1974 from the University of Wisconsin, Madison, and her M. B. A. from the Kellogg School of Business of Northwestern University.   In 1991 she was employed at the Chemical Bank, in New York.   James graduated from the University of Wisconsin, Madison in 1981 with a degree in Construction Management. His hobby is training dogs for the handicapped.

755742300   MCDONALD

	Birth	Marriage	Death
Kathryn Ann Kopp	1954 Dec 8 Milwaukee WI	1986 Aug 2 Boulder CO	
Brian McDonald			

Kathryn graduated from Metropolitan College in Denver, CO in 1984 with a B.S. in Exercise Physiology.   She is a Physical Therapist in Boulder Memorial Hospital. Brian is a Counselor.

	Birth	Marriage	Death
1 Kellyn Michael	1988 Jul 9		

755742400   WINTHEISER

	Birth	Marriage	Death
Susan Ellen Kopp	1961 Jul 1 Sheboygan WI	1991 Oct 5 Sheboygan WI	
Paul Wintheiser			

298

Serial # and Name	Birth	Marriage	Death
755743000 STOECKMANN			
James Otto Stoeckmann	1928 Mar 10 Baraboo	WI 1951 Nov 17	1970 Nov 20 Baraboo WI
Teresa Ann Repka	1933 Aug 26 Loganville	WI Thomas Paul Repka &	
		Ida Marie Maulwruf	
1 Connie Lynn	* 1952 Jun 17 Baraboo	WI	
2 John James	* 1953 Nov 22 Baraboo	WI	
3 Cathy Jean	* 1959 Sep 19 Baraboo	WI 1977 Dec 4 Baraboo WI	
4 Sandra Kay	1962 Nov 11 Baraboo	WI	
755743100 OLSON			
Connie Lynn Stoeckmann	1952 Jun 17 Baraboo	WI	
Clyde Olson			
755743200 STOECKMANN			
John James Stoeckmann	1953 Nov 22 Baraboo	WI	
Ann Hanson			
755743300 AYLESWORTH			
Cathy Jean Stoeckmann	1959 Sep 19 Baraboo	WI 1977 Dec 4 Baraboo WI	
Harvey Paul Aylsworth	1958 Mar 12 Baraboo	WI Warner Aylsworth &	
		Nora Jean Burkman	
1 Angela Marie	1978 Apr 10 Baraboo	WI	
2 Jessica Lynn	1979 May 31 Baraboo	WI	
3 Laura Kay	1982 Jun 10 Baraboo	WI	
755744000 BRAUN			
Janice Fern Stoeckmann	1930 Aug 11 Baraboo	WI 1951 Oct 20 Baraboo	WI 1986 Mar 19
Robert John Braun	1927 Mar 30 Sheboygan	WI	
1 Debra Lynn	* 1953 Dec 20 Sheboygan	WI	
2 Daniel Otto	* 1954 Nov 18 LaCrosse	WI	
3 Robert John	1958 Oct 5 LaCrosse	WI	
4 David Joseph	1963 Apr 26 Sheboygan	WI	
755744100 ANDERSON			
Debra Lynn Braun	1953 Dec 20 Sheboygan	WI	
Roger Anderson			
755744200 BRAUN			
Daniel Otto Braun	1954 Nov 18 LaCrosse	WI	
Elizabeth Ann Lorenz			
755750000 CAINE			
Hazel M. Hindes	1895 Mar 7 Ableman	WI 1921 Oct 22	1975 Nov 1 Oregon WI
Joseph M. Caine			
1 Thomas			
2 Lawrence			
3 Jack		never married	1970 Sep 4

Serial # and Name	Birth	Marriage	Death
756000000 MCILVAINE			
Andrew Jackson McIlvaine	1829 Sep 9 Wayne Co. OH		1873 Dec 7 i. Stark Co. OH
----- -----			
This family lived in Youngstown, OH.			
1 LaVern	*		
2 Cora Jane	* 1868		1943
3 Mary Waunita	*		
4 Frank H.	* 1874c		
756100000 POTTORF			
LaVern McIlvaine			
Jake Pottorf			
1 LeRoy	1878 Aug 28 Emlenton PA		
2 Fred G.	1881 Mar 2		
756200000 RUSSELL			
Cora Jane McIlvaine	1868		1943
J. E. Russell	1864		1945
1 Elden Leo			
2 Ruth	*		
756220000 GOLDSWORTHY			
Ruth Russell			
----- Goldsworthy			
756300000 LEO			
Mary Waunita McIlvaine			
C. W. Leo			
1 Eldon			
2 Harry McIlvaine			
3 Ralph Reeder			
756400000 MCILVAINE			
Frank H. McIlvaine	1874c OH		
Bertha A. Eddy	1875c PA		
Frank and Bertha lived alone in Youngstown, OH in 1920.			
1 Irene	*		1925 Feb 12
2 LaVern			1917 Sep 16
756410000 SUMMERS / HOWELL			
Irene McIlvaine			1925 Feb 12
s L. L. Summers			
t Richard Howell			
1 Beatrice Summers			
2 Dorothy Summers			

Serial # and Name	Birth	Marriage	Death

757000000 WEIDMAN

	Birth	Marriage	Death
Eleanor McIlvaine	1831 Wayne Co. OH		
Alex Weidman			
1 Samuel			

Samuel was a professor at Kansas State University.

758000000 MCILVAINE

	Birth	Marriage	Death
John McIlvaine	1835 Wayne Co. OH		
Ann -----			
1 Mariah McIntire	1859 Sep c Wayne Co. OH		

759000000 MCILVAINE

	Birth	Marriage	Death
James Greer McIlvaine	1835 May 7 Wayne Co. OH	1868 Oct 7 Wayne Co. OH	1913 Jan 9 Neosho MO
Percinda Alanca Stinson			

This family moved to Arkansas.

	Birth	Marriage	Death
1 Katie Edith	#1870 Oct 8 Wayne Co. OH	1890 Jan 29 Rockwell TX	1902 Jun 15 Newton Co. MO
2 Wilfred Oleon	#1873 Jul 19 Wayne Co. OH	1901 Nov 20	1947 Sep 16 Newton Co. MO

759100000 BALDWIN

	Birth	Marriage	Death
Katie Edith McIlvaine	1870 Oct 8 Wayne Co. OH	1890 Jan 29 Rockwell TX	1902 Jun 15 Newton Co. MO
Charles M. Baldwin			
1 Vada	1893 Nov MO		
2 Burt	1895 Nov MO		
3 Nellie	1898 Mar MO		
4 Edith Lucy	1901 Mar 12 MO		1902 Jun 23 Newton Co. MO

759200000 MCILVAINE

	Birth	Marriage	Death
Wilfred Oleon McIlvaine	1873 Jul 19 Wayne Co. OH	1901 Nov 20	1947 Sep 16 Newton Co. MO
Lillie Mae Watkins			
1 Edith May	1903		1903
2 Everett			1913
3 Walter Rosebury			1915
4 James Monroe	#1904 Apr 23 Neosho MO	1932 Nov 25	1991 Dec 15 Joplin MO
5 Nellie Lorene	#1907 Jan 10 Neosho MO	1931 Jan 12	
6 Christopher Cody	#1909 Feb 8 Neosho MO	1931 Jul 29 Neosho MO	1988 Oct 9
7 Wilfred Jethro	#1911 Mar 31 Neosho MO		
8 Emma Neoma	#1916 Mar 26 Neosho MO	1931 Jun 29 Neosho MO	
9 Mildred Valentine	#1919 Feb 14 Neosho MO	1949 Dec 25 Boise ID	
a Ruby Juanita	#1921 Jan 28 Neosho MO		
b Helen Annis	#1924 Jun 26		
c William Charley	#1927 Feb 12 Newton Co. MO	1948 Sep 2 Neosho MO	1991 Mar 1 Joplin MO
d Lilly Adave Christine	#1929 Aug 9 Newton Co. MO		

Serial # and Name	: Birth			: Marriage		: Death	

759240000   MCILVAINE

James Monroe McIlvaine	:1904 Apr 23 Neosho	MO:1932 Nov 25	:1991 Dec 15 Joplin	MO
Goldie May Lewis	:	:	:	
	:	:	:	
1 Patty Lorene	*:1933 Oct 15	:1949	:	
2 Phyllis Neoma	*:1936 Jun 8	:1956 Dec 26 Miami	OK:	
3 James William	*:1938 May 11	:1958 Aug	:	

759241000   LAUDERDALE

Patty Lorene McIlvaine	:1933 Oct 15	:1949	:
Everett Raymond Lauderdale:		:	:
	:	:	:
1 Everett Earl	*:1950 Neosho	MO:1970 Dec	:
2 Jimmy Carl	*:1951 Neosho	MO:1971	:
3 Robert Eugene	*:1952 Neosho	MO:1971	:
4 Tommy Lee	*:1953 Neosho	MO:1976	:

759241100   LAUDERDALE

Everett Earl Lauderdale	:1950 Neosho	MO:1970 Dec	:
a Marsha Long	:	:	:
b Brenda -----	:	:1980	:
	:	:	:
1 Chad Raymond	? :	:	:

759241200   LAUDERDALE

Jimmy Carl Lauderdale	:1951 Neosho	MO:1971	:
Vickie Millikin	:	:	:
	:	:	:
1 Jeffery Carl	:	:	:

759241300   LAUDERDALE

Robert Eugene Lauderdale	:1952 Neosho	MO:1971	:
s Shirley Weldon	:	:	:
t Kelly Fairchild	:	:	:
	:	:	:
1 Janelle Lea	s*:	:	:
2 Robert Jason	s :	:	:

759241310   BEAVER

Janelle Lea Lauderdale	:	:	:
Brian Beaver	:	:	:
	:	:	:
1 Melony	:	:	:

759241400   LAUDERDALE

Tommy Lee Lauderdale	:1953 Neosho	MO:1976	:
s Teresa Scroggins	:	:	:
t Elizabeth Lawson	:	:1981	:
	:	:	:
1 Michael Shane	s :	:	:
2 Patricia Rose	t :1982	:	:

Serial # and Name	Birth	Marriage	Death
759242000 SIGARS			
Phyllis Neoma McIlvaine	1936 Jun 8	1956 Dec 26 Miami	OK
Kenneth Sigars			
1 Calvin Wayne	#:1953 Dec 23 Neosho	MO:1976 Oct 27 Neosho	MO
759242100 SIGARS			
Calvin Wayne Sigars	1953 Dec 23 Neosho	MO:1976 Oct 27 Neosho	MO
Jenny Jane David			
1 Pamela Sue	1980 Feb 20 Joplin	MO	
2 David Wayne	1990 Sep 18 Joplin	MO	
759243000 MCILVAINE			
James William McIlvaine	1938 May 11	1958 Aug	
s Martha Linda Joiner			
t Hattie Irene Hainline		1963 Jul 26	
1 James William, Jr.	s#:1959 Sep 18	1979 Jun 2	
2 Kelly Lynn	t#:1964 Sep 24	1984 Apr 27	
3 Penni Jean	t :1966 Apr 20		
4 Dawn Denise	t#:1968 Oct 21	1989 Jul 29	
759243100 MCILVAINE			
James William	1959 Sep 18	1979 Jun 2	
McIlvaine, Jr.			
Alisa Roxanna Snider			
1 James William, III	1984 Apr 9		
2 Shawn Eugene	1986 Jun 22		
3 Patrick Ryan	1987 Aug 21		
4 Travis Shane	1988 Dec 9		
759243200 OXENDINE			
Kelly Lynn McIlvaine	1964 Sep 24	1984 Apr 27	
Charles Oxendine			
1 Charles Grant	1985 Aug 27		
759243400 SPEAK			
Dawn Denise McIlvaine	1968 Oct 21	1989 Jul 29	
Jeffrey Todd Speak			
1 Jeffrey Austin	1990 Jan 19		

Serial # and Name	Birth	Marriage	Death

759250000   BERRY

Nellie Lorene McIlvaine	1907 Jan 10 Neosho	MO 1931 Jan 12	
William A. Berry			
1 Joe			
2 Ila			
3 Wilma			
4 Carl			
5 Wanna Lee			
6 Jerry			

759260000   MCILVAINE

| Christopher Cody McIlvaine | 1909 Feb 8   Neosho | MO 1931 Jul 29 Neosho | MO 1988 Oct 9 |
| Frances Marie Rogers | | | |

Christopher went by the name of Cody C.   He was employed at the Wolfe Milling Co. for 3 years, and then worked 19 years at Southwest Lime. Thereafter he was a self-employed roofer for 20 years before retiring.

1 Eva Marie	* 1934 Apr 19 Newton Co.	MO 1952 Jul 19 Bensonville	AR
2 William Cody	* 1943 Mar 24 Neosho	MO 1963 Jun 16 Texarkana	TX
3 Larry Eugene	* 1946 Apr 18 Neosho	MO 1966 Jun 28 Joplin	MO

759261000   LEWIS / BAKER

Eva Marie McIlvaine	1934 Apr 19 Newton Co.	MO 1952 Jul 19 Bensonville	AR
s Russell Norman Lewis			
t William Warren Baker		1954 Aug 8	
1 Michael Charles Lewis	* 1953 Sep 28 Hoquiam	WA 1971 Jan 18 Neosho	MO
2 Gaillard Filiterra Baker	* 1955 Aug 20 San Francisco	CA 1986 Mar 22 Concord	CA
3 Panicia Marie Baker	* 1961 Mar 3 San Francisco	CA 1988 Sep 10 Concord	CA

759261100   LEWIS

Michael Charles Lewis	1953 Sep 28 Hoquiam	WA 1971 Jan 18 Neosho	MO
s Deborah Darlene Butler			
t Debra Jane Yost		1973 Jul 29	
1 Angel Dawn	s 1972 Apr 18 Gravett AR		
2 Michael Bud	s 1973 Mar 21 Neosho MO		

759261200   BAKER

Gaillard Filiterra Baker	1955 Aug 20 San Francisco	CA 1986 Mar 22 Concord	CA
Patricia Ruth McGuire			
1 Ireland Marie	1987 Jul 17 Concord CA		
2 William Brandyn	1989 Nov 18 Concord CA		

759261300   STROSKI

Panicia Marie Baker	1961 Mar 3 San Francisco	CA 1988 Sep 10 Concord	CA
James Stroski			
1 Mitchell James	1991 Aug 26 Walnut Creek CA		

Serial # and Name	Birth	Marriage	Death

759262000   MCILVAINE

Name	Birth	Marriage	Death
William Cody McIlvaine	1943 Mar 24 Neosho	MO 1963 Jun 16 Texarkana	TX
Lois Darlene Damrill	1946 Jul 24 Neosho	MO	

William and Lois are first cousins. Lois is listed also as #7592a2000.

1 Christiana Leann	1965 Feb 24		1966 Jun 25 i. Neosho MO
2 William David	*1967 Jun 29 Neosho	MO 1989 Jul 1 Neosho	MO
3 Michell Lynn	*1971 Sep 1 Neosho	MO 1992 Oct 10 Neosho	MO
4 Brian Cody	1974 Jun 20 Neosho	MO	
5 Lori Marie	1978 Mar 10 Neosho	MO	

759262200   MCILVAINE

Name	Birth	Marriage	Death
William David McIlvaine	1967 Jun 29 Neosho	MO 1989 Jul 1 Neosho	MO
Melissa Dawn Blevins			
1 Ashleigh Nicole	1987 Aug 25 Joplin	MO	
2 Emileigh	1991 Nov 6 Joplin	MO	
3 Stephen Cody	1993 Jan		

759262300   HENADY

Name	Birth	Marriage	Death
Michell Lynn McIlvaine	1971 Sep 1 Neosho	MO 1992 Oct 10 Neosho	MO
Brad Alan Henady			

759263000   MCILVAINE

Name	Birth	Marriage	Death
Larry Eugene McIlvaine	1946 Apr 18 Neosho	MO 1966 Jun 28 Joplin	MO
s Betty Lou Weems			
t Nancy Gail Malotte	1953 Sep 14	1975 Jul 26	
u Bobbie Wilson			

Larry remarried Nancy Malotte on July 17, 1986

1 Larry Eugene, Jr.	s*1968 Jan 13 Joplin	MO 1991 Jul 7 Flippin	AR
2 Jerome Ray	t*1976 Aug 10 Joplin	MO 1992 Sep 11 Joplin	MO
3 Kristi Dawn	u 1979 May 9		

759263100   MCILVAINE

Name	Birth	Marriage	Death
Larry Eugene McIlvaine, Jr.	1968 Jan 13 Joplin	MO 1991 Jul 7 Flippin	AR
Dessie Diane Mitchell			

759263200   MCILVAINE

Name	Birth	Marriage	Death
Jerome Ray McIlvaine	1976 Aug 10 Joplin	MO 1992 Sep 11 Joplin	MO
Tonia Paulette Proctor			
1 Uriah Dawn	1992 Jan 11 Joplin	MO	

759270000   MCILVAINE

Name	Birth	Marriage	Death
Wilfred Jethro McIlvaine	1911 Mar 31 Neosho	MO	
s Marie -----			
t Hazel Spoon			
1 Marsha Kay	?*		
2 Anita Faye	?		

Serial # and Name	Birth	Marriage	Death
759271000 SHEPHERD			
Marsha Kay McIlvaine			
Danny Shepherd			
759280000 FIKES			
Emma Neoma McIlvaine	1916 Mar 26 Neosho	MO 1931 Jun 29 Neosho	MO
Lawrence Joseph Fikes			
1 Veta Neoma	* 1932 Nov 14		
2 Lawrence Olean	* 1935 May 13		
3 Leo	* 1937 Feb 19	1957 Nov 7 Neosho	MO 1984 Feb 17 Kansas City MO
4 Vera Kathleen	* 1939 Jun 7		
5 Judy Ann	* 1942 Feb 20		
6 Erma Gail	* 1947 Jul 24		
7 Ernest Richard	* 1955 Oct 16		
8 Sheila Wyleen	* 1957 Nov 23		
759281000 JENNINGS			
Veta Neoma Fikes	1932 Nov 14		
LeRoy Jennings			
1 Joyce Lee	*		
2 Steven	*		
3 Veta Diane	*		
4 Cheryl Jane	*		
5 David J.	*		
6 Dena Michele	* 1961 Jul		
7 Dennis	*		
8 Kevin			
9 Keith	*		
a Brian Scott	*		
b Jill Rene	1971 Apr 18		
759281100 MUSGROVE			
Joyce Lee Jennings			
Orval Musgrove			
1 Kyle Andre			
2 Adam			
3 Chad			
759281200 JENNINGS			
Steven Jennings			
s Karen -----			
t Kathy -----			
1 Kimberly	s		
2 Stephanie	s		
3 [child]	t		
4 [child]	t		

Serial # and Name	Birth	Marriage	Death

759281300   COOPER / BASSINGER
  Veta Diane Jennings
s Lonnie Cooper
t James Basinger

1 Tammy Diane Cooper
2 Rusty Alan Cooper
3 Janet Cooper
4 Wendy Cooper
5 Shelly Cooper
6 James Basinger

759281400   THOMPSON / HILL
  Cheryl Jane Jennings
s Michael Thompson
t Gary Hill

1 Chrystal Marcella Thompson

759281500   JENNINGS
  David J. Jennings
  Vicki Daugherty

1 Michael
2 [daughter]

759281600   HUFF
  Dena Michele Jennings   1961 Jul
  Gary Huff

1 [son]
2 [son]

759281700   JENNINGS
  Dennis Jennings
  ----- -----

1 [child]
2 [child]
3 [child]

759281900   JENNINGS
  Keith Jennings
  Mary Kay -----

1 Angela Kay
2 Jennifer

759281a00   JENNINGS
  Brian Scott Jennings
  Tamara Raines

1 Amanda
2 [daughter]

Serial # and Name	Birth	Marriage	Death
759282000 FIKES			
Lawrence Olean Fikes	1935 May 13		
s Frances Long			
t Barbara Ezell			
1 Cindy	s		
2 Shelly	s		
759283000 FIKES			
Leo Fikes	1937 Feb 19	1957 Nov 7 Neosho MO	1984 Feb 17 Kansas City MO
Lola May Smith			
1 Leo Albert			
2 Lela Ann			
3 Linda			
4 Lynn Alan			
759284000 FLYNN			
Vera Kathleen Fikes	1939 Jun 7		
Jack Flynn			
1 Gregory Lynn	*		
2 Angela Denise			i. Newton Co. MO
759284100 FLYNN			
Gregory Lynn Flynn			
Evangela Ellis			
1 Jason Lynn			
2 Jarod Alan	1978 Mar		
759285000 DUNCAN			
Judy Ann Fikes	1942 Feb 20		
Darrol Duncan			
1 Darren			
2 Ronnie			
3 Donnie			
4 Johnnie			i. Newton Co. MO
5 Malissa Ann			
759286000 JOHNSON			
Erma Gail Fikes	1947 Jul 24		
Kenneth Robert Johnson			
1 Darla Gail	* 1947 Jul 14		
2 Kenny Dale	*		

Serial # and Name	Birth	Marriage	Death
759286100 HOUSE			
Barla Gail Johnson	1947 Jul 14		
Vincent House			
1 Megan			
2 Mandy			
759286200 JOHNSON			
Kenny Dale Johnson			
Shelley Hutchins			
1 [son]			
2 [son]			
759287000 FIKES			
Ernest Richard Fikes	1955 Oct 16		
Debbie Arnold			
759288000 MYERS			
Sheila Wyleen Fikes	1957 Nov 23		
Michael Myers			
1 Jana			
2 Jennifer			
3 Levi			
759290000 JACKSON / HAY			
Mildred Valentine	1919 Feb 14 Neosho	MO	
McIlvaine			
s E. R. Jackson			
t Harry William Hay	1914 Jun 14 Brooklyn	NY 1949 Dec 25 Boise	ID 1964 Aug
1 Linda Ann Hay	1954 Oct 10 Los Angeles	CA	
7592a0000 DAMRILL			
Ruby Juanita McIlvaine	1921 Jan 28 Neosho	MO	
Ralph E. Damrill			
1 Lora Juanita	* 1940 Jul 10 Newton Co.	MO	
2 Lois Darlene	* 1946 Jul 24 Neosho	MO 1963 Jun 17 Texarkana	TX

Lois married her first cousin William McIlvaine (#759262000). Her descendents are entered there.

Serial # and Name	Birth	Marriage	Death
7592a1000 BREWER			
Lora Juanita Damrill	1940 Jul 10 Newton Co.	MO	
Jerry V. Brewer			
1 Lora Teresa	* 1957 Feb 23 Tucson	AZ	
2 Jeri Vondale	1958 Jan 23 Phoenix	AZ	
3 Daniel Lewis	* 1959 Jan 17 Phoenix	AZ	
4 Dennis James	* 1960 Aug 28 Phoenix	AZ	

309

Serial # and Name	Birth	Marriage	Death
7592a1100 HAGEN / MADISON / BANHART			
Lora Teresa Brewer	1957 Feb 23 Tucson AZ		
s Randy Hagan			
t Harry Madison			
u Kenneth Banhart			
1 Stacy Lynn Hagan	1971 Sep 8		
2 Stephanie Nicole Madison			

Stacy was adopted by Lora's third husband, Kenneth Banhart.

7592a1300 BREWER			
Daniel Lewis Brewer	1959 Jan 17 Phoenix AZ		
Katherine Elaine Lowry			
1 Elaine Lee			
2 Jeryd Daniel			
7592a1400 BREWER			
Dennis James Brewer	1960 Aug 28 Phoenix AZ		
s Marlynn McWade			
t Tishia Lynn Houston			
1 Denise LaCole	t 1987 Jul 7 Rogers AR		
2 Jerry Lee Morgan	t 1989 Apr Gravette AR		
7592a2000 MCILVAINE			
Lois Darlene Damrill	1946 Jul 24 Neosho MO	1963 Jun 16 Texarkana TX	
William Cody McIlvaine	1943 Mar 24 Neosho MO		

This family appears under William Cody McIlvaine (#759262000). Lois and William were first cousins.

7592b0000 KEEN / DAMRILL			
Helen Annis McIlvaine	1924 Jun 26		
s Bob Keen			
t Ralph E. Damrill			
7592c0000 MCILVAINE			
William Charley McIlvaine	1927 Feb 12 Newton Co. MO	1948 Sep 2 Neosho MO	1991 Mar 1 Joplin MO
s Eula Jennings			
t Betty Jo Dugger			
u Phyllis Lou Cavener		1961 Jul 6	
1 Gary Dale	s*		
2 Rhonda Louise	u*		
3 Caroline Denise	u		
4 Charles William, Jr.	u*		
7592c1000 MCILVAINE			
Gary Dale McIlvaine			
s ----- -----			
t Irene -----			

Serial # and Name	Birth	Marriage	Death
7592c2000 ARMSTRONG			
Rhonda Louise McIlvaine			
Pat Armstrong			
1 [daughter]			
2 [son]			
3 [daughter]			
7592c4000 MCILVAINE			
Charles William			
McIlvaine, Jr.			
----- -----			
1 [son]			
2 [son]			
7592d0000 BARKLUND			
Lilly Adave Christine	1929 Aug 9 Newton Co. MO		
McIlvaine			
Ramon Barklund			
75a000000 HERSHEY			
Maria McIlvaine			
Amos Hershey			

    Maria and Amos moved to Kansas.

770000000 MCILVAINE			
George McIlvaine, Jr.	1793 Washington Co. PA		
Jane McIlvaine	1790	Greer McIlvaine &	
		Elizabeth Morrow	

    George and Jane were first cousins. Jane's father was the brother of George's father. In 1850 the family lived in Somerset twp., Washington Co., PA. In 1860 George and Jane lived in Somerset twp.; Ruth and Anne (Mary Ann) lived with them. In the later year George was a farmer with real estate of $7,600 and personal property of $1,500.

1 Elizabeth	1817		
2 Ruth	*1819		
3 Margaret	*1820		
4 Mary Ann	*1823		
5 Thomas M.	1826		died young
6 Sheshbazar Bentley	*1829 Feb 9 Vanceville PA	1854 Mar 31	1906 Mar 20
7 Eleanor			
8 Jane	1833		died young
772000000 CARSON			
Ruth McIlvaine	1819		
John Carson			
773000000 MCILVAINE			
Margaret McIlvaine	1820		
Smith McIlvaine	1820	John McIlvaine &	
		Margaret Smith	

    The descendents of Margaret and Smith will be found under Smith McIlvaine (#753000000).

Serial # and Name	Birth	Marriage	Death

774000000   CLARK / MCILVAINE

Mary Ann McIlvaine	1823		
s Isiah Clark			
t ----- McIlvaine			

  Mary Ann (Anne in the 1860 census) lived with her son in the home of her parents in 1850 and 1860. There
  no mention of her husband in the censuses for those years.

| 1 John McIlvaine | #:1843c | | |

774100000   MCILVAINE

| John McIlvaine | 1843c | | |
| ----- ----- | | | |

  John lived with his mother in the home of her parents in 1850 and 1860.   He was a soldier in the
  Civil War.   He became a physician.

| 1 Allie | | | |
| 2 Carson Horner | | | |

  Allie lived in Cannonsburg, PA, and Carson in Linden, PA.

776000000   MCILVAINE

Sheshbazar Bentley	1829 Feb 9 Vanceville PA:1854 Mar 31		1906 Mar 20
McIlvaine			
Catherine Hill	1830c Vanceville PA: James J. Hill &		
		Catherine Leyda	

  Sheshbazar Bentley was named for Sheshbazar Bentley, the founder of Bentleyville, PA, who was named for
  his father.   Where the original Sheshbazar got his name is difficult to say.   In 1860 and in 1880 the
  family lived in Somerset twp., Washington Co., PA.   In 1860 Shesh was a farmer (personal property $400);
  his name was given as Bentley in 1880 census. In 1910 Catherine was living with her daughter Julia Nicholl.

1 Winfield	#:1856 Jan 30		1920 Mar 12
2 Arabella	#:1857 Sep 10 Washington Co. PA:		
3 Ella LaVerne	#:1859 Sep 20 Washington Co. PA:1878 Nov 20		1946 Mar 24
4 Lena	#:1862 May 5		
5 Ulysses Grant	#:1865 Feb 9		1937 Sep 17
6 Julia	#:1868 Aug 9		
7 Edwin Linton	#:1873 Feb 12 Bentleyville PA:1900 Jul 10 Pittsburgh PA:1961		NJ

776100000   MCILVAINE

| Winfield McIlvaine | 1856 Jan 30 | PA: | 1920 Mar 12 |
| Elizabeth Stewart | 1855c | PA: | |

  In 1920 Winfield and Elizabeth lived at 362 Maisden Street, Washington, PA.   An obituary for W. A. H.
  McIlvaine (#781420000) mentions that "he read law with the late Winfield McIlvaine." The men were second
  cousins once removed.

776200000   IRVIN

Arabella McIlvaine	1857 Sep 10 Washington Co. PA:		
William W. Irvin			
1 James McIlvaine	#:		

776210000   IRVIN

| James McIlvaine Irvin | | | |
| Bessie Roberts | | | |

312

Serial # and Name	Birth	Marriage	Death
776300000 THOMAS			
Ella LaVerne McIlvaine	:1859 Sep 20 Washington Co. PA	:1878 Nov 20	:1946 Mar 24
Josiah Thomas	:1853 Jun 11	: Josiah Thomas & ----- -----	:1936 May 21
	:	:	:
1 James Bentley	#:1879 Aug 23 Washington Co. PA	:1916 Jun 14	:1948 Aug 17
2 Margaret Bell	#:1883 Jan 1	:1905 Jan 31 Washington Co. PA	:1962 Oct 8
3 Edna Berthey	#:1887 Apr 12 Washington Co. PA	:1905 Dec 21	:
4 Laura Alice	#:1889 Mar 5	:	:1959 Mar 1
5 Harry	#:1894 Apr 19 Washington Co. PA	:1915 Sep 23	:
6 Clarence	:1901 Nov 28	:	:1922 Aug 29
776310000 THOMAS			
James Bentley Thomas	:1879 Aug 23 Washington Co. PA	:1916 Jun 14	:1948 Aug 17
Minnie Daque	:	:	:
776320000 GOUGH / MCCORMICK			
Margaret Bell Thomas	:1883 Jan 1	:1905 Jan 31 Washington Co. PA	:1962 Oct 8
s Alfred Gough	:	:	:
t ----- McCormick	:	:	:
776330000 CRAWFORD			
Edna Berthey Thomas	:1887 Apr 12 Washington Co. PA	:1905 Dec 21	:
Walter S. Crawford	:1883c	PA:	:1965 Jun 10

In 1910 this couple lived with three children in Crawford Co., PA; in 1920, with their six children, they lived in Washington County, PA.

1 Oliver E	:1907c	PA:	:
2 James W.	:1909c	PA:	:
3 Leah L.	:1911c	PA:	:
4 Nellie V.	:1913c	PA:	:
5 Wallace B.	:1915c	PA:	:
6 William W.	:1918c	PA:	:
776340000 HUFF / FOWLER			
Laura Alice Thomas	:1889 Mar 5	:	:1959 Mar 1
s ----- Huff	:	:	:
t ----- Fowler	:	:	:
776350000 THOMAS			
Harry Thomas	:1894 Apr 19 Washington Co. PA	:1915 Sep 23	:
Elizabeth L. Smith	:1896c	PA:	:1950 Dec 25

In 1920 Harry and Elizabeth with their two sons lived in Washington County, PA.

1 Guy E.	:1917c	PA:	:
2 William H.	:1918c	PA:	:
776400000 NICHOLL			
Lena McIlvaine	#:1862 May 5	:	:
Robertson A. Nicholl	:	:	:

Serial # and Name	Birth	Marriage	Death

776500000   MCILVAINE

Ulysses Grant McIlvaine	1865 Feb 9		1937 Sep 17
Elizabeth Swagler	1869c PA		

In 1910 this couple with their three sons lived in Washington County, PA;   In 1920 they lived, with Judson
and Lloyd, in Washington County.   In the 1920 census Ulysses was listed as Grant U.

1 Lawrence	*1893 Washington Co. PA		1973
2 Ruth	1895 Aug 21 Washington Co. PA		
3 Judson S.	*1898 Washington Co. PA		
4 Lloyd Grant	1905 Washington Co. PA		

776510000   MCILVAINE

Lawrence McIlvaine	1893 Washington Co. PA		1973
Margaret Verna Buckingham			
1 William Blair	*1924		
2 Robert Grant	*1927 Aug 13 Washington Co. PA	1951 Jun 9 Monongahela PA	
3 Thomas Lawrence	*1929 May 8 Bentleyville PA	1961 Mar 17 Eighty Four PA	1989 May 31 Eighty Four PA
4 Carl Edwin	*1934 May 1 Bentleyville PA	1963 Jun 1 Bentleyville PA	

776511000   MCILVAINE

William Blair McIlvaine	1924		
----- -----			
1 Lawrence Allen	1956		
2 Barbara Louise	1958		
3 David William	1961		
4 Helen Marie	1965		

776512000   MCILVAINE

Robert Grant McIlvaine	1927 Aug 13 Washington Co. PA	1951 Jun 9 Monongahela PA	
Margaret Sterner	1929 Dec 17 New Eagle PA	Clifford Van Dyke Sterner &	
		Marie Francis Dickey	
1 Robert Keith	*1954 Feb 22 Washington Co. PA	1989 May 6	

776512100   MCILVAINE

Robert Keith McIlvaine	1954 Feb 22 Washington Co. PA	1989 May 6	
Traci Lynne Wirmel	1964 Mar 20 Cincinatti OH	Richard Albert Wirmel &	
		Barbara Ann Coleman	

776513000   MCILVAINE

Thomas Lawrence McIlvaine	1929 May 8 Bentleyville PA	1961 Mar 17 Eighty Four PA	1989 May 31 Eighty Four PA
Hilda Kovacicek	1931 Oct 10 Washington PA	Luka Kovacicek &	
		Frances -----	
1 Randy	1963 Feb 27 Eighty Four PA		1963 Mar 7 Eighty Four PA

776514000   MCILVAINE

Carl Edwin McIlvaine	1934 May 1 Bentleyville PA	1963 Jun 1 Bentleyville PA	
Nancy Fitch	1936 Sep 15 Finleyville PA	Sherman Fitch &	
		Bertha Leonard	
1 Paul Edwin	*1964 Oct 4 Bentleyville PA	1983 Nov 4 Bentleyville PA	
2 Scott Sherman	1969 Jul 7 Bentleyville PA		

Serial # and Name	Birth	Marriage	Death	

776514100   MCILVAINE

Paul Edwin McIlvaine	1964 Oct 4 Bentleyville PA	1983 Nov 4 Bentleyville PA	
s Sherry Lynn Matthews	1970 Feb 17 Scenery Hill PA		
t ----- -----			
1 Kevin Alan	s 1983 Nov 27 Bentleyville PA		
2 Kelly Matthew	s 1985 Dec 24 Bentleyville PA		
3 Leah Marie	t 1989 Apr 14 Monongahela PA		

776530000   MCILVAINE

Judson S. McIlvaine	1898		
----- -----			
1 Charles			

776600000   NICHOLL

| Julia McIlvaine | 1868 Aug 9 | PA | |
| Julius Nicholl | 1856c | PA | |

Julia and Julius lived in Washington County, PA in 1910.

776700000   MCILVAINE

Edwin Linton McIlvaine	1873 Feb 12 Bentleyville PA	1900 Jul 10 Pittsburgh PA	1961	NJ
Hilda Morrow	1874 West Liberty VA	James Elmore Morrow &	1954 Tenafly	NJ
		Clara Johnson		

Edwin graduated cum laude from Washington and Jefferson College in 1895 with a B. A. degree.   He received his M. A. degree from Washington and Jefferson in 1898, and an honorary Doctorate in 1920.   He graduated from Western Theological Seminary in 1898, and was ordained as a minister of the Presbyterian Church of the USA the same year. He served as minister in Castle Shannon, PA; Toronto, OH; Emlenton, PA; Ridgeway, PA; Meadville, PA; and Englewood, NJ.

1 Ruth	* 1901 Nov 19 Toronto OH		1973	
2 Rebekah	1903 Emlenton PA		1905 Mar 17 i. Emlenton PA	
3 James Morrow	* 1905 Jun 10 Emlenton PA	1938 Jul 31	1963 Jun 17	
4 Katherine	* 1907 Jun 16 Ridgeway NJ		1982	

776710000   VORHEES

| Ruth McIlvaine | 1901 Nov 19 Toronto   OH | | 1973 | |
| Frederick Vorhees | | | | |

776730000   MCILVAINE

| James Morrow McIlvaine | 1905 Jun 10 Emlenton   PA | 1938 Jul 31 | 1963 Jun 17 | |
| Virginia Fuller Tucker | 1909 Feb 7 Skaneateles NY | | | |

James graduated from Washington and Jefferson College in 1927, and received his J.D. degree from New York University in 1933. He was employed in a variety of positions by Sun Oil from 1938 until his death.

1 Susan Fuller	* 1941 Apr 28	1964 Nov 28 Skaneateles NY		
2 Patricia Morrow	1947 Feb 4			
3 Andrew Gregory	* 1948 Aug 24 Toledo OH	1976 Jun 12 Stoneleigh EN		

776731000   KENNEY

Susan Fuller McIlvaine	1941 Apr 28	1964 Nov 28 Skaneateles NY		
Edwin James Kenney		James Kenney & ----- -----		
1 James McIlvaine	1970 Aug Waterville ME			
2 Anne Morrow	1973 Jun Waterville ME			

Serial # and Name	Birth	Marriage	Death

776733000 MCILVAINE

Andrew Gregory McIlvaine	1948 Aug 24 Toledo OH	1976 Jun 12 Stoneleigh EN	
Julie Ann Penneck	1953 Apr 8 Ipswich EN	Sidney Wilfred Penneck &	
		Joan Muriel Bartlett	

Andrew graduated from Washington and Jefferson College in 1970 with a B. A. in History, and from Wharton
School of the University of Pennsylvania with an M. B. A. degree in Finance.   He has been employed since
1973 in a variety of administrative positions by the University of Pennsylvania. Andrew co-authored the
introduction to Ordway's *The House of Grimet*.

1 Sarah Ann	1978 May 5 Philadelphia PA		
2 Stephen Penneck	1981 Feb 7 Camden NJ		
3 Heather Joan	1985 Feb 14 Camden NJ		

776740000 LEIGHTON

Katherine McIlvaine	1907 Jun 16 Ridgeway NJ		1982 i. Emlenton PA
James Kenrick Leighton			

780000000 MCILVAINE

Robert McIlvaine	1795 Washington Co. PA		1864 Nov 5
Ann Stringer	1794 Washington Co. PA		1868

In 1860 Robert and Ann lived in Somerset twp., Washington Co., PA.   He was a farmer (real estate
$2000, personal property $300).

1 Matilda	*|1814 Feb 27 Washington Co. PA		1898
2 Mary Jane	*|1823c Washington Co. PA		1890
3 George W.	*|1823		1887
4 John D.	*|1824 Washington Co. PA		1918

781000000 MCILVAINE

Matilda McIlvaine	1814 Feb 27 Washington Co. PA		1898
William McIlvaine	1805 Washington Co. PA	Greer McIlvaine &	1888
		Elizabeth Morrow	

William's father, Greer, was the brother of George, Matilda's grandfather.   In 1850 Matilda and William
lived in Somerset twp., Washington Co., PA, and had real property of $5700.

1 Mary Agnes	*|1839 Dec 21 Washington Co.PA		
2 Greer Harvey	1841 Washington Co.PA		1843
3 John Addison	*|1843 Apr 13 Washington Co.PA		1929 Jun 2
4 William Robert	*|1845 Washington Co.PA	1868 Oct 29	1933
5 Mary	1847c Washington Co.PA		

781100000 JONES

Mary Agnes McIlvaine	1839 Dec 21 Washington Co.PA		
Isaac Jones	1836		1901
1 Dora Belle	*|1860 Sep 20 Washington Co. PA		1941 Sep 30
2 William Elmer	*|1862 Oct 5 Washington Co. PA		1920 May 4
3 Laurence Isaac	*|1865 Jan 22 Washington Co. PA		1918 Aug 30
4 John McIlvaine	*|1867 Jun 30 Washington Co. PA		1947 Sep 5
5 Harry Albert	*|1873 Jun 9 Washington Co. PA		1965 May 24
6 Mary Arilla	*|1876 Jun 22 Washington Co. PA		1963 May 5

781110000 MORROW

Dora Belle Jones	1860 Sep 20 Washington Co. PA		1941 Sep 30
William Morrow	1853c WV		

The Morrows lived in Washington Co., PA in 1910; no children were listed in the census for that year.

Serial # and Name	Birth	Marriage	Death
781120000 JONES			
William Elmer Jones	1862 Oct 5 Washington Co. PA		1920 May 4
----- Allen			
781130000 JONES			
Laurence Isaac Jones	1865 Jan 22 Washington Co. PA		1918 Aug 30
Annie Rettig			
1 Pauline	1893		
2 Wilbur	1894		
3 Helen	1897		
4 Russell	1899		
781140000 JONES			
John McIlvaine Jones	1867 Jun 30 Washington Co. PA		1947 Sep 5
Lottie Stratton			
1 Frank	1902		
2 Bernard	1903		
3 J. McIlvaine	1905		
4 Agnes	1906		
5 John	1908		
6 Margaret	1909		
781150000 JONES			
Harry Albert Jones	1875 Jun 9 Washington Co. PA		1965 May 24
Catherine Ruth Crawford	1881 PA		
This family lived in Washington County, PA in 1910.			
1 Catherine	1909 PA		
781160000 JONES			
Mary Arilla Jones	1876 Jun 22 Washington Co. PA		1963 May 5
Clifford H. Jones			
1 Walter	1904		
2 Robert	1907		
781300000 MCILVAINE			
John Addison McIlvaine	1843 Apr 13 Washington Co. PA		1929 Jun 2
Ada C. Shaw	1851 Nov	James T. Shaw	1929
John and Ada lived at 47 N. Wade Ave., E. Washington, PA in 1900. No children were listed in that census.			
781400000 MCILVAINE			
William Robert McIlvaine	1845 Feb 1 Washington Co. PA	1868 Oct 29	1933
Sarah B. Hamilton	1849 Jan PA		
In 1900, 1910, and 1920 William and Sarah lived in East Washington, PA. Their address was 56 Wade Ave.			
Nora (Lenora in the 1920 census) lived with her parents, unmarried, in 1900, 1910, and 1920.			
1 Nora Irene	1869 Aug 8 Washington Co. PA		1941 May 16
2 William Alexander	#1871 Mar 1 Washington Co. PA	1902	1945 Jul 31
Hamilton			
3 John Addison	#1872 Nov 17 Washington Co. PA		
4 Wilbert Greer	1877 Washington Co. PA		1880

Serial # and Name	Birth	Marriage	Death

781420000 MCILVAINE

William Alexander
Hamilton McIlvaine | 1871 Mar 1 Washington Co. PA | 1902 Sep 10 | 1945 Jul 31 Washington PA
s Annie Gertrude Wilson | 1879c   PA | | 1919 Feb 10
t Florence H. Sturgis | | 1923 Apr 3 |

William and Annie, with their three children, lived in Washington County, PA in 1910 and 1920.   In 1920 their address was 30 So. Wade St. William graduated from Washington and Jefferson College and attended Western University of Pittsburgh Law School.   In addition to practicing law, William was an executive of the Washington Union Trust Co., and the George Washington Hotel Corporation.   He was a life member of the Washington and Jefferson College Board of Trustees, was a member of the East Washington School Board, and served for a number of years on the board of the Y.M.C.A.

1 Alexander W. | s*|1904 May 29 | PA|1928 |
2 John Wilson | s*|1907 Jun 22 | PA|1930 |
3 Elizabeth | s*|1909 | PA| |

781421000 MCILVAINE

Alexander W. McIlvaine | 1904 May 29 | 1928 |
Sarah Sloan | | |

Alexander joined his father's law firm in 1938, leaving it during World War II.   He attained the rank of captain in the Army Air Corps, with the Army Transport Service.

1 William R. | 1929 Aug 24 Washington Co. PA |
2 Sarah Ann | *|1932 May 19 Washington Co. PA |

781421200 DONNAN

Sarah Ann McIlvaine | 1932 May 19 Washington Co. PA |
John Donnan | | |

1 Alvin Ewing | *|1951 Oct 16 Washington Co. PA |
2 Alexander McIlvaine | 1955 Jun 21 Burbank CA |
3 Sarah Sloan | 1956 Dec 20 Burbank CA |
4 Dorothy Griffith | *|1960 Jun 27 Glendale CA |

781421210 DONNAN

Alvin Ewing Donnan | 1951 Oct 16 Washington Co. PA |
----- ----- | | |

1 Brendan John | | |

781421240 CURNOW

Dorothy Griffith Donnan | 1960 Jun 27 Glendale CA |
----- Curnow | | |

1 Christopher John | | |

781422000 MCILVAINE

John Wilson McIlvaine | 1907 Jun 22 | 1930 |
Easie Smith | | William McKennon Smith & |
| | Lucy Butler |

John practiced law with his father's firm from 1938 until just after Pearl Harbor, when he joined the armed forces.   As a lieutenant colonel he served as Assistant Chief of Staff A-2, Army Air Force, Personnel Distribution Command.

1 John Wilson, Jr. | *|1930 Oct 22 Washington Co. PA|four times married |
2 Easie | *|1938 Oct 31 Washington Co. PA |

Serial # and Name	Birth	Marriage	Death

781422100 MCILVAINE

Serial # and Name	Birth	Marriage	Death
John Wilson McIlvaine Jr.	1930 Oct 22 Washington Co. PA		
s Dorothy Vance			
t Marilyn Coen			
u Shirley Wyne			
v Alice Lee Moses	1940 Dec 25 Washington PA	1982 May 23 Bethseda MD	

In *The House of Griget* there is a picture of John and his farm, Calydon, located in Greene County, PA, and given the same name as the original McIlvaine farm in Washington Co.   John is descended from both George and Greer through the marriage of his great³ grandparents, William the son of Greer and Matilda the granddaughter of George.

Serial # and Name	Birth	Marriage	Death
1 Dorothy Donnan	s	1956 Washington Co. PA		
2 Greta	s	1958 Washington Co. PA		
3 John Wilson, III	t	1963 May 4 Washington Co. PA		
4 Charles Coen	t	1964 Jul 23 Washington Co. PA		
5 Andrew McKennan	t	1967 Jan 18 Washington Co. PA		
6 Mark Kirkpatrick	t	1970 Mar Washington Co. PA		
7 Heather McKennan	u	1970 Nov 20 Pittsburgh PA		
8 Cynthia Lee	v	1962 Dec 13 Santa Monica CA		

Cynthia is the daughter of Alice, and was adopted by John.

781422200 PARKER

Serial # and Name	Birth	Marriage	Death
Emsie McIlvaine	1938 Oct 31 Washington Co.PA		
Leslie Parker			
1 Mark Wilson	#	1955 May 20 Elyria OH		
2 Emsie	#	1962 Dec 31 Washington PA		
3 Ian Leslie	1967 Dec 28 New Haven CT		
4 Julia Grant	1969 Nov 17 Washington PA		

781422210 PARKER

Serial # and Name	Birth	Marriage	Death
Mark Wilson Parker	1955 May 20 Elyria OH		
Judith -----			

781422220 TINKEN

Serial # and Name	Birth	Marriage	Death
Emsie Parker	1962 Dec 31 Washington PA		
Henry H. Tinken			

781423000 COOPER

Serial # and Name	Birth	Marriage	Death
Elizabeth McIlvaine	1909 PA		
William Murray Cooper			

Elizabeth and William lived in Mt. Lebanon, PA in 1945.

781430000 MCILVAINE

Serial # and Name	Birth	Marriage	Death
John Addison McIlvaine	1872 Nov 17 Washington Co. PA		
Helen Shurtliff			
1 Janet			

Serial # and Name	Birth		Marriage	Death

782000000 DRURY

Mary Jane McIlvaine	!1823c	Washington Co. PA!		!1890
William Drury	!1827c	MD!		!

Mary Jane, William, Robert, Anne, and Louise lived in Washington Co., PA in 1850; in 1860 the census named the children Robert, Jane, Anne, and Thomas. William was a shoemaker; in 1860 he owned real property worth $950 and personal property of $466.   The 1870 census lists William as a boot and shoe merchant with personal property of $3000.

1 Robert McIlvaine	#!1847c	Washington Co. PA!		!
2 Anne	#!1849c	Washington Co. PA!	Washington Co. PA!	
3 Louise Jane	#!1849c	Washington Co. PA!		!
4 Thomas	#!1854c	Washington Co. PA!		!

782100000 DRURY

Robert McIlvaine Drury	!1847c	Washington Co. PA!		!
----- Kurtz	!		!	!

Robert lived unmarried with his parents in 1870; he was a boot and shoe merchant with personal property of $2000.

782200000 DAVIDSON

Anne Drury	!1849c		PA!	Washington Co. PA!
James Davidson	!		!	!

782300000 FISHER

Louise Jane Drury	!1849c	Washington Co. PA!		!
Sanford Fisher (Rev.)	!		!	!
	!		!	!
1 Drury (Rev.)	!		TX!	!
2 Anna	!		TX!	!
3 Susan	#!		TX!	!
4 Lulu	#!		TX!	!

782330000 MILNER

Susan Fisher	!		TX!	!
----- Milner (Dr.)	!		!	!

782340000 CONNETT

Lulu Fisher	!		TX!	!
Ralph Connett	!		!	!

782400000 DRURY

Thomas Drury	!1854c	Washington Co. PA!		!
Ida Hambright	!		!	!
	!		!	!
1 Alice	!	Washington Co. PA!		!
2 Lillian	!	Washington Co. PA!		!
3 Laura	!	Washington Co. PA!		!

Serial # and Name	Birth	Marriage	Death
783000000 MCILVAINE			
George W. McIlvaine	¦1823	¦	¦1887
s Jane Robb	¦	¦	¦
t Caroline M. Rinehart	¦	¦	¦
u Ursula Tirrell	¦	¦	¦1919

George was an Ohio circuit court judge and later a Justice of the Ohio Supreme Court.

Serial # and Name	Birth	Marriage	Death
1 Wilbert R.	s*¦1844c	OH¦1866 Dec 1 Tuscarawas Co.	OH¦1908
2 Floyd N.	t*¦1857	OH¦	¦
3 Flora Belle	t*¦1859	OH¦	¦
4 Carrie R.	t*¦1865	OH¦	¦1918
783100000 MCILVAINE			
Wilbert R. McIlvaine	¦1844c	OH¦1866 Dec 1 Tuscarawas Co.	OH¦1908
Mary Wallace	¦1856c	OH¦	¦

This McIlvaine family lived in Goshen, Tuscarawas County, OH in 1880.   Anna was listed as Florence in the census.

Serial # and Name	Birth	Marriage	Death
1 George	¦1867c	OH¦	¦1921 Oct 31
2 Charles Wilbert	*¦1869	OH¦	¦1952
3 Anna	¦1872c	OH¦	¦
4 Joseph	¦1877c	OH¦	¦
783120000 MCILVAINE			
Charles Wilbert McIlvaine	¦1869	OH¦	¦
Ada Wester	¦	¦	¦
	¦	¦	¦
1 James Laurence	¦	¦	¦1910
783200000 MCILVAINE			
Floyd N. McIlvaine	¦1862 Jan	OH¦	¦
Margaret Reynolds	¦1871 Mar	OH¦	¦

Floyd, Margaret, and George, unmarried, lived in Lorain, OH in 1910 and 1920.

Serial # and Name	Birth	Marriage	Death
1 George W.	¦1890 Sep	OH¦	¦
783300000 SHOTWELL			
Flora Belle McIlvaine	¦1859 Dec	OH¦	¦
Walter Gaston Shotwell	¦1856 Dec	OH¦	¦

The Shotwells lived in Cadiz, Ohio. He was a judge in the same Ohio circuit court as his father-in-law had been.

Serial # and Name	Birth	Marriage	Death
1 Margaret McIlvaine	*¦1886 Mar Cadiz	OH¦	¦
783310000 MCLAUGHLIN			
Margaret McIlvaine	¦1886 Mar Cadiz	OH¦	¦
Shotwell	¦	¦	¦
Samuel P. McLaughlin	¦	¦	¦
783400000 SHOTWELL			
Carrie R. McIlvaine	¦1865	OH¦	¦1918
Stuart Beebe Shotwell	¦	¦	¦
	¦	¦	¦
1 Stuart McIlvaine	¦	¦	¦

Serial # and Name	Birth	Marriage	Death

784000000 MCILVAINE

John D. McIlvaine	1824 Oct Washington Co. PA		1918
s Charlotte Wilson	1830c	PA	
t Rachel Kurtz	1847 Apr	PA	

John, Charlotte, and the oldest four children were living with John's parents in Somerset township, Washington Co., PA in 1860. In 1880 John and Rachel were living in Tuscarora County, Ohio with Frank and a daughter called Bell (perhaps Rebecca). In 1900 the parents, with Frank and Florence, lived in New Philadelphia, PA. John lived in New Philadelphia in 1910. Rachel was not mentioned in the 1910 census, indicating that she had probably died.

1 George W.	s*1853	PA1885 Dec 22 Tuscarawas Co. OH1913	
2 Robert W.	s*1855	PA1883 Dec 11 Tuscarawas Co. OH	
3 Alfretta Jane	s*1857	OH1879 Apr 3	1920
4 Rebecca A.	s*1860	OH	
5 Nellie R.	t 1874	OH	1878
6 Frank O.	t*1876 Nov	OH	
7 Florence L.	t*1881 Jul	OH	

784100000 MCILVAINE

George W. McIlvaine	1853	PA1885 Dec 22 Tuscarawas Co. OH1913	
Mary E. Warner	1858c	OH	

This McIlvaine family lived in New Philadelphia, OH in 1900 and 1910, in 1900 on Commercial Street.

1 Clarence L.	1890	OH	
2 Earl W.	*1894	OH	
3 Ruth I.	1897	OH	

784120000 MCILVAINE

Earl W. McIlvaine	1894	OH	
Anne -----	1898c	OH	

This family lived at 429 West Front St. (rear) New Philadelphia, OH in 1920.

1 Audrey May	1919c		

784200000 MCILVAINE

Robert W. McIlvaine	1855 Feb	PA1883 Dec 11 Tuscarawas Co. OH	
Margaret Darst	1859 Dec	OH	

This family lived in Ohio, in New Philadelphia in 1900, in Columbus in 1900, in Richland Co. in 1910, and in Mansfield in 1920.

1 Nellie M.	1887 Jun	OH	

Nellie was living with her parents, unmarried, in 1910 and 1920.

784300000 HARNEY

Alfretta Jane McIlvaine	1857	OH1879 Apr 3	1920
John L. Harney			
1 Clara C.			
2 Myrtle O.			
3 Laura H.			
4 Earl L.	*1895c	OH	

Serial # and Name	Birth	Marriage	Death

784400000   CRAWFORD

Rebecca A. McIlvaine	1860	OH	
Theodore Crawford			
1 Edgar R.	1892		

784600000   MCILVAINE

| Frank O. McIlvaine | 1876 Nov | OH | |
| Estella J. Limbaugh | 1881c | OH | |

The McIlvaines lived in New Philadelphia, PA in 1910 and 1920.   In 1920 their address was 358 Seventh St.

| 1 Hazel A. | 1906c | OH | |
| 2 Pearl Louise | 1910c | OH | |

784700000   GIBBS

| Florence L. McIlvaine | 1881 Jul | OH | |
| David Gibbs | 1880c | OH | |

Florence was living unmarried with her parents in 1900.   In 1910 she and David lived in New Philadelphia,
Ohio.

| 1 Ethel M. | | | |
| 2 Raymond D. | | | |

7b0000000   MCILVAINE

| Greer McIlvaine | 1801 Jan 10 Washington Co. PA | 1831 Mar 6 | 1871 Nov 16 Delaware Co. OH |
| Martha Browne | 1813 Aug 20 Washington Co. PA | Samuel Browne & Nancy Bannon | |

This McIlvaine family lived in Westerville, OH.   The 1850 census gave Greer's occupation as that of
a farmer, with real estate valued at $500. Son George was also listed as a farmer.

1 George W.	1832	Licking Co. OH		1862	Stones River TN
2 Samuel	*1834	Licking Co. OH	1862 Nov 14 Delaware Co. OH	
3 Nathaniel	1835	Licking Co. OH		
4 Margaret	*1836	Licking Co. OH		
5 John F.	*1839 Mar 5 Union Co. OH		
6 Ann E.	1842 Dec 8 Union Co. OH		1860 Jul 12
7 David Greer	1844	Union Co. OH		1862
8 Joseph Thomas	*1846 Nov 22 Union Co. OH	1872 Aug 23 Franklin Co. OH	1913 Sep 3 Flint OH
9 Nancy	1849	Delaware Co. OH		
a Emily McIlvaine	*1853 Nov 22 Delaware Co. OH		

George was killed in the Civil War at the Battle of Stones River. David was also killed in the Civil War.
Nathaniel does not appear in the 1850 census.

7b2000000   MCILVAINE

| Samuel McIlvaine | 1834 | Licking Co. OH | 1862 Nov 14 Delaware Co. OH | |
| Nancy J. Bennett | | | Elijah Bennett & ----- ----- | |

7b4000000   PACE

| Margaret McIlvaine | 1836 | Licking Co. OH | | |
| ----- Pace | | | |

7b5000000   MCILVAINE

| John F. McIlvaine | 1839 Mar 5 Union Co. OH | | |
| Elizabeth Titus | | | |

Serial # and Name	Birth	Marriage	Death

7b8000000 MCILVAINE

Joseph Thomas McIlvaine	1846 Nov 22 Union Co. OH	1872 Aug 23 Franklin Co. OH	1913 Sep 3 Flint OH
Mary Marcella Hurlburt	1853 Jul 21 Franklin Co. OH	John Hurlburt &	
		Arvilla Cockerill	

Joseph and Mary lived in Franklin County, Ohio, in Sharon twp in 1880, and in Columbus in 1910.

1 Arthur Cicero	*1873 Mar 30 Franklin Co. OH		1956 Jun 2 Columbus OH
2 Johney Burr	*1874 Dec 22 Franklin Co. OH		1953 May Worthington OH
3 Clay Orville	1880 Dec 27 Franklin Co. OH	never married	1938 Mar 5 Columbus OH
4 Joseph Dwight	*1885 Oct 8 Franklin Co. OH		1965 May 13 Worthington OH
5 Ernest Hadley	*1889 Jun 19 Franklin Co. OH		1964 Oct 26 Prescott AZ

7b8100000 MCILVAINE

Arthur Cicero McIlvaine	1873 Mar 30 Franklin Co. OH		1956 Jun 2 Columbus OH
s Roberta L. Joslin	1874 Aug 21 OH	Charles C. Joslin &	1904 Nov i. Worthington OH
		Harriet C. Powers	
t Alta Grace	1881	1910<	1958 i. Dublin OH
		Benjamin F. Grace &	
		Clyda -----	

Arthur, Roberta, and their four children lived in Orange twp., Delaware Co., OH in 1900.   In 1910 Arthur
and Alta with the four children lived in Franklin County, OH. In 1920 they lived alone in Franklin County.

1 Annabelle Lee	s*1893 Dec 22 OH		
2 Fancheon	s*1895 Dec 9 Delaware Co. OH		1967 Dec 27 Denver CO
3 Maude Merrell	s*1897 Jul 15 Delaware Co. OH	1918 Aug 29 Worthington OH	1966 May 20 Worthington OH
4 Clarice Marcella	s*1900 Jan 12 Franklin Co. OH		1983 Dec 29 Worthington OH

7b8110000 MADDY

Annabelle Lee McIlvaine	1893 Dec 22		
Charles T. Maddy		Franklin Co. OH Joseph Maddy &	1944 Coral Gables FL
		Catherine Moriarity	

7b8120000 CLARK / ZAHN

Fancheon McIlvaine	1895 Dec 9 Delaware Co. OH		1967 Dec 27 Denver CO
s Charles Clark	OH		
t Edwin Zahn	1898 Mar 27	OH 1923 Jun 17	
1 Charles Clark	*1917 Mar 5		1987 May 28
2 David Clark	*1920		1982 Aug 2
3 Carolyn Zahn	*1924		
4 Catherine Zahn	*1925		
5 Mary Marcelle Zahn	*1927 Jan 1 Tulsa	OK 1947 Jun 14 Tulsa OK	
6 Clarice Zahn	*1930		

7b8121000 CLARK

Charles Clark	1917 Mar 5		1987 May 28
----- -----			
1 Gary	1944 Oct 23		
2 Patricia	1946 Oct 10		

Serial # and Name	Birth	Marriage	Death
7b8122000 CLARK			
David Clark	1920		1982 Aug 24
----- -----			
1 David Michael	1943 Jun 11		
2 Diane Margaret	19-- May 10		
3 Daniel Mark	19-- Sep 22		
7b8123000 KRAMER			
Carolyn Zahn	1924		
William Kramer			
7b8124000 RAPP			
Catherine Zahn	1925		
Joseph Rapp			
7b8125000 JEWEL			
Mary Marcelle Zahn	1927 Jan 1 Tulsa	OK 1947 Jun 14 Tulsa	OK
Clifford Jewel			
1 Kirk Allen	1951 Dec 16 Tulsa	OK	
2 Lynn Marie	1953 Sep 21 Tulsa	OK	
3 Keri Ann	1956 Jun 17 Tulsa	OK	
7b8126000 ENDAM			
Clarice Zahn	1930		
----- Endam			
7b8130000 WILLIAMS / WRIGHT			
Maude Merrell McIlvaine	1897 Jul 15 Delaware Co. OH	1918 Aug 29 Worthington OH	1966 May 20 Worthington OH
s William Dale Williams	1897 Jan 29 Gallia Co. OH	Theo Roberts Williams &	1972 Mar 4 Weirton WV
		Blanche Martindale	
t Arnold Wright			
1 William Dale	* 1919 Sep 29 Steubenville OH		1976 May 19
Williams, Jr.			i. New Manchester WV
2 Ann Elizabeth Williams	* 1924 Jan 3 Steubenville OH	1946 May 23 Columbus OH	
7b8131000 WILLIAMS			
William Dale	1919 Sep 29 Steubenville OH		1976 May 19
Williams, Jr.			i. New Manchester WV
s Bess Kock			
t Marie -----			
1 Vaun Ann	s* 1937 Nov 21 Steubenville OH		
2 Daniel	s 1939 Dec 11 Steubenville OH		
3 William Nicole	t 1963 Oct 24 Los Angeles CA		

Serial # and Name	Birth	Marriage	Death
7b8131100 COTTRELL / STROUD			
Vaun Ann Williams	1937 Nov 21 Steubenville OH		
s Harold Cottrell			
t Edward Stroud			
1 Candace Cottrell	1954 Sep 5		
2 Sue Cottrell	1957 Dec 7		
3 Stephanie Stroud	1961 Sep 21		
4 Esther M. Stroud	1963 Jun 6		
5 Edward C. Stroud	1973 Apr 30		
7b8132000 FAVRET			
Ann Elizabeth Williams	1924 Jan 3 Steubenville OH	1946 May 23 Columbus OH	
James Louis Favret	1923 Jun 11 Cincinnati	OH Louis Edward Favret &	
		Marie Anna Smyth	
1 James Louis, Jr.	*1947 Mar 11 Columbus	OH 1980 Jun 6 Meiges Co. OH	
2 John Michael	*1948 Aug 3 Columbus	OH 1986 Jul 25	
3 Mary Jocelyn	1950 May 11 Columbus	OH	1950 May 11 Columbus OH
4 Mark Edward	*1951 Aug 9 Columbus	OH 1975 May 31 Columbus OH	
5 Matthew Joseph	*1954 May 5 Columbus	OH 1985 Sep 30	
6 Mariann Patricia	*1958 Mar 17 Columbus	OH 1983 Dec 30 Columbus OH	
7 Charles Arnold	*1961 Jan 25 Columbus	OH 1984 Sep 20 Worthington OH	
7b8132100 FAVRET			
James Louis Favret, Jr.	1947 Mar 11 Columbus	OH 1980 Jun 6 Meiges Co. OH	
Alice Carol Dieter	1953 Apr 18 Youngstown	OH Donald Bender Dieter &	
		----- -----	
1 Leah Nicole	1981 Feb 14 Columbus	OH	
2 Tivon Michael	1983 Apr 20 Columbus	OH	
3 Kyla Marie	1985 Nov 7 Worthington	OH	
7b8132200 FAVRET			
John Michael Favret	1948 Aug 3 Columbus	OH 1986 Jul 25	
Cynthia McClurg	1953 Oct 14 Canton	OH	
1 [child]	1990 Nov		
7b8132400 FAVRET			
Mark Edward Favret	1951 Aug 9 Columbus	OH 1975 May 31 Columbus OH	
Margaret Mary Bonfonte	1951 Aug 9 Columbus	OH John Bonfonte &	
		Mary Gasberro	
1 David Mark	1979 Apr 17 Columbus	OH	
2 Peter Aaron	1981 Jul 15 Columbus	OH	
3 Patrick	1983 Sep 17		
7b8132500			
Matthew Joseph Favret	1954 May 5 Columbus	OH 1985 Sep 30	
----- -----			
7b8132600 METZGER			
Mariann Patricia Favret	1958 Mar 17 Columbus	OH 1983 Dec 30 Columbus OH	
Mark Metzger			

Serial # and Name	Birth	Marriage	Death
7b8132700 FAVRET			
Charles Arnold Favret	1961 Jan 25 Columbus OH	1984 Sep 20 Worthington OH	
Deborah Bolin	1962 Nov 2 Columbus OH	Edward Bolin & Sharon -----	
1 Jacklyn Christine	1987 Jan 15 Columbus OH		
2 Jacob Charles	1989 Sep 11 Columbus OH		
7b8140000 GHEEN / THRUSH / FARINA			
Clarice Marcella	1900 Jan 12 Franklin Co. OH		1983 Dec 29 Worthington OH
McIlvaine			
s Claude Gheen			
t Robert Thrush			
u Bert Farina			
7b8200000 MCILVAINE			
Johney Burr McIlvaine	1874 Dec 22 Franklin Co. OH		1953 May Worthington OH
Myrtle -----			
7b8400000 MCILVAINE			
Joseph Dwight McIlvaine	1885 Oct 8 Franklin Co. OH		1965 May 13 Worthington OH
Roxy C. Bryant	1891c OH		
7b850000 MCILVAINE			
Ernest Hadley McIlvaine	1889 Jun 19 Franklin Co. OH		1964 Oct 26 Prescott AZ
Kate Throne			
7ba000000 WHITNEY			
Emily McIlvaine	1853 Nov 22 Delaware Co. OH		
L. B. (Banks) Whitney			
7c0000000 KERR			
Eleanor McIlvaine	1805 Washington Co. PA		
Walter Kerr			
800000000 STEWART / MARTIN / MCLAUGHLIN			
Eleanor McElwain	1762c Cumberland Co. PA	1783	
s James Stewart	1752		1792
t John Martin		1792 Aug 16	
u Thomas McLaughlin			
1 James Stewart, Jr.	*1784		1845
2 Mary Stewart	*1785		1860
3 John Stewart			
4 Andrew Stewart	*1790		1824
5 Lucinda Stewart	*1792		1844
810000000 STEWART			
James Stewart, Jr.	1784		1845
Janet McElwaine			
820000000 PATTERSON			
Mary Stewart	1785		1860
Samuel Patterson			

Serial # and Name	Birth	Marriage	Death	

840000000   STEWART

| Andrew Stewart | :1790 | : | :1824 | |
| Isabella Craighead | : | : | : | |

850000000   BINGHAM

| Lucinda Stewart | :1792 | : | :1844 | |
| Thomas Bingham | : | : | : | |

900000000   MCELWAIN

| Robert McElwain | :1766 Oct   Cumberland Co. PA | :1789 Oct 7 | : | Westmoreland Co. PA |
| Elizabeth McGlaughlin | :1769 | : | : | Westmoreland Co. PA |

　　　See the History, pages 29-32, for information on the family of Robert.

a00000000   MCELWAIN

| William McElvain | :1767c   Cumberland Co. PA | : | : | Westmoreland Co. PA |
| Lydia Curren | : | :1799< | : | |

　　　See the History section, pages 29-32, for information on the family of William.

| 1 Elizabeth McElvain | #:1809   Westmoreland Co. PA | :1830 | :1873 | Westmoreland Co. PA |

a10000000   LOVE

| Elizabeth McElvain | :1809   Westmoreland Co. PA | :1830 | :1873 | Westmoreland Co. PA |
| John McIlvain Love | :1807 Apr 04 nr. Albany   NY | Peter Love & Rachel Barber | :1873 | |

　　　Elizabeth and John apparently spent much of their married life in Jefferson Co., PA.   They appear in the
　　　1850, 1860 and 1870 censuses for that place.   In 1860 their residence was in Beaver twp.   John was listed
　　　as a laborer in 1850, a farmer in 1860, and a laborer in 1870.

1 Hannah	#:1830	PA	:1884	
2 Lydia C.	:1832	:	:1853	
3 Peter J.	#:1834	:	:1904	
4 William	#:1838 Mar	PA	:1906	
5 Andrew	:1840c	:	:1862	
6 John H.	#:1843 Apr	PA	:1910	
7 Elizabeth Rachel	:1845c	:	:1931	
8 James M.	:1847c	:	:1899	
9 Isaac H.	#:1851 Jan	PA	:	
a Abigail Serena	#:1854	:	:1945	

　　　Andrew is listed as a laborer, living with his parents, in the 1860 census.

a11000000   DEETER

| Hannah Love | :1830 | PA | :1884 | |
| Daniel Deeter | :1834c | PA | : | |

　　　Daniel, a farmer, and Hannah, with George and Clara, lived in Clover twp., Jefferson Co., PA in 1860.   In 1880
　　　the family lived in Knox twp.

1 George W.	#:1855c	PA	:	
2 Clara A.	:1859c	PA	:	
3 Charles	:1860c	PA	:	
4 Andrew	:1863c	PA	:	
5 Lucy	:1866c	PA	:	
6 Magee	:1868c	PA	:	
7 William R.	:1871c	PA	:	

Serial # and Name	Birth	Marriage	Death
a11100000 DEETER			
George W. Deeter		1855 May	PA			
Fannie A. -----		1846 May	NY			
This family lived in Hastings (Cambria Co.), PA in 1900.			
1 Maggie	*	1871 Mar	PA			
a11110000 VARBINDER			
Maggie Deeter		1871 Mar				
----- Varbinder						
Maggie and the three children lived with her parents in 1900.			
1 Irene M.		1888 Apr				
2 Nettie		1897 Aug				
3 Ettie		1897 Aug				
a13000000 LOVE			
Peter J. Love		1834				1904
----- Lucas						
a14000000 LOVE			
William Love	|1838 Mar	PA|	|1906
Clementine Furman		1838 May	PA			
William was living with his parents and working as a laborer in 1860. In 1880 he and his family lived in Knox twp., Jefferson Co., and in 1900 in Rose twp.			
1 Sid Bell		1868>	PA			
2 Andrew		1869>	PA			
3 Frank E.	*	1874 Sep	PA			
4 Mary E.		1877 Nov	PA			
5 William		1879c	PA			
a14300000 LOVE			
Frank E. Love		1874 Sep	PA			
Addie M. -----		1873c	KS			
This couple lived in Jefferson Co., PA in 1910. There were no children listed in the census.			
a16000000 LOVE			
John H. Love	|1843 Apr	PA|	|1910
Nancy Ellen McKee		1845 Feb	PA			
John was living with his parents and working as a laborer in 1860; he was still living with his parents in 1870. In 1900 he, his wife, and his son lived in Licking twp., Clarion Co., PA. Nancy was living alone in Clarion Co. in 1910.			
1 John Reed	*	1886 Jun	PA			
a16100000 LOVE			
John Reed Love		1886 Jun	PA			
Beulah M. -----		1889	PA			
This Love family lived in Collinsburg, Clarion Co., PA in 1920.			
1 Charles R.		1914c	PA			
2 Grace E.		1916c	PA			
3 Ralph E.		1918c	PA			

Serial # and Name	Birth	Marriage	Death
a19000000 LOVE			
Isaac H. Love	1851 Jan	PA	
Elizabeth J. -----	1857 Oct	PA	
This family lived in Jefferson Co., PA. in 1880 (Knox twp.), 1900 (Washington twp.), and 1910.			
1 Ida	1876c	PA	
2 Elva	1877c	PA	
3 James E.	#1878c	PA	
4 Barkley B.	#1884 Jan	PA	1947
5 John L.	1891 Jan	PA	
6 Walter D.	1892 Jun	PA	
a19300000 LOVE			
James E. Love	1878c	PA	
Maude C. -----	1880c	OH	
This family lived in Jefferson Co., PA in 1910 and 1920. In 1920 their address was Taylor Ave. (town not given).			
1 Dallas C.	1902c	PA	
2 Pearle	1904c	PA	
a1940000 LOVE			
Barkley B. Love	1884 Jan	PA	1947
Emma E. -----	1886c	PA	1968
This family lived in Jefferson Co., PA in 1910 and 1920. In 1920 their address was Taylor Ave. (town not given).			
1 Doris E.	1906	PA	
2 Leah E.	1911	PA	
a1a000000 GASTON			
Abigail Serena Love	1854		1945
John Gaston			
x000000000 THOMPSON			
Eleanor McElwain	1718		1797
William Thompson	1708		1797
Eleanor is supposed by some researchers to be a McElwain, and the sister of Andrew (000000000). This is a reasonable supposition, since William was the brother-in-law of either Andrew McElwain or Robert Mickey. However, no documentation has been produced to determine which.			
1 Mary	1742 Mar		
2 Margaret	1744 May		
3 Eleanor	#1746 Nov		1817
4 Margery Ellen	#1750 May 13		
5 Matthew	#1754 Apr		1823
x30000000 MOORE			
Eleanor Thompson	1746 Nov		1817
John Moore			

Serial # and Name	Birth	Marriage	Death

x40000000 DAVIDSON

Margery Ellen Thompson	1750 May 13		1832 Jan 9 Bedford Co. PA
Samuel Davidson	1748	John Davidson & Ann -----	1803 Jun Bedford Co. PA

Samuel was member of the Bedford County Committee of Correspondence and an officer in the Bedford County militia during the Revolutionary War. He also served the County as Justice of the Peace, County Commissioner, Coroner, Wood Ranger, and member of the Council of Censors. He apparently was a large landowner, as there are fifty deeds recorded for him in Bedford County.

1 Eleanor	#|1771 Feb 3		1840 Apr<
2 John	1773 Apr 10	never married	1840 Apr<
3 William Thompson	1775 Oct 5	never married	1826 nr. Starved Rock IL
4 Samuel	1778 Jan 22 (or 27)	never married	1842 Feb 20 Bedford Co. PA
5 Matthew	#|1780 Dec 20	1814 Mar 10	1825 Sep Bedford Co. PA
6 George	1784 Jan 29	never married	
7 Margery Ellen	#|1786 Aug 26	1814 Jan 20	1838 Dec 29 Bedford Co. PA
8 Mary Ann	1788	never married	1858 Jan Bedford Co. PA
9 Margaret	1790	never married	1856 Aug 24 Bedford Co. PA

x41000000 DAILEY / PARROTT

Eleanor Davidson	1771 Feb 3		1840 Apr <
s Edward Dailey			
t John Parrott			

x45000000 DAVIDSON

Matthew Davidson	1780 Dec 20	1814 Mar 10	1825 Sep Bedford Co. PA
Mary Magdalene Filler			

x46000000 REYNOLDS

Margery Ellen Davidson	1786 Aug 26	1814 Jan 20	1838 Dec 29 Bedford Co. PA
John Reynolds			

x50000000 THOMPSON

Matthew Thompson	1754 Apr		1823
s Ann McFarland			1789
t Ruth Robinson			
1 Rosanna	s	1784 May Cumberland Co. PA		
2 William	s |1787		1823
3 Esther	t			
4 Matthew	t			
5 [child]	t			
6 [child]	t			
7 [child]	t			
8 [child]	t			

y00000000 WILLIAMSON

Prudence McElvain			
James Williamson			

Prudence is stated by some researchers to be a sister of Andrew McElvain (000000000), but no documentary evidence is known.

INDEX TO THE HISTORY

This index covers the History or narrative portion of the book; a separate Index to the Genealogy begins on page 337. Topics indexed include every reference that seemed likely to be helpful to the user.   Not indexed are non-family members in several of the genealogies and family trees, and in material on the McElwain Institute.

To increase the usefulness of the index a description is added for many of the topics.   For family members the description is the serial number assigned in the Genealogy.   Distant relatives, not in the Genealogy, are described by birth and death dates, or simply described as a "relative", a term which is applied liberally, and includes relatives by marriage.   An "ancestor" fulfills that function for one or more persons in The Genealogy. A person described as a researcher has published material used in this book.   A contributor is one who has personally submitted information for this book. Women contributors are indexed under their married name.

Individuals are indexed by surname and first name only. Groups with the same first name are ordered by their serial numbers.

TOPIC	DESCRIPTION	PAGES
Adamson, Martha	4ab000000s	71
Ager family		58
Allegheny Co., PA		65, 69, 71
Allen, Hugh	landowner	61
Allen, John	landowner	61
Anjou, Gustave	researcher	1, 2
Attiquin estate	Scotland	89
Augnacloy	Ireland	45
Baker, Samuel	servant	43
Bargany, Laird of		90
Barr, Robert	landowner	61
Bechtel, Eliza	4a6000000	71
Bell family		58
Bell family tree		38
Bell, Elizabeth	ancestor	34, 38
Bell, Margaret	400000000t	23, 24, 25, 30
Bell, Raymond M.	researcher	35, 37
Bell, Robert	1739-	36
Bell, Walter	relative	10
Bell, Walter	ancestor	37, 38
Big Spring Presbyterian Church		81-85
Big Spring cemetery		84
Blake, Sally Jo	contributor	105
block houses	Mifflin twp.	58
Bloomfield Joseph	Governor NJ	93
Boatman, Louise	contributor	105
Borland, A. A.	238530000s	75
Bourdelon, Polly	contributor	105
Braddock's Road		69
Brady family		58
Brandy Run		57
Braudel, Fernand	historian	iii
bridges	Mifflin twp.	58
Brison, Samuel	landowner	61

TOPIC	DESCRIPTION	PAGES
Brown family		58
Brown, William Jr.	executor	12, 13
Browne, Martha	7b0000000s	71
Bruner, Earle D.		75
Carnahan family		5, 58
Carnahan, Adam	2300000000s	19-20, 65, 71
Carnahan, Adam, Jr.	237000000	20, 71
Carnahan, B. N.		73
Carnahan, Carlos	237200000	71
Carnahan, Elizabeth	236000000	20 (Thompson)
Carnahan, Glenn F.	contributor	105
Carnahan, J. T.		73
Carnahan, James	neighbor	61
Carnahan, James M.	235000000	20, 68, 106
Carnahan, John	239000000	20
Carnahan, Margaret	231000000	20 (Walker)
Carnahan, Maria	234000000	20 (Rhodes)
Carnahan, Mary J.	237000000s	20, 71
Carnahan, Nancy	233000000	20
Carnahan, Ruth	238000000	20, 39
Carnahan, Vicnelia	237100000	71
Carnahan, William	23a000000	20
Carson, Alice	4b0000000	71
Carson, Elisha	relative	43
Carson, Ezekiel	relative	43
Carson, Joseph	relative	43
Carson, Margaret	relative	43
Carson, Mary	relative	43
Carson, Robert	relative	43
Carson, William	relative	43
Cassia Co., ID	migration	71
Cassilis, Gilbert,	Earl of	90
Cassilis, John,	Earl of	90
Caswell, Richard,	Governor NC	94
census	source	103-104

TOPIC	DESCRIPTION	PAGES
Church of England		100
Church of Jesus Christ of the Latter Day Saints	source	100-101
Clemens, Juliana	ancestor	39
Clum, Marjorie	contributor	105
Cochrane	researcher	4
Cokayne, Thos.	witness	46
Complete History of the McElvain-McIlvaine Family Line	source	3, 98-99
Corbin, Benjamin	4a5300000s	71
Corrie, John		90
Coweb, Samuel	witness	51
Craighead, Thomas	clergyman	81
Crawford, Douglas	contributor	105
Crawford Co., KS	migration	71
Creslip, Isaac		22
Cross, Gordon C.	contributor	105
Culbertson, Joseph		21, 38
Cumberland Co,. PA		57-64, 71
Curren, Lidey	a00000000s	30-31, 71
Decennial Census	source	103-104
distilleries		58, 59, 61
donation lands		65
Dunlap, Alexander	7550000000s	71
Earnshaw, Anna	4a9500000s	71
Emery, Arden M.	contributor	105
Emery, Raymen F.	contributor	105
Emery, William R.	contributor	105
Erwin, James Bard	421000000	71
Fairfield Presbyterian Church		106
Fallen Timbers	battle of	70
Family History Library	source	100-101
Fawside, Battle of		90
Fayette County, PA		69
Felair, Andrew	landowner	61
Fenton, Samuel	relative	43, 52
Forbes' Road		69
Fort Duquesne	PA	69
Fort Stanwix treaty		65
Fountain of Health Farm		58
Fredonia Institute		76, 77
French Creek twp.		65
Gamble, Benjamin	relative	34
Gees, Conrad	landowner	61
Gilmore, Mrs.		58
glebe land	Big Spring	84
Gordon, John	witness	42

TOPIC	DESCRIPTION	PAGES
Graduation Program	McElwain In.	80
Gray, David B. & Cheryl Cress	contributor	105
Great Trail		70
Greene Co., OH	migration	70, 71
Greene County, PA		69
Greer, Mary	ancestor	52
Grimet estate	Scotland	89
Hanna Cemetery		86
Hannah, Annabelle	source	97
Hannah, John	233000000s	20
Harrison, Mrs. Gordon	Zahniser Fd.	40
Hemphill Co., TX	migration	71
Herodotus	historian	iii
Hill, Clyde S.	contributor	105
Hill, Dorothy	contributor	105
histories, local	sources	102
History of McElwain Institute		73-74
House of Grimet	source	89, 99-100
Indians	Mifflin twp.	58
industries	Cumb. Co. PA	59
industries	Mifflin twp.	58
International Genealogical Index (IGI)	source	101
Iowa City, IA	migration	71
Jasper	researcher	4
Jefferson Co., PA	migration	71
Johnson Co., KS	migration	71
Johnston, George	contributor	104
Kansas	migration	71
Katich, Betty J.	contributor	105
Kenedy, Johnne		90
Kennedy, Gilbert		90
Kennedy, Hew		90
Ketler, Isaac C.		75
Ketler, Joseph		77
Knox Co., IL	migration	71
Kovach, Marilyn L.	contributor	105
Lamond, William	witness	50
Land Ordinance	1785	69
Laughlin family		58
Laughlin, Alexander	witness	6, 34
Laughlin, Hugh	witness	34
Law, Doris Ann	contributor	40, 105
Lawrence County		65
Licking Co., OH	migration	70, 71
Lightcap family		58
Lightcap, William	neighbor	51, 61
Lindsay, John	witness	42

TOPIC	DESCRIPTION	PAGES
Lindsey, James	executor	19
Lint, Mary	ancestor	39
local histories	sources	102
Love, John	a10000000s	30, 71
Lower Mifflin twp.	Cumb. Co. PA	57
Lusk family		58
Lusk, Robert	neighbor	29, 30, 60, 61, 82
Lusk, William	witness	11, 24
Lyons, Marion	contributor	105
Mackelvaine, Francis	witness	46
Malven (Malvern)	variant name	95
Mapps, Mary Jane	4a5000000	71
Marion Co., IN	migration	71
Marriner, John	relative	52
Martin family		58
McCalvaine, Andrew	relative	1, 2, 45, 46
McCandless, James	executor	14
McCormick, J. F.	witness	19
McCracken, Alexander	relative	42
McCracken, Anna		72
McCracken, James	relative	42
McCracken, James		73
McCracken, John	relative	42
McCracken, Joshua	ancestor	16, 39, 42
McCracken, Mary	226000000s	16-18, 39, 42
McCracken, Thomas	ancestor	42, 65
McCulloch, Letitia	witness	13
McElhenny family		58
McElhenny, Hugh	relative	43
McElhenny, Robert	relative	43
McElvain, Frank C.	researcher	4, 9, 89-90, 98-99
McElwain Family Histories		96-97
McElwain Institute		16, 72-80
McElwain Shoe Co.		95
McElwain, Adam T.	226800000	18
McElwain, Albert	24550000	71
McElwain, Alexander	226300000	18
McElwain, Alexander and Francis	KY family	95
McElwain, Andrew	000000000	1-6, 50, 58, 60, 64, 71, 91
McElwain, Andrew T.	242000000	71
McElwain, Andrew	400000000	2, 6, 22-27, 29-30, 43, 60-63, 82-83
McElwain, Andrew	450000000	44, 84
McElwain, Andrew	4a3000000	71
McElwain, Andrew	1740-1793	48, 50-53, 61
McElwain, Andrew	b. 1787	52, 54
McElwain, Anna B.	226a00000	19
McElwain, Benjamin	440000000	44
McElwain, Cyrus P.	226100000	18

TOPIC	DESCRIPTION	PAGES
McElwain, David	226200000	18
McElwain, David A.	contributor	105
McElwain, Donald	contributor	105
McElwain, Eleanor	relative	2
McElwain, Elenor	800000000	2, 6
McElwain, Elizabeth	100000000	2, 3, 6, 7
McElwain, Elizabeth	243000000	12
McElwain, Elizabeth	470000000	44
McElwain, Elizabeth	a10000000	30, 71
McElwain, Ellen	4a8000000	86
McElwain, Emma A.	226700000	18
McElwain, Florence	24550000s	71
McElwain, Forrest	226410000	97
McElwain, George	relative	1, 46-52,
McElwain, George	genealogy	53-56
McElwain, Hannah	600000000	2, 6
McElwain, Harvey	226400000	18
McElwain, Isabel	421000000	71
McElwain, Isabella	1784-1846	52, 54
McElwain, James	200000000	2-3, 6, 8-15, 60-64, 82
McElwain, James	221000000	9, 71
McElwain, James	4a5000000	71
McElwain, James	4b0000000	25, 44, 71
McElwain, James and Elinor	MA family	94
McElwain, James and Jane Heany	related family	94
McElwain, Jane	430000000	22, 25, 44, 82
McElwain, Janet	1785-1835	52
McElwain, John S.	220000000	8-10, 14-16, 34, 38, 65, 71, 82
McElwain, John T.	226000000	16-19, 39, 68, 72-73
McElwain, John C.	226220000	18
McElwain, John	4c0000000	44
McElwain, Joseph	b. 1743	48, 51-53, 61
McElwain, Lacy	4a9000000	71
McElwain, Malinda	226b00000	19
McElwain, Margaret	200000000t	8-12, 22
McElwain, Margaret	250000000	8-13
McElwain, Margery	246000000	12
McElwain, Mary	210000000	8, 9, 13-14, 34, 82
McElwain, Mary F.	226300000	79
McElwain, Mary T.	226600000	18
McElwain, Mary J.	410000000	23, 44, 82
McElwain, Mary	4a3000000s	71
McElwain, Mary	500000000	2, 6, 7
McElwain, Mary	b. 1784c	52, 54
McElwain, Nancy	4a5300000	71
McElwain, Patrick & Mary Campbell	PA family	95
McElwain, Prudence	300000000	2, 6

TOPIC	DESCRIPTION	PAGES
McElwain, Rhuhama	1786-1856	52,54
McElwain, Richard	contributor	105
McElwain, Richard	240000000	8-12, 14-16, 20-23 34, 38, 65
McElwain, Robert	420000000	10, 22-25, 44, 82-83
McElwain, Robert H.	4ab000000	71
McElwain, Robert	900000000	2-3, 6, 29-32, 82,
McElwain, Ruth	230000000	19-20, 34, 65, 71, 82
McElwain, Ruth	700000000	2, 6, 27-28, 69 71
McElwain, Sarah	480000000	44
McElwain, Sarah	490000000	25,44
McElwain, Stewart	4d0000000	25,44
McElwain, Thomas	460000000	24,25,44
McElwain, Thomas S.	4ac000000	71
McElwain, Thomas	error	3
McElwain, Watson	226500000	18
McElwain, William and Florence	contributors	105
McElwain, William Penrose	226900000	18, 19
McElwain, Wm. Bell	4a0000000	25, 44, 86
McElwain, William Bell, Jr.	4a4000000	71
McElwain, William	a00000000	2, 3, 6, 23, 29-32 60, 62-63, 69, 71
McElwain, Wm. Howe	manufacturer	95
McElwaine, Andrew	contributor	105
McElwaine, Myron M.	contributor	105
McGlaughlin, Elizabeth	900000000s	29-31, 71, 82
McIlvain, Andrew	(McCalvaine)	1
McIlvain, John and Sarah Bell	PA family	95
McIlvain, Moses and Agnes Miller	related family	94
McIlvain, Moses and Margaret Martin	related family	94
McIlvaine family of Grimet, Scotland		89-91
McIlvaine, Alan	ancestor	90
McIlvaine, Alexander	Augnacloy, Ireland	45, 52
McIlvaine, Andrew	776733000	89, 99
McIlvaine, Andrew	1669-1726	1, 4, 45-47, 52
McIlvaine, Andrew and Martha Mickey	ancestors	93
McIlvaine, Bloomfield	relative	93
McIlvaine, Bowes Reed	relative	93

TOPIC	DESCRIPTION	PAGES
McIlvaine, Charles Pettit	relative	93
McIlvaine, Daniel and Mary Smith	NH family	95
McIlvaine, George	700000000	27-28, 52, 69, 71
McIlvaine, George	783000000	71
McIlvaine, Gilbert	Laaird	90
McIlvaine, Greer	7b0000000	71
McIlvaine, James and Mary Tyson	related family	94
McIlvaine, James	1693-1754	46, 47, 52
McIlvaine, John	750000000	71
McIlvaine, John A.	781300000	27
McIlvaine, John D.	784000000	71
McIlvaine, John	b. 1691	46, 52
McIlvaine, John	d. 1789	47, 52
McIlvaine, John	Laird	45, 52
McIlvaine, John	ancestor	90
McIlvaine, Joseph and Anna Rogerson	relative	93
McIlvaine, Joseph	Rev. officer	93
McIlvaine, Joseph	Senator	93
McIlvaine, Martha	(Warriner)	46, 52
McIlvaine, Mary	(Bloomfield)	95
McIlvaine, Mary J.	755000000	71
McIlvaine, Patrick	Laird	90, 92
McIlvaine, Quentin	Laird	45, 52, 92
McIlvaine, Robert and Mary Duffield	related family	94
McIlvaine, Ruth	754000000	71
McIlvaine, W. A. H.	781420000	27
McIlvaine, William	Rev. officer	93
McIlvaine, William	relative	93
McIlwain family of Virginia	related family	95
McIlwain, Andrew & Margaret Douglas	related family	95
McIlwain, Gilbert & Jane Graham	related family	94
McIlwain, James and Katy Scott	related family	95
Mcilwean, Mary	(Caswell)	94
McKee, Andrew	heir	46
McKee, John		21, 36-37
McKee, William	heir	46
McLaughlin family		58
McQuiston, Nellie		72
McYlveyne, Nigel	Laird	90, 92
Mercer County	Pennsylvania	65-68
Mercer County, PA	migration	71
Mickey, Daniel		46, 50
Mickey, Mary	000000000s	1-6, 60, 71, 82

TOPIC	DESCRIPTION	PAGES
Mickey, Robert	ancestor	45
Mickey, Robert	relative	1, 3, 4, 5, 6, 58
Middle Spring Pres-		48, 49, 85-88
byterian Church		
Middle Sp. cemetery		85-86
Mifflin township	Cumb. Co. PA	57-58
migration patterns		70-71
Mill Creek twp.		66
Miller, Glenn, Sr.	contributor	105
Mills, Frances	(McIlvaine)	47, 52
Montgomery, William	witness	36, 37
Moody, Gatsey	relative	94
Moore, Jean	historian	89, 99
Mormon Church	source	100-101
Morrow family		58
Morrow, John	landowner	61
Morrow, Samuel	landowner	61
Mourer, Mary	ancestor	39
Muckelane,	Delaware	146
Alexander		46
Muckelvane, Francis	Delaware	1
Musical Program	McElwain In.	78
Nash, William B.	author	94
National Archives	source	103
National Road		70
New Lebanon, PA	map	67
Newville, PA		84
Newville Valley	newspaper	4
Star		
Nicholson family		5, 33-34, 58
Nicholson, Ann	relative	34
Nicholson	unidentified	12
Elizabeth		
Nicholson, Isabel	ancestor	33
Nicholson, James	relative	7, 33, 34, 61
Nicholson, James B.	researcher	7
Nicholson, John	500000000s	7
Nicholson, Margaret	relative	34
Nicholson, Margerey	relative	33
Nicholson, Mary	200000000s	8, 9, 82
Nicholson, Mary	ancestor	33, 82
Nicholson, Nancy	221000000s	71
Nicholson, Richard	ancestor	33
Nicholson, Richard	ancestor	8, 9, 33-34, 82
Nicholson, Sarah	relative	33
Nicholson, William	100000000s	7
Nicholson, William	relative	33, 34
Nickerson, John	executor	14
Nickey, Mary	4ac000000s	71
Noble Co., OK	migration	71
Northwest Ordinance		70
Ohio		69-70

TOPIC	DESCRIPTION	PAGES
Ohio Company		70
Oiler, Mrs. E. Lee	researcher	57
Ordway, William L.	755616000	91, 99, 100, 104
Patton, John	relative	43
Penn, John	PA proprietor	5
Penrod, Naldene R.	contributor	105
Pinckie, Battle of	Scotland	90
Pittsburgh, PA		69
Portage Co., OH	migration	71
Porter, Donald M.	contributor	105
Porterfield, Wm.	relative	43
Porterfield family		58
Pruitt, Penelope	contributor	105
Ralston, David	witness	12
Ramp, Harvey	4a9500000	71
Ramp, John	4a9000000s	71
Ramp, John D. &	contributors	105
Al'Louise Suthers		
Rice Co., KS	migration	71
Richards, Rita	contributor	105
Ritchvan, William	witness	22
Robb, Jane	783000000s	71
Roget, Peter	lexicographer	iii
Sandy Lake	map	68
Sauk Co., WI	migration	71
Schouler, James B.	researcher	4, 57
Scroggs, Alexander	witness	51
Scroggs, Jeanette		52
Session Minutes	Middle Sprg.	48-49, 86-88
Shannon family		5, 44, 58
Shannon, Elizabeth	400000000s	23, 43, 82
Shannon, Isaac	relative	34
Shannon, Jean	ancestor	43
Shannon, John	relative	43, 52
Shannon, Joseph	relative	43
Shannon, Mary	relative	43
Shannon, Robert	ancestor	5, 23, 43
Shannon, Robert	relative	21, 23, 43
Shannon, Samuel	relative	43
Shannon, Sarah	relative	43
Smith, Margaret	750000000s	71
Snody, John	executor	36-37
Somerset, Duke of		90
Steel, Elizabeth	21?000000	12
Steel, James	21?000000	14
Steel, Leticia	21?000000	14
Steel, Margaret	21?000000	12, 13, 14
Steel, Matthew	21?000000	14
Steel, Robert	210000000	13, 14
Steel, Robert	21?000000	14
Sterrett, Brice	witness	10
Sterrit family		58

TOPIC	DESCRIPTION	PAGES
Stevenson family		5, 58
Stevenson, James	landowner	34, 61
Stevenson, John		34
Stevenson, Mary	relative	34
Stevenson, William	relative	34
Stewart, James	landowner	61
Stewart, James	430000000s	25
Stewart, James	100000000s	2
Stewart, Janet L.	contributor	105
Sussex Co., DE		45
Swope, Belle		85
Swope, Gilbert E.		81
tanneries	in Mifflin	58
Ten Nights in a Bar-Room	McElwain Institute	79
Thomaston estate		89
Thompson, Adam	236000000	20
Thompson, Andrew	ancestor	34-37, 38, 85
Thompson, Clare		75
Thompson, Elizabeth	236000000	20
Thompson, Elizabeth	relative	36, 38
Thompson, Hannah	220000000	14, 35-38, 65, 71
Thompson, Hugh	ancestor ?	35
Thompson, Jane	relative	36, 38
Thompson, John	witness	51
Thompson, Joseph	neighbor	35
Thompson, Margaret	relative	48
Thompson, Martha	ancestor	22, 34-36, 52
Thompson, Mary	relative	35, 36, 38
Thompson, Prudence	relative	35-38
Thompson, Rosanna	240000000s	11-12, 20-21, 36-38, 71
Thompson, Sarah	relative	36, 38
Thompson, Vance		75
Thompson, W. A.		75
Thompson, William	relative	1, 2, 4, 5, 6, 50, 58
Three Square Hollow		57
Tilley, Celia J.	contributor	105
Torrence, Robert	researcher	3, 7, 48, 97-98
Treaty of Greenville		70
Tuscarawas Co., OH	migration	71
United States Direct Tax of 1798		58-59, 61
Verner, Beverly J.	contributor	105
Villa, Maryamber S. & Val	contributor	105
Walker, Margaret	232000000	20
Waltenberg, George	754000000s	71
Washington County	PA	65, 69, 71
Wayne Co., OH	migration	70, 71
Wayne, Gen. Anthony		70
Weber, Irving	contributor	105
Westmoreland County	PA	65, 69, 71
Wheatley, Nancy	242000000s	71
Whiskey Run	Cumb. Co. PA	57
Williamson Massacre		5
Williamson family		558
Williamson		2
Williamson, David	landowner	61
Wills, David	executor	36-37
Wilson, Andrew	relative	36
Wilson, Charlotte	784000000s	71
Wilson, Francis	237100000	71
Wilson, John	relative	36, 38
Wilson, Samuel		81
Womer, Jan Lynn	contributor	105
Womer, William A.		74, 75
Wyandotte Co., OH	migration	71
Zahm, Jeanne Lea	contributor	105
Zahneisen, Valentine	ancestor	39
Zahniser Foundation		39, 101
Zahniser, Charles	researcher	39
Zahniser, Kate M.	researcher	39
Zahniser, Mary	ancestor	16, 39, 42
Zahniser, Matthias	ancestor	39, 40, 65
Zahniser, Michael	ancestor	39
Zahniser, Ruth	278000000	20
Zahniser, Stuart	contributor	105
Zahniser, William	238000000s	19, 20, 39
Zahnisers, The	source	40-41
Zapolnik, Carol	contributor	104
Zeamer, Jeremy	researcher	84

INDEX TO THE GENEALOGY

The Index to the Genealogy lists every person mentioned in the Genealogy, both those descended from Andrew McElwain and Mary Mickey and those who have married into the family. The History is separately indexed beginning on page 331.

Individuals are listed, in all but a few special cases, under the surname at the time of birth. Thus women who married appear under their maiden names. Women who married into the family, but whose maiden names are not known are indexed under their married name shown in brackets and placed at the end of the section for that name.

The final "e" in McElwaine is printed but was ignored in the indexing; both those persons who changed the spelling and those who inherited the spelling are indexed intermingled with those who spell the name McElwain.

The index is arranged in a columnar form to provide easier scanning of the surname and given name columns. The violations of the column margins made for the sake of economy should not materially interfere with the scanning process.

Index listings give the full name (surname, first given name, and second given name, if any) as it appears in the Genealogy. A few names have been abbreviated when an individual has two or more given names.

There are two columns for page numbers. The first column provides the page number for the family into which the person was born, and the second that for the family resulting from his or her marriage. Thus a page number only in the second column indicates a person who married into the family. Each person born into the family (except the founding Andrew) has a page number in the first column. Those with a page number in both column are descendents of Andrew who have married or have had children.

Also indexed are a small number of persons who may be family members but are mentioned only in the biographical notes attached to some entries.

Surname	Given Name	Page	Page
Abel	Hazel		166
Abraham	Gladys Emma		288
Ackley	Newton		154
Adams	Ethel C.	185	
Adams	Jeffrey Lee	256	
Adams	Ray		256
Adams	Ray Charles	256	256
Adams	Ryan Lee	256	
Adams	William		185
Adamson	Martha Jane		227
Agins	Bret McCoy	204	
Agins	Sherman Leonard		204
Ahmed	Aliyah Yasmeen	294	
Ahmed	Arshad	294	
Ahmed	Ayoub Afzal	294	
Ahmed	Rashed Mohamed		294
Aiken	Lucinda		264
Akers	Cathy Sue		236
Albertson	Charlene June		234
Aldorf	Lois		274
Aldrich	Edna		109
Aleshire	Gary Lee		287
Aleshire	Gary Lee, Jr.	287	
Aleshire	Gordon Stephen	287	
Aleshire	Linda Lee	287	
Aleshire	Loree Linn	287	287
Allen	-----		316
Allen	Andrew Richard	273	
Allen	Benjamin David	273	
Allen	Charles William	273	274
Allen	Cynthia Gail	273	
Allen	Daniel Floyd	273	
Allen	David		146
Allen	Dominic Michael	290	
Allen	Donald Joseph	273	
Allen	Donald Wesley	273	273
Allen	Floyd Nathaniel		273
Allen	George Harold	273	
Allen	Hayden Ray	290	
Allen	Jacqueline	273	
Allen	Jill Lynn	274	
Allen	John Marty	274	
Allen	Jon Brian	274	274
Allen	Lee Jonathan	273	
Allen	Mary Jo		279
Allen	Michael James	274	
Allen	Michael Ray		290
Allen	Michael Scott		158
Allen	Patricia Ann		147
Allen	Patricia Jo	273	
Allen	Richard George	273	273
Allen	Ross Charles	274	
Allen	Scott Dale	273	
Allen	Steven Robert	274	274
Allen	Susan Rae	273	
[Allen]	-----		274
[Allen]	Rose		274
Alvarez	Isabel		171
Ambro	Dorothy		273
Ames	Arlene	164	165
Ames	Fred W., Jr.		164
Ames	Lucille	164	165
Ames	Marjory A.	164	164
Ames	Warren	164	
Anderson	-----		296
Anderson	-----		296
Anderson	Richard John		284
Anderson	Roger		298
Anderson	Ross	284	
Anderson	Sara Nicole	284	
Anderson	Wendy Sue		286
Andrews	Harold		111
Andrews	Wilma L. Johnson		145
Anthony	Anita Ruth		290
Antonacci	Susan Gale		173
Applington	Diane		293
Arket	Baule	174	
Arket	Bob	174	
Arket	James Ray	174	
Arket	W. F.		174
Arket	William McCormick	174	
Armstrong	[daughter]	310	
Armstrong	Jennie		248
Armstrong	Margaret		283
Armstrong	Pat		310
Armstrong	[son]	310	
Arnold	Debbie		308
Arnold	Mary		114
Arnold	Tamara Rose	288	
Arnold	Thomas Eugene		288
Arrott	Colleen		158
Asberry	Amy Elaine	137	
Asberry	Dennis		137
Atkinson	Jill		115
Aubihl	Sara Sue		268
Ault	-----		223
Aumack	Francine		266
Austin	Irene		182
Aylsworth	Angela Marie	298	
Aylsworth	Harvey Paul		298
Aylsworth	Jessica Lynn	298	
Aylsworth	Laura Kay	298	
Bailey	Caleb		154
Bailey	James	154	
Bailey	Oscar	154	
Baird	Joan Marie		293
Baker	Bess Lucille		240
Baker	Charles		238
Baker	Gaillard Filiterra	303	303
Baker	Ireland Marie	303	
Baker	Margaret Lynn		281
Baker	Panicia Marie	303	303
Baker	Sarah Ann		264
Baker	William Brandyn	303	
Baker	William Warren		303
Baldwin	Burt	300	
Baldwin	Charles M.		300
Baldwin	Edith Lucy	300	
Baldwin	Eleanor Mae	235	235
Baldwin	John Lloyd		235
Baldwin	Nellie	300	
Baldwin	Shirley Joanne	235	235
Baldwin	Vada	300	
Bangerter	Verna Lorna		160
Banhart	Kenneth		309
Bannon	Cora		154
Barklund	Ramon		310
Barnett	Clay		240
Barrett	Anne Elizabeth		203
Bartell	Lorraine		131
Bartocci	Paul Louis		190
Barton	Edward		283
Bashaw	Roena		133
Basil	Deloris Jean	109	
Basil	John		109
Basinger	James		306
Bassinger	James	306	
Batterbee	Ashley Marie	187	
Batterbee	Katherine Paige	187	
Batterbee	Michael Arnold		187
Baumgartner	Francis		282
Baumgartner	Howard Steven		240
Baumgartner	Michael Paul	240	
Baumgartner	Rebekah Clare	240	
Baumgartner	Steven Douglas	240	
Baylor	David Leslie		144
Baylor	Jonathan Michael	144	
Baylor	Rebecca Jean	144	
Baylor	Sharon Marie	144	
Beal	Rosetta		209
Beard	William J.		279
Beaver	Brian		301
Beaver	Melony	301	
Bechtle	Eliza Jane		223
Beckeman	Eric Byrman		205
Bell	David Patrick		218
Bell	Debra Sue		212
Bell	Florence Elma	267	267
Bell	Joyce Pauline	267	267
Bell	Margaret		192
Bell	Nicole Marie	218	
Bell	Walter William		267

Bell	William Walter	267	
Bemis	Harry C.	192	
Bemis	Helen T.	192	
Bemis	John C.		192
Bemis	Marion E.	192	192
Bennett	Carrie Elizabeth		130
Bennett	Nancy J.		322
Bennington	Judith Kay		137
Bentley	Deborah Jeanne		268
Berkompas	Linda		186
Berrdine	James		255
Berringer	Beatrice Lorinda		147
Berry	-----		150
Berry	Carl	303	
Berry	Ila	303	
Berry	Jerry	303	
Berry	Joe	303	
Berry	Wanna Lee	303	
Berry	William A.		303
Berry	Wilma	303	
Best	Darren Michael	231	
Best	Harold A.		165
Best	Kevin Randall	231	
Best	Teresa Lea	231	
Best	Terry		231
Bevington	Florence		198
Bickel	Mildred Beers		123
Bickel	Mildred Elizabeth		126
Bilesimo	David		262
Bilesimo	Michael Allen	262	
Bilesimo	Toni Ann	262	
Bingham	Thomas		327
Binkley	[son]	110	
Binkley	Joseph		110
Binkley	Suzanne	110	
Bird	Kate		155
Bisang	Janette Renee		234
Bishop	-----		129
Black	Will		184
Blake	Steve Lee		136
Blaylock	Pearl Evedna		289
Blazic	Adam Lee	235	
Blazic	Amy Lynn	235	
Blazic	Gerald Lee		235
Blazic	Jonathan Rudy	235	
Blevins	Melissa Dawn		304
Blizzard	Dorothy Lucille		196
Bloomquist	Gary Stewart	126	
Bloomquist	Jean Elizabeth	126	126
Bloomquist	Michael Ray	126	
Bloomquist	Robert Leslie		126
Bloomquist	Robert Leslie	126	126
Bloomquist	Shannon Marie	126	
Bloomquist	Valentine	126	
Boatman	Alvin Taylor		235
Boatman	Janice Rae	235	235
Boatman	Kathryn Kay	235	235
Boatman	Patricia Louise	235	235
Bodey	Laura Ann		241
Boeber	Clara		165
Boggs	Ramona Rae		237
Bolas	David Justin	191	
Bolas	Donald M.		191
Bolin	Deborah		326
Bonfonte	Margaret Mary		325
Bordelon	John Wayne		137
Bordelon	Samantha Marie	137	
Bordelon	Shantel Marie	137	
Bordonaro	Cosmo Charles		145
Bordonaro	Mary Ann	145	145
Bordonaro	Sharon Lynn	145	145
Borland	Andrew A.		170
Borland	Andrew Charles	170	170
Borland	Anthony Mega	170	
Borland	Gerald Canon	170	170
Borland	Gina Mega	170	
Borland	Kermit Marshall	170	171
Borland	Margaret Eleanor	170	171
Borland	Margaret Jane	170	171
Borland	Neil Carlos	171	
Bottlemy	Bryan M.	282	
Bottlemy	Greg		282
Bottlemy	Nicklass	282	
Boudiette	Carey		145
Bower	Catherine Dorey		209
Bowers	Anna Grace		270
Bowers	Samuel E.		194
Bowman	Cheryl Lynn	266	266
Bowman	David Adrian, Jr.		266
Bowman	Denise Ann	266	
Bowman	Dorothy Jean	288	288
Bowman	Douglas Brian	266	266
Bowman	Edward Roy		288
Boyd	Barbra	114	
Boyd	Donald	114	
Boyd	Eva	195	
Boyd	Gladys Elwain	113	114
Boyd	Hiram Elmer		195
Boyd	Joan	114	114
Boyd	John		113
Boyd	Linda Lou	114	
Boyd	Meredith Ann	114	
Boyd	Raymond DeWitt	113	114
Boyd	Russell Garner	113	114
Boyea	Douglas Paul, Jr.		240
Boyea	Keith	240	
Boyea	Luke	240	
Boyer	Carol Beth		268
Boyles	George Richard	146	146
Boyles	Jessica Renea	146	
Boyles	John Robert	146	
Boyles	John T.		146
[Boyles]	Diane Pearl		146
Bradson	Clara		254
Brandow	Connie Jean		239
Braun	Daniel Otto	298	298
Braun	David Joseph	298	
Braun	Debra Lynn	298	298
Braun	Robert John		298
Braun	Robert John	298	
Breckinridge	H.		224
Breckinridge	Ruby	224	224
Brewer	Daniel Lewis	308	309
Brewer	Denise LaCole	309	
Brewer	Dennis James	308	309
Brewer	Elaine Lee	309	
Brewer	Jeri Vondale	308	
Brewer	Jerry Lee Morgan	309	
Brewer	Jerry V.		308
Brewer	Jeryd Daniel	309	
Brewer	Lora Teresa	308	309
Bricker	Daniel Calvin	265	
Bricker	David W.		265
Bricker	Matthew David	265	
Brook	Sharon		122
Brooks	Paul Philip		292
Broomall	Dorothy Laverne	271	271
Broomall	Jesse		271
Broomall	Norris Mark	271	271
Brown	Barbara Grace		291
Brown	Courtney Marie	218	
Brown	David	223	
Brown	Donald R., Jr.		226
Brown	Emily Amelia	226	
Brown	George Edward	223	
Brown	George Washington		223
Brown	James Lester	223	
Brown	Jessie LaVerne	223	223
Brown	Kimberly Jean	145	
Brown	Oliver William	223	
Brown	Robert Wilson		145
Brown	Terry Joe		218
Brown	Wayne Hall	145	145
Browne	Martha		322
Brubaker	Janice Ann		272
Brunett	Mitchell Arthur	125	
Brunett	Timothy Edward		125
Bryant	Roxy C.		326
Buchanan	Amy Sue	123	
Buchanan	[child]	123	
Buchanan	Daniel J.		123
Buckingham	Margaret Verna		313

Bucklad	Carl Francis	116
Bucklad	Carley Marie	116
Bucklad	Jeremy Allen	116
Bucklad	Katy Elizabeth	116
Bucklad	Mark Steven	116
Bucklad	Matthew Alan	116 116
[Bucklad]	Mary	116
Buckler	Darrell Wayne	239 239
Buckler	Durward Preston	239
Buckler	Hana Kalani	239
Buckler	Melvin Douglas	239 239
Buckler	Pamela Dawn	239
Buckler	Terry Lynn	239 239
Buckler	Timothy Wayne	239
Buckler	Toni Lanatte	239
Buis	Robert	271
Bunch	Bobbie Jo	227
Bundy	June Erwin	198
Bundy	Raymond	198
Burbo	Linda Marie	190
Burge	Charles Raymond	177
Burge	Daisy Inez	177
Burge	Grace Valentine	177 177
Burge	James William	177
Burge	Marjorie Lou	177
Burge	Oka Dot	177
Burge	Vannie G.	177
Burke	Karen Elizabeth	165
Burke	Roger Ames	165
Burke	Roger Joseph	165
Burkett	M. M., Sr.	227
Burkholder	Ella Nora	213
Burt	[child]	219
Burt	David Henderson	219 219
Burt	Evan Whiteside	219
Burt	John Warren	219
Burt	Warren Brooker	219
Burton	Martha Ann	157
Butler	Deborah Darlene	303
Butler	James	131
Butler	Joshua	131
Butler	William E.	131
Butt	John	227
Butt	John W.	227
Butterfield	Nancy Queen	121
Byler	Benjamin	265
Byler	Hal	265
Byler	Peter John	265
Caine	Jack	298
Caine	Joseph M.	298
Caine	Lawrence	298
Caine	Thomas	298
Campbell	Darrel Lee	221
Campbell	Kari Lynn	221
Campbell	Kelly Ann	221
Campbell	Meighan Elizabeth	135
Campbell	Ronald Lee	135
Campbell	Ryan Lee	221
Canney	Mabel	150
Canon	Carrie Irene	169 170
Canon	Claude Ira	169
Canon	Jessie E.	169 170
Canon	John C.	169
Canon	Mabel E.	169 171
Canon	Raymie Elizabeth	169 172
Canon	Ruth Zahnise	169 172
Cansler	Amber Corcelles	212
Cansler	Grant Carlton	212
Cansler	Joel Ethan	212 212
Cansler	Loman D.	212
Cansler	Myra Annette	212 212
Cansler	Philip Trent	212 212
Cansler-Kipp	Mackenzie Devon	212
Cansler-Kipp	Zachary Adam	212
Capritz	Alice Emma	257 260
Capritz	Anna Catherine	257 258
Capritz	Gertrude	257 257
Capritz	Gertrude Agnes	257 263
Capritz	Harry George	257 257
Capritz	John	257 257
Capritz	John F.	257
Capritz	John Henry	257 260
Capritz	Rose Marie	257 262
Capritz	[son]	257
[Capritz]	Tensie	260
Carberry	Adelaide	133
Cardinelli	Donald Anthony	218
Cardinelli	Thomas Anthony	218
Carey	Lucinda Jean	140
Carlson	Charlene Marie	205
Carnahan	Adam	152
Carnahan	Adam	184
Carnahan	Adam Jr.	152 156
Carnahan	Adolphus	175
Carnahan	Amber Lee	159
Carnahan	Annette	158
Carnahan	Brenda	158
Carnahan	Buchanan Hanna	153 154
Carnahan	Caitlin Marie	159
Carnahan	Carl Jeffrey	159 159
Carnahan	Carla	158 158
Carnahan	Carlos	156 156
Carnahan	Carlos Blaine	157 158
Carnahan	Carlos Burton	157 157
Carnahan	Cassius Shields	153 155
Carnahan	Charles B.	175
Carnahan	Christine Dawn	159
Carnahan	Christopher Neil	160
Carnahan	Christopher Paul	154
Carnahan	Clara Priscilla	158
Carnahan	Clayton Patrick	159 159
Carnahan	Cleo Clinton	156 156
Carnahan	Cory Glenn	159
Carnahan	Crystal	158
Carnahan	Curtis Gregory	159 159
Carnahan	[daughter]	152
Carnahan	David	160
Carnahan	Debbie	160
Carnahan	Elizabeth	152 155
Carnahan	Elizabeth	184
Carnahan	Elmira	153 155
Carnahan	Evan Vela	159
Carnahan	Florence I.	155
Carnahan	George	175
Carnahan	Glenn Frank	157 159
Carnahan	Howard	154 154
Carnahan	Hugh	176
Carnahan	Idoletta	153
Carnahan	James M.	154 154
Carnahan	James M.	184
Carnahan	James Madison	152 153
Carnahan	James T.	153 155
Carnahan	Jeannie	158 158
Carnahan	John	152 175
Carnahan	John A.	175 175
Carnahan	John M.	176 176
Carnahan	John Milton	153 155
Carnahan	Karen	158 158
Carnahan	Kathleen	158
Carnahan	Kyle	158
Carnahan	Lacey G.	153 154
Carnahan	Lafayette Adam	156 156
Carnahan	Lafayette Earnest	156 157
Carnahan	Lafayette Kerr	176 176
Carnahan	Leo D.	155
Carnahan	LeRoy	184
Carnahan	Lewis Clare	155
Carnahan	Lola Venice	157
Carnahan	Lynn	158
Carnahan	Margaret	152 152
Carnahan	Margaret	184
Carnahan	Margorie Lee	158
Carnahan	Maria	152 153
Carnahan	Marion	154
Carnahan	Marion Carlos	156 157
Carnahan	Mary	176
Carnahan	Mary Jane	153 154
Carnahan	Mary M.	155 155
Carnahan	Melissa	184
Carnahan	Melvina	153 154
Carnahan	Merna Carlyn	157 159

Carnahan	Myrtle	176		Caryer	Carl James	119		Christie	Daisy	155	
Carnahan	Naldene Rose	157	160	Caryer	Carol Catherine	118		Christie	David	155	
Carnahan	Nancy	152	152	Caryer	[daughter 1	118		Church	James Matthew		288
Carnahan	Nettie G.	154	154	Caryer	[daughter 2	118		Church	Zachary Wallace	288	
Carnahan	Nicholas Andrew	159		Caryer	Phyllis	118	119	Ciummo	Cynthia Mary Tina	205	
Carnahan	Orvil Leon	157	157	Caryer	Robert		118	Clark	Benjamin Franklin		116
Carnahan	Orvil William	156	157	Caryer	Robert	118	119	Clark	Charles		323
Carnahan	Orville Darrell	157	158	Caryer	Ruth	118	119	Clark	Charles	323	323
Carnahan	Orville Darrell	158	158	Case	Ron		221	Clark	Daniel Mark	324	
Carnahan	Otis O.	153	155	Caskey	Elizabeth Lauren	219		Clark	David	323	324
Carnahan	Paul Carlos	158		Caskey	Lott Edward	219		Clark	David Michael	324	
Carnahan	Rita	156	157	Caskey	Wayne Joseph		219	Clark	Diane Margaret	324	
Carnahan	Roma Jean	156	157	Cassilly	Thomas C.		273	Clark	Elliott Neal	212	
Carnahan	Rosanna	153		Cavener	Phyllis Lou		309	Clark	Gary	323	
Carnahan	Rosanna	184		Cellar	Calvin M.		201	Clark	Greyser James	212	
Carnahan	Rosemary	158		Cellar	Catherine	201	201	Clark	Howard Raymond		211
Carnahan	Rulan Marion	157	160	Chaban	Larry		259	Clark	Isiah		311
Carnahan	Ruth	152	161	Chambers	Catherine C.	245	245	Clark	James Allen	211	212
Carnahan	Ruth Ann	153		Chambers	Dora	245	245	Clark	Jason Walter	116	
Carnahan	Samuel I.	155		Chambers	Dora	245	246	Clark	Judith Lee	196	
Carnahan	Steve	160		Chambers	Elizabeth	245		Clark	Linda Mae		114
Carnahan	Tamara	159	159	Chambers	John		245	Clark	Marguerite Florence		293
Carnahan	Teresa	160		Chambers	John	245		Clark	Mary Lucinda	117	117
Carnahan	Tyson Alexander	159		Chambers	John M.	245		Clark	Naomi Grace	117	118
Carnahan	Vicnelia	156	156	Chambers	Josiah	245	245	Clark	Neil Kent	211	212
Carnahan	Wanda Mary	157	157	Chambers	Margaret M.	245	245	Clark	Nettie Esther		188
Carnahan	William	152	176	Chambers	Martha	245	245	Clark	Patricia	323	
Carnahan	William	154	154	Chambers	Martha	245		Clark	Richard		117
Carnahan	William	184		Chambers	Nancy	245	246	Clark	Richard Lee		196
Carnahan	Winfield	175		Chambers	William	245		Clark	Richard Lee, Jr.	196	
[Carnahan]	-----		157	Chambers	William B.	245		Clark	Ryan Douglas	116	
[Carnahan]	Belle		175	[Chambers]	Mary		245	Clark	Steven Lee	211	
[Carnahan]	Cynthia A.		176	Chapman	Alfred		201	Clark	William		178
[Carnahan]	Eleanor		176	Chapman	Alfred McCrae	201		[Clark]	-----		324
[Carnahan]	Sarah Ann		175	Chatley	Donald Paul	123	123	[Clark]	-----		323
Carpenter	Carolyn Ann	171	171	Chatley	Edward R.	123		Classen	Rebecca		292
Carpenter	Chandra	215		Chatley	Errett Clyde	122		Clawson	Caroline Elmira		268
Carpenter	David R.	171	172	Chatley	Herbert Dale	122	123	Cleland	J. J.		143
Carpenter	Gary Lee	215	216	Chatley	Leon	122		Clemons	John C.		200
Carpenter	Gary Noel	216		Chatley	Linda	123		Cline	Doris Ellen		242
Carpenter	Janet M.	171	172	Chatley	Marian Delores	122	123	Clum	Amy Claire	117	
Carpenter	Lois		271	Chatley	Nancy Lee	123	123	Clum	Brian Curtis	117	
Carpenter	Micah Vincent	215		Chatley	Shirley Dianne	122		Clum	Gerald		117
Carpenter	Michael Alan	215	215	Chatley	Wallace Jerome		122	Clum	Sara Beth	117	
Carpenter	Michaela Katharine	215		Chowning	Anna Belle	224	224	Clum	Scott Charles	117	
Carpenter	Noel V.		215	Chowning	Eva	224		Clum	Spencer Ray	117	
Carpenter	Reynold L.		171	Chowning	Harry	224		Cockrell	Ada G.	264	264
Carr	Deborah		171	Chowning	Robert		224	Cockrell	John F.		264
Carr	Elizabeth		208	Christ	Clifford	254	254	Coen	Marilyn		318
Carrigan	Kathleen		182	Christ	Jason	254		Coffey	Bessie		140
Carson	Alice		241	Christ	Joseph		254	Coffield	Cheryl Diane		293
Carson	John		310	Christ	Leslie	254		Colella	Barbara Szokoly		205
Carter	Daisy Ora		231	Christ]	-----		254	Coleman	Alice Cecilia		257
Caryer	Bernice	118	119	Christie	Charles		155	Collins	Cathy		146

Collins	Jacqueline		273
Collins	James Ronald	280	
Collins	Ralph Aloysius, Sr.	280	
Collins	Ralph Aloysius, Jr.	280	
Collins	Vickie Rose	280	
Collins	Walter William	280	
Conley	Ellen		252
Connell	Sharon Loretta		191
Connett	Ralph		319
Converse	Mary Jane		156
Cook	Amelia Marilla		226
Cook	Carey Williamson		222
Cook	Samuel Verner	222	
Cooke	Donald Cyril		285
Cooke	Jeanette Ruth	285	285
Cooke	Lois Marie	285	286
Cooper	Janet	306	
Cooper	Lonnie		306
Cooper	Rusty Alan	306	
Cooper	Shelly	306	
Cooper	Tammy Diane	306	
Cooper	Wendy	306	
Cooper	William		282
Cooper	William Murray		318
Cope	Barry	262	
Cope	Brandy	262	
Cope	Brian	262	
Cope	Kenneth Arthur		293
Cope	Wendy Louellen	293	
Cope	William		262
Corbin	Benjamin		213
Corbin	Eva L.	213	
Corbin	George E.	213	
Corbin	Laverna	213	
Corbin	Mary E.	213	213
Corbin	Nellie F.	213	
Corbin	Ora B.	213	
Corbin	Ralph H.	213	
Corley	Jean Irene		115
Cornatzer	Letty		225
Cornfelt	-----		111
Cornwell	Christine Carol		162
Cortinovis	Pamela		142
Cortright	Michael		127
Cote	Michael A.		162
Cotner	Lola Olive		112
Cottrell	Candace	325	
Cottrell	Harold		325
Cottrell	Sue	325	
Coulson	Melinda		154
Coulson	Permelia		153
Cox	Catheryn Rebecca	172	172
Cox	Eleanor	172	
Cox	Mable Louise	172	172
Cox	Pearson Wayne	172	
Cox	Pearson		172
Cox	Ronald Eugene	172	
Cox	Roscoe Calvin	172	172
Crabtree	Butch		269
Craig	Alice	109	
Craig	Alvin B.	246	
Craig	Dale	109	
Craig	Ella M.	246	
Craig	Geneva		247
Craig	Grethel	109	
Craig	Irene	109	
Craig	James H.	246	
Craig	Joseph		246
Craig	Lloyd	109	
Craig	Margaret D.	246	
Craig	Ramsy	246	
Craig	Raymond	109	
Craig	Robert	109	
Craig	Rolla		109
Craighead	Isabella		327
Craven	Francis Sanderson		267
Crawford	Arthur		110
Crawford	Brooke Anne	110	
Crawford	Catherine Ruth		316
Crawford	Daniel Joseph	110	
Crawford	David James	110	
Crawford	Debra Kay	110	110
Crawford	Douglas Jon	110	
Crawford	Edgar R.	322	
Crawford	Gary Arthur	110	110
Crawford	Glen Alan	110	110
Crawford	Jacqueline	110	110
Crawford	James W.	312	
Crawford	Leah L.	312	
Crawford	Nellie V.	312	
Crawford	Oliver E.	312	
Crawford	Scott Jeffrey	110	110
Crawford	Theodore		322
Crawford	Wallace B.	312	
Crawford	Walter S.		312
Crawford	William W.	312	
Cress	Cheryl Elizabeth	178	179
Cress	Leighton Edward		178
Cress	Leighton Edward, Jr.	178	178
Crews	Carolyn		281
Criswell	Andrew	207	
Criswell	Andrew McElwain	207	207
Criswell	Elizabeth	207	
Criswell	Henrietta	207	
Criswell	Henry C.	207	
Criswell	Jane	207	
Criswell	John	207	207
Criswell	John R.	207	
Criswell	Julia K.	207	
Criswell	Robert		207
Criswell	Robert	207	
Criswell	Robert	207	
Criswell	Robert W.	207	
[Criswell]	Louisa		207
[Criswell]	Susan		207
Crooks	T. M.		247
Cross	Alan Ray	226	226
Cross	Caitlin Noel	226	
Cross	Emily Alice	225	225
Cross	Gordon Cooper	225	226
Cross	John Milton		225
Cross	Letty Jean	225	
Cross	Linda May	226	226
Crouch	Alexander	251	251
Crouch	Alphonso	250	
Crouch	Andrew	251	
Crouch	Anna May	250	
Crouch	Anne S.	250	
Crouch	Annie	250	
Crouch	Cooley Samuel	252	
Crouch	Daniel O.	250	252
Crouch	Daniel Ogden	251	252
Crouch	Eleanor	251	
Crouch	Eliza	250	
Crouch	Elizabeth	250	
Crouch	Elizabeth	252	
Crouch	Elizabeth A.	251	
Crouch	Ellen H.	250	
Crouch	Fern D.	252	
Crouch	Florence	250	
Crouch	Frances [?] C.	252	
Crouch	Frank Jr.	252	
Crouch	George	250	250
Crouch	George	252	
Crouch	George P.	252	
Crouch	Greta V.	252	252
Crouch	Harmon	250	
Crouch	Harriet	251	
Crouch	Harriet	252	
Crouch	Isaiah	250	
Crouch	James B.	251	
Crouch	John		244
Crouch	John	250	250
Crouch	John	250	251
Crouch	John	251	251
Crouch	John M.	252	
Crouch	Joseph	250	251
Crouch	Joseph M.	252	
Crouch	Joseph R.	252	
Crouch	Josiah B.	250	
Crouch	Laura Bell	250	
Crouch	Laura C.	252	

Surname	Given	Col A	Col B
Crouch	Linn [?]	251	
Crouch	Mary	250	
Crouch	Mary	250	
Crouch	Mary E.	252	
Crouch	Mary M.	251	
Crouch	Nancy	252	
Crouch	Nancy L.	251	
Crouch	Rachel C.	250	
Crouch	Robert	250	251
Crouch	Robert	251	
Crouch	Robert C.	250	
Crouch	Ruth	250	
Crouch	Ruth D.	252	
Crouch	Wallace Hunter	251	251
Crouch	Watson	250	
Crouch	William		250
Crouch	William	250	
Crouch	William	250	
Crouch	William	250	252
Crouch	William H.	250	250
Crouch	William H.	250	
[Crouch]	-----		250
[Crouch]	Anne		251
[Crouch]	Frances B.		251
[Crouch]	Hannah		250
[Crouch]	Isabel		250
[Crouch]	Margie C.		252
[Crouch]	Martha		251
[Crouch]	Mary		251
[Crouch]	Mary M.		251
[Crouch]	Sarah P.		251
Cullen	Caroline	197	
Cullen	Joseph F.		197
Cullen	Michael William	197	
Cullen	Robert Dean	197	
Cullen	Thomas Bruce	197	
Cunigan	Lisa Michelle		137
Cunningham	Annie May	195	196
Cunningham	Barbara Ann	196	196
Cunningham	Bruce Tracy	195	196
Cunningham	Bruce Tracy	196	197
Cunningham	Bruce Tracy, III	197	
Cunningham	Dorothy Ellen	196	196
Cunningham	George Oliver	195	198
Cunningham	George III	198	
Cunningham	Gladys May	196	197
Cunningham	June Erwin	196	197
Cunningham	June Erwin	195	198
Cunningham	Katherine Erwin	195	197
Cunningham	Lois May	196	196
Cunningham	Mary Ellen	195	196
Cunningham	Mary Jane	196	196
Cunningham	Miriam Ruth	197	
Cunningham	Samuel Roberts		195
Cunningham	Samuel R., Jr.	195	196
Cunningham	Sarah Lawson	195	198
Curnow	-----		317
Curnow	Christopher John	317	
Curren	Lydia		327
Curry	Emma		273
Custer	James Scott		130
D'Addio	Daniel F.		163
D'Addio	Francesca Camilla	163	
Dahm	Deidre	279	279
Dahm	Geoffrey Allen	279	
Dahm	George Paul	279	279
Dahm	Julie Sharon	279	279
Dahm	Margaret Miriam	279	
Dahm	Paul Emil		279
Dailey	Edward		330
Dalton	Joanna Marie	281	
Dalton	Joshua Dale	281	
Damrill	Lois Darlene		304
Damrill	Lois Darlene	308	309
Damrill	Lora Juanita	308	308
Damrill	Ralph E.		308
Damrill	Ralph E.		309
Daque	Minnie		312
Darcy	Lewis		131
Darst	Margaret		321
Dart	Harry		223
Dascomb	Arthur S.		166
Dascomb	Edmund Brooke	166	
Dash	William		257
Daugherty	Vicki		306
Davenport	Gabriel Joseph	235	
Davenport	Harold Dwayne		235
Davenport	Michael Charles	235	
David	Jenny Jane		302
Davidson	Eleanor	330	330
Davidson	George	330	
Davidson	James		319
Davidson	John	330	
Davidson	Margaret	330	
Davidson	Margery Ellen	330	330
Davidson	Mary Ann	330	
Davidson	Matthew	330	
Davidson	Samuel		330
Davidson	Samuel	330	
Davidson	William Thompson	330	
Davis	[infant]	185	
Davis	Alea Joe	291	
Davis	Andrew Thompson	185	185
Davis	Bessie Jeanette	185	186
Davis	Betty Lou	190	191
Davis	Cora Olive	185	192
Davis	David		185
Davis	Donald Page	185	191
Davis	Dorothea Lovenia	191	191
Davis	Emma	185	192
Davis	Georgia Jean		290
Davis	Greg		291
Davis	Herschel J.		166
Davis	Leslie Ray		215
Davis	Lucinda B.	185	185
Davis	Mary Jane	185	185
Davis	Mary Virginia	190	
Davis	Robert John	185	190
Davis	Robert John, Jr.	190	
Davis	Robyn		162
Davis	Scott Duane		160
Davis	Sophia D.		111
Davis	Timothy Ray	215	
Davis	Tyler William	291	
Deason	Helen Agnes		156
Deaville	John T.		296
Deem	Mark		137
Deem	Patricia Lynn	137	137
Deemer	Betty Ann	196	
Deemer	James		167
Deemer	Lester Earl		196
Deemer	Robert Erwin	196	
Deeter	Andrew	327	
Deeter	Charles	327	
Deeter	Clara A.	327	
Deeter	Daniel		327
Deeter	George W.	327	328
Deeter	Lucy	327	
Deeter	Magee	327	
Deeter	Maggie	328	328
Deeter	William R.	327	
[Deeter]	Fannie A.		328
DeFelice	Deanna		261
Del Bianco	Ashley Danielle	262	
Del Bianco	Daniel		262
Dell	Michelle Marie		291
DeMarco	Bruce Lee		191
DeMarco	Eric Lee	191	
Dent	Philip		175
Dent	Philip M.	175	
Denton	Margaret Gibbs		279
Detagle y Lozano	Mary Lou S.		226
Detwiler	Norma		273
DiBardeleben	Diane		258
Dicroce	Sheila Marie		259
Dieter	Alice Carol		325
Dill	Catherine A.	246	
Dill	John		246
Dilley	Mary L.		176
Dilley	Mathias		120
Dillon	Harry		216
Dillon	Janet Lynn	216	

Dingle	Patricia Ann		281
Dinning	Elizabeth		258
Dinsmore	Aletha H.	249	
Dinsmore	Androse T.	248	249
Dinsmore	Bettie	248	
Dinsmore	Chester	248	
Dinsmore	Delsa L.	249	249
Dinsmore	Florence Hope	248	249
Dinsmore	Frank A.	248	249
Dinsmore	Gray	249	
Dinsmore	Josiah G.	248	248
Dinsmore	Katie	248	248
Dinsmore	Lenore L.	249	
Dinsmore	Lester R.	249	
Dinsmore	Lloyd	248	248
Dinsmore	Lottie	248	
Dinsmore	May	248	249
Dinsmore	Odessa B.	248	249
Dinsmore	Robert A.	248	248
Dinsmore	Robie	248	
Dinsmore	Ward	248	
Dinsmore	William		248
Dinsmore	William	248	249
Dinsmore	William B.	248	248
Dinsmore	William B.	249	
[Dinsmore]	Adeline J.		248
Dirmeyer	Elizabeth		116
Dix	Debra Jean	119	
Dix	Lonetta Ray	119	
Dix	Roger		119
Dix	Roger Lee	119	
Dixon	David		157
Dobkowski	Joshua Francis	293	
Dobkowski	Marc Edward		293
Dobson	Aaron	239	
Dobson	Marsha Faye Brooks	239	
Donati	Benedict William, II		159
Donati	Benedict William, III	159	
Donnan	Alexander McIlvaine	317	
Donnan	Alvin Ewing	317	317
Donnan	Brendan John	317	
Donnan	Dorothy Griffith	317	317
Donnan	John		317
Donnan	Sarah Sloan	317	
[Donnan]	-----		190
Dorr	Frederick Fortson		289
Dosenberry	Ethel Janet		188
Dost	Lawrence Adam	191	
Dost	Lawrence Edward		191
Dost	Lisa Jane	191	
Douglas	Charles E.		192
Douglas	Flossye S.		282
Dowding	Jenny Kay	238	238
Dowding	Ruth Ann	238	
Dowding	Willard Paul Jr.		238
Dowty	Gary Joe		243
Drain	Jason Matthew	138	
Drain	Nathaniel Scott	138	
Drain	Racheal Dawn		
Drain	Robin Dale		138
Drain	Thomas Dale	138	
Driver	[son]	118	
Driver	Arlene	118	120
Driver	Avery M.	118	119
Driver	David Henry		118
Driver	Judith Ann	119	
Driver	Nancy Sue	119	
Driver	Rollie C.	118	
Driver	Rollie S.	119	
Driver	Ruby Ethel	118	120
Driver	Russell E.	119	
Driver	Treva Alma	118	118
Driver	Wava Marie	118	119
Drury	Alice	319	
Drury	Anne	319	319
Drury	Kathryn Annabell		234
Drury	Laura	319	
Drury	Lillian	319	
Drury	Louise Jane	319	319
Drury	Robert McIlvaine	319	319
Drury	Thomas	319	319
Drury	William		319
Drysdale	Louise		272
Dugger	Betty Jo		309
Duncan	Darren	307	
Duncan	Darrol		307
Duncan	Donnie	307	
Duncan	Johnnie	307	
Duncan	Malissa Ann	307	
Duncan	Ronnie	307	
Dunham	Keith		255
Dunlap	Alexander		280
Dunlap	Bonnie Laura	286	288
Dunlap	Christopher Loren	289	
Dunlap	Duane Charles	288	289
Dunlap	Earl Alexander	280	281
Dunlap	Elden Wayne	286	288
Dunlap	Estella Irene	286	289
Dunlap	Harriet Janette	280	281
Dunlap	Heidi Lynn	289	
Dunlap	Ian Charles	289	
Dunlap	Ida Isabel	280	280
Dunlap	Ina Grace	286	286
Dunlap	James Crosby	280	280
Dunlap	Jerry Wayne	288	289
Dunlap	John McIlvaine	280	280
Dunlap	Jory Patrick	289	
Dunlap	Laura	280	296
Dunlap	Mark	281	
Dunlap	Mary Estelle	280	289
Dunlap	Mary Ina	280	280
Dunlap	Nancy Gayle	288	289
Dunlap	Oliver C.	280	
Dunlap	Raymond	280	
Dunlap	Richard	281	
Dunlap	Richard Earl	281	281
Dunlap	Virginia Ann	281	
Dunlap	Wallace Elwood	286	288
Dunlap	Wallace Lafayette	280	286
Dunlap	William Earl	281	281
[Dunlap]	Cella		280
[Dunlap]	Nelda		288
Dunn	Myrna Ann		214
Duparc	Helene Boulley		197
Dutko	Michael Francis		122
Dwars	Milo		283
Dwyer	Joseph Charles		145
Dwyer	Rachel Ann	145	
Earnshaw	Anna Jane		225
Eaton	Mark		259
Eddy	Bertha A.		299
Edmiston	Abigail Lynne	148	
Edmiston	Benjamin Richard	149	
Edmiston	Chester Leroy		147
Edmiston	Corrin Jo	148	
Edmiston	Dale Ann	147	149
Edmiston	Elizabeth Ann	147	148
Edmiston	Evelyn Mae	147	147
Edmiston	Janet Lynn	147	147
Edmiston	Jenny Marie	148	
Edmiston	John Howard	147	148
Edmiston	Joshua Robert	148	
Edmiston	Kimberly Lynn	148	
Edmiston	Logan John	148	
Edmiston	Marilyn Jean	147	149
Edmiston	Matthew Michael	149	
Edmiston	Patricia Joan	147	148
Edmiston	Richard Bruce	147	149
Edmiston	Robert Carl	147	148
Edmiston	Sandra May	148	
Edmiston	Sarah Elizabeth	148	
Edmiston	Suanne Elaine	148	
Edmiston	Sue Ellen	147	
Edmiston	William David	147	148
Edwards	Jerry	170	
Edwards	Lowell S.		170
Ege	Christine Carol		272
Einspahr	Clayton Gregory	219	
Einspahr	Matthew Warren	219	
Einspahr	Ronald Kent		219
Elisar	Kyle		137
Elisar	Zachary Michael	137	
Ellis	Evangela		307

Ellis	Marjorie		197
Emad	Jamal		164
Emad	Jeffrey Sharif	164	
Emad	Linda Shorhreh	164	
Emad	Paul Reza	164	
Emery	Alice Anne	141	141
Emery	Amanda Rae	141	
Emery	Arden McElwain	141	142
Emery	Daniel Eric	142	
Emery	David Arden	142	143
Emery	Jacob Estes	142	
Emery	Janis Marie	142	
Emery	Jessica Ann	141	
Emery	Jill Elizabeth	142	
Emery	John Lawrence	141	
Emery	Linda Graham	142	
Emery	Michael Dymock	143	
Emery	Raymen Forrest	141	141
Emery	Raymen Graham		141
Emery	Raymen Lewis	141	141
Emery	Robert William	141	142
Emery	William George	142	142
Emery	William Reaney	141	142
Endam	-----		324
Ensign	-----		224
Erickson	Andrew Jay	133	
Erickson	George Thomas		133
Erickson	Lissa Aylene	133	
Ermlich	Florence		257
Ervin	[child]	194	081
Ervin	[twin 1]	194	
Ervin	[twin 2]	194	
Ervin	Alice	199	
Ervin	Annie May	195	195
Ervin	Catherine Poe	199	
Ervin	Charles Shannon	194	194
Ervin	Clyde	199	
Ervin	Edward Eaton B.	195	
Ervin	Elizabeth Maria	194	195
Ervin	Ellen Whalley	194	194
Ervin	Esther M.		138
Ervin	Frank H.	199	199
Ervin	Henry Bard	194	
Ervin	James Bard		194
Ervin	James Bard, Jr.	194	194
Ervin	Jane Emily	194	194
Ervin	Jane Mary	194	198
Ervin	John Dickson	195	
Ervin	John Richard	194	
Ervin	Joseph McFarland	194	
Ervin	June Tracy	195	198
Ervin	Katherine	194	
Ervin	Katherine Bruce	195	195
Ervin	Lucille Wilson	199	199
Erwin	Mary Belle	199	199
Erwin	Minnie Bell	194	194
Erwin	Rachel E.	194	
Erwin	Richard Bard	199	
Erwin	Robert McElwain	194	195
Erwin	Robert McElwain	194	
Erwin	Robert McElwain, Jr.	195	198
Erwin	Sarah Belle	194	199
Erwin	Scott Ward	199	199
Erwin	Thomas McElwain	194	199
Erwin	Walter Tracy	195	
Erwin	Wenzel W.	194	
Erwin	William Kingsley	195	
Erwin	William T.	199	
[Erwin]	Kathryn		199
Eschbach	Harold		119
Eschbach	Larry Lynn	119	
Eschbach	Linda Mae	119	
Eschbach	Marianne	119	
Eschbach	Ronald Dean	119	
Eselgroth	Constance Dawn		229
Etheridge	David Ellis	216	216
Etheridge	Ellis F.		216
Etheridge	Janet Lynn	216	216
Etheridge	Ross Lane	216	
Etheridge	Scott David	216	
Etheridge	Suzanna Lynn	216	
Evans	Anora Amanda	158	
Evans	Kevin Hyde		158
Evans	Morgan Carnahan	158	
Evansek	Fran Noreen		292
Ewing	Charles E.	270	
Ewing	Cloyd E.	270	
Ewing	Edgar		270
Ewing	Edgar Clair	270	
Ewing	Sumner	270	
Exrott	Rose		260
Ezell	Barbara		307
Failor	Susanna		208
Fairchild	Kelly		301
Fall	Ann C.	281	281
Fall	Francis Elbert		280
Fall	Francis M.	280	281
Fall	Mack Dunlap	280	281
Fall	Robert A.	281	281
Fanelli	Salvatore A.		203
Fanelli	Staci Ann	203	
Faria	Benjamin Hollis	165	
Faria	Tyler John	165	
Faria	Walter John		164
Farina	Bert		326
Farnoff	Mary Rosalind		126
Farrah	Mary		149
Farrell	Cullen		148
Farrington	-----		248
Favret	Charles Arnold	325	326
Favret	[child]	325	
Favret	David Mark	325	
Favret	Jacklyn Christine	326	
Favret	Jacob Charles	326	
Favret	James Louis		325
Favret	James Louis, Jr.	325	325
Favret	John Michael	325	325
Favret	Kyla Marie	325	
Favret	Leah Nicole	325	
Favret	Mariann Patricia	325	325
Favret	Mark Edward	325	198
Favret	Mary Jocelyn	325	
Favret	Matthew Joseph	325	325
Favret	Patrick	325	
Favret	Peter Aaron	325	
Favret	Tivon Michael	325	
[Favret]	-----		325
Feathers	Elizabeth Silverhorn		136
Fedak	Delores Jean		146
Fee	Lulu A.		190
Feldner	Frederick		113
Feldner	Joyce Ann	113	
Feldner	Nancy Sue	113	
Fergeson	Morgan Brianna	294	
Ferguson	Otis		294
Ferguson	Robert Franklin	255	
Ferguson	Rolla		255
Ferguson	Sevilla	255	256
Ferguson	Zelda Lorena	255	255
Fetter	Barbara Gaye	120	
Fetter	Beverly Grace	120	
Fetter	Mary	120	
Fetter	Paul		120
Fetter	Sharon	120	
Fetter	Shirley	120	
Field	Martha Luella		134
Fikes	Cindy	307	
Fikes	Erma Gail	305	307
Fikes	Ernest Richard	305	308
Fikes	Judy Ann	305	307
Fikes	Lawrence Joseph		305
Fikes	Lawrence Olean	305	307
Fikes	Lela Ann	307	
Fikes	Leo	305	307
Fikes	Leo Albert	307	
Fikes	Linda	307	
Fikes	Lynn Alan	307	
Fikes	Sheila Wyleen	305	308
Fikes	Shelly	307	
Fikes	Vera Kathleen	305	307
Fikes	Veta Neoma	305	305
Filler	Mary Magdalene		330

Fillwock	Patrick L.		164
Findley	William		149
Finney	-----		247
Finney	Margaret		247
Fiscus	Kathleen Jane		148
Fisher	Anna	319	
Fisher	Basil Westa		112
Fisher	Caleb Joseph	149	
Fisher	Carol Virginia		179
Fisher	Dortha Kay	112	
Fisher	Drury	319	
Fisher	Frederick Eugene	112	
Fisher	Greg		149
Fisher	Janet Ann	112	
Fisher	Lulu	319	319
Fisher	Nathaniel Jude	149	
Fisher	Sandra Sue	112	
Fisher	Sanford		319
Fisher	Susan	319	319
Fitch	Nancy		313
Fleeger	Elizabeth A.		172
Fleming	-----		249
Flickner	-----		280
Flickner	Claud	280	
Flickner	[daughter 1]	280	
Flickner	[daughter 2]	280	
Flint	Lisa Lynn		187
Flynn	Angela Denise	307	
Flynn	Gregory Lynn	307	307
Flynn	Jack		307
Flynn	Jarod Alan	307	
Flynn	Jason Lynn	307	
Fonay	Gary William		218
Fonay	Kyle William	218	
Fonay	Shelley Jean	218	
Forney	Edward J.		266
Forney	Sara A.	266	
Forrester	-----		225
Foster	Alexander		247
Foster	Alexander	247	
Foster	Charles E.		171
Foster	Gene Allen	171	
Foster	Helen		168
Foster	Helen Louise		236
Foster	John		248
Foster	Josiah	247	
Foster	Margaret Ellen	171	
Foster	Martha	247	248
Foster	Phyllis Jane	171	171
Fowler	-----		312
Fowler	Ina Estelle		183
Fowler	Lula Maxine		115
Francisco	Amy Elicia	168	
Francisco	Brad Emery	167	168
Francisco	Kerry Elizabeth	168	
Francisco	Laura Jane	168	
Francisco	Lee		167
Francisco	Marlene Faye	167	167
Francisco	Mary Lee	167	167
Franklin	Ray A.		228
Frasure	Rachel Ann		277
Freeburg	-----		208
Freeman	Gale Wanda		140
Friedel	Lynn		225
Friedhoff	Deidre Lee	288	
Friedhoff	Francis William		288
Friedhoff	Kalan Ina	288	
Friesek	Vern		178
Fryer	Alberta May	238	239
Fryer	Frank Mervin	238	238
Fryer	Harry	238	240
Fryer	Jessie	238	240
Fryer	Juanita Faye	238	239
Fryer	Kenneth Wayne	240	
Fryer	Lucy	238	238
Fryer	Opal	238	
Fryer	Ruth Helen	240	
Fryer	Thelma Marguerite	240	240
Fryer	Velma Ruth	238	238
Fryer	Virgil Dale	238	
Fryer	William A.		238
Fryer	Zona Hazel	238	238
Furman	Clementine		328
Gahr	Francis Gene		122
Gahr	Jacob Lee	122	
Gahr	Jerome Robert	122	
Gahr	Joshua Gene	122	
Galbraith	-----		245
Gallota	Ann Marie		284
Garrett	Dorothea Jean	178	178
Garrett	Eugene Thrall		178
Garrett	Eugene Thrall Jr.	178	179
Garrett	Patricia Ann		219
Gaston	John		329
Gates	Charles Arthur		236
Gates	Connie Jean	236	236
Gates	Robert Charles	236	
Gaudreau	James Arnott		287
Gearhart	Dorothy		123
Geisseheiner	Charles Augustus		194
Genter	Gregory James		125
Genter	Shaun Stewart	125	
George	Sarah		169
Gerber	Caleb J.		267
Gerber	Donna Joann		148
Gesmond	Anthony John	140	
Gezlov	Alma Rita		188
Gheen	Claude		326
Gholson	Anna Estelle		286
Gibbs	Daniel		322
Gibbs	Ethel M.	322	
Gibbs	Raymond D.	322	
Gibson	-----		196
Gibson	James		120
Gibson	Lois G.		174
Gibson	Shirley		169
Gielow	Aberdeen Jenae	285	
Gielow	Diane Lynn	285	285
Gielow	Howard L.		285
Gielow	Tad Alan	285	285
Gifford	Effie Louise		242
Giles	Ruby		221
Gillen	April	171	
Gillen	John		171
Gilleron	George E.		272
Gilliland	Alletta Ruth	121	122
Gilliland	Brooke Nichole	122	
Gilliland	Cheryl Gay	122	122
Gilliland	Edward		146
Gilliland	Jesse Brione	149	
Gilliland	Judson Rankin	121	122
Gilliland	Megan Elizabeth	122	
Gilliland	Oren Boyd		121
Gilliland	Oren Kim	122	122
Gilliland	Ronald James		149
Gilliland	Zachary Samuel	149	
Gilmore	Lucy		155
Gissal	Adam William	284	
Gissal	Alex William	284	
Gissal	Cindy Ann	283	284
Gissal	Fred Wilmer		283
Gissal	Frederick William	283	284
Gissal	Jeff Joseph	284	
Gissal	Jeffrey Joseph	283	284
Gissal	Jessie Lynn	284	
Gissal	Judy Lynn	283	284
Gissal	Marci Ann	284	
Gissal	Mary Lee	283	
Gissal	Matthew Ryan	284	
Gissal	Stephanie Lynn	284	
Gissal	Tina Marie	284	
Gissal	Wendy Jane	283	
Glandon	Alexandra Nicole	226	
Glandon	Nicholas Cooper	226	
Glandon	William		226
Glenn	Douglas Edward		149
Glenn	Melody		118
Glowacki	Judith Mary		211
Godfrey	Evan Michael	261	
Godfrey	Matthew Richard	261	
Godfrey	Nicholas	261	
Godfrey	Richard		261

Goldsworthy	-----		299	Hall	Eleanor	109	110	Hardy	Travis Leslie		160
Goodman	Jeanne Louise	141		Hall	Ester		109	Harlan	-----		243
Goodman	Silas Michael	141		Hall	Glen		271	Harney	Audrey May	321	
Goodman	Timothy Paul		141	Hall	Nevelda	109	109	Harney	Clara C.	321	
Goodnight	Maryjo		292	Hall	Ruth Odetta	109		Harney	Earl L.	321	321
Gordon	Donald Paul		286	Halliwell	Catherine C.		111	Harney	John L.		321
Gordon	Donna Lee	286	287	Ham	Carol		165	Harney	Laura H.	321	
Gordon	Patricia Diane	286		Hambright	Ida		319	Harney	Myrtle O.	321	
Gottesfeld	Marylin Lucille		239	Hamilton	Sarah B.		316	[Harney]	Anne		321
Gough	Alfred		312	Hamilton	Valeta Inone		232	Harrison	Jill Marie	211	
Grace	Alta		323	Hanks	Alan Eugene	277	278	Harrison	Paul Edward	211	
Grady	Elizabeth Deborah		194	Hanks	Brian Donald	277		Harrison	Rodger Paul		211
Graeff	Katherine		199	Hanks	John Cameron	277		Hartshorn	Harriet		252
Graff	Julia A.		278	Hanks	Melissa Dawn	277		Hartzell	Diana Sue	171	
Graney	David Thomas	147		Hanks	Philip	278		Hartzell	Jacob William	171	
Graney	Juliana Mae	147		Hanks	Philip Donald		277	Hartzell	Kathrine Andrea	171	
Graney	Richard Edward		147	Hanks	Richard Philip	277	277	Hartzell	Walter Andrew	171	171
Grant	-----		156	Hanks	Tammy Kay	278		Hartzell	William		171
Grant	Howard	156		Hanks	Tracy Jane	278		Hartzell	William Tisdale	171	171
Gratz	Linda Ellen		112	Hanna	Charles M.		150	Harvey	Frank	111	
Gray	David Barry		179	[Hanna]	Maria		152	Harvey	Mary Isabel	111	
Gray	Mame		249	[Hanna]	Mary		153	Harvey	Minnie	111	
Grayson	Jacob John	139		Hannah	Adam C.	152		Harvey	Robert		111
Grayson	Tom		139	Hannah	Alice	152		Hatfield	Harriet Patterson		274
Greenblatt	Paula Etta		197	Hannah	Andrew J.	152	153	Hauser	Roger		180
Gregory	Bobbie Jean		167	Hannah	Arthur	152		Hauser	Roger, Jr.	180	
Gridley	Samuel (Rev.)		155	Hannah	Bessie	152		Hauser	Wilton A.	180	
Griffin	Judith Kay		110	Hannah	Blanch	153		Hawley	William C.		230
Griggs	Ronnie Richard		137	Hannah	Charles	152		Hay	Harry William		308
Grill	Melissa		124	Hannah	Dora B.	152		Hay	Linda Ann	308	
Grimes	Delia		249	Hannah	Elizabeth C.	152		Hayes	George Ambrose, III		272
Gross	Catherine Ann		162	Hannah	Ella M.	153		Hayes	Mark McIlvaine	272	
Grotheer	Mary K.		236	Hannah	Evalina	152		Hays	Edith Mae		145
Groves	Dorothy Dalene		218	Hannah	Hervey B.	152		Hedges	Leroy E.	109	
Guarnieri	Elizabeth Mary		148	Hannah	James C.	152	152	Hedges	Owen H.		109
Guthrie	Gladys Maxine		114	Hannah	Jane	152		Hedges	Ralph L.	109	
Guyton	Gregory Kyle	122		Hannah	John		152	Hefner	Ethel		117
Guyton	John		122	Hannah	John, Jr.	152	153	Heilman	Rachel Ann	144	
Guyton	Lisa Michelle	122		Hannah	Lavinia	152		Heilman	Sarah Elizabeth	144	
Haagensen	Carrie	283		Hannah	Mary B.	152		Heilman	Stephen Thomas		144
Haagensen	Karen	283		Hannah	Maud R.	153		Helmick	Virginia Lee		294
Haagensen	Kenneth	283	283	Hannah	Minnie L.	153		Helser	Howard		114
Haagensen	Kenneth W.		283	Hannah	Nancy	152		Hemming	Mildred		269
Haagensen	Mark	283	283	Hannah	Olive B.	153		Henady	Brad Alan		304
Haagensen	Michael	283		Hannah	Oliver W.	152		Henderson	Aaron Marshel	276	
Haagensen	Rebecca	283		Hannah	Ruth	152		Henderson	Blake	219	
Hackett	Sharon Grace		217	Hannah	William	152		Henderson	Breck Andrew	276	
Hadley	Lucille		157	[Hannah]	Elvia [?]		153	Henderson	Breck Wenger	277	277
Haffner	Robert Michael		243	Hannigsmann	Mary		296	Henderson	Callie Rose	277	
Haffner	Robert Michael, III	243		Hanson	Ann		298	Henderson	Candace E.		230
Hagan	Randy		309	Hanson	Daniel LeRoy		291	Henderson	Carrie Louise	277	
Hagan	Stacy Lynn	309		Hanson	Julie Marie	291		Henderson	Cassandra Rene	276	
Hainline	Hattie Irene		302	Hanz	Mary Catherine		205	Henderson	Clyde Patterson		219
Hall	Beulah	109	110	Hardesty	Trina		169	Henderson	Cora Rebecca	276	

Henderson	Cynthia Jane	219 219	Hesch	Patrick Gerard	162 162	Hilty	William Arthur	263
Henderson	Edward Lee	276 276	Hesch	Richard Gerard	162	Hindes	Harriet	296 296
Henderson	Emmett Eugene	276 276	Hesch	Russell Jacob	161	Hindes	Hazel M.	296 298
Henderson	Eugene Marshel	276 276	Hesch	Russell Joseph	161 162	Hindes	Hubert John	296 296
Henderson	Garrett Robert	219	Hesch	Stephanie Carol	162	Hindes	John	296
Henderson	Gregory Eugene	276 276	Hesch	Susan Jane	163 163	Hindes	John William	296
Henderson	Haley	277	Hetrick	Lucinda Ann	263 263	Hindes	Laurena	296
Henderson	Jane	276 277	Hetrick	William	263	Hindes	Lawrence	296 296
Henderson	Jo Anne	219 219	Heuschkel	Sheri	222	Hindes	Margie	296 296
Henderson	John Breck	276 277	Hibbard	Carl J.	166	Hindes	Marguerite Estelle	296 297
Henderson	John Henry	276	Hibbard	David Allen	166	Hindes	Mary Fern	296 297
Henderson	John Herrit	276	Hibbard	Gerald Abel	166	[Hindes]	Sylvia	296
Henderson	John Marshel	277 277	Hibbard	Jafola	166 166	Hindman	Mildred	168
Henderson	Katie Eugenia	276	Hibbard	Roscoe Carl	166 166	Hitt	Harlee Rene	135
Henderson	Kezia Catherine	277	Hibbard	Wallace Carl	166	Hitt	Hunter Cole	135
Henderson	Laura Ann	276	Hicks	Jessie A.	279	Hitt	Ronald Mark	135
Henderson	Lauren Michelle	277	Hicks	John Frederick	279	Hogue	Edith	198
Henderson	Lois Arlene	219	Hicks	Ruth	279	Hollenbeak	Linda Jo	291
Henderson	Louise Elizabeth	277	Hill	Adam Paul	135	Holloway	George C.	228
Henderson	Marcus Lee	276	Hill	Allen Edward	135 136	Holm	Sarah Marion	220
Henderson	Marshel Andrew	277	Hill	Ann Michelle	135 135	Holman	Arthur Leroy	112 112
Henderson	Mary Adele	219	Hill	Catherine	311	Holman	Cale Matthew	112
Henderson	Michael Eugene	277	Hill	Clyde Samuel	174	Holman	Colleen Louise	112
Henderson	Michael Emmet	277 277	Hill	Clyde Samuel, Jr.	174 175	Holman	Kathryn Elizabeth	112
Henderson	Miles Rankin	219 219	Hill	Clyde Samuel, III	175 175	Holman	Kira Ellen	112
Henderson	Nancy Elizabeth	219 219	Hill	Darin Aaron	135	Holman	Krista Elaine	112
Henderson	Robert Edward	219 219	Hill	David Allen	135	Holman	Robert Wayne	112 112
Henderson	Shelly	277	Hill	Deborah Ann	135 136	Holman	Ronald Leroy	112
Henderson	Stephanie Jo	276	Hill	Emily Melinda	136	Holman	Ronald Wayne	112
Henderson	William Robert	276 276	Hill	Erin Alexis	136	Holty	Marcella	283
Henry	Marlene Fay	124	Hill	Gary	306	Holtz	Sherry	211
Henwood	Daniel J.	259	Hill	Jacob Kelly	136	Hook	Rebecca	243
Henwood	David P.	259	Hill	James Hulbert	174 174	Hooker	Dewey A.	116
Henwood	Jerry	259	Hill	James R.	174	Hopkins	Lou Ann	177
Henwood	Jessica B.	259	Hill	Jeane Isabelle	174 174	Hopper	Arthur Leroy	172
Hepler	Hazel D.	167	Hill	Jodi	175 175	Hopper	Carol Ruth	172
Herb	Mary Kathryn	201	Hill	Lori	175 175	Hopper	Norman Maynard	172
Herod	Camilla	163 163	Hill	Mary Dorothea	174 174	Hopper	Susan Winona	172
Herod	Catherine	163 164	Hill	Melinda Kay	135 135	Hopper	Walter C.	172
Herod	Donald M.	163	Hill	Melissa Rene	135 135	Hopperstad	Donald Robert	204 205
Herod	Donald Michael	163 164	Hill	Meredith Ashley	136	Hopperstad	Robert Donald	204
Herr	Martha Louise	113	Hill	Michael Edward	136	Hornstein	Paul Jay	284
Hershey	Amos	310	Hill	Olivia Rebecca	136	Hornstein	Philip Bryan	284
Hertia	Timothy	163	Hill	Paul Eugene	135	Hortner	Leddie Claire	142
Hesch	Barbara Jane	161 162	Hill	Paul Orion	135 135	Houghton	Hattie	269
Hesch	Carolyn Ann	162 163	Hill	Robert Aaron	135 135	House	Mandy	308
Hesch	David Gerard	162 162	Hill	Samuel P.	175	House	Megan	308
Hesch	Faith Marie	162	Hill	Sara Elizabeth	174 174	House	Vincent	308
Hesch	Jacob Gerard	162	Hill	Seth Andrew	136	Houston	Tishia Lynn	309
Hesch	Janelle Katherine	162	Hill	Susan Rae	174	Hovey	Craig Warren	288
Hesch	Janice Lynn	163	Hill	Thaddeus Joel	136	Hovey	Erin Kathleen	288
Hesch	Jean Ann	163 163	Hill	Timothy Eugene	135 136	Howarth	Jacqueline A.	259 259
Hesch	John Thomas	161 163	Hilty	Eugene Arthur	263	Howarth	John M.	259
Hesch	Lora Jane	163	Hilty	Jennifer Lynn	263	Howarth	Karla M.	259 259

Howarth	Philip J.	:259:	
Howell	Richard	: :299	
Hubbard	Brian Todd	:242:242	
Hubbard	Christopher Ryan	:242:	
Hubbard	Jane Maria	: :242	
Hubbard	William Wyatt	:242:242	
Hubbard	William Henry	: :242	
Hudak	Joyce Carol	: :164	
Hudson	David M. C.	: :111	
Hudson	Minnie	:111:	
Huff	[son]	:306:	
Huff	:-----	: :312	
Huff	Dorothy Mae	: :136	
Huff	Gary	: :306	
Hughes	Michelle Marie	: :216	
Hunsaker	Laurel	: :159	
Hunt	:-----	: :224	
Hunt	Barbara Ann	:262:263	
Hunt	Beverly Rea	:262:262	
Hunt	Karen Ann	:262:262	
Hunt	Kathleen	:262:262	
Hunt	Ray Edward	: :262	
Hurd	Mary Mildred	: :127	
Hurlburt	Mary Marcella	: :323	
Hurn	Debra Ruth	: :292	
Hutchins	Shelley	: :308	
Hutchinson	Diane Elizabeth	:144:144	
Hutchinson	Lawrence Frederick	: :144	
Hutchinson	Lawrence Fred. II	:144:	
Hutchinson	Mark David	:144:	
Hutchinson	Pamela Ann	:144:144	
Hutchinson	Robin Kay	:144:144	
Iannotti	Donna Anne	: :266	
Irvin	Clara Belle	: :271	
Irvin	James McIlvaine	:311:311	
Irvin	William W.	: :311	
Irwin	Catherine	: :257	
Iverson	Irvin J.	: :179	
Jackson	Cheryl Lynn	: :230	
Jackson	E. :R.	: :308	
Jackson	Samuel	: :248	
Jacobs	:-----	: :254	
Jacobs	Mary Ann	: :220	
Jacobs	Patricia	: :175	
James	:-----	: :146	
James	Brandon	:146:	
James	Charles B.	: :282	
James	J. E.	: :278	
James	Phyllis L.	:282:282	
Janssen	Leo Dale	: :237	
Janssen	Robin Dale	:237:	
Janssen	Tracey Lee	:237:	
Jatzak	Kenneth	: :285	
Jeffrey	Nellie Emma	: :185	
Jenkins	Alice L.	: :199	
Jenkins	Alyssa Alexandria	:242:	
Jenkins	Billi Vanessa	: :242	
Jenkins	Tina Renee	: :116	
Jennings	Amanda	:306:	
Jennings	Angela Kay	:306:	
Jennings	Brian Scott	:305:306	
Jennings	Cheryl Jane	:305:306	
Jennings	[child]	:305:	
Jennings	[child]	:306:	
Jennings	[daughter]	:306:	
Jennings	David J.	:305:306	
Jennings	Dena Michele	:305:306	
Jennings	Dennis	:305:306	
Jennings	Eula	: :309	
Jennings	Jennifer	:306:	
Jennings	Jill Rene	:305:	
Jennings	Joyce Lee	:305:305	
Jennings	Keith	:305:306	
Jennings	Kevin	:305:	
Jennings	Kimberly	:305:	
Jennings	LeRoy	: :305	
Jennings	Michael	:306:	
Jennings	Ora Ellen	: :112	
Jennings	Stephanie	:305:	
Jennings	Steven	:305:305	
Jennings	Veta Diane	:305:306	
[Jennings]	:-----	: :306	
[Jennings]	Karen	: :305	
[Jennings]	Kathy	: :305	
[Jennings]	Mary Kay	: :306	
Jernigan	Nancy E.	: :144	
Jewel	Clifford	: :324	
Jewel	Keri Ann	:324:	
Jewel	Kirk Allen	:324:	
Jewel	Lynn Marie	:324:	
Jewell	Catherine	: :131	
Jewett	John A.	:278:	
Jewett	Kent	: :278	
Jobs	:-----	: :120	
Johns	Betsy Ann	:174:	
Johns	Jay	: :174	
Johns	Jay	:174:	
Johns	Leslie	:174:	
Johns	Lynn	:174:	
Johnson	:-----	: :231	
Johnson	Cathline	: :118	
Johnson	Darla Gail	:307:308	
Johnson	Helen Carlene	: :229	
Johnson	Inez Marie	: :211	
Johnson	Jody Lynn	: :277	
Johnson	Kenneth Robert	: :307	
Johnson	Kenny Dale	:307:308	
Johnson	Pauline Wheeler	: :234	
Johnson	[son]	:308:	
Johnson	Sue Ann	: :291	
Johnston	Adam Darrell	:148:	
Johnston	Bruce Erik	:197:198	
Johnston	Darrell Edward	: :148	
Johnston	Felix George	:197:	
Johnston	George Oliver C.	:197:197	
Johnston	Ian Gregory	:198:	
Johnston	Janna Maureen	:148:	
Johnston	John Raymond	: :197	
Johnston	Julian Ross	:197:197	
Johnston	Samantha Lynn	:148:148	
Johnston	Samuel Barnaby	:197:	
Johnston	Sophy Mabel C.	:198:	
Johnston	Todd Robert	:148:	
Joiner	Martha Linda	: :302	
Jones	Agnes	:316:	
Jones	Bernard	:316:	
Jones	Catherine	:316:	
Jones	Clifford H.	: :316	
Jones	Connie Lynn	:214:	
Jones	Dora Belle	:315:315	
Jones	Frank	:316:	
Jones	Gail Laureen	:214:	
Jones	Harold Joseph	: :214	
Jones	Harry Albert	:315:316	
Jones	Helen	:316:	
Jones	Isaac	: :315	
Jones	J. McIlvaine	:316:	
Jones	John McIlvaine	:315:316	
Jones	John	:316:	
Jones	Joseph H.	: :201	
Jones	Kay	: :146	
Jones	Laurence Isaac	:315:316	
Jones	Margaret	:316:	
Jones	Mary Arilla	:315:316	
Jones	Pauline	:316:	
Jones	Robert	:316:	
Jones	Russell	:316:	
Jones	Russell Lee	:214:	
Jones	Sharon LeAnn	:214:	
Jones	Walter	:316:	
Jones	Wilbur	:316:	
Jones	William Elmer	:315:316	
Jordan	Larry	: :216	
Joslin	Roberta L.	: :323	
Judy	Benjamin Ivan	:186:188	
Judy	Bessie	:186:	
Judy	Carol Sue	:189:190	
Judy	Charles Burton, Jr.	: :186	
Judy	Charles Burton	:186:189	
Judy	Ella Mae	:186:186	
Judy	Janet Elaine	:188:189	
Judy	LaVesta Laverne	:186:186	
Judy	Mary Elizabeth	:188:188	

Judy	Mary Ellen	188	188	Kerr	Florence Catherine		203	Kucera	Rose Catherine		293
Judy	Mary Ethel	188	189	Kerr	Harold A.		173	Kuespert	Don Raymond		219
Judy	Robert John	186	188	Kerr	Walter		326	Kurpik	Russell		260
Juen	Darcy Marie	126		Kerr	William Agnew, II	173		Kurtz	-----		319
Juen	Douglas Richard		126	Kieswetter	Tammy		141	Kurtz	Rachel		321
Juen	Richard Douglas	126		Kiger	Belle		249	Kyle	-----		130
Kady	-----		245	Kiger	Florence	249		Kyle	Clement	130	
Kagy	Leona		127	Kiger	Harvey	249		Lacey	Laura Belle		210
Kampsula	Bruno Benjamin		295	Kiger	Maybelle	249		Laing	Edward Everett		287
Kampsula	Jennifer Sue	295		Kilgore	William		249	Laing	Larry Everett	287	287
Karhoff	Mark Joseph		236	Kim	Hyon Jung		290	Laing	Susan	287	287
Katich	Brent	138	139	Kimes	Lois Virginia		122	Lambrechts	Benjamin	284	
Katich	Luann	138		King	Fred		127	Lambrechts	John		284
Katich	Nick		138	King	John Nelson		278	Lance	JoAnn		135
Kaufman	Andrea Janine	295		King	Margaret Dick	278	278	Larson	Susan Ann		289
Kaufman	Carolyn Lucille	295	295	King	Ruth	278	278	Lauderdale	Chad Raymond	301	
Kaufman	Dale Stewart	295	295	Kinney	Judith K.		267	Lauderdale	Everett Earl	301	301
Kaufman	Kyle Kevan	295		Kipp	Bruce Eric		212	Lauderdale	Everett Raymond		301
Kaufman	Peter Arthur		295	Kipp	Erin Leigh	212		Lauderdale	Janelle Lea	301	301
Kaufman	Troy Dale	295		Klasen	Margaret Edith		149	Lauderdale	Jeffery Carl	301	
Kaufmann	Marc Allen		218	Klooster	Donna Gail		187	Lauderdale	Jimmy Carl	301	301
Kaufmann	Michael Benjamin	218		Klug	-----		297	Lauderdale	Michael Shane	301	
Kaufmann	Timothy	218		Knecht	Janice E.		270	Lauderdale	Patricia Rose	301	
Kaustinen	Brad William		270	Knepper	Olive		269	Lauderdale	Robert Eugene	301	301
Kaustinen	Kaitlyn Beth	270		Knight	Rachel Jeanne		233	Lauderdale	Robert Jason	301	
Kaustinen	Kelsey Leanne	270		Knok	Gregory		178	Lauderdale	Tommy Lee	301	301
Kavanaugh	William		132	Knopf	Cheryl Lyn	215	215	[Lauderdale]	Brenda		301
Kee	Mary Elizabeth		185	Knopf	Edward		215	Law	Alan Dashton	140	
Keen	Bob		309	Kobets	Brian Godfrey	233		Law	Albert William		139
Keen	Cynthia Alice	265	265	Kobets	Mary Elizabeth	233		Law	Christopher Shane	140	
Keen	David Earl	265		Kobets	Rebecca Ann	233		Law	David Alan	139	140
Keen	Earl Maynard	265	265	Kobets	Teresa Christine	233		Law	Decinda Marie	140	
Keen	Gary Paul	265		Kobets	Thomas Harvey		233	Law	Jessica Renee	140	
Keen	George Calvin		265	Koch	Denise G.		282	Law	Mary		246
Keen	George Calvin	265	265	Kock	Bess		324	Law	Robert Laverne	139	140
Keen	Janet Sue	265	265	Kolljeski	Allyson Elizabeth	261		Law	Valorie Alison	140	
Keen	Jeffrey Allen	265		Kolljeski	Brandon Edward	261		Law	William Edward	139	140
Keen	Robert George	265		Kolljeski	George		261	Lawler	Geri	263	
Keen	Thomas George	265		Kopp	James Luvern	297		Lawler	Jolene	263	
Keep	Linda Ann		140	Kopp	Kathryn Ann	297	297	Lawler	Joseph		263
Keith	Eliza Ann		238	Kopp	Luvern Van Doren		297	Lawler	Nichole	263	
Keller	Jane Elizabeth	274	274	Kopp	Mary Marguerite	297		Lawson	Elizabeth		301
Keller	Matthew David	274		Kopp	Susan Ellen	297	297	Layman	David	119	
Keller	Matthew E.		274	Kortge	Billie Jean		291	Layman	Floyd	119	
Kelly	Shanta		171	Kovach	Louis Andrew		139	Layman	John	119	
Kennedy	Bernice		296	Kovacicek	Hilda		313	Layman	Paul	119	
Kennemond	Patricia		256	Koza	Casmir		262	Layman	Ralph	119	
Kenney	Anne Morrow	314		Koza	Katie	262		Layman	Virgil C.		119
Kenney	Brittany Dale	291		Koza	Michael	262		Ledger	Ella May		132
Kenney	Edwin James		314	Kramer	William		324	Lee	Charles		238
Kenney	James McIlvaine	314		Kranz	Mark		162	Lee	Gina Michelle	238	
Kenney	John Henry, II		291	Kranz	Rebecca Michelle	162		Lee	Kristen Kay	238	
Kenney	Jon Michael	291	291	Kratzer	Sally Jane		274	Lehman	Jeffrey Andrew		189
Kenney	Justin Michael	291		Krison	Cynthia Louise		124	Lehman	Rebecca Joe	113	

Surname	Given Name		
Lehman	Theodore		113
Leighton	James Kendrick		315
Lemon	Mabel		248
Lenati	Frank		230
Lenati	Jonathan S.	230	
Lenhardt	Lance Hugh		234
Lenhardt	Rhiannon R.	234	
Lenhart	Michele Ann		149
Leo	C. W.		299
Leo	Eldon	299	
Leo	Harry McIlvaine	299	
Leo	Ralph Reeder	299	
Leonard	Rebecca	266	
Leonard	Robert John		266
Leonard	Robert John	266	
Leonard	Victoria	266	
Lesher	Albert D.		167
Lesher	Jason Douglas	167	
Lesher	Jeffrey Duane	167	167
Lesher	Lisa Elaine	167	167
Levinson	Brian Matthew	285	
Levinson	Carly Leah	285	
Levinson	Eric Michelle	285	
Levinson	Lawrence Michael		285
Lewis	Angel Dawn	303	
Lewis	Goldie May		301
Lewis	H. K.		130
Lewis	Jamie Scott		189
Lewis	Michael Bud	303	
Lewis	Michael Charles	303	303
Lewis	Russell Norman		303
Lichtenberg	Dianna		220
Lieber	Barbara		184
Lieber	Daniel	118	
Lieber	Dennis Lynn	118	118
Lieber	Richard Paul		118
Lieber	Roger Lee	118	
Lien	Egil		279
Lien	Justin Tyler	279	
Lien	Matthew Allen	279	
Lien	Megin Elizabeth	279	
Limbaugh	Estella J.		322
Lindsey	Alta May		200
Lininger	Howard		114
Linter	Nellis Dewitt		272
Little	Martha Louise		195
Livingston	Margaret Mae		130
Lloyd	Janis		159
Lock	Andrew John	220	
Lock	Donald J.		220
Lock	Lloyd Leslie	220	
Lock	Sara Rae	220	
Lock	Stephen Kent	220	220
Lock	William Donald	220	
Lockhart	Emma C.	257	257
Lockhart	John B.		257
Long	Frances		307
Long	Marsha		301
Long	Penelope Jane		180
Longhofer	Harriet Austin		227
Lorenz	Elizabeth Ann		298
Loutzenhiser	Theodore Raymond		130
Love	Abigail Serena	327	329
Love	Andrew	328	
Love	Andrew	327	
Love	Barkley B.	329	329
Love	Charles R.	328	
Love	Dallas C.	329	
Love	Doris E.	329	
Love	Elizabeth Rachel	327	
Love	Elva	329	
Love	Frank E.	328	328
Love	Grace E.	328	
Love	Hannah	327	327
Love	Ida	329	
Love	Isaac H.	327	329
Love	James E.	329	329
Love	James M.	327	
Love	John H.	327	328
Love	John L.	329	
Love	John McIlwain		327
Love	John Reed	328	328
Love	Leah E.	329	
Love	Lydia C.	327	
Love	Mary E.	328	
Love	Pearle	329	
Love	Peter J.	327	328
Love	Ralph E.	328	
Love	Sid Bell	328	
Love	Walter D.	329	
Love	William	327	328
Love	William	328	
[Love]	Addie M.		328
[Love]	Beulah M.		328
[Love]	Elizabeth J.		329
[Love]	Emma E.		329
[Love]	Maude C.		329
Lovelady	Harold		295
Lowers	Dorothy Lynn		124
Lowry	Katherine Elaine	309	
Lucas	-----		328
Lundquist	Donnie E.	180	
Lundquist	Eddie H.		180
Lundquist	Gary D.	180	
Lyle	Marion		116
Lyman	Ann	231	
Lyman	Joannie L.		289
Lyman	John	231	
Lyman	Richard "Dick"		231
Lynch	Matthew	145	
Lynch	William		145
Lyon	Marjorie		138
Lyons	Ashley Marie	189	
Lyons	Jacob Lee	189	
Lyons	John Lee		189
Lyons	Martha		225
Lyons	Nicholas Lee	189	
MacDonald	Lane Ellen	147	148
MacDonald	Shay Douglas	147	
Mackey	Gary L.		171
Madison	Harry		309
Madison	Stephanie Nicole	309	
Magnusson	Margori Lee		158
Maier	Susanna Francesca		197
Main	Stephen Michael		188
Makovecki	Edith		115
Malinas	Judy		117
Malm	Gerald		220
Malm	Heather	220	
Malm	Joshua	220	
Malm	Meredith	220	
Malotte	Nancy Gail		304
Mapps	Mary Jane		210
March	George		254
March	Rex Smiley	254	
Marcozzi	Ernest		253
Marcozzi	Joellen	253	253
Marcozzi	Raymond Paul	253	
Marcus	Sue		186
Mark	Russell		240
Markley	Carol	272	
Marsh	Anna		264
Marshall	Alice		170
Marshall	Diane Elizabeth		218
Marshel	Leila		276
Martin	Annis		263
Martin	Barbara Ruth		203
Martin	Heather J.		164
Martin	Jacqueline K.		124
Martin	James		246
Martin	James	246	247
Martin	John		326
Martin	Josiah	246	246
Martin	Joyce Lydia		269
Martin	Lulu	246	247
Martin	Margaret	246	247
Martin	Mary Catherine	246	246
Martin	Rose	246	247
Martin	Sadie	246	247
Martin	Samuel	246	246
Martin	William	246	247
Martineau	Wendy		226

Mason	Frank E.		224
Mason	Ruby Mae	224	224
Masten	Frank		157
Matthews	Dale LeRoy		186
Matthews	Julie Marie	189	189
Matthews	Kryslyn Saige	189	
Matthews	Sherry Lynn		314
Matthews	Victor Monroe		189
Matthews	Victor Monroe Jr.	189	189
Mattingly	Cleo Marie	214	215
Mattingly	Douglas Lee	215	
Mattingly	Evelyn Mae	214	214
Mattingly	Galen Wayne	214	214
Mattingly	Joseph A.		214
Mattingly	Joseph Michael	214	
Mattingly	Kenneth Wayne	214	
Mattingly	Kir-Lee	215	
Mattingly	Lawrence Logan	214	214
Mattingly	Leonard LaDean	214	215
Mattingly	Nancy Belle	214	214
Mattingly	Patrick Galen	214	
Mattingly	Richard	214	
Mattingly	Robert James	214	
Mattingly	Scott Allen	214	
Mattingly	Tawnya Rae	214	
[Mattingly]	Donna Jean		215
[Mattingly]	Helen		214
[Mattingly]	Terry		215
Mattis	Mildred		256
Maw	Elizabeth Mary	191	
Maw	John Connell	191	
Maw	John Davis	191	191
Maw	Johnson Ebert		191
Maw	Loretta Louis	191	
Maxwell	Clara		168
Maxwell	Emily		179
May	Carolyn Jean	218	218
May	Donald Boyd		218
May	Douglas	218	
May	Gregory Donald	218	
May	Laurinda Lea	218	218
Mayer	Dittie Jo		115
Mayher	Mike		273
Maynard	Karen Lynne		143
McCall	------ [Dr.]		225
McCalmont	------		210
McCartney	Albert		130
McCartney	James		196
McCartney	Mary Margaret	130	131
McClimans	------		132
McClimans	Frederick	132	132
[McClimans]	Leona		132
McCloy	------		246
McClurg	Cynthia		325

McConnell	Shari Lee		187
McCormick	-----		312
McCoy	Albert Shannon	202	202
McCoy	Alice	202	
McCoy	Amber Regina	203	204
McCoy	Anna	202	
McCoy	Bertrand S.	202	
McCoy	Carrie Bell	202	
McCoy	Daniel		202
McCoy	Harry E.	202	
McCoy	John	202	
McCoy	Louella D.	202	202
McCoy	Margaret E.	202	
McCoy	Mary M.	202	205
McCoy	Maurice C.	202	
McCoy	Michael Moore	203	204
McCoy	Miriam Rebecca	203	205
McCoy	Rachel W.	202	
McCoy	Raymond W.	202	202
McCoy	Robert W.	202	
McCoy	Stewart	202	
McCoy	Susan Lynn	203	203
McCoy	William Barrett	203	203
McCoy	William Daniel	202	203
McCoy	William Kerr	203	203
McCracken	Mary		129
McCracken	Roger Earl		235
McCrae	William H.		201
McCrea	Barbara Snyder	201	
McCrea	Elizabeth Norcross	201	
McCrea	John	201	201
McCrea	Katherine Jane	201	201
McCrea	Margaret Ballantyne	201	201
McCrea	Sara McElvain	201	201
McCrea	William Henry		201
McCrea	William Henry, Jr.	201	201
McCroskey	Lois Ann		281
McCullick	Dora		266
McCullough	Agnes	177	
McCullough	Audrey Marie	169	169
McCullough	Bessie Ida	166	167
McCullough	Carl Plummer	168	
McCullough	David Harold	169	
[McCullough]	Ellen		177
McCullough	Harold Elliot	168	169
McCullough	Henry B.		177
McCullough	Jared Paul	169	
McCullough	Jessie	177	
McCullough	Jessie Ira	166	168
McCullough	John B.		166
McCullough	John Ira	168	168
McCullough	John Mark	169	
McCullough	John R.	177	
McCullough	Joyce Kathryn	168	168

McCullough	Karen Lynn	168	168
McCullough	Leonard D.	166	
McCullough	Linda Mae	169	169
McCullough	Michael Plummer	166	168
McCullough	Nancy Lou	169	169
McCullough	Ora Belle	177	
McCullough	Patricia Ann	168	
McCullough	Paul Wilson	168	169
McCullough	Paul Wilson, Jr.	169	169
McCullough	Paxton Kerr	166	
McCullough	Thomas P.	168	168
McCullough	William L.	177	177
McCullough	William Thomas	168	
McCullough	William Zahniser	166	
McCumber	Kathy		215
McCurdy	William M.		205
McDermott	Betty Veronica		268
McDonald	Amanda Kaye	136	136
McDonald	Brian		297
McDonald	David Neil		147
McDonald	English Brenna	147	
McDonald	Kane Eric	147	
McDonald	Kellyn Michael	297	
McDonald	Lloyd Robert	136	137
McDonald	Lloyd Emerson		136
McDonald	Randall David	147	147
McDonnell	George		120
McElvain	Adarene	108	
McElvain	Alice E.	108	109
McElvain	Delia	111	111
McElvain	Emmet	111	
McElvain	John		108
McElvain	Wilbert E.	108	111
McElvain	Adam Clair	117	
McElvain	Adam Keith	211	
McElvain	Adam Norbert	178	179
McElvain	Adam T.	129	149
McElvain	Adrienne Muriel	133	134
McElvain	Agnes	200	
McElvain	Agnes Matilda	176	177
McElvain	Alan Clair	117	117
McElvain	Albert	180	183
McElvain	Albert Barnes	210	
McElvain	Alexander	129	131
McElvain	Alice	209	
McElvain	Alice B.	223	
McElvain	Alison Eaton	133	133
McElvain	Allen	108	151
McElvain	Alyssa	220	
McElvain	Amy	115	
McElvain	Andrew		107
McElvain	Andrew	107	192
McElvaine	Andrew	184	184
McElvain	Andrew	192	207

McElwain	Andrew	193 200	McElwain	Daisy Ruth	231 231	McElwain	Etta G.	209
McElwain	Andrew	208 209	McElwain	[daughter]	111	McElwain	Eugene	180 184
McElwain	Andrew	209 209	McElwain	[daughter]	150	McElwain	Eugene	209
McElwain	Andrew	209	McElwain	[daughter]	193	McElwain	Evangeline	115
McElwain	Andrew	243	McElwain	[daughter]	193	McElwain	Fay Etta	228
McElwain	Andrew Craig	234	McElwain	David	129 129	McElwain	Florence G.	129
McElwain	Andrew McKinney	241 241	McElwain	David Allen	220	McElwain	Florence Woodburn	200
McElwain	Andrew T.	108	McElwain	Dean Robert	115 115	McElwain	Floyd	183
McElwain	Andrew Thomas	108 111	McElwain	Deborah Rae	229 229	McElwain	Floyd Miller	132
McElwain	Andrew Thompson	176 176	McElwain	Dennis	209 209	McElwain	Forest Glen	228
McElwain	Andrew Thompson	178 179	McElwaine	Donald	183 183	McElwain	Forest John	178 179
McElwain	Andrew Walter	115 116	McElwain	Donald James	133 134	McElwain	Forrest Chetwynd	140 140
McElwain	Andrew William	117	McElwaine	Donald Jr.	183	McElwain	Francis Marion	228 229
McElwain	Ann Cecelia	223 223	McElwain	Donald Ray	115 115	McElwain	Frank	151
McElwain	Ann Marie	117	McElwaine	Donna	183	McElwain	Frank	209
McElwain	Anna Bell	129 150	McElwain	Donna Marie	220	McElwain	Frank L.	183
McElwain	Anna Belle	200 200	McElwain	Doris Ann	139 139	McElwain	Fred B.	209 209
McElwain	Anna Mae	229 229	McElwain	Doris Anne	216 217	McElwain	Fred G.	183
McElwain	Audrey Fay	114 116	McElwain	Doris Jean	116 117	McElwain	Gale K.	213
McElwain	Benjamin	192	McElwain	Dorothy Mae	134 135	McElwain	Gary Ray	234 111
McElwain	Bertha Artemisia	111 113	McElwain	Edgar Marshall	112 112	McElwain	George Roscoe	228
McElwain	Beva Jean	130 130	McElwain	Edith Irene	211 211	McElwain	Gertrude	209
McElwain	Beverly Jane	179	McElwain	Edward Harrison	210 210	McElwain	Grace L.	183 183
McElwain	Beverly Jean	221 222	McElwaine	Edward L.	181	McElwain	Grace Viorqua	111 113
McElwain	Beverly Kay	131 131	McElwain	Edward Lenore	131 132	McElwaine	Guy	183
McElwain	Blake Edward	222 222	McElwain	Eileen Ruth	216 216	McElwain	Hannah	107 243
McElwain	Bonnie Lynn	179	McElwain	Eleanor	107 326	McElwain	Hannah	108 150
McElwain	Brad	184	McElwain	Eleanor Edith	220 220	McElwain	Hannah A.	108 108
McElwain	Brandon J.	234	McElwain	Eleanor Grace	112 112	McElwain	Harley	213
McElwain	Buchanan	180	McElwain	Eleanor J.	209	McElwain	Harold Carter	231
McElwain	Burton D.	209 209	McElwain	Eliza	108 120	McElwain	Harry D.	130 130
McElwain	Caley Jean	115	McElwain	Eliza	208	McElwain	Harry E.	183
McElwain	Carl Willard	112	McElwain	Eliza B.	108 120	McElwain	Harvey	129 140
McElwain	Carol Diane	137 138	McElwain	Elizabeth	107 107	McElwain	Hazel	183 183
McElwain	Carol Marie	229 231	McElwain	Elizabeth	192 207	McElwain	Helen Edith	211 211
McElwain	Carolyn Joyce	116 117	McElwain	Elizabeth	327 327	McElwain	Henry	108
McElwain	Carrie	180 184	McElwain	Elizabeth A.	208 227	McElwain	Herbert Lee	231 234
McElwain	Carrie Biantha	111 117	McElwain	Elizabeth Ann	193	McElwain	Herbert Lyle	116 116
McElwain	Cass B.	180	McElwain	Elizabeth Bell	108 120	McElwain	Herman Lee	180
McElwain	Cathie Jean	115 115	McElwain	Elizabeth Bell	176	McElwain	Howard Russell	140
McElwain	Charles R.	206 206	McElwain	Ella	151	McElwain	Ira C.	108
McElwain	Charles Robert	115 115	McElwain	Ellen	208	McElwain	Isaac W.	241 243
McElwain	Charles Ross	228 231	McElwain	Ellen	241	McElwain	Isabel McKee	193 194
McElwain	Charles Wesley	231 234	McElwain	Ellen May	228	McElwain	Izora C.	132
McElwaine	child	181	McElwain	Elmer Edward	228 228	McElwain	J. B. Robert	180
McElwain	Christopher James	242	McElwain	Elsie Alberta	140 141	McElwaine	Jack	181
McElwain	Clark Wallace	179	McElwain	Elsie Alberta	140	McElwain	Jacob Orion	137
McElwaine	Claude M.	181 181	McElwain	Emily	241	McElwain	James	107 107
McElwain	Connie Jean	234 234	McElwain	Emily Marie	131	McElwain	James	108 108
McElwain	Corley	115	McElwain	Emma A.	129 149	McElwain	James	108 108
McElwain	Cynthia	108 151	McElwain	Eric Henry	211	McElwain	James	176 180
McElwain	Cyrus	129 129	McElwain	Ernest Eugene	111 112	McElwain	James	192 241
McElwain	Daisy Marie	114 114	McElwain	Ethel Lorena	140 143	McElwain	James	208 223
						McElwain	James Alexander	134

McElwain	James Arthur	231		McElwain	Keith Edward	211 211		McElwain	Martha Belle	235 235
McElwain	James C.	243		McElwain	Kiersten Alyssa	116		McElwain	Martha Grace	140 143
McElwain	James H.	223 224		McElwain	L. J. Simpson	231		McElwain	Martha Jane	176
McElwain	James P.	108		McElwain	Lacy Ralston	208 224		McElwain	Martha L.	227 228
McElwain	James R.	241 241		McElwain	Laura	151		McElwain	Martin William	220 220
McElwain	James Roger, Jr.	241 242		McElwain	Laura B.	209		McElwain	Marva Lee	216 218
McElwain	James Roger, Sr.	241 241		McElwain	Laura Belle	140 143		McElwain	Marvin Glenister	231
McElwain	James Roger, III	242 243		McElwain	Laura June	211 212		McElwain	Mary	107 107
McElwain	James Roger, IV	243		McElwain	Laverna Kate	209 210		McElwain	Mary	107 243
McElwain	James S.	241		McElwain	Lawrence	184		McElwain	Mary	193
McElwain	James Shannon	193 206		McElwain	Lawrence Edward	231 232		McElwain	Mary	208 224
McElwain	James Thompson	176		McElwain	Lee Penrose	149 150		McElwain	Mary	227 228
McElwain	Jan LeRoy	230		McElwain	Leola	178 179		McElwain	Mary A.	223 223
McElwain	Jane	192 206		McElwain	LeRoy Edward	221 222		McElwain	Mary Arline	179
McElwain	Jane	241		McElwain	Lester Corley	115 115		McElwain	Mary B.	241
McElwaine	Janet	326		McElwain	Lester Leroy	114 115		McElwain	Mary Belle	200
McElwain	Janet Lou	115 116		McElwain	Liberty McKinney	193		McElwain	Mary Charlotte	231 231
McElwaine	Jay B.	181 181		McElwain	Lillian Grace	235 237		McElwain	Mary E.	209
McElwain	Jaye Ellen	133 134		McElwain	Lillie Alice	200 200		McElwaine	Mary Elizabeth	182 182
McElwain	Jean Ellen	112 113		McElwain	Lillie Hannah	223 223		McElwain	Mary Ella	200
McElwain	Jeanette E.	178 180		McElwain	Lilly	213		McElwain	Mary Ellen	221 221
McElwain	Jeanna Lea	232 232		McElwain	Lilly B.	206		McElwain	Mary Florence	131 132
McElwain	Jeannette Viola	211		McElwain	Linda Louise	132 138		McElwain	Mary Hazel	178 180
McElwain	Jeffrey Joe	230		McElwain	Lindsey L.	200		McElwain	Mary Jane	108
McElwain	Jennie	176		McElwain	Lisa Diane	230 230		McElwain	Mary Jane	108
McElwain	Jennie	210		McElwain	Lloyd Delford	213 215		McElwain	Mary Jane	153
McElwain	Jennifer Nichole	137		McElwain	Lori Lee	230 230		McElwain	Mary Jane	192 193
McElwain	Jerry Lee	242 242		McElwain	Lori Sheree	242		McElwain	Mary Jane	210
McElwain	Jesse Bowen	176 178		McElwain	Lorna Diane	220 221		McElwain	Mary Katherine	220 220
McElwain	Jessie Ellen	223 223		McElwain	Louie Robert	228 231		McElwain	Mary Louise	179
McElwain	Jessie Marie	178 178		McElwain	Lucille Eunice	216 216		McElwain	Mary Nicholson	176
McElwain	Jo Ann	221		McElwain	Lucy A.	108 120		McElwaine	Mary Sheila	182
McElwain	John	151 151		McElwain	Luella Virginia	235 236		McElwaine	Mary Therese	129
McElwain	John	192		McElwain	Luke Spencer	234		McElwain	Maud	129 129
McElwain	John Clair	129 130		McElwain	Mabel	213		McElwain	Maxine	150
McElwain	John Edward	211 211		McElwain	Mabel Janice	213 215		McElwain	Maxine Edna	112 112
McElwain	John Kerr	228		McElwain	Malinda F.	129 150		McElwain	Melanie Jean	243 243
McElwain	John Paul	231		McElwain	Malinda Louise	235 235		McElwain	Melody	220
McElwain	John Roop	176		McElwain	Margaret	107		McElwain	Mervin LeRoy	229 230
McElwain	John S.	107 108		McElwain	Margaret	108 120		McElwain	Michael Guy	136
McElwain	John S.	108		McElwain	Margaret A.	108 111		McElwain	Mildred Louise	228
McElwain	John Thomas	242		McElwain	Margaret Ann	211 211		McElwain	Minnie E.	243
McElwain	John Thompson	108 129		McElwain	Margaret Bell	241 241		McElwain	Minor Leroy	111 114
McElwain	John Wilson	210		McElwain	Margaret Elinor	193 202		McElwain	Molly Jo	115 116
McElwain	Joseph Edward	132 139		McElwaine	Margaret Ellen	182		McElwain	Monica Lea	243 243
McElwain	Joseph Robert	136 137		McElwain	Margaret J.	208 208		McElwain	Montgomery Leroy	132
McElwain	Joseph Robert, Jr.	137		McElwain	Margaret Joan	112		McElwaine	Montgomery Monroe	181 181
McElwain	Justin Lee	222		McElwain	Margery Ellen	176 184		McElwaine	Montgomery Murdoch	180 181
McElwain	Kammy Lee	222 222		McElwain	Marian P.	229 230		McElwaine	Myron Monroe	182 182
McElwain	Katherine	178		McElwain	Marjorie	206		McElwaine	Myron Murdoch	181 182
McElwain	Katherine Ella	213 214		McElwain	Marjorie Anne	117 117		McElwain	Nancy Elizabeth	243 243
McElwain	Kathryn E.	130 130		McElwain	Mark	213 221		McElwain	Nancy Owen	210 213
McElwain	Kathryn Louise	117		McElwaine	Mark Lieber	184		McElwain	Nellie T.	140
McElwain	Kathy Lynn	234 234		McElwain	Martha	151		McElwain	Orion Roosevelt	132 134

McElwain	Ortie Lacy	210	211	McElwain	Sara Jane	193	200	[McElwain]	-----		184
McElwain	Ottie Ethel	111	118	McElwain	Sarah	192		[McElwain]	-----		242
McElwain	Otto Galen	213	213	McElwain	Sarah	192	208	[McElwain]	Bessie		210
McElwain	Pauline Esther	231	231	McElwain	Sarah	206		[McElwain]	-----		150
McElwain	Pearl D.	243		McElwain	Sarah Ann	208	200	[McElwain]	Debra		220
McElwain	Penelope Sue	136	137	McElwain	Sarah Ella	180	182	[McElwain]	Edna L.		209
McElwain	Percy	213	216	McElwain	Sarah Parrot	176	178	[McElwain]	Elizabeth		206
McElwain	Peter Alan	117		McElwain	Sean Andrew	115		[McElwain]	Elizabeth		209
McElwain	Peter Leigh	133	134	McElwain	Shelly Kay	220	221	[McElwain]	Emma		241
McElwain	Phyllis Kay	232	233	McElwain	Shirley Vivian	228	235	[McElwain]	Ethel		209
McElwain	Polly Ann	136	137	McElwain	[son]	111		[McElwain]	Florence		183
McElwain	Prudence	107	192	McElwain	[son]	117		[McElwaine]	Helen F.		181
McElwain	Prudence		330	McElwain	[son]	193		[McElwaine]	Jennie		181
McElwain	Ralph Andrew	112		McElwain	Steven W.	234		[McElwain]	Lulu E		206
McElwain	Ralph Gerald	114	116	McElwain	Stewart	192		[McElwaine]	Margaret		107
McElwain	Randall Robert	220	220	McElwain	Stewart	243		[McElwaine]	Marie		181
McElwain	Rebecca A.	208	238	McElwain	Susan	208		[McElwaine]	Mary		181
McElwain	Rebecca Joan	116	116	McElwain	Terry Lynn	138	138	[McElwain]	Mary		209
McElwain	Richard	107	176	McElwain	Thomas	192		[McElwain]	Matilda		151
McElwain	Richard Allen	134	137	McElwain	Thomas Challen	200		[McElwain]	Nancy		228
McElwain	Richard Allen II	137	137	McElwain	Thomas Earl	228	107	[McElwain]	Ruth		134
McElwain	Richard Allen III	137		McElwain	Thomas Edward	137	138	[McElwaine]	Sandra C.		184
McElwain	Richard Clair	114	117	McElwain	Thomas Evan	138		[McElwaine]	Una M.		181
McElwain	Rita Lucille	242	242	McElwain	Thomas Field	134	138	McFarland	Ann		330
McElwain	Robert	107	327	McElwain	Thomas Jackson	241	242	McGlaughlin	Elizabeth		327
McElwain	Robert	184		McElwain	Thomas Ralph	227	228	McGregor	-----		278
McElwain	Robert	192	193	McElwain	Thomas Simpson	208	228	McGuire	Patricia Ruth		303
McElwain	Robert	228		McElwain	Tyson Matthew	234		McHale	Joseph R.		131
McElwain	Robert Douglas	131	131	McElwain	Urva Cleda	178	179	McHale	Kari Janelle	131	
McElwain	Robert G.	108		McElwain	Vance	149	150	McHale	Kevin Joseph	131	
McElwain	Robert H.	206	206	McElwain	Vernelle C.	215	215	McIlvaine	-----		311
McElwain	Robert Henderson	208	227	McElwain	Virginia Rae	179		McIlvaine	-----		313
McElwaine	Robert John	184		McElwain	Watson	129		McIlvaine	Alexander Jentes	268	
McElwaine	Robert Marshall	183	184	McElwain	Wesley Joe	234	234	McIlvaine	Alexander W.	317	317
McElwaine	Robert McCachran	193		McElwain	Wilbur Jay	132	133	McIlvaine	Alfretta Jane	321	321
McElwaine	Robert Morris	115	115	McElwain	Wilbur Jay	133	133	McIlvaine	Alice		
McElwain	Robert N.	178	180	McElwain	William	107	327	McIlvaine	Alice Jean	270	270
McElwain	Robert Orion	134	136	McElwain	William	180		McIlvaine	Allie	311	
McElwain	Robert Shannon	200	200	McElwain	William Bell	192	208	McIlvaine	Anderson L.	275	
McElwain	Rock S.	227	228	McElwain	William Bell, Jr.	208	210	McIlvaine	Andrew	244	
McElwain	Rosanna	176	177	McElwain	William E.	229		McIlvaine	Andrew Gregory	314	315
McElwain	Roscoe H.	140		McElwain	William H.	108		McIlvaine	Andrew Jackson	263	299
McElwain	Roy	228		McElwain	William Harley	220	220	McIlvaine	Andrew McKennan	318	
McElwain	Roy Eugene	231	234	McElwain	William Henry	210	213	McIlvaine	Andrew S.	268	
McElwain	Ruth	107	152	McElwain	William John	130	131	McIlvaine	Anita Faye	304	
McElwain	Ruth	107	244	McElwain	William Penrose	129	150	McIlvaine]	Ann		300
McElwain	Ruth	178	180	McElwain	William Ray	229	229	McIlvaine	Ann E.	322	
McElwain	Ruth	209		McElwain	William Stewart	241		McIlvaine	Anna	320	
McElwain	Ruth C.	108	121	McElwain	William Thomas	200		McIlvaine	Annabelle Lee	323	323
McElwain	Ruth Ellen	111	108	McElwain	William Wren	213	220	McIlvaine]	Anne		321
McElwain	Ruth Rosanna	176	185	McElwain	William Wright	210		McIlvaine	Arabella	311	311
McElwain	Sally Jo	136	136	McElwain	Winifred Frances	213	219	McIlvaine	Arthur Cicero	323	323
McElwain	Samuel	180		McElwain]	-----		150	McIlvaine	Arthur Franklin	264	275
McElwain	Sandra Jo	232	233	McElwain]	-----		228	McIlvaine	Ashleigh Nicole	304	

McIlvaine	Audrey May	321	
McIlvaine	Barbara Louise	313	
McIlvaine	Benjamin M.	264 267	
McIlvaine	Brian Andrew	270	
McIlvaine	Brian Cody	304	
McIlvaine	Brian Matthew	272 272	
McIlvaine	Carl Allen	273	
McIlvaine	Carl Edwin	313 313	
McIlvaine	Carmen	269	
McIlvaine	Caroline Denise	309	
McIlvaine	Carrie R.	320 320	
McIlvaine	Carson Horner	311	
McIlvaine	Catherine	244 244	
McIlvaine	Charles	314	
McIlvaine	Charles Coen	318	
McIlvaine	Charles Wilbert	320 320	
McIlvaine	Charles Wm, Jr.	309 310	
McIlvaine	Christiana Leann	304	
McIlvaine	Christopher Cody	300 303	
McIlvaine	Clarence Bruce	270 270	
McIlvaine	Clarence L.	321	
McIlvaine	Clarice Marcella	323 326	
McIlvaine	Clay Orville	323	
McIlvaine	Cloyd Almont	269 269	
McIlvaine	Cora Jane	299 299	
McIlvaine	Cynthia	275	
McIlvaine	Cynthia Lee	318	
McIlvaine	Dale Irvin	271 272	
McIlvaine	Daniel Webster	264 269	
McIlvaine	Danielle Rae	272	
McIlvaine	David Ellsworth	264 271	
McIlvaine	David Ellsworth II	274 275	
McIlvaine	David Ellsworth III	275	
McIlvaine	David Eugene	273 273	
McIlvaine	David Greer	322	
McIlvaine	David William	313	
McIlvaine	Dawn Denise	302 302	
McIlvaine	Dean Alton	264 269	
McIlvaine	Dean William	272 272	
McIlvaine	Donald	268 269	
McIlvaine	Donald Irvin	271 271	
McIlvaine	Doris Irene	273 273	
McIlvaine	Doris Isabel	271	
McIlvaine	Dorothy Donnan	318	
McIlvaine	Earl Eugene	268 268	
McIlvaine	Earl W.	321 321	
McIlvaine	Earle	264	
McIlvaine	Edith May	300	
McIlvaine	Edwin Linton	311 314	
McIlvaine	Eleanor	244 326	
McIlvaine	Eleanor	244	
McIlvaine	Eleanor	263 300	
McIlvaine	Eleanor	310	
McIlvaine	Elinor Narcine	267 267	
McIlvaine	Elizabeth	244 250	
McIlvaine	Elizabeth	310	
McIlvaine	Elizabeth	317 318	
McIlvaine	Ella LaVerne	311 312	
McIlvaine	Ellen Christine	272	
McIlvaine	Emileigh	304	
McIlvaine	Emily	322 326	
McIlvaine	Emma Neoma	300 305	
McIlvaine	Emsie	317 318	
McIlvaine	Ernest Hadley	323 326	
McIlvaine	Eva Marie	303 303	
McIlvaine	Everett	300	
McIlvaine	Fancheon	323 323	
McIlvaine	Flora Belle	320 320	
McIlvaine	Flora Gail	271 273	
McIlvaine	Florence L.	321 322	
McIlvaine	Floyd N.	320 320	
McIlvaina	Frances Elevan	265	
McIlvaine	Frank H.	299 299	
McIlvaine	Frank O.	321 322	
McIlvaine	Gary Dale	309 309	
McIlvaine	George	244	
McIlvaine	George	320	
McIlvaine	George Andrew	264 264	
McIlvaine	George B.	263 264	
McIlvaine	George Ellsworth	271 274	
McIlvaine	George Jr.	244 310	
McIlvaine	George W.	315 320	
McIlvaine	George W.	320	
McIlvaine	George W.	321 321	
McIlvaine	George W.	322	
McIlvaine	Gilbert	275	
McIlvaine	Greer	244 322	
McIlvaine	Greer	244	
McIlvaine	Greer Harvey	315	
McIlvaine	Gregg Allen	272 272	
McIlvaine	Greta	318	
McIlvaine	Hannah Eleanor	264 264	
McIlvaine	Hazel A.	322	
McIlvaine	Heather Joan	315	
McIlvaine	Heather McKennan	318	
McIlvaine	Helen Annis	300 309	
McIlvaine	Helen M.	265 265	
McIlvaine	Helen Marie	313	
McIlvaine	Ian Moffett	272	
McIlvaine	Irene	299 299	
McIlvaine	Iris P.	265 267	
McIlvaine	Jacob Ross A.	268	
McIlvaine	James Bruce	270 270	
McIlvaine	James Buchanan	264	
McIlvaine	James Greer	263 300	
McIlvaine	James Laurence	320	
McIlvaine	James M.	265	
McIlvaine	James Monroe	300 301	
McIlvaine	James Morrow	314 314	
McIlvaine	James Ross	268 268	
McIlvaine	James William	270 270	
McIlvaine	James William	301 302	
McIlvaine	James William, Jr.	302 302	
McIlvaine	James William, III	302	
McIlvaine	Jane	310	
McIlvaine	Jane	310	
McIlvaine	Janet	318	
McIlvaine	Jean	268 269	
McIlvaine	Jerome Ray	304 304	
McIlvaine	Joan Alice	274 275	
McIlvaine	Joe Donald	271 272	
McIlvaine	John	244 263	
McIlvaine	John	263 300	
McIlvaine	John	311 311	
McIlvaine	John Addison	315 316	
McIlvaine	John Addison	316 318	
McIlvaine	John D.	315 321	
McIlvaine	John F.	322 322	
McIlvaine	John H.	275	
McIlvaine	John Haldane	268 269	
McIlvaine	John Jay	264	
McIlvaine	John Tyler	269	
McIlvaine	John Wilson	317 317	
McIlvaine	John Wilson, Jr.	317 318	
McIlvaine	John Wilson, III	318	
McIlvaine	Johney Burr	323 326	
McIlvaine	Jonathan Franklin	268	
McIlvaine	Joseph	320	
McIlvaine	Joseph Dwight	323 326	
McIlvaine	Joseph Thomas	322 323	
McIlvaine	Judson S.	313 314	
McIlvaine	Julia	311 314	
McIlvaine	Karen Barbara	268	
McIlvaine	Karen Jeanne	268	
McIlvaine	Katherine	314 315	
McIlvaine	Katherine Erin	268	
McIlvaine	Katie Edith	300 300	
McIlvaine	Keith Welles	269	
McIlvaine	Kelly Lynn	302 302	
McIlvaine	Kelly Matthew	314	
McIlvaine	Kevin Alan	314	
McIlvaine	Kristi Dawn	304	
McIlvaine	Larry Eugene	303 304	
McIlvaine	Larry Eugene Jr.	304 304	
McIlvaine	LaVern	299	
McIlvaine	LaVern	299 299	
McIlvaine	Laverne	269 270	
McIlvaine	Lawrence	275	
McIlvaine	Lawrence	313 313	
McIlvaine	Lawrence Allen	313	
McIlvaine	Leah Marie	314	
McIlvaine	Lena	311 312	

McIlvaine	Lloyd Grant	313
McIlvaine	Lois Irene	270 271
McIlvaine	Lori Marie	304
McIlvaine	Luanne	270 271
McIlvaine	Lynne M.	268 269
McIlvaine	Margaret	263
McIlvaine	Margaret	275
McIlvaine	Margaret	310 310
McIlvaine	Margaret	322 322
McIlvaine	Margaret Jane	264
McIlvaine	Maria	263 310
McIlvaine	Mariah McIntire	300
McIlvaine	Mark George	270
McIlvaine	Mark Kirkpatrick	318
McIlvaine	Marquis	275
McIlvaine	Marsha Kay	304 305
McIlvaine	Mary	244 244
McIlvaine	Mary	269 271
McIlvaine	Mary	315
McIlvaine	Mary Agnes	315 315
McIlvaine	Mary Alice	264
McIlvaine	Mary Ann	310 311
McIlvaine	Mary Jane	263 280
McIlvaine	Mary Jane	273 273
McIlvaine	Mary Jane	315 319
McIlvaine	Mary Kathleen	271 272
McIlvaine	Mary Waunita	299 299
McIlvaine	Matilda	315 315
McIlvaine	Maude Merrell	323 324
McIlvaine	Meredith	265 266
McIlvaine	Michael	267
McIlvaine	Michael Griffith	275
McIlvaine	Michael Terry	268 269
McIlvaine	Michell Lynn	304 304
McIlvaine	Mildred Valentine	300 308
McIlvaine	Nancy	322
McIlvaine	Nathaniel	322
McIlvaine	Neal George	265
McIlvaine	Nellie Lorene	300 303
McIlvaine	Nellie M.	321
McIlvaine	Nellie R.	321
McIlvaine	Nora Irene	316
McIlvaine	Patricia	267
McIlvaine	Patricia Morrow	314
McIlvaine	Patrick Ryan	302
McIlvaine	Patrick William	268
McIlvaine	Patty Lorene	301 301
McIlvaine	Paul Edwin	313 314
McIlvaine	Pearl Louise	322
McIlvaine	Penni Jean	302
McIlvaine	Perry E.	265 267
McIlvaine	Phyllis Neoma	301 302
McIlvaine	Randy	313
McIlvaine	Rebecca A.	321 322
McIlvaine	Rebekah	314
McIlvaine	Rex Gibson	268 268
McIlvaine	Rhonda Louise	309 310
McIlvaine	Robert	244 315
McIlvaine	Robert Bruce	269 270
McIlvaine	Robert Bruce Jr.	270
McIlvaine	Robert Grant	313 313
McIlvaine	Robert Keith	313 313
McIlvaine	Robert W.	321 321
McIlvaine	Ronald James	273
McIlvaine	Ross C.	264 268
McIlvaine	Roy Emmett	264 265
McIlvaine	Ruby Juanita	300 308
McIlvaine	Ruth	244 252
McIlvaine	Ruth	263 275
McIlvaine	Ruth	310 310
McIlvaine	Ruth	313
McIlvaine	Ruth	314 314
McIlvaine	Ruth Eleanor	271 272
McIlvaine	Ruth I.	321
McIlvaine	Samuel	322 322
McIlvaine	Sandra Lee	270 270
McIlvaine	Sarah Ann	315
McIlvaine	Sarah Ann	317 317
McIlvaine	Sarah Catherine	264
McIlvaine	Sarah Ruth	272
McIlvaine	Scott Sherman	313
McIlvaine	Shawn Eugene	302
McIlvaine	Sheril Anne	273
McIlvaine	Sheshbazzar B.	310 311
McIlvaine	Smith	263 275
McIlvaine	Smith	310
McIlvaine	[son]	310
McIlvaine	Stephen Brownlee	268 268
McIlvaine	Stephen Cody	304
McIlvaine	Stephen Penneck	315
McIlvaine	Susan Fuller	314 314
McIlvaine	Susan Grace	271 274
McIlvaine	Susan Ruth	272 272
McIlvaine	Thomas Lawrence	313 313
McIlvaine	Thomas M.	310
McIlvaine	Timothy Earl	268
McIlvaine	Travis Shane	302
McIlvaine	Ulysses Grant	311 313
McIlvaine	Uriah Dawn	304
McIlvaine	Wallace Jay	271 273
McIlvaine	Walter Rosebury	300
McIlvaine	Wayne	269
McIlvaine	Wilbert Greer	316
McIlvaine	Wilbert R.	320 320
McIlvaine	Wilfred Jethro	300 304
McIlvaine	Wilfred Oleon	300 300
McIlvaine	William	315
McIlvaine	William A. H.	316 317
McIlvaine	William Andrew	268 268
McIlvaine	William Blair	313 313
McIlvaine	William Charley	300 309
McIlvaine	William Cody	303 304
McIlvaine	William Cody	309
McIlvaine	William David	304 304
McIlvaine	William R.	317
McIlvaine	William Robert	315 316
McIlvaine	Winfield	311 311
[McIlvaine]	-----	269
[McIlvaine]	-----	275
[McIlvaine]	-----	299
[McIlvaine]	-----	309
[McIlvaine]	-----	310
[McIlvaine]	-----	311
[McIlvaine]	-----	314
[McIlvaine]	-----	314
[McIlvaine]	Ann	300
[McIlvaine]	Anne	321
[McIlvaine]	Irene	309
[McIlvaine]	Jean	267
[McIlvaine]	Kim	269
[McIlvaine]	Leona	272
[McIlvaine]	Marie	304
[McIlvaine]	Myrtle	326
McIntire	Helen	268
McKay	David Alan	294
McKee	Nancy Ellen	328
McKeefrey	Jane Ervin	198
McKeefrey	Neil	198
McKim	James	243
McKim	James	243
McKim	Ruth	243 243
McKinney	Mary	207
McKissick	Florence	224
McKnight	Levi A.	199
McLaughlin	Eleanor Ann	196
McLaughlin	Frank Parnell	196
McLaughlin	Frank Parnell Jr.	196
McLaughlin	Samuel P.	320
McLaughlin	Thomas	326
McLean	Robert	192
McLeod	Keith Allen	136
McManus	Carl L.	109 109
McManus	Cora	109 109
McManus	Estella	109 109
McManus	Eva	109 111
McManus	John	109
McManus	Lenore	109
McManus	Maggie M.	109 109
McManus	Patricia Ann	240
McMaster	Mary E.	199
McMaster	Robert B. Jr.	199

Surname	Given			Surname	Given			Surname	Given		
McMeans	Sarah Elizabeth		227	Miller	Clyde McElwain	150	150	Mizicko	Dolores Jean		164
McMillen	Patricia Lea		243	Miller	Elizabeth Lucille		241	Moffett	Luanne		272
McMurray	Cassie Elissa	125		Miller	George S.		150	Montgomery	Nettie Maud		132
McMurray	James Wilbur	124	124	Miller	James Aaron, Jr.		187	Montroy	Lawrence H.		186
McMurray	Janet Louise	123	125	Miller	James Aaron, III	187		Moody	Vickie Barbara		217
McMurray	Jeffrey Lee	124		Miller	Jay E.	150		Mook	Florence		155
McMurray	John Stewart		123	Miller	Jay George	150	150	Moon	Traci Lynn		110
McMurray	John Stewart Jr.	123	124	Miller	Jennifer		110	Mooney	Clinton		296
McMurray	Margaret E.	123	126	Miller	Jo Ann		134	Moore	Edna Florence	132	132
McMurray	Mark Stewart	124		Miller	Joel Alexander	187		Moore	Elizabeth		156
McMurray	Paul William	123	124	Miller	Marcie	262	262	Moore	F. Richard		204
McMurray	Paula Lynne	124		Miller	Mark	262	262	Moore	Harriet Ann	258	259
McMurray	Rodney Eugene	124	124	Miller	Michael	262		Moore	Henry George		258
McMurray	Ryan Patrick	124		Miller	Regis		262	Moore	James Reed		132
McMurray	Steven Craig	124		Miller	Shane David		160	Moore	Joan Josephine	258	259
McMurray	Terry Wayne	124	124	Miller	Virgil		226	Moore	John		329
McNamara	Mary Elizabeth		150	[Miller]	-----		150	Moore	Marguerite		234
McQuiston	Bonnie Jane	146	146	[Miller]	Ida		150	Moore	Martha		249
McQuiston	Carl David	143	149	Millikin	Vickie		301	Moore	Maryellen Morton		203
McQuiston	Carol Jane	145	146	Milner	----- (Dr.)		319	Moore	Patricia Irene	258	258
McQuiston	David Jon	146		Milner	Bertha	128		Moore	Robin Marie		222
McQuiston	David William		143	Milner	Charles	121	128	Moose	Gerald	172	
McQuiston	Dorothy Mae	143	147	Milner	Clarence	128		Moose	John	172	
McQuiston	Fred Eugene	145	146	Milner	Clyde	128	128	Moose	Richard		172
McQuiston	Glen Lee	145		Milner	Elmer	121		Moquin	Austin David	148	
McQuiston	Kathie Jean	149	149	Milner	Eugene W.	121		Moquin	Jeffrey Thomas		148
McQuiston	Kevin Paul	149		Milner	Floyd	128	128	Morgan	Dale		261
McQuiston	Marion Rose	143		Milner	Geraldine E.	128		Morgan	Frank		278
McQuiston	Patty Jean	146	146	Milner	Grace	128		Morgan	James Anthony		165
McQuiston	Paul B.	143		Milner	Hannah Mariah	121		Morgan	Kay		270
McQuiston	Paula Jean	146		Milner	Helen	128		Morris	John E., Jr.		201
McQuiston	Rita Margaret	143	143	Milner	Hester Jane	121		Morrison	-----		222
McQuiston	Robert J.	143	145	Milner	James	128	128	Morrison	Jamieson Cory	222	
McQuiston	Susan Kay	146		Milner	John A.	128		Morrow	Hilda		314
McQuiston	Thomas Robert	146		Milner	Leroy	128		Morrow	William		315
McQuiston	Tom Albert	145	146	Milner	Levi		121	Moser	Sandra		269
[McQuiston]	Bobbie		146	Milner	Levi	121	128	Moses	Alice Lee		318
McReynolds	Marie Frances		216	Milner	Mary Melvina	121	121	Motor	[daughter]	114	
McWade	Marlynn		309	Milner	Pearl	128		Motor	-----		114
Means	Lawrence Allen		198	Milner	Vance	128		Mountain	Wanda Lee		189
Means	Sarah Katherine	198		[Milner]	Daisy C.		128	Moye	Linda Lou		276
Means	Thomas Allen	198		[Milner]	Emma		128	Muck	Sharon Elizabeth		190
Mederios	Janice		261	[Milner]	Mary		128	Mucke	Linda Lee		198
Mega	Darlene		170	Minnis	Kay Ann	143	145	Mullen	Malinda Dale		237
Meiksel	-----		120	Minnis	Marilyn Jean	143	144	Murphy	Betty Virginia	236	236
Mettheis	Arvid	213		Minnis	Maureen Lee	144	144	Murphy	Calvin Lynn	236	236
Mettheis	Edward P.		213	Minnis	Paul Ramon	143	144	Murphy	Carol Diane	236	236
Mettheis	Nadene	213		Minnis	Paul Wayne		143	Murphy	Donald Dean	236	236
Metzger	Mark		325	Minnis	Rita Lynn	144	145	Murphy	Jesse Allen	236	
Mickey	Mary		107	Minor	Ona Belle		220	Murphy	Joseph Dean	236	
Mikolaizik	Mary Jane		163	Mitchell	Dessie Diane		304	Murphy	Karen LeAnn	236	
Miles	Marilouise		219	Mitchell	Judith Ann		236	Murphy	Kenneth Marvin	236	
Miles	Mary		130	Mitchell	Robert J.	180		Murphy	Lawrence		236
Miller	Abigail Marie	187		Mitchell	Vernon J.		180	Murphy	Lisa Rae	237	

Surname	Given name		
Murphy	Lori Lynn	237	
Murphy	Mandy Lynn	236	
Murphy	Marvin Lawrence	236	236
Murphy	Mathew Dean	236	
Murphy	Michael David	236	
Murphy	Richard Allen	236	237
Murphy	Scott Richard	237	
Murray	Kandice K.		142
Musgrove	Adam	305	
Musgrove	Chad	305	
Musgrove	Kyle Andre	305	
Musgrove	Orval		305
Musto	Ann	110	
Musto	Christina	110	
Musto	Regina	110	
Musto	Richard		110
Musto	Vincent	110	
Myers	Jana	308	
Myers	Jennifer	308	
Myers	Levi	308	
Myers	Michael		308
Naddy	Charles T.		323
Neal	Alma Venora		265
Neal	Cleo Patricia		229
Neal	Mae Eunice		179
Neeley	Louanne		124
Neemes	Jennie Calhoun		199
Neil	Patricia Joan		230
Nelson	Barbara Lou	288	288
Nelson	Candice	158	
Nelson	Gillian	158	
Nelson	Guy Buford		288
Nelson	James Randy		158
Nelson	Laura Lee	288	
Nelson	Shannon	158	
Nesbit	James	244	
Nesbit	John		244
Nesbit	Maria Jane	244	245
Nesbit	Mary	244	
Netzler	Jeneen Dawn	122	122
Netzler	Robert Edward		122
Netzler	Soni Sue	122	122
Neubauer	-----		155
Neubauer	Ardelle	155	
Neubauer	Robert	155	
Newbold	Mary Elizabeth		185
Newhall	Katherine Mary		179
Newman	Jan		293
Nicholas	Mary Violet		179
Nichols	Brenda Gayle		242
Nicholson	Bessie M.		228
Nicholson	John		243
Nicholson	Mary		107
Nicholson	Nancy Judith		108
Nicholson	William		107
Nickey	Mary Martha		228
Nicodemus	Edgar		243
Nicol	Sandra		165
Nicoll	Julius		314
Nicoll	Robertson A.		312
Noble	Florence		131
Nordstrom	Cally Arlen	215	
Nordstrom	Carl Andrew		215
Nordstrom	Chris Alden	215	
Nordstrom	Clinton Andrew	215	
Nordstrom	Curt Allen	215	
Norman	Brandon Aaron	136	
Norman	John E.		136
Norris	Adam Douglas	169	
Norris	Douglas		169
Norris	Edith Caroline		189
Norris	Tyler Douglas	169	
Nuckolls	Desmond, III		240
Nuckolls	Desmond, IV	240	
Nuckolls	Drew Tyler	240	
Nuckolls	Lauren Carol	240	
O'Kane	Gerald		115
O'Kane	Patrick Gabriel	115	
Olinger	Henri Caesar		201
Oliver	David		131
Olson	Clyde		298
Ordway	Alta Fern	289	294
Ordway	Amy Lee	294	
Ordway	Angeline Estelle	294	
Ordway	Arlo Blaylock	289	293
Ordway	Bryan Michael	291	
Ordway	Bryon Alan	294	
Ordway	Carey	292	
Ordway	Christian Russell	290	
Ordway	Christopher W. S.	292	
Ordway	Danny Joe	290	292
Ordway	David Glen	294	
Ordway	Doris Irene	289	292
Ordway	Duane Lee	293	
Ordway	Earl	289	289
Ordway	Earl Clark	293	293
Ordway	Edith	289	295
Ordway	Edna Lucille	289	
Ordway	Floy	289	296
Ordway	Gary Lynn	290	291
Ordway	Gayle Anthony	290	
Ordway	Gayle Arthur	290	290
Ordway	Glen	289	296
Ordway	Heather LeAnn	290	290
Ordway	Ingrid Jo	291	291
Ordway	James Russell	290	290
Ordway	Janice Terrell	290	291
Ordway	Jean Ann	293	293
Ordway	Jennifer Lee	294	294
Ordway	Jennifer Marie	293	
Ordway	Jeremy Russell	291	
Ordway	Jessica Lynn	291	
Ordway	John Malcolm	292	292
Ordway	Jolie Lynn	293	
Ordway	Julie Marie	292	
Ordway	Kamala Cassandra	292	
Ordway	Katrina Sue	292	
Ordway	Kenneth Raymond	289	
Ordway	Kristal Ruth	292	
Ordway	Kyle Jo	292	
Ordway	Laura Ann	290	291
Ordway	Lillian	296	296
Ordway	Linda Marie	290	291
Ordway	Linda Marie	293	294
Ordway	Lloyd Arthur	289	290
Ordway	Lois Jean	294	294
Ordway	Lori Kay	294	294
Ordway	Malcolm Earl	289	292
Ordway	Mark Edward	292	292
Ordway	Nicholas Noel	293	
Ordway	Raymond Keith	290	292
Ordway	Robert James	291	
Ordway	Robert Wayne	289	293
Ordway	Robert William		289
Ordway	Russell Edwin	290	290
Ordway	Scott Jeremy	292	
Ordway	Sebastian James	290	
Ordway	Sondra Estelle	293	
Ordway	Stanley Allen	293	293
Ordway	Stephen Blaylock	292	
Ordway	Susan Carol	290	
Ordway	Todd Owen	290	291
Ordway	William Leslie	289	294
Ormsby-Bristol	Barbara Nell		222
Osterle	Charlotte Loretz		276
Otto	Eve		133
Oxendine	Charles		302
Oxendine	Charles Grant	302	
Oxley	Edna A.	192	
Oxley	John H.		192
Oxley	Ray D.	192	
Pace	-----		322
Pachello	Donald Michael		214
Pachello	Greg James	214	
Pachello	Jerry Joseph	214	
Pachello	Terri Marie	214	
Paff	Russell D.		282
Parker	Emsie	318	318
Parker	Ian Leslie	318	
Parker	Julia Grant	318	
Parker	Leslie		318
Parker	Mark Wilson	318	318

[Parker]	Judith		318
Parks	Carol Anne	225	
Parks	Frank Gary	225	225
Parks	Fredrick Andrew	225	225
Parks	Michael Allen	225	
Parks	Robert		225
Parks	Shannon Nicole	225	
Parrott	John		330
Parsons	Michelle Susan		233
Passarelli	Julie Ann		205
Patterson	Chester LaVerne	113	113
Patterson	Elizabeth Louise	113	
Patterson	Frederick	113	
Patterson	Gilda Mary	113	113
Patterson	Harry Leicester	113	113
Patterson	Ilo May	113	113
Patterson	John	113	
Patterson	John N.		113
Patterson	Leo May	113	006
Patterson	Samuel		326
Patton	Charles V.		173
Patton	Mary Elizabeth	173	174
Patton	Rita Imelda	173	173
Paul	Minnie		154
Payne	David Wallace		289
Payne	Emalee Suzanne	289	
Payne	Matt David	289	
Payne	Roxanne	289	
Payne	Todd David	289	
Pearch	Brianna Leigh	266	
Pearch	Dan Scott	266	
Pearch	David Neal	266	266
Pearch	Edith Ann	266	266
Pearch	Franklin David		266
Pearch	Karen Sue	266	266
Pearch	Steven Dale	266	266
Pearson	Bertha Lucille		139
Peck	Alysse Amber	294	
Peck	Paul John		294
Pefley	Rosa May		228
Penneck	Julie Ann		314
Pennington	Paul		270
Pennock	Della B.	223	
Pennock	Florence E.	223	
Pennock	Gertrude L.	223	
Pennock	Lois	223	
Pennock	Nathaniel		223
Pennock	William	223	
Penrod	Eileen Amber	160	160
Penrod	Laurie Jane	160	160
Penrod	Lawrence Owen		160
Penrod	Nelda Ann	160	160
Penrod	Pamela Kay	160	160
Penrod	Rosemarie	160	
Perkins	Gladys Irene		290
Perrin	Thomas Wesley		188
Perrine	Hazel E.		137
Peters	Mildred B.		191
Peterson	Sarah		151
Petri	Jane Kathryn		295
Phillips	Amy		124
Phillips	Burt J.		283
Phillips	David Michael	123	123
Phillips	Dorothy Mae	283	283
Phillips	Gloria Diane	123	123
Phillips	Harriet Ann	283	283
Phillips	Kenneth Eugene	123	
Phillips	Kevin John	123	
Phillips	Warren		123
Piccinelli	Robert James		235
Pigoni	Charles George		258
Pigoni	Charles George, Jr.	258	260
Pigoni	Donna	260	260
Pigoni	Sharon	260	260
Pigoni	Stephen	260	260
Polansky	Eleanor		127
Porter	Betty Jeanne	138	138
Porter	Celia Jane	138	139
Porter	Donald Moore	138	138
Porter	Drew Erwin	138	
Porter	James Lawrence		138
Porter	Marilyn Louise	138	139
Porter	Mark Wayne	138	
Porter	Nancy Ann	138	
Porter	Patricia Ann	138	139
Postma	Marcia		187
Potter	Brandie	282	
Potter	Claude		282
Potter	Crystal	282	
Potter	DeBlaine	282	
Potter	Eric	282	
Potter	Landry C.	282	
Potter	Laurie F.	282	282
Potter	Laverne G.	282	282
Potter	Leon J.	282	282
Potter	LeRoy C.	282	
Potter	Leslie Jacinta		276
[Potter]	Ruby		282
Pottorf	Fred G.	299	
Pottorf	Jake		299
Pottorf	LeRoy	299	
Powell	Amanda Jo	110	
Powell	Dennis		110
Powell	Heather Dawn	110	
Powell	Jodi Denise	110	
Prater	Pearl E.		280
Prather	Frank		183
Pruitt	Hubert Royce		137
Price	Phoebe		129
Pritchard	John		194
Proctor	Tonia Paulette		304
Protsman	Cora		227
Prouty	Lenna Claire		150
Putnam	Leola Pearl		157
Pyle	Charles David		271
Pyle	Charles David	271	
Pyle	Lindsey Ann	271	
Quijada	Vilma Mercedes		159
Rackley	Joanne		256
Raiff	Nancy M.		126
Raines	D. W.		223
Raines	Tamara		306
Ralston	Andrew		200
Ramp	Andrew Mervin	224	227
Ramp	Cindy Nell	227	
Ramp	Ella E.	224	224
Ramp	Harvey Leroy	225	227
Ramp	Harvey McElwain	224	225
Ramp	Harvey Robert	227	227
Ramp	Ida Mae	224	225
Ramp	Jacob Rupley	224	
Ramp	Jake William	227	
Ramp	James Harvey	227	227
Ramp	John		224
Ramp	John Clifford	225	
Ramp	John Dale	227	227
Ramp	Karlyn Beth	227	
Ramp	Laura Belle	224	224
Ramp	Letta Cornatzer	225	225
Ramp	Peggy Joan	226	226
Ramp	Ruby Fern	227	227
Ramp	Susan Lynn	227	
Ramp	Velma Lacy	225	226
Ramp	Vicki Jo	227	
Ramp	William Earnshaw	225	226
Ramsey	Charlotte	244	248
Ramsey	Eleanor	244	246
Ramsey	Elizabeth	244	248
Ramsey	George	244	246
Ramsey	Josiah		244
Ramsey	Josiah A.	244	247
Ramsey	Katherine	244	245
Ramsey	Maria	244	
Ramsey	Martha	244	247
Ramsey	Mary	244	
Ramsey	Mary Jane	244	246
Ramsey	Ruth	244	244
Ramsey	William	244	
[Ramsey]	Annie		246
[Ramsey]	Emeline E.		247
Randolph	Nancy		275
Rangel	Nancy		234

Rankin	Frank		238	Riley	Andrew Jay	167	Royse	Rose Mary	287	288
Rapp	Joseph		324	Riley	Angela Marie	167	Royse	Wallace Dunlap	286	287
Ray	Judy Marie		285	Riley	John J., Jr.		167	Runkle	Susie		154
Reddin	April Michelle		145	Riley	Matthew Lee	167	Rupert	Alice Marion	164	164
Redman	Wallace		204	Riley	Michael Sean	167	Rupert	David Fred Ames	164	164
Reed	Shannon Elaine		214	Rinehart	Caroline M.		320	Rupert	David Fred A. Jr.	164	
Reeves	Betty Lee	179	179	Ring	Ernest Harvey Jr,		188	Rupert	Ernest Victor		164
Reeves	Harry		179	Rinker	Alice M.	241	Rupert	Evelyn Joyce	164	164
Rehn	Bruce		169	Rinker	George Washington		241	Rupert	Marjory Almaretta	164	165
Reifstock	Christine Anne		284	Rinker	James A.	241	Rupert	Mark Zahniser	164	165
Reinhart	Cheryl Lynn		115	Rinker	John McElwain	241	Rupert	Mildred Arlene	164	165
Remaley	Kelly Marie	168	Rinker	William H.	241	Rupert	Queene	164|
Remaley	Terrance		168	Roark	Cindy Jane		232	Rupert	Stacey Nicol	165	
Rengo	Phil		188	Robb	Jane		320	Rupert	Susan Renee	164	165
Rennie	Joseph		256	Roberts	Bessie		311	Russell	Elden Leo	299	
Repka	Teresa Ann		298	Robertson	Christopher	260	Russell	J. E.		299
Rettig	Annie		316	Robertson	David		260	Russell	Ruth	299	299
Retzel	-----		246	Robinson	Ruth		330	Russell	Sarah Jane		140
Reynolds	Camilla B.	163	163	Rodgers	Donald Tracy		261	Rust	David	225	
Reynolds	John		330	Rodgers	Leah	261	Rust	Paul L.	224	
Reynolds	Joseph L.		163	Rodriguez	Sandra		160	Rust	Ralph G.		224
Reynolds	Margaret		320	Rogers	Frances Marie		303	Rust	Ralph Mason	224	225
Rhoads	Malinda		206	Rollya	Alice J.		128	Rust	Robert	225	
Rhodes	-----		143	Rollya	Ruth A.		128	[Rust]	Arlene		225
Rhodes	-----		153	Romo	-----		182	Ruth	Ezemiah Jane		202
Rhodes	Clara May	170	170	Rose	Casey Lee	237	Rutherford	Mary Janis		141
Rhodes	Claude O.	170	170	Rose	Charles Leroy	237	237	Ruthrauff	Susan Nan		237
Rhodes	Doris Elaine	170		Rose	Dustin Charles	237	Ruzika	-----		254
Rhodes	Otis M.		170	Rose	Jeffrey Lee	237	Sabila	Diana		261
Rhodes	William Lawrence	170	170	Rose	Jerry Lee	237	237	Sage	David Carleton		221
Rhodes	William Lawrence Jr.	170|	Rose	Judy Anneira	237|237	Sage	Jeffrey Carlton	221
Richards	Alexander	193	Rose	Nancy Darlene	237|237	Sage	Lindsay Gail	221
Richards	Andrew	193	Rose	Richard Allen	237	Sandusky	Danielle Marie	178
Richards	Andrew James	123	Rose	Roy Lee		237	Sandusky	Leslie		178
Richards	Elizabeth	193	Rose	Sonny Todd	237	Sassaman	Avary Gale	191
Richards	Harry		123	Ross	Carita Beryl	130	130	Sassaman	Stephen Harry		191
Richards	James		193	Ross	Clement Valindingham		129	Sawhill	Elizabeth Jane	247
Richards	James	193	Ross	David S.	129	Sawhill	Elmer C.	247
Richards	James, Jr.	193	Ross	Elizabeth E.		129	Sawhill	Ina M.	247
Richards	Jamie Ellen	123	Ross	Franklin Clair	129	130	Sawhill	John		247
Richards	Lydia	193	Ross	Harold C.	129	Sawhill	John M.	247
Richards	Margaret	193	Ross	Hortense	129	Sawhill	Mary Jane	247
Richards	Mary	193	Ross	Lela E.	129|130	Sawhill	Oscar H.	247
Richards	Mary Jane	200	Ross	Marilyn Grace	130|130	Sawhill	Sadie M.	247
Richards	Michael Wilson	123	Ross	Thelma		170	Sawhill	William S.	247
Richards	Richard	193	Ross	William	129	Sberna	Laurie		175
Richards	Robert	193	193	Rost	Earl A.		180	Scammon	Jed		234
Richards	Sarah	193	Rost	Richard J.	180	Scanlon	Mary Jane	174
Richards	Thomas	193	Royse	Barbara Jean	287	288	Scanlon	W. E.		174
Richards	Thomas	193	Royse	Bernita Madeline	286|286	Scheer	Christopher James	125
Richards	Timothy Wayne		242	Royse	Betty Jean	286	Scheer	Lindsey Diane	125
[Richards]	Susan		193	Royse	Judith Ann	287	288	Scheer	Mark Walter		125
Richter	Vincent		238	Royse	Lucille Isabel	286	287	Schick	Kenneth Lee	296
Riddle	Helen Faye		175	Royse	Martin Jefferson	286	Schick	Raymond Wallace		296

Surname	Given Name	Pg	Pg
Schmidt	Carol Ann	113	
Schmidt	Daniel		229
Schmidt	David Thomas	113	
Schmidt	Lynn Louise	113	
Schmidt	Susan Jean	113	
Schmidt	Thomas Loren		113
Schmitz	Carole		144
Schneidmiller	John		221
Schneidmiller	Joie Marie	221	
Schneidmiller	Kurtis	221	
Schnoes	Diane Marie	162	162
Schnoes	James Thomas	162	
Schnoes	Karen Jane	162	162
Schnoes	Mark Joseph	162	
Schnoes	Paul Joseph		162
Schnoes	Paul Joseph	162	162
Schnoes	Paul Vincent	162	
[Schnoes]	Mindy		162
Schultise	Edwin		254
Scoby	Helen		181
Scorupan	Colton William	148	
Scorupan	Donald William		148
Scorupan	Hayvn Michael	148	
Scott	Beth Ann		276
Scroggins	Teresa		301
Sealand	Amanda Mae	169	
Sealand	David		169
Sears	CLurtis J.		131
Seaver	Jeffrey Alan	189	189
Seaver	Jodi Lynn	189	189
Seaver	Jordan Lemuel	189	
Seaver	Marah Eleanor	189	
Seaver	Thomas Martin		189
Sefzik	David Lester	260	
Sefzik	Diane	260	261
Sefzik	Gustave William Jr.		260
Sefzik	Linda Lou	260	261
Sefzik	Susan Ann	260	261
Sefzik	Tracy Lee	260	261
Seibold	Nancy		146
Sellers	Daniel F.	208	
Sellers	James A.	208	
Sellers	John W.	208	
Sellers	Mary F.	208	208
Sendek	Matilda		198
Sewell	Clair D.		221
Sewell	Janet Gail	221	221
Sewell	Jo Ann Clare	221	221
Sewell	Judy Lynn	221	221
Shadley	Lois Carol		266
Shannon	Barbara Jean	127	127
Shannon	Bette	127	
Shannon	Catherine Eleanor		127
Shannon	Elizabeth		192
Shannon	Jane		193
Shannon	Judson Clyde	127	127
Shannon	Kenneth Leroy	127	127
Shannon	Martha	127	
Shannon	Raymond	127	
Shannon	William Earl		127
Shannon	William Russell	127	127
Shaw	Ada C.		316
Shaw	Jacqueline Lee	204	
Shaw	James Albert		204
Shaw	James Albert Jr.	204	
Shaw	Maryamber Florence	204	204
Shaw	Ruth Ellen	204	
Shaw	Shirley Jane	204	205
Shearer	Mary Jean		265
Sheldon	Gregory J.	259	
Sheldon	Michael R.	259	
Sheldon	Robert		259
Shepard	------		196
Shepherd	Danny		305
Shinerberry	Edith		113
Shipley	Cleo		213
Shockley	Charles		249
Shook	Oliver		154
Shoop	Mary Matilda		178
Shotwell	Margaret McIlvaine	320	320
Shotwell	Stuart Beebe		320
Shotwell	Stuart McIlvaine	320	
Shotwell	Walter Gaston		320
Shreccgart	Albert		252
Shuler	Christian Lee	230	
Shuler	Don		230
Shurtliff	Helen		318
Sias	David Lester	260	
Sias	Gayle Alice	260	260
Sias	James Russell	261	
Sias	Joan Delane	260	261
Sias	John Dando		260
Sias	John Dando, Jr.	260	261
Sias	Melia Kathleen	261	
Sickenberger	Georgia Carol		295
Sigars	Calvin Wayne	302	302
Sigars	David Wayne	302	
Sigars	Kenneth		302
Sigars	Pamela Sue	302	
Simcox	Florence		155
Simmons	Bryonite Elizabeth	144	
Simmons	Douglas Herbert		144
Simmons	Joy Brandon		277
Simmons	Mary		277
Simpson	Beth Ann	275	
Simpson	Carol Jean		187
Simpson	Mitchell Nolan	275	
Simpson	Robert Scott	275	
Simpson	Robert W.		275
Simpson	Sarah Jean	275	
Simpson	Terri Lynn	275	
Singleton	Ramon Asa	144	
Singleton	Robert Jerome		144
Singleton	Robert Jerome	144	
Skinker	Mary Caroline		286
Slaper	Frank Milton		229
Slaper	Frank Thomas	229	
Slaper	Jessica Constance	229	
Slaper	Larry	229	
Slaper	Lloyd	229	
Slaper	Lonnie	229	229
Slaper	Lynette	229	229
Slater	Bruce Richard	173	173
Slater	Charlotte		173
Slater	Douglas D.	173	
Slater	Gary Alan	173	
Slater	H. Clay		172
Slater	Jennifer Susan	173	
Slater	John Canon	172	173
Slater	John Clinton	173	
Slater	Lena Jane	173	
Slater	Lois Patricia	172	
Slater	Richard Bruce	173	
Slater	Richard Watson	172	173
[Slater]	------		173
Slichter	Rebecca		201
Slike	------		231
Sloan	Sarah		317
Sloper	Lucy		154
[Smaroff]	Lori		255
Smarroff	Jennifer	255	
Smarroff	John		255
Smarroff	John	255	255
Smarroff	Lisa	255	
Smarroff	Sherri	255	255
Smiley	------		254
Smiley	Georgia	254	254
Smiley	Irene	253	254
Smiley	Joella	253	253
Smiley	John		253
Smiley	John		254
Smiley	Rex	253	
Smiley	Ruth	254	254
Smith	Amy Jo	239	
Smith	Byron	120	
Smith	Cameron	120	
Smith	Carol May	239	
Smith	Charlotte L.	120	
Smith	Cheryl Lynne	159	
Smith	Chester R.		120
Smith	Connie Leola	159	
Smith	Denise Ann	159	

Smith	Diane Ellen	120
Smith	Douglas	269
Smith	Elizabeth L.	312
Smith	Elizabeth L.	120
Smith	Elizabeth Evelyn	159
Smith	Emma Josephine	235
Smith	Emsie	317
Smith	Ethel	175
Smith	Ethel	195
Smith	Gail Ann	239 240
Smith	Grace Alice	233
Smith	Inez Ann	231
Smith	John L.	195
Smith	Joseph	154
Smith	Juanita Irene F.	146
Smith	Kristen McIlvaine	269
Smith	LeRoy C.	264
Smith	Leslie Renee	239
Smith	Leslie Kathleen	233
Smith	Lola May	307
Smith	Lynda Fay	239 240
Smith	Margaret	263
Smith	Marsha	120
Smith	Mary Elizabeth	294
Smith	Paige Kathleen	233
Smith	Ray Wesley	120
Smith	Richard	117
Smith	Robert Samuel	159
Smith	Rodney Douglas	239
Smith	Rodney Martin	233
Smith	Rodney Dale	239 240
Smith	Ryan Douglas	240
Smith	Sandra Dee	159
Smith	Scott Martin	233 233
Smith	Scott Douglas	269
Smith	Sharol Kay	239 240
Smith	Stacy Lynne	233 233
Smith	Steven	117
Smith	Teresa	120
Smith	Thelma P.	279
Smith	Thomas William	159
Smith	Virginia	120
Smith	William A.	182
Smith	William Samuel	159
Smithyman	Austin	258
Smithyman	Christal	258
Smithyman	Daniel Raymond	258 258
Smithyman	Drew	258
Smithyman	Jennifer	258
Smithyman	Jesse	258
Smithyman	John Leo	258
Smithyman	John	258 258
Smithyman	Michael Joseph	258 258
Smithyman	Owen	258
Smithyman	Patricia Jean	258 258
Smithyman	Tracy	258
Smoyer	Barbara Jean	124
Snider	Alisa Roxanna	302
Snyder	Greg	138
Snyder	James Wesley	138
Snyder	Patricia Ann	276
Sonka	Chenney Rebecca	237
Sonka	Daniel Craig	237
Sonka	Travis Darin	237
Sopira	Christine	258
Southworth	Archie Clark	161
Southworth	Dean LaVerne	217
Southworth	Dean	218
Southworth	Donna Leanne	217 218
Southworth	Duane LaVerne	217 218
Southworth	Frances Eleanor	161 161
Southworth	Jessica Elizabeth	218
Southworth	Joy Melissa	218
Southworth	Julia Ann	218
Southworth	Lee C.	161
Southworth	Lettie Camilla	161 163
Southworth	Linda Loree	217 218
Southworth	Terry John	218
Sowash	Ruth Garnet	271
Sowers	-----	245
Spaulding	Albert D.	282
Spaulding	Albert Ross	281
Spaulding	Annie Byrd	225
Spaulding	Bernice Hazel	281 284
Spaulding	Eunice H.	282 282
Spaulding	Flossye Irene	281 283
Spaulding	Golden	282 283
Spaulding	Lenore R.	282
Spaulding	Raymond B.	282 283
Spaulding	Ross	281
Spaulding	Roy M.	281 282
Spaulding	Ruth Marie	281 285
Spaulding	Viva B.	282 283
Speak	Jeffrey Austin	302
Speak	Jeffrey Todd	302
Speiser	Lloyd	119
Spencer	Elisabeth Shaw	134
Spencer	Ian Douglas	134
Spencer	Kathleen	168
Spencer	Terence Richard	134
Sphar	Sarah Ann	253
Spilker	Linda	285
Spitzer	Raymond	179
Spitzer	Raymond E.	179
Spitzer	Sherrion Lee	179
Sponsler	Andrew	154
Spoon	Hazel	304
Sprague	Allen	117 118
Sprague	Donald Norbert	117 118
Sprague	Donald	117
Sprague	Frank E.	127
Sprague	Matthew Donald	118
Sprague	Timothy Joseph	118
Stafford	Audrey	157
Staley	Rhonda Delane	137
Staley	Rita Louise	112
Stearn	Donald Leroy	116
Stearn	Milton	116
Stearn	William Robert	116
Steel	Robert	107
Steffan	-----	143
Steffan	Thomas	143
Stegall	William	221
Steiner	Alexander Eun	134
Steiner	Annie Riggs	134
Steiner	David Denison	134
Stephen	Pat	272
Steppe	Joseph	143
Steppe	Laura Belle	143 143
Sterner	Margaret	313
Stevenot	Helen Margaret	292
Stevens	Carolyn Rosa	136
Stewart	Andrew	326 327
Stewart	Andrew	206
Stewart	Caroline R.	207
Stewart	Charles LeRoy	166
Stewart	Charles Arthur	125
Stewart	Clara B.	207
Stewart	Cynthia Sue	125 125
Stewart	Douglas	188
Stewart	Eleanor	206
Stewart	Eliza J.	206
Stewart	Elizabeth	311
Stewart	Elizabeth	206
Stewart	Ellen	182
Stewart	Evaline A.	207
Stewart	James	206
Stewart	James Jr.	326 326
Stewart	James	326
Stewart	Jane A.	207
Stewart	Janelle Kay	295 295
Stewart	John	206 207
Stewart	John M.	207
Stewart	John	326
Stewart	Jonathan	168
Stewart	Karen Ann	125 125
Stewart	Kate	257
Stewart	Kathryn Elizabeth	168
Stewart	Kathy Ann	295 295
Stewart	Kevin Charles	125
Stewart	Laura C.	207
Stewart	Lucinda	326 327

Stewart	Lucy	206	Stringer	Freda Belle	255	Szokoly	Angela	205	
Stewart	Margaret L.	207	Stringer	George	252 253	Szokoly	Jason	205	
Stewart	Mary	326 326	Stringer	Harry	256	Tadajski	Bernard John		139
Stewart	Mary E.	207	Stringer	Harry Elmer	255 256	Tadajski	Christine	139 139	
Stewart	Mary Frances	294 295	Stringer	Jacqueline Kay	254 254	Talbott	Patricia Ann	130 131	
Stewart	Mary Jane	206	Stringer	James	252 253	Talbott	William		130
Stewart	Robert	206	Stringer	John	252 257	Talkington	Alexa Jane	135	
Stewart	Russell William	294 295	Stringer	Justin	257	Talkington	Mark Edward		135
Stewart	Samuel	206 206	Stringer	Martha Ruth	255 256	Talkington	Mark Edward II	135	
Stewart	Susan E.	207	Stringer	Mary Alice	255 255	Tanner	Ruby Joyce		158
Stewart	Thomas	206	Stringer	Nelson Dewey	253 254	Taylor	Bryan		145
Stewart	Trevor	188	Stringer	Patty	256	Taylor	Casey William	295	
Stewart	William Francis	295	Stringer	Ray	256 256	Taylor	Cody Lawrence	295	
Stewart	William McD.	206	Stringer	Robert		252	Taylor	James Benjamin	267	
Stewart	William Thompson	294	Stringer	Robert	252	Taylor	James Nelson		267
[Stewart]	Margaretta		206	Stringer	Ruth	252	Taylor	Lynn Stanley	267 267	
[Stewart]	Rebecca		207	Stringer	Theodore	254	Taylor	Michael Joseph	145	
Stickel	Daniel		202	Stringer	Thomas	254 254	Taylor	Raymond Earl		295
Stickel	Edward E.	202	Stringer	Thomas Dwayne	254	Taylor	Rebecca Lynn	267	
Stickel	Mildred V.	202	Stringer	Timothy	254	Taylor	Theodore Merle	267	
Stickel	Percy L.	202	Stringer	Tracy	254	Teeters	Mary J.		253
Stickel	William A.	202	[Stringer]	-----		254	Terrell	John	261 261	
Stinson	Percinda Alanca		300	[Stringer]	-----		256	Terrell	Joseph M.	261 262	
Stoeckmann	Cathy Jean	298 298	[Stringer]	-----		257	Terrell	Pamela	261 262	
Stoeckmann	Connie Lynn	298 298	[Stringer]	Diannah		253	Terrell	Richard	261 261	
Stoeckmann	George	297 297	[Stringer]	Julia		256	Terrell	William		261
Stoeckmann	James Otto	297 298	[Stringer]	Virginia		256	Terrell	William	261	
Stoeckmann	Janice Fern	297 298	Strock	Karen Dawn		212	Terry	George C.		179
Stoeckmann	John James	298 298	Stroski	James		303	Terry	Harold Wilmer		160
Stoeckmann	Marguerite E.	297 297	Stroski	Mitchell James	303	Terry	Robert C.	179	
Stoeckmann	Otto		297	Stroud	Edward		325	Thomas	Brenda Lee		159
Stoeckmann	Sandra Kay	298	Stroud	Edward C.	325	Thomas	Clarence	312	
Stokes	Ora Delphine		156	Stroud	Esther M.	325	Thomas	Edna Berthey	312 312	
Stone	Jerry		281	Stroud	Stephanie	325	Thomas	Guy E.	312	
Strait	Debbie		123	Sturges	Phineas M.		198	Thomas	Harry	312 312	
Strampher	Cecil William		240	Sturgis	Florence H.		317	Thomas	Helen Ann		293
Stratton	Lottie		316	Summerhill	Bradley P., III	165	Thomas	James Bentley	312 312	
Strawn	Brent Allen		222	Summerhill	Craig Alan	165	Thomas	Josiah		312
Stricker	Althea Grace	191 191	Summerhill	George A.	165	Thomas	Laura Alice	312 312	
Stricker	Bonita Lee	191 191	Summerhill	George A. Jr.		165	Thomas	Margaret Bell	312 312	
Stricker	Carol Jean	191 191	Summers	Beatrice	299	Thomas	William H.	312	
Stricker	Charles Andrew		191	Summers	Dorothy	299	Thompson	Adam		155
Stright	Elizabeth		173	Summers	Helen		156	Thompson	Addison E.	151 151	
Stringer	Albert Melville	253 253	Summers	L. L.		299	Thompson	Albert O.	151	
Stringer	Ann		315	Surrell	John		295	Thompson	Augustus M.	151	
Stringer	Barry	256 257	Surrell	John Junior	295	Thompson	Benjamin A.		151
Stringer	Blanche	253 253	Surrell	Mildred Geraldine	295 296	Thompson	Bessie T.	151	
Stringer	Charles Boyd	255 257	Suthers	Al'Louise		227	Thompson	Brandi Renee		233
Stringer	Clara Josephine	255	Swagler	Elizabeth		313	Thompson	[child]	330	
Stringer	Emma J.	257 257	Swayze	Horace George	198	Thompson	Chrystal Marcella	306	
Stringer	Florence	255 256	Swayze	Jason Clark		198	Thompson	Douglas DeWayne		242
Stringer	Frances	253 254	Swayze	Jason Clark	198	Thompson	Eleanor	329 329	
Stringer	Frank Vernon	255 256	Swigert	Ida		119	Thompson	Emma L.	151	
Stringer	Franklin Elmer	253 255	Swoveland	Devon Ray		188	Thompson	Esther	330	

Thompson	Hannah	|	|108	Tyler	|Daniel Elwain	|216|217	Verner	|Jordan Reese	|222|
Thompson	Harry S.	|151|		Tyler	|Donald Wayne	| |216	Verner	|Reese Allan	|222|222
Thompson	Henry A.	|151|		Tyler	|Jennifer Lynn	|217|	Verner	|Riley Allen	|222|
Thompson	James T.	|151|151		Tyler	|Joyce Elaine	|216|	Verner	|Tracey Ann	|222|222
Thompson	Margaret	|329|		Tyler	|Karli Lee	|217|	Vernor	|Reese	| |222
Thompson	Margery Ellen	|329|330		Tyler	|Kathleen Marie	|216|217	Villa	|Angelo Sanchez	| |204
Thompson	Marietta	|151|		Tyler	|Michael Wayne	|217|	Villa	|Donald Robert	|204|205
Thompson	Mary	|329|		Tyler	|Nathan Brian	|217|	Villa	|Francesca Carmel|205|
Thompson	Matthew	|329|330		Tyler	|Philip Wayne	|217|	Villamagna	|Robert	| |139
Thompson	Matthew	|330|		Tyler	|Ida	|257|	Vincent	|Charles	| |238
Thompson	Michael	| |306		Tynan	|Ida	|257|	Vogan	|[child]	|121|
Thompson	Rosanna	| |176		Tynan	|Thomas	| |257	Vogan	|Anna Bernice	|121|122
Thompson	Rosanna	|330|		Tynan	|Thomas, Jr.	|257|	Vogan	|Carl Alvin	|126|127
Thompson	Vance E.	|151|		Ullman	|Carl Tracy	|197|	Vogan	|Cecile Elizabeth|121|123
Thompson	William	| |329		Ullman	|Christine Ann	|197|	Vogan	|Daryl Gene	|126|126
Thompson	William	|330|		Ullman	|Curtis Alan	|197|	Vogan	|Gloria Faith	|167|
[Thompson]	Anna M.	| |151		Ullman	|Gregory Ernst	|197|	Vogan	|Harry Benton	| |167
[Thompson]	Emma	| |151		Ullman	|Gretchen	|197|	Vogan	|Harry Roscoe	|167|
Thordell	Josephine Pauline|	|215		Ullman	|Myron Edward Jr.|	|197	Vogan	|Hazel Anita	|121|
Thornhill	David L.	| |138		Ullman	|Myron Edward III|197|	Vogan	|Jessie Raymond	|167|167
Thornhill	David Nicholas	|138|		Unico	|Christopher Vincent|259|	Vogan	|Jessie Raymond Jr.|167|
Throne	Kate	| |326		Unico	|Daniel Vincent	| |259	Vogan	|Judson Clyde	|121|121
Thrush	Robert	| |326		Unico	|Kenneth Anthony	|259|259	Vogan	|Kathy	|126|127
Tidd	Karen	| |146		Unico	|Lisa Marie	|259|260	Vogan	|Mary Elizabeth	|167|167
Tilger	Shannon	| |262		Unico	|Mark Daniel	|259|259	Vogan	|Mary Lucille	|121|121
Tilley	Jane Ann	|139|139		Unico	|Renee Ann	|259|259	Vogan	|Patricia Ann	|167|
Tilley	Jason Lloyd	|139|		Unico	|Shannon Theresa	|259|	Vogan	|Paul Eugene	|121|
Tilley	Neil William	| |139		[Unico]	|-----	| |259	Vogan	|Peggy	|126|127
Timmons	Floyd A.	| |296		Urber	|Minerva	| |202	Vogan	|Ruth Pearl	|121|
Timmons	Mary Frances	| |281		Vacel	|John	| |285	Vogan	|Samuel Judson	|126|126
Tinken	Henry H.	| |318		Vance	|Dorothy	| |318	Vogan	|Sandra Joy	|167|
Tirrell	Ursula	| |320		Vandervort	|Bonnie Lee	|149|	Vogan	|Thomas Floyd	|121|126
Titus	Elizabeth	| |322		Vandervort	|Patty Ann	|149|	Vogan	|Thompson James	| |121
Todd	Angie	| |170		Vandervort	|Paul Tim	| |149	Vogan	|Timmy	|126|
Townley	[child]	|185|		Vandervort	|Scott David	|149|	Vogan	|Vesta Viola	|121|127
Townley	John Brown	|185|185		Varbinder	|-----	| |328	[Vogan]	|-----	| |126
Townley	Nina Ruth	|185|		Varbinder	|Ettie	|328|	[Vogan]	|-----	| |127
Townley	Thomas Jefferson|	|185		Varbinder	|Irene M.	|328|	Voll	|Cheryl	|285|285
Tracy	Ann Ecca	| |195		Varbinder	|Nettie	|328|	Voll	|Gerry Worden	|284|285
Trimpey	Paul E.	| |174		Veenstra	|Flora	| |186	Voll	|James	|285|
Tropah	Shirley	| |118		Vela	|Anna Bertha	| |159	Voll	|Nancy	|285|
Trotter	Laurel Lynn	|217|		Venning	|Jesse C.	| |199	Voll	|Noreen	|284|284
Trotter	Nancy Lee	|217|		Venning	|Jesse Neemes	|199|	Voll	|S. Leonard	| |284
Trotter	Richard Donald	| |217		Venning	|Margaret Hamilton|199|199	Voll	|Sarah	|285|
Trotter	Terri Marie	|217|		Venning	|Richard E.	|199|	Vorhees	|Frederick	| |314
Tucker	Kelly Lee	| |138		Vento	|Christi Lynn	|205|	Vornheder	|Judith Ann	| |287
Tucker	Virginia Fuller	| |314		Vento	|David Allen	|205|205	Vos	|Jason	|188|
Tuggle	Ruthann	| |262		Vento	|David Allen, Jr.|205|	Vos	|Martin	|188|
Turchich	Karen Lynn	| |139		Vento	|Diane Marie	|205|	Vos	|Scott	|188|
Turner	Evaline	| |181		Vento	|Joseph Albert	|205|205	Vos	|Traci	|188|188
Turner	Julie Sue	| |136		Vento	|Joseph Nicholas	| |205	Vos	|Wayne	| |188
Tuttle	Candace Amy	| |267		Vento	|Matthew David	|205|	Vozar	|Ann	| |260
Tyler	Brett Daniel	|217|		Vento	|Valerie Ann	|205|	Wadolny	|Donald	| |284
Tyler	Brian Wayne	|216|217		Verner	|Christopher Mark|222|	Wadolny	|Donette	|284|284

Wadolny	Lynette	284 285
Wake	Gladys Marie	196
Walker	-----	153
Walker	Anna Jane	226 226
Walker	Glenn William	226
Walker	Jason William	148
Walker	Lilly Irene	211
Walker	Wilkes	152
Walker	William Patrick	226 226
Wallace	Mary	320
Walser	Gwendolyn Lee	226
Waltenberg	Breck Henry	275 278
Waltenberg	Edna R.	278 278
Waltenberg	Elizabeth Smith	279 280
Waltenberg	Fred	278
Waltenberg	George Henry	275
Waltenberg	George James	275 278
Waltenberg	James E.	278
Waltenberg	John Andrew	275
Waltenberg	Lulu E.	278 278
Waltenberg	Mary Jane	275 276
Waltenberg	Menzo Romaine	275 279
Waltenberg	Miriam Denton	279 279
Waltenberg	Orminda Ruth	275 279
Waltenberg	Pearl	278
Waltenberg	Rebecca Frances	275 278
Waltenberg	Romaine George	279 279
Waltenberg	Stella V.	278
Walter	Alyssa	253
Walter	Cara	253
Walter	Paul	253
Walton	Darwin	157
Walton	Judith	182 182
Walton	Lawrence C.	182
Walton	Lawrence C., Jr.	182
Wambold	Michael Alan	291
Wambold	Shauna Lynn	291
Ward	Myrtle	182
Warner	Mary E.	321
Warrick	George R.	245
Warrick	John W.	245
Warrick	John W., Jr.	245
Warrington	Bethany Allen	279
Warrington	Lucas Emerson	279
Warrington	Ross	279
Watkins	Lillie Mae	300
Way	Becky	278
Weaver	Bernice	114
Weaver	Beryl	114
Weaver	Catherine Rose	268
Weaver	Dale	114
Weaver	Helen	114 114
Weaver	Ruth	114
Weber	Ann Nicole (Ott Lynne)	177
Weber	Edward H.	177
Weber	Ingrid Margaret	177 178
Weber	Irving Burge	177 177
Weber	John Philip	177
Weber	Melissa Jean	123
Weber	Michiko Winona	177 178
Weber	Willis Edward	177 177
Weems	Betty Lou	304
Weidman	Alex	300
Weidman	Samuel	300
Weigand	Barbara	285
Weinert	Catherine Michelle	189
Weiss	Cindy	283
Weist	Catherine Jane	200 201
Weist	Leonard	200
Weist	Mary L.	200 201
Weisz	Kara	175
Weisz	Rachel	175
Weisz	Robert	175
Welch	Carol	178
Weldon	Shirley	301
Weliver	David	274
Weliver	Matthew	274
Wellington	Richard	256
Wells	Florence Estelle	255
Wells	Martha Alice	270
Wenger	Rosemary	277
Wenzel	Alice	194
Werner	Frederick Andreas	287
West	Mary	247
Wester	Ada	320
Westmoreland	Adam Ross	163
Westmoreland	Austin Reed	163
Westmoreland	Dakota Bennett	163
Wetzel	Glen Alan	286 286
Wetzel	Nathan Richard	286 286
Wetzel	Richard Alan	286
Wetzel	Ruth Helen	286
Whalen	Kaitlyn Jane	163
Whalen	Kirk James	163
Wheatley	Nancy A.	176
Whirley	Alexandria Michelle	230
Whirley	Bernard L.	230
Whirley	Bradley Lynn	230 230
Whirley	Carmella Kay	230
Whirley	Crystal	230
Whirley	Douglas L.	230 230
Whirley]	Margaret	230
[Whirley]	Yvonne	230
White	Emma	195
White	Esther	195
White	Janice	157
White	John Wesley	199
White	John Wesley, Jr.	199
White	Kathryn	195
White	William H.	195
White	William Harbaugh	195
Whiteman	Sue	248
Whiteside	Audrey	219
Whiteside	Martha Thoren	177
Whitney	L. B. (Banks)	326
Whitt	----- (Rev.)	287
Widyolar	Bennett Kuang Tai	144
Widyolar	Delaney McQuiston	144
Widyolar	Keith Kirati	144
Wienmann	Catherine Marie	135
Wiggins	Kevin	256
Wiggins	Lynne	255 255
Wiggins	Shane	256
Wiggins	Todd	255 256
Wiggins	Virgil	255
[Wiggins]	Cynda	256
Wilcox	Lyle	283
Wilcox	Mary Lou	142
Wild	Laura Lynn	243
Wiley	Frank	247
Wilkens	Kenneth I.	281
Willard	Gerald W.	297
Willard	Margie	297 297
Willard	Michael	297
Williams	Addison Grace	232
Williams	Ann Elizabeth	324 325
Williams	Brett Stephen	232
Williams	Daniel	324
Williams	Lauren Jeanna	232
Williams	Lyle	211
Williams	Marian Rae	253 253
Williams	Ray	253
Williams	Rosetta Jane	156
Williams	Vaun Ann	324 325
Williams	William Dale	324
Williams	William Dale Jr.	324 324
Williams	William Nicole	324
[Williams]	Marie	324
Williamson	James	330
Wilmoth	Rhetta	227
Wilson	Andrew	208
Wilson	Annie Gertrude	317
Wilson	Arthur	245
Wilson	Bernard	245
Wilson	Bobbie	304
Wilson	Charles (Dr.)	211
Wilson	Charlotte	321
Wilson	Cyrus	208
Wilson	Edna Mae	126
Wilson	Elizabeth	246
Wilson	Francis Marion	156
Wilson	John	245

Wilson	Julie Marie	211
Wilson	Lula	156 156
Wilson	Margaretta	208
Wilson	Mary	153
Wilson	Mary Kathryn E.	168
Wilson	Morgan Lee	211
Wilson	Samuel	245
Wilson	William	245
Wilt	Ellen Jane	135
Wintheiser	Paul	297
Wirmel	Traci Lynne	313
Wise	Alice M.	278
Wolf	Catherine	210
Wolf	Charles Raymond	210 210
Wolf	Cheryl	216
Wolf	Frank J.	210
Wolf	Frank A.	210 210
Wolf	Frank	210
Wolf	Laura K.	210
Wolf	Laverna Louise	210
Wolf	Margaret	210 210
Wolf	Michael	126
Wolf	Robert E.	210
Wolf	William	210
[Wolf]	Helen S.	210
Womer	Brandon Paul	147 147
Womer	David Edward	147
Womer	Heidi Sue	147
Womer	Leanna Beth	147 147
Womer	Mara Renee	147
Woodley	James Robert	292
Woodley	Priscilla Ruth	292
Woods	Joan	172
Wright	Arnold	324
Wright	Frank	110
Wright	Hilda	198
Wright	Willard W.	165
Wutke	Ronald Dean	235
Wyne	Shirley	318
Wynsma	Benjamin Joel	186
Wynsma	Betty Lou	186 188
Wynsma	Brandon Richard	187
Wynsma	Brianne Nichole	187
Wynsma	[daughter]	186

Wynsma	Debra Sue	187 187
Wynsma	Dee Ann Elayne	186 186
Wynsma	Jonathan Luke	186
Wynsma	Kathy Jo	187 188
Wynsma	Kevin John	186
Wynsma	Kristin Kay	187
Wynsma	Mark Adam	187
Wynsma	Miles Burton	186 187
Wynsma	Philip Marcus	186
Wynsma	Rachel Lynn	187
Wynsma	Ralph William	186 187
Wynsma	Rick Alan	187 187
Wynsma	Roger Allen	187 187
Wynsma	Ronald Burton	187 187
Wynsma	Sherri Lynn	187 187
Wynsma	Steven Paul	186 186
Wynsma	Thomas M.	186
Wynsma	Thomas M. Jr.	186 186
Wynsma	Thomas Victor	187
Wynsma	Timothy Jay	186 186
Wynsma	Wendy Marie	187
Yatchyshyn	Kathrine	287
Yates	Edward	131
Yoho	Carol Beth	236
Yoho	Charles LeRoy	236
Yoho	Jennifer Dawn	236
Yost	Debra Jane	303
Yost	Laura	196
Young	------	183
Young	Alma	161
Young	Martha	183
Young	Sarah Emma	166
Zahm	Clark Lynn	232
Zahm	Curtis Paul	232
Zahm	Jacob Ryan	232
Zahm	Jonathan Q. Cousil	233
Zahm	Lawrence William	232 232
Zahm	Michael Alan	232 233
Zahm	Nicholas Lawrence	232
Zahm	Philip Edward	232 233
Zahm	Susan Linn	232 232
Zahm	Taylor Renee	233
Zahn	Carolyn	323 324
Zahn	Catherine	323 324

Zahn	Clarice	323 324
Zahn	Edwin	323
Zahn	Mary Marcella	323 324
Zahniser	Clover	161
Zahniser	Cora Mabel	161 161
Zahniser	Edna V.	173 173
Zahniser	Eleanor G.	166 166
Zahniser	Fidella	161
Zahniser	Frederick Boeber	165 165
Zahniser	Ira Condit	161 173
Zahniser	J. Wilbur	173 175
Zahniser	Margaret	161 169
Zahniser	Mary Elizabeth	161 166
Zahniser	Mary Jane	173 174
Zahniser	Michael Carnahan	161 166
Zahniser	Philip Kearney	161
Zahniser	Queene Alice	161 164
Zahniser	Roscoe Conkling	161 165
Zahniser	Ruth Ella	161
Zahniser	Ruth Delia	161 166
Zahniser	Ruth Emma	161
Zahniser	Thompson	161 161
Zahniser	William	161
Zahniser	William Plummer	161 173
Zahniser	William Matthew	161
Zahniser	William Frederick	165
Zapolnik	Charyl Marie	190 190
Zapolnik	Daniel James	190
Zapolnik	Gerald Lee	190 190
Zapolnik	Judy Rae	190
Zapolnik	Sara Elizabeth	190
Zapolnik	Theresa Lynn	190
Zeller	Sharon	119
Zellers	John	208
Zielke	Jeannine Ann	212
Zimmer	Julie E.	173
Zimmerman	Eugene	117
Zito	John Joseph	258
Zito	Lisa	258
Zito	Matthew	258
Zonke	Doris	180
Zook	Alice Katherine	265
Zurat	Michael A.	172
Zurheide	Lois	297

www.ingramcontent.com/pod-product-compliance
Lightning Source LLC
Chambersburg PA
CBHW082350270326
41935CB00013B/1573